Computer Networks: Design and Implementation

Computer Networks: Design and Implementation

Edited by
Akira Hanako

WILLFORD PRESS

www.willfordpress.com

Published by Willford Press,
118-35 Queens Blvd., Suite 400,
Forest Hills, NY 11375, USA

ISBN: 978-1-68285-476-1

Cataloging-in-Publication Data

Computer networks : design and implementation / edited by Akira Hanako.
p. cm.
Includes bibliographical references and index.
ISBN 978-1-68285-476-1
1. Computer networks. 2. Computer networks--Design and construction.
3. Computer networks--Management. I. Hanako, Akira.
TK5105.5 .C66 2018
004.6--dc23

For information on all Willford Press publications
visit our website at www.willfordpress.com

Contents

Preface

Every book is a source of knowledge and this one is no exception. The idea that led to the conceptualization of this book was the fact that the world is advancing rapidly; which makes it crucial to document the progress in every field. I am aware that a lot of data is already available, yet, there is a lot more to learn. Hence, I accepted the responsibility of editing this book and contributing my knowledge to the community.

Computer network helps in sharing of data, files and other types of information. It is applied in numerous machines such as fax machines, printers, etc. Computer networks have changed the way businesses work. The most commonly used computer network is the Internet. This book contains some path-breaking studies in the field of computer networks. Also included in this book is a detailed explanation of the various concepts and applications of the subject. For all those who are interested in computer networks, this book can prove to be an essential guide.

While editing this book, I had multiple visions for it. Then I finally narrowed down to make every chapter a sole standing text explaining a particular topic, so that they can be used independently. However, the umbrella subject sinews them into a common theme. This makes the book a unique platform of knowledge.

I would like to give the major credit of this book to the experts from every corner of the world, who took the time to share their expertise with us. Also, I owe the completion of this book to the never-ending support of my family, who supported me throughout the project.

Editor

Decision Support for Personalized Cloud Service Selection through Multi-Attribute Trustworthiness Evaluation

Shuai Ding[1,2]*, **Chen-Yi Xia**[3]*, **Kai-Le Zhou**[1,2], **Shan-Lin Yang**[1,2], **Jennifer S. Shang**[4]

1 School of Management, Hefei University of Technology, Hefei, P.R. China, **2** Key Laboratory of Process Optimization and Intelligent Decision-Making, Ministry of Education, Hefei, P.R. China, **3** Tianjin Key Laboratory of Intelligence Computing and Novel Software Technology and Key Laboratory of Computer Vision and System (Ministry of Education), Tianjin University of Technology, Tianjin, P.R. China, **4** The Joseph M. Katz Graduate School of Business, University of Pittsburgh, Pittsburgh, Pennsylvania, United States of America

Abstract

Facing a customer market with rising demands for cloud service dependability and security, trustworthiness evaluation techniques are becoming essential to cloud service selection. But these methods are out of the reach to most customers as they require considerable expertise. Additionally, since the cloud service evaluation is often a costly and time-consuming process, it is not practical to measure trustworthy attributes of all candidates for each customer. Many existing models cannot easily deal with cloud services which have very few historical records. In this paper, we propose a novel service selection approach in which the missing value prediction and the multi-attribute trustworthiness evaluation are commonly taken into account. By simply collecting limited historical records, the current approach is able to support the personalized trustworthy service selection. The experimental results also show that our approach performs much better than other competing ones with respect to the customer preference and expectation in trustworthiness assessment.

Editor: Peter Csermely, Semmelweis University, Hungary

Funding: This work was supported by the National Natural Science Foundation of China through grant Nos. 61374169, 71131002, and 71201042, the National Key Basic Research Program of China through grant No. 2013CB329603 and the Specialized Research Fund for the Doctoral Program of Higher Education of MOE of China through grant No. 20120111110020. These funders had no role in study design, data collection and analysis, decision to publish, or preparation of the manuscript.

Competing Interests: The authors have declared that no competing interests exist.

* Email: dingshuai@hfut.edu.cn (SD); xialooking@163.com (CYX)

Introduction

Cloud computing has become the driver for innovation in the recent years, from startups (e.g. Dropbox, Instagram) to established enterprises (Samsung). They are all using cloud computing to better serve their customers around the world [1]. Cloud service is also gaining wide acceptance and becoming popular to individuals as it reduces hardware and licensing costs, and it is scalable and allows users to work from any computer anywhere.

Several leading IT enterprises including Google, IBM, Microsoft, and Amazon have started to offer cloud services to their customers [2–4]. While many small and medium-sized enterprises (SMEs) and individual customers prefer to apply cloud services to build their business system or personal applications, they are often facing two major challenges at the selection time: (1) multiple cloud services are often available by different venders providing similar functional properties (i.e., "functionally-equivalent"). Customers usually lack appropriate, qualified, sufficient information and benchmarks to assess cloud services with regard to individual preferences and market dynamics [5]; (2) although cloud service vendors are struggling to improve service quality and performance, cloud computing are not necessarily trustworthy – unhandled exceptions and crashes may cause cloud service to

deviate dramatically from the expectation [6,7]. Therefore, there is an increasing demand to help the non-expert customers with the selection of trustworthy cloud service.

The trustworthiness of cloud service affects customers' perception towards service quality, which has significant bearing on customer satisfaction and royalty. The trustworthy attributes include reliability, scalability, availability, safety, security, etc [8–10]. Designing a general and comprehensive analytical model for trustworthiness evaluation is challenging, as the model needs the assessor to achieve, in reasonable time, useful results to determine the best service option. Due to their commercial value (similar to online recommendation system), several evaluation models [11–14] have been proposed by academia and industry lately. These models focus on quantitative analysis and evaluate trustworthiness through a collectively exhaustive dataset.

Except for some specific cases, the assessment dataset remains very sparse due to the costly and time-consuming nature of cloud service invocation. Intuitively, without sufficient data, fair review of cloud services cannot be achieved by existing evaluation methods [9,15]. Fortunately, cloud vendors can collect historical records (QoS values, customer ratings, etc) from different cloud applications in cloud computing environment. With the vast amount of collaborative filtering (CF) technologies available in the field of online recommendation system, we believe there is a strong theoretical foundation to derive a generic trustworthiness model to support the evaluation of cloud service.

There have been some attempts to improve the accuracy of cloud service assessment by a CF process. However, very little attention is paid to the trustworthiness of cloud service, and no interest is given to the case when significant attribute values are missing. The lack of general and formal methodology can be attributed to the large process gap between the cloud service recommenders and trustworthiness researchers. To deal with this challenge, we propose a new CF approach to make use of hidden information (i.e. experience usability, value distribution) to measure the similarity between different services. Moreover, to support personalized selection of cloud services, we also provide a natural treatment for multi-attribute aggregation taking into account customer's preference and expectation.

Background

In the current market, multiple cloud services of similar functions are often available for specific domains. For example, in cloud storage service (e.g. data service, online file system, online backup plan), over 100 functionally-equivalent cloud services are offered by vendors. Some typical examples can be found in Table 1. Given the lack of cloud computing experience of non-expert customers, it is tedious to manually select an appropriate candidate from a set of functionally-equivalent services. Therefore, cloud service evaluation through quality analysis has gained much attraction among service-oriented computing and cloud computing communities over the past two decades.

Given the intricate interactions among QoS (Quality of Service) attributes, customer preferences and market dynamics that jointly influence the perceived quality of cloud services, developing a market-relevant analytical model is crucial to cloud service selection [16–18]. Due to their commercial value and the associated research challenges, many researchers and practitioners have studied the topics. Two types of service selection models are widely examined: evaluation-focused service selection models and prediction-focused service selection models.

By achieving market-relevant evaluations, customers can identify risks and benefits of each cloud service application and choose the best for adoption. The most employed evaluation models include: AHP-based cloud service ranking [19], reputation-aware service rating [20], trust-aware service selection [21], brokerage-based selection [22], SLA-based cloud trustworthiness estimation [11], trustworthy service selection [23]. Although these techniques can accurately and exhaustively estimate service quality, their implementation is time-consuming and costly.

Instead of real-world cloud service invocations, the prediction-focused service selection models can produce QoS values or service ranking using collaborative filtering (CF). The CF approaches for cloud service selection can be categorized as: item-based approaches [24], customer-based approaches [25], their fusion approaches [26], model-based approaches [27], and ranking-oriented approaches [28], where the first three categories are rating-oriented approaches. These approaches help assessors predict the missing attribute values by exploiting neighbors' usage experiences. Several collaborative filtering approaches for cloud service selection have been studied, but they did not consider customer preference and expectation in trustworthiness assessment.

In the prediction process, similar neighbors (customers or services) are identified to generate useful collaborative information. Popular choices for similarity estimation include Pearson correlation coefficient (PCC) [29] and vector similarity (VS) [30]. Since these measures only consider the numerical relationship between different ratings, they remain imprecise and confusing for estimating the neighbor similarity to support missing value

Table 1. Online cloud storage services.

Vender	Cloud Service	Feature	Pricing
Amazon	EBS	Storage Service	$0.1 per GB-month, $0.1 per 1 million I/O requests
Amazon	S3 Standard	Storage Service	$0.095 per GB-month, $0.005 per 1000 requests
Google	Google Cloud Storage	Storage Service	$0.085 per GB-month, $0.01 per 1000 ops-month
IBM	SoftLayer Object Storage	Storage Service	$0.1 per GB-month
Microsoft	Azure Data Service	Storage Service	$0.095 per GB-month, $0.01 per 100000 I/O requests
Apple	iCloud	Storage Service	$20 for 10 GB upgrade
GoGrid	GoGrid Cloud Storage	Storage Service	$0.12 per GB-month
JustCloud	JustCloud Cloud Storage	Storage Service	$3.95 per month, unlimited storage
ZipCloud	ZipCloud Online Storage	Storage Service	$6.95 per month, unlimited storage
AT&T	Synaptic Storage	Storage Service	Unknown
LiveDrive	Livedrive Backup Plan	Backup System	$6 per month, 2 TB storage space
CrashPlan	CrashPlan Backup Plan	Backup System	$5.99 per month, unlimited storage
Carbonite	Cloud Backup Services	Backup System	$59.99 per year, unlimited storage
FlexiScale	FlexiScale Public Cloud	Platform Service	$17 per 1000 unit-hour
AppNexus	AppNexus Cloud	Platform Service	Unknown
Rackspace	Mosso cloud files	File System	$0.75 per GB-month
HighTail	HighTail	File System	$15.99 per month, unlimited storage
Amazon	SimpleDB	Database	$0.12 per GB-month

prediction. Concerned that PCC may overestimate the similarities of negative services, Zheng et al. [26] propose a significance weight and modify PCC to improve the accuracy of similarity computation in service recommendation. However, the significance weight affects the similarity computation of positive services with more usage experiences. To address this problem, Ding et al. [31] define a convex function (usage structure factor) to reflect the usability of customer experience.

While a great number of researchers have focused on the trust-aware service selection and recommendation, little attention has been devoted to the role of customer preference and expectation in multi-attribute trustworthiness evaluation [32]. In addition, large quantities of works offer some valuable clues to discern between different services, the significances arising from value distribution is seldom considered. Thus, we will here combine evaluation-focused and prediction-focused approaches to propose a novel trustworthiness evaluation method which will fully utilize the information of similar services and customer's experience, and take into account both the missing attribute value prediction and the multi-attribute trustworthiness evaluation at the same time.

Methods and Materials

Based on the fact that the size and rate of growth in customers outweigh the expansion of delivered services in the cloud computing market, we employ item-based CF approach rather than the user-based or their fusion approach to produce the missing attribute values in trustworthiness evaluation. Motivated by the observation that experience usability and value distribution could provide valuable insight and distinctive information in the CF process, we create a new similarity measure for enhancing the prediction performance.

Pearson Correlation Coefficient

To make an accurate prediction, we first estimate the similarity between different cloud services. Given a service selection problem consisting of M customers and N services, the customer-service matrix for missing value prediction is denoted as

$$\begin{bmatrix} q_{1,1} & \cdots & q_{1,N} \\ \vdots & \ddots & \vdots \\ q_{M,1} & \cdots & q_{M,N} \end{bmatrix} \quad (1)$$

where the entry $q_{m,n}$ denotes a historical record (QoS value or customer rating) of cloud service cs_n made by customer u_m, "$q_{m,n} = null$" states that u_m didn't invoke cs_n yet.

Pearson Correlation Coefficient (PCC). [29] Taking use of numerical distance to estimate the correlation between different services, PCC has been successfully adopted for recommendation system evaluations. Let cs_n and cs_v be two services, $U_{n,y}$ be the subset of customers who have invoked both cs_n and cs_v, then PCC is applied to calculate the similarity between cs_n and cs_v by

$$Sim\left(cs_n, cs_y\right) = \frac{\sum_{m \in U_{n,y}} (q_{m,n} - \bar{q}_n)(q_{m,y} - \bar{q}_y)}{\sqrt{\sum_{m \in U_{n,y}} (q_{m,n} - \bar{q}_n)^2} \sqrt{\sum_{m \in U_{n,y}} (q_{m,y} - \bar{q}_y)^2}} \quad (2)$$

where $Sim(cs_n, cs_v)$ is in the interval of $[-1, 1]$, $\bar{q}_n$ and $\bar{q}_y$ stand for the average values of cs_n and cs_v made by different customers. However, as noted in Ref. [26], PCC always overestimate the

similarities of negative services, which are actually not similar but happen to have similar usage experience made by few customers. Table 2 shows a simple customer-service matrix which contains six customers (u_1 to u_6) and ten cloud services (cs_1 to cs_{10}). When utilizing Eq. (2), we calculate the PCC values between the services, and get the following relation: $Sim(cs_1, cs_3) > Sim(cs_1, cs_4) > Sim(cs_1, cs_2)$, which indicates cs_3 is more similar to cs_1 than cs_2 and cs_4. It is clearly contrary to the reality due to the limited usage experience. Therefore, it is necessary to reinforce the similarity information in the CF process.

Significance estimation

It seems logical to believe that some cloud services in customer-service matrix may have high significances in making recommendations [33,34]. For instance, a cloud service, which has more useful historical records, may be regarded as more important compared with a negative service. PCC is only related to the numerical distance between different services, but it has nothing to do with the statistical features of historical records. For this case, we introduce two types of significances arising from the experience usability and value distribution of historical records, respectively.

Estimating the experience usability. To determine the significance of neighbors in a CF process, one often assumes a linear relationship between usage experiences and neighbor significances [26,31]. One difference of our work from traditional CF approaches is that we apply a distance measurement method to estimate the experience usability in customer-service matrix. During the distance measurement, Jaccard's coefficient [35] is frequently employed to estimate the discrimination of asymmetric information on binary variables. Before integrating Jaccard's coefficient into our similarity measure, we map the original customer-service matrix into a rectangular binary matrix as follows:

$$\begin{bmatrix} q_{1,1} & \cdots & q_{1,N} \\ \vdots & \ddots & \vdots \\ q_{M,1} & \cdots & q_{M,N} \end{bmatrix} \xrightarrow[\substack{IF(q_{m,n}=null)THEN(b_{m,n}=0) \\ ELSE(b_{m,n}=1)}]{} \begin{bmatrix} b_{1,1} & \cdots & b_{1,N} \\ \vdots & \ddots & \vdots \\ b_{M,1} & \cdots & b_{M,N} \end{bmatrix} \quad (3)$$

where the entry $b_{m,n} = 1$ denotes the customer u_m has invoked the service cs_n previously, whereas $b_{m,n} = 0$ denotes that u_m didn't invoke cs_n. Let $|U_n|$ be the number of customers who has invoked cs_n before, and $|U_{n,y}|$ be the number of customers who invoked both cs_n and cs_v. We use the Jaccard's coefficient $J_{n,y}$ to reflect the rise of significance due to the experience usability, which can be expressed mathematically as:

$$J_{n,y} = \frac{|U_{n,y}|}{|U_n| + |U_y| - |U_{n,y}|} = \frac{\sum_{m=1}^{M} (b_{m,n} \wedge b_{m,y})}{\sum_{m=1}^{M} (b_{m,n} \vee b_{m,y})}, \quad (4)$$

where $J_{n,y}$ is in the interval of $[0, 1]$, and a larger $J_{n,y}$ value indicates that the historical records made over cs_v is more useful in the CF process. $J_{n,y} = J_{y,n}$ holds for all services, which is consistent with the intuition that the similarity between cs_v and cs_n is only related to the subset of historical records made by the customers who have invoked both cs_n and cs_v.

Based on the customer-service matrix in Table 2, we get the significances arising from the experience usability for each service, as shown in Table 3. The values shown in grey are calculated for the negative service cs_3. As observed from Table 2, cs_3 has only been invoked twice. Consequently, his experience usability values

Table 2. A simple customer-service matrix.

	cs_1	cs_2	cs_3	cs_4	cs_5	cs_6	cs_7	cs_8	cs_9	cs_{10}
u_1	0.9	0.7	null	1	0.8	0.6	0.4	0.7	null	null
u_2	0.8	0.7	0.8	0.4	0.6	0.6	0.7	null	0.9	0.8
u_3	0.9	0.8	null	0.6	0.5	0.5	0.5	null	null	1
u_4	0.8	0.9	null	1	null	0.8	0.6	0.7	0.6	null
u_5	0.7	0.6	null	0.5	0.7	null	0.8	null	0.4	0.9
u_6	null	0.8	0.9	0.6	null	null	0.9	0.8	0.8	0.7

are significantly lower than other services (e.g. $J_{1,3} \ll J_{1,2}$). We can infer that integrating $J_{n,y}$ into similarity measure will notably reduce the influence of negative service. It is worth noting that neither PCC nor $J_{n,y}$ can distinguish between cs_2 and cs_4, since they do not have sufficient power to detect the crucial difference in value distributions.

Estimating the value distribution. The neighbors which have the same PCC similarity may have different value distributions. It is necessary to detect more hidden information in the customer-service matrix for significance estimation. For this case, we propose a method to discriminate neighbors' significances arising from their unique value distributions. In practice, the customer-service matrix is very sparse due to limited usage experiences. Therefore, we will ignore the historical records made by the customer u, where $u \notin U_{n,y}$. Let $D_n = \{q_{m,n} \mid u_m \in U_{n,y}\}$ and $D_y = \{q_{m,y} \mid u_m \in U_{n,y}\}$ be the historical records in similarity computation made over cs_n and cs_v, and $|D_y|$ be the cardinality of D_n, and $dom(D_n)$ be the domain of D_n subject to the following constraints:

$$dom(D_n) \rightarrow [q_n^-, q_n^+] \sim \begin{cases} q_n^- = MIN\left(q_{m,n} | u_m \in U_{n,y}\right), \\ q_n^+ = MAX\left(q_{m,n} | u_m \in U_{n,y}\right). \end{cases} \quad (5)$$

Following $dom(D_n)$, the dataset D_y can be grouped into three categories:

$$\begin{cases} D_y^{<n} = \left\{q_{m,y} | u_m \in U_{n,y}, q_{m,y} \in (-\infty, q_n^-)\right\}, \\ D_y^{=n} = \left\{q_{m,y} | u_m \in U_{n,y}, q_{m,y} \in [q_n^-, q_n^+]\right\}, \\ D_y^{>n} = \left\{q_{m,y} | u_m \in U_{n,y}, q_{m,y} \in (q_n^+, +\infty)\right\}. \end{cases} \quad (6)$$

Since D_y is a finite discrete dataset, the probability of each category can be computed as:

$$\left\{p_y^1 = \frac{|D_y^{<n}|}{|D_y|}, p_y^2 = \frac{|D_y^{=n}|}{|D_y|}, p_y^3 = \frac{|D_y^{>n}|}{|D_y|}\right\}, \quad (7)$$

where $\sum_{k=1}^{3} \left(p_y^k\right) = 1$, and $|D_y^{<n}| + |D_y^{=n}| + |D_y^{>n}| = |D_y|$. From the information entropy aspect, we use the following expression to detect the difference between the value distributions of cs_n and cs_y:

$$VD_{n,y} = 1 - \frac{H_{n,y}}{H_{max}}, \quad (8)$$

where $H_{n,y} = \sum_{p_y^k \neq 0} \left(-p_y^k \log_2(p_y^k)\right)$ denotes the information entropy of D_y, and H_{max} denotes the maximal entropy in customer-service matrix, respectively. $VD_{n,y}$ is a linear function defined in [0, 1]. From the maximum entropy principle [36], we have $H_{max} = \log_2(3)$. Thus, Eq.(8) can be rewritten as

$$VD_{n,y} = 1 - \frac{\sum_{p_y^k \neq 0} \left(-p_y^k \log_2(p_y^k)\right)}{\log_2(3)}, \quad (9)$$

where $VD_{n,y}$ attains its unique global minimum $VD_{n,y}^{MIN} = 0$ if $p_y^1 = p_y^2 = p_y^3 = 1/3$; otherwise it attains global maximum $VD_{n,y}^{MAX} = 1$ when $\exists p_y^k = 1$.

We can thus calculate the significances $VD_{n,y}$ arising from the value distribution using Eq.(9) over the customer-service matrix in

Table 3. Significances arising from the experience usability.

	cs_1	cs_2	cs_3	cs_4	cs_5	cs_6	cs_7	cs_8	cs_9
cs_2	0.833								
cs_3	0.167	0.333							
cs_4	0.833	1	0.333						
cs_5	0.8	0.667	0.2	0.667					
cs_6	0.8	0.667	0.2	0.667	0.6				
cs_7	0.833	1	0.333	1	0.667	0.667			
cs_8	0.333	0.5	0.25	0.5	0.167	0.4	0.5		
cs_9	0.5	0.667	0.5	0.667	0.333	0.333	0.667	0.4	
cs_{10}	0.5	0.667	0.5	0.667	0.6	0.333	0.667	0.167	0.6

Table 4. Significances arising from the value distribution.

	cs_1	cs_2	cs_3	cs_4	cs_5	cs_6	cs_7	cs_8	cs_9	cs_{10}
cs_1		1	1	1	0.488	0.369	0.387	1	1	0.421
cs_2	0.545		0.685	1	1	0.488	1	0.421	1	0.488
cs_3	1	0.369		1	1	1	1	1	1	0.369
cs_4	0.387	0	1		0.054	0.054	0.079	0.421	0.488	1
cs_5	0.369	0.488	1	1		0.421	1	1	1	1
cs_6	0.488	0.488	1	1	1		0.488	1	1	1
cs_7	0.387	0.421	0.369	1	0.488	0.488		1	1	0.369
cs_8	1	1	1	1	1	1	1		1	1
cs_9	0.421	0.488	1	1	1	0.369	0.421	0.369		0.421
cs_{10}	0.421	0.421	1	1	1	1	1	1	0.685	

Table 2. Table 4 shows the values of these significances. The values shown in grey are calculated for the cloud services cs_2 and cs_4.

Similarity measurement adopting significance. After we have defined the two types of significance for each service, we can then create the similarity measure, $Sim^s(cs_n, cs_v)$, which takes into account the significance previously defined. To estimate the significance as accurately as possible, we identify the significance of cs_v with respect to cs_n as a linear combination of $J_{n,y}$ and $VD_{n,y}$, such that:

$$SIG_{n,y} = \alpha \times J_{n,y} + (1 - \alpha) \times VD_{n,y}, \qquad (10)$$

where α is defined to determine how much our significance relies on experience usability and value distribution. If $\alpha = 0$, we only extract the experience usability for conducting significance estimation, and if $\alpha = 1$, we consider only the value distribution. Hence, the similarity measure can be written in standard form:

$$Sim^s(cs_n, cs_y) = SIG_{n,y} \times Sim(cs_n, cs_y) \qquad (11)$$

where $SIG_{n,y}$ denotes the significance of cs_v with respect to cs_n, and $Sim(cs_n, cs_v)$ denotes the PCC value between cs_n and cs_v. Different from existing similarity measures, our approach employs not only numerical distance but also usage experience as well as value distribution to determine the similarity between different services. With the definition of similarity measure defined in Eq.(11), for every cloud service in customer-service matrix, we rank their neighbors and select the top-k most similar services to make missing value prediction. Following the top-k similar service defined in [26], we get

$$CS_n^k = \{cs_y | cs_y \in CS_n,\ Sim^S(cs_n, cs_y) > 0, y \neq n\}, \qquad (12)$$

where CS_n denotes the neighbor set of cs_n in customer-service matrix, and $Sim^S(cs_n, cs_v)$ denotes the similarity between cs_n and cs_v. For the customer-service matrix in Table 2, we set α to 0.8 to obtain the similarity measures between different services (see Table 5). The top 3 neighbors of each service are marked in grey areas as seen in each column.

Missing value prediction. With the exponential growth of cloud service on the Internet, service recommendation techniques like QoS-aware CF approaches have become increasingly important and popular [37]. Based on our similarity measure, we propose an enhanced item-based CF approach (named as JV-PCC) to reinforce the prediction performance. To predict the missing value $\hat{q}_{m,n}$ of service cs_n for customer u_m, we first determine the objective weight of each similar neighbor:

Table 5. Similarities between different services.

	cs_1	cs_2	cs_3	cs_4	cs_5	cs_6	cs_7	cs_8	cs_9	cs_{10}
cs_1		0.361	0.334	0.366	−0.099	−0.421	−0.663	−0.24	0.402	0.141
cs_2	0.323		0.403	0.484	−0.379	0.376	−0.153	0	0.213	−0.081
cs_3	0.334	0.34		0.223	0.36	0.36	0.259	0.4	−0.165	−0.212
cs_4	0.314	0.387	0.223		0.336	0.303	−0.494	−0.347	−0.166	0.046
cs_5	−0.096	−0.326	0.36	0.453		0.324	−0.099	−0.334	−0.464	−0.432
cs_6	−0.435	0.376	0.36	0.408	0.39		0.145	−0.312	−0.208	−0.405
cs_7	−0.663	−0.135	0.189	−0.605	−0.085	0.146		0.549	0.032	−0.451
cs_8	−0.24	0	0.4	−0.43	−0.334	−0.312	0.549		0.518	−0.334
cs_9	0.324	0.184	−0.165	−0.193	−0.464	−0.152	0.027	0.393		−0.395
cs_{10}	0.14	−0.079	−0.268	0.04	−0.432	−0.405	−0.544	−0.334	−0.432	

Table 6. Predicted attribute values.

	cs_1	cs_2	cs_3	cs_4	cs_5	cs_6	cs_7	cs_8	cs_9	cs_{10}
u_1			0.843						0.609	1
u_2								0.808		
u_3			0.865					0.74	0.842	
u_4			0.85		0.8					0.887
u_5			0.831			0.593		0.76		
u_6	0.865				0.703	0.749				

$$\omega_{n,y} = \frac{Sim^S(cs_n,cs_y)}{\sum_{q_{m,y} \neq null} Sim^S(cs_n,cs_y)}, \quad (13)$$

where $cs_v \in CS_n^k$ denotes a similar neighbor of cs_n, while $Sim^S(cs_n, cs_v)$ denotes the similarity between cs_n and cs_v. The objective weights define the relative importance of each similar neighbor in the CF process. Next, we attain a prediction by a classic aggregation function:

$$\hat{q}_{m,n} = \sum_{q_{m,y} \neq null} (q_{m,y} \times \omega_{n,y}), \quad (14)$$

where $q_{m,y}$ denotes the historical record of cs_y made by customer u_m. In practice, local runtime environment (e.g. network bandwidth) and customer's rating style may significantly influence the historical records over delivered services. However, the above function deems inappropriate as it is calculated through only one customer. To address this problem, JV-PCC predicts the missing attribute value by the following equation:

$$\hat{q}_{m,n} = q_n^+ + (q_n^+ - q_n^-) \sum_{\substack{cs_y \in CS_n^k, \\ q_{m,y} \neq null}} \omega_{n,y} \times \left(\frac{q_{m,y} - q_y^-}{q_y^+ - q_y^-} \right), \quad (15)$$

where $\omega_{n,y}$ denotes the objective weight of cs_y with respect to cs_n, while q_y^- and q_y^+ denote the minimum and maximum values of service cs_y, respectively. Table 6 displays the values estimated for the missing records in Table 2. In the experimental examples, both customer-based and service-based neighborhood information were adopted for approximating the missing value.

Trustworthiness-aware service selection

Several models, focusing on the quantitative measurement of service trustworthiness, have been proposed in Refs. [9,18,38]. However, different customers have different preference and expectation in service selection. A thorough understanding into these factors is essential to ensure effective evaluation finding. Here, we introduce a cloud service evaluation model, which helps aggregate trustworthy attributes by considering customer's preference and expectation.

Attribute utility determination. To make use of observed or estimated values, we need to know that different attributes may have inconsistent dimensions. The results in [32] show that utility can be used to identify an entity's trustworthiness. Therefore, we first derive the utility from the customer-service matrix so as to ensure their values are in the range of [0, 1]. Trustworthy

attributes are often divided into quantitative and qualitative attributes, of which the former are objective measures (e.g. QoS value), and the latter are subjective customer ratings. In addition, quantitative trustworthy attributes can be grouped into two classes: "benefit" and "cost". For "benefit" ("cost") attribute, e.g. *throughput (response-time)*, the higher (lower) its value is, the greater the possibility that a customer would choose it becomes. In our model, qualitative attributes are also considered as "benefit" attributes. Let $q_{m,n}$ be the attribute value of cs_n, and the attribute utility (risk-neutral) $H_{m,n}$ has the following form:

$$H_{m,n} = \begin{cases} \dfrac{q_{m,n} - q_m^-}{q_m^+ - q_m^-}, & q_{m,n} \in ''benefit'', \\ \dfrac{q_m^+ - q_{m,n}}{q_m^+ - q_m^-}, & q_{m,n} \in ''cost'', \end{cases} \quad (16)$$

where q_m^- and q_m^+ denote the minimum and maximum attribute values for customer u_m, and they are subject to the following constraints:

$$\begin{cases} q_m^- = MIN(q_{m,n}|n=1,...,N), \\ q_m^+ = MAX(q_{m,n}|n=1,...,N). \end{cases} \quad (17)$$

The attribute utility $H_{m,n}$ is in the range of [0, 1], where a larger $H_{m,n}$ indicates that customer u_m is more satisfied with the service cs_n.

Customer satisfaction estimation. From influential theory in marketing science, we consider that the perception of cloud service trustworthiness is a customer satisfaction function, which includes customer preference and expectation attributes. In general, customer satisfaction function should exhibit two characteristics: (1) given the same expectation, a trustworthy cloud service is weighed much more heavily than an untrustworthy service. This effect is reflected in the derivation of attribute utility; (2) customer satisfaction slightly increases when attribute utility surpasses a certain value (expectation), and significantly decreases when attribute utility falls below expectation [39]. We formalize this interaction as a piecewise linear function:

$$C_{m,n} = \begin{cases} H_{m,n}, & H_{m,n} \geq H^{exp}, \\ H_{m,n}(H_{m,n} - H^{exp} + 1)^{\delta}, & H_{m,n} \leq H^{exp}, \end{cases} \quad (18)$$

where $C_{m,n}$ is constrained to $0 \leq C_{m,n} \leq 1$; the parameter δ regulates the impact of customer preference on perceived trustworthiness; and H^{exp} denotes the customer expectation with regard to selecting trustworthy cloud service. As shown in Fig. 1, $C_{m,n}$ is continuous (i.e. the piecewise function converges at $H_{m,n} = H^{exp}$).

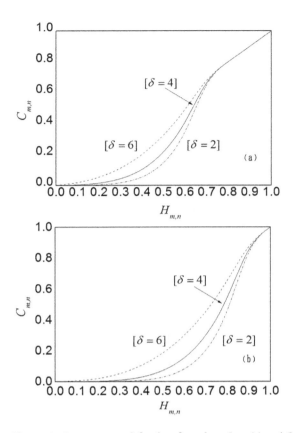

Figure 1. Customer satisfaction function $C_{m,n}$. (a) and (b) depict the distributions of customer satisfaction as recorded at the fixed expectation $H^{exp} = 0.7$ and $H^{exp} = 0.9$, where the parameter δ is varied from 2 to 6 in increment of 2. It can be observed that the rate of change in customer satisfaction differs significantly when $H_{m,n}$ falls below and exceeds the expectation.

The severity and rate of satisfaction (controlled by H^{exp} and δ, respectively) reflect different customer's tolerance to untrustworthy candidates. Let $H^{exp} = 0.7$, and $\delta = 2$. Table 7 shows the customer satisfaction for each attribute value (historical record or predicted value), which corresponds to the original customer-service matrix in Table 2 and the predicted missing values given in Table 6.

Trustworthy attribute aggregation. After estimating customer satisfaction and ensuring the value of $C_{m,n}$ in the interval of $[0, 1]$, the degree of trustworthiness (alias "trust value" [40]) of each cloud service in customer-service matrix can be achieved by aggregating trustworthy attributes. Let $C_{m,n}^1 .. C_{m,n}^J$ be the customer

satisfaction on a set of specified attributes $A_1..A_J$, then the trust value of cs_n is computed as:

$$trust_n = \frac{\sum_{j=1}^{J} \omega_j \times C_{m,n}^j}{J},\qquad(19)$$

where ω_j denotes the weight of trustworthy attribute A_j, $\sum_{j=1}^{J} \omega_j = 1$.

The trust value gives the comprehensive perception of cloud service trustworthiness, while the weights modify this trust value based on the relative importance of trustworthy attributes. Actually, a set of specified trustworthy attributes can be easily weighted by applying existing technologies such as those discussed in [32]. We omit the details for brevity.

Decision support for personalized service selection. Multi-attribute trustworthiness evaluation is an important step for making accurate service selection. We suppose that u_m is the active customer, who requires trustworthy cloud service. While the evaluation results have arrived, a set of appropriate service candidates can be identified for u_m by:

$$CS^m = \{cs_n | trust_n > \varepsilon_m, n = 1,...,N\},\qquad(20)$$

where $trust_n$ denotes the trust value of cs_n, ε_m denotes the selection threshold determined by u_m. We aim to remedy the shortcomings of evaluation-focused selection methods by avoiding the costly and time-consuming real-world service invocations. Note that when $CS^m = \varnothing$ the service selection for the active customer u_m needs to be degrade by decreasing the parameter ε_m.

Let $\varepsilon_1 = ... = \varepsilon_6 = 0.85$, a set of trustworthy cloud services can be recommended for $u_1...u_6$ as

$$CS^1 = \{cs_1, cs_4, cs_5\}, \quad CS^2 = \{cs_8, cs_9\}, \quad CS^3 = \{cs_1, cs_9, cs_{10}\},$$
$$CS^4 = \{cs_2, cs_4, cs_5, cs_6\}, \quad CS^5 = \{cs_7\}, \quad CS^6 = \{cs_7, cs_8\},\qquad(21)$$

where the customer satisfaction for each attribute value is presented in Table 7. In practice, our approach makes it possible to deal with various types of trustworthiness-aware cloud service selections by combing the evaluation-focused and the prediction-focused methods. Note that if trustworthiness is not the only issue that affects customer's decision making, it is necessary to extend the selection process of our approach, e.g., price-oriented service filtering, into other attributes or indexes.

Results

In this section, abundance of experiments are conducted to show how to recommend trustworthy cloud service in the context

Table 7. Customer satisfaction.

	cs_1	cs_2	cs_3	cs_4	cs_5	cs_6	cs_7	cs_8	cs_9	cs_{10}
u_1	1	0.134	0.229	1	1	0.134	0	0	0.215	1
u_2	0.32	0.134	0	0	0.134	0.134	0.486	1	1	0.134
u_3	1	0.623	0.587	0.134	0	0	0.05	0.166	0.884	1
u_4	0.32	1	0.32	1	1	1	0.196	0	0.196	0.531
u_5	0	0	0.115	0.036	0.623	0.115	0.8	0.407	0	0.623
u_6	0.825	0.623	1	0.134	0.645	0.83	1	0.926	0.8	0

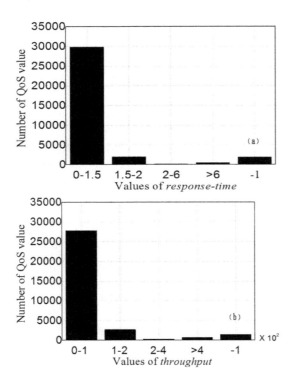

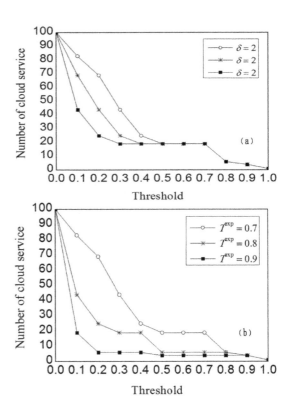

Figure 2. QoS value distributions. (a) and (b) depict the value distributions of *response-time* and *throughput* in our customer-service matrices, where "−1" indicates that the service invocation failed due to an http error. The ranges of *response-time* and *throughput* are 0–16.053 seconds and 0–541.546 kbps, respectively.

Figure 4. Impact of preference and expectation. (a) and (b) depict the experimental results of preference parameter δ and expectation H^{exp}, respectively. They indicates that δ regulates the elimination rate of untrustworthy cloud services, whereas H^{exp} controls the degree of customer's tolerance to untrustworthy service.

of large sparse assessment dataset, and to verify the efficiency of our CF approach.

Prototype implementation and results

To demonstrate the effectiveness of the proposed service selection approach, we use Microsoft C# .NET to develop a prototype system. Based on literature [8,41,42], we find *Availability* and *Performance* are two commonly used trustworthy attributes. We utilize them to conduct trustworthiness-aware service selection, by including two types of historical records: *response-time* and *throughput*. Their evaluation styles and weights are summarized as Table 8.

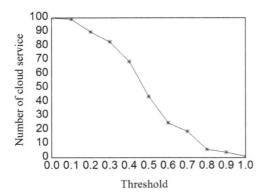

Figure 3. The number of recommended services for u_{339}. Results are presented for the proposed cloud service selection approach, where the parameter ε_{339} is varied from 0 to 1 in increment of 0.1.

We employ an open QoS research dataset [43] to simulate the historical records of Performance and Availability in cloud service market. The QoS values for *response-time* and *throughput* were collected from 339 users over 5825 web services in a real-world environment. Since it is impractical to discover and distinguish all functionally-equivalent services at the selection time, we randomly select 100 services' QoS records, and construct two 339×100 customer-service matrices for our experiment. Figure 2 shows the value distribution of *response-time* and *throughput* in *user-service* matrix. We cannot simply utilize these QoS records to analyze and rank the cloud services since these customer-service matrices are sparse assessment datasets, and cannot accurately interpret the trustworthiness status of all services. Suppose u_{339} is the active customer. The historical records made by u_{339} contains 9 and 7 missing values (on *response-time* and *throughput*, respectively) which will potentially affect his cloud service selection decision. Therefore, the proposed CF approach is employed to predict the missing attribute values. At this simulation experiment, the similarity parameter α is set to 0.8 and remains so until the trust values for u_{339} are reported. Once the prototype system obtains the customer satisfactions by utilizing Eqs.(12)–(14), where the parameter $\delta = 2$ and the expectation $H^{exp} = 0.7$, the active customer will receive the trust values of each service. We vary the selection parameter ε_{339} from 0 to 1 in increment of 0.1, and count the cloud services whose trust values surpass ε_{339} (the number of recommended services for u_{339}, i.e. $|CS^{339}|$). The experiment results are shown in Figure 3. Although we only study two trustworthy attributes in the

Table 8. Trustworthy attributes of cloud service.

Attribute	A_j	Evaluation style	Weight	q_{339}^-	q_{339}^+
Availability	A_1	"cost" QoS value	0.65	0	16.053
Performance	A_2	"benefit" QoS value	0.35	0	541.546

experiment, the proposed approach can be easily extended to other trustworthiness-aware service selection problems. When selecting the optimal trustworthy services from a set of functionally-equivalent candidates, the entry data of our approach are the corresponding historical records (i.e., QoS values or customer ratings), the active customer's preference and expectation towards service trustworthiness, and the selection parameter.

Impact of δ and T^{exp}

Different customers have different preference and expectation in trustworthy service selections. Instead of risk-neutral attribute utility, we use the customer satisfaction $C_{m,n}$ to identify the perceived trustworthiness of delivered services. To evaluate the impact of customer's preference and expectation, we have conduct additional experiments with variable parameters δ and H^{exp}. In these experiments, we first vary δ from 2 to 6 in increment of 2, where the expectation H^{exp} is fixed at 0.7 first. Later, we set δ to 2,

and vary H^{exp} from 0.7 to 0.9 in increment of 0.1. Figure 4 (a) shows the experimental results of preference parameter δ and Figure 4 (b) shows the experimental results of expectation H^{exp}. The parameters δ and H^{exp} jointly determine how to derive the customer satisfaction from attribute utility to approximate the active customer's attitude towards profit and risk.

Performance comparison of CF approaches

In this work, we present an enhanced item-based CF approach (i.e., JV-PCC) to predict the missing attribute values for cloud service selection. Our approach engages the significances ($J_{n,y}$ and $VD_{n,y}$) to improve the accuracy of similarity estimation. To study the prediction performance, we compare JV-PCC with two existing item-based approaches: Item-based CF adopting PCC (IPCC) [44], and Extended PCC approach (f-PCC) [31].

Evaluation metric. We use Mean Absolute Error (MAE) and Root Mean Square Error (RMSE) to evaluate the prediction

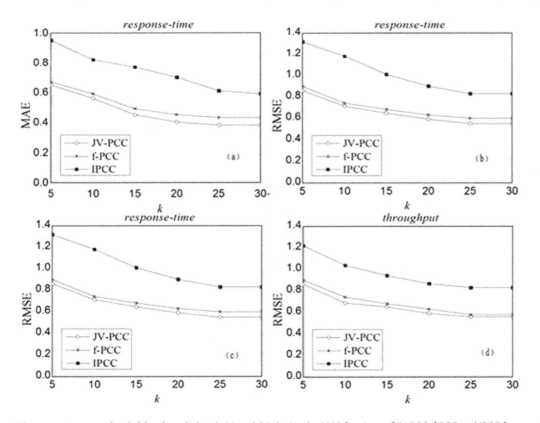

Figure 5. Impact of neighborhood size k. (a) and (b) depict the MAE fractions of JV-PCC, f-PCC and IPCC for *response-time* and *throughput*, while (c) and (d) depict the RMSE fractions. It can be observed that JV-PCC achieves smaller MAE and RMSE consistently than f-PCC for both *response-time* and *throughput*. Regardless of JV-PCC or f-PCC, as k increases, MAE and RMSE drop at first, indicating that better performance can be achieved by employing more similar services' records to generate the predictions. However, when k surpasses a specific level (i.e. $k = 25$), they fail to drop with a further increase in k, which were caused by the limited number of similar neighbors.

performance of our approach in comparison with other approaches. MAE and RMSE are defined as:

$$
\begin{cases}
MAE = \dfrac{\sum_{m,n} |\hat{q}_{m,n} - q_{m,n}|}{Q} \\[2ex]
RMSE = \sqrt{\dfrac{\sum_{m,n} (\hat{q}_{m,n} - q_{m,n})^2}{Q}}
\end{cases}
\tag{22}
$$

where $\hat{q}_{m,n}$ and $q_{m,n}$ are the predicted QoS value and the actual value, respectively.

Experimental setup and results. The size of top-k similar service set plays an important role in CF approach, which determines how many neighbors' historical records are employed to generate predictions. To study the impact of neighborhood size k, we separate the customer-service matrices into two parts: training set (80% historical records in the matrix) and test set (the remaining 20% records). We set the density to 50%, the significance parameter α to 0.7, and vary k from 5 to 30 in increment of 5. Figure 5 shows the experimental results for *response-time* and *throughput*. Under the same simulation condition, JV-PCC and f-PCC significantly outperform IPCC. The observations also suggest that better accuracy can be achieved by our model when more historical records are available in the service selection study.

Conclusions

Trustworthiness-aware service selection is a critical issue among cloud computing and service-oriented architecture communities.

In this paper, we propose a personalized service selection approach which takes into account the missing value prediction and the multi-attribute evaluation requirements. We find that the proposed approach can tackle various types of trustworthiness-aware selection problems in cloud service market. Meanwhile, the experimental results demonstrate that the proposed CF approach significantly improves the prediction performance as compared with other competing item-based approaches.

Employing untrustworthy cloud service will expose users to high-risk IT structure, resulting in a host of intra-organizational hazards that detriment the organization and disrupt the normal operations [45]. In the present work, we can only look into the static approach for trustworthy service selection, and we will investigate more types of trustworthiness evaluation models (e.g. probability model, dynamic model, etc) in the future since different cloud service applications may have different selection criteria and data structures.

Acknowledgments

We would like to thank Prof. Youtao Zhang, from University of Pittsburgh, for giving detailed and valuable comments on the paper.

Author Contributions

Conceived and designed the experiments: SD CYX KLZ SLY JSS. Performed the experiments: SD. Analyzed the data: SD JSS CYX. Contributed reagents/materials/analysis tools: SD CYX. Contributed to the writing of the manuscript: SD CYX.

References

1. Katzan H (2011) Cloud software service: concepts, technology, economics. Service Science 1(4): 256–269.
2. Stolyar AL (2013) An infinite server system with general packing constraints. Operations Research 61(5): 1200–1217.
3. Chen PY, Wu SY (2013) The impact and implications of on-demand services on market structure. Information Systems Research 24(3): 750–767.
4. Sunyaev A, Schneider S (2013) Cloud services certification. Communications of the ACM 56(2): 33–36.
5. Sanjukta D, Anna YD (2011) Risk management and optimal pricing in online storage grids. Information Systems Research 22(4): 756–773.
6. Marston S, Li Z, Bandyopadhyay S, Zhang JH, Ghalsasi A (2011) Cloud computing – The business perspective. Decision Support Systems 51: 176–189.
7. Cusumano M (2010) Cloud computing and SaaS as new computing platforms. Communications of the ACM, 53(4): 27–29.
8. Alhamad M, Dillon T, Chang E (2011) A trust-evaluation metric for cloud applications. International Journal of Machine Learning and Computing 1(4): 416–421.
9. Yao JH, Chen SP, Wang C, Levy D, Zic J (2011) Modelling collaborative services for business and QoS compliance. IEEE International Conference on Web Services (ICWS), pp.299–306.
10. Tao F, Zhao DM, Hu YF, Zhou ZD (2010) Correlation-aware resource service composition and optimal-selection in manufacturing grid. European Journal of Operational Research 201(1): 129–143.
11. Grag SK, Versteeg S, Buyya R (2013) A framework for ranking of cloud computing services. Future Generation Computer Systems 29(4): 1012–1023.
12. Limam N, Boutab R (2010) Assessing software service quality and trustworthiness at selection time. IEEE Transactions on Software Engineering 36(4): 559–574.
13. Hang CW, Singh MP (2011) Trustworthy service selection and composition. ACM Transactions on Autonomous and Adaptive Systems 6(1): 1–17.
14. Chakraborty S, Roy K (2012) An SLA-based framework for estimating trustworthiness of a cloud. IEEE 11th International Conference on Trust, Security and Privacy in Computing and Communications, pp. 937–942.
15. Mehdi M, Bouguila N, Bentahar J (2012) Trustworthy web service selection using probabilistic models. IEEE 19th International Conference on Web Services (ICWS), Honolulu, HI, pp.17–24.
16. Hackney R, Xu HN, Ranchhod A (2006) Evaluating web services: Towards a framework for emergent contexts. European Journal of Operational Research 173(3): 1161–1174.
17. Ding S, Yang SL, Zhang YT, Liang CY, Xia CY (2014) Combining QoS prediction and customer satisfaction estimation to solve cloud service trustworthiness evaluation problems. Knowledge-Based Systems, 56(1): 216–225.
18. Lecue F (2010) Combing collaborative filtering and semantic content-based approaches to recommend web services. IEEE Fourth International Conference on Semantic Computing, pp. 200–205.
19. Tserpes K, Aisopos F, Kyriazis D, Varvarigou T (2012) A recommender mechanism for service selection in service-oriented environments. Future Generation Computer Systems, 28(8): 1285–1294.
20. Zheng ZB, Ma H, Lyu MR, King I (2011) QoS-aware web service recommendation by collaborative filtering. IEEE Transactions on Services Computing, 4(2): 140–152.
21. Chen X, Liu XD, Huang ZC, Sun HL (2010) Region KNN: A scalable hybrid collaborative filtering algorithm for personalized web service recommendation. IEEE International Conference on Web Service (ICWS), pp.9–16.
22. Zheng ZB, Wu XM, Zhang YL, Lyu MR, Wang JM (2013) QoS ranking prediction for cloud services. IEEE Transactions on Parallel and Distributed Systems, 24(6): 1213–1222.
23. Pal R, Hui P (2013) Economic models for cloud service markets: Pricing and capacity planning. Theoretical Computer Science, 496(22): 113–124.
24. Sundarewaran S, Squicciarini A, Lin D (2012) A brokerage-based approach for cloud service selection. IEEE Fifth International Conference on Cloud Computing, pp.558–565.
25. Resnick P, Iacovou N, Suchak M, Bergstrom P, Riedl J (1994) Grouplens: An open architecture for collaborative filtering of networks. Proceeding of ACM Conference on Computer Supported Cooperative Work, pp.175–186.
26. Breese JS, Heckerman D, Kadie C (1998) Empirical analysis of predictive algorithms for collaborative filtering. Proceedings of 14th Annual Conference on Uncertainty in Artificial Intelligence, 43–52.
27. Ding S, Ma XJ, Yang SL (2012) A software trustworthiness evaluation model using objective weight based evidential reasoning approach. Knowledge and Information Systems 33(1): 171–189.
28. Jin R, Chai J, Si L (2005) An automatic weighting scheme for collaborative filtering. SIGIR, 337–344.
29. Bobadilla J, Hernando A, Ortega F, Gutierrez A (2012) Collaborative filtering based on significances. Information Sciences 185: 1–17.
30. Seifoddini H, Djassemi M (1991) The production data-based similarity coefficient versus Jaccard's similarity coefficient. Computer & Industrial Engineering 21(1–4): 263–266.

31. Cheng HD, Chen JR (1997) Automatically determine the membership function based on the maximum entropy principle. Information Sciences 96(4): 163–182.
32. Shao LS, Zhang J, Wei Y, Zhao JF, Xie B, et al. (2007) Personalized QoS Prediction for Web Services via Collaborative Filtering. IEEE International Conference on Web Services (ICWS), pp.439–446.
33. Dozelli P, Basili V (2006) A practical framework for eliciting and modeling system dependability requirements: Experience from the NASA high dependability computing project. Journal of Systems and Software 79(1): 107–119.
34. Hwang SY, Lee CH (2013) Reliable web service selection in choreographed environments, Decision Support Systems 54(3): 1463–1476.
35. Anderson EW, Sullivan MW (1993) The antecedents and consequences of customer satisfaction of firms. Marketing Science 12(2).
36. Karaoglanoglou K, Karatza H (2011) Resource discovery in a Grid system: Directing requests to trustworthy virtual organizations based on global trust values. Journal of Systems and Software 84(3): 465–478.
37. Cruz JM, Liu ZG (2012) Modeling and analysis of the effects of QoS and reliability on pricing, profitability, and risk management in multiperiod grid-computing networks. Decision Support Systems 52(3): 562–576.
38. Rosario S, Benveniste A, Haar S, Jard C (2008) Probabilistic QoS and soft contracts for transaction-based web services orchestrations. IEEE Transactions on Services Computing 1(4): 187–200.

39. Zheng ZB, Zhang YL, Lyu MR (2010) Distributed QoS evaluation for real-world web services. Proceedings of the 8th International Conference on Web Services (ICWS), Miami, Florida, USA, pp. 83–90.
40. Deshpande M, Karypis G (2004) Item-based top-N recommendation. ACM Transactions on Information System 22(1): 143–177.
41. Benlian A, Hess T (2011) Opportunities and risks of software-as-a-service: Findings from a survey of IT executives. Decision Support Systems 52: 232–246.
42. Demirkan H, Cheng HK, Bandyopadhyay S (2010) Coordination strategies in a SaaS supply chain. Journal of Management Information Systems 26(4): 119–143.
43. Tsesmetzis D, Roussaki I, Sykas E (2008) QoS-aware service evaluation and selection. European Journal of Operational Research 191: 1101–1112.
44. Wang Q, Wang C, Ren K, Lou KJ, Li J (2011) Enabling public auditability and data dynamics for storage security in cloud computing. IEEE Transactions on Parallel and Distributed Services 22(5): 847–859.
45. Iosup A, Ostermann S, Yigitbasi MN, Prodan R, Fahringer T, et al. (2011) Performance analysis of cloud computing services for many-tasks scientific computing. IEEE Transactions on Parallel and Distributed Systems 22(6): 931–945.

2

STORMSeq: An Open-Source, User-Friendly Pipeline for Processing Personal Genomics Data in the Cloud

Konrad J. Karczewski[1,2]*, **Guy Haskin Fernald**[1,2], **Alicia R. Martin**[1,2], **Michael Snyder**[2], **Nicholas P. Tatonetti**[3], **Joel T. Dudley**[4]*

1 Biomedical Informatics Training Program, Stanford University School of Medicine, Stanford, California, United States of America, 2 Department of Genetics, Stanford University School of Medicine, Stanford, California, United States of America, 3 Department of Biomedical Informatics, Columbia University, New York, New York, United States of America, 4 Department of Genetics and Genomic Sciences, Mount Sinai School of Medicine, New York, New York, United States of America

Abstract

The increasing public availability of personal complete genome sequencing data has ushered in an era of democratized genomics. However, read mapping and variant calling software is constantly improving and individuals with personal genomic data may prefer to customize and update their variant calls. Here, we describe STORMSeq (Scalable Tools for Open-Source Read Mapping), a graphical interface cloud computing solution that does not require a parallel computing environment or extensive technical experience. This customizable and modular system performs read mapping, read cleaning, and variant calling and annotation. At present, STORMSeq costs approximately $2 and 5–10 hours to process a full exome sequence and $30 and 3–8 days to process a whole genome sequence. We provide this open-access and open-source resource as a user-friendly interface in Amazon EC2.

Editor: I. King Jordan, Georgia Institute of Technology, United States of America

Funding: KJK is funded by the National Science Foundation (NSF) Graduate Research Fellowship. KJK and GHF are funded by National Institutes of Health (NIH) Training Grant LM007033. ARM is funded by NIH Training Grant GM007790. MS is funded by grants from the NIH. The funders had no role in study design, data collection and analysis, decision to publish, or preparation of the manuscript.

Competing Interests: The authors have declared that no competing interests exist.

* E-mail: konradjkarczewski@gmail.com (KJK), joel.dudley@mssm.edu (JTD)

Introduction

Individuals are now empowered to obtain and explore their full personal genome and exome sequences owing to declining costs in genome sequencing, and direct-to-consumer genetic testing companies have begun to provide sequencing services: in 2011, 23andMe conducted a pilot exome sequencing program for $999, while at the time of this writing, DNADTC provides the service for $895. Software and algorithms for short read mapping and variant calling are an active area of development and individuals may prefer to customize which software or parameters to use to process their raw genetic data. However, as these programs require significant computational resources, such a task is generally intractable without access to large-scale computing resources. Furthermore, execution of the required software pipeline requires proficiency in command-line programming, or alternatively, expensive commercial software options geared towards experts. These concerns can be ameliorated by use of intuitive open-source software operating in a cloud-computing environment.

A number of solutions enabling researchers to process sequencing data using cloud computing are available. The majority of open-source, cloud-based tools for genomic data are command-line based and require substantial technical skills to use. Notable exceptions are Galaxy, Crossbow, and SIMPLEX. Galaxy aims to provide a reproducible environment for genome informatics accessible to non-technical investigators[1], but offers a vast array of tools beyond those typically used for processing personal genomic data and requires knowledgeable use of its workflow system. Crossbow provides a scalable framework for mapping and variant calling[2], but is limited to the Bowtie suite, while SIMPLEX requires command-line proficiency[3]. Ideally, by our definition, a user-friendly solution would employ a simple, unified graphical user interface for uploading reads, setting parameters, executing analyses, and downloading and visualizing results.

Implementation

Thus, we created STORMSeq (Scalable Tools for Open-source Read Mapping) to fill the need for a user-friendly processing pipeline for personal human whole genome and exome sequence data. STORMSeq utilizes the Amazon Web Services (http://aws.amazon.com) cloud-computing environment for its implementation, and offers an intuitive interface enabling individuals to perform customized read mapping and variant calling with personal genome data. STORMSeq dissociates the backend computational pipeline from the end-user and provides a simplified point-and-click interface for setting high-level parameters, and the system initiates with an optimized default configuration using recent versions of BWA (0.7.5a) and GATK Lite (2.1) as of 11/1/13. Users can then access final processed data and visualize summary statistics without having to load the data into a statistical software package. STORMSeq is a highly secure system entirely encapsulated within the user's Amazon account space, thereby ensuring that only the user has the ability to gain or grant access to their genetic data and results.

STORMSeq's cloud-based architecture is illustrated in Figure 1. The user uploads their reads in FASTQ or BAM formats to Amazon S3 (Simple Scalable Storage) through a graphical interface provided by Amazon Web Services. The STORMSeq website (www.stormseq.org) provides instructions for starting the STORMSeq webserver machine image (AMI v1.0: ami-b35b7cda) within the Amazon cloud computing environment. This STORMSeq webserver is then the entry point for the user to choose software packages and set parameters for the analysis (Figure S1). The system currently offers a complete short read processing pipeline, including:

- Read mapping software packages, including BWA[4], BWA-MEM[5], and SNAP[6]
- Read cleaning pipeline with GATK[7]
- Variant (SNP and indel) calling packages, GATK and Samtools[8]
- Annotation using VEP[9]

The system backend is modular, and designed to be easily expandable by researchers wishing to add additional functionality or incorporate other software packages.

Once the user has set the relevant parameters (or uses the default set provided) and clicked "GO," the system starts a compute cluster on the Amazon Elastic Compute Cloud (with the number of machines started related to the number of files

uploaded and whether exome or genome analyses are selected) and runs the relevant software. The use of the software is free, and the user simply pays for compute time and storage on the Amazon servers, which as of 11/1/13 (for spot instances) costs $0.026 per hour for the (large) systems required for BWA, and $0.14 per hour for the (quadruple extra-large) high-memory systems required for SNAP, and $0.095 per GB-month for persistent storage of reads and variant call results. As the pipeline progresses, a progress bar is updated on the webserver and once the pipeline is finished, summary statistics, such as depth of coverage and other variant information, and visualizations using ggbio[10] and d3[11], are displayed on the webserver (Figure 2). Processing is parallelized where possible using Starcluster (http://mit.edu/star/cluster) and Sun Grid Engine. The results are then uploaded back to Amazon S3 for persistent storage.

Results and Discussion

We tested the STORMSeq system using two paired-end 100 bp read datasets: a personal genome sequence dataset with 1.1B reads (approximately 38X coverage), and a personal exome sequence data set with 90M reads (approximately 45X coverage; available in STORMSeq's demo functionality). For the personal exome data, the pipeline cost approximately $2 USD using spot pricing and took 10 hours using BWA and 5 hours using SNAP (Table 1; Figure S2). For personal genome sequence data, BWA and SNAP

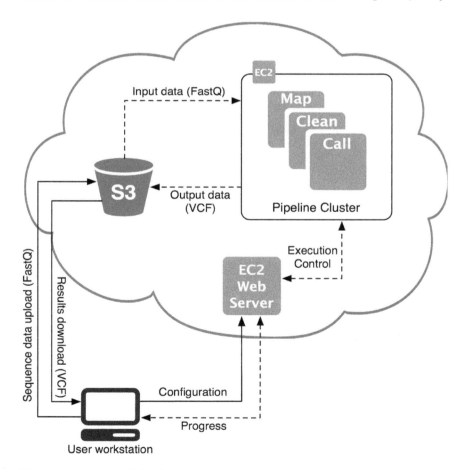

Figure 1. Overview of the STORMSeq system. The user uploads short reads to Amazon S3 and starts a webserver on Amazon EC2, which controls the mapping and variant calling pipeline. Progress can be monitored on the webserver and results are uploaded to persistent storage on Amazon S3.

A

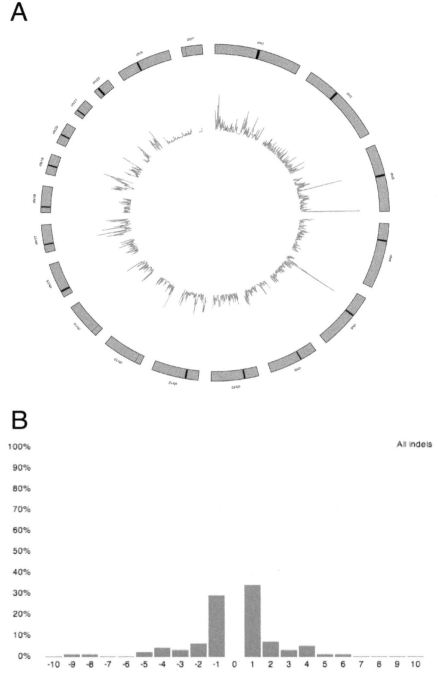

B

100%   All indels

90%

80%

70%

60%

50%

40%

30%

20%

10%

0%
   -10 -9 -8 -7 -6 -5 -4 -3 -2 -1 0 1 2 3 4 5 6 7 8 9 10

Figure 2. Sample output. STORMSeq provides basic visualization for summary statistics, such as (A) genome-wide SNP density and (B) size distribution of short indels.

took 176 and 82 hours for processing, respectively, and each at a cost of approximately $30 USD (Table 1; Figure S3). Note that these values do not include storage costs, and are highly dependent on a number of factors, including the number and size of files provided by the user, as the software dynamically determines a cluster size based on this information. Additionally, STORMSeq was developed to support current cost savings of spot instances, and so, on-demand costs for the pipeline are much higher (Table 1).

We offer STORMSeq free for public use, where users pay only for compute time on the Amazon cloud. The source code for the STORMSeq software is available for download from www.github. com/konradjk/stormseq under an open-source license. We expect that the majority of STORMSeq users will be individuals from academia and the broader lay public interested in analyzing personal genomic information. In addition, those without access to large computing clusters, such as clinicians wishing to process patient data for clinical studies, as well as small research groups

Table 1. Approximate costs for STORMSeq.

Analysis Type	Exome		Genome	
Pipeline	SNAP	BWA	SNAP	BWA
Cost (Spot)	$2.26	$1.90	$26.42	$32.76
Cost (On-demand)	$19.68	$8.16	$254.20	$129.12
Time	5 h	10 h	176 h	98 h

Note that these costs are approximate and may depend on a number of factors related to the input files.

with genome sequence projects may seek to use the system to process genomic data for their patients and subjects. The system is modular and can be easily expanded and integrated with other tools. In the future, it will be crucial to integrate such tools with genome interpretation services, such as Interpretome[12].

Supporting Information

Figure S1 The STORMSeq webserver allows users to set parameters and start the pipeline using a graphical interface.

Figure S2 Time and cost estimates (spot pricing) for a personal exome sequence (90M reads, or 45X coverage)

for BWA (red) and SNAP (blue). These figures are estimates only and results may vary. The merged step includes initial aligned BAMs, while final includes cleaned, sorted, and re-calibrated BAMs, as well as annotated variant calls (VCF). The stats step includes GATK's VariantEval and other VCF statistics, and depth is the completed GATK's DepthOfCoverage process.

Figure S3 Time and cost estimates for a personal genome sequence (1.1B reads, or 38X coverage) for BWA (red) and SNAP (blue). These figures are estimates only and results may vary. The merged step includes initial aligned BAMs, while final includes cleaned, sorted, and re-calibrated BAMs, as well as annotated variant calls (VCF). The stats step includes GATK's VariantEval and other VCF statistics, and depth is the completed GATK's DepthOfCoverage process.

Acknowledgments

We would like to acknowledge the individuals who helped in the design of the system at the BioCurious hackathon in July 2012, in particular David Dehghan for his insights on cloud computing.

Author Contributions

Conceived and designed the experiments: KJK GHF ARM NPT JTD. Performed the experiments: KJK GHF ARM JTD. Contributed reagents/materials/analysis tools: KJK GHF ARM MS NPT JTD. Wrote the paper: KJK JTD.

References

1. Goecks J, Nekrutenko A, Taylor J, Galaxy Team (2010) Galaxy: a comprehensive approach for supporting accessible, reproducible, and transparent computational research in the life sciences. Genome Biol 11: R86. doi:10.1186/gb-2010-11-8-r86.

2. Langmead B, Schatz MC, Lin J, Pop M, Salzberg SL (2009) Searching for SNPs with cloud computing. Genome Biol 10: R134. doi:10.1186/gb-2009-10-11-r134.

3. Fischer M, Snajder R, Pabinger S, Dander A, Schossig A, et al. (2012) SIMPLEX: cloud-enabled pipeline for the comprehensive analysis of exome sequencing data. PLoS ONE 7: e41948. doi:10.1371/journal.pone.0041948.

4. Li H, Durbin R (2009) Fast and accurate short read alignment with Burrows-Wheeler transform. Bioinformatics 25: 1754–1760. doi:10.1093/bioinformatics/btp324.

5. Li H (2013) Aligning sequence reads, clone sequences and assembly contigs with BWA-MEM. arXiv.

6. Faster and More Accurate Sequence Alignment with SNAP (2011) Faster and More Accurate Sequence Alignment with SNAP. arXiv.

7. DePristo MA, Banks E, Poplin R, Garimella KV, Maguire JR, et al. (2011) A framework for variation discovery and genotyping using next-generation DNA sequencing data. Nat Genet 43: 491–498. doi:10.1038/ng.806.

8. Li H, Handsaker B, Wysoker A, Fennell T, Ruan J, et al. (2009) The Sequence Alignment/Map format and SAMtools. Bioinformatics 25: 2078–2079. doi:10.1093/bioinformatics/btp352.

9. McLaren W, Pritchard B, Rios D, Chen Y, Flicek P, et al. (2010) Deriving the consequences of genomic variants with the Ensembl API and SNP Effect Predictor. Bioinformatics 26: 2069–2070. doi:10.1093/bioinformatics/btq330.

10. Yin T, Cook D, Lawrence M (2012) ggbio: an R package for extending the grammar of graphics for genomic data. Genome Biology 13: R77. doi:10.1186/gb-2012-13-8-r77.

11. Bostock M, Ogievetsky V, Heer J (2011) D³ Data-Driven Documents. Visualization and Computer Graphics, IEEE Transactions on 17: 2301–2309. doi:10.1109/TVCG.2011.185.

12. Karczewski KJ, Tirrell RP, Cordero P, Tatonetti NP, Dudley JT, et al. (2012) Interpretome: a freely available, modular, and secure personal genome interpretation engine. Pac Symp Biocomput: 339–350.

3

Evolution Characteristics of the Network Core in the Facebook

Jian-Guo Liu[1]*, Zhuo-Ming Ren[1,2], Qiang Guo[1], Duan-Bing Chen[2,3]

1 Research Center of Complex Systems Science, University of Shanghai for Science and Technology, Shanghai, People's Republic of China, **2** Department of Physics, University of Fribourg, Chemin du Musée 3, Fribourg, Switzerland, **3** Web Sciences Center, University of Electronic Science and Technology of China, Chengdu, People's Republic of China

Abstract

Statistical properties of the static networks have been extensively studied. However, online social networks are evolving dynamically, understanding the evolving characteristics of the core is one of major concerns in online social networks. In this paper, we empirically investigate the evolving characteristics of the Facebook core. Firstly, we separate the Facebook-link(FL) and Facebook-wall(FW) datasets into 28 snapshots in terms of timestamps. By employing the k-core decomposition method to identify the core of each snapshot, we find that the core sizes of the FL and FW networks approximately contain about 672 and 373 nodes regardless of the exponential growth of the network sizes. Secondly, we analyze evolving topological properties of the core, including the k-core value, assortative coefficient, clustering coefficient and the average shortest path length. Empirical results show that nodes in the core are getting more interconnected in the evolving process. Thirdly, we investigate the life span of nodes belonging to the core. More than 50% nodes stay in the core for more than one year, and 19% nodes always stay in the core from the first snapshot. Finally, we analyze the connections between the core and the whole network, and find that nodes belonging to the core prefer to connect nodes with high k-core values, rather than the high degrees ones. This work could provide new insights into the online social network analysis.

Editor: Satoru Hayasaka, Wake Forest School of Medicine, United States of America

Funding: This work is partially supported by Natural Science Foundation of China (NSFC, 61374177, 71371125, and 71171136), the Ministry Of Education (MOE) Project of Humanities and Social Science (13YJA630023), and the Shanghai First-class Academic Discipline Project (S1201YLXK). The funders had no role in study design, data collection and analysis, decision to publish, or preparation of the manuscript.

Competing Interests: The authors have declared that no competing interests exist.

* Email: liujg004@ustc.edu.cn

Introduction

Online social networks are organized around participating users who create interactions with whom they associate [1–3]. As online social networks are gaining more attentions, more than a billion people have been integrated to make friends, communicate with friends, share interests, spread ideas and so on [4,5]. An in-depth investigation of the evolving network core is very important for deeply understanding the evolving characteristics of online social networks [6,7], where the core could be identified by the k-core decomposition method [8]. Carmi *et al.* [9], Zhang *et al.* [10], and Orsini *et al.* [11] investigated the topological properties of the internet at the autonomous system level, and found that the internet core was a small and well connected subgroup, specifically its size was approximately stable over time. Kitsak *et al.* [12] employed the k-core decomposition method to identify the most influential spreaders which is defined as the nodes with the highest k-core value(i.e. core). Miorandi *et al.* [13], Ren *et al.* [14] extended the k-core decomposition method to identify the node spreading influence in networks, and Garas *et al.* [15] presented a generalized method for calculating the k-core structure of weighted networks. These works have similar conclusions that nodes belonging to the core are the most influential spreaders. Regarding to the internet network analysis, little attention has been paid to the core properties of the online social networks. In this paper, we empirically analyze the evolution characteristics of

the Facebook's core, and the statistical results indicate that (1) The core sizes of the Facebook-link(FL) and Facebook-wall(FW) networks are approximately stable around 672 nodes and 373 nodes respectively. (2) Nodes belonging to the core get more interconnected, and their k-core values increase correspondingly. (3) The life span analysis of the nodes belonging to the core reveals that more than 50% nodes stay in the core for more than one year, and 19% nodes always stay in the core from the first snapshot. (4) The nodes in the core prefer to connect to high k-core nodes, regardless of the high degree ones.

Materials and Methods

Datasets

The Facebook datasets [16] are investigated in this paper, which consist of two different components. The first one is the Facebook-link(FL) that spans from September 5, 2006 to January 22, 2009. The timestamp of each link indicates the time when one pair of users become friends. The other one is the Facebook-wall(FW) that spans from September 14, 2004 to January 22, 2009. It should be noticed that a user can post comments on his/her friends' walls, and these comments can be seen by visitors. In this paper, we treat these interactions as undirect links. The information of each link in the FW network consists three parts: The wall owner, the user who posted and the corresponding posted time. In order to compare the evolution characteristics of the network core between the FL and FW networks, the period investigated in this paper is set from September 2006 to December 2008.

Firstly, we separate the FL network into pieces with the interval of one month. Since approximately 41% timestamps of links could not be determined, we set this kind of links as the initial network S_0. The first piece S_1 is set from September 1, 2006 to September 30, 2006. The second one S_2 is set from October 1, 2006 to October 31, 2006, and the last one S_{28} is set from December 1, 2008 to December 31, 2008. Based on the initial network S_0 and 28 pieces, we can construct 28 corresponding snapshots. The first snapshot is defined by merging S_0 and S_1. The second one consists of S_0, S_1 and S_2. The last one consists of the initial network S_0 and all pieces $S_1, S_2, \cdots$ and S_{28}. Similarly, the FW network can also be separated into 28 snapshots. It is emphasized that in the FW network, the initial network S_0 corresponds to September 14, 2004 to August 31, 2006.

Methods

Identifying the network core has been extensively investigated [9–13, 15, 17–19]. For example, the core might be defined as the set of all nodes with degree higher than some threshold. But this method requires setting a free parameter, the degree threshold. Other methods [18] like k-clique, k-clan and some improved methods based k-core methods like k-dense [11], Medusa-model [9] are used to identify the AS network core. In this paper, we focus on investigating the set of most influential nodes in online social networks, which is defined as the nodes with the highest k-core value [12]. We employ the k-core decomposition method to obtain the cores of different snapshots. The k-core decomposition method could be implemented as shown in Fig. 1. Firstly, remove all 1-degree nodes, and then keep pruning these nodes until no more such nodes remaining, the remained nodes form the node set named 2-core. In the similar manner, repeat the pruning process in a similar way for other nodes in the network which have assigned to the corresponding cores(denoted as k_s). The nodes with the largest k-core value is defined as the network core.

The following definitions are given to analyze the evolutional characteristics. The relative growth rate $\rho(t)$ is defined to measure the core growth comparing with the network growth.

$$\rho(t) = \frac{\sum_{i=1}^{N(t)} \delta(i,t) - \sum_{i=1}^{N(t-1)} \delta(i,t-1)}{N(t) - N(t-1)}, \quad t = 1, 2, \cdots, 28, \quad (1)$$

where $\delta(i,t) = 1$ if node i exists in the core of the tth snapshot; Otherwise $\delta(i,t) = 0$. $N(t)$ is the number of nodes in the tth snapshot, and $t \in [1,28]$. If $|\rho(t)| = 1$, the size change of the cores is the same as that of the network. If $|\rho(t)| < 1$, the size change of cores is less in compared with that of the network, otherwise $|\rho(t)| > 1$.

To give the life span definition, we need to measure the existing times $L(i)$ and the continues lifetime $M(j, s)$. The existing times $L(i)$ quantifies the number of snapshots that node i exists in the 28 cores. The continues lifetime $M(j, s)$ quantifies the number of nodes staying in the cores from the jth snapshot to the sth one, which could be defined as follows.

$$L(i) = \sum_{t=1}^{t_n} \delta(i,t), \quad (2)$$

$$M(j,s) = \sum_{i=1}^{N(s)} \prod_{t=j}^{s} \delta(i,t). \quad (3)$$

If $L(i) = 0$, the node i never appears in any core, and $L(i) = 28$ means that the node i stays in all 28 cores. $M(j,s) = 1$ means that there is one node stays in the core from the jth snapshot to the sth one, and $M(j,s) \in [0, N(t_n)]$. According the above definitions, we can give the distribution $P(L)$ of the existing times $L(i)$ and the distribution $P(M)$ of the nodes who exists in the cores from the tth snapshot to the last one.

$$P(L) = \frac{L}{\sum_{L=1}^{28} L}, \quad (4)$$

$$P(M) = \frac{M(t,t_n)}{n(t_n)}, \quad (5)$$

where the $n(t_n)$ is the core size of the last snapshot. To investigate the connection patterns from the viewpoints of the k-core(k_s) and the degree(k), the correlation between the k_s value of the core element and the k_s values of its neighbors and corresponding $P(k,t)$ are defined as follows.

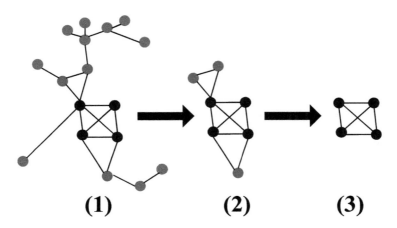

(1)   **(2)**   **(3)**

Figure 1. (Color online) Illustration of k-core decomposition. (1) is 1-core, (2) is 2-core, (3) is 3-core, i.e. core of the network.

$$P(k_s,t) = \frac{\sum_{j=1}^{N(t)} k_s(j,t)}{\sum_{i=1}^{n(t)} k(i,t)}, \qquad (6)$$

$$P(k,t) = \frac{\sum_{j=1}^{N(t)} k(j,t)}{\sum_{i=1}^{n(t)} k(i,t)}, \qquad (7)$$

where $k_s(j,t)$ is the k_s value of node j in the tth snapshot. $k(j,t)$ is the degree of node j in the tth snapshot. The node j is one of the core neighbors. $k(i,t)$ is the degree of the core node i in the tth snapshot. The $n(t)$ is the core size of the tth snapshot.

Additional methods

The properties of the core including assortative coefficient ($r(t)$) [23], clustering coefficient ($c(t)$) [24], and the average shortest path lengths ($l(t)$) are detailed as follows. The assortative coefficient is a measure of the likelihood for nodes which connect to other nodes with similar degrees. A general measure of assortative coefficient is given by [23].

$r(t) =$

$$\frac{E(t)^{-1}\sum_i j(i,t)h(i,t) - [E(t)^{-1}\sum_i \frac{1}{2}(j(i,t)+h(i,t))]^2}{E(t)^{-1}\sum_i \frac{1}{2}(j(i,t)^2+h(i,t)^2) - [E(t)^{-1}\sum_i \frac{1}{2}(j(i,t)+h(i,t))]^2}, \qquad (8)$$

where $j(i,t)$, $h(i,t)$ are the degrees of the nodes of the ith link in the core of the tth snapshot, for $i = 1,2,\ldots,E(t)$. The assortative coefficient value ranges between -1 and 1. By construction, this formula yields $r=0$ when the amount of assortative mixing is the same as that expected independently at random i. A positive assortative coefficient value means that nodes tend to connect to the nodes with similar degree, while a negative assortative coefficient value means that nodes likely connect to nodes with very different degrees from their own.

The clustering coefficient is calculated as follows [24],

$$c(t) = \frac{1}{n(t)}$$

$$\sum_{i=1}^{n(t)} \frac{\text{(number of pairs of neighbors of } i \text{ that are connected)}}{\text{(number of pairs of neighbors of } i\text{)}}. \qquad (9)$$

To understand how the shortest path lengths of the network core change in the evolving process, the average shortest path lengths l is used to express as follows.

$$l(t) = \frac{\sum_{i \neq j} d(i,j,t)}{n(t)}. \qquad (10)$$

where $d(i,j,t)$ is the shortest path distance between node i and j in the core of the tth snapshot.

Results

The size stability of the core

As shown in Fig. 2(a), the sizes of the FL and FW networks grow exponentially with $N(t) \sim 10^{\lambda t}$, where the parameters λ are 0.078 and 0.028 respectively. However, as shown in Fig. 2(b), the core sizes of the FL and FW networks are approximately stable over time. The core relative growth rate $\rho(t)$ of both the FW and the FL(after $March-07$) networks fluctuate around zero with time when is as shown in Fig. 2(c). In addition as shown in Tab. 1, we statistics the average core size $\bar{n}$ which are equal to 672 and 373 respectively, and the average core relative growth rate value $\bar{\rho}$ which are equal to 0.040 and 0.009 respectively. That is to say, the size of the core keep stable comparing with the rapid growth of the whole network. Our results suggest that as the Facebook becomes increasingly popular and attracts more and more users, the size of the network grows fast, while the size of core still maintains a stable level.

The evolving topological properties of the core

From Fig. 3, we could find that the k_s values of cores increase quickly, which indicates that the nodes of cores connect each other more closely. Figure 4 presents the evolving topological properties of the core. In Fig. 4(a), the assortative coefficient $r(t)$ of the FL core is always lower than 0.05, while the $r(t)$ of the FW core keeps decreasing from 0.25 to 0. The results indicate that the users in the Facebook core choose friends to post their comments in walls of their friends independently. They do not care their friends who have be or not be most popular or influential. From Fig. 4(b), one can find that the clustering coefficient $c(t)$ gets larger with time, which indicates the core becomes more interconnected. As shown in Figure 4(c), the shortest path lengths of core gently decreases to 3 in the FL network, and to 4.5 in the FW network as time varying. The decreasing trend also manifests that the core is becoming more interconnected over time.

The life span of nodes in the core

Figure 5(a) shows the distribution of the existing times $P(L)$, which has a 'U' shaped feature. There are lots of nodes whose existing times are less than 6 or more than 24. Meanwhile, we analyze the number of nodes that stay in the core from one snapshot to last snapshot. Figure 5(b) indicates that over 50% nodes stay in the core for more than one year, and 19% nodes always stay in the core from the first snapshot. We suggest that when the Facebook quickly becomes popular and attracts large amounts of users, the most influential and active users will inhabit in the Facebook core for long time.

The connections between the nodes of core and their neighbors

Online social interactions have provided plentiful evidence of their influence for information diffusion. Unfortunately, it is difficult to understand the tendency for individuals who connect to friends with similar tastes or popular preferences [20]. A well-known tendency is that new connections are made preferentially to more popular nodes [21]. Nonetheless, Papadopoulos et al. [22] pointed out that the connections should be formed by the trade-off optimization between the popularity and similarity. Here we analyze the core connections from the viewpoints of the k_s values and degree respectively. As shown in Fig. 6(a) and (b), from which we observe that the correlation between the k_s value of the core nodes and the k_s values of its neighbors increases with the k_s values in the FL and FW networks. We could find that the nodes

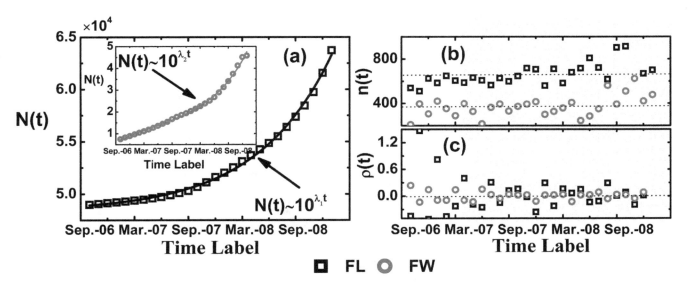

Figure 2. (Color online) Statistical properties of the network size $N(t)$ (a) and the corresponding network core sizes $n(t)$ (b), as well as the relative growth rate $\rho(t)$ (c). (a) The growing tendency of the size $N(t)$ of the FL and FW networks obey an exponential form with exponent $\lambda_1 = 0.078 \pm 0.002$ (inset $\lambda_2 = 0.028 \pm 0.002$). (b) The core sizes $n(t)$ are around 672 and 373. (c) The core relative growth rate $\rho(t)$ fluctuates around 0.

with larger k_s values are more likely to connect to the core. However, as time increasing, the correlation between the k_s value of the core nodes and the k_s values of its neighbors has fallen with the k_s values. Figure 6(c) and (d) show the correlation between the degree k of the core element and the degree of its neighbors, from which we could see that nodes in the network have a high probability to connect to core even if they do not have largest degrees. We could conclude that nodes in the core prefer to connect to nodes with higher k_s values, rather than the degrees ones.

Conclusions and Discussions

In this article, we empirically investigate the evolving characteristics of the core of the Facebook. We separate the Facebook-link(FL) and Facebook-wall(FW) networks into 28 snapshots in terms of timestamps, and employ the k-core decomposition method to identify the core of each snapshot. The empirical results show the number of users grows exponentially in the evolving process, while the core sizes approximately keep stable levels about 672 and 373 for the FL and FW networks respectively. We also analyze topological properties of the core including the k_s values, assortative coefficient $r(t)$, clustering coefficient $c(t)$ and the average shortest path length $l(t)$ versus time t. The k_s values of cores increase quickly. The assortative coefficient $r(t)$ of the FL

core is always lower than 0.05, while the $r(t)$ of the FW core keeps decreasing from 0.25 to 0. The clustering coefficient $c(t)$ gets larger with time, which indicates the core becomes more interconnected. The shortest path length of core gently decreases from 3.5 to 3 in the FL network and from 5.7 to 4.5 in the FW network. From these topological properties of the core, we could conclude that the users in the core become more interconnected. Furthermore, we analyze the life span of nodes belonging to the core. The distribution of the existing times $P(L)$ indicates that there are lots of nodes whose existing times are less than 6 or more than 24. Specially the distribution of the continues lifetime $P(M,t)$ indicates that more than 50% nodes stay in the core for more than one year, and 19% nodes always belong to the core from the first snapshot. We estimated that the most influential users stay in the Facebook core for a long time. Finally, we analyze the connections of individuals in the core. The correlations between the k_s value(k) of the core element and the $k_s(k)$ values of its neighbors indicate that the users in core prefer to make interactions with network users with higher k-core values, regardless of the high degree ones.

Our analysis only focused on the evolutional characteristics of the network core in the Facebook, but some additional researches are necessary to complete our findings. First, in this paper, we investigate the evolution properties of the Facebook core with the time interval one month. However, the identification of the network core is affected by the time interval, therefore we also

Table 1. The comparisons between the results obtained by the time interval two month (14 snapshots) and the ones obtained by only one month (28 snapshots).

Parameters	λ		$\bar{n}$		$\bar{\rho}$	
Time Interval	1	2	1	2	1	2
FL	0.078	0.076	672	673	0.040	0.06
FW	0.028	0.030	373	377	0.009	−0.003

The average value $\bar{n}$ is defined as $\bar{n} = \Sigma_{t=1} n(t)/28$; The average value $\bar{\rho}$ is defined as $\bar{\rho} = \Sigma_{t=1} \rho(t)/28$.

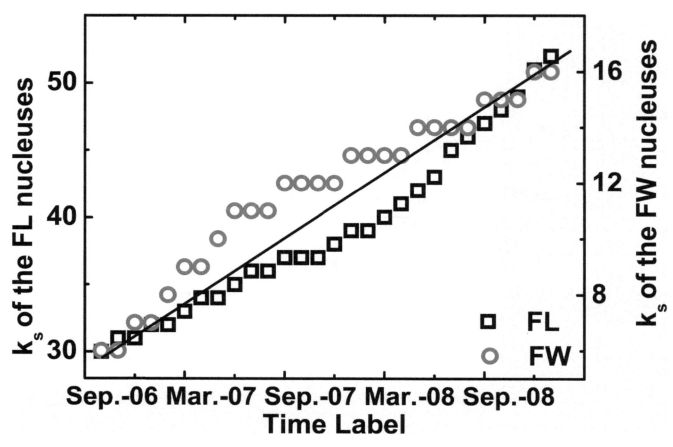

Figure 3. (Color online) The k_s values of each core in the FL and FW networks.

investigated the corresponding results with the time interval two month as shown in the Fig. 7 and Tab. 1, and find that the core size, relative growth rate and other statistical characteristics are robust with the time interval, which suggests that the results obtained in the paper is independent with the time interval. It also should be emphasized that the interactions in online social networks are evolving rapidly, therefore, how to model the temporal relationship between each pair of users and identify the corresponding network core is still an open question for the online

social network analysis.Second, although the k-core definition of the undirect network core is parameter-free and effective to implement, a lot of online social networks are directed weighted networks which are not suitable for the implementation of the k-core decomposition method. To further validate the work presented here, our work will develop a reliable identification of core for directed weighted networks.

In addition, our research could supple some important criteria for modeling the core of the online social networks. In a broader

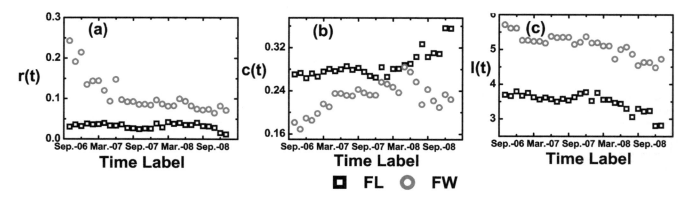

Figure 4. (Color online) The topological properties of the cores. (a) the assortative coefficient $r(t)$ is decreasing from 0.25 to 0.1 in the FL network, and fluctuating around 0.05. (b) the average clustering coefficient $c(t)$ is increasing slightly. (c) the average shortest path length of the core $l(t)$ are decreasing from 3.5 to 3 in the FL network and from 5.7 to 4.5 in the FW network.

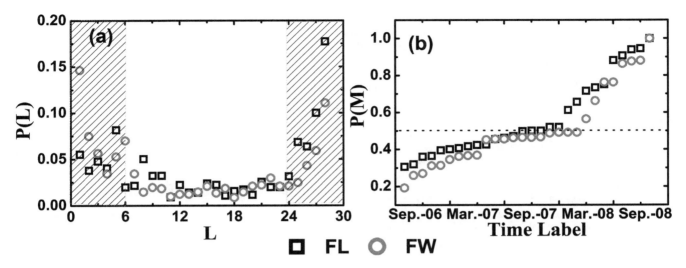

Figure 5. (Color online) The life span of nodes staying in the cores. (a) The distribution P(L) has 'U' shaped feature. There are lots of nodes whose existing times are less than 6 or more than 24, and less users whose existing times are larger than 6 and smaller than 24. (b) The distribution P(M) of the nodes who exists in the cores from the tth snapshot to the last one. There are more than 50% nodes belong to the cores for more than one year, 19% nodes always belong to the cores from the first snapshot.

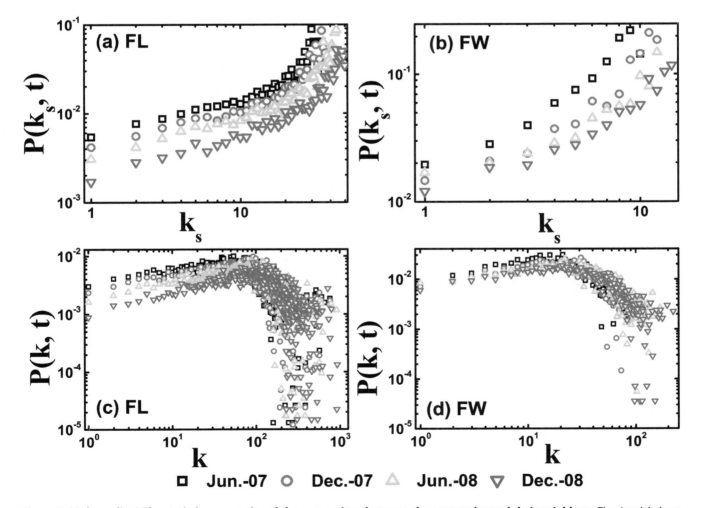

Figure 6. (Color online) The statistics properties of the connections between the core nodes and their neighbors. The time labels are set to Jun. 2007, Dec. 2007, Jun. 2008, and Dec. 2008 which are interval of six months. [(a) and (b)] The correlation between the k_s value of the core element and the k_s values of its neighbors increases with the k_s values in the FL and FW networks. [(c) and (d)] The correlation between the degree k of the core element and the degree of its neighbors, from which we could see that nodes in the network have a high probability to connect to core even if they have not largest degrees.

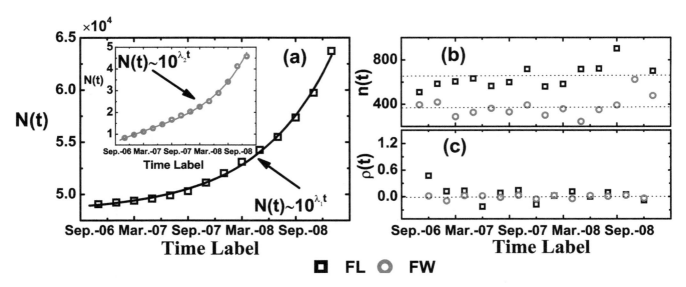

Figure 7. (Color online) Statistical properties of the network size *N(t)* (a) and the corresponding network core sizes *n(t)* (b), as well as the relative growth rate *p(t)* (c). (a) The growing tendency of the size *N(t)* of the FL and FW networks obey an exponential form with exponent $\lambda_1 = 0.076 \pm 0.002$ (inset $\lambda_2 = 0.030 \pm 0.002$). (b) The core sizes *n(t)* are around 672 and 373. (c) The core relative growth rate *p*(t) fluctuates around 0.

context, our work may be relevant to construct dynamical core model to understand the evolution of the online social network core deeply. User interactions on the online social networks also affect the user behaviors, thus the user behaviors should not just consider the influence of the online societies, but also the influence of offline societies. Specially, the offline social influence could change the user behavior, and then may cause users to leave, which may trigger further leaves of others who lost connections to their friends. This may lead to cascades of users leaving and change the online social network topological structures dramatically. Hence, How to quantify the influence of the offline societies

in these online systems can also be an interesting and important open problem.

Acknowledgments

We acknowledge Dr Tsikerdekis M. for his assistance.

Author Contributions

Conceived and designed the experiments: JGL ZMR. Performed the experiments: ZMR. Analyzed the data: JGL ZMR QG. Wrote the paper: JGL ZMR QG DBC.

References

1. Centola D (2010) The spread of behavior in an online social network experiment. Science 329: 1194–1197.
2. Goel S, Watts DJ, Goldstein DG (2012) The structure of online diffusion networks. In Proceedings of the 13th ACM Conference on Electronic Commerce. pp 623–638.
3. Ugander J, Backstrom L, Marlow C, Kleinberg J (2012) Structural diversity in social contagion. Proc Natl Acad Sci USA 109: 5962–5966.
4. Williams AL, Merten MJ (2008) A review of online social networking profiles by adolescents: Implications for future research and intervention. Adolescence 43: 253–274.
5. Onnela JP, Reed-Tsochas F (2010) Spontaneous emergence of social influence in online systems. Proc Natl Acad Sci USA 107: 18375–18380.
6. Wilson RE, Gosling SD, Graham LT (2012) A review of Facebook research in the social sciences. Perspectives on Psychological Science 7: 203–220.
7. Ellison NB (2007) Social network sites: Definition, history, and scholarship. Journal of Computer-Mediated Communication 13: 210–230.
8. Seidman SB (1983) Network structure and minimum degree. Social networks 5: 269–287.
9. Carmi S, Havlin S, Kirkpatrick S, Shavitt Y, Shir E (2007) A model of Internet topology using k-shell decomposition. Proc Natl Acad Sci USA 104: 11150–11154.
10. Zhang GQ, Zhang GQ, Yang QF, Cheng SQ, Zhou T (2008) Evolution of the Internet and its cores. New J Phys 10: 123027.
11. Orsini C, Gregori E, Lenzini L, Krioukov D (2013) Evolution of the Internet k-Dense structure. Networking, IEEE/ACM Transactions on 99: 1.
12. Kitsak M, Gallos LK, Havlin S, Liljeros F, Muchnik L, et al. (2010) Identification of influential spreaders in complex networks. Nat Phys 6: 888–893.
13. Miorandi D, De Pellegrini F (2010) K-shell decomposition for dynamic complex networks. In Modeling and Optimization in Mobile, Ad Hoc and Wireless Networks (WiOpt), 2010 Proceedings of the 8th International Symposium on. pp 488–496.
14. Ren ZM, Zeng A, Chen DB, Liao H, Liu JG (2014) Iterative resource allocation for ranking spreaders in complex networks. Europhys Lett 106: 48005.
15. Garas A, Schweitzer F, Havlin S (2012) A k-shell decomposition method for weighted networks. New J Phys 14: 083030.
16. Viswanath B, Mislove A, Cha M, Gummadi KP (2009) On the evolution of user interaction in facebook. In Proceedings of the 2nd ACM workshop on Online social networks. pp 37–42.
17. Feige U, Peleg D, Kortsarz G (2001) The dense k-subgraph problem. Algorithmica 29: 410–421.
18. Palla G, Barabási A L, Vicsek T (2007) Quantifying social group evolution. Nature 446: 664–667.
19. Siganos G, Tauro SL, Faloutsos M (2006) Jellyfish: A conceptual model for the as internet topology. Journal of Communications and Networks 8: 339–350.
20. Aral S, Muchnik L, Sundararajan A (2009) Distinguishing influence-based contagion from homophily-driven diffusion in dynamic networks. Proc Natl Acad Sci USA 106: 21544–21549.
21. Barabási AL, Albert R (1999) Emergence of scaling in random networks. Science 286: 509–512.
22. Papadopoulos F, Kitsak M, Serrano MA, Boguna M, Krioukov D (2012) Popularity versus similarity in growing networks. Nature 489: 537–540.
23. Newman MEJ (2002) Assortative mixing in networks. Phys Rev Lett 89: 208701.
24. Watts DJ, Strogatz SH (1998) Collective dynamics of 'small-world' networks. Nature 393: 440–442.

4

Unraveling Spurious Properties of Interaction Networks with Tailored Random Networks

Stephan Bialonski[1,2,3]*, **Martin Wendler**[4], **Klaus Lehnertz**[1,2,3]

1 Department of Epileptology, University of Bonn, Bonn, Germany, **2** Helmholtz Institute for Radiation and Nuclear Physics, University of Bonn, Bonn, Germany, **3** Interdisciplinary Center for Complex Systems, University of Bonn, Bonn, Germany, **4** Fakultät für Mathematik, Ruhr-Universität Bochum, Bochum, Germany

Abstract

We investigate interaction networks that we derive from multivariate time series with methods frequently employed in diverse scientific fields such as biology, quantitative finance, physics, earth and climate sciences, and the neurosciences. Mimicking experimental situations, we generate time series with finite length and varying frequency content but from independent stochastic processes. Using the correlation coefficient and the maximum cross-correlation, we estimate interdependencies between these time series. With clustering coefficient and average shortest path length, we observe unweighted interaction networks, derived via thresholding the values of interdependence, to possess non-trivial topologies as compared to Erdös-Rényi networks, which would indicate small-world characteristics. These topologies reflect the mostly unavoidable finiteness of the data, which limits the reliability of typically used estimators of signal interdependence. We propose random networks that are tailored to the way interaction networks are derived from empirical data. Through an exemplary investigation of multichannel electroencephalographic recordings of epileptic seizures – known for their complex spatial and temporal dynamics – we show that such random networks help to distinguish network properties of interdependence structures related to seizure dynamics from those spuriously induced by the applied methods of analysis.

Editor: Michal Zochowski, University of Michigan, United States of America

Funding: MW and SB were supported by the German National Academic Foundation. SB and KL acknowledge support from the German Science Foundation (LE 660/4-2). The funders had no role in study design, data collection and analysis, decision to publish, or preparation of the manuscript.

Competing Interests: The authors have declared that no competing interests exist.

* E-mail: bialonski@gmx.net

Introduction

The last years have seen an extraordinary success of network theory and its applications in diverse disciplines, ranging from sociology, biology, earth and climate sciences, quantitative finance, to physics and the neurosciences [1–4]. There is now growing evidence that research into the dynamics of complex systems profits from a network perspective. Within this framework, complex systems are considered to be composed of interacting subsystems. This view has been adopted in a large number of modeling studies and empirical studies. It is usually assumed that the complex system under study can be described by an *interaction network*, whose nodes represent subsystems and whose links represent interactions between them. Interaction networks derived from empirical data (multivariate time series) have been repeatedly studied in climate science (climate networks, see [5–9] and references therein), in seismology (earthquake networks, see, e.g., [10–13]), in quantitative finance (financial networks, see e.g. [14–18] and references therein), and in the neurosciences (brain functional networks, see [19,20] for an overview). Many interaction networks have been reported to possess non-trivial properties such as small-world architectures, community structures, or hubs (nodes with high centrality), all of which have been considered to be characteristics of the dynamics of the complex system.

When analyzing empirical data one is faced with the challenge of defining nodes and inferring links from multivariate noisy time series with only a limited number of data points due to stationarity requirements. Different approaches varying to some degree across disciplines have been proposed. For most approaches, each single time series is associated with a node and inference of links is based on time series analysis techniques. Bivariate time series analysis methods, such as the correlation coefficient, are used as estimators of signal interdependence which is assumed to be indicative of an interaction between different subsystems. Inferring links from estimates of signal interdependence can be achieved in different ways. Weighted interaction networks can be derived by considering estimated values of signal interdependence (sometimes mapped via some function) as link weights. Since methods characterizing unweighted networks are well-established and readily available, such networks are more frequently derived from empirical data. Besides approaches based on constructing minimum spanning trees (see, e.g., reference [14]), on significance testing [21–23], or on rank-ordered network growth (see, e.g., reference [15]), a common practice pursued in many disciplines is to choose a threshold above which an estimated value of signal interdependence is converted into a link ("thresholding", see, e.g., references [5,12,16,20]). Following this approach, the resulting unweighted interaction networks have been repeatedly investigated employing various networks characteristics, among which we mention the widely-used clustering coefficient C and average shortest path length L to assess a potential small-world characteristic, and the node degrees in order to identify hubs.

As studies employing the network approach grow in numbers, the question arises as to how informative reported results are with respect to the investigated dynamical systems. To address this issue, properties of interaction networks are typically compared to those obtained from network null models. Most frequently, Erdös-Rényi random networks [24] or random networks with a predefined degree distribution [25,26] serve as null models; network properties that deviate from those obtained from the null model are considered to be characteristic of the investigated dynamical system. Only in a few recent studies, results obtained from network analyses have been questioned in relation to various assumptions underlying the network analysis approach. Problems pointed out include: incomplete data sets and observational errors in animal social network studies [27]; representation issues and questionable use of statistics in biological networks (see [28] and references therein); challenging node and link identification in the neurosciences [29–31]; the issue of spatial sampling of complex systems [31–33]. This calls not only for a careful interpretation of results but also for the development of appropriate null models that incorporate knowledge about the way networks are derived from empirical data.

We study – from the perspective of field data analysis – a fundamental assumption underlying the network approach, namely that the multivariate time series are obtained from interacting dynamical processes and are thus well represented by a model of mutual relationships (i.e., an interaction network). Visual inspection of empirical time series typically reveals a perplexing variety of characteristics ranging from fluctuations on different time scales to quasi-periodicity suggestive of different types of dynamics. Moreover, empirical time series are inevitably noisy and finite leading to a limited reliability of estimators of signal interdependencies. This is aggravated with the advent of time-resolved network analyses where a good temporal resolution often comes at the cost of diminished statistics. Taken together, it is not surprising that the suitability of the network approach is notoriously difficult to judge prior to analysis.

We here employ the above-mentioned thresholding-approach to construct interaction networks for which we estimate signal interdependence with the frequently used correlation coefficient and the maximum cross correlation. We derive these networks, however, from multivariate time series of finite length that are generated by independent (non-interacting) processes which would a priori not advocate the notion of a representation by a model of mutual relationships. In simulation studies we investigate often used network properties (clustering coefficient, average shortest path length, number of connected components). We observe that network properties can deviate pronouncedly from those observed in Erdös-Rényi networks depending on the length and the spectral content of the multivariate time series. We address the question whether similar dependencies can also be observed in empirical data by investigating multichannel electroencephalographic (EEG) recordings of epileptic seizures that are known for their complex spatial and temporal dynamics. Finally, we propose random networks that are tailored to the way interaction networks are derived from multivariate empirical time series.

Methods

Interaction networks are typically derived from N multivariate time series x_i ($i \in \{1, \ldots, N\}$) in two steps. First, by employing some bivariate time series analysis method, interdependence between two time series $x_i(t)$ and $x_j(t)$ ($t \in \{1, \ldots, T\}$) is estimated as an indicator for the strength of interaction between the underlying systems. A multitude of estimators [34–40], which differ in concepts, robustness (e.g., against noise contaminations), and statistical efficiency (i.e., the amount of data required), is available. Studies that aim at deriving interaction networks from

field data frequently employ the absolute value of the linear correlation coefficient to estimate interdependence between two time series. The entries of the correlation matrix $\boldsymbol{\rho}^c$ then read

$$\rho_{ij}^c := \left| T^{-1} \sum_{t=1}^{T} (x_i(t) - \bar{x}_i)(x_j(t) - \bar{x}_j) \hat{\sigma}_i^{-1} \hat{\sigma}_j^{-1} \right| =: \left| corr(x_i, x_j) \right|, (1)$$

where $\bar{x}_i$ and $\hat{\sigma}_i$ denote mean value and the estimated standard deviation of time series x_i. Another well established method to characterize interdependencies is the cross correlation function. Here we use the maximum value of the absolute cross correlation between two time series,

$$\rho_{ij}^m := \max_{\tau} \left\{ \left| \frac{\xi(x_i, x_j)(\tau)}{\sqrt{\xi(x_i, x_i)(0)\xi(x_j, x_j)(0)}} \right| \right\}, (2)$$

with

$$\xi(x_i, x_j)(\tau) := \begin{cases} \sum_{t=1}^{T-\tau} x_i(t+\tau)x_j(t) & , \tau \geq 0 \\ \xi(x_j, x_i)(-\tau) & , \tau < 0 \end{cases} (3)$$

to define the entries of the cross correlation matrix $\boldsymbol{\rho}^m$. As practiced in field data analysis, we normalize the time series to zero mean before pursuing subsequent steps of analysis. Note that ρ_{ij}^m is then the maximum value of the absolute cross covariance function. Both interdependence estimators are symmetric ($\rho_{ij}^c = \rho_{ji}^c$ and $\rho_{ij}^m = \rho_{ji}^m$) and are confined to the interval [0,1]. High values indicate strongly interdependent time series while dissimilar time series result in values close to zero for T sufficiently large.

Second, the adjacency matrix $\mathbf{A}$ representing an unweighted undirected interaction network is derived from $\boldsymbol{\rho}^c$ (or $\boldsymbol{\rho}^m$) by thresholding. For a threshold $\theta \in [0,1]$ entries A_{ij} and A_{ji} of $\mathbf{A}$ are set to 1 (representing an undirected link between nodes i and j) for all entries $\rho_{ij}^c > \theta$ ($\rho_{ij}^m > \theta$, respectively) with $i \neq j$, and to zero (no link) otherwise. In many studies θ is not chosen directly but determined such that the derived network possesses a previously specified mean degree $\bar{k} := N^{-1} \sum_i k_i$, where k_i denotes the degree of i, i.e., the number of links connected to node i. More frequently, θ is chosen such that the network possesses a previously specified link density $\epsilon = \bar{k}(N-1)^{-1}$. We will follow the latter approach and derive networks for fixed values of ϵ.

To characterize a network as defined by $\mathbf{A}$, a plethora of methods have been developed. Among them, the clustering coefficient C and the average shortest path length L are frequently used in field studies. The local clustering coefficient C_i is defined as

$$C_i := \begin{cases} \frac{1}{k_i(k_i-1)} \sum_{j,m} A_{ij}A_{jm}A_{mi}, & \text{if } k_i > 1 \\ 0, & \text{if } k_i \in \{0,1\}. \end{cases} (4)$$

C_i represents the fraction of the number of existing links between neighbors of node i among all possible links between these neighbors [1,2,41]. The clustering coefficient C of the network is defined as the mean of the local clustering coefficients,

$$C := \frac{1}{N} \sum_{i=1}^{N} C_i. (5)$$

C quantifies the local interconnectedness of the network and $C_i, C \in [0,1]$.

The average shortest path length is defined as the average shortest distance between any two nodes,

$$\tilde{L} := \frac{2}{N(N+1)} \sum_{i \leq j} l_{ij}, \qquad (6)$$

and characterizes the overall connectedness of the network. l_{ij} denotes the length of the shortest path between nodes i and j. The definition of the average shortest path length varies across the literature. Like some authors, we here include the distance from each node to itself in the average $(l_{ii} = 0 \forall i)$. Exclusion will, however, just change the value by a constant factor of $(N+1)/(N-1)$.

If a network disintegrates into a number N_c of different connected components, there will be pairs of nodes (i,j), for which no connecting path exists, in which case one usually sets $l_{ij} = \infty$ and thus $\tilde{L} = \infty$. In order to avoid this situation, in some studies l_{ij} in equation (6) is replaced by l_{ij}^{-1}. The quantity defined this way is called efficiency [42,43]. Another approach, which we will follow here and which is frequently used in field studies, is to exclude infinite values of l_{ij} from the average. The average shortest path length then reads

$$L := \frac{1}{|S|} \sum_{(i,j) \in S} l_{ij}, \qquad (7)$$

where

$$S := \{(i,j) | l_{ij} < \infty; i, j = 1, \ldots, N\} \qquad (8)$$

denotes the set of all pairs (i,j) of nodes with finite shortest path. The number of such pairs is given by $|S|$. Note that $L \to 0$ for $N_c \to N$.

In field studies, values of C and L obtained for interaction networks are typically compared with average values obtained from an ensemble of random Erdös-Rényi (ER) networks [24]. Between every pair of nodes is a link with probability ϵ, and links for different pairs exist independently from each other. The expectation value of the clustering coefficient of ER networks is $C_{ER} = \epsilon$ [2]. The dependence of the average shortest path length L_{ER} of ER networks on ϵ and N is more complicated (see references [2,44]). Almost all ER networks are connected, if $\epsilon \gg \ln N/(N-1)$. ER networks with a predefined number of links (and thus link density) can also be generated by successively adding links between randomly chosen pairs of nodes until the predefined number of links is reached. During this process, multiple links between nodes are avoided.

Results

Simulation studies

We consider time series z_i, $i \in \{1, \ldots, N\}$, whose entries $z_i(t)$ are drawn independently from the uniform probability distribution $\mathcal{U}$ on the interval $(0,1)$. We will later study the impact of different lengths T of these random time series on network properties. In order to enable us to study the effects of different spectral contents on network properties, we add the possibility to low-pass filter z_i by considering

$$x_{i,M,T}(t) := M^{-1} \sum_{l=t}^{t+M-1} z_i(l), \qquad z_i(l) \sim \mathcal{U}, \qquad (9)$$

where $t \in \{1, \ldots, T\}$, and $1 \leq M \ll T$. By definition $x_{i,1,T}(t) = z_i(t) \forall t$. With the size M of the moving average we control the

spectral contents of time series. We here chose this ansatz for the sake of simplicity, for its mathematical treatability, and because the random time series with different spectral contents produced this way show all properties we want to illustrate.

In the following we will study the influence of the length T of time series on network properties by considering $x_{i,1,T}$ for different T. For a chosen value of T we determine R realizations of $x_{i,1,T}$ and we denote each realization r with $x_{i,1,T}^{(r)}$. When studying the influence of the spectral content we will consider $x_{i,M,T'}$ with different M and with $T' = 500$. We chose this value of T' because we are interested in investigating time series of short length as typically considered in field studies. For a chosen value of M we determine R realizations of $x_{i,M,T'}$ and we denote realization r with $x_{i,M,T'}^{(r)}$.

In order to keep the line of reasoning short and clear, we will present supporting and more rigorous mathematical results in Appendix S1 and refer to them in places where needed. In addition, since we observed most simulation studies based on ρ^m to yield qualitatively the same results as those based on ρ^c, we will present results based on ρ^c only and report results of our studies based on ρ^m whenever we observed qualitative differences.

Clustering coefficient. Let $\rho_{ij,1,T}^{(r)} := \rho^c(x_{i,1,T}^{(r)}, x_{j,1,T}^{(r)})$ denote the absolute value of the empirical correlation coefficient estimated for time series $x_{i,1,T}^{(r)}$ and $x_{j,1,T}^{(r)}$, and let us consider R realizations, $r \in \{1, \ldots, R\}$. Because of the independence of processes generating the time series and because of the symmetry of the correlation coefficient, we expect the R values of the empirical correlation coefficient calculated for finite and fixed T to be distributed around the mean value 0. The variance of this distribution will be higher the lower we choose T. If we sample one value $\rho_{ij,1,T}^{(r)}$ out of the R values it is almost surely that $\rho_{ij,1,T}^{(r)} > 0$. Thus there are thresholds $0 < \theta < \rho_{ij,1,T}^{(r)}$ for which we would establish a link between the corresponding nodes i and j when deriving a network. Let us now consider a network of N nodes whose links are derived from N time series as before. For some $\theta > 0$ the network will possess links and $\epsilon > 0$. We expect to observe ϵ for some fixed $\theta > 0$ to be higher the larger the variance of the distribution of $\rho_{ij,1,T}^{(r)}$. Likewise, for fixed values of ϵ we expect to find θ to be higher the lower we choose a value of T.

As a first check of this intuition we derive an approximation ϵ_{al} for the edge density by making use of the asymptotic limit $(T \to \infty$, see Appendix S1, Lemma 2 for details),

$$\epsilon_{al}(\theta, T) = 2\Phi(-\sqrt{T}\theta), \qquad (10)$$

where Φ denotes the cumulative distribution function of a standard normal distribution. In figure 1 (top left) we show the dependence of $\epsilon_{al}(\theta, T)$ on θ for exemplary values of T. Indeed, $\epsilon_{al}(\theta, T)$ is decreasing in θ and T.

The concession of taking the asymptotic limit when deriving equation (10) may limit its validity in the case of small values of T in which we are especially interested. Thus, we approach this case by simulation studies. Let us consider $R = 10^6$ values of $\rho_{12,M,T}^{(r)}$ obtained for R realizations of two time series $x_{i,M,T}$, $i \in \{1,2\}, r \in \{1, \ldots, R\}$. We estimate the edge density $\hat{\epsilon}(\theta, M, T)$ by

$$\hat{\epsilon}(\theta, M, T) := R^{-1} \sum_r H_{12,M,T}^{(r)}(\theta), \qquad (11)$$

where $H_{ij,M,T}^{(r)}(\theta) = 1$ for $\rho_{ij,M,T}^{(r)} > \theta$, and 0 else. Note that $\hat{\epsilon}(\theta, M, T)$ does not depend on N. This is because $\hat{\epsilon}(\theta, M, T)$ represents the (numerically determined) probability that there is a link between two vertices. The dependence of $\hat{\epsilon}(\theta, 1, T)$ on θ for

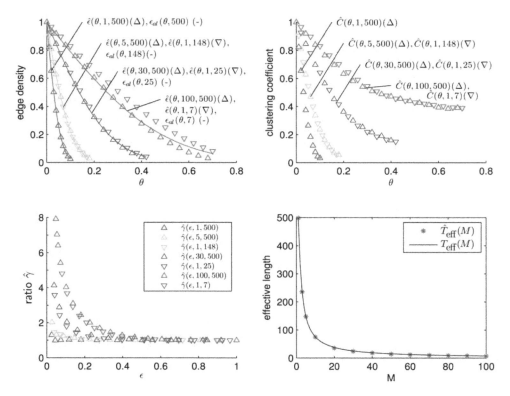

Figure 1. Simulation results for the edge density, the clustering coefficient, and the effective length. Top row: Dependence of edge density $\hat{\epsilon}(\theta,M,T)$ (left) and of clustering coefficient $\hat{C}(\theta,M,T)$ (right) on the threshold θ for different values of the size M of the moving average and of the length T of time series. Values of edge density $\epsilon_{al}(\theta,T)$ obtained with the asymptotic limit (equation (10)) are shown as lines (top left). Bottom left: Dependence of the ratio $\hat{\gamma}(\epsilon,T,M) = \hat{C}_{M,T}(\epsilon)/C_{ER}(\epsilon)$ on edge density ϵ. Note, that we omitted values of estimated quantities obtained for $\theta \in \{\theta : (R^{-1}\sum_r H_{12,M,T}^{(r)}(\theta)H_{13,M,T}^{(r)}(\theta)) < 10^{-3}\}$ since the accuracy of the statistics is no longer guaranteed. Bottom right: Dependence of effective length T_{eff} as determined by equation (14) (black line) and its numerical estimate $\hat{T}_{eff}$ (red markers) on M.

different values of T shown in figure 1 (top left) indicates a good agreement between $\epsilon_{al}(\theta,T)$ and $\hat{\epsilon}(\theta,1,T)$ for larger values of T but an increasing difference for $T < 30$.

We proceed by estimating the clustering coefficient $\hat{C}$ for our model using R realizations of three time series $x_{i,M,T}$, $i \in \{1,\dots,3\}$ by

$$\hat{C}(\theta,M,T) := \frac{\sum_r H_{12,M,T}^{(r)}(\theta)H_{13,M,T}^{(r)}(\theta)H_{23,M,T}^{(r)}(\theta)}{\sum_r H_{12,M,T}^{(r)}(\theta)H_{13,M,T}^{(r)}(\theta)}. \quad (12)$$

The dependence of $\hat{C}(\theta,1,T)$ on θ for various T is shown in the top right part of figure 1. For fixed T, $\hat{C}(\theta,1,T)$ decreases from 1 with increasing values of θ which one might expect due to the decrease of ϵ. However, we also observe for $\theta > 0$ that $\hat{C}(\theta,1,T)$ takes on higher values the lower T.

In order to investigate whether the clustering coefficients of our networks differ from those of Erdös-Rényi networks we use equation (11) and obtain $\hat{C}_{M,T}(\epsilon) = \hat{C}(\hat{\theta}(\epsilon,M,T),M,T)$ with $\hat{\theta}(\epsilon,M,T) = \inf\{\theta : \hat{\epsilon}(\theta,M,T) \geq \epsilon\}$. This allows the comparison with $C_{ER}(\epsilon) = \epsilon$ by considering the ratio $\hat{\gamma}(\epsilon,M,T) := \hat{C}_{M,T}(\epsilon)/C_{ER}(\epsilon)$. Remarkably, $\hat{\gamma}(\epsilon,1,T) \gg 1$ for a range of values of ϵ and T (cf. lower left part of figure 1). $\hat{\gamma}(\epsilon,1,T)$ even increases for small ϵ and T. This indicates that there is a relevant dependence between the three random variables $\rho_{ij,M,T}$, $\rho_{il,M,T}$, and $\rho_{jl,M,T}$ for different indices i,j,l and small T. For $T \to \infty$ and fixed edge density, C converges to C_{ER} because the dependence between the random variables $\rho_{ij,M,T}$, $i,j \in \{1,\dots,N\}$, vanishes (i.e., the

random variables will converge in distribution to independent normal random variables).

In order to gain deeper insights into the influence of the spectral contents of random time series on the clustering coefficient, we repeat the steps of analysis with time series $x_{i,M,T'}$, where $T' = 500$ is kept fix, and we choose different values of M. Figure 1 (top panels and lower left) shows that the higher the amount of low-frequency contributions (large M) the higher $\hat{\epsilon}(\theta,M,T')$ and $\hat{C}(\theta,M,T')$ (for $\theta > 0$), and the higher $\hat{\gamma}(\epsilon,M,T')$ (for $\epsilon \ll 1$). The difference between Erdös-Rényi networks and our time series networks becomes more pronounced ($\hat{\gamma}(\epsilon,M,T') \gg 1$) the smaller ϵ and the higher M.

Given the similar dependence of $\hat{\gamma}$, $\hat{C}$, and $\hat{\epsilon}$ on T and M, we hypothesize that the similarity can be traced back to similar variances of $\rho_{ij,1,T}$ and $\rho_{ij,M,T}$ for some values of T and M. By making use of the asymptotic variance of the limit distributions of $T \to \infty$, we derive an expression relating $\text{Var}(\rho_{ij,1,T})$ and $\text{Var}(\rho_{ij,M,T})$ to each other (see Appendix S1, Lemma 1),

$$\text{Var}(\rho_{ij,M,T}) \approx g(M)\text{Var}(\rho_{ij,1,T}), \; with \; g(M) = \frac{2}{3}M + \frac{1}{3M}. \quad (13)$$

We are now able to define an effective length T_{eff} of time series,

$$T_{eff}(M) := \frac{T'}{g(M)}, \quad (14)$$

for which $\text{Var}(\rho_{ij,1,T_{eff}}) \approx \text{Var}(\rho_{ij,M,T'})$. In the lower right part of figure 1 we show $T_{eff}(M)$ in dependence on M. To investigate whether equation (14) also holds for small values of T, we determine numerically, for different values of θ, $\hat{C}(\theta,1,T)$ for $T \in \{3,\ldots,T'\}$ as well as $\hat{C}(\theta,M,T')$ for some chosen values of M. Eventually, we determine for each value of M a value of T, for which $\hat{C}(\theta,1,T)$ and $\hat{C}(\theta,M,T')$ curves match in a least-squares sense, and denote this value with $\hat{T}_{\text{eff}}$ (see the lower right part of figure 1). We observe a maximum deviation $\left| T_{\text{eff}} - \hat{T}_{\text{eff}} \right| \approx 2$ and conclude that equation (14) indeed holds for small length T of time series. Moreover, numerically determined dependencies of $\hat{\epsilon}$ on θ, $\hat{C}$ on θ, as well as $\hat{\gamma}$ on ϵ for pairs of values (M,T') show a remarkable similarity to those dependencies obtained for pairs of values $(1,\hat{T}_{\text{eff}})$.

Thus, the clustering coefficient of networks derived from random time series of finite length and/or with a large amount of low-frequency contributions is higher than the one of Erdös-Rényi (ER) networks – independently of the network size N (cf. equation (12)). This difference becomes more pronounced the lower the edge density ϵ, the lower the length T of time series, and the larger the amount of low-frequency contributions. These results point us to an important difference between ER networks and our model networks: possible edges in ER networks are not only (1) equally likely but also (2) independently chosen to become edges. While property (1) is fulfilled in our model networks, property (2) is not.

Average shortest path length. Next we study the impact of the length of time series and of the amount of low-frequency contributions on the average shortest path length L of our model networks by employing a similar but different simulation approach as used in the previous section. To estimate L, we consider $R = 100$ networks with a fixed number of nodes ($N = 100$). We derive our model networks by thresholding $\rho_{ij,M,T}^{(r)}$, $i,j \in \{1,\ldots,N\}$, $r \in \{1,\ldots,R\}$. Let $L^{(r)}(\epsilon,1,T)$ denote the average shortest path length for network r with $M = 1$ and different values of T, and $L^{(r)}(\epsilon,M,T')$ the average shortest path length for network r with fixed value of T ($T = T' = 500$) and different values of M. With $L_{\text{ER}}^{(r)}(\epsilon)$ we refer to the average shortest path length obtained for the r-th ER network of size N and edge density ϵ. Mean values over realizations will be denoted as $\hat{L}(\epsilon,1,T)$, $\hat{L}(\epsilon,M,T')$, and $\hat{L}_{\text{ER}}(\epsilon)$ respectively. Finally, we define $\hat{\lambda}(\epsilon,1,T) := \hat{L}(\epsilon,1,T)/\hat{L}_{\text{ER}}(\epsilon)$ and $\hat{\lambda}(\epsilon,M,T') := \hat{L}(\epsilon,M,T')/\hat{L}_{\text{ER}}(\epsilon)$.

In figure 2 we show the dependence of $\hat{L}$ and $\hat{\lambda}$ on ϵ for various values of M and T. All quantities decrease as ϵ increases which can be expected due to additional edges reducing the average distances between pairs of nodes of the networks. For fixed $\epsilon \ll 1$, $\hat{L}$ takes on higher values the higher M or the lower T. With equation (14) we have $\hat{L}(\epsilon,1,T_{\text{eff}}) \approx \hat{L}(\epsilon,M,T')$ which resembles the results obtained for the clustering coefficient. Differences between the average shortest path lengths of our model networks and ER networks (as characterized by $\hat{\lambda}$) become more pronounced the higher M and the lower T. For edge densities typically reported in field studies ($\epsilon \approx 0.1$), however, differences are less pronounced ($\hat{\lambda} \lesssim 1.2$, cf. figure 2 right) than the ones observed for the clustering coefficient ($\hat{\gamma} > 2$ for selected values of M and T, cf. figure 1 bottom left). We obtained qualitatively similar results for small ($N = 50$) and large numbers of nodes ($N = 500$).

Number of connected components and degree distribution. Since the number of connected components of a given network might affect network characteristics such as the average shortest path length (see equation (7)), we investigate the impact of different length of time series and of the amount of low-frequency contributions on the average number of connected components $\hat{N}_c(\epsilon,M,T)$ of the networks derived from $x_{i,1,T_{\text{eff}}}$ and $x_{i,M,T'}$. We determine $\hat{N}_c(\epsilon,M,T)$ as the mean of R realizations of

the corresponding networks and with $\hat{N}_{c,\text{ER}}(\epsilon)$ we denote the mean value of the number of connected components in R realization of ER networks. For the edge densities considered here we observe ER networks to be connected (cf. figure 3), $N_{c,\text{ER}} \approx 1$, which is in agreement with the connectivity condition for ER networks, $\epsilon \gg \ln N/(N-1) \approx 0.05$ (for $N = 100$). Similarly, we observe $\hat{N}_c(\epsilon,1,T_{\text{eff}}) \approx 1$, even for small values of T (cf. figure 3 right). In contrast, $\hat{N}_c(\epsilon,M,T')$ takes on higher values the lower ϵ and the higher M (cf. figure 3 left). In order to achieve a better understanding of these findings, we determine degree probability distributions of our model networks. Let $\hat{p}_k$ denote the estimated probability of a node to possess a degree k, i.e., $\hat{p}_k = \#\{i^{(r)} : k_i^{(r)} = k, r \in \{1,\ldots,R\}\}/(NR)$. With $\hat{p}_k(\epsilon,M,T)$ we will denote the estimated degree distribution for networks derived from $x_{i,M,T}$. We briefly recall that the degree distribution of ER networks $p_{k,N,\text{ER}}$ follows a binomial distribution,

$$p_{k,N,\text{ER}}(\epsilon) = \binom{N-1}{k} \epsilon^k (1-\epsilon)^{N-k-1}, \qquad (15)$$

which we show in figure 4 for $N = 100$ and various ϵ (top panels and lower left panel). In the same figure we present our findings for $\hat{p}_k(\epsilon,M,T)$ for various values of $T = T_{\text{eff}}$ and M. We observe $\hat{p}_k(\epsilon,1,T_{\text{eff}})$ to be equal to $\hat{p}_{k,N,\text{ER}}(\epsilon)$ within the error to be expected due to the limited sample size used for the estimation. For $\hat{p}_k(\epsilon,M,T')$, however, we observe striking differences in comparison to the previous degree distributions. In particular, for decreasing ϵ and higher M, the probability of nodes with degree $k = 0$ increases, which leads to networks with disconnected single nodes, thereby increasing the number of connected components of the network.

We hypothesize that the observed differences in the number of connected components as well as in the degree distributions are related to differences in the spectral content of different realizations of time series $x_{i,M,T'}^{(r)}$ for $M > 1$. In particular, a node i with a low degree k_i might be associated with a time series $x_{i,M,T'}^{(r)}$, which possesses, by chance, a small relative amount of low frequency contributions (or, equivalently, a large relative amount of high frequency contributions).

In order to test this hypothesis, we generate R realizations of $N = 100$ time series $x_{i,M,T'}^{(r)}$ and estimate their periodograms $\hat{P}_{i,M}^{(r)}(f)$ for frequencies $f \in \{0,\ldots,f_{\text{Nyq}}\}$ using a discrete Fourier transform [45]. f_{Nyq} denotes the Nyquist frequency, and periodograms are normalized such that $\sum_f \hat{P}_{i,M}^{(r)}(f) = 1$. From the same time series, we then derive the networks using $\epsilon = 0.1$ and determine the degrees $k_i^{(r)}$. For some fixed $f' > 0$ we define the total power above f' (upper frequency range) as $\hat{P}_{i,M}^{\text{H},(r)} = \sum_{f'}^{f_{\text{Nyq}}} \hat{P}_{i,M}^{(r)}(f)$, and the total power below f' (lower frequency range) as $\hat{P}_{i,M}^{\text{L},(r)} = \sum_{f=0}^{f'-1} \hat{P}_{i,M}^{(r)}(f)$. For each realization r we estimate the correlation coefficients between the degrees and the corresponding total power contents in upper and lower frequency range, $\kappa_{\text{L}}^{(r)} = corr(k^{(r)},\hat{P}_M^{\text{L},(r)})$ and $\kappa_{\text{H}}^{(r)} = corr(k^{(r)},\hat{P}_M^{\text{H},(r)})$, respectively, and determine their mean values, $\kappa_{\text{L}}(M) = R^{-1}\sum_r \kappa_{\text{L}}^{(r)}$ and $\kappa_{\text{H}}(M) = R^{-1}\sum_r \kappa_{\text{H}}^{(r)}$. Note that $\kappa_{\text{L}}(M) = -\kappa_{\text{H}}(M)$ by construction. We choose $f' = f'(M)$ such that 40% of the total power of the filter function associated with the moving average is contained within the frequency range $f \in [0,f']$.

For increasing M we observe in the lower right panel of figure 4 the degrees to be increasingly correlated with $\hat{P}_M^{\text{L},(r)}$, which corresponds to an anti-correlation of degrees with $\hat{P}_M^{\text{H},(r)}$. Thus, as hypothesized above, the observed differences in the degree distributions can indeed be related to the differences in the power content of the time series. We mention that the exact choice of f'

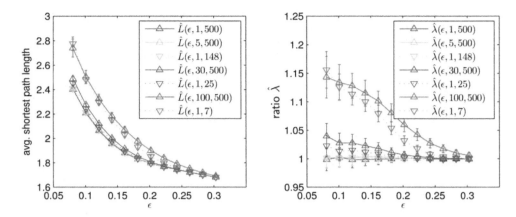

Figure 2. Simulation results for the average shortest path length. Dependence of the average shortest path length $\hat{L}(\epsilon,M,T)$ (left) and of the ratio $\hat{\lambda}(\epsilon,M,T) = \hat{L}(\epsilon,1,T)/L_{ER}(\epsilon)$ (right) on edge density ϵ for different values of the size M of the moving average and of the length T of time series. Lines are for eye-guidance only.

does not sensitively affect the observed qualitative relationships as long as $0 < f' \ll f_{Nyq}$ is fulfilled.

We briefly summarize the results obtained so far, which indicate a striking difference between networks derived from independent random time series using ρ^c or ρ^m (cf. equations (1) and (2)) and corresponding ER networks. First, we observed the clustering coefficient C and the average shortest path length L of our networks to be higher the lower the length T of the time series (cf. figures 1 and 2). Second, for some fixed T we observed C and L to be higher the larger the amount of low frequency components (as parametrized by M) in the time series. In addition, these contributions led to an increasing number of connected components in our networks and to degree distributions that differed strongly from those of the corresponding ER networks (cf. figures 3 and 4). We mention that L as defined here (cf. equation (7)) tends to decrease for networks with an increasing number N_c of connected components, and $L \to 0$ for $N_c \to N$. L thus depends non-trivially on the amount of low frequency components in the time series. Third, for small edge densities ϵ and for short time series lengths or for a large amount of low frequency components, the clustering coefficient deviates more strongly from the one of corresponding ER networks ($\hat{\gamma} > 2$) than the average shortest path

length ($\hat{\lambda} \lesssim 1.2$; cf. figure 2 right and figure 1 (bottom left)). Networks derived from independent random time series can thus be classified as small world networks if one uses $\gamma \gg 1$ and $\lambda \approx 1$ as practical criterion, which is often employed in various field studies (cf. [31] and references therein).

Field data analysis

The findings obtained in the previous section indicate that strong low frequency contributions affect network properties C and L in a non-trivial way. We now investigate this influence in electroencephalographic (EEG) recordings of epileptic seizures that are known for their complex spatial and temporal changes in frequency content [46–49]. We analyze the multichannel ($N = 53 \pm 21$ channels) EEGs from 60 patients capturing 100 epileptic seizures reported in reference [50]. All patients had signed informed consent that their clinical data might be used and published for research purposes. The study protocol had previously been approved by the ethics committee of the University of Bonn. During the presurgical evaluation of drug-resistant epilepsy, EEG data were recorded with chronically implanted strip, grid, or depth electrodes from the cortex and from within relevant structures of the brain. The data were sampled at

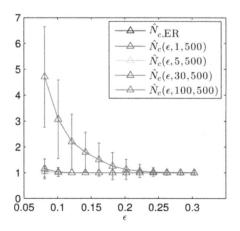
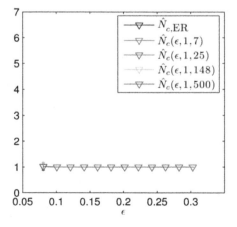

Figure 3. Simulation results for the number of connected components. Dependence of the number of connected components $\hat{N}_c(\epsilon,M,T)$ on the edge density ϵ for different values of the size M of the moving average (left, for $T = 500$) and of the length T of time series (right, for $M = 1$). Lines are for eye-guidance only.

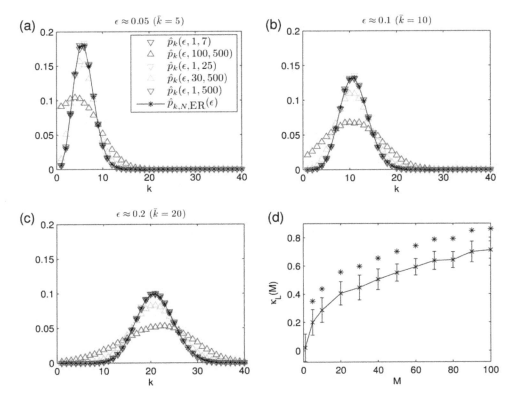

Figure 4. Simulation results for the degree distribution. (a–c) Degree distributions $\hat{p}_k(\epsilon,M,T)$ estimated for $R=1000$ realizations of networks derived from time series $x_{i,M,T}$ ($N=100$) via thresholding using various edge densities $\epsilon=\bar{k}(N-1)^{-1}$ and for selected values of the size M of the moving average and of the length T of time series. The symbol legend in (a) also holds for (b) and (c). (**d**) Dependence of correlation ($\kappa_L(M)$) between node degrees and power content in the lower frequency range on the size M of the moving average. Mean values of correlations obtained for $R=100$ realizations of networks for each value of M are shown as crosses and standard deviations as error bars. Stars indicate significant differences in comparison to $\kappa_L(1)$ (Bonferroni corrected pair-wise Wilcoxon rank sum tests for equal medians, $p<0.01$). Lines are for eye-guidance only.

200 Hz within the frequency band $0.5-70$ Hz using a 16-bit analog-to-digital converter. Electroencephalographic seizure on-sets and seizure ends were automatically detected [51], and EEGs were split into consecutive non-overlapping windows of 2.5 s duration ($T=500$ sampling points). Time series of each window were normalized to zero mean and unit variance. We determined ρ^c and ρ^m for all combinations of EEG time series from each window and derived networks with a fixed edge density $\epsilon=0.1$ in order to exclude possible edge density effects. With L_c and C_c as well as L_m and C_m we denote characteristics of networks based on ρ^c and ρ^m, respectively. In order to simplify matters, we omit the window indexing in the following.

We investigate a possible influence of the power content of EEG time series on the clustering coefficient and the average shortest path length by comparing their values to those obtained from ensembles of random networks that are based on properties of the EEG time series at two different levels of detail. For the first ensemble and for each patient we derive networks from random time series with a power content that approximately equals the mean power content of all EEG time series within a window. Let $\hat{P}_i(f)$ denote the estimated periodogram of each EEG time series i, and with $P(f)=N^{-1}\sum_i \hat{P}_i(f)$ we denote the mean power for each frequency component f over all N time series. We normalize $P(f)$ such that $\sum_f P(f)=1$. We generate N random time series of length $T=500$ whose entries are independently drawn from a uniform probability distribution, and we filter these time series in the Fourier domain using $\sqrt{P(f)}$ as filter function. We normalize

the filtered time series to zero mean and unit variance and derive a network based on ρ^c or ρ^m ($\epsilon=0.1$). We use 20 realizations of such networks per window in order to determine the mean values of network characteristics $C_c^{(1)}$ and $L_c^{(1)}$ as well as $C_m^{(1)}$ and $L_m^{(1)}$ based on ρ^c or ρ^m, respectively. Since the power spectra of all time series equal each other, these random networks resemble the ones investigated in the previous section.

With the second ensemble, we take into account that the power content of EEG time series recorded from different brain regions may differ substantially. For this purpose we make use of a well established method for generating univariate time series surrogates [52,53], which have power spectral contents and amplitude distributions that are practically indistinguishable from those of EEG time series but are otherwise random. Amplitudes are iteratively permuted while the power spectrum of each EEG time series is approximately preserved. Since this randomization scheme destroys any significant linear or non-linear dependencies between time series, it has been successfully applied to test the null hypothesis of independent linear stochastic processes. For each patient, we generated 20 surrogate time series for each EEG time series from each recording site and each window, and derived networks based on either ρ^c or ρ^m ($\epsilon=0.1$). Mean values of characteristics of these random networks are denoted as $C_c^{(2)}$ and $L_c^{(2)}$ as well as $C_m^{(2)}$ and $L_m^{(2)}$, respectively.

We begin with an exemplary recording of a seizure of which we show in figure 5 (left) the temporal evolution of the relative amount of power in the δ- ($0-4$ Hz, P_δ), ϑ- ($4-8$ Hz, P_ϑ), α- ($8-12$ Hz, P_α),

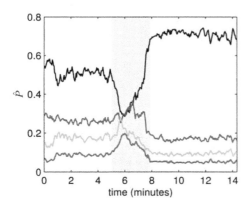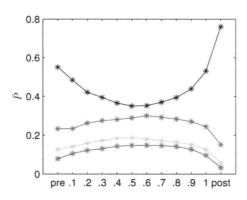

Figure 5. Evolving relative amount of power during epileptic seizures. (Left) Relative amount of power $\hat{P}$ contained in the δ- ($\hat{P}_\delta$, black), ϑ- ($\hat{P}_\vartheta$, blue), α- ($\hat{P}_\alpha$, green), and β- ($\hat{P}_\beta$, red) frequency bands during an exemplary seizure. Profiles are smoothed using a four-point moving average. Grey-shaded area marks the seizure. (Right) Mean values ($\bar{P}_\delta$, $\bar{P}_\vartheta$, $\bar{P}_\alpha$, $\bar{P}_\beta$) of the relative amount of power averaged separately for pre-seizure, discretized seizure, and post-seizure time periods of 100 epileptic seizures. Lines are for eye-guidance only.

and β- (12–20 Hz, P_β) frequency bands. Prior to the seizure the δ-band contains more than 50% of the total power which is then shifted towards higher frequencies and back towards low frequencies at seizure end. P_δ is even higher after the seizure than prior to the seizure.

In figure 6 we show the temporal evolution of network properties obtained for this recording based on ρ^c (top panels) and ρ^m (bottom panels). During the seizure both the clustering coefficients C_c and C_m and the average shortest path lengths L_c and L_m show pronounced differences to the respective properties obtained from the random networks. These differences are less pronounced prior to and after the seizure, where $C_m^{(2)}$ and $L_m^{(2)}$ even approach the values of C_m and L_m, respectively. $C_c^{(1)}$ and $C_m^{(1)}$ decrease during the seizure and already increase prior to seizure end, resembling the changes of P_δ (cf. figure 5 (left)). This is in accordance with results of our simulation studies: there we observed the clustering coefficient to be higher the larger the amount of low frequency components in the time series; this could also be observed, but to a much lesser extent, for the average shortest path length. Indeed, $L_m^{(1)}$ and $L_c^{(1)}$ vary little over time, and $L_c^{(1)}$ is only slightly increased after the seizure, reflecting the high amount of power in the δ-band.

We only observe small deviations between $C_c^{(1)}$ and $C_c^{(2)}$ as well as between $L_c^{(1)}$ and $L_c^{(2)}$, which appear to be systematic (for many windows $C_c^{(1)} \lesssim C_c^{(2)}$ and $L_c^{(1)} \gtrsim L_c^{(2)}$). These suggest that for interaction networks derived from ρ^c, both random network ensembles appear appropriate to characterize the influence of power in low frequency bands on clustering coefficient and the average shortest path length. In contrast, we observed differences between $C_m^{(1)}$ and $C_m^{(2)}$, as well as between $L_m^{(1)}$ and $L_m^{(2)}$. These differences were most pronounced during the seizure and for $L_m^{(1)}$ and $L_m^{(2)}$ also after the seizure. This finding indicates that the clustering coefficient and average shortest path length of interaction networks derived from ρ^m depend sensitively on the power contents of EEG time series recorded from different brain regions. Thus, for these interaction networks only the random networks that account for the complex changes in frequency content of different brain regions prior to, during, and after seizures appear appropriate to characterize the influence of power in low frequency bands on clustering coefficient and the average shortest path length.

We continue by studying properties of networks derived from the EEG recordings of all 100 focal onset seizures. Due to the different durations of seizures (mean seizure duration: 110 ± 60 s)

we partitioned each seizure into 10 equidistant time bins (see reference [50] for details) and assigned the time-dependent network properties to the respective time bins. For each seizure we included the same number of pre-seizure and post-seizure windows in our analysis and assigned the corresponding time-dependent network properties to one pre-seizure and one post-seizure time bin. Within each time bin we determined the mean value (e.g., $\bar{C}_c$) and its standard error for each property. In figure 5 (right), we show for each time bin the mean values of the relative amount of power in different frequency bands of all seizure recordings ($\bar{P}_\delta$, $\bar{P}_\vartheta$, $\bar{P}_\alpha$, $\bar{P}_\beta$). Similar to the exemplary recording (cf. figure 5 (left)), we observe a shift in the relative amount of power in low frequencies prior to seizures towards higher frequencies during seizures and back to low frequencies at seizure end. The amount of power in the δ-band is on average higher in the post-seizure bin than in the pre-seizure bin.

In figure 7 we show the mean values of properties of networks in each time bin for all seizures. We observe $\bar{C}_c^{(1)}$, $\bar{C}_c^{(2)}$, $\bar{L}_c^{(1)}$, $\bar{L}_c^{(2)}$, $\bar{C}_m^{(1)}$, and $\bar{L}_m^{(1)}$ to decrease during seizures and to increase prior to seizure end thereby roughly reflecting the amount of power contained in low frequencies (cf. figure 5 (right), $\bar{P}_\delta$). $\bar{C}_c^{(1)}$ and $\bar{C}_c^{(2)}$ and to a lesser extent also $\bar{L}_c^{(1)}$ and $\bar{L}_c^{(2)}$ roughly follow the same course in time, however, with a slight shift in the range of values as already observed in the exemplary recording of a seizure (cf. figure 6). Differences between both random network ensembles are most pronounced in network properties based on ρ^m, i.e., between $\bar{C}_m^{(1)}$ and $\bar{C}_m^{(2)}$ as well as between $\bar{L}_m^{(1)}$ and $\bar{L}_m^{(2)}$. This corroborates the observation that the clustering coefficient and the average shortest path length of the random networks based on ρ^m depend more sensitively on the power contents of EEG time series recorded from different brain regions than the respective quantities derived from ρ^c. While $\bar{L}_c$ and $\bar{L}_m$ show a similar course in time, reaching a maximum in the middle of the seizures, we observe a remarkable difference between $\bar{C}_c$ and $\bar{C}_m$ prior to end of the seizures, where the amount of power in low frequencies is large. While $\bar{C}_m$ decreases at the end of the seizures, $\bar{C}_c$ does not and remains elevated after seizures. Interestingly, considering the corresponding quantities obtained from the second random network ensemble, $\bar{C}_m^{(2)}$ fluctuates around 0.3 ± 0.01 and does not increase at the end of seizures, while, in contrast, $\bar{C}_c^{(2)}$ increases at the end of the seizures, traversing an interval of values roughly three times larger than the interval containing values of $\bar{C}_m^{(2)}$. Taken together these findings suggest that the pronounced

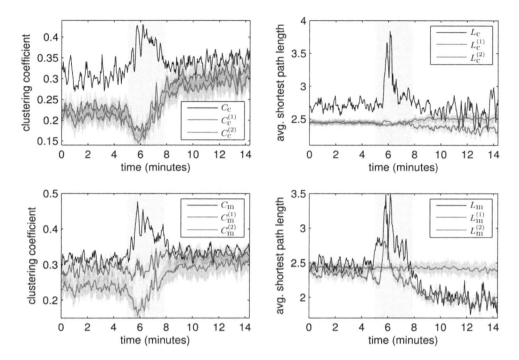

Figure 6. Evolving network properties during an exemplary epileptic seizure. Network properties C_c and L_c (top row, black lines) as well as C_m and L_m (bottom row, black lines) during an exemplary seizure (cf. figure 5 (left)). Mean values and standard deviations of network properties obtained from surrogate time series ($C_c^{(2)}$, $L_c^{(2)}$, $C_m^{(2)}$, $L_m^{(2)}$) are shown as blue lines and blue shaded areas, respectively, and mean values and standard deviations of network properties obtained from the overall power content model ($C_c^{(1)}$, $L_c^{(1)}$, $C_m^{(1)}$, $L_m^{(1)}$) are shown as red lines and red shaded areas, respectively. Profiles are smoothed using a four-point moving average. Grey-shaded area marks the seizure. For corresponding Erdős-Rényi networks $C_{ER} \approx 0.1$ and $L_{ER} \approx 2.4$ for all time windows.

changes of the frequency content of EEG time series seen during epileptic seizures influence the values of the clustering coefficient and the average shortest path length.

A comparison of some value of a network property with the one obtained for a random network with the same edge density and number of nodes is typically achieved by calculating their ratio. If ER networks are used for comparison, the value of a network property is rescaled by a constant factor. In this case, the time-dependent changes of network properties shown in figure 7 will be shifted along the ordinate only. In order to take into account the varying power content of EEG time series recorded from different brain regions we instead normalize the clustering coefficients and the average shortest path lengths with the corresponding quantities from the second random network ensemble $\bar{C}_c^{(2)}$, $\bar{C}_m^{(2)}$, $\bar{L}_c^{(2)}$, and $\bar{L}_m^{(2)}$ (cf. figure 8). We observe the normalized network properties to describe a concave-like movement over time indicating a reconfiguration of networks from more random (before seizures) towards a more regular (during seizures) and back towards more random network topologies. This is in agreement with previous observations using a different and seldom used thresholding method [50].

Discussion

The network approach towards the analysis of empirical multivariate time series is based on the assumption that the data is well represented by a model of mutual relationships (i.e., a network). We studied interaction networks derived from finite time series generated by independent processes that would not advocate a representation by a model of mutual relationships. We observed the derived interaction networks to show non-trivial network

topologies. These are induced by the finiteness of data, which limits reliability of estimators of signal interdependence, together with the use of a frequently employed thresholding technique. Since the analysis methodology alone can already introduce non-trivial structure in the derived networks, the question arises as to how informative network analysis results obtained from finite empirical data are with respect to the studied dynamics. This question may be addressed by defining and making use of appropriate null models. In the following, we briefly discuss two null models that are frequently employed in field studies.

Erdős-Rényi (ER) networks represent one of the earliest and best studied network models in mathematical literature and can be easily generated. They can be used to test whether the network under consideration complies with the notion of a random network in which possible edges are equally likely and independently chosen to become edges. We observed that clustering coefficient C and average shortest path length L for interaction networks derived from finite random time series differed pronouncedly from those obtained from corresponding ER networks, which would likely lead to a classification of interaction networks as small-world networks. Since the influence of the analysis methodology is not taken into account with ER networks, they may not be well suited for serving as null models in studies of interaction networks derived from finite time series.

Another null model is based on randomizing the network topology while preserving the degrees of nodes [26,54,55]. It is used to evaluate whether the network under consideration is random under the constraint of a given degree sequence. Results of our simulation studies point out that the structures induced in the network topology by the way how networks are derived from empirical time series cannot be related to the degree sequence

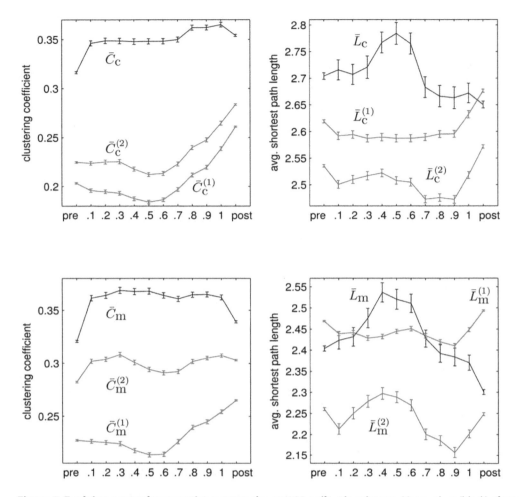

Figure 7. Evolving network properties averaged over 100 epileptic seizures. Mean values (black) of network properties C_c (top left), L_c (top right), C_m (bottom left), and L_m (bottom right) averaged separately for pre-seizure, discretized seizure, and post-seizure time periods of 100 epileptic seizures. Mean values of corresponding network properties obtained from the first and the second ensemble of random networks are shown as red and blue lines, respectively. All error bars indicate standard error of the mean. Lines are for eye-guidance only.

only. We observed that C and L from interaction networks remarkably depended on the finiteness of the data, while the degree distribution did not (cf. figure 4 (a–c), $M=1$). The usefulness of degree-preserving randomized networks has also been subject of debate since they do not take into account different characteristics of the data and its acquisition [56,57]. Moreover, the link-switching algorithm frequently employed for generating such networks has been shown to non-uniformly sample the space

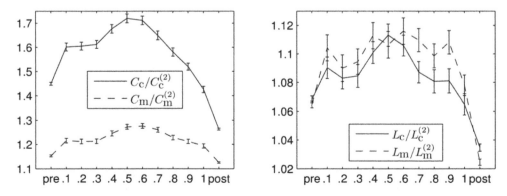

Figure 8. Evolving normalized network properties averaged over 100 epileptic seizures. Mean values of $C_c/C_c^{(2)}$ and $C_m/C_m^{(2)}$ (left) as well as $L_c/L_c^{(2)}$ and $L_m/L_m^{(2)}$ (right) averaged separately for pre-seizure, discretized seizure, and post-seizure time periods of 100 epileptic seizures. All error bars indicate standard error of the mean. Lines are for eye-guidance only.

of networks with predefined degree sequence (see, e.g., references [25,58]). This deficiency can be addressed by using alternative randomization schemes (see, e.g., [58–60] and references therein).

We propose to take into account the finite length and the frequency contents of time series when defining null models. For this purpose we applied the same methodological steps as in field data analysis (estimation of signal interdependence and thresholding of interdependence values to define links) but used surrogate time series [53] to derive random networks (second ensemble). These surrogate time series comply with the null hypothesis of independent linear stochastic processes and preserve length, frequency content, and amplitude distribution of the original time series. For these random networks, we observed (in our simulation studies) dependencies between properties of networks and properties of time series: the clustering coefficient C, and, to a lesser extent, the average shortest path length L are higher the higher the relative amount of low frequency components, the shorter the length of time series, and the smaller the edge density of the network. Results obtained from an analysis of interaction networks derived from multichannel EEG recordings of one hundred epileptic seizures confirm that the pronounced changes of the frequency content seen during seizures influence the values of C and L. Comparing these network characteristics with those obtained from our random networks allowed us to distinguish aspects of global network dynamics during seizures from those spuriously induced by the applied methods of analysis.

Our random networks will likely be classified as small-world networks when compared to ER networks which might indicate that small-world topologies in networks derived from empirical data as reported in an ever increasing number of studies can partly or solely be related to the finite length and frequency content of time series. If so, small-world topologies would be an overly complicated description of the simple finding of finite time series with a large amount of low frequency components. In this context, our approach could be of particular interest for studies that deal with short time series and low frequency contents, as, for example, is the case in resting state functional magnetic resonance imaging studies (see, e.g., references [61–65]). In such studies, taking into account potential frequency effects could help to unravel information on the network level that would be otherwise masked.

We observed the degrees of nodes of our random networks to be correlated with the relative amount of power in low-frequencies in the respective time series (cf. figure 4). The degree of a node has been used in field studies as an indicator of its centrality in the network (see, e.g., [2,66] and references therein). Particular interest has been devoted to nodes which are highly central (hubs). In this context it would be interesting to study whether findings of hubs in interaction networks can partly or solely be explained by the various frequency contents of time series entering the analysis. In such a case, hubs would be a complicated representation of features already present on a single time series level. We are confident that our random networks can help to clarify this issue.

Our simulation studies were based on the simplified assumption that power spectra of all time series from which a network is derived are approximately equal. The dependencies of C and L on the power content could also be observed qualitatively for networks derived from EEG time series – that were recorded from different brain regions and whose power spectra may differ substantially among each other – but only if link definition was based on thresholding the values of the correlation coefficient (ρ^c). Thus, estimating mean power spectra of multivariate time series can provide the experimentalist with a rule of thumb for the potential relative increase of C and L in different networks based on the correlation coefficient. This rule of thumb, however, might not be helpful if the maximum value of the absolute cross correlation (ρ^m) is used to estimate signal interdependencies. In this case, C and L depended sensitively on the heterogeneity of power spectra (see the second random network ensemble). It would be interesting to investigate in future studies, which particular properties of ρ^c and ρ^m can be accounted for these differences.

We close the discussion with two remarks, the first being of interest for experimentalists. Our findings also shed light on a network construction technique that relies on significance testing in order to decide upon defining a link or not [21]. For this purpose, a null distribution of a chosen estimator of signal interdependence (ρ^m) is generated for each pair of time series and a link is established if the null hypothesis of independent processes generating the time series can be rejected at a predefined significance level. It was suggested in Ref. [21] to use a limited subset of time series in order to minimize computational burden when generating null distributions. Our findings indicate that networks constructed this way will yield an artificially increased number of false positive or of false negative links which will depend on the frequency contents of time series being part or not part of the subset. Our second remark is related to network modeling. By choosing some threshold and generating time series that satisfy the relation between the size of the moving average and the length of time series, networks can be generated which differ in their degree distributions but approximately equal in their clustering coefficient and average shortest path length. This property could be of value for future modeling studies.

To summarize, we have demonstrated that interaction networks, derived from finite time series via thresholding an estimate of signal interdependence, can exhibit non-trivial properties that solely reflect the mostly unavoidable finiteness of empirical data, which limits the reliability of signal interdependence estimators. Addressing these influences, we proposed random network models that take into account the way interaction networks are derived from the data. With an exemplary time-resolved analysis of the clustering coefficient C and the average shortest path length L of interaction networks derived from multichannel electroencephalographic recordings of one hundred epileptic seizures, we demonstrated that our random networks allow one to gain deeper insights into the global network dynamics during seizures. Here we concentrated on C and L but we also expect other network characteristics to be influenced by the methodologies used to derive interaction networks from empirical data. Analytical investigations of properties of our random networks and the development of formal tests for deviations from these networks may be regarded as promising topics for further studies. Other research directions are related to the framework we proposed to generate random networks from time series. For example, parts of the framework may be exchanged in order to study network construction methodologies other than thresholding (e.g., based on minimum spanning trees [14] or based on allowing weighted links) or other widely used linear and nonlinear methods for estimating signal interdependence [34,35,39]. Other surrogate concepts [67–72] may allow for defining different random networks tailored to various purposes. We believe that research into network inference from time series and into random network models that incorporate knowledge about the way networks are derived from empirical data can decisively advance applied network science. This line of research can contribute to gain a better understanding of complex dynamical systems studied in various scientific fields.

Supporting Information

Appendix S1 Mathematical proofs.

Acknowledgments

We thank Marie-Therese Kuhnert, Gerrit Ansmann, and Alexander Rothkegel for their helpful comments and Paula Daniliuc for proofreading the manuscript.

Author Contributions

Conceived and designed the experiments: SB MW KL. Performed the experiments: SB. Analyzed the data: SB. Wrote the paper: SB MW KL. Mathematical proofs: MW.

References

1. Newman MEJ (2003) The structure and function of complex networks. SIAM Rev 45: 167–256.
2. Boccaletti S, Latora V, Moreno Y, Chavez M, Hwang DU (2006) Complex networks: Structure and dynamics. Phys Rep 424: 175–308.
3. Arenas A, Díaz-Guilera A, Kurths J, Moreno Y, Zhou C (2008) Synchronization in complex networks. Phys Rep 469: 93–153.
4. Barrat A, Barthélemy M, Vespignani A (2008) Dynamical Processes on Complex Networks. New York, USA: Cambridge University Press.
5. Tsonis AA, Roebber PJ (2004) The architecture of the climate network. Physica A 333: 497–504.
6. Yamasaki K, Gozolchiani A, Havlin S (2008) Climate networks around the globe are significantly affected by El Niño. Phys Rev Lett 100: 228501.
7. Donges JF, Zou Y, Marwan N, Kurths J (2009) Complex networks in climate dynamics. Eur Phys J–Spec Top 174: 157–179.
8. Tsonis AA, Wang G, Swanson KL, Rodrigues FA, da Fontura Costa L (2010) Community structure and dynamics in climate networks. Clim Dynam, in press.
9. Steinhaeuser K, Chawla NV, Ganguly AR (2011) Complex networks as a unified framework for descriptive analysis and predictive modeling in climate science. Statistical Analysis and Data Mining 4: in press.
10. Abe S, Suzuki N (2004) Small-world structure of earthquake network. Physica A 337: 357–362. 23.
11. Abe S, Suzuki N (2006) Complex-network description of seismicity. Nonlinear Proc Geoph 13: 145–150.
12. Jiménez A, Tiampo KF, Posadas AM (2008) Small world in a seismic network: the California case. Nonlinear Proc Geoph 15: 389–395.
13. Krishna Mohan TR, Revathi PG (2011) Network of earthquakes and recurrences therein. J Seismol 15: 71–80.
14. Mantegna RN (1999) Hierarchical structure in financial markets. Eur Phys J B 11: 193–197.
15. Onnela JP, Kaski K, Kertesz J (2004) Clustering and information in correlation based financial networks. Eur Phys J B 38: 353–362.
16. Boginski V, Butenko S, Pardalos PM (2005) Statistical analysis of financial networks. Comput Stat An 48: 431–443.
17. Qiu T, Zheng B, Chen G (2010) Financial networks with static and dynamic thresholds. New J Phys 12: 043057.
18. Emmert-Streib F, Dehmer M (2010) Influence of the time scale on the construction of financial networks. PLoS ONE 5: e12884.
19. Reijneveld JC, Ponten SC, Berendse HW, Stam CJ (2007) The application of graph theoretical analysis to complex networks in the brain. Clin Neurophysiol 118: 2317–2331.
20. Bullmore E, Sporns O (2009) Complex brain networks: graph theoretical analysis of structural and functional systems. Nat Rev Neurosci 10: 186–198.
21. Kramer MA, Eden UT, Cash SS, Kolaczyk ED (2009) Network inference with confidence from multivariate time series. Phys Rev E 79: 061916.
22. Donges JF, Zou Y, Marwan N, Kurths J (2009) The backbone of the climate network. Europhys Lett 87: 48007.
23. Emmert-Streib F, Dehmer M (2010) Identifying critical financial networks of the DJIA: Toward a network-based index. Complexity 16: 24–33.
24. Erdős P, Rényi A (1959) On random graphs I. Publ Math Debrecen 6: 290–297.
25. Rao AR, Jana R, Bandyopadhyay S (1996) A Markov chain Monte Carlo method for generating random (0,1)-matrices with given marginals. Sankhya Ser A 58: 225–242.
26. Maslov S, Sneppen K (2002) Specificity and stability in topology of protein networks. Science 296: 910–913.
27. James R, Croft DP, Krause J (2009) Potential banana skins in animal social network analysis. Behav Ecol Sociobiol 63: 989–997.
28. Lima-Mendez G, van Helden J (2009) The powerful law of the power law and other myths in network biology. Mol Biosyst 5: 1482–1493.
29. Ioannides AA (2007) Dynamic functional connectivity. Curr Opin Neurobiol 17: 161–170.
30. Butts CT (2009) Revisiting the foundations of network analysis. Science 325: 414–416.
31. Bialonski S, Horstmann MT, Lehnertz K (2010) From brain to earth and climate systems: Small-world interaction networks or not? Chaos 20: 013134.
32. Antiqueira L, Rodrigues FA, van Wijk BCM, da F Costa L, Daffertshofer A (2010) Estimating complex cortical networks via surface recordings–a critical note. Neuroimage 53: 439–449.
33. Gerhard F, Pipa G, Lima B, Neuenschwander S, Gerstner W (2011) Extraction of network topology from multi-electrode recordings: Is there a small-world effect? Front Comp Neuroscience 5: 4.
34. Brillinger D (1981) Time Series: Data Analysis and Theory. San Francisco, USA: Holden-Day.
35. Pikovsky AS, Rosenblum MG, Kurths J (2001) Synchronization: A universal concept in nonlinear sciences. Cambridge, UK: Cambridge University Press.
36. Boccaletti S, Kurths J, Osipov G, Valladares DL, Zhou CS (2002) The synchronization of chaotic systems. Phys Rep 366: 1–101.
37. Kantz H, Schreiber T (2003) Nonlinear Time Series Analysis. Cambridge, UK: Cambridge Univ. Press, 2nd edition.
38. Pereda E, Quian Quiroga R, Bhattacharya J (2005) Nonlinear multivariate analysis of neurophysiological signals. Prog Neurobiol 77: 1–37.
39. Hlaváčková-Schindler K, Paluš M, Vejmelka M, Bhattacharya J (2007) Causality detection based on information-theoretic approaches in time series analysis. Phys Rep 441: 1–46.
40. Lehnertz K, Bialonski S, Horstmann MT, Krug D, Rothkegel A, et al. (2009) Synchronization phenomena in human epileptic brain networks. J Neurosci Methods 183: 42–48.
41. Watts DJ, Strogatz SH (1998) Collective dynamics of 'small-world' networks. Nature 393: 440–442.
42. Latora V, Marchiori M (2001) Efficient behavior of small-world networks. Phys Rev Lett 87: 198701.
43. Latora V, Marchiori M (2003) Economic small-world behavior in weighted networks. Eur Phys J B 32: 249–263.
44. Chung F, Lu L (2001) The diameter of sparse random graphs. Adv Appl Math 26: 257–279.
45. Press WH, Teukolsky SA, Vetterling WT, Flannery BP (2002) Numerical Recipes in C. Cambridge, UK: Cambridge University Press, 2nd edition.
46. Franaszczuk PJ, Bergey GK, Durka PJ, Eisenberg HM (1998) Time-frequency analysis using the matching pursuit algorithm applied to seizures originating from the mesial temporal lobe. Electroencephalogr Clin Neurophysiol 106: 513–521.
47. Schiff SJ, Colella D, Jacyna GM, Hughes E, Creekmore JW, et al. (2000) Brain chirps: spectrographic signatures of epileptic seizures. Clin Neurophysiol 111: 953–958.
48. Jouny CC, Franaszczuk PJ, Bergey GK (2003) Characterization of epileptic seizure dynamics using Gabor atom density. Clin Neurophysiol 114: 426–437.
49. Bartolomei F, Cosandier-Rimele D, McGonigal A, Aubert S, Regis J, et al. (2010) From mesial temporal lobe to temporoperisylvian seizures: A quantified study of temporal lobe seizure networks. Epilepsia 51: 2147–2158.
50. Schindler K, Bialonski S, Horstmann MT, Elger CE, Lehnertz K (2008) Evolving functional network properties and synchronizability during human epileptic seizures. Chaos 18: 033119.
51. Schindler K, Leung H, Elger CE, Lehnertz K (2007) Assessing seizure dynamics by analysing the correlation structure of multichannel intracranial EEG. Brain 130: 65–77.
52. Schreiber T, Schmitz A (1996) Improved surrogate data for nonlinearity tests. Phys Rev Lett 77: 635–638.
53. Schreiber T, Schmitz A (2000) Surrogate time series. Physica D 142: 346–382.
54. Roberts JM (2000) Simple methods for simulating sociomatrices with given marginal totals. Soc Networks 22: 273–283.
55. Maslov S, Sneppen K, Zaliznyak A (2004) Detection of topological patterns in complex networks: correlation profile of the internet. Physica A 333: 529–540.
56. Artzy-Randrup Y, Fleishman SJ, Ben-Tal N, Stone L (2004) Comment on "Network Motifs: Simple building blocks of complex networks" and "superfamilies of evolved and designed networks". Science 305: 1107.
57. Milo R, Itzkovitz S, Kashtan N, Levitt R, Alon U (2004) Response to comment on "Network Motifs: Simple building blocks of complex networks" and "superfamilies of evolved and designed networks". Science 305: 1107.
58. Artzy-Randrup Y, Stone L (2005) Generating uniformly distributed random networks. Phys Rev E 72: 056708.
59. Del Genio CI, Kim H, Toroczkai Z, Bassler KE (2010) Efficient and exact sampling of simple graphs with given arbitrary degree sequence. PLoS ONE 5: e10012. 27.
60. Blitzstein J, Diaconis P (2010) A sequential importance sampling algorithm for generating random graphs with prescribed degrees. Internet Mathematics 6: 489–522.

61. Eguiluz VM, Chialvo DR, Cecchi GA, Baliki M, Apkarian AV (2005) Scale-free brain functional networks. Phys Rev Lett 94: 018102.
62. van den Heuvel MP, Stam CJ, Boersma M, Hulshoff Pol HE (2008) Small-world and scale-free organization of voxel-based resting-state functional connectivity in the human brain. Neuroimage 43: 528–539.
63. Hayasaka S, Laurienti PJ (2010) Comparison of characteristics between region-and voxel-based network analyses in resting-state fMRI data. Neuroimage 50: 499–508.
64. Fransson P, Åden U, Blennow M, Lagercrantz H (2011) The functional architecture of the infant brain as revealed by resting-state fMRI. Cereb Cortex 21: 145–154.
65. Tian L, Wang J, Yan C, He Y (2011) Hemisphere- and gender-related differences in small-world brain networks: A resting-state functional MRI study. Neuroimage 54: 191–202.
66. Guye M, Bettus G, Bartolomei F, Cozzone PJ (2010) Graph theoretical analysis of structural and functional connectivity MRI in normal and pathological brain networks. Magn Reson Mater Phy 23: 409–421.
67. Small M, Yu D, Harrison RG (2001) Surrogate test for pseudoperiodic time series data. Phys Rev Lett 87: 188101.
68. Breakspear M, Brammer M, Robinson PA (2003) Construction of multivariate surrogate sets from nonlinear data using the wavelet transform. Physica D 182: 1–22.
69. Nakamura T, Small M (2005) Small-shuffle surrogate data: Testing for dynamics in fluctuating data with trends. Phys Rev E 72: 056216.
70. Keylock CJ (2006) Constrained surrogate time series with preservation of the mean and variance structure. Phys Rev E 73: 036707.
71. Suzuki T, Ikeguchi T, Suzuki M (2007) Algorithms for generating surrogate data for sparsely quantized time series. Physica D 231: 108–115.
72. Romano MC, Thiel M, Kurths J, Mergenthaler K, Engbert R (2009) Hypothesis test for synchronization: Twin surrogates revisited. Chaos 19: 015108.

5

Resources and Costs for Microbial Sequence Analysis Evaluated Using Virtual Machines and Cloud Computing

Samuel V. Angiuoli[1,2]*, **James R. White**[1], **Malcolm Matalka**[1], **Owen White**[1], **W. Florian Fricke**[1]*

1 Institute for Genome Sciences (IGS), University of Maryland Baltimore, Baltimore, Maryland, United States of America, 2 Center for Bioinformatics and Computational Biology, University of Maryland, College Park, Maryland, United States of America

Abstract

Background: The widespread popularity of genomic applications is threatened by the "bioinformatics bottleneck" resulting from uncertainty about the cost and infrastructure needed to meet increasing demands for next-generation sequence analysis. Cloud computing services have been discussed as potential new bioinformatics support systems but have not been evaluated thoroughly.

Results: We present benchmark costs and runtimes for common microbial genomics applications, including 16S rRNA analysis, microbial whole-genome shotgun (WGS) sequence assembly and annotation, WGS metagenomics and large-scale BLAST. Sequence dataset types and sizes were selected to correspond to outputs typically generated by small- to midsize facilities equipped with 454 and Illumina platforms, except for WGS metagenomics where sampling of Illumina data was used. Automated analysis pipelines, as implemented in the CloVR virtual machine, were used in order to guarantee transparency, reproducibility and portability across different operating systems, including the commercial Amazon Elastic Compute Cloud (EC2), which was used to attach real dollar costs to each analysis type. We found considerable differences in computational requirements, runtimes and costs associated with different microbial genomics applications. While all 16S analyses completed on a single-CPU desktop in under three hours, microbial genome and metagenome analyses utilized multi-CPU support of up to 120 CPUs on Amazon EC2, where each analysis completed in under 24 hours for less than $60. Representative datasets were used to estimate maximum data throughput on different cluster sizes and to compare costs between EC2 and comparable local grid servers.

Conclusions: Although bioinformatics requirements for microbial genomics depend on dataset characteristics and the analysis protocols applied, our results suggests that smaller sequencing facilities (up to three Roche/454 or one Illumina GAIIx sequencer) invested in 16S rRNA amplicon sequencing, microbial single-genome and metagenomics WGS projects can achieve cost-efficient bioinformatics support using CloVR in combination with Amazon EC2 as an alternative to local computing centers.

Editor: Sarah K. Highlander, Baylor College of Medicine, United States of America

Funding: This research was supported by funds from the National Human Genome Research Institute (NHGRI), National Institutes of Health (NIH), ARRA under Grant No. RC2 HG005597-01, the National Science Foundation (NSF), under Grant No. 0949201 and the Amazon Web Services in Education Research Grants program. The funders had no role in study design, data collection and analysis, decision to publish, or preparation of the manuscript.

Competing Interests: The authors have declared that no competing interests exist.

* E-mail: angiuoli@umiacs.umd.edu (SVA); wffricke@som.umaryland.edu (WFF)

Introduction

Genome sequencing has found widespread applications, including basic science, biosafety and biomedical research, and is expected to become part of the service sector, e.g. in the form of personalized health care [1–3]. The popularity of genomics applications has largely been driven by the introduction of new sequencing technologies that offer increasing sequencing throughput at a decreasing cost per nucleotide. As third-generation sequencing platforms [4] are becoming available, the cost of sequence generation is likely to decrease even further. Moreover, the introduction of "benchtop" sequencing that aims at integrating medium-scale, affordable sequence generation into the standard laboratory equipment [5] is following this decentralization trend where sequencing facilities are becoming available for any size laboratory. As a result, genomics projects no longer depend on the large sequencing centers for sequence generation.

As production of sequence data continues to expand, sequence processing and bioinformatics is increasingly becoming a bottleneck for utilizing genomics approaches. So far, the decentralization of sequence production has not been accompanied by a simultaneous decentralization in computational resources and bioinformatics expertise [6]. The generation of new sequence data is increasing faster than the capacity to computationally analyze it [7], making the feasibility and affordability of future genomics projects increasingly dependent on bioinformatics components rather than on sequence generation. The resulting "bioinformatics bottleneck" describes the problem where the time and cost of basic sequence analysis may far exceed the costs of sequence generation for many researchers.

In this context, cloud computing provides an attractive model with a recognized potential for genomics and bioinformatics to meet the increasing demands for decentralized large-scale computational resources [8]. Following the definition of the National Institute of Standards and Technology (NIST), cloud computing is a "model for enabling convenient, on-demand network access to a shared pool of configurable computing resources (e.g., networks, servers, storage, applications, and services) that can be rapidly provisioned and released with minimal management effort or service provider interaction" (http://www.nist.gov/itl/cloud/upload/cloud-def-v15.pdf).

A key technology available with the cloud is the Virtual Machine (VM). A virtual machine is an operating system that can be pre-packaged with all software needed for a particular analysis. Critically, the VM is portable and can be deployed across institutions and platforms, including desktops, laptops, servers, and remote clouds. The use of VMs aims to overcome difficulties distributing analysis software that have numerous dependencies and hinders usage. This not only addresses technical challenges of deployment and installation but also enables performance comparisons and ultimately cost comparisons across institutions and architectures.

Cloud computing plus virtualization provides a model to develop and evaluate the computational infrastructure necessary for bioinformatics processing. The availability of cloud computing platforms with transparent pricing has generated an opportunity to attach real dollar costs to bioinformatics workflows and to model the associated costs for genomics applications. The Amazon Elastic Compute Cloud (EC2; http://aws.amazon.com/ec2/) provides on-demand compute (priced per CPU hour) and charges additionally for network transfers to and from the cloud (bandwidth priced per GB) and persistent data storage (priced per GB and per month). Academic clouds are also emerging that aim to offer similar services at no cost to academic researchers (e.g., DIAG, http://diag.igs.umaryland.edu/; Magellan, http://magellan.alcf.anl.gov/).

While there is considerable enthusiasm in the bioinformatics community about cloud computing [7–10], only a few tools and examples are available [7,11–14] that demonstrate the usability of cloud services to support large-scale sequence processing. Bioinformatics case studies have been published with varying results, e.g., favoring cloud-based over local computing in both performance and cost for microarray-based transcriptomic analysis [15] or demonstrating comparable performance parameters for cloud-based and local computing and cost advantages of local executions for metagenomics BLAST analysis [14].

In order to initiate, budget and manage genomics projects the following questions need to be considered and adequately addressed beforehand: (i) What are the available methods to analyze the sequence data in order to generate publishable results in standards-conforming formats? (ii) What are the required computational requirements? (iii) What are the real dollar costs to perform the analysis? (iv) Given the amount of sequence data to be analyzed, does it make more sense to use Infrastructure as a Service (IaaS) models, such as the Amazon EC2 cloud, or to invest in a local grid network? The work presented here is intended to address these questions and provide guidelines for researchers, service providers and funding agencies, who invest in microbial genomics projects.

To evaluate the requirements for common bioinformatics applications in microbial genomics, we utilize the Cloud Virtual Resource (CloVR) package (http://clovr.org/) [16]. This software consists of a single virtual machine (CloVR VM), which contains pre-installed and pre-configured open source programs bundled into fully automated sequence analysis pipelines. CloVR supports a broad variety of small to large-scale microbial genomics applications of current and next-generation sequencing platforms

with four automated pipelines: (i) 16S rRNA-based microbial community composition analysis of Sanger and 454 sequence data (CloVR-16S) [17]; (ii) taxonomic and functional community composition analysis of metagenomic whole-genome shotgun (WGS) sequence data (CloVR-Metagenomics) [18]; (iii) bacterial single-genome WGS Sanger, 454 or Illumina sequence assembly and annotation using the IGS Annotation Engine (CloVR-Microbe) [19]; and (iv) large-scale BLAST searches of Sanger, 454 or Illumina sequence data (CloVR-Search).

Methods

Analysis protocols

Four analysis protocols (CloVR pipelines) were utilized in this study, including (i) a parallelized BLAST [20] search protocol (CloVR-Search 1.0); (ii) a comparative 16S rRNA sequence analysis pipeline (CloVR-16S 1.0) [17]; (iii) a comparative metagenomic sequence analysis pipeline (CloVR-Metagenomics 1.0) [18]; and (iv) a single microbial genome assembly and annotation pipeline (CloVR-Microbe 1.0) [19]. Figure 1 gives an overview of the processes involved in the CloVR-16S, CloVR-Metagenomics and CloVR-Microbe pipelines. Detailed pipeline descriptions, including pipeline version numbers, lists of programs used by the pipeline program version numbers and applied options if different from the defaults, can be found in the supplementary material (Text S1).

The 16S rRNA protocol allows for intra- and inter-group comparative analysis (α- and β-diversity), and is based on methods from Mothur [21], Qiime [22], the RDP Bayesian classifier [23], and Metastats [24]. CloVR-16S calculates the number of non-redundant sequences within the total dataset and uses a threshold of 50,000 above which the computationally expensive distance matrix calculation, which is part of the Mothur component of the pipeline, is not performed. The metagenomics protocol performs clustering of redundant sequences, a BLAST-based taxonomic assignment against the NCBI microbial genome Reference Sequence collection (RefSeq) [25] (BLASTN) and a functional assignment against the Clusters of Orthologous Genes (COGs) [26] databases (BLASTX) and further allows for comparative composition analyses between different sequence datasets, using Metastats. The single microbial genome analysis protocol is based on the IGS Annotation Engine [27] (http://ae.igs.umaryland.edu), with the addition that sequence assembly is performed using Celera Assembler [28] for Roche/454 and Sanger platforms-derived sequence data and Velvet [29] for Illumina platform-derived sequence data. This protocol performs a comprehensive annotation including CDS prediction with Glimmer3 [30], ribosomal RNA (rRNA) gene identification with RNAmmer [31], transfer RNA (tRNA) gene identification with tRNAscan-SE [32], and two types of homology searches using BLASTX against UniRef100 and HMMER [33] against the Pfam [34] and TIGRFAM [35] domain databases.

Pipeline execution

All analyses to evaluate the resources and costs associated with several typical analysis protocols in microbial genomics were performed using the CloVR VM version beta-0.5 (build clovr-standard-2011-12-04-22-00-04) downloaded from the CloVR project website (http://clovr.org). The technical details of the CloVR VM implementation are described in detail in a separate publication [16]. Briefly, CloVR is a VM image based on Ubuntu Linux 10.10 that runs on a local computer and optionally utilizes the cloud, where a distributed architecture allows for high-throughput parallel processing using multiple CPUs. Pipelines are

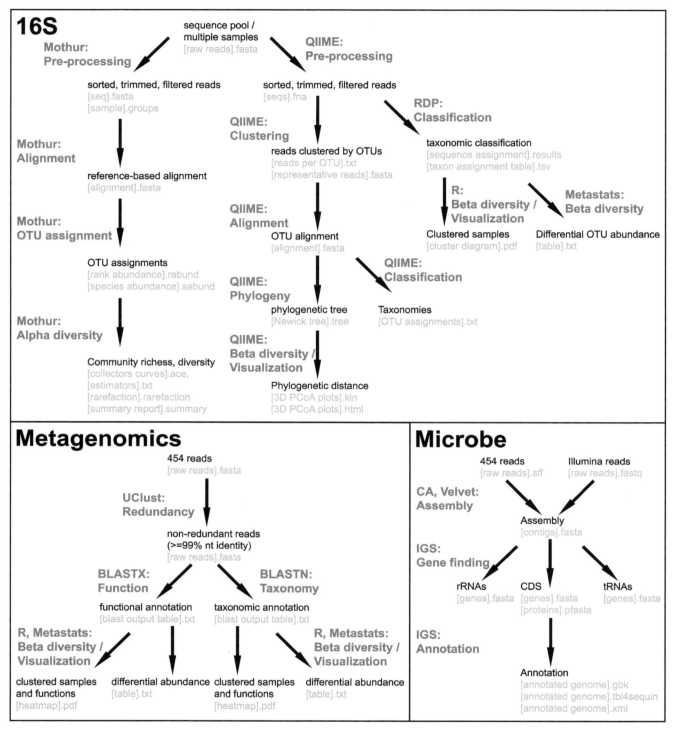

Figure 1. Overview of the CloVR-supported microbial sequence analysis protocols. 1. CloVR-16S supports analysis of pyrotagged amplicon pool sequence data as well as individual samples sequence data, using components from the Mothur [21] package for preprocessing, alignment, operational taxonomic unit (OTU) assignment and alpha diversity estimation. QIIME [22] components are used for sequence clustering, alignment, phylogenetic inference and beta diversity estimation. Sequence reads are assigned to taxonomies using the RDP classifier [23]. Additional visualizations are generated with R script implemented in CloVR. Differentially abundant taxa determined with Metastats [24]. 2. CloVR-Metagenomics supports functional and taxonomic assignments of non-redundant whole-genome shotgun (WGS) sequence data from metagenomic samples. Reads are classified based on BLASTX and BLASTN searches against functional (COG [26], optionally KEGG [46], eggNOG [47]) and taxonomic (RefSeq [25]) reference databases, respectively. The results are statistically evaluated using Metastats and visualized using R scripts implemented in CloVR. 3. CloVR-Microbe supports microbial whole-genome sequencing projects, including Illumina and 454 or Sanger sequence assembly with Velvet [29] and Celera assembler (CA) [28], respectively. Gene predictions and annotations are performed using the complex IGS standard operating procedure for automated prokaryotic annotation (IGS) [27].

executed using the Ergatis workflow system [36] and utilize Sun Grid Engine (http://wikis.sun.com/display/GridEngine/Home) for job scheduling.

Computational resources

The local computer used for evaluation was a 64-bit quad core (Intel Xeon E5520 2.27 GHz CPU) with 4 gigabytes of RAM. For local execution, CloVR was run using VMware Player version 2.0.5 build-109488 (http://vmware.com) configured to use a single CPU core and 2012 MB of memory. Amazon EC2 provides numerous instance types with varying CPU speeds, available RAM and storage (http://aws.amazon.com/ec2/#instance). Previous work in [14] showed the choice of c1.xlarge to be most cost efficient amongst the choices for applications such as BLAST. The c1.xlarge instances provide 8 virtual CPU cores, 8 GB RAM per instance, and 400 GB of local temporary disk storage. In this study, each pipeline was run on a separate cluster of instances within the cloud consisting of one master instance and zero or more worker instances. All master instances utilized the c1.xlarge instance type, except for CloVR-Microbe runs on Illumina sequence data that utilized m2.2×large and m2.xlarge instance types. All worker instances utilized c1.xlarge instances, which at the time of preparing this manuscript were priced at $0.68 per CPU hour (CPU hr). Assembly and annotation of Illumina sequence data required master instances with RAM in excess of the c1.xlarge instance capacity. In the case of the assembly and annotation run on single-read Illumina sequence data, the corresponding master instance was an m2.2×large instance ($1.00/CPU hr), while for the paired-end Illumina run we requested an m2.xlarge master Instance ($0.50/CPU hr). Associated pipeline costs on Amazon EC2 were calculated using cluster performance charts, visualized with the Ganglia tool (http://ganglia.sourceforge.net/), which describe the number of instances utilized in each cluster over time. Pipeline runtimes were obtained from the Ergatis workflow system [36].

Spot market bid-price simulations

To simulate runtime distributions within the Amazon EC2 spot market, we first collected corresponding hourly spot prices for the c1.xlarge instance type from October 20, 2010 to January 24, 2011. Assuming a hypothetical pipeline runtime of 120 CPU hours and a range of bid prices ($0.27/CPU hr to $0.80/CPU hr), we simulated the actual (wall-clock) runtime of a pipeline from random starting points in the collected spot market price data. Given a bid price β and a CPU hr requirement γ, 500 random starting points were picked between October 20, 2010 and January 24, 2011, and the runtime was calculated assuming no processes were running whenever the spot price was above the bid price β. For example, if the bid price was constantly greater than or equal to the spot price, the actual runtime would be γ, because the requested price was always met. Alternatively, if the bid price fell below the spot price for a single hour, then no work was done in that hour and the total actual runtime was γ +1. In these simulations, if a simulated pipeline extended beyond January 24, 2011, the remaining runtime was calculated as continued from the beginning of the time-series. Runtime distributions were visualized in R (http://www.r-project.org/). To support the dynamic nature of the spot market, CloVR utilizes a workflow system that supports resuming pipelines from point of failure [36], allowing for reprocessing of work units that fail on hosts that are terminated due to rising spot market prices.

Results

Computational requirements of microbial genomics applications

Representative datasets from two next-generation sequencing platforms, the Roche/454 GS (GS FLX and GS FLX Titanium) and Illumina GAIIx (Table 1), were processed with several pipelines for microbial sequence analysis (CloVR-16S, -Microbe, -Metagenomics, and -Search) (Fig. 1, see also Tables S1, S2, S3) to determine processing requirements for typical microbial genome projects (Table 2). This data provides guidelines that can help identify applications that are amenable to execution on a local computer and determine those that benefit particularly from additional resources of the cloud. The datasets evaluated include typical outputs of single or multiple sequencing reactions of the Roche/454 and Illumina platforms or fractions thereof and stem from published data from sequencing projects that received wide recognition in the microbial genomics field [37–42] as well as unpublished data from ongoing sequencing projects at the Institute for Genome Sciences (Table 1).

CloVR-16S was always run on a single CPU, either on a local desktop or on the c1.xlarge instance of the Amazon EC2. All runs finished in less than three hours (see Table S1 for a comparison of local and EC2-based runs). Processed datasets included up to ~900 K Roche/454 GS FLX reads from ~400 samples. Besides the dataset size, runtimes were mostly affected by the species diversity within the dataset. The 530 K humanized mouse gut sequences from 215 different samples [41], for example, which contain a total of 14,363 operational taxonomic units (OTUs), were processed in about the same time as the 901 K human vaginal sequences from 392 samples [40], which only contain 4,967 OTUs.

CloVR-Microbe and CloVR-Metagenomics analyses of all datasets were performed exclusively on Amazon EC2 where all runs finished in less than 24 hours (Table 2). Dataset sizes for CloVR-Metagenomics ranged from ~600 K reads (454 GS FLX Titanium), corresponding to 1.2 full sequencing plates, to 5.8 million reads (454 GS FLX), corresponding to 11.6 full sequencing plates, all of which were processed in less than six hours on Amazon EC2. Additional time due to upload of input and download of output was consistently less than one hour. Input data sizes for CloVR-Microbe were representative of typical microbial genome project work loads and included sequence read numbers corresponding to a quarter (250 K) or a half (500 K) plate of 454 GS FLX Titanium and 1/5 (8 million) of an Illumina GAIIx lane (single read and paired-end read libraries). Pipeline outputs were found to be in agreement with results from previously processed similar projects in terms of number of detected OTUs, relative OTU compositions, principal coordinate analysis plots of OTU assignments (CloVR-16S), number of functionally and taxonomically assigned reads (CloVR-Metagenomics), number and lengths of contigs, number and functional annotation of genes (CloVR-Microbe). Cluster sizes on Amazon EC2 were configured automatically based on input data sizes using BLAST and other runtime predictions as implemented in CloVR [16]. The estimates for our evaluation ranged from 14 to 15 machine instances, comprising up to 160 virtual CPUs (Table 2).

BLASTN searches of metagenomic WGS sequence data against the NCBI RefSeq collection were performed on Amazon EC2 using CloVR-Search. Using the multi-CPU support of Amazon EC2, ~600 K reads of 454 GS FLX Titanium, corresponding to 0.6 full plates could be processed in less than two hours (64 CPUs maximum usage). In comparison, a BLASTX search of a similar number (500 K) of shorter (75 bp) Illumina GAIIx reads against

Table 1. Example datasets used for CloVR pipeline benchmarking.

Dataset	Data type	Sequencing platform	Library type[1]	Total reads	Units[2]	Avg. read length [bp]	Size [MB]	Samples
CloVR-Search								
Infant gut WGS [38]	WGS	454 Titanium	SE	595816	0.6 plates	244	145.3	12
Metahit 500 K [39]	WGS	Illumina GAII	-	500000[3]	1/80 channels	75	37.5	1
CloVR-16S								
Humanized mice [41][4]	Amplicon	454 GS FLX	SE	530030	1.1 plates	232	122.5	215
Infant gut 16S [38]	Amplicon	454 GS FLX	SE	399127	0.8 plates	179	95.1	63
Human vagina [40]	Amplicon	454 GS FLX	SE	901264	1.8 plates	223	200.6	392
CloVR-Metagenomics								
Obese twins [42]	WGS	454 GS FLX	SE	999990	2 plates	219	218.9	18
Infant gut WGS[4]	WGS	454 Titanium	SE	595816	0.6 plates	244	145.3	12
Nine biomes [37]	WGS	454 GS FLX	SE	5785371	11.6 plates	109	631.2	45
CloVR-Microbe								
Escherichia coli 250 K	WGS	454 Titanium	PE (3 kbp)	250000[3]	0.25 plates	279	69.7	1
Escherichia coli 500 K[4]	WGS	454 Titanium	PE (8 kbp)	500000[3]	0.5 plates	367	183.9	1
Escherichia coli 8 M SE	WGS	Illumina GAII	SE	8000000[3]	0.2 channels	36	288	1
Escherichia coli 8 M PE	WGS	Illumina GAII	PE (3 kbp)	8000000[3]	0.2 channels	49	392	1
Acinetobacter baylyi 250 K	WGS	454 Titanium	PE (8 kbp)	250000[3]	0.25 plates	338	84.7	1

[1]Abbreviations: bp, basepairs; SE, single-end; PE, paired-end (in parentheses: insert size); WGS, whole-genome shotgun.
[2]References for unit sizes: Roche/454 GS GS FLX, 500 K reads per plate (two half plates); Roche/454 GS GS FLX Titanium, 1 M reads per plate (two half plates); Illumina GAII, 40 M reads per channel (eight channels per flowcell).
[3]Trimmed datasets.
[4]Dataset used for Figures 2 and 3.

the non-redundant protein database at NCBI (NCBI-NR comprising 14.7 M sequences, ~5000 M residues), which produced about the same percentage of matches (3.2% vs. 3.4%) took about 10 times longer to complete (~11 hours), using 2.5 times the amount of CPUs (160 CPUs maximum usage). For the Illumina GAIIx platform, 500 K reads correspond to only 1/6 of the average sequencing output of a single channel (eight lanes per flow cell).

The impact of different analysis protocols on runtime and cost for metagenomic WGS analysis was determined by comparing an assembly-based (CloVR-Microbe), a gene-prediction-based and a gene prediction-independent (CloVR-Metagenomics) protocol and a BLAST search (CloVR-Search) on the same dataset (Table S2).

Real dollar values of bioinformatics sequence analysis applications

Real dollar costs were calculated for all microbial sequence analyses performed with the CloVR protocols on Amazon EC2, in order to provide guidelines for costs associated with microbial genomics projects (Table 2). The costs include overhead introduced by the CloVR VM to make use of the cloud environment, e.g. time for data upload and download and to prepare input and output data. Table 2 also provides example network transfer times for upload to and download from Amazon EC2, although such times can vary substantially based on the network environment. Several large datasets that are used as reference data for the CloVR pipelines, e.g. the UniRef100 protein database for CloVR-Microbe comprising 3.4 GB of compressed data, were hosted permanently on the Amazon Simple Storage Service (http://aws.amazon.com/s3/). This service provides data storage inside the cloud network and was used to reduce the need for data transfer over the Internet when

executing in the cloud. During the pipeline execution, the free ephemeral instance storage was used as temporary storage and all output data was compressed and downloaded to the local desktop upon pipeline completion. CloVR is configured to automatically shut down all CloVR VMs on the cloud upon pipeline completion in order to avoid charges for idle instances and persisting storage.

Based on the CloVR runs on Amazon EC2, the cost of each 16S rRNA community analysis was less than $10. For the sequence data generated with the short amplicon 454 sequencing protocol, costs ranged from less than $1 to $2.72. Since all pipelines finished in less than two hours, the costs associated with Amazon EC2 charges for instances being active during upload and download times constitute a significant fraction of the total cost (Table 2), but are nominally small at $0.68 per EC2 c1.xlarge instance hour.

All CloVR-Metagenomics and CloVR-Microbe runs were completed at costs of less than $100. Sequence analyses with the CloVR-Metagenomics pipeline had an associated cost of between ~$23 and ~$56; CloVR-Microbe runs had costs of between ~$39 and ~$62.

Capacity and optimization of processing pipelines

The multi-CPU capabilities of the cloud allow for decreased runtime for pipelines involving analysis steps that can be parallelized, such as CloVR-Microbe and CloVR-Metagenomics, which contain BLASTX and BLASTN sequence comparisons (Fig. 1). At the same time, partitioning the analysis with CloVR into multiple parallel processes on different CPUs of the same instance or even across different instances of the same cluster involves copying of reference data, increases the amount of data transfer between instances and incurs additional processing overhead [16]. To determine differences in the CloVR-Microbe

Table 2. Cost and runtime parameters of CloVR pipeline runs on example datasets.

Dataset	Upload time	Pipeline runtime	Download time	Total cost[1]	Max. VM instances[2]	Max. CPUs	QC		
CloVR-Search							RefSeq matches		
Infant gut WGS [38], BLASTN against RefSeq	3 min	1 hr 26 min	20 min	$11	8	64	34.3		
Metahit 500 K [39], BLASTX against NR	11 min	10 hr 42 min	17 min	$151	20	160	3.2%		
CloVR-16S							OTUs		
Humanized mice [41]	42 min	1 hr 30 min	12 min	$3	1	8	14363		
Infant gut 16S [38]	3 min	42 min	10 min	$1	1	8	3447		
Human vagina [40]	1 hr 17 min	1 hr 51 min	14 min	$3	1	8	4967		
CloVR-Metagenomics[3]							nr reads	RefSeq matches	COG matches
Obese twins [42]	8 min	2 hr 25 min	24 min	$30	20	160	93.6%	33.3%	29.6%
Infant gut WGS	7 min	2 hr 17 min	29 min	$24	15	120	98.2%	35.2%[4]	33.5%
Nine biomes [37]	15 min	5 hr 35 min	39 min	$56	20	160	89.9%	9.3%	5.6%
CloVR-Microbe							Scaffolds/Contigs	N50[5]	CDS[6]
Escherichia coli 250 K	24 min	16 hr 21 min	52 min	$55	14	112	8/414	25 kbp	6313
Escherichia coli 500 K	20 min	20 hr 23 min	50 min	$60	15	120	37/141	183 kbp	5827
Escherichia coli 8 M SE	12 min	15 hr 44 min	37 min	$62	15	120	553/553	17 kbp	4803
Escherichia coli 8 M PE	16 min	15 hr 2 min	44 min	$44	15	120	481/481	18 kbp	4464
Acinetobacter baylyi 250 K	20 min	9 hr 46 min	37 min	$39	15	120	4/38	262 kbp	3417

[1]Rounded to the next full dollar.
[2]VM instances are linked together as a cluster for parallel processing on the cloud. The number of instances in a cluster can change during pipeline execution. The master instance is included.
[3]The standard CloVR-Metagenomics pipeline refers to the gene prediction-independent protocol.
[4]For the CloVR-Metagenomics pipeline sequence reads are clustered, representative reads for each cluster searched against the reference database, and matches of the representative reads assigned back to all reads from the cluster, resulting in a slightly larger number of overall matches than for the comparable CloVR-Search pipeline.
[5]Scaffold or contig N50 is a weighted median statistic such that 50% of the entire assembly is contained in scaffolds or contigs equal to or larger than this value.
[6]CDS, coding sequences.

runtimes and associated costs depending on the number of CPUs used, the same 454 GS FLX Titanium dataset, 500 K reads corresponding to one full plate of 8 kbp paired-end sequences, was run with different cluster sizes on Amazon EC2 (Fig. 2, Table S3). Based on this example, the lowest runtimes and costs achieved fell between 72 CPUs (23 hours, $58) and 120 CPUs (20 hours, $60). These numbers represent a runtime and cost improvement of up to 36 hours and $16 compared to a 56 hour-run with 16 CPUs for $74. A further increase of the cluster size to 172 CPUs did not result in runtime improvements but resulted in increased cost ($82) due to payment for under-utilized instances. Inefficiencies in pipeline implementation resulted in increased competition for resources, longer runtimes, and thus increased costs for clusters containing two and three instances (16 and 24 CPUs, respectively). Future work on optimizing the CloVR pipelines is expected to reduce runtimes and costs on smaller clusters. A local run on a single-CPU machine was canceled after 14 days and was extrapolated to require in excess of 24 days runtime.

To estimate the amount of sequence analysis that is affordable for a given dollar value, the number of analysis runs using three different protocols (CloVR-16S, CloVR-Metagenomics and CloVR-Microbe) was plotted against the corresponding cost, using results from Table 2 (Fig. 3). These costs were compared to the $130 K estimated as average annual cost to set up and maintain a local cluster of 240 CPUs for three years as described by Dudley *et al.* [15]. Using the Dudley estimates, for the cost of a local cluster, 43,333 runs of CloVR-16S; 5,416 runs of CloVR-Metagenomics; and 2,166 runs of CloVR-Microbe can be processed each year on Amazon EC2. For single whole-genome microbial sequencing projects, with a theoretical annual output of 730 datasets per 454 GS FLX Titanium sequencer (one full plate per day, two single-genome datasets per plate), up to three sequencing machines can be supported using Amazon EC2 at current prices, using CloVR-Microbe benchmark protocols, before the estimated cost of a local cluster is reached. It should be noted that the interpretation of these results is limited by the fact that the comparison does not consider utilization rates on the local cluster, which is likely to be used for a different applications, rather than to exclusively support a single protocol.

Realizing cost savings using excess capacity in the Amazon EC2 spot market

The Amazon EC2 spot market allows customers to place bids on unused cloud resources and utilize instances for as long as the bid exceeds the current spot price (http://aws.amazon.com/ec2/spot-instances/). During periods of weak demand, the spot market provides the ability to utilize excess resources at a discounted price. Over the period of the past year, the spot market price for the

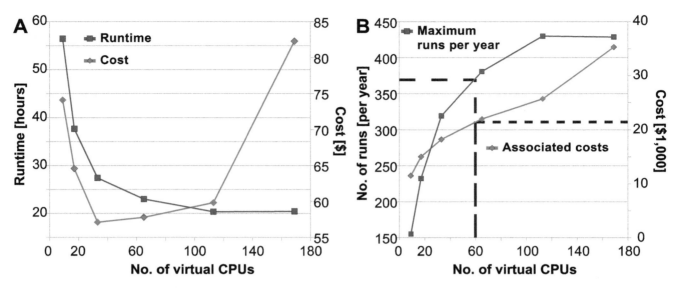

Figure 2. Cost and performance of CloVR-Microbe using different cluster sizes. A) Steps of the CloVR-Microbe pipeline can be executed in parallel to improve performance as shown by plotting pipeline runtimes (blue) and associated costs (red) against the number of CPUs used to perform the analysis on Amazon EC2. B) Using this data, the theoretical maximum throughput per year (blue) as well as associated costs (red) of analysis can be extrapolated. As an example, the output of a single 454 GS FLX Titanium machine, run every other day with two single microbial genomes per sequencing plate (365 total runs), can be processed on Amazon EC2 using 60 CPUs (or eight Amazon EC2 c1.xlarge instances) for less than $25,000, as indicated by the dashed red and blue lines. Inefficiencies in pipeline implementation resulted in increased competition for resources, longer runtimes, and thus increased costs for clusters containing 2 and 3 instances (16 and 24 CPUs, respectively).

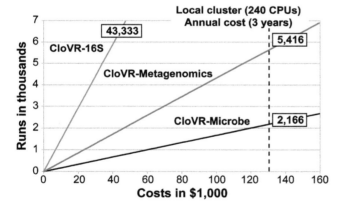

Figure 3. Costs and throughput of CloVR-16S, CloVR-Metagenomics and CloVR-Microbe analysis runs. Costs for single CloVR-16S (blue), CloVR-Metagenomics (red) and CloVR-Microbe (black) runs of comparable datasets (~500 K 454 GS FLX or GS FLX Titanium reads, see Table 1) on Amazon EC2 were extrapolated to calculate the number of runs that are obtainable for a given dollar value. The black dashed line represents the average annual cost ($130 K) to set up and maintain a local cluster of 240 CPUs for a three years from Dudley *et al.* [15]. Numbers in boxes show how many runs of CloVR-16S, -Metagenomics, and -Microbe can be afforded for the same cost. As an example, approximately three 454 GS FLX Titanium sequencers (two genomes per sequencing plate and one run per day, adding up to 2,190 datasets) or one Illumina GAIIx sequencer (five genomes per lane, eight lanes per sequencing flow cell and one run per week, adding up to 2,080 datasets) can be processed with CloVR-Microbe on Amazon EC2 annually for the same cost as estimated to set up and maintain the 240 CPU local cluster. The local cluster would, however, provide resources exceeding those required for each of the projected analysis protocols.

c1.xlarge instance averaged $0.26 compared to an on-demand price of $0.68. This variable pricing is well-suited to processing needs that are not time critical, since analyses purchased under this model will only proceed when the provided bid price is above the current market price for the resource. This market model also provides the ability to predict the expected completion time of a pipeline for a particular bid price using historical pricing data.

To evaluate potential cost savings and associated runtime increases that could be achieved with the Amazon EC2 spot market, the expected completion times were estimated for bids of $0.27 to $0.80 using a hypothetical analysis requiring 120 c1.xlarge instance hours (960 c1.xlarge CPU hours) for completion (Fig. 4). The expected completion time was predicted for each bid price using the recorded pricing data for the past month. Based on this model, at a bid price of $0.68 the analysis was expected to execute in ~120 hours, while never taking longer than ~145 hours. By comparison, a $0.27 bid, which during the recorded month was not fulfilled during times of peak demand, when the market price rose above the bid, realized savings of 40% for the user. A bid of $0.27 was estimated to result in an average runtime of ~185 hours, 50% more than when using the full on-demand price. Altogether, predicted runtimes for this bid ranged from ~155 hours (29% slower) to ~225 hours (87% slower). In this example, runtimes were estimated based on a task that was executed on a single CPU, whereas many bioinformatics pipelines utilize multiple CPUs in parallel across several instances, thereby reducing the actual pipeline runtime.

Discussion

In this study, we explore the costs and resources required for microbial sequence analysis using pre-packaged protocols in CloVR [16]. By packaging these pipelines into a single automated framework, the CloVR virtual machine, the performance of protocols between platforms and costs on commercial clouds can easily be compared and evaluated.

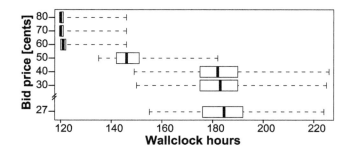

Figure 4. Predicted runtimes using varying bid prices for the Amazon EC2 spot market. An analysis requiring 120 CPU hours was used an example to estimate the expected completion time for different bid prices for the Amazon EC2 c1.xlarge instance, ranging from $0.27 to $0.80 (on-demand price: $0,68).

The automated pipelines in CloVR were selected with the intention of packaging existing community-supported analysis protocols. The protocol, CloVR-Microbe, combines a sequence assembly step with the IGS Annotation Engine [27]. With the support of a large local grid cluster, the IGS Annotation Engine was designed to be thorough for genome annotation but not optimized for speed or efficient CPU usage, and many alternative genome annotation protocols exist, e.g. RAST [43], DIYA [44]. To our knowledge, CloVR-Microbe represents the first automated pipeline that combines sequence assembly and annotation in an automated pipeline that runs on the desktop.

The CloVR-16S pipeline was designed to combine components of several widely used 16S rRNA sequence analysis protocols, without making the entire workflow computationally too complex to process even large sequence datasets (>200 samples, >500 K sequences). The current implementation of CloVR-16S supports a distance matrix-based operational taxonomic unit (OTU) assignment and α-diversity analysis with Mothur [21], direct taxonomic classifications of sequence reads with the RDP classifier tool [23] and microbial community analysis with the QIIME tool, which has a strong focus on tree-based metric for β-diversity analysis [22]. A critical component of CloVR-16S in its current implementation is the threshold of 50,000 non-redundant sequences above which the Mothur component with its computationally expensive distance matrix calculation is not carried out.

Metagenomics projects are usually designed to generate the most sequence data per invested dollar and, thus, often involve large-scale next-generation sequencing. Due to the resulting dataset sizes, metagenomics analysis protocols often rely on the direct classification of individual sequence reads by BLAST, instead of using sequence assembly, which is computationally demanding. Similarly, the CloVR-Metagenomics pipeline was built to examine and compare taxonomic and functional microbial community compositions within and between metagenomic samples using two BLAST searches against a bacterial genome database (BLASTN against NCBI's RefSeq) and against a functionally annotated protein database (BLASTP against NCBI's COG). The CloVR-Search pipeline was designed to provide support for large-scale BLAST comparisons using the cloud multi-processor architecture. A direct BLASTN comparison of each sequence read against the NCBI RefSeq nucleotide database with CloVR-Search was shown to provide runtime improvements albeit without producing the visual and statistical evaluations of the results that are generated by the CloVR-Metagenomics pipeline. BLAST search results alone can be used in downstream

applications, e.g. with the MEGAN tool, which utilizes pre-computed BLAST result to calculate taxonomic classifications of metagenomic sequence data [45].

The comparison of two pipelines for processing metagenomics WGS data demonstrates that the choice of analysis protocols is most critical and will be the primary determinant of performance rather than the execution environment. Runtimes and costs for the same dataset differed significantly, depending on whether the data was processed using assembly-based, gene prediction-based or gene prediction-independent protocols (Table S2). A recent publication suggests that for the analysis of metagenomics WGS data, an exhaustive translated BLASTX against NCBI-NR may be prohibitively time-consuming and expensive on the cloud [14]. Similarly, based on our calculations, the BLASTX protocol is expensive for searching Illumina short read data (11 hours, $150 for 500 K reads), such as those generated from the recent MetaHIT study on the human gut microbiota [39]. In summary, these results support the notion that the bioinformatics bottleneck of next-generation sequence data will not be completely addressed simply by scaling up the computational resources without utilization of methods specifically designed for large data volumes.

Cloud computing has caused notable excitement in the bioinformatics community as a potential solution to the so-called "bioinformatics bottleneck", resulting from the increasing production of second- and third-generation sequence data with high computational demands for analysis [7,8]. There is, however, concern and uncertainty over the costs of using commercial cloud resources. We decided to use the popular Amazon EC2 cloud as a model for evaluating analysis costs. Importantly for budgeting, the costs at Amazon EC2 are transparent and directly obtainable for any workload, allowing for attaching real dollar costs to computational analyses. Our results show that bioinformatics support for microbial genomics can be provided at a competitive price, provided analysis protocols are chosen carefully. In addition, as many analysis needs are not time-critical and can wait for off-peak hours, a bidding market for computational resources, such as the Amazon EC2 Spot Market, provides an intriguing model for further cost savings. Since these costs depend substantially on the choice of analysis protocol, the results in this study can also be used as benchmarks for comparing costs and resources of other analysis protocols.

The Amazon EC2 cloud can also serve as a model to evaluate the computational infrastructure needed to perform common microbial genomics applications. Our tests with the CloVR protocols show that typical workloads of small to midsize sequencing facilities are economically processed either locally, on a single desktop machine (CloVR-16S), or online using the Amazon EC2 cloud (CloVR-Metagenomics, -Microbe, -Search). The computational resources deployed for the evaluation were modest, utilizing no more than 20 virtual machine instances, eight CPUs per instance and 152 CPUs at a maximum, indicating that use of comparable resources through shared local computing infrastructures is also feasible. As multi-core CPUs are increasingly becoming accessible on the desktop computer market, the ability to process larger data on local desktops is also likely to increase in the future.

Our evaluation datasets were small (631 MB maximum) and network transfers were not prohibitively long (<1.5 hours maximum), although we do expect that network transfer can contribute significantly to overall runtime for larger datasets or lower speed connections. Although raw data output sizes may increase from new sequencing platforms, in the case of single-genome projects, the amount of raw sequence data necessary for whole genome assembly and annotation is not expected to grow dramatically in the near future. The overhead costs resulting from data transfers, either because Amazon EC2 charges directly for the transfer itself ($0.1 per GB of inbound and $0.15 per GB of outbound data transfer, April 2011) or for the instance, which is online during the transfer, are insignificant in our evaluations, totaling no more than a few dollars. It is noteworthy that Amazon allows for data import using physical storage devices sent to the Amazon Web Services (http://aws.amazon.com/importexport/).

In a recent publication the Amazon EC2 cloud was reviewed favorably as an alternative to local compute clusters for large-scale microarray data analysis [15]. In the same publication the cost to set up a local compute cluster (240 CPUs) was estimated as about $130 K per year (for three years total). Using our example calculations and an average of two datasets per 454 GS FLX Titanium sequencing run (500 K reads each) 59, 7 and 3 454 GS FLX Titanium sequencers running daily could be supported with the CloVR-16S, CloVR-Metagenomics and CloVR-Microbe protocols, respectively. However, it should be noted that the capacities of the local compute cluster used for the comparison would exceed those required for the analysis examples. The excess in computational capacities provided by the local cluster would allow for resource sharing with additional users to reduce overall costs or provide computational support for bioinformatics research and development, which can be critical especially in the academic environment.

In general, local cluster setups and cloud computing services are best compared when taking into account average utilization rates and expectations on process runtimes. The on-demand model of the cloud makes it most attractive when compared to a local cluster that is under-utilized since paying for idle cycles is avoided. Local clusters, on the other side, can be better designed to meet the exact requirements for particular analysis types, for example by providing high memory machines or fast networking, which may be unavailable on the cloud. In academic or other research settings, cost savings for local setups are realized by integrating the local compute cluster into a core facility, allowing for multiple user support, shared expenses for maintenance, and operation at levels closer to maximum capacities. In cases where a local resource achieves a very high utilization rate, the benefits and cost savings of an on-demand model may disappear. However, there is a considerable challenge in right-sizing the resource to both achieve a high utilization rate and deliver results in a reasonable amount of time.

The microbial genomics field is in the middle of experiencing a fundamental re-organization, as sequence generation is increasingly becoming decentralized and introduced as a standard application not only in smaller research laboratories but also the clinical and public health sector. This development requires a concomitant decentralization of the sequencing-associated bioinformatics, i.e. widespread access to bioinformatics expertise and computing infrastructures, as well as improved transparency of associated cost and required infrastructures. The CloVR project aims at closing the bioinformatics gap by providing automated pipelines and support for cloud computing from the local desktop (http://clovr.org). The results presented, which use CloVR in combination with the Amazon cloud, attach transparent cost and runtime calculations to common microbial genomics applications. All benchmarks provided here are specifically tied to the CloVR analysis protocols, CloVR implementation, Amazon cloud hardware, and size of data sets, and changes in any of these areas may alter the benchmarks. Users should therefore consider carefully if the examples provided will apply to a particular

sequence analysis task. However, the results presented here show that microbial sequence analysis is generally affordable to the broad user community and that cloud computing provides an economical resource for microbial genomics analysis pipelines, such as those implemented in CloVR. As virtualization and cloud computing have found widespread applications in sequence analysis, we expect the ability to evaluate and compare the cost and scalability of bioinformatics applications will increase in the future.

Supporting Information

Text S1 Detailed descriptions, including pipeline version numbers, lists of programs used by the pipeline program version numbers and applied options if different from the defaults for CloVR-16S v1.0, CloVR-Metagenomics v1.0 and CloVR-Microbe v1.0.

Table S1 Comparison of CloVR-16S runtimes executed locally and on Amazon EC2.

Table S2 Variations in cost and runtime parameters of different CloVR pipeline runs on the same metagenomics WGS dataset (Infant gut WGS). Three different analysis protocols (CloVR-Microbe, CloVR-Metagenomics and CloVR-Search) were evaluated for their impact on runtime and cost for metagenomic WGS analysis. All analyses were run on the Infant Gut Microbiome WGS input dataset [38], corresponding to 0.6 full plates of single-end 454 GS FLX Titanium sequences. The CloVR-Microbe pipeline was included to provide a comparison of assembly-based and assembly-free analysis methods. We note that the Glimmer gene finding tool [30], which is part of the CloVR-Microbe protocol, was optimized for large contiguous assembled sequence data and is known to perform less optimally on short sequence fragments that contain a large number of truncated coding sequences. Two variations were used of the CloVR-Metagenomics protocol: i) The first searches each nucleotide sequence read against the COG database [26] by BLASTX, using all six nucleotide sequence frames translated into protein sequences, whereas ii) the second first runs a gene prediction with Metagene [48], before translating the identified genes into protein sequences and running a BLASTP search against the COG database. A BLASTN comparison of each read against NCBI's RefSeq database performed with CloVR-Search was used as the most basic analysis protocol.

Table S3 Runtime and cost comparisons of CloVR-Microbe executions on the same input dataset run with different Amazon EC2 cluster sizes.

Acknowledgments

We thank Anup Mahurkar, Michelle Giglio and the entire CloVR team (Cesar Arze, Kevin Galens, Stephen Mekosh, David Riley, Mahesh Vangala) at the Institute for Genome Sciences, Baltimore, MD, for their invaluable support of this project.

Author Contributions

Conceived and designed the experiments: SVA WFF. Performed the experiments: SVA JRW MM. Analyzed the data: SVA JRW WFF. Contributed reagents/materials/analysis tools: SVA JRW MM OW WFF. Wrote the paper: SVA WFF.

References

1. Bailey RC (2010) Grand challenge commentary: Informative diagnostics for personalized medicine. Nat Chem Biol 6: 857–859.
2. Green ED, Guyer MS (2011) Charting a course for genomic medicine from base pairs to bedside. Nature 470: 204–213.
3. Guttmacher AE, McGuire AL, Ponder B, Stefansson K (2010) Personalized genomic information: preparing for the future of genetic medicine. Nat Rev Genet 11: 161–165.
4. Chin CS, Sorenson J, Harris JB, Robins WP, Charles RC, et al. (2011) The origin of the Haitian cholera outbreak strain. N Engl J Med 364: 33–42.
5. Rusk N (2011) Torrents of sequence. Nature Methods 8: 44.
6. Field D, Tiwari B, Booth T, Houten S, Swan D, et al. (2006) Open software for biologists: from famine to feast. Nat Biotechnol 24: 801–803.
7. Schatz MC, Langmead B, Salzberg SL (2010) Cloud computing and the DNA data race. Nat Biotechnol 28: 691–693.
8. Stein LD (2010) The case for cloud computing in genome informatics. Genome Biol 11: 207.
9. Bateman A, Wood M (2009) Cloud computing. Bioinformatics 25: 1475.
10. Dudley JT, Butte AJ (2010) In silico research in the era of cloud computing. Nat Biotechnol 28: 1181–1185.
11. Langmead B, Hansen KD, Leek JT (2010) Cloud-scale RNA-sequencing differential expression analysis with Myrna. Genome Biol 11: R83.
12. Langmead B, Schatz MC, Lin J, Pop M, Salzberg SL (2009) Searching for SNPs with cloud computing. Genome Biol 10: R134.
13. Schatz MC (2009) CloudBurst: highly sensitive read mapping with MapReduce. Bioinformatics 25: 1363–1369.
14. Wilkening J, Wilke A, Desai N, Meyer DF (2009) Using Clouds for Metagenomics: A Case Study. IEEE Cluster 2009. New OrleansLA: IEEE.
15. Dudley JT, Pouliot Y, Chen R, Morgan AA, Butte AJ (2010) Translational bioinformatics in the cloud: an affordable alternative. Genome Med 2: 51.
16. Angiuoli SV, Matalka M, Gussman A, Galens K, Vangala M, et al. (2011) CloVR: A virtual machine for automated and portable sequence analysis from the desktop using cloud computing. BMC Bioinformatics 12: 356.
17. White JR, Arze C, Matalka M, Team TC, White O, et al. (2011) CloVR-16S: Phylogenetic microbial community composition analysis based on 16S ribosomal RNA amplicon sequencing – standard operating procedure, version1.0. Nature Precedings.
18. White JR, Arze C, Matalka M, Team TC, Angiuoli SV, et al. (2011) CloVR-Metagenomics: Functional and taxonomic microbial community characterization from metagenomic whole-genome shotgun (WGS) sequences – standard operating procedure, version 1.0. Nature Preceding.
19. Galens K, White JR, Arze C, Matalka M, Giglio MG, et al. (2011) CloVR-Microbe: Assembly, gene finding and functional annotation of raw sequence data from single microbial genome projects – standard operating procedure, version 1.0. Nature Preceding.
20. Altschul SF, Gish W, Miller W, Myers EW, Lipman DJ (1990) Basic local alignment search tool. J Mol Biol 215: 403–410.
21. Schloss PD, Westcott SL, Ryabin T, Hall JR, Hartmann M, et al. (2009) Introducing mothur: open-source, platform-independent, community-supported software for describing and comparing microbial communities. Appl Environ Microbiol 75: 7537–7541.
22. Caporaso JG, Kuczynski J, Stombaugh J, Bittinger K, Bushman FD, et al. (2010) QIIME allows analysis of high-throughput community sequencing data. Nat Methods 7: 335–336.
23. Wang Q, Garrity GM, Tiedje JM, Cole JR (2007) Naive Bayesian classifier for rapid assignment of rRNA sequences into the new bacterial taxonomy. Appl Environ Microbiol 73: 5261–5267.
24. White JR, Nagarajan N, Pop M (2009) Statistical methods for detecting differentially abundant features in clinical metagenomic samples. PLoS Comput Biol 5: e1000352.
25. Pruitt KD, Tatusova T, Klimke W, Maglott DR (2009) NCBI Reference Sequences: current status, policy and new initiatives. Nucleic Acids Res 37: D32–36.
26. Tatusov RL, Fedorova ND, Jackson JD, Jacobs AR, Kiryutin B, et al. (2003) The COG database: an updated version includes eukaryotes. BMC Bioinformatics 4: 41.
27. Galens K, Orvis J, Daugherty S, Creasy HH, Angiuoli S, et al. (2011) The IGS Standard Operating Procedure for Automated Prokaryotic Annotation. Stand Genomic Sci 4: 244–251.
28. Adams MD, Celniker SE, Holt RA, Evans CA, Gocayne JD, et al. (2000) The genome sequence of Drosophila melanogaster. Science 287: 2185–2195.
29. Zerbino DR, Birney E (2008) Velvet: algorithms for de novo short read assembly using de Bruijn graphs. Genome Res 18: 821–829.
30. Delcher AL, Bratke KA, Powers EC, Salzberg SL (2007) Identifying bacterial genes and endosymbiont DNA with Glimmer. Bioinformatics 23: 673–679.
31. Lagesen K, Hallin P, Rodland EA, Staerfeldt HH, Rognes T, et al. (2007) RNAmmer: consistent and rapid annotation of ribosomal RNA genes. Nucleic Acids Res 35: 3100–3108.
32. Lowe TM, Eddy SR (1997) tRNAscan-SE: a program for improved detection of transfer RNA genes in genomic sequence. Nucleic Acids Res 25: 955–964.
33. Eddy SR (2009) A new generation of homology search tools based on probabilistic inference. Genome Inform 23: 205–211.
34. Finn RD, Mistry J, Tate J, Coggill P, Heger A, et al. (2010) The Pfam protein families database. Nucleic Acids Res 38: D211–222.
35. Haft DH, Selengut JD, White O (2003) The TIGRFAMs database of protein families. Nucleic Acids Res 31: 371–373.
36. Orvis J, Crabtree J, Galens K, Gussman A, Inman JM, et al. (2010) Ergatis: a web interface and scalable software system for bioinformatics workflows. Bioinformatics 26: 1488–1492.
37. Dinsdale EA, Edwards RA, Hall D, Angly F, Breitbart M, et al. (2008) Functional metagenomic profiling of nine biomes. Nature 452: 629–632.
38. Koenig JE, Spor A, Scalfone N, Fricker AD, Stombaugh J, et al. (2010) Microbes and Health Sackler Colloquium: Succession of microbial consortia in the developing infant gut microbiome. Proc Natl Acad Sci U S A.
39. Qin J, Li R, Raes J, Arumugam M, Burgdorf KS, et al. (2010) A human gut microbial gene catalogue established by metagenomic sequencing. Nature 464: 59–65.
40. Ravel J, Gajer P, Abdo Z, Schneider GM, Koenig SS, et al. (2010) Microbes and Health Sackler Colloquium: Vaginal microbiome of reproductive-age women. Proc Natl Acad Sci U S A.
41. Turnbaugh P, Ridaura V, Faith J, Rey FE, Knight R, et al. (2009) The Effect of Diet on the Human Gut Microbiome: A Metagenomic Analysis in Humanized Gnotobiotic Mice. Sci Transl Med 1: 6ra14.
42. Turnbaugh PJ, Hamady M, Yatsunenko T, Cantarel BL, Duncan A, et al. (2009) A core gut microbiome in obese and lean twins. Nature 457: 480–484.
43. Aziz RK, Bartels D, Best AA, DeJongh M, Disz T, et al. (2008) The RAST Server: rapid annotations using subsystems technology. BMC Genomics 9: 75.
44. Stewart AC, Osborne B, Read TD (2009) DIYA: a bacterial annotation pipeline for any genomics lab. Bioinformatics 25: 962–963.
45. Huson DH, Auch AF, Qi J, Schuster SC (2007) MEGAN analysis of metagenomic data. Genome Res 17: 377–386.
46. Kanehisa M, Goto S, Furumichi M, Tanabe M, Hirakawa M (2010) KEGG for representation and analysis of molecular networks involving diseases and drugs. Nucleic Acids Res 38: D355–360.
47. Muller J, Szklarczyk D, Julien P, Letunic I, Roth A, et al. (2010) eggNOG v2.0: extending the evolutionary genealogy of genes with enhanced non-supervised orthologous groups, species and functional annotations. Nucleic Acids Res 38: D190–195.
48. Noguchi H, Park J, Takagi T (2006) MetaGene: prokaryotic gene finding from environmental genome shotgun sequences. Nucleic Acids Res 34: 5623–5630.

6

CloudDOE: A User-Friendly Tool for Deploying Hadoop Clouds and Analyzing High-Throughput Sequencing Data with MapReduce

Wei-Chun Chung[1,2,3], Chien-Chih Chen[1,2], Jan-Ming Ho[1,3], Chung-Yen Lin[1], Wen-Lian Hsu[1], Yu-Chun Wang[1], D. T. Lee[1,2,4], Feipei Lai[2], Chih-Wei Huang[1], Yu-Jung Chang[1]*

1 Institute of Information Science, Academia Sinica, Taipei, Taiwan, 2 Department of Computer Science and Information Engineering, National Taiwan University, Taipei, Taiwan, 3 Research Center for Information Technology Innovation, Academia Sinica, Taipei, Taiwan, 4 Department of Computer Science and Information Engineering, National Chung Hsing University, Taichung, Taiwan

Abstract

Background: Explosive growth of next-generation sequencing data has resulted in ultra-large-scale data sets and ensuing computational problems. Cloud computing provides an on-demand and scalable environment for large-scale data analysis. Using a MapReduce framework, data and workload can be distributed via a network to computers in the cloud to substantially reduce computational latency. Hadoop/MapReduce has been successfully adopted in bioinformatics for genome assembly, mapping reads to genomes, and finding single nucleotide polymorphisms. Major cloud providers offer Hadoop cloud services to their users. However, it remains technically challenging to deploy a Hadoop cloud for those who prefer to run MapReduce programs in a cluster without built-in Hadoop/MapReduce.

Results: We present CloudDOE, a platform-independent software package implemented in Java. CloudDOE encapsulates technical details behind a user-friendly graphical interface, thus liberating scientists from having to perform complicated operational procedures. Users are guided through the user interface to deploy a Hadoop cloud within in-house computing environments and to run applications specifically targeted for bioinformatics, including CloudBurst, CloudBrush, and CloudRS. One may also use CloudDOE on top of a public cloud. CloudDOE consists of three wizards, i.e., Deploy, Operate, and Extend wizards. Deploy wizard is designed to aid the system administrator to deploy a Hadoop cloud. It installs Java runtime environment version 1.6 and Hadoop version 0.20.203, and initiates the service automatically. Operate wizard allows the user to run a MapReduce application on the dashboard list. To extend the dashboard list, the administrator may install a new MapReduce application using Extend wizard.

Conclusions: CloudDOE is a user-friendly tool for deploying a Hadoop cloud. Its smart wizards substantially reduce the complexity and costs of deployment, execution, enhancement, and management. Interested users may collaborate to improve the source code of CloudDOE to further incorporate more MapReduce bioinformatics tools into CloudDOE and support next-generation big data open source tools, e.g., Hadoop BigTop and Spark. Availability: CloudDOE is distributed under Apache License 2.0 and is freely available at http://clouddoe.iis.sinica.edu.tw/.

Editor: Christophe Antoniewski, CNRS UMR7622 & University Paris 6 Pierre-et-Marie-Curie, France

Funding: This research is partially supported by Digital Culture Center, Academia Sinica (http://www.sinica.edu.tw/main_e.shtml) under the project "System Management and Content Retrieval Technologies for Supporting Cloud-based Digital Archive Systems and Services," and National Science Council (http://web1.nsc.gov.tw/mp.aspx?mp=7), Taiwan, under 102-2221-E-001-013-MY3 dubbed as "Next Generation Content Delivery Network: Cloud and Mobile Internet." The hicloud CaaS computing resources are supported by Chunghwa Telecom Co. and Networked Communications Program of Taiwan under the project "A Cloud-Based DNA Analysis Platform." The Microsoft Azure computing resources are supported by Microsoft Co. and National Science Council of Taiwan under the project "World Cloud Research Collaboration Project hosted by Microsoft Research: Electronic Laboratory Notebook (Elegance) for Biomedical Research Community on Sharing, Co-working and Inspiriting in the Cloud" to Chung-Yen Lin. The funders had no role in study design, data collection and analysis, decision to publish, or preparation of the manuscript.

Competing Interests: The authors have declared that no competing interests exist.

* E-mail: yjchang@iis.sinica.edu.tw

Introduction

Progress in computer science and technology has vastly promoted the development of genetic research in the past few decades. Next-generation sequencing (NGS) is a particularly notable technology for genetics and computational biology research. The explosive growth of NGS data has already resulted in ultra-large-scale datasets and various computational problems for conventional NGS tools; for instance, insufficient computation resources and undesirably long execution times [1]. To overcome the issues associated with processing of large-scale data, MapReduce [2] and its Java implementation, Hadoop [3], were introduced. MapReduce is a framework that processes huge datasets in parallel by utilizing a large number of computers simultaneously, in which the computing resources can be allocated dynamically. In the programming model of MapReduce, devel-

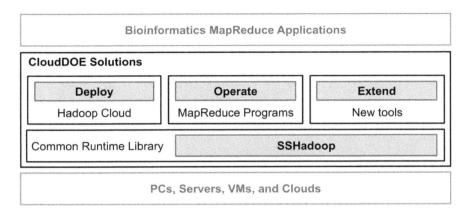

Figure 1. Software solutions of CloudDOE. A user can deploy a Hadoop Cloud, operate the supported bioinformatics MapReduce programs, and extend cloud functions through installing new tools.

opers only need to focus on implementing their programs by writing appropriate mapper and reducer procedures. Data and computations within the framework are automatically stored and executed across all computers to obtain redundancy, fault tolerance, parallelization, and load balance. Therefore, an increasing number of tools in bioinformatics [1,4] are successfully being adapted to fit within the MapReduce programming model in order to analyze large biological datasets using cloud computing, e.g., mapping reads to human genomes [5], calculating expression of RNA data [6], finding single nucleotide polymorphisms [7], performing *de novo* genome assembly [8], and achieving error correction of reads [9]. Some bioinformatics tools have also been developed for Hadoop ecosystems [10,11,12]. However, usability remains one of the main obstacles for cloud computing [13]. The prerequisite procedures of running MapReduce programs, including deploying Hadoop environments on computer clusters and executing programs through a series of technical Hadoop commands, pose considerable challenges for biological research laboratories that are interested in using MapReduce.

Several existing approaches have been developed in an attempt to ease the burden of deploying and managing a Hadoop cloud. The hicloud-hadoop [14] open-source project focuses on automatically deploying a Hadoop environment on Hinet hicloud [15]. Apache Whirr [16] provides a unified application programming interface for users to initiate cloud services from providers, e.g., Amazon EC2 [17] and Rackspace Cloud Servers [18]. Amazon EMR [19] is a well-known service for renting MapReduce computing resources on demand. Puppet [20] is designed as an automation software that aids system administrators in managing and quickly deploying critical applications on large-scale servers. Cloudera Manager [21] is targeted for deploying Hadoop ecosystems for enterprise-class requirements, including additional enterprise management components and security enhancement packages. Apache Ambari [22] is designed to simplify Hadoop management. Although these tools and services are useful, some common functionalities required for using Hadoop computing clouds, hereafter referred to as Hadoop clouds, are not user-friendly for scientists without computer science expertise and relevant technical skills. Such examples include constructing a Hadoop cloud on idle computers of a laboratory and integrating bioinformatics MapReduce tools for a Hadoop cloud or users.

In this study, we present CloudDOE, a software package for deploying an on-demand computing cloud with minimal user intervention. CloudDOE integrates available MapReduce pro-

grams within a unified graphical interface, and extends their functions with the addition of new MapReduce programs. In addition, smart features are included in CloudDOE, e.g., an auto-configuring algorithm of the Deploy wizard and an isolation method of the Operate wizard. CloudDOE encapsulates the complicated and niggling procedures of manipulating a Hadoop cloud, and is hence suitable for users of MapReduce cloud computing tools.

Results

CloudDOE aims at providing an open and integrated platform for biology/bioinformatics laboratories seeking to analyze big data via cloud computing with Hadoop/MapReduce (Figure 1). CloudDOE provides straightforward and user-friendly graphical interfaces, and covers most of the complicated, technical, and difficult command-line operations a user may encounter in traditional approaches (Figure 2). Several MapReduce programs are currently integrated into CloudDOE (Table 1). Since CloudDOE is implemented in Java, users can run it on various operating systems, e.g., Windows, Linux, and Mac OS, with Java runtime environments installed. Prerequisites of CloudDOE are provided in Supplementary section 1 of File S1.

Deploying a Hadoop Computing Cloud

The Hadoop cloud deployment procedure involves installing runtime environments and configuring system parameters. A Java runtime environment and Hadoop distributions are the basic requirements for constructing a Hadoop cloud. To improve usability and to simplify the installation processes, we developed Deploy wizard, which guides users to build their own Hadoop cloud in only three steps. Users simply need to provide user credentials and network connection settings of each computer upon installation of the cloud. Thus, the otherwise complicated installation procedure is completed automatically.

Configuring a functional Hadoop cloud requires a computer science background and relevant operating skills, since improper parameter settings may affect cloud performance and incorrect system settings may lead to a malfunctioning system. To minimize the complexity of configuring a Hadoop cloud, we designed an auto-configuring algorithm in the Deploy wizard. The algorithm generates Secure Shell (SSH) certificates for internal communication and a set of cloud settings. This information is stored in files distributed to the cloud nodes as well as in the local PC for further use, e.g., for modifying cloud settings and re-deploying the cloud.

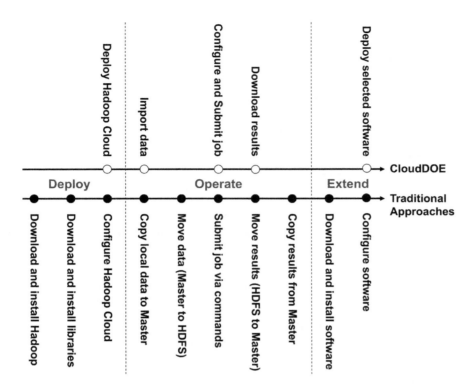

Figure 2. Comparison of CloudDOE and traditional approaches. CloudDOE encapsulates complicated procedures of traditional approaches into graphical user-friendly interfaces. Nearly 50% of the manipulating steps are reduced compared to traditional approaches.

A Hadoop cloud consists of a master node and multiple slave nodes (Figure 3A). A user is prompted to fill in the IP address and user account/password for the master node (Figure 3B) and each slave node (Figure 3C). The deployment process often takes 10–15 minutes (Figure 3D). Users can also undeploy a Hadoop cloud installed by CloudDOE, and restore configurations using the uninstallation function of Deploy wizard. To understand the process quickly, users can watch the supplementary video of Deploy wizard for step-by-step instructions and useful tips (File S2).

In addition, CloudDOE is applicable for use in multiple deployment environments, e.g., hybrid and private/public clouds. An in-depth discussion of Deploy wizard is provided in Supplementary section 2 of File S1, including a list of necessary service ports used by Hadoop services and CloudDOE (Table S1 in File S1), an example of simulated machine information of a hybrid cloud on Windows Azure [23] (Figure S1 and Table S2 in File S1), and a list of files and directories affected during deployment (Table S3 in File S1). Advanced users can also download the development branches or manually change the configuration for deploying a

Hadoop cloud with different Hadoop releases (Table S4 in File S1).

Operating with Existing MapReduce Programs

Several NGS data analysis tools have been implemented on the MapReduce framework. To overcome the hurdle of manipulating a MapReduce program with complicated command-line interfaces, we proposed a graphical wizard dubbed Operate. Users can manipulate a program with customized interfaces generated from necessary information in a configuration file, which is composed by the program's author or an advanced user (Figure 4). An isolation method is also introduced to create a dedicated workspace for storing experimental data, i.e., programs, input files, and experimental results, of each execution. With Operate wizard, users can benefit from (1) a graphical interface for the MapReduce program, (2) a streamlined method for manipulating input/output data and setting up program parameters, and (3) a status tracker and progress monitor for execution.

The user can fill out or load the stored login information to log in to the Master node of a Hadoop cloud (Figure 5A). After a

Table 1. Currently integrated MapReduce programs.

Name	Description
CloudBurst	Highly sensitive short read mapping.
CloudBrush	A *de novo* genome assembler.
CloudRS	An error corrector of substitution sequencing.
Hadoop-Examples	Hadoop example applications, including WordCount and Grep programs. The streaming mode of WordCount program is also available.

A B C D

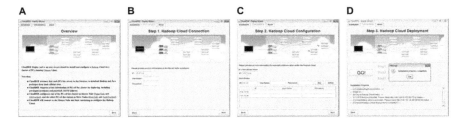

Figure 3. Screenshots of Deploy wizard. (A) Brief instructions to explain the system requirements and procedures that Deploy wizard will perform. A user is prompted (B) to provide information of the connection between the local PC and the Hadoop cloud and (C) to set up information of the Hadoop cloud, including IP addresses and a username/password. (D) Settings and configurations of the target cloud are generated automatically. The installation progress and logs can also be monitored on the wizard.

successful login, the user can upload data files to the Hadoop cloud (Figure 5B), select supported MapReduce programs, and specify parameters for execution (Figure 5C). We also designed two progress bars for monitoring the execution progress of the ongoing MapReduce step and the entire program. After the program execution is completed, the user can download experimental results to a local computer for further processing (Figure 5D). To understand the process quickly, users can watch the supplementary video of Operate wizard for step-by-step instruction and useful tips (File S3).

In addition, the tool-adding process of CloudDOE, which requires the MapReduce jar files and their configuration files in the same directory under the target Hadoop cloud, could only be carried out by advanced users. To further simplify the burden of adding tools to CloudDOE, we presented Extend wizard, which is an extension management center of a Hadoop cloud (Figure S2 in File S1). Note that the Extend wizard is currently a prototype, and detailed information is provided in Supplementary section 3 of File S1.

Discussion

Hadoop/MapReduce supports large-scale computing in a distributed parallel and robust manner, thus ushering in a new era of bioinformatics data analysis. More bioinformatics tools are adopting the Hadoop/MapReduce framework. However, there are only a few software packages that currently provide bottom-tier support of MapReduce applications for general audiences, including developers, system administrators, and users. We thus developed CloudDOE, which provides cross-platform and user-friendly graphical interfaces, allowing a wider user base to manipulate a Hadoop cloud.

Strengths and Limitations

CloudDOE is suitable as a unified console to Hadoop clouds among various computing environments, e.g., an in-house private cloud or rented machines from public cloud providers. CloudDOE is also useful and applicable across different scenarios: (1) deploying a workable Hadoop cloud with the auto-configuring algorithm within three steps, (2) manipulating a supported MapReduce program with the isolation method, and (3) integrating a MapReduce program with the program configuration file.

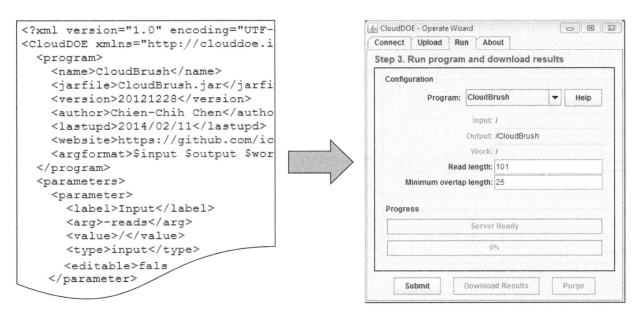

Figure 4. A structured XML configuration file and the generated wizard. The configuration file contains a metadata section on general program information, a set of parameters and its default values that are necessary to execute the program, and sections on log files and result download methods. CloudDOE loads a configuration file and generates the specific wizard required.

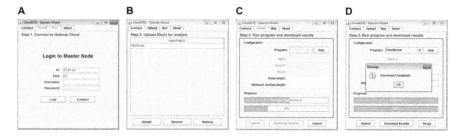

Figure 5. Screenshots of Operate wizard. A user can (A) log in to their Hadoop cloud, (B) upload and manage input data, (C) configure program parameters, and thus submit and monitor an execution, and (D) download the results after execution is completed.

There are nonetheless several limitations of the current CloudDOE release. The auto-configuring algorithm is performed sequentially, and only supports Ubuntu Linux distribution. Program integration does not support constructing pipelines for multiple programs. The deploy function only supports deploying the most common Hadoop releases on machines without Hadoop-integrated environments (Table 2). Note that the support of deploying Apache Hadoop version 2 is released as a development branch of CloudDOE.

Comparison with Similar Deploying Tools

Several existing projects aim at easing the burden of deploying and managing a Hadoop cloud. Table 3 shows a comparison of the main features of current projects. The hicloud-hadoop, Apache Whirr, and Puppet projects are based on command-line interface, whereas the Cloudera manger, Apache Ambari, and CloudDOE projects provide graphical user interfaces. Apache Whirr supports deploying a Hadoop cloud through composing proper deployment files, thus initiating machine instances from infrastructure-as-a-service providers. Puppet supplies functions for deploying, enhancing, and managing a Hadoop cloud through executing appropriate modules developed by experts. Cloudera Manager and Apache Ambari provide functions for manipulating a Hadoop cloud. However, computer science expertise is still necessary to accomplish technical operations, e.g., generate and exchange SSH key pairs and adapt system configuration files. CloudDOE presents functions for deploying and undeploying a Hadoop cloud for administrators, and encapsulates technical operations using wizards. It also supports the manipulation of available bioinformatics MapReduce programs on a Hadoop cloud for a bioinformatician.

Future Work

Parallel processing utilizes non-blocking operations and job overlapping to reduce waiting latency, and has been applied to different situations. We would like to accelerate deploying progress by introducing a parallel dispatcher and a monitor mechanism in future CloudDOE releases. One of the most successful characteristics of the existing workflow or execution platforms is the ability for users to construct analysis pipelines from available programs. Thus, incorporating the MapReduce programs into a pipeline with stand-alone programs to replace time-consuming processes is a promising future direction. We plan to implement wrapper functions or tools to integrate the MapReduce programs into workflows of existing bioinformatics platforms, e.g., Galaxy [24]. To enhance and keep up with technology trends, we plan to support state-of-the-art big data computing platforms, e.g., Hadoop BigTop [25] and Spark [26]. We also welcome community efforts to collaborate in future developments and in the maintenance of CloudDOE for integrating more MapReduce bioinformatics tools, providing multivariate deploying environment support, e.g., Cloud BioLinux [27], and supporting next-generation big data open source tools.

Conclusion

We have presented CloudDOE, a software package with user-friendly graphical wizards. CloudDOE supports users without an advanced computer science background in manipulating a Hadoop cloud, and thus reduces operation costs by encapsulating technical details and niggling command-line processes. Cloud-DOE also improves the usability of existing bioinformatics MapReduce programs by integrating these programs into a unified graphical user interface. We have also demonstrated that

Table 2. Supports of CloudDOE for various deployment environments.

Deployment Environments				
Category	Examples	Hadoop Installed?	Hadoop Configured?	Supported by CloudDOE[#]?
Generic machines	PCs, servers, or VMs	No	No	Yes
Cloud providers	Amazon EC2	No	No	Yes
	RackSpace			
	Microsoft Azure			
	Hinet hicloud			
Hadoop-integrated environments	Cloud BioLinux	Yes	No	No

[#]CloudDOE supports deploying Apache Hadoop version 0.20.203 in the current release. The supports of deploying Apache Hadoop 1.2.1 and 2.2.0 are released as development branches.

Table 3. Features comparison of CloudDOE and similar deploying tools.

Project	Function[#]			User Interface[#]	IaaS Only?[#]
	Deploy	Operate	Extend		
hicloud-hadoop	√	N/A	N/A	CLI	No
Apache Whirr	√	N/A	N/A	CLI	Yes
Puppet	√	N/A	√	CLI	No
Cloudera Manager	√	N/A	√	GUI (Web)	No
Apache Ambari	√	N/A	√	GUI (Web)	No
CloudDOE	√	√	√	GUI (Java)	No

[#]N/A, not available in the current release of the project; IaaS, infrastructure-as-a-service; CLI, command-line interface; GUI, graphical-user interface.

CloudDOE is useful and applicable for different scenarios and targeted users, including ordinary users, developers, and administrators. CloudDOE is an open-source project distributed under Apache License 2.0 and is freely available online.

Materials and Methods

To operate a Hadoop cloud remotely, we employed the client-server model as the system architecture of CloudDOE. Client-side applications were developed by Java and encapsulated as Java archive (JAR) executable files designed to be executed smoothly across different operating systems and environments, e.g., Windows, Linux, and Mac OS. Server-side deploying agents were written in GNU Bourne-Again Shell (BASH) script language because of its flexibility and good support for most Linux distributions. Figure 6 shows the system architecture of Cloud-DOE. Further details about the interaction of CloudDOE and a Hadoop cloud are provided in Supplementary section 4 of File S1, including the Deploy, Extend (Figure S3 in File S1), and Operate (Figure S4 in File S1) wizards.

Communications between clients and the server were conducted through SSH channels in a reliable and secure manner. SSH is a cryptographic network protocol that aims to communicate securely within an insecure network environment. We developed SSHadoop, a library inherited from JSch [28], to establish secure communication channels and execute commands. It also enables the ability to complete basic demands and operations of CloudDOE, including remote program execution and job monitoring, data import and management, and downloading of experimental results.

An auto-configuring algorithm was a major component necessary for deploying a Hadoop cloud from CloudDOE.

Runtime environments and dependent libraries were installed through our server-side agents, currently applied to the Ubuntu Linux distribution. A set of security credentials (e.g., SSH key pair) was generated for internal usage, e.g., communication and services control, for configuring a Hadoop cloud. Moreover, pre-formatting cloud settings were also produced and applied globally. The configuration files contain role types of a Hadoop cloud in each computer (i.e., master or slave), a number of data replicas and relevant configurations of Hadoop Distributed File System, and operating system-related settings.

A unique isolation identifier (IID) was the core concept of the isolation method, which is aimed at constructing independent workspaces and distinguishing the operation scope of executions. An IID is composed of a magic number and a user identifier, i.e., a timestamp followed by the current username. It is generated and applied to Hadoop cloud the first time an integrated program is initiated. We also exploited the IID to implement a stateful interaction environment, e.g., execution status recovery, to improve the reliability of connection and usability.

A structured extensible markup language (XML) configuration file was utilized to integrate a MapReduce program into CloudDOE. This XML file is composed of various information blocks, i.e., program, parameters, logs, and downloads (Figure S5 in File S1). The *program* block expresses general information of the program. In the *parameters* block, parameters and their default values are defined. The *logs* block lists a program log file provided by authors that can be used to monitor program execution. Output files and their corresponding download methods are defined in the *downloads* block. Detailed information of each configuration field is given in Supplementary section 5 of File S1 for interested users.

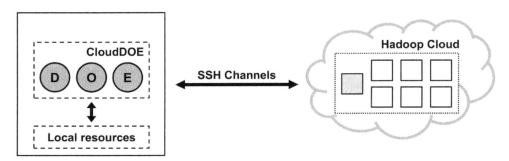

Figure 6. System architecture of CloudDOE. The solid square represents a machine or a computing resource, and the gray solid square is the master of the Hadoop cloud. CloudDOE establishes Secure Shell (SSH) channels for communication and acquires local resources for operations.

Supporting Information

File S1 Supplementary information, figures, and tables. Figure S1. A Hadoop cloud environment simulated from real Microsoft Azure machine data. Figure S2. Screenshots of Extend wizard. Figure S3. Interactions between CloudDOE, Hadoop cloud and Internet when manipulating a Hadoop cloud with Deploy or Extend function. Figure S4. Interactions between CloudDOE and Hadoop cloud when manipulating a Hadoop cloud with Operate function. Figure S5. Format of the program integration configuration file of CloudDOE.

File S2 A step-by-step video of Deploy wizard with useful tips.

File S3 A step-by-step video of Operate wizard with useful tips.

Acknowledgments

The authors wish to thank anonymous reviewers, Dr. Laurent Jourdren, Dr. Christophe Antoniewski, Jazz Yao-Tsung Wang (National Center for High-Performance Computing, Taiwan), Dr. Laurent H. Lin and Jen-Hao Cheng (Institute of Information Science, Academia Sinica, Taiwan) for their help, suggestions, and valuable comments. They also wish to thank Dr. Dennis Gannon and Dr. Nien-Chen Liu from Microsoft Co. on World Cloud Research Collaboration Projects for helping this research through the project to Chung-Yen Lin.

Author Contributions

Conceived and designed the experiments: WCC CCC JMH CYL WLH YCW DTL FL YJC. Performed the experiments: WCC CCC YCW YJC. Analyzed the data: WCC CCC JMH CYL WLH YJC. Contributed reagents/materials/analysis tools: JMH CYL WLH. Wrote the paper: WCC CCC JMH CYL WLH YCW DTL FL YJC. Developed the software and web: WCC CCC YCW CWH YJC.

References

1. Zou Q, Li XB, Jiang WR, Lin ZY, Li GL, et al. (2013) Survey of MapReduce frame operation in bioinformatics. Brief Bioinform.
2. Dean J, Ghemawat S (2008) MapReduce: simplified data processing on large clusters. Commun ACM 51: 107–113.
3. Welcome to Apache Hadoop! Available: http://hadoop.apache.org/.Accessed 2014 May 5.
4. Taylor RC (2010) An overview of the Hadoop/MapReduce/HBase framework and its current applications in bioinformatics. BMC Bioinformatics 11 Suppl 12: S1.
5. Schatz MC (2009) CloudBurst: highly sensitive read mapping with MapReduce. Bioinformatics 25: 1363–1369.
6. Langmead B, Hansen KD, Leek JT (2010) Cloud-scale RNA-sequencing differential expression analysis with Myrna. Genome Biol 11: R83.
7. Langmead B, Schatz MC, Lin J, Pop M, Salzberg SL (2009) Searching for SNPs with cloud computing. Genome Biol 10: R134.
8. Chang YJ, Chen CC, Chen CL, Ho JM (2012) A de novo next generation genomic sequence assembler based on string graph and MapReduce cloud computing framework. BMC Genomics 13: 1–17.
9. Chen CC, Chang YJ, Chung WC, Lee DT, Ho JM (2013) CloudRS: An error correction algorithm of high-throughput sequencing data based on scalable framework. 6–9 Oct. 2013. 717–722.
10. Nordberg H, Bhatia K, Wang K, Wang Z (2013) BioPig: a Hadoop-based analytic toolkit for large-scale sequence data. Bioinformatics 29: 3014–3019.
11. Schumacher A, Pireddu L, Niemenmaa M, Kallio A, Korpelainen E, et al. (2014) SeqPig: simple and scalable scripting for large sequencing data sets in Hadoop. Bioinformatics 30: 119–120.
12. Jourdren L, Bernard M, Dillies MA, Le Crom S (2012) Eoulsan: a cloud computing-based framework facilitating high throughput sequencing analyses. Bioinformatics 28: 1542–1543.
13. Schatz MC, Langmead B, Salzberg SL (2010) Cloud computing and the DNA data race. Nat Biotechnol 28: 691–693.
14. hicloud-hadoop. Available: https://github.com/jazzwang/hicloud-hadoop. Accessed 2014 May 5.
15. Hinet hicloud. Available: http://hicloud.hinet.net/. Accessed 2014 May 5.
16. Apache Whirr. Available: http://whirr.apache.org/. Accessed 2014 May 5.
17. Amazon Elastic Compute Cloud (Amazon EC2). Available: http://aws.amazon.com/ec2/. Accessed 2014 May 5.
18. Rackspace Cloud Servers. Available: http://www.rackspace.com/cloud/servers/. Accessed 2014 May 5.
19. Amazon Elastic MapReduce (Amazon EMR). Available: http://aws.amazon.com/elasticmapreduce/. Accessed 2014 May 5.
20. Puppet Open Source. Available: http://puppetlabs.com/puppet/puppet-open-source. Accessed 2014 May 5.
21. Cloudera Manager. Available: http://www.cloudera.com/content/cloudera/en/products-and-services/cloudera-enterprise/cloudera-manager.html. Accessed 2014 May 5.
22. Apache Ambari. Available: http://ambari.apache.org/. Accessed 2014 May 5.
23. Windows Azure. Available: http://www.windowsazure.com/. Accessed 2014 May 5.
24. Goecks J, Nekrutenko A, Taylor J, Team G (2010) Galaxy: a comprehensive approach for supporting accessible, reproducible, and transparent computational research in the life sciences. Genome Biology 11.
25. Apache Bigtop. Available: http://bigtop.apache.org/. Accessed 2014 May 5.
26. Zaharia M, Chowdhury M, Das T, Dave A, Ma J, et al. (2012) Resilient distributed datasets: a fault-tolerant abstraction for in-memory cluster computing. Proceedings of the 9th USENIX conference on Networked Systems Design and Implementation. San Jose, CA: USENIX Association. 2–2.
27. Krampis K, Booth T, Chapman B, Tiwari B, Bicak M, et al. (2012) Cloud BioLinux: pre-configured and on-demand bioinformatics computing for the genomics community. Bmc Bioinformatics 13.
28. JSch - Java Secure Channel. Available: http://www.jcraft.com/jsch/. Accessed 2014 May 5.

7

A Lightweight Distributed Framework for Computational Offloading in Mobile Cloud Computing

Muhammad Shiraz[1]*, Abdullah Gani[1], Raja Wasim Ahmad[1], Syed Adeel Ali Shah[1], Ahmad Karim[1], Zulkanain Abdul Rahman[2]

1 Center for Mobile Cloud Computing (C4MCC), Faculty of Computer Science and Information Technology, University of Malaya, Kuala Lumpur, Malaysia, **2** Department of History, Faculty of Arts and Social Sciences, University of Malaya, Kuala Lumpur, Malaysia

Abstract

The latest developments in mobile computing technology have enabled intensive applications on the modern Smartphones. However, such applications are still constrained by limitations in processing potentials, storage capacity and battery lifetime of the Smart Mobile Devices (SMDs). Therefore, Mobile Cloud Computing (MCC) leverages the application processing services of computational clouds for mitigating resources limitations in SMDs. Currently, a number of computational offloading frameworks are proposed for MCC wherein the intensive components of the application are outsourced to computational clouds. Nevertheless, such frameworks focus on runtime partitioning of the application for computational offloading, which is time consuming and resources intensive. The resource constraint nature of SMDs require lightweight procedures for leveraging computational clouds. Therefore, this paper presents a lightweight framework which focuses on minimizing additional resources utilization in computational offloading for MCC. The framework employs features of centralized monitoring, high availability and on demand access services of computational clouds for computational offloading. As a result, the turnaround time and execution cost of the application are reduced. The framework is evaluated by testing prototype application in the real MCC environment. The lightweight nature of the proposed framework is validated by employing computational offloading for the proposed framework and the latest existing frameworks. Analysis shows that by employing the proposed framework for computational offloading, the size of data transmission is reduced by 91%, energy consumption cost is minimized by 81% and turnaround time of the application is decreased by 83.5% as compared to the existing offloading frameworks. Hence, the proposed framework minimizes additional resources utilization and therefore offers lightweight solution for computational offloading in MCC.

Editor: Rongrong Ji, Xiamen University, China

Funding: This research is carried out as part of the Mobile Cloud Computing research project funded by the Malaysian Ministry of Higher Education under the University of Malaya High Impact Research Grant with reference UM.C/HIR/MOHE/FCSIT/03. The funders had no role in study design, data collection and analysis, decision to publish, or preparation of the manuscript.

Competing Interests: The authors have declared that no competing interests exist.

* Email: muh_shiraz@um.edu.my

Introduction

Recent developments in mobile computing technology have changed user preferences for computing. Smart Mobile Devices (SMDs) have replaced a number of portable computing and communication devices as all-in-one device [1], [2]. Human dependency on the smartphones is increasing in different fields of life including e-business, e-education, entertainment, gaming, management information systems, and healthcare [3]. The consumer and enterprise market for cloud based mobile applications is expected to raise $9.5 billion by 2014 [4], which predicts the growth of applications for Mobile Cloud Computing (MCC). SMDs are predicated to employ computational intensive applications identical to the station based computers [5]; however, mobile applications on the latest generation of smartphones and tablets are still constrained by battery power, CPU potentials and memory capacity of the SMDs [6]. Therefore, MCC is employed to leverage the services of computational clouds for mitigating resources limitations in SMDs [7,8].

Computational clouds facilitate to increase the computing capabilities of resources constrained client devices by offering on demand access to the widespread services and resources of cloud datacenters [9]. Computational clouds offer different service models for the provisioning of computing services [10]. For example, Elastic Cloud Compute (EC2) is employed for application processing services and Simple Storage Service (S3) of Amazon Web Services (AWS) is utilized for off-device storage [9]. MCC employs the services of computational clouds for enabling computational intensive and ubiquitous mobile applications on SMDs. For instance, the application processing services of computational clouds are utilized for augmenting application processing potentials of SMDs. Recently, a number of computational offloading frameworks are proposed for enabling intensive mobile applications on SMDs [5]. For instance, Apple iCloud [11] and Amazon Silk [12] browser are two latest mobile applications which leverage the services of computational cloud for application processing.

Traditional computational offloading frameworks employ application partitioning and component migration for computational offloading to the computational clouds. Elastic mobile applications are partitioned at different granularity levels and the intensive partitions of the applications are migrated at runtime for computational offloading. Therefore, current frameworks involve the overhead of application partitioning and additional cost of transferring the application binary code and corresponding data file(s) of the running instances of mobile application to the remote server node. Existing computational offloading frameworks lack of considering the intensity of runtime application partitioning and component migration. Therefore, resources intensive platform is established at runtime for the distributed processing of intensive mobile application. Such frameworks result in larger data transmission cost, high energy consumption and longer turnaround time of the mobile applications in accessing the application processing services of computational clouds [5,13–15]. The resources constrained nature of SMDs requires deploying lightweight procedures for leveraging the application processing services of computational clouds. Lightweight computational offloading techniques require minimal resources utilization on SMDs in accessing the application processing services of cloud server nodes [6]. Therefore, mobile users are enabled to utilize distributed services with lower computational load on mobile devices, shorter turnaround time of the application and relatively long lasting battery lifetime.

This paper presents a lightweight Distributed Computational Offloading Framework (DCOF) for computational offloading in MCC. DCOF employs distributed approach for the configuration of intensive mobile application between mobile device and cloud server node. It eradicates the overhead of application partitioning and component migration at runtime, as a result the amount of data transmission, energy consumption cost and turnaround time of the application is reduced in cloud based processing of mobile application. The framework is evaluated by testing prototype application in real MCC environment. The lightweight nature of the proposed framework is validated by comparing results of employing DCOF and latest computational framework [16–18] for computational offloading in MCC. Analysis of the results shows that by employing DCOF for computational offloading the size of data transmission is minimized 91%, energy consumption cost is reduced 81% and turnaround time of the application is decreased 83.5%. Hence, the proposed framework minimizes resources utilization in leveraging the application processing services of computational clouds and offers lightweight procedure for computational offloading in mobile cloud computing.

The paper is classified into the following sections. Section 2 discusses related work in computational offloading for MCC. Section 3 presents the architecture of proposed framework and explains the operating procedure of DCOF. Section 4 describes methodology used for the evaluation of proposed framework. Section 5 presents results and discusses experimental findings. Finally, section 6 draws concluding remarks and future directions.

Related Work

In the recent years, a number of cloud server based application offloading frameworks are introduced for outsourcing computational intensive components of the mobile applications to cloud datacenters [5]. Elastic applications are partitioned at runtime for the establishment of distributed processing platform. The offloading frameworks for MCC employ static or dynamic application partitioning mechanism. The static application partitioning mechanism [19] involves single time application partitioning for

the distribution of workload between SMD and cloud server node, wherein the intensive components of the application are partitioned and transferred to the remote server node. For example, the primary functionality offloading [20] mechanism involves partitioning and offloading of the intensive components at runtime. Static application partitioning is simple mechanism for the distribution of computational load; however, it lacks of coping with the dynamic processing load on SMDs. Dynamic application partitioning [21–23] involves runtime profiling mechanism for determining the intensive components of the application which need to be offloaded to the clouds server node. Dynamic application partitioning is a robust technique for coping with the dynamic processing loads on SMD. Current dynamic partitioning approaches analyze the resources consumption of SMDs, computational requirements of the mobile application and search for runtime solving of the problem of resource limitations on SMD [24].

A number of frameworks employ Virtual Machine (VM) migration based computational offloading, wherein the running instance of mobile application is encapsulated in the virtual machine image [13]. It includes creation of VM instance, encapsulation of the running mobile application in the VM instance and transmission of the VM image on the wireless medium to the remote server node. On the cloud server node, a fresh VM instance is created and the delegated VM instance is cloned onto the newly created VM instance. Mobile application resumes its running state and application is executed on remote server node. However, VM migration based computational offloading requires additional computing resources for the deployment and management of VM and migration of VM instance to remote server node [13]. As a result, the execution cost and turnaround time of the application is increased. Furthermore, the migration of running application along with its data and active states is susceptible to security breaches and attacks.

Computational offloading is composed of three phases including initialization, computational offloading and remote application execution. (a) In the initialization phase, the availability of services on the cloud server node are discovered, context information reports are collected from various sensor modules. Furthermore, application characteristics such as security level and QoS demands are also gathered. The information collected in this phase is used for the offloading mechanisms. (b) The computational offloading process involves decision of application partitioning and offloading of an application, user authentication and authorization, VM instance creation on mobile and cloud server, migration of VM clone, QoS parameter negotiation and resources reservation. (c) Once the delegated application is configured, the running state of the application is resumed on the remote virtual device instance and application is executed on remote server node. Recently, a number of mobile cloud applications employ cloud computing to alleviate resources constraints of SMDs. For instance, Apples iCloud [11] provides applications such as music, photos, apps, calendars, documents automatically on demand basis. Apples iCloud employs the PaaS (Microsoft Azure) and IaaS (EC2) of Amazon for hosting the application store. Similarly, Silk application [12] is released by Amazon, which is a cloud-accelerated web browser. Silk is a split browser which resides on both Kindle Fire and EC2. For each web page request, Silk dynamically determines distribution of computational load between the local SMD and remote Amazon EC2. Silk considers the objective functions of network conditions, page complexity and the location of any cached content.

Existing frameworks [16,22,23,25] employ application partitioning and component migration for computational offloading to the cloud server nodes. Mobile applications are partitioned at different granularity levels and the intensive partitions of the applications are migrated at runtime for computational offloading [24]. The mechanism of runtime application partitioning and component migration results in longer turnaround time of the application and larger size of data transmission. The timing cost of runtime computational offloading includes preferences saving time (T_{ps}), binary code offloading time of the application (T_{cm}), time taken in uploading the data states of the mobile application to remote server node (T_{pu}), application download time to remote virtual device instance on the cloud server node (T_{dv}), application reconfiguration and resuming time on the remote server node (T_{rr}), remote application execution time (T_{re}) and time taken in returning the resultant data file to local mobile device (T_{pr}). Therefore, the turnaround time of a single component of the mobile application which is offloaded at runtime is given by equation (1).

$$TT = T_{ps} + T_{cm} + T_{pu} + T_{dv} + T_{rr} + T_{re} + T_{pr} \qquad (1)$$

The Size of Data transmission (D_s) in runtime computational offloading involves the size of application binary file migrated at runtime (D_m), the size of preferences file uploaded to cloud server node (D_{pu}) and the size of resultant preferences file downloaded to the local (D_{pd}). The total size of data transmission of a single component of the mobile application which is offloaded at runtime is given by equation (2).

$$D_s = D_m + D_{pu} + D_{pd} \qquad (2)$$

Therefore, current frameworks [16,22,25–30] involve the overhead of application partitioning and additional cost of transferring the application binary code and corresponding data file(s) of the running instances of mobile application to the remote server node. As a result, a resources intensive and time consuming distributed platform is established for the distributed processing of intensive mobile applications.

Proposed Distributed Computational Offloading Framework (DCOF)

We propose as a lightweight alternative for the processing of intensive mobile applications in MCC. DCOF enables intensive mobile applications on the SMDs and reduces the additional overhead of computational offloading to the cloud server nodes. DCOF aims at leveraging the application processing services of cloud datacenters with minimal resources utilization on SMD. DCOF employs the SaaS model of computational clouds for accessing the services of cloud server nodes on demand basis. It focuses on dynamic computational task offloading to the cloud server node instead of dynamic intensive partition migration. The configuration of resources intensive components of the mobile application on the cloud server nodes results in eradication of the overhead of transmitting the application binary files and data files to the cloud server node at runtime. Computational load of the intensive mobile application is distributed by eliminating the overhead of migrating application binary file and active states of the application at runtime.

However, relying on the preconfigured services of the cloud server nodes lead to the problem of dependency on the centralized services and reduced offline usability. Similarly, it leads to the

employment of thin client applications such as traditional web and email applications, wherein the processing logic of the application is hosted on the remote server nodes and client applications provide user interface. In order to address such issues, the proposed framework employs replication of the intensive components of the mobile application on mobile device and cloud server node. DCOF employs two distinct operating modes (offline mode and online mode) for the execution of mobile application. The offline mode of the application execution indicates an ideal situation wherein, sufficient computing resources are available on the local mobile device for the execution of mobile application. Therefore, in the offline mode all the components of mobile application are enabled to be scheduled for execution on the local mobile device. The profiler mechanism dynamically evaluates availability of resources (RAM, CPU and battery power) and future demands of the execution of mobile applications on SMD. Mobile application switches to online mode in the critical condition wherein the application processing services of computational clouds are used for the execution of intensive components of the mobile application. The required input data are transmitted to the cloud server node and upon the successful execution of the task on the cloud server node, resultant data are returned back to mobile device.

DCOF implements method level granularity for computational task offloading. Traditional computational offloading frameworks employ additional library which is coupled with the compiler support for tagging the intensive components of the mobile application (as remote) at compile time. Such frameworks [22,23,25,31–33] involve the overhead of code generator module which is executed against the modified code, takes the source le as input and generates necessary remote-able method wrappers and utility functions. The remotely tagged methods are used as potential candidate methods for computational offloading. However, DCOF does not require the annotation of individual methods of the mobile application as local and remote. Therefore, DCOF reduces the developmental efforts for the distribution of execution load between mobile device and cloud server node. Furthermore, DCOF eliminates the additional overhead of distributed application deployment for leveraging the application processing services of cloud datacenters in MCC. Fig 1 shows architecture of the proposed framework.

The computational intensive components of the mobile application which do not require users interaction are configured on the cloud server node, which is provided access on demand basis in the online mode of application execution. DCOF based mobile application is based on the conventional application framework for mobile devices. However, mobile application is

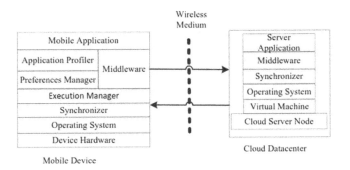

Figure 1. Architecture of the Proposed Distributed Computational Offloading Framework.

enabled to switch dynamically between online and offline mode. The dual operation modes of the mobile application enables to dynamically switch between online and offline mode. Applications are capable to operate with full functionalities on local mobile device in the situations of remote server access problems. Application is enabled to operate as a standalone application in the offline mode and to access distributed cloud services in the online mode. DCOF is composed of the following components.

Application Profiler

Application profiling mechanism is implemented for automating the mechanism of application partitioning and computational offloading [24]. Prolers are important part of computational offloading frameworks. Computational offloading frameworks employ different types of profilers. For instance, application profiling dynamically evaluates availability of resources (CPU, RAM) on mobile device and computational requirements of mobile application [25]. Similarly, network profiling mechanism determines accessibility of network and quality of signal strengths while accessing the wireless access medium in MCC. Energy profiler examines utilization of battery power during the processing of mobile application. Memory profiler assesses the memory allocated to applications running on the mobile device and availability of memory for future allocations [22,34]. The accurate and light weight nature of the profiling mechanism results in correct decisions for computational offloading [25,35]. Profiling mechanism is significant for the reason that it determines the feasibility of application partitioning and component offloading. Profiler decides the destination location for the execution of mobile application. Based on the objective function considered by the computational offloading framework, profiler decides either to execute the component locally or remotely. DCOF employs application profiling for dynamically switching between online and offline mode of execution. Application profiler dynamically evaluates resources utilization on SMD and it works in coordination with the execution manager for switching the application between online and offline modes.

Execution Manager

Execution manager monitors the execution modes of the mobile application. In the critical conditions, application is switched to the online mode wherein the running instance of the component of the application is terminated after saving the running state of the application. Execution manager is responsible for the configuration of the mobile application on SMD in the dual operating mode. In the online mode execution manager enables mobile application on the local device to access the services on the cloud server node for remote application processing, whereas in the offline mode all the components of the application are executed on local mobile device. Preferences Manager: The execution manager component is assisted by the preferences manager component for saving data states of the running instance of the application (in the online mode) and resuming the active state of the application on the local mobile device (in the offline mode). Preferences manger provides access to the preferences file of the application. Active data state of the application is written to the preferences while switching to the online mode. Similarly, data is read from preferences file while switching back to the offline mode of the execution. Synchronizer component of DCOF accesses the preferences for the exchange of data files between SMD and remote server node.

Synchronizer

The synchronizer component of DCOF monitors synchronization of data transmission between local mobile device and cloud server node. It is responsible for the synchronization of the distributed components of the application. Synchronizer provides different types of services in the online mode of the application execution. Synchronizer coordinates for the synchronization between the application running on local mobile device and the application running on the cloud server node.

Middleware

Mobile applications require distributed services access features and the configuration of middleware services for enabling access to the distributed services of cloud server nodes. DCOF provides a transparent distributed application execution environment in the online mode. In the online mode the services of distributed middleware are employed for computational task offloading. The execution manager saves the execution states of the identified intensive component by using preferences manager component of DCOF framework. The running instance of the executing component is terminated and the allocated resources are released to reduce the execution load on local mobile device. DCOF employs middleware services for accessing the services of cloud server node. Application running on mobile device activates the services of cloud server node by employing Inter Process Communication (IPC) mechanism such as RPC or RMI [6]. Mobile devices implement different middleware services [36] based upon the operating system platform. Middleware hides the complications of the communication between the local mobile application and cloud server application. DCOF provides a transparent distributed application execution environment in the online mode and therefore, mobile users are provided the notion as all the components of the mobile application are executed locally on SMD. For instance, we employ kSOAP2 API [37] for accessing the application processing services on the cloud server

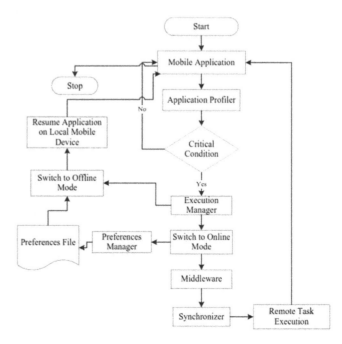

Figure 2. Illustration of the Interaction of the Components of EECOF Framework in POP and SOP.

node. kSOAP2 is a lightweight SOAP client library for the Android platform [38]. Similarly, we employ Web Service Definition Language (WSDL) [39] middleware on the cloud server node for enabling access to the services of cloud server node.

Fig 2 shows the flowchart for the interaction of the components of DCOF framework in the execution of mobile application. Mobile application is employed on the mobile device and is capable to access cloud server node for computational task offloading. The application profiler evaluates resources utilization on mobile device continuously. In the critical conditions (for instance low battery), application execution manager switches the application to the online mode. Execution manager considers the execution history of the running instances of the components of mobile application for making the decision of computational offloading. The running states of the component of the application which is executing for a longer period of time and which utilizes abundant processing potential of the mobile device are saved by using the preferences manager. Mobile application accesses the services of cloud server node and the required input parameters are transferred for remote application execution. It is important to highlight that only the resources intensive tasks of the application are offloaded to the cloud server node, whereas the rest of the application continues execution on the mobile device. The synchronizer component of DCOF is responsible for the synchronization between mobile application running on the local mobile device and components of the application running on the cloud server node. Once the computational task is performed successfully on the cloud server node, final results are returned to the application running on mobile device. The services of the cloud server node always remain in the active mode. In the meanwhile, whenever remote services become inaccessible for the reason of interruption in network connectivity, execution manager is capable to switch back to the offline mode and to resume the running state of the application on local mobile device. However, the decision of resuming to the offline mode is based up on the feasibility of application execution on local mobile device. Execution manager makes the decision of resuming running state of the interrupted component on the basis of the input from the application profiler.

To reduce the dependency on the remote server node, DCOF involves the replication of computational intensive components of the application on mobile device and cloud server node. Application replication involves the complexities of consistency and synchronization in the distributed processing of the application between mobile device and remote cloud server node. However, the replication of intensive components of the mobile application assists in achieving the goals of minimal resources utilization in computational offloading, rich user experiences and offline usability. Resources utilization is reduced by eliminating the overhead of runtime application partitioning and partition migration at runtime. Similarly, rich user experience and offline usability is ensured by dynamically switching mobile application between online and offline mode. Therefore, application on the mobile device can resume the interrupted running state of the intensive component of the application in the situations of unavailability of remote services on the cloud server node.

DCOF employs traditional client/server architecture in the online mode of the application. However, the architecture and operation procedure of DCOF are different from the traditional client/server applications. The traditional client/server applications are thin client applications, wherein client applications are dependent on the server component of the application. The client applications provide user agents for interaction with the local computer and the processing logic is implemented on the server

machines. Examples of such applications include web application, email application, social network applications such as Facebook, and video conferencing applications such as Skype application. Therefore in the traditional client/server model, client component of the application becomes inactive in the situations of inaccessibility of the server application. DCOF addresses such issues by enabling the operation of mobile application in two distinct modes. The application on the mobile device remains operational even though the services of computational clouds are inaccessible. Similarly, the components of the application can be executed on the local mobile device in the online mode.

Evaluation

This section discusses the methodology used for the evaluation of proposed framework and explains experimental findings.

Methodology

Experimental Setup. The proposed framework is evaluated by testing the prototype application for Android devices in the real mobile cloud computing environment. The server machine is configured for the provisioning of services to the mobile device in the online mode. SaaS model of computational clouds is employed for the provision of services to mobile devices. Mobile device accesses the wireless network via Wi-Fi wireless network connection of radio type 802.11 g, with the available physical layer data rates of 54 Mbps. Java based Android software development toolkit (Android SDK) is deployed for the development of the prototype application. Power Tutor tool [40] is used for the measurement of battery power consumption in distributed application processing.

Prototype Application. The Service Oriented Architecture (SOA) of Android application framework is employed for the development of prototype application. The prototype application is composed of three computational intensive components. (a) Sorting service component implements the logic of bubble sort for sorting liner list of integer type values. The sorting operation is tested with 30 different computational intensities (11000–40000). (b) The matrix multiplication service of the application implements the logic of computing the product of 2-D array of integer type values. Matrix multiplication logic of the application is tested with 30 different computational intensities by varying the length of the 2-D array between 160*160 and 450*450. c) The power compute service of the application implements the logic of computing $b \wedge e$, whereas b is the base and e is the exponent. The power compute logic of the application is tested for 30 different computational intensities by varying the exponent between 1000000 and 200000000. Empirical data are collected by sampling all computational intensities of the application in 30 different experiments and the value of sample mean is shown with 99% confidence for the sample space of 30 values in each experiment.

Data are collected by running the prototype application in three different scenarios. In the first scenario, the components of the mobile application are executed on the local mobile device to analyze resources utilization and turnaround time of the application on mobile device. In the second scenario, the intensive components of the mobile application are offloaded at runtime by implementing the latest techniques [16], [18] which involve entire component migration for computational offloading in MCC. In this scenario, we analyze size of data transmission and turnaround time of the mobile application. In the third scenario, DCOF is employed for evaluating resources utilization on mobile device and turnaround time of the application in cloud based application processing. The evaluation parameters include RAM allocation on mobile device (MB), CPU utilization on mobile device (MIPS), the size of data transmission (KB), and Turnaround Time (TT) of the application (ms). RAM allocation shows the amount of memory allocated to a particular component of the application on mobile device. CPU utilization indicates the percent CPU utilization during the execution of the component of mobile application on mobile device. TT parameter represents the total time taken in the execution of the component of mobile execution. The size of data transmission parameter represents the amount of data transmitted over the wireless network medium for offloading the components of mobile applications. The amount of data transmission affects the cost (energy consumption and turnaround time) of computational offloading for MCC.

Results and Discussion

This section discusses experimentation findings of evaluating DCOF by employing the prototype application. It presents analysis of turnaround time, amount of data transmission, and energy consumption cost of the application from the perspective of local and remote application execution. Remote execution of the application is evaluated by employing the latest component offloading frameworks [16], [18] and DCOF based computational offloading for MCC.

As shown in the equation (1) the turnaround time (TT) of each component of the application in traditional computational offloading includes preferences saving time (T_{ps}), binary code offloading time of the application (T_{cm}), time taken in uploading the data states of the mobile application to remote server node (T_{pu}), application download time to remote virtual device instance on the cloud server node (T_{dv}), application reconfiguration and resuming time on the remote server node (T_{rr}), remote application execution time (T_{re}) and time taken in returning the resultant data file to local mobile device (T_{pr}). However, DCOF employs computational task migration rather than application partitioning and intensive components migration at runtime. Therefore, the TT of each component of the application in DCOF based computational offloading involves time taken in task offloading (T_{cm}), remote application processing time (T_{re}) and preferences download time (T_{pr}).

$$TT = T_{cm} + T_{pu} + T_{pr} \quad (3)$$

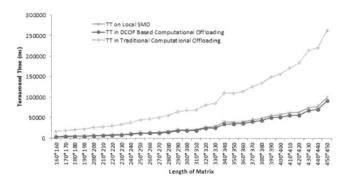

Figure 4. Comparison of the Turnaround Time of the Matrix Multiplication Service Execution in Local and Remote Execution.

It shows that DCOF eliminates the additional delay incurred during component migration (T_{ps}, T_{pu}) and reconfiguration (T_{dv}, T_{rr}) on the remote server node. Therefore, the TT of the intensive operation is reduced in each instance of computational offloading of the prototype application. Fig 3 shows the comparison the TT of sorting service execution in different scenarios. It is found that for sorting service execution the TT and resources utilization on SMD varies with the varying intensities of the sorting operation. For instance, the TT is found 4876 ms for list size 11000, 16950 ms for list size 25000, and 31207 ms for list size 40000. We found that TT for sort service execution on SMD increases by 84.3% for sorting list of 40000 values as compared to sorting list of 11000 values. The comparison of TT for sorting operation in local execution and traditional offloading techniques shows that TT of the sorting service increases considerably in runtime component offloading. It is observed in offloading sorting service component the TT of the sorting operation increases by: 80% for sorting list of 11000 values, 75% for sorting list 17000 values, 80% for sorting list of 30000 values and 81% for sorting list of 40000 values.

The comparison of sorting service execution on local mobile device and the DCOF based computational offloading shows decrease in TT of the sorting operation in the online mode of DCOF. We examined that by accessing the services of cloud server on in the online mode of DCOF, the TT of sorting services reduces by: 48% for sorting list of 11000 values, 60% for sorting list of 25000 values and 57% for sorting list of 40000 values. The overall reduction in TT value for sorting service is found by 57.8(+/−) 2% with 99% confidence in the sample space of 30

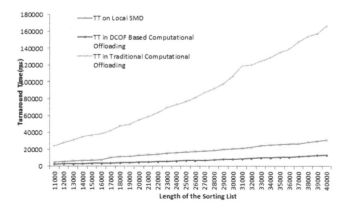

Figure 3. Comparison of the Turnaround Time of the Sorting Service Execution in Local and Remote Execution.

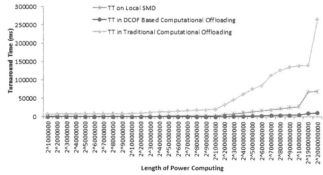

Figure 5. Comparison of the Turnaround Time of Power Compute Operation in in Local and Remote Execution.

values. The comparison of TT for the sorting operation in the DCOF based computational offloading and traditional offloading shows the lightweight nature of DCOF framework for computational offloading. The decrease in DCOF based offloading of sorting service as compared to traditional runtime component offloading is found 89% for sorting list of 11000 values, 91% for sorting list of 20000 values, 92% for sorting list of 31000 values and 92% for sorting list of 40000 values.

Fig 4 shows the comparison of the TT of matrix multiplication service execution in different scenarios. It is observed that for matrix multiplication operation the execution time is 3653 ms for matrices length 160*160, 21185 ms for matrices length 310*310 and 99286 ms for matrices length 450*450. It shows that the execution time increases 96.3% for multiplying matrices of length 450*450 as compared to matrices of length 160*160. TT of the matrix multiplication increases considerably in runtime component offloading. It is observed in offloading matrix multiplication service the TT of the matrix multiplication service in remote processing compared to local execution on mobile device increases by: 78% for multiplying matrices of length 160*160, 70% for multiplying matrices of length 250*250, 66% for multiplying matrices of length 300*300 and 65% for multiplying matrices of length 450*450.

DCOF based computational offloading however, reduces the TT of the matrix multiplication operation as compared to both local and traditional computational offloading based execution. It is observed that DCOF based computational offloading reduces the TT of matrix multiplication operation by: 10% for matrices of length 160*160, 9% for multiplying matrices of length 350*350 and 8% for multiplying matrices of length 450*450. The overall reduction in TT for matrix multiplication service in DCOF based offloading of matrix multiplication operation is found 10.3(+/−) 0.5% with 99% confidence in the sample space of 30 values. The decrease in TT of matrix multiplication operation in DCOF based offloading as compared to traditional runtime component offloading is examined 74% for multiplying matrices of length 160*160, 72% for multiplying matrices of length 230*230, 64% for multiplying matrices of length 350*350 and 63% for multiplying matrices of length 450*450.

Fig 5 shows the comparison of turnaround time of the power compute service execution for local and remote execution. It shows that the turnaround time of power compute operation increases with the increase in the intensity of power compute operation. For example, the TT on local mobile device is found

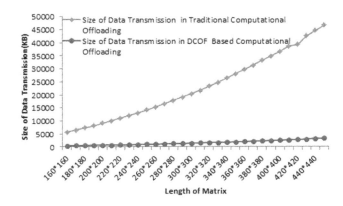

Figure 7. Comparison of the Size of Data Transmission in Traditional Offloading and DCOF Based Offloading for Matrix Multiplication Operation.

51 ms for computing 2 ^1000000, 1767 ms for computing 2 ^60000000 and 69044 ms for computing 2 ^2000000000. It shows the TT for power compute service execution increases by 99.9 for computing 2 ^2000000000 as compared to computing 2 ^1000000. The comparison of TT for power compute operation in local execution and traditional offloading technique shows that TT of the power computing increases considerably in runtime component migration. We found that in runtime component offloading the TT of power computing increases by: 99.3% for computing 2 ^1000000, 96.2% for computing 2 ^20000000, 81.4% for computing 2 ^400000000 and 74% for computing 2 ^2000000000.

The comparison of TT of power compute operation in local and remote execution shows that DCOF based computational offloading is insignificant for lower intensities of the application. For instance, the TT of power compute operation for computing 2 ^1000000 is 33% higher in DCOF based computational offloading as compared to the local execution of power compute operation. It is for the reason of additional delays incurred in the process of computational offloading. However for higher intensive operations, DCOF based computational offloading reduces the TT of the power compute operation as compared to both local execution and traditional computational offloading. It is observed that DCOF based computational offloading reduces the TT of power compute operation 6.3% for computing 2 ^2000000, 47.7% for

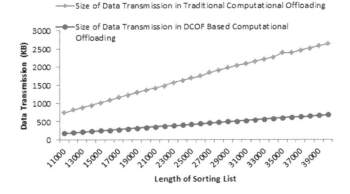

Figure 6. Comparison of the Size of Data Transmission in Traditional Offloading and DCOF Based Offloading for Sorting Operation.

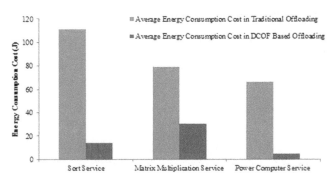

Figure 8. Comparison of Energy Consumption Cost in Traditional and DCOF based Computational Offloading.

computing 2 ^20000000 and 84.2% for computing 2 ^2000000000. The overall reduction in TT in DCOF based offloading as compare to local execution of power compute operation is found 65(+/−) 10.8%. Similarly, the decrease in TT of power compute operation in DCOF based offloading as compared to traditional runtime component offloading is examined by: 99% for computing 2 ^2000000, 98% for computing 2^20000000 and 95.9% for computing 2 ^2000000000. The overall reduction in TT of power compute operation in DCOF based offloading as compare to traditional runtime component offloading is found 97(+/−) 0.6%.

As shown in equation (2) the amount of data transmission in runtime computational offloading involves the size of application binary file migrated at runtime, the size of preferences file uploaded to cloud server node and the size of resultant preferences file downloaded to the local mobile device. However, the size of data transmission in DCOF based computational offloading of each component of the application involves the amount of data transmitted to remote server node as input parameter and amount of data transmitted as the final result returned from remote server node to the local mobile device. DCOF eliminates the additional data transmitted in migrating application binary code and preferences files. Therefore, the size of data transmission is reduced in each instance of computational offloading of the prototype application.

Fig 6 shows the size of data transmission in offloading sort service component of the application at runtime. It is examined that in all instances of offloading sorting service, the size of binary application file (.apk) remains 44.4 KB for sort service; whereas, the size of preferences file uploaded to the cloud server node and the size of the resultant preferences file downloaded to the local mobile device varies for different intensities of the sorting operation. The size of data transmission for offloading sort service component with the list of 11000 values is found 752.4 KB, whereas the size of data transmission in accessing sorting service of DCOF server application is examined 83 KB. Similarly, the size of data transmission is examined 2645.4 KB for list of 40000 values in traditional computational offloading, whereas the size of data transmission by employing DCOF is found 692 KB. It shows that by employing DCOF based computational offloading; the size of data transmission is reduced 76% for sorting list of 1100 values and 74% for sorting list of 40000 values. The average reduction of data transmission is found 74.7% by employing DCOF based computational offloading for the sorting list of 11000–40000 values.

Fig 7 shows the comparison of data transmission in traditional runtime application offloading and proposed DCOF based computational offloading for matrix service component of the application. It is examined that in all instances of matrix multiplication service offloading the size of binary application file (.apk) remains 46 KB; whereas, the total size of data transmission in runtime offloading of matrix multiplication service is examined: 5739.4 KB for matrices length 160*160, 15426.5 KB for matrices length 260*260 and 46740 KB for matrices length 450*450. The average size of data transmission for offloading matrix multiplication service with the matrices length 160*160–450*450 is determined 11474.3 KB. However, the size of data transmission by employing DCOF for offloading matrix multiplication operation is found 463 KB for matrices of length 160*160, 1979 KB for matrices of length 350*350 and 3308 KB for matrices of length 450*450. It shows that the size data transmission is reduced by 91.9% for matrix size 160*160 and by 92.2% for matrix size of 450*450 values by employing DCOF for offloading matrix multiplication operation. The average reduction of data transmis-

sion over the wireless network medium is by 92% in DCOF based computational offloading for the matrices of size 160*160–450*450.

The size of data transmission for offloading power compute service by employing traditional computational offloading is evaluated in 30 different experiments. It is examined that in all instances of offloading power compute service the size of binary application file (.apk) is 42.7 KB; whereas, the size of preferences file uploaded to the cloud server node is 1 KB and the size of the resultant preferences file downloaded to the local is 1 KB. Therefore, the total size of data transmission is observed as 44.7 KB for offloading power compute service at runtime; whereas, the size of data transmission in employing DCOF for power compute service is found 2KB. It shows that the overhead of offloading the binary file of the power compute service is eliminated; therefore, the size of data transmission reduces 95.5% which results in the reduction of energy consumption cost and turnaround time of the application in cloud based application processing. The total size of data transmission in traditional computational offloading for the mobile application is observed as 24761 KB; whereas, the size of data transmission in DCOF based computational offloading is found 2074.6 KB. It shows that the amount of data transmission is reduced 95.6% in employing DCOF for offloading the intensive components of the application.

The energy consumption cost is evaluated in 30 different experiments for all the three components of the application by employing traditional and DCOF base computational offloading. It is found that the energy consumption cost reduces considerably by implementing DCOF for offloading computational task to cloud server nodes. The decrease in the energy consumption cost is for the reason of reducing the overhead of additional resources utilization in the establishment of distributed application processing platform at runtime. Fig 8 compares the average decrease in energy consumption cost of offloading the components of the application in traditional and DCOF based computational offloading. It is examined that energy consumption cost reduces by: 85.1% for sorting 11000 values, 85.2% for sorting 20000 values, 87.8% for sorting 30000 values and 88.6% for sorting 40000 values.

The decrease in the energy consumption cost by employing DCOF for offloading sorting operation is found by 86.7% with 30 different intensities of the sorting operation. Similarly, it is examined that by employing DCOF based offloading, the energy consumption cost of matrix multiplication operation reduces by: 73% for matrices of length 160*160, 66.3% for matrices of length 300*300, 56.8% for matrices of length 400*400 and 50.4% for matrices of length 450*450. The average decrease in the energy consumption cost by employing DCOF for offloading matrix multiplication operation is found 64.3% with 30 different intensities of matrix multiplication operation. Similarly, the energy consumption cost of power compute operation reduces by 63% for computing 2 ^1000000, 76.8% for computing 2 ^30000000, 91.8% for computing 2 ^200000000 and 96.8% in computing 2 ^2000000000.

The employment of DCOF results in minimal resources utilization on SMD for computational offloading in MCC. It is observed that the additional cost of application binary code migration and active data state migration to the cloud server node is reduced by employing DCOF for cloud based processing of computationally intensive mobile applications. Therefore, turnaround time, size of data transmission and energy consumption cost is reduced in processing intensive mobile application on cloud server node. For instance, by employing DCOF the size of data transmission for sorting service is reduced by 74.8%, turnaround time of the sorting operation reduces by 91.3% and the energy consumption cost is reduced by 87.5% as compared to the traditional computational offloading technique [16], [18]. Similarly, the size of data transmission for matrix multiplication operation is reduced by 92.8%, turnaround time is reduced by 72% and energy consumption cost is reduced by 61.6% compared to the traditional computational offloading technique. In the same way, the size of data transmission for power compute operation is reduced by 95.5%, turnaround time is reduced by 97% and energy consumption cost is reduced by 93%.

Conclusions

The mechanism of application partitioning at runtime and component migration increases data traffic, energy consumption cost and turnaround time of the application. Therefore, resources intensive and time consuming distributed application execution environment is established for computational offloading in MCC. DCOF is proposed to minimize the overhead of load distribution between mobile devices and cloud server node in leveraging the application processing services of computational clouds. DCOF employs lightweight operating procedures for computational offloading and leverages the SaaS model for the deployment of computationally intensive mobile applications in MCC. The incorporation of distributed services access technique for computational offloading facilitates in the optimal deployment procedure with minimal resources utilization for the establishment of distributed platform in MCC. The dual operating nature contributes to the versatility and robustness of the distributed framework for enabling intensive applications on resources constrained SMDs. Mobile applications are enabled to operate independently on the local mobile device in the offline mode; whereas, the services of computational clouds are employed on demand basis in the online mode for conserving computing resources of SMDs.

Analysis of the results signifies the lightweight nature of DCOF, which reduces the energy consumption cost, size of data transmission and turnaround time of the application in cloud based processing of the intensive component of mobile application. The additional cost of application binary code migration and active data state migration to the cloud server node is reduced by employing DCOF for computational offloading. It is found that by employing the DCOF for computational offloading, the size of data transmission is minimized by 91%, energy consumption cost is reduced by 81% and turnaround time of the application is decreased by 83.5% as compared to the contemporary offloading frameworks. Hence, the DCOF minimizes additional resources

utilization and therefore offers lightweight solution for computational offloading in MCC. The future research includes extending the scope this research to address the issues of consistency of simultaneous application execution between local mobile device and remote cloud server node, and seamless application execution in leveraging application processing services of computational clouds in MCC.

Supporting Information

Table S1   Comparison of Application Processing Time (ms) of the Sort Service Component.

Table S2   Comparison of Application Processing Time of Matrix Multiplication Service.

Table S3   Comparison of Application Processing Time (ms) on SMD in Processing Application locallay and by implenting the POP of DEAP Model.

Table S4   Summary of Data Transmission in Traditional and Proposed Framework Based Computational Offloading.

Table S5   Summary of Data Transmission in Traditional and Proposed Framework Based Computational Offloading.

Table S6   Comparison of ECC.

Acknowledgments

This research is carried out as part of the Mobile Cloud Computing research project funded by the Malaysian Ministry of Higher Education under the University of Malaya High Impact Research Grant with reference UM.C/HIR/MOHE/FCSIT/03.

Author Contributions

Conceived and designed the experiments: RWA SAS AK AG ZBA. Performed the experiments: RWA SAS AK ZBA AG. Analyzed the data: RWA SAS AK ZBA AG. Contributed reagents/materials/analysis tools: RWA SAS AK ZBA AG. Contributed to the writing of the manuscript: MS RWA SAS AK ZBA AG.

References

1. Prosper mobile insights website. Available: http://www.prospermobile.com/mobileuser-august11. pdf. Accessed 2014 June 19.
2. Shiraz M, Whaiduzzamn M, Gani A (2013) A Study on Anatomy of Smartphone. Computer Communication & Collaboration 1: 24–31.
3. Pc magazine website. Available: http://www.pcmag.com/article2/0,2817,2379665,00.asp. Accessed 2014 June 19.
4. Juniper research website. Available: http://www.juniperresearch.com/analyst-xpress-blog/2010/01/26/mobile-cloud-application-revenues-to-hit-95-billion-by-2014-driven-by-converged-mobile-services/. Accessed 2014 June 19.
5. Shiraz M, Gani A, Khokhar RH, Buyya R (2013) A review on distributed application processing frameworks in smart mobile devices for mobile cloud computing. Communications Surveys & Tutorials, IEEE 15: 1294–1313.
6. Shiraz M, Gani A, Khokhar R (2012) Towards Lightweight Distributed Applications for Mobile Cloud Computing. In: Computer Science and Automation Engineering (CSAE), 2012 IEEE International Conference on. volume 1, pp. 89–93. doi:10.1109/csae.2012.6272555.
7. Hoang T, Dinh, Chonho L, Dusit, NPing w (2011) A Survey of Mobile Cloud Computing: Architec-ture, Applications, and Approaches. Wireless Communications and Mobile Computing.

8. Abolfazli S, Sanaei Z, Gani A (2012) Mobile Cloud Computing: A Review On Smartphone Augmentation Approaches. 1st International Conference on Computing, Information Systems and Communications.
9. Buyya R, Yeo CS, Venugopal S, Broberg J, Brandic I (2009) Cloud Computing and Emerging IT Platforms: Vision, Hype, and Reality for Delivering Computing as the 5th Utility. Future Generation Computer Systems 25: 599–616.
10. Armbrust M, Fox A, Grifth A, Joseph DA, Katz HR, et al. (2009) Above the Clouds: A Berkeley View of Cloud Computing. Electrical Engineering and Computer Sciences University of California at Berkeley.
11. Apple website. Available: www.apple.com/icloud/. Accessed 2014 June 19.
12. Amazonsilk website. Available: http://amazonsilk.wordpress.com/2011/09/28/introducing-amazon-silk/. Accessed 2014 June 19.
13. Shiraz M, Abolfazli S, Sanaei Z, Gani A (2013) A study on virtual machine deployment for application outsourcing in mobile cloud computing. The Journal of Supercomputing 63: 946–964.
14. Khan AN, Mat Kiah ML, Khan SU, Madani SA (2012) Towards Secure Mobile Cloud Computing: A Survey. Future Generation Computer Systems.

15. Rongrong J, Hongxun Y, Wei L, Xiaoshuai S, Qi T (2012) Task Dependent Visual Codebook Compression. IEEE Transactions on Image Processing 21: 2282–2293.

16. Hung SH, Shih CS, Shieh JP, Lee CP, Huang YH (2012) Executing Mobile Applications on the Cloud: Framework and Issues. Comput Math Appl 63: 573–587.

17. T G, Y H, J G, J Y, J Y (2013) On-Device Mobile Visual Location Recognition by Integrating Vision and Inertial Sensors. IEEE Transactions on Multimedia 15, no7: 1688–1699.

18. Shiraz M, Gani A (2014) A lightweight active service migration framework for computational offloading in mobile cloud computing. The Journal of Supercomputing 68: 978–995.

19. Dou A, Kalogeraki V, Gunopulos D, Mielikainen T, Tuulos VH (2010). Misco: A MapReduce Framework for Mobile Systems. doi:10.1145/1839294.1839332.

20. Satyanarayanan M, Bahl P, Ram, #243, Caceres n, et al. (2009) The Case for VM-Based Cloudlets in Mobile Computing. IEEE Pervasive Computing 8: 14–23.

21. Kovachev D, Klamma R (2012) Framework for Computation Offloading in Mobile Cloud Computing. International Journal of Interactive Multimedia and Artificial Intelligence 1: 6–15.

22. Cuervo E, Balasubramanian A, Cho Dk, Wolman A, Saroiu S, et al. (2010). MAUI: Making Smartphones Last Longer with Code Offload. doi:10.1145/1814433.1814441.

23. Zhang X, Jeong S, Kunjithapatham A, Gibbs S (2010) Towards an Elastic Application Model for Augmenting Computing Capabilities of Mobile Platforms. In: Mobile Wireless Middleware, Operating Systems, and Applications, Springer Berlin Heidelberg, volume 48, chapter 12. pp. 161–174. doi:10.1007/978-3-642-17758-3_12. URL http://dx.doi.org/10.1007/978-3-642-17758-3_12.

24. Shiraz M, Ahmed E, Gani A, Han Q (2014) Investigation on runtime partitioning of elastic mobile applications for mobile cloud computing. The Journal of Supercomputing 67: 84–103.

25. Kosta S, Aucinas A, Hui P, Mortier R, Zhang X (2012) Thinkair: Dynamic resource allocation and parallel execution in the cloud for mobile code offloading. In: INFOCOM, 2012 Proceedings IEEE. IEEE, pp. 945–953.

26. Abebe E, Ryan C (2012) Adaptive Application Offloading using Distributed Abstract Class Graphs in Mobile Environments. Journal of Systems and Software 85: 2755–2769.

27. Chun BG, Ihm S, Maniatis P, Naik M, Patti A (2011). CloneCloud: Elastic Execution Between Mobile Device and Cloud.

28. Chun BG, Maniatis P (2009). Augmented Smartphone Applications through Clone Cloud Execution.

29. Iyer R, Srinivasan S, Tickoo O, Zhen F, Illikkal R, et al. (2011) CogniServe: Heterogeneous Server Architecture for Large-Scale Recognition. Micro, IEEE 31: 20–31.

30. Kumar K, Lu YH (2010) Cloud computing for mobile users: Can offloading computation save energy? Computer 43: 51–56.

31. Rongrong J, Ling-Yu D, Jie C, Tiejun H, Wen G (2014) Mining compact 3d patterns for low bit rate mobile visual search. IEEE Transactions on Image Processing.

32. Rongrong J, Ling-Yu D, Hongxun Y, Lexing X, Yong R, et al. (2013) Learning to Distribute Vocabulary Indexing for Scalable Visual Search. IEEE Transactions on Multimedia 15(1): 153–166.

33. Messer A, Greenberg I, Bernadat P, Milojicic D, Chen D, et al. (2002). Towards a Distributed Platform for Resource-Constrained Devices Hewlett-Packard Company.

34. T G, YF H, LY D, JQ Y (2014) Efficient Bag-of-Features Generation and Compression for On-Device Mobile Visual Location Recognition. IEEE Multimedia 21(2): 32–41.

35. Bineng Z, Hongxun Y, Sheng C, Rongrong J, Tat-Jun C, et al. (2014) Visual tracking via weakly supervised learning from multiple imperfect oracles. Pattern Recognition 47(3): 1395–1410.

36. Shiraz M, Gani A, Khokhar RH, Ahmed E (2012) An Extendable Simulation Framework for Modeling Application Processing Potentials of Smart Mobile Devices for Mobile Cloud Computing. In: Frontiers of Information Technology (FIT), 2012 10th International Conference on. IEEE, pp. 331–336.

37. Sourceforge website. Available: http://ksoap2.sourceforge.net/. Accessed: 2014 June 19.

38. Android website. Available: http://developer.android.com/. Accessed 2014 June 19.

39. W3c website. Available: ttp://www.w3.org/TR/wsdl. Accessed 2014 June 19.

40. Powertutor website. Available: http://powertutor.org/. Accessed 2014 June 19.

8

Attack Resilience of the Evolving Scientific Collaboration Network

Xiao Fan Liu[1]*, **Xiao-Ke Xu**[1,2], **Michael Small**[1], **Chi K. Tse**[1]

1 Department of Electronic and Information Engineering, The Hong Kong Polytechnic University, Hung Hom, Kowloon, Hong Kong, **2** School of Communication and Electronic Engineering, Qingdao Technological University, Qingdao, People's Republic of China

Abstract

Stationary complex networks have been extensively studied in the last ten years. However, many natural systems are known to be continuously evolving at the local ("microscopic") level. Understanding the response to targeted attacks of an evolving network may shed light on both how to design robust systems and finding effective attack strategies. In this paper we study empirically the response to targeted attacks of the scientific collaboration networks. First we show that scientific collaboration network is a complex system which evolves intensively at the local level – fewer than 20% of scientific collaborations last more than one year. Then, we investigate the impact of the sudden death of eminent scientists on the evolution of the collaboration networks of their former collaborators. We observe in particular that the sudden death, which is equivalent to the removal of the center of the egocentric network of the eminent scientist, does not affect the topological evolution of the residual network. Nonetheless, removal of the eminent hub node is exactly the strategy one would adopt for an effective targeted attack on a stationary network. Hence, we use this evolving collaboration network as an experimental model for attack on an evolving complex network. We find that such attacks are ineffectual, and infer that the scientific collaboration network is the trace of knowledge propagation on a larger underlying social network. The redundancy of the underlying structure in fact acts as a protection mechanism against such network attacks.

Editor: Petter Holme, Umeå University, Sweden

Funding: XKX was supported by the PolyU Postdoctoral Fellowships Scheme (G-YX4A) and the Research Grants Council of Hong Kong (BQ19H). XKX also acknowledges the National Natural Science Foundation of China (61004104, 60802066). The funders had no role in study design, data collection and analysis, decision to publish, or preparation of the manuscript.

Competing Interests: The authors have declared that no competing interests exist.

* E-mail: xfliu@eie.polyu.edu.hk

Introduction

Many natural and man-made complex systems such as biological networks, the WWW, airport network and stock markets network, evolve intensively at the local level [1–3]. In fact, local level evolution is both characteristic and typical of human dynamics, where people constantly change their affinity, cooperation strategies and communication patterns [4–6]. There are now several notable models of network evolution including the preferential attachment model [7] and the adaptive network models in which network topology evolves as a feedback to the state change of nodes [8]. However in the real world, both network nodes and edges may appear and disappear through a variety of other mechanisms. For example, none of the above mentioned models consider the life span of connections among nodes, which may naturally have a broad distribution uncorrelated with their topological properties.

On the other hand, it has been widely observed that many stationary networks are robust to random failure but vulnerable to targeted attacks [9,10]. For example, the analysis of the North America blackout in 2003 shows that disturbances affecting key transmission substations greatly reduce the grid's ability to function [11]. Immunization strategies based on the network vulnerability have also been proposed to stop epidemic spreading on complex networks [12]. The scientific collaboration network, which bears the same statistical properties as many stationary complex networks [13], has also been shown, in numerical simulations, to be vulnerable to targeted removal of important nodes [9]. However, exactly how the intensively evolving scientific collaboration network responds to such attacks in the real world has not been carefully studied.

In this paper we analyze the collaboration network of US-based life scientists to address two main topics. First, we examine the topological evolution of the network and show that the scientific collaboration network is intensively evolving. When compared to recently proposed theoretical models of such networks [14–18] we find that the data is consistent with changes in link configuration being driven by an autonomous process, rather than in response to the change of state of adjacent nodes. Second, we analyze the impact of unanticipated death of high profile scientists to their collaborators' collaboration network building. We use sudden death within the network as an observed experimental proxy for targeted attack on an evolving complex network. We find the network to be very robust against the removal of even these hub nodes. Furthermore, we conjecture that the scientific collaboration network should be considered the trace of knowledge spreading on a larger and denser mapping of hidden social ties among scientists. That is, not only is there a network of active collaboration, but there is a secondary larger hidden network of latent potential collaborations. When nodes in the active collaboration network are removed, this latent network helps to replace that structure in a robust manner.

Results

Topological evolution on the networks

Collaborations between scientists do not last forever. In the scientific collaboration network – where nodes are scientists and links are collaborations – the network can therefore have drastically different constitution when sampled in different time intervals. In this section we study the topological evolution on the collaboration network first by examining the life span of scientific collaborations. Five thousand scientists are sampled from the AAMC Faculty Roster according to the criteria that their academic life spans are longer than 10 years and each of them has more than 10 collaborators. By using this criterion, we actually assure that the life span of collaboration will not be restricted by the observation period. Then by retrieving their publications from PubMed, the life span and productivity (in term of numbers of journal articles published) of each pair of collaboration can be studied.

Figs. 1A and B show the distribution of life span s and the distribution of collaboration productivity r of all pairs of scientific collaborations. The extremely skewed distributions indicate that most of the scientific collaborations last for only one year and have only one research article published. Fig. 1C shows the correlation between scientific collaboration life span and output. There is no clear evidence that collaborations with long life span will have higher productivity than those with short life span. Notice from Fig. 1A that fewer than 20% of scientific collaboration last more than one year, indicating that long term collaborations are actually fairly infrequent. We define the "long term" collaborations of a researcher as those last longer than half of the scientist's academic life span. As shown in Fig. 2A, the probability $P(l)$ of a scientist having $l-1$ long term collaborators roughly decays with a power law, where most of the scientists have no long term collaborators. Fig. 2B shows that the number of long term collaborators to total number of collaborators ratio l/d stays stationary for all degrees, which means that no matter how big the collaboration network a scientist has, approximately among every 50 of his/her collaborators, only one will turn out to be a long term collaboration. Hence, the dominance of short life span collaborations characterizes the scientific collaboration network as an intensively evolving network. The lack of competitive advantage of long term collaborations to short term ones in both productivity and team building actually implies that when selecting collaborators, short term collaborations are intrinsically preferred over long term long term co-operation.

To fully characterize the dynamics of the topological network evolution, egocentric scientific collaboration networks are constructed based on a sliding window. The egocentric network of a scientist contains the scientist and his/her first tier collaborators, i.e. the scientists co-authored papers with him/her, and/or the second tier collaborators, i.e. the co-authors of the first tier collaborators excluding the center scientist him/her-self, within a certain period of time. Here we consider the egocentric networks in two different scales:

1. T-1 network: (i) the center node (the scientist) and (ii) its first tier neighbors;
2. T-2 network: (i) the center node (the scientist), (ii) its first tier neighbors and (iii) second tier neighbors.

Then we define the *academic age* of a scientist as the number of years since his/her first academic publication. Starting from age 0, for every age y of a scientist, the egocentric network is constructed using the co-authorship of research articles published from age y to

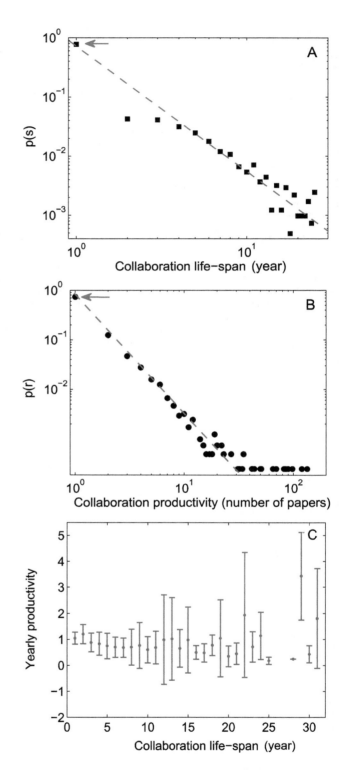

Figure 1. Statistics of scientific collaboration life span and productivity. (A) The probability distribution $p(s)$ of collaboration life span s. Most collaborations lasts for only one year. The dashed line is a power law with exponent -2.3. (B) The probability distribution $p(r)$ of number of journal articles r published by each collaboration. The dashed line is a power law with exponent -2.4. (C) Average yearly productivity for collaboration of different life spans. The average publications produced by each pair in a collaboration stays a bit lower than 1 per year, whereas for collaborations with longer life spans, the productivity varies.

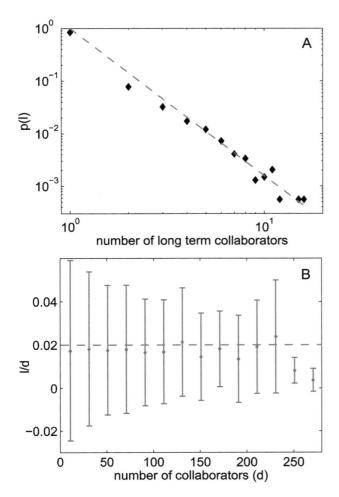

Figure 2. Statistics of long term scientific collaborations. (A) The probability distribution $p(l)$ of number of long term collaborations $l-1$ a scientist can have. The average number of long term collaborations the 5000 selected scientists have is 0.73. Most of the scientists do not have long term collaborations with peer researchers. The dashed line is a power law with exponent -2.4. (B) The correlation between the a scientist's number of collaborators d and probability of having long term collaborators (denoted by the proportion of long term ones in all the collaborators l/d). Each point on the graph shows the average l/d ratio of scientists with $d \pm 10$ collaborators.

y+4 (both inclusive, hence forming a window of 5 years). Figs. 3A and B illustrate the egocentric scientific collaboration networks of the same scientist (the red dot) in two consecutive non-overlapping time windows.

Once the egocentric networks of all windows are formed, we measure the scale and connectivity of the networks with four parameters: numbers of nodes N, number of edges M, clustering coefficient c and network efficiency e. The clustering coefficient c is calculated as follows:

$$c = \frac{3 \times \text{number of triangles in the network}}{\text{number of connected triples of nodes}}. \qquad (1)$$

The clustering coefficient measures the conditional probability that two scientists may collaborate if they both collaborate with same (third-party) scientist. The network efficiency e is obtained by:

$$e = \frac{1}{N(N-1)} \sum_{i \neq j} \frac{1}{d_{ij}}, \qquad (2)$$

where d_{ij} is the shortest path distance between node i and j. The network efficiency of a fully connected network is 1, whereas for a network of isolated nodes, its efficiency will be 0. Fig. 4 shows the measure of sizes and connectivity of the egocentric collaboration networks of two scientists in the first 20 windows of their academic careers.

Previous research of the US airport network [2] indicates that large complex system can display stationary "macroscopic" structure properties but retain intensive "microscopic" evolution over time. Despite of the ubiquitous global structure of scientific collaboration networks in different fields [13,14,18], our analysis shows that same to the airport network, the collaboration network is also intensively evolving at the local scale, where collaborations between scientists are rather temporal than stationary. Furthermore, Fig. 4 also shows that the scientists may have their egocentric collaboration networks evolving in entirely different tracks. The different patterns of evolution can be caused by the fact that in a certain period of time the scientist switches his/her work emphasis to (for example) clinical duties or that at some time the scientist is granted a large amount of money and is able to make more collaborations with peer researchers. Hence we argue that when elaborating a model of the evolving scientific collaboration network and other social networks, except for considering the growing mechanism based on existing topology [14,18] and modifying connections as a feedback of the dynamical process on the network [8], future study should also take the ability of nodes attracting connections and the life spans of links as intrinsic properties embedded in the systems.

Targeted attacks on the networks

Recent studies have shown that, following the death of an eminent life scientist ("superstar"), collaborators experience a 5% to 8% decline in their publication rates [19]. Yet, apart from numerical simulations [9], there are few reports regarding the structural response to real life "attacks" on the scientific collaboration networks (or in any other application domain). In this section we evaluate the impact of sudden deaths of superstars to their former collaborators' scientific collaboration networks in order to capture the robustness and resilience of these naturally evolving complex systems.

Twenty one superstars who died unexpectedly are selected as the subject of our study. We define the "former collaborators" of a dead superstar as the superstar's direct collaborators in five years preceding death. To study the impact of the superstars' sudden death, we compare the collaboration networks of the former collaborators in the last 5 years before the superstar's death and in the first 5 years afterwards. The T-1 and T-2 egocentric networks of the dead superstars in the last window characterize, respectively, the collaboration among the former collaborators and their collaboration networks right before the death of the superstar. Then, in the first 5-year window after the superstar's death, two new networks T'-1 and T'-2 are constructed analogously to T-1 and T-2 networks, as shown in Fig. 3C, but with the publications of the former collaborators in this certain period. The before and after-death networks T-1 and T'-1 have almost identical nodes, while for the T-2 and T'-2 networks, the network components can be quite different.

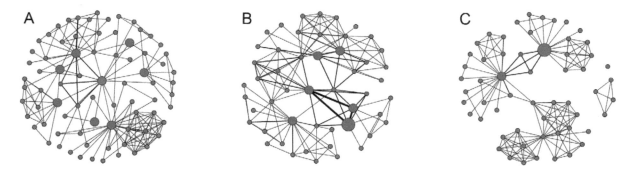

Figure 3. Illustration of egocentric scientific collaboration network evolution. (A) and (B) are the T-2 egocentric scientific collaboration networks of the same eminent scientist in two consecutive non-overlapping time windows (window size = 5 years). The red node is the center of the network, i.e. the superstar. The blue and gray nodes are the first and second tier neighbors of the superstar in that particular time window. The sizes of the nodes and thickness of the edges in the figure are proportional to the numbers of journal articles published by the scientists and the numbers of journal articles co-authored by the pairs of collaborations. (C) is the T'-2 network after the superstar's death. The blue nodes are the dead superstar's first tier neighbors in the last window before his death (the former collaborators). The gray nodes are the neighbors of the former collaborators in the first window after the superstar's death.

Having constructed the former collaborators' collaboration networks in two consecutive windows, we measure the changes (ΔN, ΔM, Δc, and Δe) of the number of nodes N, number of edges M, clustering coefficient c (Eqn. 1) and network efficiency e (Eqn. 2). Table 1 presents the average values of the parameters of the networks before and after the sudden deaths of the superstars as well as the average change of parameters as a percentage. The results show that in comparison with the T-1 networks, the number of nodes in the T'-1 networks only decreases by about two while the number of edges decreases sharply and along with the disappearance of edges, the clustering coefficient and network efficiency have both dropped significantly. Comparing to the T-2

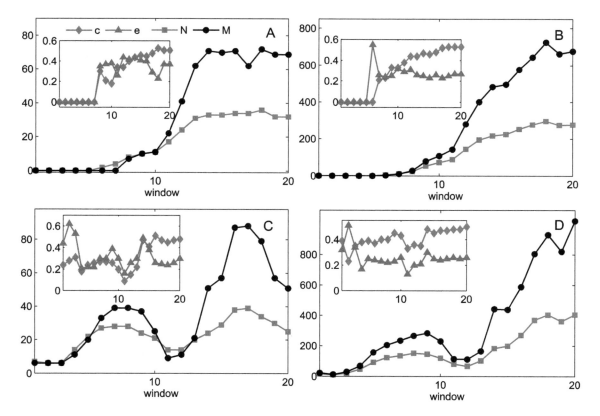

Figure 4. Measures of parameters of two egocentric scientific collaboration networks in their first 20 windows. Figures labeled A–B and C–D represent two scientists respectively. A and C: Numbers of nodes N, number of edges M, clustering coefficient c and network efficiency e in T-1 networks. B and D: Numbers of nodes N, number of edges M, clustering coefficient c and network efficiency e in T-2 networks in each window. The two scientists have their collaboration networks evolve in two different patterns. The egocentric networks of the first scientist (A and B) have a boost in size during window 10 to 13, while the egocentric networks of the second scientist (C and D) have two peaks of their sizes around window 7 and 16.

Table 1. Parameter changes of the former collaborators' networks after superstars' deaths.

	N	M	c	e
T-1 (before death)	12.57	28.24	0.48	0.75
T'-1 (after death)	10.33	4.57	0.08	0.11
Change in %	−18%	−84%	−83%	−86%
T-2 (before death)	81.57	203.90	0.48	0.43
T'-2 (after death)	105.29	306.81	0.51	0.21
Change in %	+29%	+50%	+7%	−50%

Average values of network parameters (i.e. number of nodes N, number of edges M, clustering coefficient c and network efficiency e) and the changes of these parameters in the collaboration networks of superstars' former collaborators. Assuming a superstar died in year y, $T-1$ and $T-2$ networks are his egocentric networks containing only the first tier neighbors and both the first and second tier neighbors from year $y-4$ to y. $T'-1$ and $T'-2$ networks are the former collaborators' collaboration networks of themselves and with their first tier collaborators from year $y+1$ to $y+5$. After the superstars' death, the former collaborators tend to disconnect with each other and find other collaborations elsewhere.

Table 2. Results of Test 1 and Test 2.

	Change between	ΔN	ΔM	Δc	Δe
Test 1 (P)	T'-1 and T-1	21/21	20/21	21/21	21/21
	T'-2 and T-2	21/21	20/21	20/21	21/21
Test 2 (p-value)	T'-1 and T-1	0.52	0.45	0.68	0.36
	T'-2 and T-2	0.27	0.24	0.22	0.53

The test results of Test 1 (P) and Test 2 (p-value) for the changes of numbers of nodes ΔN, number of edges ΔM, clustering coefficient Δc and network efficiency Δe in $T'-1$ and $T'-2$ networks comparing to $T-1$ and $T-2$ networks. The large values of P's (close to 1) and p-value's (larger than 0.05) indicate that the deaths of superstars did not have significant impact on the way of evolving of their collaborators.

networks, in the T'-2 networks the number of nodes and number of edges have increased by certain amount while the clustering coefficient varies by a small proportion and the network efficiency of the networks decreases by a half.

This result suggests that the sudden deaths of the superstars have stimulated their former collaborators to rearrange their networks in an efficient manner. To determine whether the impact of sudden death is significantly different from the natural network evolution (i.e. without the sudden death of the superstar), two non-parametric statistical tests are conducted.

Test 1: 77 scientists are selected from a group of eminent life scientists as the control group. Having a superstar suddenly died in age y, we first find all the scientists in the control group who were still active in research in age $y+5$. Then we measure the properties of T-1 and T-2 networks of control groups scientists in the window of age $y-4$ to y and the properties of T'-1 and T'-2 networks in the window of age $y+1$ to $y+5$. For each change of the parameters, say θ, of each suddenly died scientist, we want to know whether it falls into the range of all the θ's of the control group. Of the active superstars, let $U=max(\theta)$ and $V=min(\theta)$. For each of the dead scientists i, if $U\geq\theta_i\geq V$, let $d_i=1$ (else $d_i=0$). Then the probability of any dead superstars' θ fall inside U and V is:

$$P(U\geq\theta\geq V)=\frac{\sum d_i}{21}.$$

The results of the measured parameters are summarized in Table 2. Almost all the parameter changes of individual egocentric networks after the sudden death of superstars fall in range of the parameter changes due to normal evolution of the collaboration networks.

In **Test 2** the Wilcoxon's two-sided rank sum test is used. The observed data is the parameter changes θ of all the 21 sudden deaths; the control group is the θ of 42 normal superstars, who are also in the control group in Test 1 and are removed from their egocentric networks at ages following the same academic "age-of-death" distribution as the observed data. For each θ, we test the observed data and control group for the null hypothesis: observed and control group data are independent samples from identical

continuous distributions with equal medians, against the alternative that they do not have equal medians. The p-values for each parameter is presented in Table 2. Let significance level be 95%, then all the changes of network parameters of dead superstars are actually not different (i.e. p-values are all larger than 0.05) from the change of network evolutions of active scientists.

Our statistical tests show that there is no evidence that the sudden death of a superstar may have a significant impact on the evolution of its collaborators' scientific collaboration networks. Previous research shows that improving the robustness of diverse networks often involves increasing the redundancy of the network at critical positions [20]. Our findings of the evolving scientific collaboration network reveal, on the other hand, that the network with intensive evolution also show great resilience even under attacks on important nodes, which could severely disrupt the functionality of stationary networks.

Discussion

Of course, the premature deaths of eminent scientists may be considered a great loss to their particular discipline. Nonetheless, it is known that after the (unanticipated) deaths of some eminent scientists, the scientific productivity of collaborators suffer from a 5% − 8% drop. In this paper we have examined, from another aspect, the impact of the sudden deaths of these superstars to the structure evolution of their former collaborators' collaboration networks. We have firstly shown that the scientific collaboration network is a complex system which intensively evolves at the local level. Most collaborations among scientists have short life spans and the relative incidence of long term collaboration is very low. We have compared the behavior of network evolution between collaborators of suddenly deceased eminent scientists and active ones. Surprisingly, statistics show that the evolution of collaborators' networks are not affected by the sudden deaths of the superstars.

In particular, we have observed that the egocentric scientific collaboration networks evolve in such a manner that: direct collaborators of a superstar in one period of time tends not to collaborate with each other in the next, whereas the collaborators' own egocentric networks grow bigger. This evolution pattern is actually an analogy to the diffusion process on an arbitrary form of network, where nodes can generate a stimulus and spread it out to their first then second tier neighbors and so on. Hence we conjecture that, rather than mapping the social networks of scientists, the scientific collaboration network is actually the "trace" of information propagation on a larger and denser invisible social network than the trace itself.

Actually the trace of information propagating and disease spreading in human society share the same evolution mechanism with scientific collaboration network and that the redundancy of the underlying social structure in fact acts as a protection mechanism when these networks are under attack. From this perspective, future study of effective network attacks (such as immunization strategies) should consider the underlying rapid evolving social structure. Moreover, the designing of robust information transmission systems could also gain from the robust system formed by human social and collaborative endeavors. For example in the Internet, routing strategies with constantly changing paths between nodes might give extra robustness to the system even under targeted attacks.

Materials and Methods

In this paper the collaborations of three groups of US based life scientists are studied. The first group are the scientists listed in the Faculty Roster of the Association of American Medical Colleges until the end of 2010. The second group contains 77 eminent life scientists ("superstars"), including (i) current members of National Academy of Sciences major in life science; (ii) emeritus members of National Academy of Sciences major in life science; (iii) top 500 highly cited life scientists retrieved from ISI Web of Knowledge until the end of 2010. Moreover all of the 77 scientists had been active in their academic life for not less than 10 years and had collaborated with not less than 20 other scientists in the Faculty Roster. The third group of scientists are 21 life scientists who died unexpectedly and prematurely in the early stage of their scientific career and had comparable academic achievements with the previous group of superstars at the time of their death [19]. These 21 scientists had also been active in their academic life for not less than 10 years and had collaborated with not less than 20 other scientists in the Faculty Roster.

Scientists are connected only when they co-author a journal article. The publication information are retrieved from online database PubMED, which is provided by the National Library of Medicine and stores intact biomedical research literature. The authors' names in PubMED are stored in the form of name identifier which takes the initials of the first names and the whole last name, i.e. Xiao Fan Liu is stored as XF Liu. However in the Faculty Roster which stores the full names of all the faculties, some of the names may have the same identifiers. For example the identifiers of John Doe and Jane Doe are all J Doe. Hence from the information provided by PubMED we cannot determine whether a paper published by J Doe is actually written by John Doe or Jane Doe. In our work, different names with the same identifiers are eliminated from the Faculty Roster, thereby reducing the size of the Faculty Roster to 112,753.

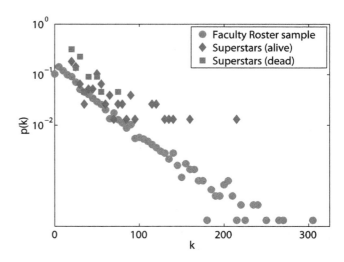

Figure 5. Degree distributions of three groups of scientists. The degree distributions of 7555 samples from the Faculty Roster, 77 eminent life scientists and 21 suddenly died eminent life scientists are shown in the figure. The average degree of the three groups are 31.83, 56.56 and 35.29.

The superstars are not only excellent in their academic achievements but also important in terms of network measure in the network of scientists. Constructing a scientific collaboration network covering all the publications the scientists have in their life time, Fig. 5 shows the degree distribution of the three groups of scientists. The degree distribution of scientists in the Faculty Roster follows an exponential distribution and has an average degree of 31.83; the average degree of the 77 eminent life scientists is 56.56, which is almost twice as much as that of all the scientists in the Roster; and the average degree of the 21 scientists who died suddenly is 35.29. Note that the 21 scientists died in their early ages and had obtained comparable academic achievements with the 77 eminent ones at the time of death, we can assume that their collaboration network would also have continued to grow to comparable sizes as the ones alive.

Author Contributions

Conceived and designed the experiments: XFL XKX MS CKT. Performed the experiments: XFL. Analyzed the data: XFL XKX MS CKT. Contributed reagents/materials/analysis tools: XFL. Wrote the paper: XFL XKX MS.

References

1. Dorogovtsev S, Mendes J (2003) Evolution of networks: From biological nets to the Internet and WWW. Oxford University Press, USA.
2. Gautreau A, Barrat A, Barthélemy M (2009) Microdynamics in stationary complex networks. Proceedings of the National Academy of Sciences 106: 8847–8852.
3. Liu XF, Tse CK (2011) A network perspective of world stock markets: synchronization and volatility. International Journal of Bifurcation and Chaos in press.
4. Zachary W (1977) An information flow model for conflict and fission in small groups. Journal of anthropological research 33: 452–473.
5. Grujić J, Fosco C, Araujo L, Cuesta J, Sanchez A, et al. (2010) Social experiments in the mesoscale: Humans playing a spatial prisoner's dilemma. PloS one 5: e13749.
6. Palla G, Barabási AL, Vicsek T (2007) Quantifying social group evolution. Nature 446: 664–667.
7. Albert R, Barabási AL (2002) Statistical mechanics of complex networks. Reviews of Modern Physics 74: 47–97.
8. Gross T, Blasius B (2008) Adaptive coevolutionary networks: a review. Journal of the Royal Society Interface 5: 259.
9. Holme P, Kim BJ, Yoon CN, Han SK (2002) Attack vulnerability of complex networks. Physical Review E 65: 056109.
10. Albert R, Jeong H, Barabási A (2000) Error and attack tolerance of complex networks. Nature 406: 378–382.
11. Albert R, Albert I, Nakarado G (2004) Structural vulnerability of the north american power grid. Physical Review E 69: 25103.
12. Cohen R, Havlin S, Ben-Avraham D (2003) Efficient immunization strategies for computer networks and populations. Physical Review Letters 91: 247901.
13. Newman MEJ (2001) The structure of scientific collaboration networks. Proceedings of the National Academy of Sciences of the United States of America 98: 404–409.
14. Jin E, Girvan M, Newman M (2001) Structure of growing social networks. Physical Review E 64: 046132.
15. Holme P, Kim BJ (2002) Growing scale-free networks with tunable clustering. Physical Review E 65: 026107.

16. Guimerà R, Sales-Pardo M, Amaral LAN (2007) Classes of complex networks defined by role-to-role connectivity profiles. Nat Phys 3: 63–69.

17. Kumpula JM, Onnela JP, Saramäki J, Kaski K, Kertész J (2007) Emergence of communities in weighted networks. Physical Review Letters 99: 228701.

18. Lee D, Goh K, Kahng B, Kim D (2010) Complete trails of coauthorship network evolution. Physical Review E 82: 026112.

19. Azoulay P, Graff Zivin JS, Wang J (2010) Superstar extinction. The Quarterly Journal of Economics 125: 549–589.

20. Schneider CM, Moreira AA, Andrade JS, Havlin S, Herrmann HJ (2011) Mitigation of malicious attacks on networks. Proceedings of the National Academy of Sciences 108: 3838–3841.

9

Bioinformatics on the Cloud Computing Platform Azure

Hugh P. Shanahan[1]*, Anne M. Owen[2], Andrew P. Harrison[2,3]

1 Department of Computer Science, Royal Holloway, University of London, Egham, Surrey, United Kingdom, **2** Department of Mathematical Sciences, University of Essex, Wivenhoe Park, Colchester, United Kingdom, **3** Department of Biological Sciences, University of Essex, Wivenhoe Park, Colchester, United Kingdom

Abstract

We discuss the applicability of the Microsoft cloud computing platform, Azure, for bioinformatics. We focus on the usability of the resource rather than its performance. We provide an example of how R can be used on Azure to analyse a large amount of microarray expression data deposited at the public database ArrayExpress. We provide a walk through to demonstrate explicitly how Azure can be used to perform these analyses in Appendix S1 and we offer a comparison with a local computation. We note that the use of the Platform as a Service (PaaS) offering of Azure can represent a steep learning curve for bioinformatics developers who will usually have a Linux and scripting language background. On the other hand, the presence of an additional set of libraries makes it easier to deploy software in a parallel (scalable) fashion and explicitly manage such a production run with only a few hundred lines of code, most of which can be incorporated from a template. We propose that this environment is best suited for running stable bioinformatics software by users not involved with its development.

Editor: Shyamal D. Peddada, National Institute of Environmental and Health Sciences, United States of America

Funding: The research for this paper was made possible by funding from the VENUS-C EU network. The funders had no role in study design, data collection and analysis, decision to publish, or preparation of the manuscript.

Competing Interests: HS has read the journal's policy and the authors have the following conflicts. Microsoft is a partner in the VENUS-C collaboration which provided the funding for this project.

* Email: Hugh.Shanahan@rhul.ac.uk

Introduction

There has been a rapid increase in the number of cloud computing solutions across the computational biology community. For example, cloud computing has already been utilised for bioinformatics workflows [1], comparative genomics [2], gene set analysis for biomarkers [3], identifying epistatic interactions between single-nucleotide polymorphisms [4], microbial sequence analysis [5], multiple sequence alignment algorithms [6], pandemic simulations [7], personal genome variant annotation [8], protein annotation [9], proteomics analysis [10] and systems biology [11].

The community has explored different cloud solutions, such as hybrid clouds [12,13], Hadoop-like architectures [14], and the Google App Engine [15]. However, despite the wide variety of different cloud computing platforms available, most of the existing work in computational biology has focussed on Amazon Web Services (AWS) as provided by Amazon, in particular their Elastic Cloud Computing (EC2) service [16].

In this paper we will consider an alternative type of cloud computing platform: namely Azure the cloud computing platform provided by Microsoft. The rest of this paper will be organised as follows. We shall briefly explain the qualitative difference between this platform and the more traditional platforms such as Amazon EC2. We will explain the importance of coordinating large numbers of Virtual Machines (VM's) using Job Management software for researchers. We will explain the features of Azure and contrast them with those of other cloud computing platforms, pointing out strengths and weaknesses. We will present results based on a typical bioinformatics workflow using R to analyse microarray data computed on Azure, initially to determine if it reproduces locally computed results and then to determine if its performance is comparable to running the same task locally. Finally we draw conclusions about the applicability of Azure and draw some general lessons on how cloud computing would ideally evolve for bioinformatics.

Cloud computing fundamentals

There exists an extensive literature providing definitions of cloud computing [17]. We refer the reader to table 1 with cloud computing related definitions. In essence clouds are large server farms which make extensive use of virtualisation to provide outside users with effectively arbitrarily large numbers of Virtual Machines (VM's) and in some respects they can be seen as an extension of the idea of utility computing that was carried forward by Grid Computing in the 1990's [18].

The most commonly used cloud computing infrastructures in bioinformatics, such as Amazon EC2, are referred to as Infrastructure as a Service (IaaS), where each VM can be accessed directly via a command line interface. Others, such as Azure, Google AppEngine and Heroku [19] are referred to as Platform as a Service (PaaS) as they supply additional services and programmatic access to each VM. It should be noted that the divisions between these different types of platforms are becoming increasingly blurred - Azure also provides an IaaS and Amazon provides a PaaS built on EC2 called Elastic Beanstalk [20].

Nevertheless there is a substantial difference between using Azure and using IaaS infrastructures which translates into a steep learning curve particularly for bioinformatics developers who typically have a background in writing software for Linux systems.

Table 1. Definitions of Cloud Computing Terms.

Term	Explanation	Example
VM	Virtual Machine - a piece of software that emulates the behaviour of a separate computer running an Operating System.	
IaaS	Infrastructure as a Service - VM's can be accessed directly via a command line interface.	EC2, RackSpace, OpenStack
PaaS	Platform as a Service - VM's can only be accessed programmatically	Azure, AppEngine, Elastic BeanStalk, Heroku
Job manager	Software which manages the submission of an arbitrary number of executables (jobs) over a large number of computers which typically vary in their parameters. Job Management software will typically include the creation of log files for each run in a systematic fashion and deal with failures in an orderly way.	StarCluster, Generic Worker, Condor, Oracle Grid Engine
Software stack	A set of software that communicate with each other in a hierarchical fashion. In the context of cloud computing, this allows the decoupling of issues that are relevant to each local computer with global issues such as their overall management.	
Image	Bit-for-bit copy of the state of a particular VM which can then be deployed elsewhere. As a result, one can use a VM which runs locally or on a cloud which is configured precisely with the software and data the user requires.	
MapReduce	A protocol for distributed systems that notes that in the analysis of large data sets distributed over many VM's require one (Map) step that has to be executed by all the VM's on the data it has, followed by another (Reduce) step where the results of the Map step are then collated in some fashion to one VM.	Hadoop, HDInsight, Greenplum

The above are consistent with formal definitions that are provided by, for example, NIST [21]. It should be noted that these definitions do not necessarily imply that a PaaS is built upon an IaaS. The functional construction of these clouds is complex and beyond the scope of this article.

The basic issues for cloud computing and its application in bioinformatics have already been discussed in detail elsewhere [16,22]. In brief, the key advantage of cloud computing for bioinformatics researchers is the ability to scale an analysis up and complete the task in as short a period of time as possible. Many bioinformatics researchers do not use high-throughput computing resources to carry out this phase on a frequent basis and hence it is efficient to lease time on a cloud computing platform for a comparatively small sum of money (e.g. hundreds of U.S. dollars) that can be readily absorbed into the day to day costs of a project.

Batch mode submission

While it is often possible to consider problems which require a high level of parallelisation (using message passing or threading) [23,24], the prohibitive amount of development time and resource required to do this tends to direct researchers into pursuing the "low lying fruit" and doing analysis which can be trivially decomposed into a set of jobs that run in parallel with each other [25]. Schematically (using the example of an R script analysing a set of differently-sized data sets) such a batch mode of operation is shown in Figure 1.

For many calculations the number of cores required is much larger than can be allocated onto a single computer. Hence, apart from access to the cloud platform itself, job management software is essential. Job managers will do a variety of tasks to aid the above, in particular submitting the tasks to the allocated VMs, creating appropriately named log files and managing failures of individual VMs during the running of the job. This is not trivial to carry out on Amazon EC2. Software such as StarCluster http://star.mit.edu/cluster/ can do this on EC2 but the configuration of StarCluster is a not an easy task and requires a level of familiarity with shell scripts. As a result the full power of these resources can only be employed by computational biologists with extensive experience of shell-scripting as well as expertise in the software

they wish to use. This excludes the large number of individuals without those skills whose research could benefit from access to such resources. Cloud computing platforms represent very large software stacks but surprisingly do not by default include this type of job management software.

Azure provides a set of C# libraries referred to as the Generic Worker (GW) to perform a similar set of tasks as a Job Manager. This provides a framework to write C# software to perform the tasks that a Job Manager can do for tailored set of software. Hence it is possible to develop a bespoke interface for users to manage batch jobs for a particular set of software.

Azure features and comparison

In this section we will provide a more detailed explanation of the Azure infrastructure with comparisons where possible with the Amazon EC2 service. The reader is referred to Table 2 for comparisons of features at a glance. In particular, we will discuss the computational services they provide, disk space, and their ease of use from the perspective of a typical bioinformatics developer with extensive experience of developing software on a Linux architecture and of a biologist with little or no scripting experience. We will also make comparisons from the perspective of costing.

Computational Services

As noted previously, Azure provides an IaaS and PaaS - which Microsoft refer to, respectively, as Virtual Machines and Cloud services. The IaaS offering allows one to deploy VM's which run either pre-built Windows Server 2008 or Linux images, or to upload one's own customized image. This service is similar to the one offered by other IaaS providers but does not make use of the GW libraries discussed above for job management and hence we will not focus further on it here.

The Azure PaaS provides programmatic access from .NET (including C#), Java, node.js, PHP, Ruby and Python though at present the GW libraries are only available for C# and hence the other languages are largely for data transfer. It is comprised of two "roles": the Web Role designed for setting up a web-based service and the Worker Role which is designed to run applications in a batch production mode. Frequently these can be in parallel with

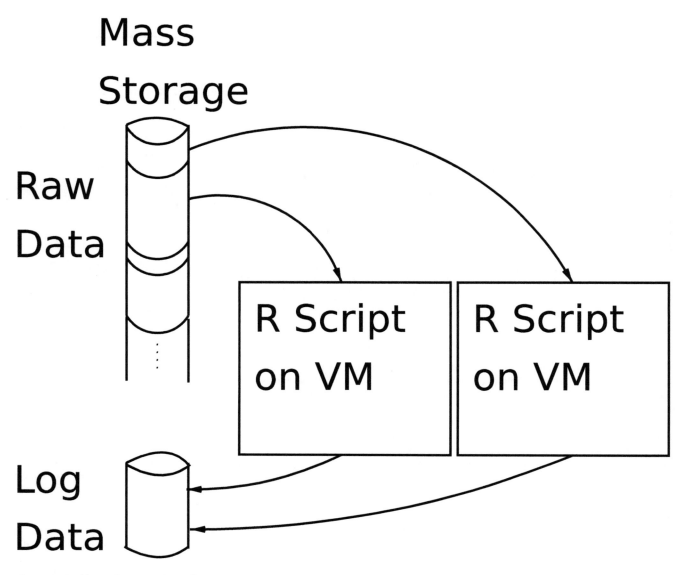

Figure 1. Batch mode operation schematic.

Table 2. Comparison of Cloud Computing Features.

Feature	Microsoft Azure	Amazon EC2
Infrastructure provision	PaaS (Cloud Service) and IaaS (Virtual Machines)	IaaS, also PaaS via Elastic Beanstalk
Job Manager?	Via Generic Worker libraries	Yes.
Operating Systems available	Windows Server 2008 on PaaS Windows and Linux on IaaS	Linux and Windows
Data Storage	Mass store	S3 Storage
MapReduce available?	Yes	Yes
SQL available?	Yes	Yes
Ease of use for Linux developer	Learning curve to get familiar with C#; authentication methods not yet trivial	Provision of excellent tutorials plus extensive community support.
Ease of use for user	GW allows development of tailored tools	Requires experience of scripting or workflow software such as Galaxy or Taverna.

each other, with a web role passing on tasks to a worker role. Both roles use fixed-configuration VMs that are based on a Windows Server Operating System. The major difference between the roles is that the web role has IIS (Microsoft's web server software) installed on it. VMs (and the roles) can vary from the equivalent of 1 CPU with 760 Mbyte memory and 20 Gbyte disk space running nominally on 1 GHz CPU to 8 CPU with 56 Gbyte memory and 2 Tbyte storage running nominally on a 1.6 GHz CPU.

We note that a MapReduce service is also available on Azure called HDInsight.

Worker Role

The worker role is designed for running large numbers of jobs. Efficient use of this type of role has been improved significantly by the provision of an additional set of libraries from Microsoft called the Generic Worker (GW) which can be accessed from http://resources.venus-c.eu. In particular these libraries can be used within a C# program to submit and efficiently manage jobs submitted to a set of worker roles, as illustrated in Figure 2. In this framework the software runs in two modes. In the first mode an application (which can be a simple executable or a more complex workflow of executables) is uploaded to Azure storage along with a description of the application (in particular the expected list of parameters that will be used in the application). In the second mode the application is transferred from storage and called with a specific set of parameters. The GW provides efficient job management and hence allows a straightforward means to scaling a task. Activation or deactivating of instances of the worker roles can be called within a Windows power shell script or via the code. Additional software can be installed silently at the start of each run. It is possible to construct a workflow where the output from one worker role running one type of executable passes the data onto another worker running another executable and so on, though we have not explored this option. In addition to the demos provided by Microsoft we have developed code that uses the GW

to run an R script which can access data that is on Azure storage. The source code for this can be downloaded from http://gene.cs.rhul.ac.uk/RAzure/GWydiR.zip. Details for setting up and using the GW for a sample R script are given in Appendix S1.

Web Role

As the name suggests the Web Role is designed for setting up web services on Azure. These services can be set up using ASP.NET and C# to create web pages through which a user can interact with programs and data. Web Roles are not designed to run large production runs but can act as a front end by passing data onto worker roles. Obviously this is not optimal for a standard production run where individual failures should be detected and rerun on an as-required rather than as-expected basis. Nonetheless, they can be used to implement tasks such as large uploads of data to the Azure mass storage facilities.

Data storage and Transfer

Long term storage of data is provided via a mechanism that is similar to Amazon's S3 system. Data is stored in containers which are effectively a single layer of a directory. Individual files are referred to as blobs. It is possible to recreate a pseudo-directory hierarchy by appropriate naming of the blobs with slash characters as in a data path. Microsoft also provides the Azure Marketplace (http://datamarket.azure.com/) where data sets and applications for Azure can be made available.

It is possible to set up a SQL database within Azure for both IaaS and PaaS. The *Azure Storage Explorer* from Neudesic (http://azurestorageexplorer.codeplex.com) allows data to be browsed or transferred to or from Azure storage. We have provided a set of simple Java executables and an R script that enable data transfer to Azure storage within a VM in Azure or on a local machine based on examples provided with Microsoft's documentation. This can be found at https://github.com/hughshanahan/RAzureEssentials.

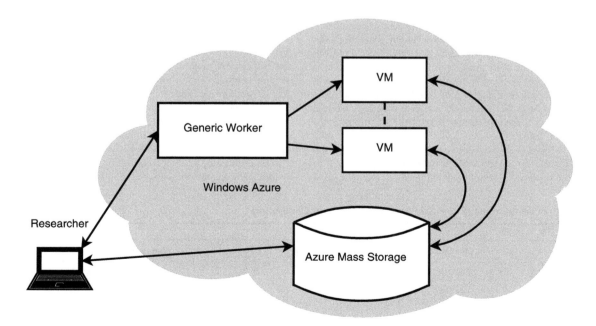

Figure 2. Using Azure with the Generic Worker. Shows that a number of Virtual Machines (VMs) created for the worker roles can be scaled up and down as needed.

Ease of use for Developers

As noted previously, for a developer who is experienced in using Linux systems and is not familiar with a .NET software architecture, designing software using the GW libraries can represent a steep learning curve. On the other hand for a batch mode submission there are templates that can make this substantially easier. The source code for the package corresponds to roughly 400 lines of code, much of which can be taken from the templates available from http://resources.venus-c.eu and the GWydiR github site. As one can see from the walk through for installing the software in Appendix S1, getting initially configured is still not trivial though there is no technical impediment to this being made substantially easier.

Ease of use for users

From the perspective of the user the same issue of initial configuration is a stumbling block. On the other hand the web resources for managing the VM's and data storage being used are excellent and the user is able to inspect results from the runs via a web interface. Because of the bespoke nature of this it is possible to create an interface that is highly tailored to a specific task and could be substantially easier to use than generic workflow software such as Galaxy and Taverna [26].

Cost

In Table 3 we provide a comparison of costings between Azure and Amazon EC2. We are not quite comparing like with like in that the pricing for Amazon is using the Linux OS while Azure is using Windows Server 2008 but we are focussing on the cheapest possible option in all cases. We note that pricing can be highly dynamic - for example earlier on in 2013 prices for CPU time on the Azure PaaS were twice that of Amazon EC2. Despite this we can see that market forces influence prices to be roughly comparable (i.e. within the same order of magnitude).

Materials and Methods

In this work we focus on a real world example to demonstrate the use of R in Azure, namely how G-stacks (probes with runs of 4 or more guanine bases) bias the experiment data for the Affymetrix Human GeneChip called HG_U133A. This GeneChip was studied with a wide scale analysis both because much data is publicly available and because it has the highest ratio of G-stack probes among the Affymetrix Human GeneChips available. It is more beneficial to bioinformaticians to use real data and a useful study than to use an artificial example to evaluate the use of R for bioinformatics in Azure.

The data for many microarray experiments that utilise the HG_U133A GeneChip are available at public repositories such as NCBI Gene Expression Omnibus (GEO) [27], and the EBI ArrayExpress [28]. Each experiment or data set consists of a set of measurements that are stored in CEL files, which can be either binary or character text, depending on the choices of the researcher. We used the data from 576 HG_U133A experiments that were deposited before May, 2012.

The HG_U133A GeneChip contains 22,283 annotated probe sets and about one third of these contain one or more probes with a G-stack in them. Our analysis compared normalised expression values of all probe sets with normalised expression values of probe sets with G-stacks removed. We previously predicted that because probes containing runs of guanine are systematically correlated with each other [29], due to the coherent formation of G-stacks [30], then the difference in normalised expression data between the two sets of results will show a bias. Our analysis also compared correlations of each probe set of the two groups with every other probe set.

The analysis that was carried out on six data sets in GEO [29] on a locally-based computer was repeated on the Azure cloud. The results computed on Azure were the same as those computed locally, hence we are confident of reproducibility. The full analysis on the 576 experiments was performed on Azure. In this paper we will focus on timings, scale and load. Date and time stamp output was written to a log at the beginning and end of loading each set of CEL files, i.e. transferring the files from Azure storage to R working storage. Similar date and time stamp output was also written to the log at the beginning and end of performing the main normalisation and G-stack comparison analyses.

Results

It is important to understand how the run times on Azure compare with a locally-run calculation. In addition to the time taken to run the script on Azure there is the additional issue of loading the data from the mass storage to the VM. We consider each of these elements in turn.

Load time

The uploading of the publicly available experiment datasets to Azure mass storage was achieved in two ways. The first method was to use a customised webpage that was initiated and processed by an Azure Webrole (discussed previously). With this method a list of datasets could be passed to the uploading routine. The second method used to upload a few individual experiments was the *Azure Storage Explorer* from Neudesic (mentioned above). This provides a direct link between Azure mass storage accounts and the user's local machine. It can be used to examine files and data in Azure storage and to upload or download individual files. It was less useful when long lists of datasets needed to be uploaded.

The timings for loading data files from Azure mass storage to R working storage are shown for all 576 HG_U133A experiments in

Table 3. Cost of some features of Azure and Amazon Cloud Computing.

Feature	Microsoft Azure	Amazon EC2
VM (Small Instance)	$ 0.08 hr^{-1} PaaS – Windows	$ 0.06 hr^{-1} U.S. East - Linux
	$ 0.06 hr^{-1} IaaS - Linux	
Ingress	Nothing	Nothing (from Internet)
Egress	$ 119.40 $Tbyte^{-1}$	$ 122.88 $Tbyte^{-1}$
Storage	$ 95 $Tbyte^{-1}Month^{-1}$ (Mass storage - Globally redundant)	$ 97.28 $Tbyte^{-1}Month^{-1}$ (S3 Standard)

Figure 3. The elapsed time for loading an experiment comprising 2 CEL files (about 23 KBytes for text CEL files) was typically about 2 seconds, and for an experiment comprising 200 CEL files (about 2.25 MBytes for text CEL files) was around 45 seconds. CEL files can be stored in either a text-based or binary format with the text-based format clearly requiring more space. The size of particular CEL files also varies on other factors; for example, how many masks and/or biological outliers the researcher has chosen to record after the intensity data for the array. The outlier experiments in Figure 3 depend on whether the CEL files were stored in binary (shorter load times than the trend) or text-based (longer run times than the trend). The largest outlier had a combination of these formats.

Run time

The timings of the 576 analysis runs (i.e. how long the R scripts ran on an individual VM once the data was loaded) are shown in Figure 4. The outliers below the trend of the data are experiments with binary format CEL files, which are a little quicker to process than the text-format ones.

Once the GW software had been set up and tested, it was a simple matter to scale up the number of VMs to run these analysis jobs. Each experiment was submitted as a separate job. Earlier in our use of Azure we had submitted lists of experiments for analysis runs. It was found that the list approach was less easy to control and scale because sometimes an experiment within the list would fail through a shortage of disk space. By starting each experiment as a new job with fresh disk space this problem was minimised.

Comparison with using R in a local machine

A set of experiments was chosen to repeat the analyses, which had been done on the Azure cloud, on local machines. The experiments had a range of numbers of CEL files to ensure they were representative of different lengths of jobs. In particular, they had 4, 8, 16, 32, 64 and 128 CEL files.

As it is difficult to reproduce exactly the configuration of an Azure VM, a variety of different local computers were used: -

- Local1 has a 2.13 GHz processor.

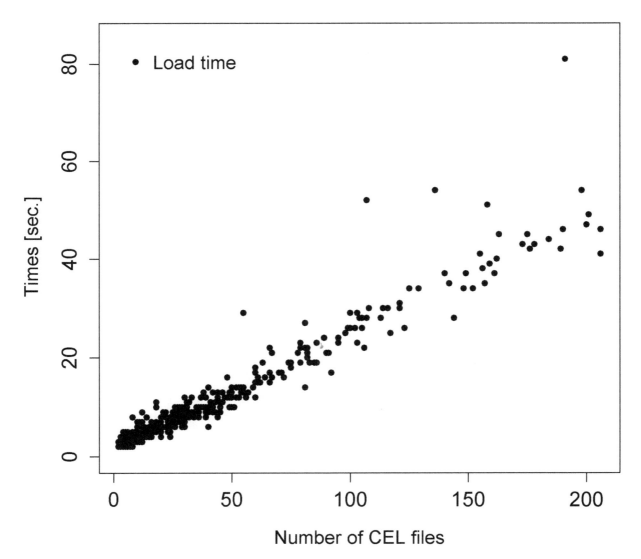

Figure 3. Time taken to load microarray data from Azure mass storage to R working storage. Plot showing the time in seconds taken to load each of 576 datasets from Azure blob storage to local VM disk space, in terms of the number of CEL files in each GSE experiment.

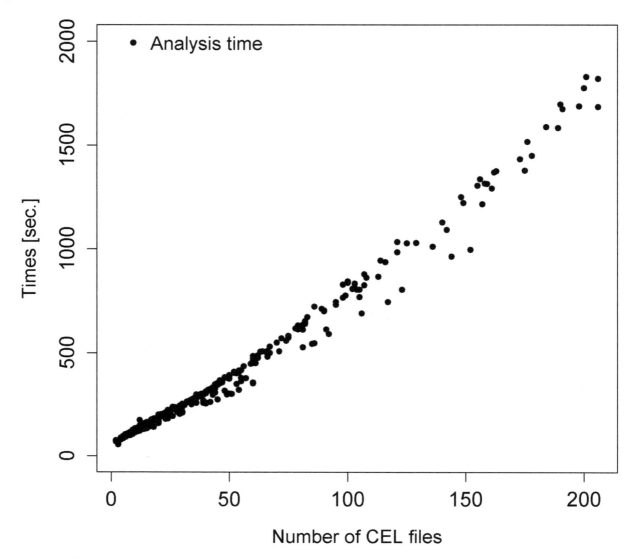

Figure 4. Time taken to analyse data with R script. Shows the time in seconds taken to analyse each of 576 datasets, in terms of the number of CEL files in each GSE experiment.

- Local2 has a 2.24 GHz processor that runs Windows as a virtual machine.
- As Local2 is run as a virtual machine it is also run with a 70% execution cap to crudely reproduce the nominal VM processor frequency.

The results are shown in Figure 5. In all cases the Azure VM runs more slowly than the local machines, taking roughly a factor of two times as long as the slowest local case.

Discussion

The wide-spread adoption of cloud computing platforms within bioinformatics has made a major impact on the capability of researchers whose work intermittently requires large amounts of CPU time (or simply large memory) for tasks which can be carried out in a trivially parallel way. The cloud computing paradigm will be of increasing importance for users, particularly as data sets continue to expand in size and hence the analysis will have to come to the data and not the other way around. Up to this point,

the majority of bioinformaticians who use cloud computing have made use of Amazon's EC2. It provides a stable software stack with an associated large community of users who can provide support and solutions specific to a researcher's domain. Nonetheless, it is clear that Amazon is no longer the only possible provider of cloud-based solutions and that other approaches should be explored.

In this paper we have specifically examined Microsoft's Azure platform, but we note that many other alternatives exist. The utility of all of these approaches should be considered, if only to ensure that each of the commercial providers remain under pressure to provide as economical a solution as possible.

We have noted that the PaaS infrastructure provided by Azure allows one to develop bespoke interfaces for specific executables that run in a batch mode. Despite the learning curve for developers who do not have a background in writing C# code, these can be put together with a little effort requiring approximately 400 lines of code, much of which can be appropriated from templates. The initial configuration is complex but this could be fixed at first by those developing the bioinformatics pipelines

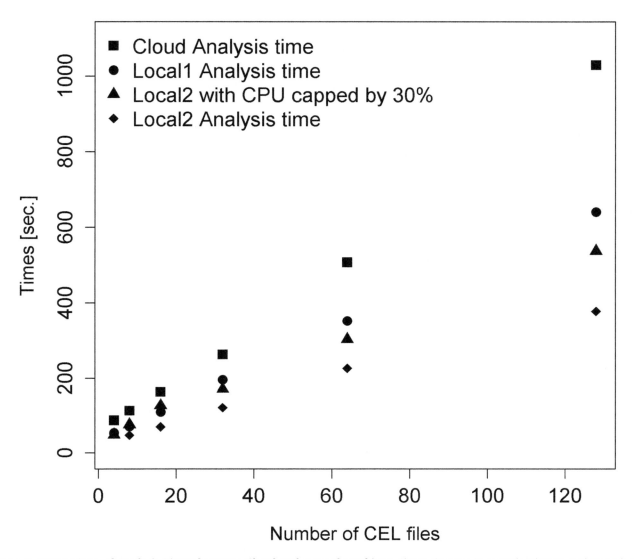

Figure 5. Comparison of Analysis Times between Cloud and 2 Local machines. Shows the time in seconds taken to analyse each of 6 particular experiments, in terms of the number of CEL files in each experiment. The particular experiments were chosen because they had 4, 8, 16, 32, 64 and 128 CEL files, to give a range of experiment data amounts. The machine labelled Local1 had a CPU clock speed of 2.13 GHz, and the machine labelled Local2 had a CPU clock speed of 2.24 GHz. The 70% CPU cap was added to the Local2 machine to crudely estimate the slower 1.60 GHz stated clock speed of the Azure VM.

though it is clear that the process could be streamlined further by Azure developers in later releases. In this light, and given the fact that the Worker roles can only run the Windows Server OS it is apparent that the present offering is not a viable solution for bioinformatics software with analyses which are still being developed. On the other hand a substantial set of stable bioinformatics software such as that available via EMBOSS or BioLinux could be deployed very successfully using Azure and its PaaS.

We have shown that the pricing of Azure is comparable with other clouds (at least to within an order of magnitude) though this is highly dynamic. We have also shown that results generated locally are reproduced by equivalent Azure runs and that performance is not substantially affected. Run times suggest that Azure is slower by roughly a factor of 2–3 than local PCs though one has to be careful since we were not able to make a like-for-like comparison using precisely the same CPU-type, memory and exact version of the Windows Operating System.

We have not discussed the general upload of public data as this is a global issue for any public cloud. In tests on a University network we estimated that uploading 1 Tbyte would take approximately 26 hours. This is a rough estimate and is highly dependent on the network connection. However, it is clear that at the very least the large amounts of publicly available data should not be uploaded on an individual basis. The cloud providers that can support this will have a substantial advantage over their competitors. We note that Amazon have made steps in this direction by providing a number of relevant datasets available free of charge such as the data from the modENCODE project [31].

Looking forward the continued blurring between IaaS and PaaS will enable developers and users to make use of the best features of both. Developers can port images created locally to a cloud with precisely the configuration they require, while still being able to run them programmatically so that scaling can be achieved easily with an intuitive interface. If we draw an analogy with web-development, it is possible to imagine an equivalent of Ruby-on-

Rails [32] and Django [33]. Both of these enable the easy development of dynamic web sites to be started, that can run using different web server technologies and the underlying scripting languages of Ruby and Python. In the same way one can envisage a similar framework allowing specific executables to be deployed on a cloud (not fixed to any one vendor) and which are run in a batch mode and have an easy interface.

Supporting Information

Appendix S1   Scaling an R script on Azure using the Generic Worker.

Acknowledgments

The authors would like to express their thanks to Graham Upton for advice on the analysis and providing feedback on the installation of the Generic Worker software. We acknowledge the support of the British Council INSPIRE award to the Universities of Essex and Sindh to develop bioinformatics in Sindh.

Author Contributions

Conceived and designed the experiments: HS AO AH. Performed the experiments: HS AO AH. Analyzed the data: HS AO AH. Contributed reagents/materials/analysis tools: HS AO AH. Wrote the paper: HS AO AH.

References

1. Abouelhoda M, Issa SA, Ghanem M (2012) Tavaxy: Integrating Taverna and Galaxy workflows with cloud computing support. BMC bioinformatics 13: 77.
2. Wall DP, Kudtarkar P, Fusaro VA, Pivovarov R, Patil P, et al. (2010) Cloud computing for comparative genomics. BMC bioinformatics 11: 259.
3. Zhang L, Gu S, Liu Y, Wang B, Azuaje F (2012) Gene set analysis in the cloud. Bioinformatics (Oxford, England) 28: 294–5.
4. Wang Z, Wang Y, Tan KL, Wong L, Agrawal D (2011) eCEO: an efficient Cloud Epistasis cOmputing model in genome-wide association study. Bioinformatics (Oxford, England) 27: 1045–51.
5. Angiuoli SV, White JR, Matalka M, White O, Fricke WF (2011) Resources and costs for microbial sequence analysis evaluated using virtual machines and cloud computing. PloS one 6: e26624.
6. Di Tommaso P, Orobitg M, Guirado F, Cores F, Espinosa T, et al. (2010) Cloud-Coffee: implementation of a parallel consistency-based multiple alignment algorithm in the T-Coffee package and its benchmarking on the Amazon Elastic-Cloud. Bioinformatics (Oxford, England) 26: 1903–4.
7. Eriksson H, Raciti M, Basile M, Cunsolo A, Fröberg A, et al. (2011) A cloud-based simulation architecture for pandemic influenza simulation. AMIA Annual Symposium proceedings/AMIA Symposium AMIA Symposium 2011: 364–73.
8. Habegger L, Balasubramanian S, Chen DZ, Khurana E, Sboner A, et al. (2012) VAT: A computational framework to functionally annotate variants in personal genomes within a cloud-computing environment. Bioinformatics (Oxford, England): bts368–.
9. de Lima Morais DA, Fang H, Rackham OJL, Wilson D, Pethica R, et al. (2011) SUPERFAMILY 1.75 including a domain-centric gene ontology method. Nucleic acids research 39: D427–34.
10. Halligan BD, Geiger JF, Vallejos AK, Greene AS, Twigger SN (2009) Low cost, scalable proteomics data analysis using Amazon's cloud computing services and open source search algorithms. Journal of proteome research 8: 3148–53.
11. Ropella GEP, Hunt CA (2010) Cloud computing and validation of expandable in silico livers. BMC systems biology 4: 168.
12. Kim H, Parashar M, Foran DJ, Yang L (2009) Investigating the Use of Cloudbursts for High-Throughput Medical Image Registration. Proceedings of the IEEE/ACM International Conference on Grid Computing IEEE/ACM International Conference on Grid Computing 2009: 34–41.
13. Qiu J, Ekanayake J, Gunarathne T, Choi JY, Bae SH, et al. (2010) Hybrid cloud and cluster computing paradigms for life science applications. BMC bioinformatics 11 Suppl 1: S3.
14. Taylor RC (2010) An overview of the Hadoop/MapReduce/HBase framework and its current applications in bioinformatics. BMC bioinformatics 11 Suppl 1: S1.
15. Widera P, Krasnogor N (2011) Protein Models Comparator: Scalable Bioinformatics Computing on the Google App Engine Platform. CoRR: 10.
16. Fusaro VA, Patil P, Gafni E, Wall DP, Tonellato PJ (2011) Biomedical cloud computing with Amazon Web Services. PLoS computational biology 7: e1002147.
17. Grandison T, Maximilien EM, Thorpe S, Alba A (2010) Towards a Formal Definition of a Computing Cloud. In: 2010 6th World Congress on Services. IEEE, pp. 191–192. doi:10.1109/SERVICES.2010.111. URL http://www.computer.org/csdl/proceedings/services/2010/4129/00/4129a191-abs.html.
18. Foster I, Zhao Y, Raicu I, Lu S (2008) Cloud Computing and Grid Computing 360-Degree Compared. In: 2008 Grid Computing Environments Workshop. IEEE, pp. 1–10. doi:10.1109/GCE.2008.4738445. URL http://ieeexplore.ieee.org/lpdocs/epic03/wrapper.htm?arnumber = 4738445.
19. Leite AF, Magalhaes Alves de Melo AC (2012) Executing a biological sequence comparison application on a federated cloud environment. In: 2012 19th International Conference on High Performance Computing. IEEE, pp. 1–9. doi:10.1109/HiPC.2012.6507500. URL http://ieeexplore.ieee.org/lpdocs/epic03/wrapper.htm?arnumber = 6507500.
20. Firdhous M, Ghazali O, Hassan S (2011) A trust computing mechanism for cloud computing. In: Kaleidoscope 2011: The Fully Networked Human? - Innovations for Future Networks and Services (K-2011), Proceedings of ITU. pp. 1–7.
21. Mell P, Grance T (2011) Final Version of NIST Cloud Computing Definition Published. In: National Institute of Standards and Technology Special Publication SP 800-145. URL http://csrc.nist.gov/publications/nistpubs/800-145/SP800-145.pdf.
22. Stein LD (2010) The case for cloud computing in genome informatics. Genome biology 11: 207.
23. Feng W (2004) Green destiny + mpiBLAST = Bioinformagic. In: GR . Joubert WE, Nagel FJP, Walter WV, editors, Parallel Computing Software Technology, Algorithms, Architectures and Applications, North-Holland, volume 13 of Advances in Parallel Computing. pp. 653–660. doi:10.1016/S0927-5452(04)80081-9. URL http://www.sciencedirect.com/science/article/pii/S0927545204800819.
24. Zhu H, Chen S, Wu J (2010) Paralleling Clonal Selection Algorithm with OpenMP. In: Intelligent Networks and Intelligent Systems (ICINIS), 2010 3rd International Conference on. pp. 463–466. doi:10.1109/ICINIS.2010.41.
25. Stockinger H, Pagni M, Cerutti L, Falquet L (2006) Grid Approach to Embarrassingly Parallel CPU-Intensive Bioinformatics Problems. In: 2006 Second IEEE International Conference on e-Science and Grid Computing (e-Science'06). IEEE, pp. 58–58. doi:10.1109/E-SCIENCE.2006.261142. URL http://ieeexplore.ieee.org/xpl/articleDetails.jsp?arnumber = 4031031\#.
26. Afgan E, Chapman B, Jadan M, Franke V, Taylor J (2012) Using cloud computing infrastructure with CloudBioLinux, CloudMan, and Galaxy. Current protocols in bioinformatics/editoral board, Andreas D Baxevanis [et al] Chapter 11: Unit11.9.
27. Barrett T, Troup DB, Wilhite SE, Ledoux P, Rudnev D, et al. (2006) NCBI GEO: mining tens of millions of expression profiles–database and tools update. Nucleic acids research 35: D760–765.
28. Parkinson H, Kapushesky M, Kolesnikov N, Rustici G, Shojatalab M, et al. (2009) ArrayExpress update–from an archive of functional genomics experiments to the atlas of gene expression. Nucleic Acids Research 37: D868.
29. Shanahan HP, Memon FN, Upton GJG, Harrison AP (2011) Normalized Affymetrix expression data are biased by G-quadruplex formation. Nucleic acids research.
30. Langdon WB, Upton GJG, Harrison AP (2009) Probes containing runs of guanines provide insights into the biophysics and bioinformatics of Affymetrix GeneChips. Briefings in bioinformatics 10: 259–277.
31. Contrino S, Smith RN, Butano D, Carr A, Hu F, et al. (2012) modMine: flexible access to modENCODE data. Nucleic acids research 40: D1082–8.
32. Bachle M, Kirchberg P (2007) Ruby on rails. Software, IEEE 24: 105–108.
33. Rodriguez-Martinez M, Seguel J, Greer M (2010) Open source cloud computing tools: A case study with a weather application. In: Cloud Computing (CLOUD), 2010 IEEE 3rd International Conference on. pp. 443–449. doi:10.1109/CLOUD.2010.81.

10

Completely Anonymous Multi-Recipient Signcryption Scheme with Public Verification

Liaojun Pang[1,2]*, Huixian Li[2,3], Lu Gao[1], Yumin Wang[1]

1 School of Life Sciences and Technology, Xidian University, Xi'an, China, **2** Department of Computer Science, Wayne State University, Detroit, Michigan, United States of America, **3** School of Computer Science and Engineering, Northwestern Polytechnical University, Xi'an, China

Abstract

Most of the existing multi-recipient signcryption schemes do not take the anonymity of recipients into consideration because the list of the identities of all recipients must be included in the ciphertext as a necessary element for decryption. Although the signer's anonymity has been taken into account in several alternative schemes, these schemes often suffer from the *cross-comparison attack* and *joint conspiracy attack*. That is to say, there are few schemes that can achieve complete anonymity for both the signer and the recipient. However, in many practical applications, such as network conference, both the signer's and the recipient's anonymity should be considered carefully. Motivated by these concerns, we propose a novel multi-recipient signcryption scheme with complete anonymity. The new scheme can achieve both the signer's and the recipient's anonymity at the same time. Each recipient can easily judge whether the received ciphertext is from an authorized source, but cannot determine the real identity of the sender, and at the same time, each participant can easily check decryption permission, but cannot determine the identity of any other recipient. The scheme also provides a public verification method which enables anyone to publicly verify the validity of the ciphertext. Analyses show that the proposed scheme is more efficient in terms of computation complexity and ciphertext length and possesses more advantages than existing schemes, which makes it suitable for practical applications. The proposed scheme could be used for network conferences, paid-TV or DVD broadcasting applications to solve the secure communication problem without violating the privacy of each participant. Key words: Multi-recipient signcryption; Signcryption; Complete Anonymity; Public verification.

Editor: Francesco Pappalardo, University of Catania, Italy

Funding: National Natural Science Foundation of China under grant numbers 61103178, 61103199 and 60803151; the Research Fund for the Doctoral Program of Higher Education of China under grant number 20096102120045; Basic Science Research Fund in Xidian University under grant number K5051310006. The funders had no role in study design, data collection and analysis, decision to publish, or preparation of the manuscript.

Competing Interests: The authors have declared that no competing interests exist.

* E-mail: liaojun.pang@wayne.edu

Introduction

With development of network technology and its applications, a lot of group-oriented network services such as network multicasting or broadcasting have been proposed. Usually, in these services, a message sender is required to securely send the same messages to a group of recipients, such that only a certain number of recipients can read the messages while unauthorized recipients can extract nothing useful from these messages [1]. Therefore, the concept of multi-recipient encryption was put forward [2–6], and it has been considered as one of most promising solutions to solve the security problem of securing multicasting or broadcasting. Later, combining the concept of multi-recipient encryption with the idea of Zheng's signcryption [7], Duan *et al.* [8] proposed the first multi-recipient signcryption scheme. In their scheme, to achieve the goal of sending the same message to all authorized recipients confidentially, the sender only needs to execute one signcryption operation, and at the same time, each recipient can verify the validity of messages. Since then, many excellent multi-recipient signcryption schemes [9–11] were proposed, which take more security properties into consideration than Duan *et al.*'s scheme. In general, multi-recipient signcryption can be used in many important applications, such as paid-TV or DVD broad-

casting systems [10], where only authorized or paying users should be able to access such services.

Nevertheless, today, more and more people are concerned regarding personal privacy, thus participant anonymity should be taken into account when designing multi-recipient signcryption [12]. For example, in paid-TV and DVD broadcasting application systems, service providers do not want others to obtain the real identities from the ciphertext messages. Therefore, multi-recipient signcryption with the sender (or called the signer) anonymity had been introduced. In literature, there have been several multi-recipient signcryption schemes [13–17] which try to assure anonymity of the sender. The concept of anonymous signature was firstly proposed by Rivest *et al.* [18]. In 2005, Huang *et al.* [19] proposed the first anonymous signcryption scheme, which used an ID-based ring signature to assure anonymity of the signer. However, their scheme is only a single-recipient scheme. Later, based on similar thoughts, Lal *et al.* [13] extended this method for multi-recipient environments. Furthermore, a multi-recipient scheme with anonymity of the sender [14–17] was proposed. Although these schemes [13–17] provide solutions for assuring signer anonymity, there are still some unsolved issues. For example, they suffer from two new attacks known as the *cross-comparison attack* [20] and the *joint conspiracy attack* [21]. Based on the ring signature, schemes [13–17] construct a list which includes the real signer and several valid participants which are chosen randomly by the signer hiding the real signer in this list. Although this perfectly works to some extent, an attacker can obtain a number of different ciphertexts from the same message source by closely monitoring network traffic, thus by comparing the signers' identities from different lists an attacker can narrow down the scope of the target signer. Using this scheme, an attacker can directly obtain the identity of the real signer. Even if the attacker does not directly obtain the real signer's identity, he/she has narrowed down the scope of the attacker's guess. In addition, it is still possible for such an attacker to retrieve a list which includes the real signer. Then, he/she can cooperate with some participants in the list to narrow down the scope and guess the real signer with a larger probability. In addition, the list of chosen participants can increase the length of the ciphertext quite significantly, potentially reducing the transmission efficiency. More important, the identities of all the authorized recipients are usually included in the ciphertext of these anonymous schemes in plaintext [13–19], which is not always wanted.

Generally speaking, anonymity of participants includes both the sender's and the recipient's anonymity. Besides the anonymity of the sender, the anonymity of the recipient is often equally important so that designers of multi-recipient signcryption schemes should pay attention. For example, in paid-TV and DVD broadcasting application systems, no user should accept that his/her subscription of these services is publicly viewable to others especially when the service is quite sensitive. However, unfortunately, almost none of the existing schemes take the anonymity of recipients into consideration because the identity of each recipient must be included in the ciphertext as a necessary element for decryption. The list of the authorized recipients' identities in the ciphertext is used to show who are the authorized recipients and how each authorized recipient gets his/her person-specific data for encryption from the ciphertext during the decryption process. Thus, schemes [9–11] directly expose the recipient's identity and therefore violate their privacy. Also, the fact that different recipients have different person-specific data for decryption can lead to decryption unfairness. This means that if some recipient's person-specific data are damaged due to communication errors, he/she cannot decrypt the ciphertext but the others can still decrypt the ciphertext correctly [12]. Therefore, it is urgent and challenging for researchers to solve the recipient anonymity issue of multi-recipient signcryption.

Following the arguments above, it is known that almost none of the existing multi-recipient signcryption schemes take the full anonymity of recipients and senders into account. Although there are several schemes that provide a solution for anonymity of the signer, they are not perfect, that is, they suffer from the *cross-comparison attack* and the *joint conspiracy attack*. Therefore, existing schemes cannot deal with the anonymity of the sender or the recipient properly. Furthermore, these schemes are not suitable for applications that need complete anonymity for the sender and the recipient. For example, in a network conference application, every conference participant often wants to be kept anonymous when he/she is taking part in the conference discussion. Furthermore, if a participant (i.e. sender) wants to publish criticism or objections, he/she hopes that others (i.e. recipients) do not know his/her identity. At the same time, the recipient cannot want the other recipients to reveal that he/she is an authorized recipient. In fact, today, anonymity is one of the most important prerequisites for people to talk freely and make objective decisions.

Motivated by the above, this paper proposes a completely anonymous multi-recipient signcryption scheme which meets: (1) The identity of the sender is kept secret; (2) The identities of all the recipients are kept secret; (3) Each recipient can easily judge whether the received message is from an authorized source, but he/she cannot determine the real identity of the sender; (4) Each recipient can easily judge whether he/she is an authorized recipient, but he/she cannot determine the identity of any other authorized recipient; (5) The validity of ciphertext can be verified publicly. Speaking of practical applications, the proposed scheme can be in principle used for network conference, paid-TV or DVD broadcasting application systems to assure secure communication among authorized participants, while at the same time, providing complete anonymity for all participants.

To facilitate the description of our scheme, notations used throughout the document are summarized in Table 1.

Preliminaries

Complexity Assumptions

The security of the proposed scheme is based on the following problems and security assumptions.

Let G_1 and G_2 be two cyclic groups of prime order q and let P be a generator of G_1. Let e: $G_1 \times G_1 \rightarrow G_2$ be a bilinear mapping. The DBDH, CDH and DBDH-M problems can thus be defined as:

(1) **Decisional Bilinear Diffie-Hellman (DBDH) Problem:** Given (P, aP, bP, cP, Ψ), for $\Psi \in G_2$ and unknown $a, b, c \in Z_q^*$, determine whether $\Psi = e(P, P)^{abc}$ holds.

   Definition 1: *The advantage of any probabilistic polynomial time (PPT) algorithm B in solving the DBDH Problem is defined as:* $Adv_B^{DBDH} = |\Pr[B(P, aP, bP, e(P, P)^{abc}) = 1] - \Pr[B(P, aP, bP, \Psi) = 1]|.$

   DBDH assumption: For any PPT algorithm B, Adv_B^{DBDH} is negligible.

(2) **Computational Diffie-Hellman (CDH) Problem:** Given $(P, aP, bP) \in G_1$, for some $a, b \in Z_q^*$, compute abP.

Table 1. Notations.

Name	meaning
q	Large prime integer
G_1	Additive group of order q
G_2	Multiplicative group of order q
Z_q^*	The set of positive integers which are less than q
P	Generator of G_1
e	Bilinear mapping, i.e. e:$G_1 \times G_1 \rightarrow G_2$
H_i	Cryptographic hash function, $i = 1, 2, 3, 4$
ID_i	The identity of the participant i
Q_i	Public key of ID_i
D_i	Private key of ID_i
PKG	Private key generator
s	The master key of PKG
P_{pub}	The system master public key
CDH	Computational Diffie-Hellman Problem
DBDH	Decisional Bilinear Diffie-Hellman Problem
DBDH-M	Modified Decisional Bilinear Diffie-Hellman Problem
PPT	Probabilistic polynomial time
Pr	The probability of an event
Adv	The advantage of one algorithm in solving a problem

Definition 2: *The advantage of any PPT algorithm* B *in solving the CDH Problem is defined as:* $Adv_B^{CDH} = \Pr[B(P,aP,bP) = abP, a,b \in Z_q^*]$.

CDH assumption: For any PPT algorithm B, Adv_B^{CDH} is negligible.

(3) **Modified Decisional Bilinear Diffie-Hellman (DBDH-M) Problem:** Given (P,aP,bP,Γ), for $\Gamma \in G_1$ and unknown $a,b \in Z_q^*$, determine whether $\Gamma = a^2 bP$ holds.

Definition 3: *The advantage of any PPT algorithm* B *in solving the* DBDH-M Problem *is defined as:* $Adv_B^{DBDH-M} = |\Pr[B(P,aP,bP,a^2bP) = 1] - \Pr[B(P,aP,bP,\Gamma) = 1]|$.

DBDH-M assumption: For any PPT algorithm B, Adv_B^{DBDH-M} is negligible.

Algorithm Model

Our identity(ID)-based multi-recipient signcryption scheme with complete anonymity consists of four algorithms, namely: Setup, Extract, Anony-signcrypt and De-signcrypt, shown as follows:

Setup. Private Key Generator (PKG) runs this algorithm to generate a master key s and public parameters *params*. Note that the public parameters are publicly known while the master key must be kept secret.

Extract. This algorithm is run by PKG to extract the private key of the user. With a user's identity ID, PKG's master key s and the public parameter *params* as input, it outputs the private key D associated with ID, namely $D = $ Extract(ID, s, *params*). The private key D must be kept secret.

Anony-signcrypt. This algorithm is run by the signer ID_S. With PKG's public parameter *params*, a plaintext message M, a list of recipients' identity $L = \{ID_1,ID_2,...,ID_n\}$ as input, the signer ID_S runs this algorithm to generate a ciphertext C associated with M, namely $C = $ Anony-signcrypt (*params*, M, L, D_S), which satisfies $L \notin C$ and $ID_S \notin C$.

De-signcrypt. With the ciphertext C, PKG's public parameter *params*, the recipient's identity $ID_i(i \in \{1,2,...,n\})$ and its private key D_i as input, the recipient can run this algorithm to decrypt the ciphertext. The recipient can first judge whether he/she is an authorized recipient. If not, he/she outputs an error message $\perp$ and exits the algorithm. Otherwise, he/she continues to carry out the decryption process and outputs the plaintext M associated with C, namely $M = $ De-signcrypt (C, *params*, D_i).

Message Confidentiality

The security model of ciphertext indistinguishability under chosen ciphertext attack was first proposed by Canetti *et al.* [20]. Later, Duan *et al.* [8] extended this security model for the multi-recipient environments, called as indistinguishability of ciphertexts under selective multi-ID, chosen ciphertext attack (IND-sMIBSC-CCA) shown as Definition 4.

Definition 4. IND-sMIBSC-CCA: Let A be a polynomial-time attacker and Π be an ID-based multi-recipient scheme. Consider that A interacts with a Challenger B in the following game:

Setup. Challenger B runs this algorithm to generate master key s and public parameters params, sends params to A, and keeps the master key s secret. Upon receiving public parameters, A outputs n target identities $L^* = \{ID_1^*,ID_2^*,...,ID_n^*\}$.

Phase 1. A performs a number of queries to B:

Extraction query: Upon receiving private key extraction query about an identity ID, $ID \neq ID_i^*$, $i = 1,2,...,n$, B runs the Extract algorithm to get $D = $ Extract(ID, s, params).

Anony-signcrypt*ion* query: A chooses a target plaintext M, a list of recipients' identity information $L = \{ID_1,ID_2,...,ID_n\}$ and gives them to B. B randomly chooses an identity ID_S, computes the private key D_S, and generates the ciphertext C = Anony-signcrypt (params,M,L, D_S) and returns it to A.

De-signcrypt*ion* query: *A generates the list of target identities* $L^* = \{ID_1^*,ID_2^*,...,ID_n^*\}$ and a ciphertext C. B randomly chooses an identity $ID_j \in L$ and computes its private key D_j. If C is a valid ciphertext, B decrypts it to obtain the corresponding plaintext M = De-signcrypt (C, params, D_j) and returns it to A; otherwise, B outputs an error message $\perp$.

Challenge. A outputs a target plaintext pair (M_0, M_1) and an arbitrary identity ID_S with its private key D_S. Upon receiving (M_0, M_1) and D_S, B picks *up a random bit* $\beta \in \{0,1\}$ and creates a target ciphertext $C^* = Anony - signcrypt(params,M_\beta,L^*,D_S)$, and then returns C^* to A.

Phase 2. A performs a number of queries like Phase 1. Note that A cannot query the identity information in L^* in the Extraction query, and cannot query C^* in the De-signcryption query.

Guess. Finally, A outputs its guess $\beta' \in \{0,1\}$. If $\beta' = \beta$, he wins this game.

An attacker A mentioned above is referred to as an IND-sMIBSC-CCA attacker. We define A's guessing advantage as follows:

$$Adv_\Pi^{IND-sMIBSC-CCA}(A) = |\Pr[\beta = \beta'] - 1/2| \qquad (1)$$

The scheme Π is said to be (t,ε)-IND-sMIBSC-CCA secure, if for any IND-sMIBSC-CCA attacker A, its guessing advantage is less than ε within polynomial running time t.

Unforgeability

This security model has been proposed by Duan *et al.* [8] and is called strong existential unforgeability under selective multi-ID, chosen message attack (SUF-MIBSC-CMA) shown as Definition 5.

Definition 5. SUF-sMIBSC-CMA: Suppose F is a forger, and let Π be an ID-based multi-recipient scheme. Consider that F interacts with a Challenger B in the following game:

Setup. B runs this algorithm to generate a master key s and a public parameter params. B gives the params to F and keeps s secretly. Upon receiving this parameter, F outputs n target identities $L^* = \{ID_1^*,ID_2^*,...,ID_n^*\}$.

Attack. F performs a number of queries to B as described in Definition 4.

Forgery. F finally outputs a new ciphertext message C^*, a list of recipient identities $L = \{ID_1,ID_2,...,ID_n\}$. If C^* is the ciphertext of the message M generated by $ID_i^* i \in \{1,2,...,n\}$ and can be decrypted by any of recipients in L, C^* is a valid ciphertext and F wins this game. The restriction here is that F cannot ask for private key extraction on ID_i^*, and C^* cannot be produced by the Anony-signcrypt algorithm.

The scheme Π is said to be (t,ε)-SUF-sMIBSC-CMA secure, if for any SUF-sMIBSC-CMA attacker F, its guessing advantage is less than ε within polynomial running time t.

Recipient Anonymity

This security model has been proposed by Fan *et al.* [5] and is called anonymous indistinguishability of encryptions under selective ID, chosen ciphertext attack (ANON-sID-CCA) and shown as Definition 6.

Definition 6. ANON-sID-CCA: Let A be a polynomial-time attacker. Let Π be an ID-based multi-recipient scheme. Consider that A interacts with a Challenger B in the following game:

Setup. Challenger B runs the Setup algorithm to generate the master key s and public parameters params. Then, B sends params to A and keeps s secret.

Phase 1. A outputs a target identity pair (ID_1^*, ID_2^*). Upon receiving (ID_1^*, ID_2^*), the Challenger B randomly chooses $\beta \in \{1,2\}$.

Phase 2. A issues private key extraction queries. Upon receiving a private key extraction query, denoted by ID_j, Challenger B runs the private key extraction algorithm to get $D_j = Extract(ID_j, s, params)$. The constraint here is that $ID_j \neq ID_i^*$, $i = 1, 2$.

Phase 3. A issues de-signcryption queries for the target identities. Upon receiving a de-signcryption query about (C^*, ID_i^*), $i = 1, 2$, Challenger B returns $M^* = De\text{-}signcrypt (C^*, params, D_i^*)$ to A, where D_i^* is the private key of ID_i^*.

Challenge. A outputs a target plaintext M to B. Then, Challenger B creates a related ciphertext $C = Anony\text{-}signcrypt$ $(params, M, ID_\beta)$ and returns it to A.

Phase 4. A issues private key extraction queries as those in Phase 2 and de-signcryption queries for target identities as those in Phase 3. The restriction here is that $C \neq C^*$.

Guess. Finally, A outputs its guess $\beta' \in \{1,2\}$. If $\beta = \beta'$, A wins the game.

An attacker A mentioned above is referred to as an ANON-sID-CCA attacker. We define A's guessing advantage as follows:

$$Adv_\Pi^{ANON\text{-}sID\text{-}CCA}(A) = |Pr[\beta = \beta'] - 1/2| \qquad (2)$$

The scheme Π is said to be (t,ε)-ANON-sID-CCA secure, if for any ANON-sID-CCA attacker A, its guessing advantage is less than ε within polynomial running time t.

Methods

The proposed scheme is composed of the following four algorithms. And at the same time, we shall take the network conference application as an example to show how to use our scheme.

Setup Algorithm

PKG performs the following process:

(1) Let G_1 be an additive group and G_2 be a multiplicative group with the same prime order q, $(q \geq 2^k$, k is a long integer). Let P be a generator of G_1. Choose a bilinear mapping e: $G_1 \times G_1 \rightarrow G_2$.

(2) Define four one-way hash functions: $H_1 : \{0,1\}^* \rightarrow G_1$; H_2: $G_2 \rightarrow \{0,1\}^{|M|}$; $H_3 : \{0,1\}^* \rightarrow Z_q^*$; $H_4 : \{0,1\}^{|M|} \times G_1 \times ... \times G_1 \rightarrow Z_q^*$, where $|M|$ is the length of the plaintext message.

(3) Choose a random number $s \in Z_q^*$ as the master key, and set $P_{pub} = sP \in G_1$ as the system's public key. Publish the system parameter $params = <G_1, G_2, q, e, P, P_{pub}, H_1, H_2, H_3, H_4>$ and keep the master key s secret.

Practically speaking, PKG is acted by some authority. For example, in a network conference application, the organizer of a conference should deal with the PKG, which is responsible for developing the system parameters as the steps mentioned above.

Extract Algorithm

With *params*, s, and an identity $ID \in \{0,1\}^*$ as input, PKG performs this algorithm to generate the private key of the identity ID:

(1) Compute ID's public key $Q_{ID} = H_1(ID)$.

(2) Compute ID's private key $D_{ID} = sH_1(ID) = sQ_{ID}$.

Each participant, the sender or the recipient, should register himself/herself at PKG and obtain his/her private key from PKG by this algorithm. For example, in a network conference application, if someone wants to attend a conference and talk with other participants, he/she must firstly send his/her ID information to the organizer PKG to get his/her own private key computed by PKG.

Anony-signcrypt Algorithm

With *params*, a plaintext M and his/her private key D_S as input, the signer ID_S chooses a list of recipients' identity $L = \{ID_1, ID_2, ..., ID_n\}$ and performs this algorithm to generate the ciphertext C of the plaintext M:

(1) Randomly choose two secret integers $r, \alpha \in Z_q^*$ and a secret element $P_1 \in G_1$, and then compute $Y = rQ_s$, $U = \alpha P$, $X = \alpha Y$, $\omega = e(P_{pub}, P_1)^\alpha$ and $\sigma = H_2(\omega) \oplus M$, where Q_S is the public key of ID_S.

(2) For $i = 1, 2, ..., n$, compute $x_i = H_3(ID_i)$ and $y_i = \alpha(P_1 + Q_i)$, where Q_i is the public key of ID_i.

(3) For $i = 1, 2, ..., n$, compute $f_i(x) = \prod\limits_{1 \leq i \neq j \leq n} \dfrac{x - x_j}{x_i - x_j} = a_{i,1} + a_{i,2}x + ... + a_{i,n}x^{n-1}$, where $a_{i,1}, a_{i,2}, ..., a_{i,n} \in Z_q$.

(4) For $i = 1, 2, ..., n$, compute $T_i = \sum\limits_{j=1}^{n} a_{j,i}y_j$ and then let $T = \{T_1, T_2, ..., T_n\}$.

(5) Compute $h = H_4(\sigma, X, U, T)$, and then compute $W = (\alpha + h) \cdot rD_S$, where D_S is the private key of ID_S.

(6) Generate the ciphertext: $C = <Y, X, U, \sigma, W, T>$.

After obtaining the private key, each participant can securely and anonymously send messages to other participants that he/she selects. For example, in a network conference application, any participant can freely select some participants as expected recipients to receive his/her messages. What he/she needs to do is to encrypt the messages by this algorithm and then broadcast the ciphertext.

De-signcrypt Algorithm

The algorithm is carried out by the recipient. With $C = <Y, X, U, \sigma, W, T>$, *params*, the recipient's identity ID_i and his/her private key D_i as input, the recipient ID_i decrypts C as follows:

Public verification. The one, who has not registered himself/herself with PKG to get his/her private key, can use the following steps to check the integrity or validity of the ciphertext. The registered participant can skip this process and directly jump to the following judgement algorithm:

(1) Compute $h = H_4(\sigma, X, U, T)$.

(2) Verify whether the equation $e(W, P) = e(X + hY, P_{pub})$ holds. If yes, the ciphertext is valid. Otherwise, the ciphertext is invalid or has been damaged during transmission.

Judgement. The one, who has registered himself/herself with PKG to get his/her private key, can use the following steps to check whether the ciphertext is valid and whether he/she is an authorized recipient before the following encryption process:

(1) Compute $h = H_4(\sigma, X, U, T)$.

(2) Check whether the equation $e(W, Q_i) = e(X + hY, D_i)$ holds. If yes, it means that ID_i is one of the recipients designated by the signer and the ciphertext is valid. Otherwise, the recipient quits the decryption process.

De-signcryption. The authorized user can recover the plaintext by the following steps:

(1) Compute $x_i = H_4(ID_i)$ and then compute $\eta_i = T_1 + x_i T_2 + ... + (x_i^{n-1} \bmod q)T_n$.

(2) Compute $\omega' = e(P_{pub}, \eta_i)(U, D_i)^{-1}$ and then get the plaintext as $M' = \sigma \oplus H_2(\omega')$.

The one who receives the broadcasting ciphertext can verify the validity of the message and judge whether he/she is authorized by the public verification or judgement algorithm. If necessary, he/she can use the de-signcrypt algorithm to decrypt the ciphertext. In a network conference application, due to the nature of the broadcast communication, anyone, authorized recipients or unauthorized ones, can easily receive the ciphertext and check the validity of the message and the authorization of the decryption. But, only the authorized recipients can decrypt it correctly.

Results and Discussion

Correctness Analyses

Theorem 1. The public verification algorithm in the De-signcrypt algorithm is correct.

Proof.

$$
\begin{aligned}
e(W, P) &= e((\alpha + h) \cdot r D_S, P) \\
&= e((\alpha + h) \cdot r Q_S, sP) \\
&= e(\alpha Y + hY, sP) \\
&= e(X + hY, P_{pub})
\end{aligned}
\tag{3}
$$

In our scheme, although the identity of the real signer is not included in the ciphertext, his/her private key is definitely necessary in the signcryption process, which ensures that only legal participants who have registered himself/herself with PKG can generate a valid ciphertext. That is to say, through this algorithm, anyone can check whether a ciphertext is generated by an authorized participant, but he/she cannot determine the real identity of the signer.

Theorem 2. The judgement algorithm in the De-signcrypt algorithm is correct.

Proof. For each authorized ID_i where $i \in \{1, 2, ..., n\}$, we have

$$
\begin{aligned}
e(W, Q_i) &= e((\alpha + h) \cdot r D_S, Q_i) \\
&= e((\alpha + h) \cdot r Q_S, sQ_i) \\
&= e(\alpha Y + hY, D_i) \\
&= e(X + hY, D_i)
\end{aligned}
\tag{4}
$$

Similarly, because the private key of the real signer is necessary in the signcryption process, this algorithm can also be used to check the validity of ciphertext. At the same time, this algorithm can help a participant, who has registered himself/herself with PKG, to judge whether himself/herself is an authorized recipient, because the private key of the recipient is also necessary in the judgement.

Theorem 3. The decryption algorithm in the De-signcrypt algorithm is correct.

Proof. The authorized ID_i, $i \in \{1, 2, ..., n\}$, can compute η_i as follows:

$$
\begin{aligned}
\eta_i &= T_1 + x_i T_2 + ... + x_i^{i-1} T_i + ... + x_i^{n-1} T_n \\
&= (a_{1,1}\alpha(P_1 + Q_1) + ... + a_{n,1}\alpha(P_1 + Q_n)) \\
&\quad + (x_i a_{1,2}\alpha(P_1 + Q_1) + ... + x_i a_{n,2}\alpha(P_1 + Q_n)) + ... \\
&\quad + (x_i^{i-1} a_{1,i}\alpha(P_1 + Q_1) + ... + x_i^{i-1} a_{n,i}\alpha(P_1 + Q_n)) + ... \\
&\quad + (x_i^{n-1} a_{1,n}\alpha(P_1 + Q_1) + ... + x_i^{n-1} a_{n,n}\alpha(P_1 + Q_n)) \\
&= (a_{1,1} + a_{1,2}x_i + ... + a_{1,n}x_i^{n-1})\alpha(P_1 + Q_1) \\
&\quad + (a_{2,1} + a_{2,2}x_i + ... + a_{2,n}x_i^{n-1})\alpha(P_1 + Q_2) + ... \\
&\quad + (a_{i,1} + a_{i,2}x_i + ... + a_{i,n}x_i^{n-1})\alpha(P_1 + Q_i) + ... \\
&\quad + (a_{n,1} + a_{n,2}x_i + ... + a_{n,n}x_i^{n-1})\alpha(P_1 + Q_n) \\
&= \alpha(P_1 + Q_i)
\end{aligned}
\tag{5}
$$

Thus, we can get $\omega' = e(P_{pub}, \eta_i)(U, D_i)^{-1} = \omega$, because

$$
\begin{aligned}
\omega' &= e(P_{pub}, \eta_i) \cdot e(U, D_i)^{-1} \\
&= e(P_{pub}, \alpha(P_1 + Q_i)) \cdot e(\alpha P, sQ_i)^{-1} \\
&= e(P_{pub}, \alpha P_1) \cdot e(P_{pub}, \alpha Q_i) \cdot e(sP, \alpha Q_i)^{-1} \\
&= e(P_{pub}, P_1)^{\alpha} \cdot e(P_{pub}, \alpha Q_i) \cdot e(P_{pub}, \alpha Q_i)^{-1} \\
&= e(P_{pub}, P_1)^{\alpha} = \omega
\end{aligned}
\tag{6}
$$

Then, we can get the plaintext through the computations $H_2(\omega') = H_2(\omega)$ and $M = H_2(\omega) \oplus \sigma$.

Security Analyses

We shall give security proof of the proposed scheme on confidentiality, unforgeability and anonymity under the random oracle model.

Theorem 4. In the IND-sMIBSC-CCA security model, if an adversary A has an advantage ε against the game defined in Definition 4 within running time t (where A makes at most q_e private key extraction queries, q_s anony-signcryption queries, q_d de-signcryption queries and $q_{H_1}, q_{H_2}, q_{H_3}, q_{H_4}$ queries to the Hash functions H_1, H_2, H_3 and H_4, respectively), then there is a algorithm B in solving the DBDH problem in the time $t' \leq t$ with an advantage $\varepsilon' \geq \varepsilon - nq_d/2^k$.

Proof. The challenger B is challenged with an instance (P, aP, bP, cP) of the DBDH problem. Assume that there is an adversary A who is capable of breaking the IND-sMIBSC-CCA security with a non-negligible advantage ε. B makes use of A to solve the DBDH instance. B simulates the system with various oracles H_1, H_2, H_3 and H_4 and allows A to make polynomially bounded number of queries, adaptive to these oracles. The game between A and B is demonstrated below:

Setup. B sets $P_1 = cP$, $P_{pub} = bP$, and gives $<G_1, G_2, q, e, P, P_{G_1}, G_2, q, e, P, P_{pub}, H_1, H_2, H_3, H_4>$ to the attacker A as the public parameters. Upon receiving the system parameters, A outputs n target identities $(ID_1^*, ID_2^*, ..., ID_n^*)$.

Phase 1. A performs a number of queries to B:

Let H_1, H_2, H_3 and H_4 be random oracles controlled by B as follows. The results of querying H_1, H_2, H_3 and H_4 are stored in H_1-list, H_2-list, H_3-list and H_4-list, respectively.

H_1-query. Input an identity ID_j,$j \in \{1,2,...,n\}$, to H_1. If there exists $\langle ID_j, l_j, Q_j \rangle$ in H_1-list, B returns Q_j; othzerwise, does as follows:

(1) Choose an integer $l_j \in Z_q^*$ at random;
(2) If $ID_j \neq ID_i^*$,$i \in \{1,2,...,n\}$, compute $Q_j = l_j P$; otherwise, compute $Q_j = l_j P - P_1$;
(3) Put $\langle ID_j, l_j, Q_j \rangle$ into H_1-list;
(4) Return Q_j.

H_i-query. $i \in \{2,3,4\}$: To answer these inquiries, B searches the corresponding list H_i-list($i = 2,3,4$). If the corresponding answer has existed already, B returns the answer to A. Otherwise, B randomly chooses an element in proper scope as the result and returns it to A, and at the same time, B adds the inquiry and the result into the corresponding list.

Extraction query. Upon receiving private key extraction query on identity ID_j ($ID_j \neq ID_i^*$, $i = 1,2,...,n$), B searches for $\langle ID_j, l_j, Q_j \rangle$ in H_1-list. B recovers triple $\langle ID_j, l_j, Q_j \rangle$ in H_1-query and computes his private key $D = l_j P_{pub} = l_j bP$, and returns it to A. If $ID_j = ID_i^*$, B aborts and outputs "failure".

Anony-signcryption query. Upon receiving A's anony-signcryption query (M, ID_S, L), B checks if $ID_S \neq ID_i^*(i = 1,2,...,n)$. If $ID_S \neq ID_i^*(i = 1,2,...,n)$, B shall get the private key of ID_S through the Extraction query. After that, B can run the Anony-signcryption query to generate the ciphertext M. An alternative to this is:

(1) B randomly chooses two secret integers $r,\alpha \in Z_q^*$, and then computes $Y = rl_S P$, $X = \alpha Y$, $U = \alpha P$, $\omega = e(P_{pub}, P_1)^\alpha$ and $\sigma = H_2(\omega) \oplus M$.
(2) For $i = 1, 2, ...,n$, compute $x_i = H_3(ID_i)$ and $y_i = \alpha(P_1 + Q_i)$, where Q_i is the public key of ID_i.
(3) For $i = 1,2,...,n$, compute: $f_i(x) = \prod\limits_{1 \leq i \neq j \leq n} \dfrac{x - x_j}{x_i - x_j} = a_{i,1} + a_{i,2}x + ... + a_{i,n}x^{n-1}$, where $a_{i,1}, a_{i,2}, ..., a_{i,n} \in Z_q$.
(4) For $i = 1,2,...,n$, compute $T_i = \sum\limits_{j=1}^n a_{j,i} y_j$ and then let $T = \{T_1, T_2, ..., T_n\}$.
(5) B randomly chooses an integer $h' \in Z_q^*$, where h' is set as the output for the random oracle query $H_4(\sigma, X, U, T)$(This is possible because the random oracles are manipulated by B). Then, B computes $W = (\alpha + h')l_S P_{pub}$.
(6) B gets the ciphertext $C = \langle Y, X, U, \sigma, W, T \rangle$ and returns it to A.

De-signcryption query. On receiving the De-signcryption query of the ciphertext C together with an identity ID_j, B proceeds as follows:

(1) If $ID_j = ID_i^*$, B shall return that the ciphertext C is invalid because B does not know the private key of ID.
(2) If $ID_j \neq ID_i^*$, B computes $h = H_4(\sigma, X, U, T)$, and verifies whether the equation $e(W, P) = e(X + hY, P_{pub})$ holds. If it does not hold, the ciphertext is not valid and then B outputs $\bot$. If it holds, B does the following steps:

(a) Find the secret key D corresponding to ID from the H_1-list.
(b) Compute η_j according to T.
(c) Compute $\omega' = e(P_{pub}, \eta_j)(U, D)^{-1}$ and then get the plaintext as $M' = \sigma \oplus H_2(\omega')$.

If all the above verifications are true, then B outputs the message M'. Otherwise, the ciphertext is invalid, and B outputs $\bot$.

Challenge. A outputs a target plaintext pair (M_0, M_1) and a private key D_S. Upon receiving (M_0, M_1) and D_S, B picks up a random bit $\beta \in \{0,1\}$ and signcrypts the message M_β. Firstly, B searches H_1-list to get l_i^* related to ID_i^*,$i \in \{1,2,...,n\}$, and their public key $Q_i = l_i^* P - P_1$, then computes $y_i^* = a(P_1 + Q_i) = a(P_1 + l_i^* P - P_1) = al_i^* P$ to get T_i^*,$i \in \{1,2,...,n\}$. B finally creates the target ciphertext $C^* = \langle Y, X, U, W, T^* \rangle$ where $X = al_S P$, $U = aP$, $W = (a+h)l_S bP$ and $P_1 = cP$, and then returns C^* to A.

Phase 2. A performs a number of queries as Phase 1. Note that A cannot query the identity information of $(ID_1^*, ID_2^*, ..., ID_n^*)$ in extraction query, and cannot query C^* in de-signcryption query.

Guess. Finally, A outputs its guess $\beta' \in \{0,1\}$. If $\beta' = \beta$, B wins this game and outputs 1 as the answer of DBDH problem because $\Psi = e(P_{pub}, P_1)^\alpha = e(bP, cP)^a = e(P,P)^{abc}$. Otherwise, B outputs 0.

From the above discussion, we shall analyze the advantages of B in the following. For q_d de-signcryption queries, the probability to reject a valid ciphertext is not greater than $nq_d/2^k$. If A wins the IND-sMIBSC-CCA game, the advantage of B is

$$\varepsilon' = |\Pr[B(bP, cP, rP, \omega) = 1]|$$
$$- \Pr\left[B(bP, cP, rP, e(P,P)^{bcr} = 1\right]$$
$$\geq |\varepsilon + 1/2 - nq_d/2^k - 1/2| \geq |\varepsilon$$
$$+ 1/2 - nq_d/2^k - 1/2| = \varepsilon - nq_d/2^k$$

Theorem 5. *In the* SUF-sMIBSC-CMA *security model*, if there is an adversary F who can win the game in the time t with a non-negligible advantage ε as described in the definition 5, there will exist an algorithm B which can solve the CDH problem in the time $t' \leq t$ with an advantage $\varepsilon' \geq \varepsilon - q_s/2^k$, where F can ask at most q_e extraction queries, q_s anony-signcryption queries and $q_{H_1}, q_{H_2}, q_{H_3}, q_{H_4}$ queries to H_1, H_2, H_3, H_4, respectively.

Proof. The challenge B is given (P, aP, bP) as an instance of the CDH problem. Assume that there is an adversary F who has a non-negligible advantage ε in breaking the SUF-sMIBSC-CMA security. Then, B uses F to solve the CDH problem. Firstly, B simulates the system with the various oracles H_1, H_2, H_3 and H_4, and then allows F to adaptively ask polynomially bounded number of queries to these oracles. The game between B and F is demonstrated below:

Setup. B sets $P_{pub} = bP$, and gives $\langle G_1, G_2, q, e, P, P_{pub}, H_1, H_2, H_3, H_4 \rangle$ to the attacker F as the public parameters. Upon receiving the system parameters, F outputs n target identities $L^* = \{ID_1^*, ID_2^*, ..., ID_n^*\}$.

Attack. F adaptively performs polynomially bounded number of queries to the various oracles in this phase, which are similar to those in Theorem 4.

Forgery. F generates a target ciphertext $C^* = \langle Y^*, X^*, U^*, \sigma^*, W^*, T^* \rangle$. If the forgery is successful, the equation $e(W^*, P) = e(X^* + h \cdot rQ_S^*, P_{pub})$ holds. Define $Q_S^* = l_S^* P = aP$, and then we have $W^* = (h+\alpha) \cdot rD_S^* = (h+\alpha)l_S^* bP = (h+\alpha)abP$. Now, it will be very easy to extract the CDH problem's solution $abP = W^*(\alpha + h)^{-1}$.

We consider the advantage of F's success here. As in the anony-signcryption query, the probability for B to answer a failure signcryption query is not greater than $q_s/2^k$, and then the advantage is $\varepsilon' \geq \varepsilon - q_s/2^k$.

Theorem 6. *In the ANON-sID-CCA security model, if an adversary A has advantage ε against the game defined in Definition 6 within running time t (where A makes at most* q_e *private key extraction queries,* q_s *anony-signcryption queries,* q_d *de-signcryption queries and* $q_{H_1}, q_{H_2}, q_{H_3}, q_{H_4}$ *queries to the Hash functions* H_1, H_2, H_3 *and* H_4, *respectively), then there is an algorithm B in solving the DBDH-M problem with an advantage* $ε' \geq ε$.

Proof. The challenger B is challenged with an instance (P, aP, bP, Γ) of the DBDH-M problem. Assume that there is an adversary A who is capable of breaking the ANON-sID-CCA security with a non-negligible advantage ε. B makes use of A to solve the DBDH-M instance. B simulates the system with hash functions H_1, H_2, H_3 and H_4, and allows A to make polynomially bounded number of queries. The game between B and A is demonstrated below:

Phase 1. Suppose that A outputs a target identity pair $(\mathrm{ID}_1^*, \mathrm{ID}_2^*)$.

Setup. B sets the public key $P_{pub} = \gamma_1 bP$ and lets $P_1 = aP$, where $\gamma_1, \gamma_2 \in Z_q^*$, and aP and bP are given from the instance of the DBDH-M problem. Here, B does not know a and b. A performs polynomially bounded number of queries to H_1, H_2, H_3 and H_4, which are similar to those in Theorem 4.

Phase 2. Upon receiving the private key extraction query of an identity ID_j such that $\mathrm{ID}_j \neq \mathrm{ID}_i^*$, for $i \in \{1, 2\}$, according to $Q_j = l_j P = aP$, B computes $D_j = l_j P_{pub}$.

Phase 3. Upon receiving a decryption query about (C^*, ID_i^*) $i = 1, 2$ and $C^* = <Y^*, X^*, U^*, \sigma^*, W^*, T_1^*>$. Challenger B performs the following steps:

(1) Compute $\eta = T_1^*$.
(2) Compute $\omega' = e(P_{pub}, \eta) e(U^*, D_\beta)^{-1}$.
(3) Judge whether $H_2(\omega') = H_2(\omega)$ holds. If not, return "reject" to A, otherwise return $M^* = H_2(\omega) \oplus \sigma$ to A.

Challenge. A outputs a target plaintext M. Upon receiving M, B does the following steps:

(1) Compute $U = abP - \gamma_1 P$.
(2) Compute $\omega = e(P_{pub}, P_1)^{\gamma_2}$.
(3) Create a target ciphertext $C = <Y, X, U, \sigma, W, T_1>$ and return it to A.

Phase 4. A issues private key extraction queries as those in Phase 2 and decryption queries for target identities as those in Phase 3, where a restriction here is that $C \neq C^*$.

Guess. Finally, A outputs its guess $\beta' \in \{1, 2\}$. If $\beta' = \beta$ holds, B outputs 1. Otherwise, B outputs 0. If $T_1 = a^2 bP$, then

$$
\begin{aligned}
\omega &= e(P_{pub}, P_1)^{\gamma_2} = e(\gamma_1 bP, \gamma_2 aP) \\
&= e(\gamma_1 bP, \gamma_2 aP + a^2 bP - a^2 bP) \\
&= e(\gamma_1 bP, a^2 bP) e((abP - \gamma_2 P), \gamma_1 abP)^{-1} \\
&= e(P_{pub}, \delta) e(U, D_\beta)^{-1}
\end{aligned}
\tag{7}
$$

Thus, we have $M = H_2(\omega) \oplus \sigma$.

Here, C is the valid ciphertext. We can get $|\Pr[B(P, aP, bP, a^2 bP) = 1]| = \Pr[\beta = \beta']$ where $|\Pr[\beta = \beta'] - 1/2| \geq ε$, and $|\Pr[B(P, aP, bP, \Gamma) = 1]| = \Pr[\beta = \beta'] = 1/2$ where Γ is randomly chosen from G_1. Therefore, we have $ε = |\Pr[B(P, aP, bP, a^2 bP) = 1]| - |\Pr[B(P, aP, bP, \Gamma) = 1]| \geq |(1/2 \pm ε) - 1/2| = ε$, that is, $ε' \geq ε$.

Efficiency Analysis

We compare our scheme with existing signcryption schemes [9,10,11,12,13,15,17,19] in terms of calculation costs and communication traffic (ciphertext length). In order to facilitate the description, we define the following symbols shown in Table 2:

First, we talk about the signcryption process. In the proposed scheme, the operation about Lagrange interpolation can also be pre-processed, so these operations can be excluded when considering computational complexity. In order to signcrypt a message M, our scheme needs 1 bilinear operation, 2 addition operations in G_1, 6 scalar multiplications in G_1, 1 exponentiation in G_2 and 2 hash operations. The length of the ciphertext is $(n+4)|G_1| + |M|$. The specific comparison results are shown in Table 3, from which one can see that our scheme performs much better than most of the existing schemes in terms of number of parameters, computation complexity and the ciphertext length.

Regarding the de-signcryption in our scheme, some calculations of the de-signcryption algorithm are used to judge the validity of ciphertext and the authorization of the recipient, which is important for broadcast-based communications to avoid receiving unwanted information (e.g. SPAM). Note that although the schemes [9,10,11,13,15] directly provide the recipients' true identities in the ciphertext, in fact the recipient cannot absolutely ensure whether he/she is authorized before checking the validity of the ciphertext. The number of pair operations (T_p, the most time-consuming operation in the existing schemes and our scheme) in our decryption algorithm is smaller than those of the existing schemes, which makes our scheme more attractive in terms of computation performance. Table 4 shows a comparison between the proposed scheme and the existing ones [9,10,11,12,13,15,17,19].

Discussion of Merit and Demerit

Compared to existing schemes, our scheme has some advantages. To achieve the signer's anonymity, the identity of the signer is no longer included in the ciphertext, although the private key of the signer is necessary for signcryption. The recipients can therefore only judge if the ciphertext received is from a trusted signer, but they cannot determine the real identity of the signer. To achieve the recipient's anonymity, the ID information of all authorized recipients is mixed by the Lagrange interpolation polynomial during the signcryption process, which prevents the recipient's ID from being exposed. This method also ensures that only the recipient, who has got the entire ciphertext, can decrypt the ciphertext, thus achieving the decryption fairness. The ID-based cryptography enables one user to confidentially send messages to other users, despite of whether the latter is a registered user, and the public verification property of our scheme enables unregistered users to judge the validity of the received

Table 2. Symbol Definition.

Symbols	Meaning
T_p	Time for bilinear pair operation
T_a	Time for addition operation
T_m	Time for scalar multiplication operation
T_e	Time for exponentiation operation
T_h	Time for Hash operation
T_s	Time for symmetric encryption algorithm

Table 3. Signcryption Efficiency Comparison.

Schemes	Number of parameters	Computation Complexity	Ciphertext length
Yu et al.'s [9]	10	$T_p+(n+1)T_a+(n+5)T_m+T_e+2T_h$	$(n+2)\|G_1\|+\|G_2\|+\|M\|+n\|ID\|$
Shamila et al.'s [10]	$n+9$	$(n+1)T_a+(n+3)T_m+T_e+2T_h$	$3\|G_1\|+\|M\|+n\|ID\|$
Elkamchouchi [11]	8	$2T_p+(n+1)T_a+(n+4)T_m+2T_e+2T_h+T_s$	$(n+2)\|G_1\|+\|M\|+n\|ID\|+\|Z_q\|$
Pang et al.'s [12]	12	$T_p+(3m-2)T_a+(2m+1)T_m+T_e+(m+1)T_h$	$(m+n+2)\|G_1\|+\|M\|+m\|ID\|$
Lal et al.'s [13]	11	$(3m+n-2)T_a+(2m+n+2)T_m+T_e+(m+2)T_h$	$(m+n+2)\|G_1\|+\|M\|+(m+n)\|ID\|$
Zhang B et al.'s [15]	13	$T_p+(m+n+1)T_m+(2m+n+3)T_e+2T_h$	$(m+n+2)\|G_1\|+\|M\|+m\|ID\|$
Zhang J et al.'s [17]	10	$T_p+(4m)T_m+(4m-2)T_a+(m+2)T_h$	$(m+2)\|G_1\|+\|M\|$
Huang et al.'s [19]	10	$T_p+(2m-3)T_a+(2m+2)T_m+(m+2)T_h$	$2\|G_1\|+m\|G_2\|+2\|M\|+m\|ID\|+m\|Z_q\|$
Ours	10	$T_p+2T_a+6T_m+T_e+2T_h$	$(n+4)\|G_1\|+\|M\|$

$\|G_1\|$: the length of the elements in G_1; $\|ID\|$: the length of ID; $\|M\|$: the length of the plaintext M;
m: the number of signers ($m=1$ in schemes [9–11] and our scheme); n: the number of recipients.

ciphertext before having to register himself/herself with PKG. The merit/demerit comparison between the existing schemes and our scheme is summarized in Table 5.

From Table 5, we can see: (1) The schemes [12,13,15,17,19] have taken anonymity of the sender into account. However, they are all prone to the *cross-comparison attack* and *joint conspiracy attack*. In these schemes, in order to protect the privacy of the sender, the sender randomly chooses some legitimate participants to hide the true identity. But in practice, these schemes are vulnerable to the *cross-comparison attack* and *joint conspiracy attack* mentioned above. (2) The schemes [9,10,11] cannot assure the anonymity of the sender because the identity of the sender is directly given in the ciphertext. (3) The schemes [9,10,11,13,15,17,19] cannot assure the anonymity of the recipient. In these schemes, the ciphertext includes two parts: a recipient identity list and each recipient's specific data. A recipient identity list is required so that an authorized recipient is able to find his/her specific data required for decryption of the ciphertext. Because the recipient identity list is given in plaintext, the ID information of each recipient is exposed, and thus the anonymity of recipients is not assured. This has the advantage that, as long as an authorized recipient receives his/her specific data correctly, he/she can decrypt the ciphertext to retrieve the corresponding message even if other recipients' specific data are invalidated during transmission. While this seems

to represent an advantage on the first sight, it also represents a problem regarding decryption fairness. Decryption unfairness can cause the sender to cheat some recipients actively by just sending incorrect recipient-specific data. (4) In all the existing schemes, public verification is not considered because the identity of the sender or the recipient must be given in the ciphertext in plaintext form, thus there are no requirements for public verification. But in a completely anonymous scheme, public verification is a necessity for recipients so that receiving or operating on unwanted messages is prevented.

To summarize, the ciphertext in our scheme no longer contains the real identity information of all participants, thus our scheme meets anonymity of the sender and recipients at the same time, and efficiently protects the privacy of all involved participants. Even more important, this scheme possesses fair decryption and public verification properties. Furthermore, our scheme is easy to implement in exsiting applications. Here, we also take a network conference application as an example. In such a case, a message sender needs only to transform the plaintext message to a ciphertext message using our encryption algorithm and then broadcasts it through the broadcast communication channel, while a message recipient simply needs to decrypt the ciphertext using our decryption algorithm. Our scheme requires only extra encryption or decryption operations for each participant and

Table 4. De-signcryption Efficiency Comparison.

Schemes	Ciphertext validity or integrity	Authorized or not	Decryption
Yu et al.'s [9]	$3T_p+2T_a+3T_m+3T_h$	$3T_p+2T_a+3T_m+3T_h$	$3T_p+2T_a+3T_m+3T_h$
Shamila et al.'s [10]	$3T_p+2T_a+(3n+3)T_m+2T_e+(n+1)T_h$	$3T_p+2T_a+(3n+3)T_m+2T_e+(n+1)T_h$	$3T_p+2T_a+(3n+3)T_m+2T_e+(n+1)T_h$
Elkamchouchi et al.'s [11]	$2T_p+T_e+T_m+2T_h$	$2T_p+T_e+T_m+2T_h$	$4T_p+2T_a+T_e+3T_h+T_s$
Pang et al.'s [12]	$2T_p+(2m-1)T_a+mT_m+mT_h$	$(2m-1)T_a+(m+2)T_m+mT_h$	$4T_p+(2m+n-2)T_a+(m+n+1)T_m+(m+2)T_h$
Lal et al.'s [13]	$2T_p+(2m-1)T_a+mT_m+mT_h$	$4T_p+2mT_a+(m+1)T_m+(m+1)T_h$	$4T_p+2mT_a+(m+1)T_m+(m+1)T_h$
Zhang B et al.'s [15]	$(m+5)T_p+T_a+(m+\|M\|+2)T_m+2T_h$	$(m+5)T_p+T_a+(m+\|M\|+2)T_m+2T_h$	$(m+5)T_p+T_a+(m+\|M\|+2)T_m+2T_h$
Zhang J et al.'s [17]	$4T_p+2mT_a+mT_m+(m+2)T_h$	N/A	$4T_p+2mT_a+mT_m+(m+2)T_h$
Huang et al.'s [19]	$3T_p+(m+1)T_a+2mT_m+(m+2)T_h$	N/A	$3T_p+(m+1)T_a+2mT_m+(m+2)T_h$
Ours	$2T_p+T_a+T_m+T_h$	$2T_p+T_a+T_m+T_h$	$2T_p+nT_a+(n-1)T_m+2T_h$

$\|M\|$: the length of the plaintext M; m: the number of signers ($m=1$ in schemes [9–11] and our scheme); n: the number of recipients.
Note: N/A refers to a single-recipient scheme where the message is transmitted using a unicast communication channel, thus it is unnecessary for the recipient to judge whether he/she is authorized.

Table 5. Comparison of merits and demerits.

Scheme	Signer anonymity	Recipient anonymity	Decryption fairness	Public Verification
Yu *et al.*'s [9]	No	No	No	No
Shamila *et al.*'s [10]	No	No	No	No
Elkamchouchi *et al.*'s [11]	No	No	No	No
Pang *et al.*'s [12]	Yes (*)	Yes	Yes	No
Lal *et al.*'s [13]	Yes (*)	No	No	No
Zhang B *et al.*'s [15]	Yes (*)	No	No	No
Zhang J *et al.*'s [17]	Yes (*)	No	No	No
Huang *et al.*'s [19]	Yes (*)	No	No	No
Ours	Yes	Yes	Yes	Yes

Note: (*) refers to schemes prone to the *cross-comparison attack* and *joint conspiracy attack*.

leaves the original implementation untouched, which in fact should represent an easy implementation of our scheme. While our scheme has the advantages mentioned above, it also has some disadvantages, namely its application, which increases the costs for the implementation. For example, it probably takes a great deal to establish PKG and maintain it, which may affect routine application of our scheme to some extent.

Conclusions

Due to the nature of broadcasting communications, the anonymity of both the sender and the recipient is of upmost importance in multi-recipient signcryption. However, almost none of the existing multi-recipient signcryption schemes take the anonymity of recipients into account. Although there are several schemes that provide a solution to the anonymity of the signer, they have known limitations. Owing to practical application requirements, a completely anonymous multi-recipient signcryption becomes more and more important. Aiming at the participants' anonymity, a completely anonymous multi-recipient signcryption is proposed in this paper. The new scheme ensures anonymity of all participants, the sender and all recipients. Furthermore, each recipient can easily judge whether the received message is from an authorized source, but he/she cannot determine the true identity of the sender. Each recipient can easily judge whether he/she is an authorized recipient, but he/she

cannot determine the identity of any other authorized recipient. At the same time, the validity of the ciphertext can be verified publicly. The confidentiality, unforgeablity and anonymity of our scheme are formally proven using the random oracles model. Compared to existing schemes, our scheme is more efficient in computation and ciphertext length, and possesses more merits, which makes our scheme suitable for practical applications. Our scheme is important in group-oriented network applications, such as the network conference, paid-TV or DVD broadcasting. The proposed scheme solves the secure communication problem among authorized participants, while at the same time, it provides complete anonymity for all involved participants.

Acknowledgments

The authors would like to thank the anonymous reviewers of this paper for his/her objective comments and helpful suggestions while at the same time helping us to improve the English spelling and grammar throughout the manuscript.

Author Contributions

Proved the security of the scheme: LP HL LG. Conceived and designed the experiments: LP HL. Analyzed the data: LP HL LG YW. Wrote the paper: LP HL LG YW.

References

1. Pang LJ, Li HX, Pei QQ (2012) Improved multicast key management of Chinese wireless local area network security standard. IET Communications 6: 1126–1130. doi:10.1049/iet-com.2010.0954.
2. Pang L, Li H, Jiao L, Wang Y (2009) Design and analysis of a provable secure multi-recipient public key encryption scheme. Journal of Software 20: 2739–2745. doi:10.3724/SP.J.1001.2009.03552.
3. Malone-Lee J (2002) Identity based signcryption. Cryptology ePrint Archive. Report 2002/098. Available: http://eprint.iacr.org/2002/098.pdf.
4. Baek J, Safavi-Naini R, Susilo W (2005) Efficient multi-receiver identity-based encryption and its application to broadcast encryption. Proc. the 8th International Workshop on Theory and Practice in Public Key Cryptography. Les Diablerets, Switzerland: 380–397. doi:10.1007/978-3-540-30580-4_26.
5. Fan C, Huang L, Ho P (2010) Anonymous multireceiver identity-based encryption. IEEE Transactions on Computers 59: 1239–1249. doi:10.1109/TC.2010.23.
6. Wang X, Wang A, Wang L (2009) Efficient ID-based secure encryption scheme for anonymous receivers. Academy Publisher 4: 1239–1249. doi:10.4304/jnw.4.7.641–648.
7. Zhang B, Xu Q (2010) An ID-based anonymous signcryption scheme for multiple receivers secure in the standard model. Proc. the Advances in Computer Science and Information Technology Japan: 15–27. doi:10.1007/978-3-642-13577-4_2.

8. Duan S, Cao Z (2006) Efficient and provably secure multi receiver identity based signcryption. Proc. the Information Security and Privacy 11th Australasian Conference. Melbourne, Australia: 195–206. doi:10.1007/11780656_17.
9. Yu Y, Yang B, Huang X, Zhang M (2007) Efficient identity-based signcryption scheme for multiple receivers. Proc. the Autonomic and Trusted Computing 4th International Conference. Hong Kong, China: 13–21. doi:10.1007/978-3-540-73547-2_4.
10. Sharmila S, Sree S, Srinivasan R, Pandu C (2009) An efficient identity-based signcryption scheme for multiple receivers. Proc. the Advances in Information and Computer Security 4th International Workshop on Security. Toyama, Japan: 71–88. doi:10.1007/978-3-642-04846-3_6.
11. Elkamchouchi H, Abouelseoud Y (2009) MIDSCYK: An efficient provably secure multirecipient identity-based signcryption scheme. Proc. the International Conference on Networking and Media Convergence. Cairo, Egypt: 70–75. doi:10.1109/ICNM.2009.4907192.
12. Pang L, Cui J, Li H, Pei Q, Jiang Z, et al (2011) A new multi-receiver ID-based anonymous signcryption. Chinese journal of computer 34: 2104–2113. doi:10.3724/SP.J.1016.2011.02104.
13. Lal S, Kushwah P (2009) Anonymous ID based signcryption scheme for multiple receivers. Cryptology ePrint Archive. Available: http://eprint.iacr.org/2009/345.pdf.

14. Qin H, Dai Y, Wang Z (2011) Identity-based multi-receiver threshold signcryption scheme. Security and Communication Networks 4: 1331–1337. doi:10.1002/sec.259.

15. Zhang B, Xu Q (2010) An ID-based anonymous signcryption scheme for multiple receivers secure in the standard model. Proc. of the AST/UCMA/ISA/CAN conferences. Miyazaki, Japan: 15–27. doi:10.1007/978-3-642-13577-4_2.

16. Zheng Y (1997) Digital signcryption or how to achieve cost (signature & encryption)<<cost (signature)+cost (encryption) Proc. the 17th Annual International Cryptology Conference on Advances in Cryptology. London, UK: 165–179. doi:10.1007/BFb0052234.

17. Zhang J, Gao S, Chen H, Geng Q (2009) A novel ID-based anonymous signcryption scheme. Proc. the Advances in Data and Web Management Joint International Conferences. Suzhou, China: 604–610. doi:10.1007/978-3-642-00672-2_58.

18. Rivest R, Shamir A, Tauman Y (2001) How to leak a secret: Theory and applications of ring signatures. Proc. the 7th International Conference on the Theory and Application of Cryptology and Information Security: Advances in Cryptology. London, UK: 552–565. doi:10.1007/11685654_7.

19. Huang X, Susilo W, Mu Y, Zhang F (2005) Identity based ring signcryption scheme: Cryptographic primitive for preserving privacy and authenticity in the ubiquitous world. Proc. the 19th International Conference on Advanced Information Networking and Applications. Taipei, Taiwan: 649–654. doi:10.1109/AINA.2005.205.

20. Gafurov D, Snekkenes E, Buvarp T (2006) Robustness of biometric gait authentication against impersonation attack. Proc. The OTM Workshops. Montpellier, France: 479–488. doi:10.1007/11915034_71.

21. Xie Q, Yu X (2005) A new (t, n) threshold signature scheme withstanding the conspiracy attack. Wuhan University Journal of Natural Sciences 10: 107–110. doi:10.1007/BF02828628.

11

Weighted Multiplex Networks

Giulia Menichetti[1], Daniel Remondini[1], Pietro Panzarasa[2], Raúl J. Mondragón[3], Ginestra Bianconi[4]*

1 Department of Physics and Astronomy and INFN Sez. Bologna, Bologna University, Bologna, Italy, **2** School of Business and Management, Queen Mary University of London, London, United Kingdom, **3** School of Electronic Engineering and Computer Science, Queen Mary University of London, London, United Kingdom, **4** School of Mathematical Sciences, Queen Mary University of London, London, United Kingdom

Abstract

One of the most important challenges in network science is to quantify the information encoded in complex network structures. Disentangling randomness from organizational principles is even more demanding when networks have a multiplex nature. Multiplex networks are multilayer systems of N nodes that can be linked in multiple interacting and co-evolving layers. In these networks, relevant information might not be captured if the single layers were analyzed separately. Here we demonstrate that such partial analysis of layers fails to capture significant correlations between weights and topology of complex multiplex networks. To this end, we study two weighted multiplex co-authorship and citation networks involving the authors included in the American Physical Society. We show that in these networks weights are strongly correlated with multiplex structure, and provide empirical evidence in favor of the advantage of studying weighted measures of multiplex networks, such as multistrength and the inverse multiparticipation ratio. Finally, we introduce a theoretical framework based on the entropy of multiplex ensembles to quantify the information stored in multiplex networks that would remain undetected if the single layers were analyzed in isolation.

Editor: Yamir Moreno, University of Zaragoza, Spain

Funding: DR and GM acknowledge support by the Italian Ministry of Education and Research through the Flagship (PB05) InterOmics and the European Methods for Integrated analysis of multiple Omics datasets (MIMOmics) (305280) projects. The funders had no role in study design and analysis, decision to publish, or preparation of the manuscript.

Competing Interests: The authors have declared that no competing interests exist.

* E-mail: ginestra.bianconi@gmail.com

Introduction

Network theory investigates the global topology and structural patterns of the interactions among the constituent elements of a number of complex systems including social groups, infrastructure and technological systems, the brain and biological networks [1–4]. Over the last fifteen years, a large body of literature has attempted to disentangle noise and stochasticity from non-random patterns and mechanisms, in an attempt to gain a better understanding of how these systems function and evolve. More recently, further advances in the study of complex systems have been spurred by the upsurge of interest in multiplex networks in which pairs of interacting elements are represented as nodes connected through multiple types of links, at multiple points in time, or at multiple scales of resolution [5]. More specifically, a multiplex network is a set of N nodes interacting in M layers, each reflecting a distinct type (or time or resolution) of interaction linking the same pair of nodes. Examples of multiplex networks include: social networks, where the same individuals can be connected through different types of social ties originating from friendship, collaboration, or family relationships [6]; air transportation networks, where different airports can be connected through flights of different companies [7]; and the brain, where different regions can be seen as connected by the functional and structural neural networks [8].

Most of the studies so far conducted on multiplex networks have been concerned with the empirical analysis of a wide range of systems [6,7,9,10], the modeling of their underlying structures [11–13], and the description of new critical phenomena and

processes occurring on them [14–17]. Despite the growing interest in multiplex networks, a fundamental question still remains largely unanswered: What is the advantage of a full-fledged analysis of complex systems that takes all their interacting layers into account, over more traditional studies that represent such systems as single networks with only one layer? To answer this question, one should demonstrate that novel and relevant information can be uncovered only by taking the multiplex nature of complex systems directly into account, and would instead remain undetected if individual layers were analyzed in isolation. In this paper, an attempt is made to offer a possible solution to this problem within the context of weighted multiplex networks.

Just as with single networks, links between nodes may have a different weight, reflecting their intensity, capacity, duration, intimacy or exchange of services [18]. The role played by the weights in the functioning of many networks, and especially the relative benefits of weak and strong ties in social networks, have been the subject of a longstanding debate [18–20]. Moreover, it has been shown that, in single networks, the weights can be distributed in a heterogeneous way, as a result of the non-trivial effects that the structural properties of the networks have on them [21–24]. In particular, correlations between weights and structural properties of single networks can be uncovered by the analysis of strength-degree correlations [21] and by the distribution of the weights of the links incident upon the same node [23]. To characterize weighted networks, it is common practice to measure the following quantities: i) the average strength of nodes of degree k, i.e. $s = s(k)$, describing how weights are distributed in the network; and ii) the average inverse participation ratio of the weights of the links incident upon nodes of degree k, i.e. $Y = Y(k)$, describing how weights are distributed across the links incident upon nodes of degree k. Here we show that these two quantities do not capture the full breadth of the information encoded in multiplex networks. Indeed, a full-fledged analysis of the properties of multiplex networks is needed that takes the multiple interacting and co-evolving layers simultaneously into account.

For a multiplex network, a *multilink* $\vec{m} = (m_1, m_2, \ldots, m_M)$ between nodes i and j indicates the set of all links connecting these nodes in the different layers [25]. In particular, if $m_\alpha = 1$, there is a link between nodes i and j in layer α, whereas if $m_\alpha = 0$ nodes i and j are not connected in layer α. Multilink $\vec{m} = \vec{0}$ between two nodes refers to the case in which no link exists between the two nodes in all layers of the multiplex network. Thus, multilinks indicate the most straightforward type of correlation between layers, and provide a simple generalization of the notion of overlap. In fact, if nodes i and j are connected by a multilink $\vec{m}$, with $m_\alpha = m_{\alpha'} = 1$, it follows that there is an overlap of links between i and j in layers α and α'. Figure 1 shows a multiplex network with $M = 2$ layers and $N = 5$ nodes with different types of multilinks.

Here we will define two new measures, *multistrength* and the *inverse multiparticipation ratio*, which are, respectively, the sum of the weights of a certain type of multilink incident upon a single node and a way for characterizing the heterogeneity of the weights of multilink $\vec{m}$ incident upon a single node. To provide empirical evidence that weighted properties of multilinks are fundamental for properly assessing weighted multiplex networks, we focus on the networks of the authors of papers published in the journals of the American Physical Society (APS), and analyze the scientific collaboration network and the citation network connecting the same authors. These networks are intrinsically weighted since any two scientists can co-author more than one paper and can cite each other's work several times. A large number of studies have analyzed similar bibliometric datasets drawing upon network theory [26–30]. Unlike these studies, here we investigate the APS bibliometric dataset using the framework of multiplex networks that allows us to explore novel properties of the collaboration and citation networks. In particular, we show that multistrength and the inverse multiparticipation ratio enable new relevant information to be extracted from the APS dataset and that this information extends beyond what is encoded in the strength and inverse participation

ratio of single layers. Finally, based on the entropy of multiplex ensembles, we propose an indicator Ξ to evaluate the additional amount of information that can be extracted from the weighted properties of multilinks in multiplex networks over the information encoded in the properties of their individual layers analyzed separately.

Weighted Multiplex Networks

2.1 Definition

A weighted multiplex network is a set of M weighted networks $G_\alpha = (V, E_\alpha)$, with $\alpha = 1, \ldots, M$. The set of nodes V is the same for each layer and has cardinality $|V| = N$, whereas the set of links E_α depends on the layer α. A multiplex network is represented formally as $\vec{G} = (G_1, G_2, \ldots, G_\alpha, \ldots G_M)$. Each network G_α is fully described by the adjacency matrix $\mathbf{a}^\alpha$ with elements a_{ij}^α, where $a_{ij}^\alpha = w_{ij}^\alpha > 0$ if there is a link with weight w_{ij}^α between nodes i and j in layer α, and $a_{ij}^\alpha = 0$ otherwise. From now on, in order to simplify the formalization of weighted multiplex networks, we will assume that the weight of the link between any pair of nodes i and j, $a_{ij}^\alpha = w_{ij}^\alpha$, can only take integer values. This does not represent a major limitation because in a large number of weighted multiplex networks the weights of the links can be seen as multiples of a minimal weight.

2.2 Structural Properties of Individual Layers

We indicate the degree of node i in layer α with k_i^α, defined as $k_i^\alpha = \sum_{j=1}^{N} \theta(a_{ij}^\alpha)$, where function $\theta(x) = 1$ if $x > 0$, and $\theta(x) = 0$ otherwise. In complex weighted networks, weights can be distributed across links more or less heterogeneously. A way to evaluate this heterogeneity is to introduce local properties such as the *strength* s_i^α [21] and the *inverse participation ratio* Y_i^α of node i in layer α [22,23]:

$$s_i^\alpha = \sum_{j=1}^{N} a_{ij}^\alpha,$$

$$Y_i^\alpha = \sum_{j=1}^{N} \left(\frac{a_{ij}^\alpha}{s_i^\alpha}\right)^2. \tag{1}$$

As with single networks, in any given layer α, the strength s_i^α of a node indicates the sum of the weights of the links incident upon node i in layer α, whereas the inverse participation ratio Y_i^α indicates how unevenly the weights of the links of node i are distributed in layer α. The inverse of Y_i^α characterizes the effective number of links of node i in layer α. Indeed, $(Y_i^\alpha)^{-1}$ is greater than one and smaller than the degree of node i in layer α, i.e., $(Y_i^\alpha)^{-1} \in (1, k_i^\alpha)$. Moreover, if the weights of the links of node i are distributed uniformly, i.e., $w_{ij}^\alpha = s_i^\alpha/k_i^\alpha$, we have $(Y_i^\alpha)^{-1} = k_i^\alpha$. Conversely, if the weight of one link is much larger than the other weights, i.e., $w_{ir}^\alpha \gg w_{ij}^\alpha$ for every $j \neq r$, then $(Y_i^\alpha)^{-1} = 1$.

In network theory, it is common practice to evaluate the conditional means of the strength and of the inverse participation ratio of the weights of links against the degree of nodes [21–23]. In a multiplex network, we will then consider the quantities $s^\alpha(k) = \langle s_i^\alpha \delta(k_i^\alpha, k) \rangle$ and $Y^\alpha(k) = \langle Y_i^\alpha \delta(k_i^\alpha, k) \rangle$, where the average is calculated over all nodes with degree k in layer α, and $\delta(a,b)$ indicates the Kronecker delta. As in single networks [21], s_k^α is expected to scale as

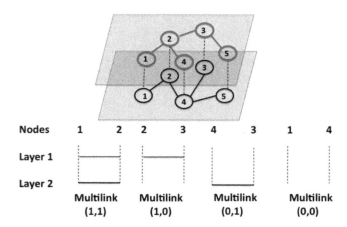

Figure 1. Example of all possible multilinks in a multiplex network with $M = 2$ layers and $N = 5$ nodes. Nodes i and j are linked by one multilink $\vec{m} = (m_\alpha, m_{\alpha'})$.

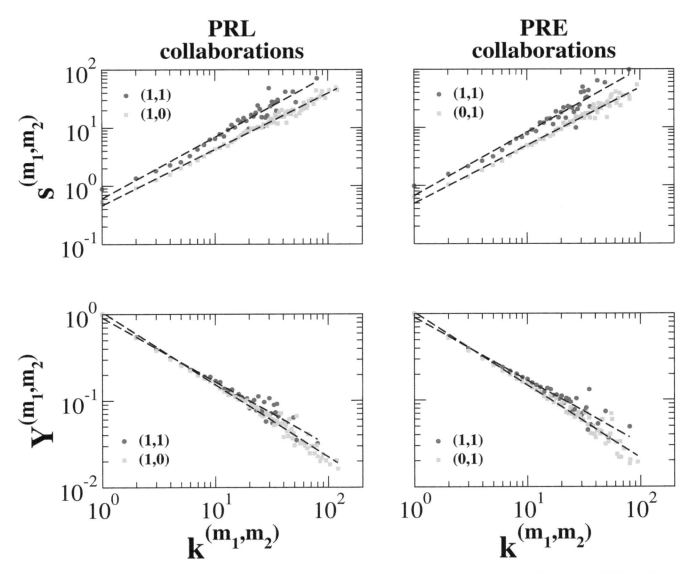

Figure 2. Average multistrength and average inverse multiparticipation ratio versus multidegree in the CoCo-PRE/PRL multiplex network. The average multistrengths and the average inverse multiparticipation ratios are fitted by a power-law distribution of the type described in Eq. (8) (fitted distributions are here indicated by black dashed lines). Statistical tests for the collaboration network of PRL suggest that the exponents $\beta_{\vec{m},1}$ defined in Eq. (8) are the same, while exponents $\lambda_{\vec{m},PRL}$ are significantly different. Similar results can be obtained for the exponents in the PRE collaboration layer. Nevertheless, multistrengths $s^{(1,1),\alpha}$ are always larger than multistrengths $s^{(1,0),PRL}$ and $s^{(0,1),PRE}$, when multistrengths are calculated over the same number of multilinks, i.e., $k^{(1,1)} = k^{(1,0)} = k^{(0,1)}$ (see Text S1 for the statistical test on this hypothesis).

$$s^{\alpha}(k) \propto k^{\beta_{\alpha}}, \tag{2}$$

with $\beta_{\alpha} \geq 1$. We can distinguish between two scenarios. In the first one, the average strength of nodes with degree k increases linearly with k, i.e., $\beta_{\alpha} = 1$. This indicates that, on average, the weights of the links incident upon the hubs do not differ from the weights of the links of less connected nodes. In the second scenario, the strength of the nodes with degree k increases super-linearly with k, i.e., $\beta_{\alpha} > 1$, thus indicating that, on average, the weights of the links incident upon the hubs are larger than the weights of the links of less connected nodes. In a multiplex network, it may be the case that weights are distributed in different ways across the layers. For instance, some layers may be characterized by a super-linear

growth of s_k^{α}, while other layers may show a linear dependence. Finally, the inverse participation ratio can be used in order to characterize the heterogeneity of the weights of the links incident upon nodes with a certain degree. In particular, it has been observed that, in many single weighted networks, the inverse participation ratio scales as an inverse power-law function of the degree of nodes. In a multiplex network, this would imply

$$Y^{\alpha}(k) \propto \frac{1}{k^{\lambda_{\alpha}}}, \tag{3}$$

where exponent $\lambda_{\alpha} \leq 1$ is layer-dependent.

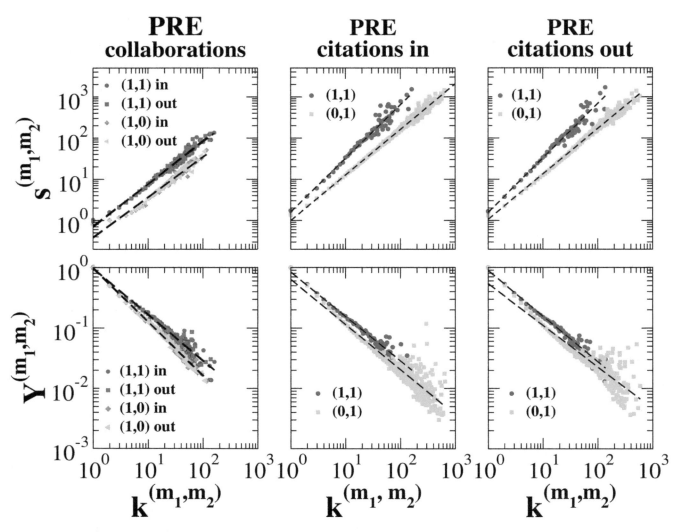

Figure 3. Properties of multilinks in the weighted CoCi-PRE multiplex network. In the case of the collaboration network, the distributions of multistrengths versus multidegrees always have the same exponent, but the average weight of multilinks (1,1) is larger than the average weight of multilinks (1,0). Moreover, the exponents $\lambda_{(1,0),col,in}$, $\lambda_{(1,0),col,out}$ are larger than exponents $\lambda_{(1,1),col,in}$, $\lambda_{(1,1),col,out}$. In the case of the citation layer, both the incoming multistrengths and the outgoing multistrengths have a functional behavior that varies depending on the type of multilink. Conversely, the average inverse multiparticipation ratio in the citation layer does not show any significant change of behavior when compared across different multilinks.

2.3 Multilink, Multistrength, and Inverse Multiparticipation Ratio

A number of multiplex networks are characterized by a significant overlap of links across the different layers [6,7]. In order to generalize the notion of overlap to weighted multiplex networks, in what follows we will draw on the concept of multilink [25]. Let us consider the vector $\vec{m} = (m_1, m_2, \ldots, m_\alpha, \ldots, m_M)$, in which every element m_α can take only two values $m_\alpha = 0,1$. We define a *multilink* $\vec{m}$ as the set of links connecting a given pair of nodes in the different layers of a multiplex network, and connecting them in the generic layer α only if $m_\alpha = 1$. In particular, any two nodes i and j are always linked by a single multilink of type $\vec{m} = \vec{m}^{ij} = (\theta(a_{ij}^1), \theta(a_{ij}^2), \ldots, \theta(a_{ij}^M))$, where $\theta(x) = 1$ if $x > 0$, and $\theta(x) = 0$ otherwise. The multilink $\vec{m} = \vec{0}$ between two nodes represents the situation in which in all the layers of the multiplex network the two nodes are not directly linked.

We can now introduce the multiadjacency matrices $\mathbf{A}^{\vec{m}}$ with elements $A_{ij}^{\vec{m}}$ equal to 1 if there is a multilink $\vec{m}$ between node i and node j and zero otherwise. In terms of the weighted adjacency matrices $\mathbf{a}^\alpha$ of the multiplex network, the elements $A_{ij}^{\vec{m}}$ of the multiadjacency matrix $\mathbf{A}^{\vec{m}}$ are given by

$$A_{ij}^{\vec{m}} = \prod_{\alpha=1}^{M} [\theta(a_{ij}^\alpha)m_\alpha + (1 - \theta(a_{ij}^\alpha))(1 - m_\alpha)], \quad (4)$$

where $\theta(x) = 1$ if $x > 0$, otherwise $\theta(x) = 0$. Even though there are 2^M multiadjacency matrices, only $2^M - 1$ of them are independent because the normalization condition, $\sum_{\vec{m}} A_{ij}^{\vec{m}} = 1$, must be satisfied for any pair of nodes i and j. Based on multi-adjacency matrices, we can define the *multidegree* $k_i^{\vec{m}}$ of node i as

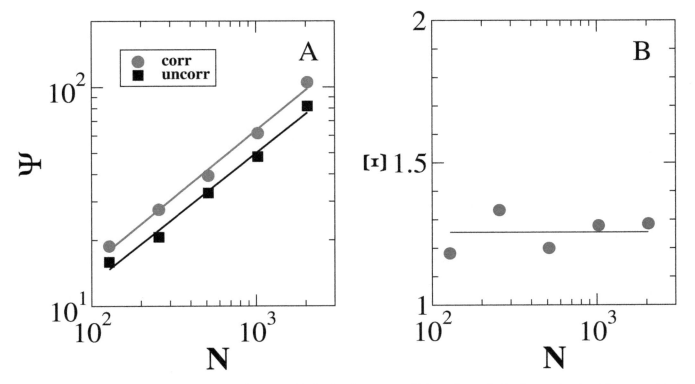

Figure 4. (A) Value of the indicator Ψ defined in Eq. (10) indicating the amount of information carried by the correlated and the uncorrelated multiplex ensembles of N nodes with respect to a null model in which the weights are distributed uniformly over the multiplex network. (B) Value of the indicator Ξ defined in Eq. (12) indicating the additional amount of information encoded in the properties of multilinks in the correlated multiplex ensemble with respect to the corresponding uncorrelated multiplex ensemble. The solid line refers to the average value of Ξ over the different multiplex network sizes.

$$k_i^{\vec{m}} = \sum_{j=1}^{N} A_{ij}^{\vec{m}}, \tag{5}$$

which indicates how many multilinks $\vec{m}$ are incident upon node i.

To study weighted multiplex networks, we now introduce two new measures. For layer α associated to multilinks $\vec{m}$, such that $m_\alpha > 0$, we define the multistrength $s_{i,\alpha}^{\vec{m}}$ and the inverse multiparticipation ratio $Y_{i,\alpha}^{\vec{m}}$ of node i, respectively, as

$$s_{i,\alpha}^{\vec{m}} = \sum_{j=1}^{N} a_{ij}^{\alpha} A_{ij}^{\vec{m}}, \tag{6}$$

$$Y_{i,\alpha}^{\vec{m}} = \sum_{j=1}^{N} \left(\frac{a_{ij}^{\alpha} A_{ij}^{\vec{m}}}{\sum_r a_{ir}^{\alpha} A_{ir}^{\vec{m}}} \right)^2. \tag{7}$$

Since multistrength $s_{i,\alpha}^{\vec{m}}$ can be non-zero only if $m_\alpha = 1$, for each layer α the number of non-trivial multistrengths is 2^{M-1}, and therefore the number of multistrengths that can be defined in a multiplex network of M layers is $K = M2^{M-1}$. Similarly, the number of inverse multiparticipation ratios $Y_{i,\alpha}^{\vec{m}}$ is given by $K = M2^{M-1}$. The average multistrength of nodes with a given multidegree, i.e., $s^{\vec{m},\alpha}(k^{\vec{m}}) = \langle s_i^{\vec{m},\alpha} \delta(k_i^{\vec{m}}, k^{\vec{m}}) \rangle$, and the average

inverse multiparticipation ratio of nodes with a given multidegree, i.e., $Y^{\vec{m},\alpha}(k^{\vec{m}}) = \langle Y_i^{\vec{m},\alpha} \delta(k_i^{\vec{m}}, k^{\vec{m}}) \rangle$, are expected to scale as

$$s^{\vec{m},\alpha}(k^{\vec{m}}) \propto (k^{\vec{m}})^{\beta_{\vec{m},\alpha}}$$

$$Y^{\vec{m},\alpha}(k^{\vec{m}}) \propto \frac{1}{(k^{\vec{m}})^{\lambda_{\vec{m},\alpha}}}, \tag{8}$$

with exponents $\beta_{\vec{m},\alpha} \geq 1$ and $\lambda_{\vec{m},\alpha} \leq 1$. The use of multilinks $\vec{m}$ to describe multiplex properties is numerically feasible if the number of layers is smaller than the number of nodes, i.e., $M \ll \log(N)$. If this condition is not satisfied, then the following quantities can be measured: the *overlap multiplicity*, $v(\vec{m}) = \sum_\alpha m_\alpha$, which indicates that multilink $\vec{m}$ connects two nodes through $v(\vec{m})$ links; $s^\alpha(v) = \langle s_{i,\alpha}^{\vec{m}} \rangle_{v(\vec{m})=v}$; and $Y^\alpha(v) = \langle Y_{i,\alpha}^{\vec{m}} \rangle_{v(\vec{m})=v}$, where $v = 1, 2 \ldots,$ M.

Empirical Evidence of Weighted Properties of Multilinks

In this section, we will draw on the measures introduced above and provide empirical evidence that, in weighted multiplex networks, weights can be correlated with the multiplex structure in a non-trivial way. To this end, we analyze the bibliographic dataset that includes all articles published in the APS journals (i.e., Physical Review Letters, Physical Review, and Reviews of Modern Physics) from 1893 to 2009. Of these articles, the dataset includes their citations as well as the authors. Here, we restrict our study only to articles published either in Physical Review Letters (PRL) or in Physical Review E (PRE) and written by ten or fewer authors, $n_p \leq 10$. We constructed multiplex networks in which the nodes are the authors and links between them have a two-fold nature: scientific collaborations with weights defined as in [28] (see Text S1), and citations with weights indicating how many times author i cited author j.

In particular, we created the following two duplex networks (i.e., multiplex networks with $M = 2$):

1. **CoCo-PRL/PRE:** *collaborations among PRL and PRE authors.* The nodes of this multiplex network are the authors with articles published both in PRL and PRE (i.e., 16,207 authors). These nodes are connected in layer 1 through weighted undirected links indicating the strength of their collaboration in PRL (i.e., co-authorship of PRL articles). The same nodes are connected in layer 2 through weighted undirected links indicating the strength of their collaboration in PRE (i.e., co-authorship of PRE articles).

2. **CoCi-PRE:** *collaborations among PRE authors and citations to PRE articles.* The nodes of this multiplex network are the authors of articles published in PRE (i.e., 35,205 authors). These nodes are connected in layer 1 through weighted undirected links indicating the strength of their collaboration in PRE (i.e., co-authorship of PRE articles). The same nodes are connected in layer 2 through weighted directed links indicating how many times an author (with articles in PRE) cited another author's work, where citations are limited to those made to PRE articles.

Both these multiplex networks show a significant overlap of links and a significant correlation between degrees of nodes as captured by the Pearson correlation coefficient ρ (see Text S1). This finding supports the hypothesis that the two layers in each of the multiplex networks are correlated. That is, the existence of a link between two authors in one layer is correlated with the existence of a link between the same authors in the other layer. Moreover, the multidegrees of the multiplex networks are broadly distributed, and the hubs in the scientific collaboration network tend to be also the hubs in the citation network (see Text S1).

In the case of the CoCo–PRL/PRE network, multilinks $\vec{m} = (1,0)$, $\vec{m} = (0,1)$ and $\vec{m} = (1,1)$ refer to collaborations only in PRL, only in PRE, and in both PRL and PRE, respectively. Moreover, to distinguish between the weights used when evaluating multistrength, we have $\alpha = PRL$ or $\alpha = PRE$. Results indicate that multistrength and the inverse multiparticipation ratio behave according to Eq. (8) (see Fig. 2). The difference between exponents $\beta_{\vec{m},PRL}$ for $\vec{m} = (1,0)$ and $\vec{m} = (1,1)$ is not statistically significant. Nevertheless, there is a statistically significant difference between the average weights of multilinks (1,0) and (1,1) in the PRL layer. As to the inverse multiparticipation ratio, there is a significant variation in the exponents, $\lambda_{(1,0),PRL} = 0.84 \pm 0.03$ and $\lambda_{(1,1),PRL} = 0.74 \pm 0.05$ (see Fig. 2, bottom left panel). This suggests that the weights of the collaborative links between co-authors of both PRL and PRE articles are distributed more heterogeneously than the weights of collaborative links between co-authors of articles published only in PRL (see Text S1 for details on the statistical tests). Similar results were found for multistrengths evaluated in the PRE layer (see Fig. 2, right panels).

These findings clearly indicate that the partial analysis of individual layers would fail to uncover the fact that the average weight of the link between authors that collaborated both on PRL and PRE articles is significantly larger than the average weight of the link between authors that collaborated only on articles published in one journal. Moreover, the difference in functional behavior of the multipartition ratio across layers could not be captured if layers were analyzed separately.

In the case of the CoCi-PRE network, there are even more significant differences between the properties of the multilinks than in the previous network. In the CoCi-PRE network the functional behavior of multistrength also depends on the type of multilink. Figure 3 shows the average multistrength in the CoCi-PRE network. To distinguish between the weights used to measure multistrength, we have layer $\alpha = col$, which refers to the collaboration network constructed on PRE articles, and layer $\alpha = cit$, which refers to the citation network between PRE articles, where a distinction is also made between incoming (*in*) and outgoing (*out*) links. First, in the scientific collaboration network, exponents $\beta_{\vec{m},col}$ are not statistically different, but the average weight of multilink (1,1) is larger than the average weight of multilinks $(1,0),in$ and $(1,0)out$. Moreover, exponents $\lambda_{(1,0),col,in}$ and $\lambda_{(1,0),col,out}$ are larger than exponents $\lambda_{(1,1),col,in}, \lambda_{(1,1),col,out}$, indicating that the weights of authors' collaborative links with other cited/citing authors are distributed more heterogeneously than the weights of authors' collaborative links with other authors with whom there are no links in the citation network. Second, in the citation network multistrengths follow a distinct functional behavior depending on the different type of multilink, and are characterized by different $\beta_{\vec{m},cit,in/out}$ exponents. In fact the fitted values of these exponents are given by $\beta_{(1,1)cit,,in} = 1.30 \pm 0.07, \beta_{(1,1),cit,out} = 1.32 \pm 0.08, \beta_{(0,1),cit,in} = 1.11 \pm 0.01$, and $\beta_{(0,1),cit,out} = 1.10 \pm 0.02$. This implies that, on average, highly cited authors are cited by their co-authors to a much greater extent than is the case with poorly cited authors. A similar, though much weaker effect was also found for the citations connecting authors that are not collaborators. Furthermore, in the citation layer the inverse multiparticipation ratio for multilink (1,1) is always larger than the inverse multiparticipation ratio for multilinks (1,0) and (0,1) (see Text S1 for details on the statistical test). Finally, when single layers were analyzed separately, we found $\beta_{col} = 1.03 \pm 0.04$ in the collaboration network, and $\beta_{cit,in} = 1.13 \pm 0.02$ and $\beta_{cit,out} = 1.14 \pm 0.03$ in the citation network. This indicates that in the citation network strength grows super-linearly as a function of degree, i.e., weights are not distributed uniformly. Nevertheless, correlations between weights and types of multilinks cannot be captured if the two individual layers are studied separately.

3.1 Assessing the Informational Content of Weighted Multilinks

Recent research on single networks has shown that the entropy of network ensembles provides a very powerful tool for quantifying their complexity [31–34]. Here, we propose a theoretical framework based on the entropy of multiplex ensembles for assessing the amount of information encoded in the weighted properties of multilinks. Multiplex weighted network ensembles can be defined as the set of all weighted multiplex networks satisfying a given set of constraints, such as the expected degree sequence and the expected strength sequence in every layer of the multiplex network, or the expected multidegree sequence and the expected multistrength sequence. A set of constraints imposed upon the multiplex network ensemble uniquely determines the probability $P(\vec{G})$ of the multiplex networks in the ensemble (see Materials and Methods). The entropy $\mathcal{S}$ of the multiplex ensemble can be defined in terms of $P(\vec{G})$ as

$$\mathcal{S} = -\sum_{\vec{G}} P(\vec{G}) \log P(\vec{G}), \qquad (9)$$

where $\mathcal{S}$ indicates the logarithm of the typical number of multiplex networks in the ensemble. The smaller the entropy, the larger the amount of information stored in the constraints imposed on the network. The entropy can be regarded as an unbiased way to evaluate the informational value of these constraints.

In order to gauge the information encoded in a weighted multiplex network with respect to a null model, we define the indicator Ψ, which quantifies how much information is carried by the weight distributions of a weighted multiplex ensemble. In particular, Ψ compares the entropy of a weighted multiplex ensemble $\mathcal{S}$ with the entropy of a weighted multiplex ensemble in which the weights are distributed homogeneously. Therefore, Ψ can be defined as

$$\Psi = \frac{|\mathcal{S} - \langle \mathcal{S} \rangle_{\pi(w)}|}{\langle (\delta \mathcal{S})^2 \rangle_{\pi(w)}}, \qquad (10)$$

where $\langle (\delta \mathcal{S})^2 \rangle_{\pi(w)}$ is the standard deviation, and the average $\langle \ldots \rangle_{\pi(w)}$ is calculated over multiplex networks with the same structural properties but with weights distributed homogeneously. In particular, when the weight distribution is randomized, the multiplex networks are constrained in such a way that each link must have a minimal weight (i.e., $w_{ij} \geq 1$), while the remaining of the total weight is distributed randomly over the links. In all the considered network ensembles we have assumed that the weights of the links can only take values that are multiple of a minimal weight. This assumption is by no means a limitation of this approach because for every finite network, there is always a minimal weight in the network such that this hypothesis is verified.

In order to evaluate the amount of information encoded in the weight of links in single layers and compare it to the information supplied by multistrength, we consider the following undirected multiplex ensembles:

- *Correlated weighted multiplex ensemble.* In this ensemble, we fix the expected multidegree sequence $\{k_i^{\vec{m}}\}$, and we set the expected multistrength sequence $\{s_i^{\vec{m},\alpha}\}$ to be

$$s_i^{\vec{m},\alpha} = c_{\vec{m},\alpha} (k^{\vec{m},\alpha})^{\lambda_{\vec{m},\alpha}} \qquad (11)$$

for every layer α. We call Ψ^{corr} the Ψ calculated from this ensemble.

- *Uncorrelated weighted multiplex ensemble.* In this ensemble, we set the expected degree k_i^{α} of every node i in every layer $\alpha = 1,2$ to be equal to the sum of the multidegrees (with $m_{\alpha} = 1$) in the correlated weighted multiplex ensemble. We set the expected strengths s_i^{α} of every node i in every layer α to be equal to the sum of the multistrengths of node i in layer α in the correlated weighted multiplex ensemble. We call Ψ^{corr} the Ψ calculated from this ensemble.

In the correlated weighted multiplex ensemble the properties of the multilinks are accounted for, while in the uncorrelated weighted multiplex ensemble the different layers of the multiplex networks are analyzed separately (see Text S1 for the details). Finally, to quantify the additional amount of information carried by the correlated weighted multiplex ensemble with respect to the uncorrelated weighted multiplex ensemble, we define the indicator Ξ as

$$\Xi = \frac{\Psi^{corr}}{\Psi^{uncorr}}. \qquad (12)$$

As an example of a possible application of the indicator Ξ, we focus on a case inspired by the CoCi-PRE multiplex network, where we consider different exponents $\beta_{\vec{m},\alpha,in/out}$ for different multilinks. First, we created the correlated multiplex ensemble with power-law multidegree distributions $P(k^{\vec{m}}) = C(k^{\vec{m}})^{-\gamma_{\vec{m}}}$ with exponents $\gamma_{(1,m_2)} = 2.6$ for $m_2 = 0,1$ and $\gamma_{(0,1),(in/out)} = 1.9$ (where for multidegree $(0,1)$ we imposed a structural cut-off). Multi-strengths satisfy Eq. (11), with $c_{\vec{m},\alpha} = 1$ and $\beta_{(1,m_2),1} = 1$, for $m_2 = 0,1$; $\beta_{(1,1),2} = 1.3$, and $\beta_{(0,1),2} = 1.1$. Second, for the second layer, we created the uncorrelated version of the multiplex ensemble which is characterized by a super-linear dependence of the average strength on the degree of the nodes. We then measured Ψ as a function of network size N for these different ensembles. Numerically, the average $\langle \ldots \rangle_{\pi(w)}$ was evaluated from 100 randomizations. Figure 4 shows that Ψ increases with network size N as a power law, and that Ξ fluctuates around an average value of 1.256. These findings indicate that a significant amount of information is contained in multistrength and cannot be extracted from individual layers separately. Similar results, not shown here, were obtained with a correlated weighted multiplex ensemble characterized by non-trivial inverse multiparticipation ratios.

Conclusions

In this paper, we have shown that weighted multiplex networks are characterized by significant correlations across layers, and in particular that weights are closely correlated with the multiplex network structure. To properly detect these correlations, we introduced and defined two novel weighted properties of multiplex networks, namely multistrength and the inverse multiparticipation ratio, that cannot be reduced to the properties of single layers. These weighted multiplex properties capture the crucial role played by multilinks in the distribution of weights, i.e., the extent to which there is a link connecting each pair of nodes in every layer of the multiplex network. To illustrate an example of weighted multiplex networks displaying non-trivial correlations between weights and topology, we analyzed the weighted properties of multilinks in two multiplex networks constructed by combining the co-authorship and citation networks involving the authors included in the APS dataset. Finally, based on the entropy of multiplex ensembles, we developed a theoretical framework for evaluating the information encoded in weighted multiplex networks, and proposed the indicator Ψ for quantifying the information that can be extracted from a given dataset with respect to a null model in which weights are randomly distributed across links. Moreover, we proposed a new indicator Ξ that can be used to evaluate the additional amount of information that the weighted properties of multilinks provide over the information contained in the properties of single layers. In summary, in this paper we have provided compelling evidence that the analysis of multiplex networks cannot be simplified to the partial analysis of single layers, and in particular that non-trivial information can be uncovered only by shifting emphasis on a number of weighted properties of multilinks.

Materials and Methods

We can build a multiplex ensemble by maximizing the entropy $\mathcal{S}$ of the ensemble given by Eq. (9) under the condition that the constraints imposed upon the multiplex networks are satisfied on average over the ensemble (soft constraints). We assume there are

K of such constraints determined by the conditions.

$$\sum_{\vec{G}} P(\vec{G}) F_\mu(\vec{G}) = C_\mu, \qquad (13)$$

for $\mu = 1, 2 \ldots, K$, where $F_\mu(\vec{G})$ determines one of the structural constraints that we want to impose on average on the multiplex network. The most unbiased multiplex ensemble satisfying the constraints given by Eqs. (13) maximizes the entropy $\mathcal{S}$ under these constraints. In this ensemble, the probability $P(\vec{G})$ for a multiplex network $\vec{G}$ of the ensemble is given by

$$P(\vec{G}) = \frac{1}{Z} \exp\left[-\sum_\mu \omega_\mu F_\mu(\vec{G}) \right], \qquad (14)$$

where the normalization constant Z is called the "partition function" of the canonical multiplex ensemble, and is fixed by the normalization condition imposed on $P(\vec{G})$, whereas ω_μ are the Lagrangian multipliers enforcing the constraints in Eq. (13). The values of the Lagrangian multipliers ω_μ are determined by

imposing the constraints given by Eq. (13), while for the probability $P(\vec{G})$ the structural form given by Eq. (14) is assumed. We refer to the entropy $\mathcal{S}$ given by Eq. 9 calculated using the probability $P(\vec{G})$ given by Eq. (14) as the Shannon entropy of the multiplex ensemble. For all the details on the derivation of the entropy for these ensembles, we refer the interested reader to the Text S1.

Supporting Information

Text S1   Supporting Information Text.

Acknowledgments

GM acknowledges the kind hospitality of Queen Mary University of London.

Author Contributions

Conceived and designed the experiments: GM DR RJM PP GB. Performed the experiments: GM. Analyzed the data: GM DR. Wrote the paper: GM DR RJM PP GB.

References

1. Albert R, Barabási A-L (2002) Statistical mechanics of complex networks. Reviews of Modern Physics 74: 47–97.
2. Newman MEJ (2003) Structure and function of complex networks. SIAM Review 45: 167–256.
3. Boccaletti S, Latora V, Moreno Y, Chavez M, Hwang D-U (2006) Complex networks: Structure and dynamics. Physics Reports 424: 175–308.
4. Fortunato S (2010) Community detection in graphs. Physics Reports 486: 75–174.
5. Kivelä M, Arenas A, Barthélemy M, Gleeson JP, Moreno Y, et al. (2013) Multilayer networks. arXiv: 1309.7233.
6. Szell M, Lambiotte R, Thurner S (2010) Multirelational organization of large-scale social networks in an online world. PNAS 107: 13636–13641.
7. Cardillo A, Gómez-Gardeñes J, Zanin M, Romance M, Papo D, et al. (2013) Emergence of network features from multiplexity. Sci. Rep. 3: 1344.
8. Bullmore E, Sporns O (2009) Complex brain networks: Graph theoretical analysis of structural and functional systems. Nat Rev Neurosci 10: 186–198.
9. Donges J, Schultz H, Marwan N, Zou Y, Kurths J (2011) Complex networks in climate dynamics. Eur. Phys. Jour. B 84: 635–651.
10. Morris RG, Barthélemy M (2012) Transport on coupled spatial networks. Phys. Rev. Lett. 109: 128703 (2012)
11. Battiston F, Nicosia V, Latora V (2014) Structural measures for multiplex networks. Phys. Rev. E 89: 032804.
12. Halu A, Mondrágon RJ, Panzarasa P, Bianconi G (2013) Multiplex PageRank. PLoS ONE 8: e78293.
13. Mucha PJ, Richardson T, Macon K, Porter MA, Onnela J-P (2010) Community structure in time-dependent, multiscale, and multiplex networks. Science 328: 876–878.
14. Buldyrev SV, Parshani R, Paul G, Stanley HE, Havlin S (2010) Catastrophic cascade of failures in interdependent networks. Nature 464: 1025–1028.
15. Baxter GJ, Dorogovtsev SN, Goltsev AV, Mendes JFF (2012) Avalanche collapse of interdependent networks. Phys. Rev. Lett. 109: 248701.
16. Gómez S, Díaz-Guilera A, Gómez-Gardeñes J, Pérez-Vicente CJ, Moreno Y, et al. (2013) Diffusion dynamics on multiplex networks. Phys. Rev. Lett. 110: 028701.
17. Brummitt CD, D'Souza RM, Leicht EA (2012) Suppressing cascades of load in interdependent networks. PNAS 109: E680–E689.
18. Granovetter MS (1973) The strength of weak ties. American Journal of Sociology 78: 1360–1380.
19. Onnela J-P, Saramäki J, Hyvönen J, Szabó G, Lazer D, et al. (2007) Structure and tie strengths in mobile communication networks. PNAS 104: 7332–7336.
20. Karsai M, Perra N, Vespignani A (2013) The emergence and role of strong ties in time-varying communication networks. arXiv: 1303.5966.
21. Barrat A, Barthélemy M, Pastor-Satorras R, Vespignani A (2004) The architecture of complex weighted networks. PNAS, 101: 3747–3752.
22. Barthélemy M, Gondran B, Guichard E (2003). Spatial structure of the Internet traffic. Physica A 319: 633–642.
23. Almaas E, Kovacs B, Vicsek T, Oltvai ZN, Barabási AL (2004). Global organization of metabolic fluxes in the bacterium Escherichia coli. Nature 427: 839–843.
24. Serrano MA, Boguñá M, Vespignani A (2009) Extracting the multiscale backbone of complex weighted networks. PNAS 106: 6483–6488.
25. Bianconi G (2013) Statistical mechanics of multiplex networks: Entropy and overlap. Phys. Rev. E 87: 062806.
26. Redner S (1998) How popular is your paper? An empirical study of the citation distribution. Eur. Phys. J. B 4: 131–134.
27. Newman MEJ (2001) The structure of scientific collaboration networks. PNAS 98: 404–409.
28. Newman MEJ (2001) Scientific collaboration networks. II. Shortest paths, weighted networks, and centrality Phys. Rev. E 64: 016132.
29. Radicchi F, Fortunato S, Markines B, Vespignani A (2009) Diffusion of scientific credits and the ranking of scientists. Phys. Rev. E 80: 056103.
30. Radicchi F, Fortunato S (2008) Universality of citation distributions: Toward an objective measure of scientific impact. PNAS 105: 17266–172172.
31. Park J, Newman MEJ (2004) Statistical mechanics of networks. Phys. Rev. E 70: 066117.
32. Johnson S, Torres JJ, Marro J, Muñoz MA (2010) Entropic origin of disassortativity in complex networks. Phys. Rev. Lett. 104: 108702.
33. Bianconi G, Pin P, Marsili M (2009) Assessing the relevance of node features for network structure. PNAS 106: 11433–11438.
34. Sagarra O, Vicente CP, Díaz-Guilera A (2013) Statistical mechanics of multiedge networks Phys. Rev. E 88: 062806.

12

GIANT: A Cytoscape Plugin for Modular Networks

Fabio Cumbo[1], Paola Paci[1,2], Daniele Santoni[1], Luisa Di Paola[3]*, Alessandro Giuliani[4]

1 Institute for System Analysis and Computer Science "Antonio Ruberti", National Research Council, Rome, Italy, **2** SysBio Centre for Systems Biology, Milan and Rome, Italy, **3** Faculty of Engineering, Università CAMPUS BioMedico, Roma, Italy, **4** Environment and Health Department, Istituto Superiore di Sanità, Rome, Italy

Abstract

Network analysis provides deep insight into real complex systems. Revealing the link between topological and functional role of network elements can be crucial to understand the mechanisms underlying the system. Here we propose a Cytoscape plugin (GIANT) to perform network clustering and characterize nodes at the light of a modified Guimerà-Amaral cartography. This approach results into a vivid picture of the a topological/functional relationship at both local and global level. The plugin has been already approved and uploaded on the Cytoscape APP store.

Editor: Baldo Oliva, Universitat Pompeu Fabra, Barcelona Research Park of Biomedicine (PRBB), Spain

Funding: The manuscript has been produced thanks to the financial support from SysBioNet, Italian Roadmap Research Infrastructures 2012 and from The Epigenomics Flagship Project (Progetto Bandiera Epigenomica) EPIGEN funded by Italian Ministry of Education, University and Research (MIUR) and the National Research Council of Italy (CNR). The funders had no role in study design, data collection and analysis, decision to publish, or preparation of the manuscript.

Competing Interests: The authors have declared that no competing interests exist.

* Email: l.dipaola@unicampus.it

Introduction

The network paradigm helps modeling the multiscale character of biological systems: "networks" is the generic name for graphs, which represent a set of nodes linked by edges. Complex systems are, thus, easily represented by graphs, whose nodes are the system elements and edges represent the relation between them.

The network structure allows for a natural combination of different scales: each node inherits its role in the system by its location in the network (top-down causation), while the global properties of the whole network depend upon the edges (bottom-up causation).

Biological networks (e.g., protein-protein interaction networks, protein contact maps, gene expression networks,) very often display a scale-free architecture lying halfway between random networks, whose wiring is assigned according to a Gaussian distribution of link probability, and regular networks, whose nodes all show the same degree (number of edges pertaining to a single node). One of the most challenging tasks for biological scale-free networks analysis is to assign a functional role to each node depending on its location in the network.

In their innovative work, Han *et al.* [1] estimated the dynamics of hubs (high-degree nodes) from the analysis of messenger RNA expression profiles. The authors examined how much hubs in the yeast interactome are co-expressed with their interaction partners, computing the average Pearson correlation coefficient (APCC) between the hub mRNA expression and its nearest neighbors. They found APCC distribution follows a bimodal distribution singling out two distinct hub populations: they called "party hubs" those nodes that are highly correlated in expression with their partners (high APCC) and "date hubs" those showing more limited co-expression with their own partners (lower APCC). This distinction matches with permanent (party hubs) and transient interactions (date hubs) [1]. Eventually, the authors showed that a

link exists between this hub classification and the network tolerance against node breakdown: scale-free networks are particularly resilient to random node removal (failure), albeit extremely sensitive to the targeted removal of hubs (attack) [2,3].

The work by Han et al. [1] is just one out of many applications of network approach in the biology and biotechnology realm (see [4] for a comprehensive review). The by far most part of the network applications deals with the mesoscopic properties of the graphs representing a link between structural and functional properties of systems.

In their seminal work [5], Guimerà and Amaral developed a methodology for the multiscale network analysis passing by the network module identification (network clustering): they classified nodes according to their inter and intra-module connectivity, by identifying two descriptors, the participation coefficient P and the within-module z-score z, for the inter and intra-module connectivity, respectively. This method has been largely applied in many different fields, from metabolic networks [5] to brain functionality [6,7], passing by non biological application [8]. The analysis of P,z space shows peculiar features when derived for protein contact networks [9–12], providing a meaningful functional characterization of local and global network properties.

Here we propose a Cytoscape plugin, GIANT (GuImerà Amaral NeTwork) implementing our modified interpretation of the Guimerà and Amaral cartography. This plugin identifies modules in a network by three different clustering methods: spectral, k-means and MCL (Markov CLuster) algorithm. The proposed approach fits with any clustering algorithm, such as those implemented in clusterMaker [13]. The output is the network cartography in the P,z plane, highlighting nodes role according to our modified Guimerà and Amaral classification.

We show the application to two case studies of biological relevance: the protein contact network of hemoglobin and the co-expression network of *Vitis Vinifera*. The color map superimposed to the Cytoscape network view shows a clear relation between the nodes role and their *P*,*z* description.

Materials and Methods

The plugin runs through the Cytoscape software [14] and allows the developers to use it as an independent Java library and to implement custom software. The installation of GIANT is possible directly via the Cytoscape plugin manager (menu Plugin > Manage Plugins, section Clustering, selecting the latest version of GIANT); alternatively, the plugin, along with the source code and video tutorials, is directly accessible for download from the GIANT official website http://www.iasi.cnr.it/~dsantoni/ GIANT/giant.html. GIANT has been developed following the classical MVC (Model-View-Controller) pattern. Figure 1 shows the GIANT *UML* class diagram and the process execution when clustering analysis is launched. The *Main* class provides the integration with the Cytoscape environment and drives the plugin user interface (*GUI*) (GIANT class implements the generic interface *Application*). Each *GUI* event, provided by the plugin, connects to a controller that maps it to a specific action. All classes that represent an action extend the abstract class *Action* (and all its methods). Figure 1 reports the action classes, corresponding to the clustering algorithms in the plugin. Each clustering action class starts the related algorithm. The clustering algorithms are developed in the *JavaML* library included in GIANT: the library is written in Java and is available from www.java-ml.sourceforge. net/under the GNU GPL license. The library implements a collection of machine learning and data mining algorithms, readily usable and easily extensible *API* for both software developers and research scientists. The algorithms strictly follow their respective interfaces, that are user-friendly and simple.

GIANT has been accepted by the Cytoscape community and is presently available for the download on the official Cytoscape APP Store http://apps.cytoscape.org/apps/giant. The plugin was successfully tested on the 2.8 and 3 releases of Cytoscape and it

was tested on Windows, Linux and OS X operating systems (in 5 or higher version of the Java Runtime Environment).

2.1 Clustering algorithms

The plugin implements three clustering algorithms: spectral Meila-Shi [15], MCL [16] and k-means [17]. It is worth noting the cartography is totally independent from clustering algorithm: the user can upload an already determined partition.

2.1.1 Spectral clustering algorithm. The spectral clustering algorithm takes as input the unweighted adjacency matrix of the network and the number *k* of clusters. Graph nodes are partitioned according to the components of the first *k* eigenvectors.

The first step is to compute the Laplacian matrix *L* depending on the unweighted adjacency matrix *A*:

$$L = D - A$$

D is the diagonal degree matrix, whose generic element D_{ii} is the i-th node degree. The algorithm applies either to the unnormalized or the normalized Laplacian matrix.

Once the eigenvectors $u_1, u_2, ..., u_n$ of the Laplacian matrix *L* are computed, a matrix $U \in \mathbf{R}^{n \times k}$ is built, whose i^{th} column corresponds to the ith eigenvector. The rows of matrix *U* correspond to nodes, partitioned into clusters according to their coordinates in matrix *U* by means of the k-means algorithm (see next subsection).

2.1.2 k-means algorithm. k-means is an unsupervised learning and partitioning clustering algorithm. The algorithm aims at minimizing the objective function Sum of the Squared Error (SSE), i.e. the sum of the squared distances of each node from the closest cluster centroid:

$$SSE = \sum_{i=1}^{k} \sum_{x \in C_i} dist(c_i, x)^2$$

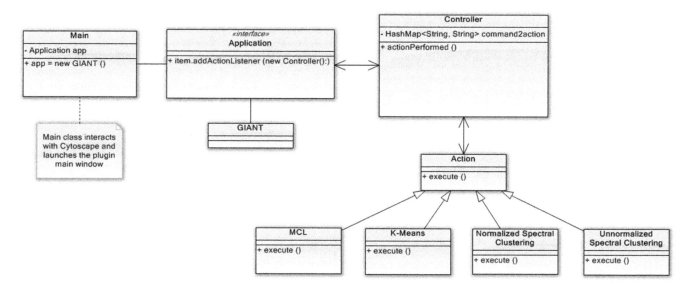

Figure 1. GIANT classes flow chart. Action classes are shown for the clustering algorithms implemented in the plugin: spectral clustering, MCL and k-means. Spectral clustering can be run in two mode, normalised and unnormalized. Each clustering action class starts the related algorithm in a new thread to maximize the performance.?

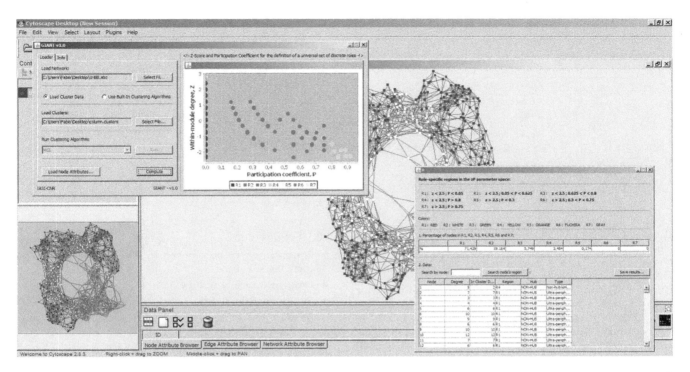

Figure 2. Screenshot of GIANT plugin. GIANT outcome to the hemoglobin (PDB code 1HBB) protein contact network application: the Guimerà-Amaral cartography, the protein contact network and the output table are reported. The nodes color corresponds to their role in the cartography (see Table 1).

where k is the number of the clusters, C_i is the ith cluster, x is an object (*i.e.* a point in the ith cluster), *dist* is the standard Euclidean (L2) distance between two objects in a Euclidean space and c_i is the centroid of the ith cluster. It is easy to demonstrate the best centroid (minimum cluster's SSE) is the cluster center of mass:

$$c_i = \frac{1}{m_i} \sum_{x \in C_i} x_i$$

m_i being the number of nodes in the ith cluster. The abscissa of the elbow in the SSE vs. k plot represents the optimal number of clusters. In GIANT, k-means acts on distances between nodes adopting as metrics the shortest paths and the Hamming distances computed on the adjacency matrix.

2.1.3 Markov Cluster algorithm. The MCL algorithm is a fast and scalable unsupervised cluster algorithm for networks based on simulation of (stochastic) flow in graphs. The algorithm simulates a flow on the graph to compute next powers of the associated adjacency matrix. At each iteration, an inflation step is applied to enhance the contrast between regions of strong and weak flow in the graph. The process converges towards a partition of the graph, with a set of high-flow regions (the clusters), parted by boundaries with no flow. The value of the inflation parameter strongly influences the number of clusters.

2.2 Node classification

Once the modules (clusters) are identified, the intra and inter-module connectivities are represented respectively by:

• the within-module z-score [18]

$$z_i = \frac{k_i^{in} - \overline{k}}{\sigma}$$

where k_i^{in} is the the number of links of node i with nodes in its own module, C_i, $\overline{k}$ and $\sigma_{C_i}^{in}$ are, respectively, the average value and the standard deviation of the overall degree distribution;

• the participation coefficient (modified with respect to its original definition [18]) describes the attitude of the node to connect to nodes in modules other than theirs:

$$P_i = 1 - \left(\frac{k_i^{in}}{k_i}\right)^2$$

k_i being the total degree of node i.

We adopted a modified version of Guimerà and Amaral participation coefficient P [18], that has helped us to identify nodes in the R4 region of the Guimerà-Amaral cartography (work in progress) not detectable by the original algorithm. R4 region collects nodes with fewer than 35% of their links within their own module, *i.e.*, with a strong inter-cluster connectivity character ($P \geq 0.75$).

The original Guimerà and Amaral definition of P [18] approaches to an upper threshold corresponding to node links uniformly distributed among modules (*i.e.*, $P_{max} = 1 - 1/N$, where N is the number of modules). Thus, for instance, when we part the hemoglobin contact network into 4 modules, 0.75 is the maximum value for P, corresponding to the lower bound of the R4 region. Therefore, if we had used the original definition of P, we could not

Table 1. Guimerà - Amaral cartography: nodes role.

	Regions	Within-module z-score	Participation coefficient
module non-hubs	R1: Ultra-peripheral node	$z < 2.5$	$P < 0.05$
	R2: Peripheral node	$z < 2.5$	$0.05 < P < 0.625$
	R3: Non-hub connectors	$z < 2.5$	$0.625 < P < 0.8$
	R4: Non-hub kinless nodes	$z < 2.5$	$P > 0.8$
module hubs	R5: Provincial hubs	$z > 2.5$	$P < 0.3$
	R6: Connector hubs	$z > 2.5$	$0.3 < P < 0.75$
	R7: Kinless hubs	$z > 2.5$	$P > 0.75$

highlight the R4 nodes corresponding to the sub-units contacts, which in turn have a high functional relevance in the protein structure (connector nodes colored in black in Figure 2C).

According to P,z values, the plugin reports the node classification (see Table 1): 'module hubs' ($z \geq 2.5$, *i.e.* hubs within their own module), 'module non hubs' ($z < 2.5$, *i.e.* node that are not hubs within their module but that can still have a hub role in the whole network). According to the participation coefficient P, the non-hubs nodes can be divided into four regions (R1, R2, R3, R4) and the hubs nodes into three regions (R5, R6, R7).

2.3 User's Guide

As a first step, the user must upload the network in.abc format: this file format requires two fields separated by a white space on each line. The first and second fields are labels specifying source and destination node, respectively. The file can contain an optional third column representing the nodes interaction. A file containing clusters data can be loaded, if available. The file to upload must be .idx type, containing two columns with the ID of the nodes and the relative cluster indication; alternately, the user can use the built-in clustering algorithms. K-means algorithm is based on two different metrics: shortest paths and Hamming distances, computed on the nodes adjacency vectors. Spectral clustering relies on two running modes: normalized and un-normalized.

Once the network is uploaded, the user must check the *Use Built-in Clustering Algorithm* option and choose the *kMeans* algorithm. In the *KMEANS INITIALIZER* left panel, there are two options: in the *Cluster Validation* section, once defined the minimum *k_min* and the maximum *k_max* number of clusters, within this range the Sum Square Error as a function of k (number of clusters) is displayed. The second option is that the user can directly decide the number of clusters k. The user can also upload, if any, a file with node attributes as required by Cytoscape environment for network visualization.

Once data are loaded and clusters made available, the Guimerà-Amaral cartography is computed (see previous section). Results are provided as a table containing a summary of P,Z values associated to each node as well as node degree, the region R (according to Guimerà-Amaral cartography) and all other features uploaded as node attributes. Practical video tutorials can be downloaded from the web site http://www.iasi.cnr.it/~dsantoni/ GIANT/giant.html. GIANT is downloadable directly from Cytoscape APP store http://apps.cytoscape.org/apps/giant or from its official web site: http://www.iasi.cnr.it/~dsantoni/ GIANT/giant.html, where a video tutorial is also available.

2.3.1 Requirements.

- **Operating system(s)**: tested on Windows, Linux and OSx operating systems
- **Programming language**: Java
- **Other requirements**: Java Runtime Environment 5.0 or higher

Results and Discussion

We applied the GIANT plugin to two different scenarios of biological relevance: the contact network of hemoglobin structure and the co-expression network of *Vitis Vinifera*. These two different networks allow to study the relation between topology and function at two different levels of biological organization: structural and gene expression regulation level.

3.1 Scenario 1: Hemoglobin structure

Hemoglobin occupies a unique niche in the proteome: this multimeric protein drives the delicate balance of oxygen and carbon monoxide exchanges between blood and tissues. Hemoglobin, at odds with other molecular systems, essentially works by alone with any relevant interaction with other biomolecular systems. This implies we can fully trace back its functional properties from its structure, as witnessed by the large amount of literature dealing with the link between hemoglobin mutations and functional properties [19].

Human hemoglobin structure (PDB code 1HBB) is made up of four sub-units (see Figure 3A), whose mutual spatial relations are at the basis of the so-called allosteric effect, due to the shift between two different configurations (T and R) at the basis of the cooperative binding and release of oxygen and carbon dioxide [20]. The identification of a peculiar topological role of the residues that connect the four sub-units can be considered a strong proof of the relevance of the GIANT approach.

Figure 2 reports the GIANT output for the analysis of the hemoglobin contact network. We transformed the protein structure data (spatial position of atoms) into a contact networks by putting an edge between residues (the nodes of the network) whose spatial distance of the corresponding α - carbons is comprised within 4 and 8 A, thus including only non-covalent intramolecular interactions [9,12,21].

Spectral clustering parts the contact network into four clusters, roughly corresponding to protein sub-units. Relying on this partition GIANT builds the modified Guimerà-Amaral cartography (see Figure 3B) and gives a pictorial representation of the network (see Figure 3C). Node colors correspond to their role in the modified Guimerà-Amaral cartography. R4 nodes ($P \geq 0.8$,

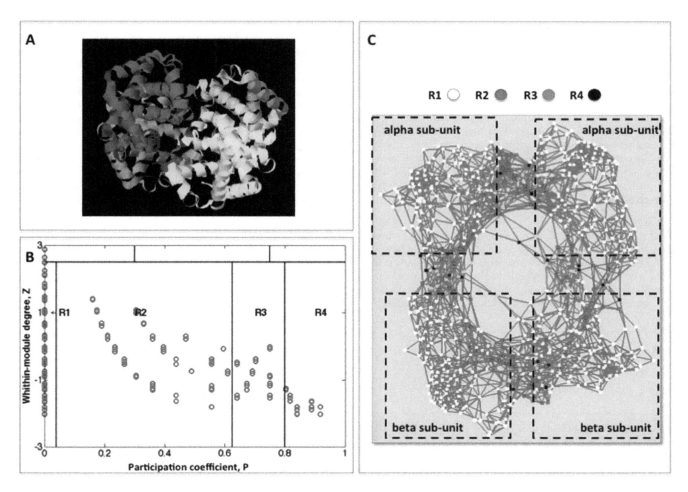

Figure 3. Guimerà-Amaral cartography for hemoglobin. A) X-ray-resolved molecular structure of hemoglobin protein (source Protein Data Bank PDB). B) Guimerà-Amaral cartography for hemoglobin; clusters are computed by spectral clustering algorithm. C) Hemoglobin protein contact network. The nodes colors correspond to their Guimerà-Amaral role.

black colored) correspond to residues placed at the boundaries of the hemoglobin sub-units. White nodes correspond to region R1 ($P \sim 0$, ultra-peripheral nodes). These nodes communicate only within their own module, remaining confined within the core of the hemoglobin sub-units. The unbiased identification of connector nodes by the algorithm is a proof-of-concept of the relation between structure topology and protein function. Spectral clustering of protein contact network produces characteristic P,z diagrams, ("dentist's chair", due to their shape [9]); this shape has been tested to be strongly invariant across a 1420 protein molecules dataset [9]: the invariance of the protein cartography suggests the chance to extend the observed topology-function relation of hemoglobin to other protein systems. 4A). Notice that the quasi-parallel lines of the graph do not correspond to clusters and still defy a simple explanation.

3.2 Scenario 2: Gene co-expression network in *Vitis vinifera*

Fruit ripening processes involve an highly coordinated set of events at both macroscopic and molecular levels. In order to check the crucial steps in ripening, the genome-wide gene co-expression could give some important hints. The shift between different development patterns is mediated by specific genes, namely transcription factors [22], able to activate (inactivate) different development modules (clusters of co-expression genes).

We make the hypothesis that a similar model applies to *Vitis vinifera* ripening: genes co-expressed across different modules could be responsible for the activation of different plant development stages.

The gene expression dataset used to build the co-expression network comes from the Gene Expression Omnibus under the series entry GSE36128 [23]. It consists of 29550 genes of *Vitis vinifera* whose expression value has been measured using microarrays from 54 samples taken from different tissues and stages. Two samples refer to leaves senescence and to pollen, while the other 52 samples can be divided into two groups: 25 samples of red/mature/woody organs and 27 samples of green/vegetative organs.

In the plant co-expression network, a link occurs if the absolute value of the correlation between the gene expression profiles is greater than 0.8; this threshold minimizes the number of connected components for both green and red tissues.

We built two co-expression networks, one for the green tissues and one for the red tissues (see Figure 4C): the cartography of these networks resembles the 'dentist's chair' we described above for hemoglobin contact network. To test the nature of the shape invariance of the P,z plane, we compared the co-expression networks with two simulated architectures corresponding to a random (Erdos-Renyi [24] Figure 4A) and a scale-free (Baràbasi) network with 1000 nodes and two clusters [25] (see Figure 4B).

In both scale-free Barabàsi and the *Vitis Vinifera* co-expression networks, we found again the characteristic dentist's chair in the P,z plane but not for random network. The strong invariance of the P,z portraits is extremely intriguing, given it suggests the existence of still hidden mesoscopic principles of scale-free networks.

The R4 region of co-expression network for red tissues (ripened fruit) is enriched in transcription factors for the post-harvest development stage. Given the green tissues do not partecipate into fruit ripening and are made up of only one developmental stage, they do not show any relevant enrichment in transcription factors.

Conclusions

It is noteworthy that a purely topological description of nodes, by the agency of the intermediate mesoscopic layer through modules identification, allows for the elucidation of the functional role of the biological network elements. This is particularly evident in the case of hemoglobin molecule where the network description exactly matched the structural role of the corresponding amino acid residues in terms of between- within- subunits location.

In the case of co-expression network, the topology function relationship is still hypothetical but suggests important lines of experimentation The Cytoscape plugin GIANT provides a powerful tool for an accurate analysis of complex networks, offering a multiscale perspective from nodes local properties to general network architecture. This integration was possibile thanks to the quantitative description of the network at a mesoscopic (clustering) level, allowing a prompt view of nodes role. The plugin interface is simple and user-friendly and a practical video tutorials can be downloaded from the web site http://www.iasi.cnr.it/~dsantoni/GIANT/giant.html. Moreover, Cytoscape community accepted GIANT plugin, which is actually available for the download on the official Cytoscape APP Store. The modular architecture of the plugin allows to expand the system so to include other clustering algorithms.

Author Contributions

Conceived and designed the experiments: PP DS. Performed the experiments: FC. Analyzed the data: PP DS LDP AG. Contributed reagents/materials/analysis tools: LDP AG. Wrote the paper: FC PP DS LDP AG.

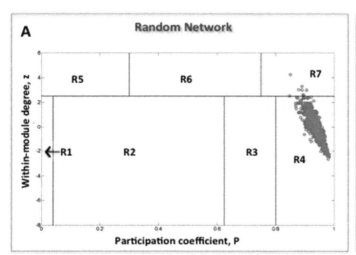
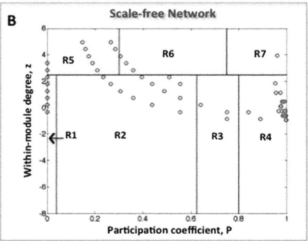
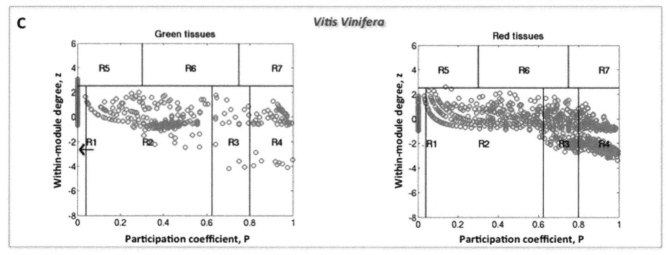

Figure 4. Guimerà-Amaral cartography. Guimerà-Amaral cartography for different networks: A) the random network of Erdos-Renyi with 1000 nodes and 50.000 edges [24]; B) the scale-free network of Barabàsi [25] with 1000 nodes and two clusters; C) the *Vitis Vinifera* co-expression network for vegetative (left) and woody organs (right).

References

1. Han J, Bertin N, Hao T, Goldberg DS, Berriz GF, et al. (2004) Evidence for dynamically organized modularity in the yeast protein protein interaction network. Nature 430: 88–93.
2. Jeong H, Mason S, Barabàsi A, Oltvai Z (2001) Lethality and centrality in protein networks. Nature 411: 41–42.
3. Oliva G, Di Paola L, Giuliani A, Pascucci F, Setola R (2013) Assessing protein resilience via a complex network approach. In: Network Science Workshop (NSW), 2013 IEEE 2nd. IEEE, pp. 131–137.
4. Csermely P, Korcsmáros T, Kiss H, London G, Nussinov R (2013) Structure and dynamics of molecular networks: a novel paradigm of drug discovery: a comprehensive review. Pharmacol Ther 138: 333–408.
5. Guimerà R, Amaral LAN (2005) Functional cartography of complex metabolic networks. Nature 433: 895–900.
6. Bassett D, Meyer-Lindenberg A, Achard S, Duke T, Bullmore E (2006) Adaptive reconfiguration of fractal small-world human brain functional networks. Nat Rev Neurosci 103: 19518–19523.
7. Pessoa L (2008) On the relationship between emotion and cognition. Nat Rev Neurosci 9: 148–158.
8. Guimerà R, Mossa S, Turtschi A, Amaral L (2005) The worldwide air transportation network: Anomalous centrality, community structure, and cities' global roles. PNAS 102: 7794–7799.
9. Di Paola L, De Ruvo M, Paci P, Santoni D, Giuliani A (2013) Proteins contact networks: an emerging paradigm in chemistry. Chem Rev 113: 1598–1613.
10. De Ruvo M, Giuliani A, Paci P, Santoni D, Di Paola L (2012) Shedding light on protein-ligand binding by graph theory: The topological nature of allostery. Biophys Chem 165–166: 21–29.
11. Krishnan A, Zbilut JP, Tomita M, Giuliani A (2008) Proteins as networks: usefulness of graph theory in protein science. Curr Protein Pept Sc 9: 28–38.
12. Tasdighian S, Di Paola L, De Ruvo M, Paci P, Santoni D, et al. (2013) Modules identification in protein structures: the topological and geometrical solutions. J Chem Inf Model 54: 159–168.
13. Morris J, Apeltsin L, Newman A, Baumbach J, Wittkop T, et al. (2011) clusterMaker: a multi-algorithm clustering plugin for cytoscape. BMC Bioinformatics 12.
14. Shannon P, Markiel A, Ozier O, Baliga N, Wang J, et al. (2003) Cytoscape: a software environment for integra ted models of biomolecular interaction networks. Genome Res 13: 2498–2504.
15. Meila M, Shi J (2001) Learning segmentation by random walks. Neural Information Processing Systems 13: 873–879.
16. Dongen SV (1997) Graph Clustering by Flow Simulation. Ph.D. thesis, University of Utrecht, The Netherlands.
17. Jain A (2009) Data clustering: 50 years beyond k-means. Pattern Recogn Lett 31: 651–666.
18. Guimerà R, Sales-Pardo M, Amaral LAN (2006) Classes of complex networks defined by role-to-role connectivity profiles. Nat Phys 3: 63–69.
19. Hardison R, Chui D, Giardine B, Riemer C, Patrinos G, et al. (2002) HbVar: A relational database of human hemoglobin variants and thalassemia mutations at the globin gene server. Human mutation 19: 225–233.
20. Monod J, Wyman J, Changeux J (1965) On the nature of allosteric transitions: a plausible model. J Mol Biol 12: 88–118.
21. Paci P, Di Paola L, Santoni D, De Ruvo M, Giuliani A (2012) Structural and functional analysis of hemoglobin and serum albumin through protein long-range interaction networks. Curr Proteomics 9: 160–166.
22. Takahashi K, Yamanaka S (2006) Induction of pluripotent stem cells from mouse embryonic and adult fibroblast cultures by defined factors. Cell 126: 663–76.
23. Fasoli M, Santo SD, Zenoni S, Tornielli G, Farina L, et al. (2012) The grapevine expression atlas reveals a deep transcriptome shift driving the entire plant into a maturation program. The Plant Cell 24: 3489–3505.
24. Bollobas B (1985) Random Graphs. Cambridge Studies in Advanced Mathematics. New York: Academic Press.
25. Barabàsi A, Albert R (1999) Emergence of scaling in random networks. Science 286: 509.

13

Applying Pebble-Rotating Game to Enhance the Robustness of DHTs

LiYong Ren, XiaoWen Nie*, YuChi Dong

School of Computer Science & Engineering, University of Electronic Science and Technology of China, ChengDu, China

Abstract

Distributed hash tables (DHTs) are usually used in the open networking environment, where they are vulnerable to Sybil attacks. Pebble-Rotating Game (PRG) mixes the nodes of the honest and the adversarial randomly, and can resist the Sybil attack efficiently. However, the adversary may have some tricks to corrupt the rule of PRG. This paper proposes a set of mechanisms to make the rule of PRG be obliged to obey. A new joining node must ask the Certificate Authority (CA) for its signature and certificate, which records the complete process on how a node joins the network and obtains the legitimacy of the node. Then, to prevent the adversary from accumulating identifiers, any node can make use of the latest certificate to judge whether one identifier is expired with the help of the replacement property of RPG. This paper analyzes in details the number of expired certificates which are needed to store in every node, and gives asymptotic solution of this problem. The analysis and simulations show that the mean number of the certificates stored in each node are $O(\log^2 n)$, where n is the size of the network.

Editor: Tobias Preis, University of Warwick, United Kingdom

Funding: This work is not only sponsored by National Natural Science Foundation of China under Contract number 61073181, but also sponsored by CNGI of the Peoples Republic of China under Contract number CNGI-04-12-1D. The funders had no role in study design, data collection and analysis, decision to publish, or preparation of the manuscript.

Competing Interests: The authors have declared that no competing interests exist.

* E-mail: niexiaowen@uestc.edu.cn

Introduction

Due to its high scalability, DHT [1–4] has won wide attention. But for its actual deployment, scalability is just one aspect of concerns, and security is another problem that cannot be avoided.

The traditional security mainly focuses on such fields as information integrity, tamper-resistance, and nonrepudiation, while things may be a little different in DHT. Generally, the DHT algorithm itself has some redundancy, and random attacks on DHT will not cause great damage. However, if the adversary can gain a great quantity of IDs and use them to start so-called Sybil attack, the redundancy of DHT will not help. Douceur [5] argues that the fundamental issue of security in DHT is how to distinguish different entities. To achieve this, we should either ensure each node can be verified directly, or build a certification authority (CA) to confirm the identities of nodes. Because the method of directly verifying nodes has poor scalability, an explicit or an implicit CA is often used in DHT. For example, the node ID is the hash value of the IP address in CFS [6], while EMBASSY [7] takes advantage of the encryption key of hardware.

Sybil attack poses a dilemma for the design of DHT: either preserving the openness to allow newcomers can easily join the network, or raising the entry barrier to enhance the security of system. Does there exist a tradeoff between the two choices? In this paper, we argue that Pebble-Rotating Game [8] or Cuckoo rule [9] proposed by Scheideler and Awerbuch may be helpful.

PRG is such a game: place black and white pebbles in a ring, white pebble for honest nodes, black pebble for attacking nodes. Assuming that all black pebbles are controlled by the adversary, she has two choices: either inserting a new black pebble into the

ring, or removing any black pebble out of the ring. In this game, to insert a pebble into the ring, each participant must follow the *K-rotation* rules: in the first round, the participant randomly replaces a new pebble with an existing one. The replaced pebble then randomly replaces another one in the ring in the second round, …, until the Kth round, the pebble which is replaced in the previous round is randomly inserted into the ring.

Scheideler [8] proves that: in PRG, when $k=3$, if the adversary could control no more than $1/4$ of the total pebbles, then in any continuous sequence of $\Theta(\log n)$ pebbles, white pebbles will win a majority over the black with high probability. When the network size is very large, the premise of this conditional statement is easy to satisfy. But in the practical application of the PRG algorithm, the adversary may try every means to interrupt the *K-rotation* rules by placing the attacking node to the position as she wishes. So there must be some ways to confirm the *K-rotation* rules to be carried out. To solve this problem, we propose an explicit CA to authenticate the K-rotation process, which guarantees that ID can not be forged and the legality of a node can be verified without CA's participation. Furthermore, to prevent the adversary from accumulating IDs, we use recent certificates to judge whether an ID has expired or not.

Materials

Security needs to be considered at the beginning of the DHT algorithm's design. Castro [10] devides the security of DHT into four areas: security for allocation of node ID, security for maintaining the routing table, security for message forwarding, and security for data. Among them, security for allocation of node

ID is the foundation of others. To protect the security of DHT, Castro suggests that the node should pay for its ID or bind the ID to the identity in the real world, but this may limit the applications of DHT.

Sybil attack was first defined by Douceur [5]. As Douceur argues, if we cannot distinguish the identity of a remote node through an explicit or implicit CA, a large part of P2P system will be mastered by the adversary. Furthermore, for a system which relies on an implicit CA, we must be soberly aware how much security such an implicit CA can provide. For example, in IPv6 network, the adversary can easily aquire a lot of addresses, so an implicit CA which is bound to the IPv6 address can not provide sufficient security.

Yu et al. [11] proposes an algorithm called SybilGuard which makes use of the in-and-out degree of social relationship in the real world to distinguish the identity of a remote user. SybilGuard believes there exists a small cut between honest and adversary nodes, and Random-Walk algorithm is used to find this cut. SybilGuard algorithm is suitable for unstructured P2P networks.

In DHT algorithm, before joining DHT network, a node must know an online node in advance and then enter the network with its introduction. According to this bootstrap relations, nodes in the network make up a bootstrap tree. The closer is a node to the root, the higher probability is it to be honest. Danezis [12] takes advantage of this phenomenon and presents some methods to resist Sybil attack, which is more suitable to the hierarchical DHT network.

The consideration of Bazi et al. [13] is more fundamental. He studies how to distinguish the remote entities with network measurement. The lighthouses measure the remote entities, and there exists a lower limit in the measurement values according to the "triangle inequality". Unfortunately this algorithm is still under development.

Rowaihy [14] tries to build a hierarchical adaptive node management system in the DHT network. In this system, if one leaf node wants to be prompted as a management node, i.e., the internal node of the tree, it must answer puzzles of all its child nodes. These puzzles will occupy a lot of computing resources, which increases the difficulty for the adversary to control other nodes. But at the same time it will waste a lot of computing resources.

Fireflies [15] is an interesting design. In Fireflies, network topology is made up with $2t+1$ Chord rings, and each physical node joins $2t+1$ networks simultaneously. The $2t+1$ precedings of one node make up the arbitor set of this node, and accusation/rebuttal mechanism is introduced to regulate the behaviors of nodes.

Condie [16] presents a solution similar to PRG and Cuckoo rules. The algorithm adopts a random number generating server as CA, which generates random numbers periodically. The ID of every node is the function of a random number. After every period of time, node IDs will change. Therefore, the locations of the nodes randomly change. Since the node ID can not be predicted from the random number, the adversary can neither pre-select an ID nor accumulate IDs, so the honest and attacking nodes are uniformly mixed. The disadvantage of this solution is that it's not suitable in storage circumstance because the network is changed frequently.

Similar to PRG [8], Cuckoo [9] is designed with replacement operation. When a new node is joining, it will replace all nodes within the distance of $c \log n/n$. The replaced nodes then will be re-inserted into the network. Awerbuch and Scheideler have proved that under Cuckoo rules, the honest and the attacking nodes are evenly mixed with high probability. Compared to PRG,

Cuckoo rules also have the advantage of load balancing. We argue that the load balancing of DHT and Sybil attacks are two orthogonal issues, and other methods can be used to compensate the load balancing in PRG.

Based on PRG, Fiat [17] has imported the Byzantine protocol to handle the cheating of the adversary. Fiat can not only solve Sybil attack, but also is able to handle routing security and data security issues. However, the cost of this proposal is expensive. If it may be tolerable to afford the cost when nodes join the network, it is not affordable for every message to be verified by the arbitor set.

Similar to the design of Fiat, King [18] proposes a security algorithm based on Byzantine protocol and leader selection protocol. However, the cost limits its application.

Methods

Without loss of generality, we choose Chord [1] as the DHT model in this paper, and apply PRG on it.

ID generating scheme

To defend the Sybil attack, the first problem to handle is to provide a secure ID generation scheme. If the adversary is able to select any desired ID, then she can put the attacking node to the position as she wishes. So we must deprive her ability to select position in address space, or limit the address space from which she can select. The PRG algorithm makes all nodes to be mixed randomly, which eventually limits the space the adversary can select.

A secure ID generation scheme has several meanings. Firstly, the ID can not be forged. This is easy to understand. If the adversary can forge ID, which means she is able to arbitrarily select a random position, it will undermine the foundation of DHT security. Secondly, the ID should be verifiable, and it is actually another aspect of the former. For one node, how can we determine whether its ID is forged? We argue that the ID should be self-verified. Finally, the ID applied by the node should be constantly changing. If one node always receives the same ID, then the adversary can collect a lot of IDs by different identities, and choose one of them to put the attacking node to the position which she prefers. For example, the adversary can use different IPv6 addresses to register a lot of IDs, then selects a preferred position, which is called adaptive joining attack [9]. So we should restrict the adversary to select an ID in a constantly changing set.

Our ID generation scheme is to make use of an explicit CA. Assuming that every node has a pair of keys K^+ and K^-, K^+ represents the public key, and K^- represents the private key. We define the cryptographic operation as $E[x,k]$, in which the plaintext x is encrypted into ciphertext by the key k. When a node p joins the network, it must apply a signature from the CA u. The signature is defined as $sig(p) = E[K^+\|T, K^-(u)]$, where K^+ is the public key of p, T is a timestamp, $\|$ represents the string concatenation operator, and $K^-(u)$ is the private key of the CA u. The node ID is defined as the hash value of signature: $id(p) = hash(sig(p))$.

In this scheme, unless the private key of CA is intercepted, it is difficult to forge a node ID. All nodes can acquire $K^+(u)$, i.e., the public key of CA u, with some methods of out-of-band or Key exchange protocol(IKE). When a node p shows its signature, other nodes first use the public key $K^+(u)$ of CA to verify the signature and then use the hash function to calculate the node ID. Finally, since the signature contains a timestamp, it will make the current signature of one node different from the past. So the adversary can not predicate the change of signature and ID.

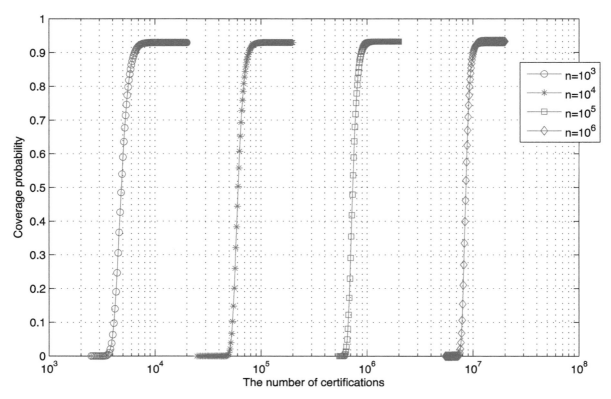

Figure 1. Under different network size, the probability changes with the increasing of λ. By formula (17), where $\tilde{\gamma} = -nW(-2\delta e^{-2\delta})$, $\delta = \lambda/n$, the Coverage Probability changes with the increasing of λ under different network size.

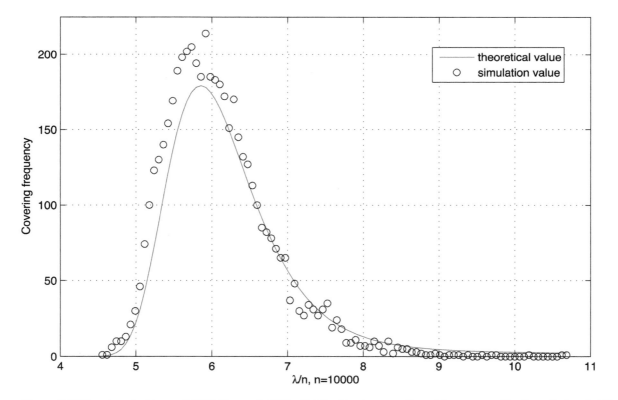

Figure 2. With network size $n = 10000$, **the probability distribution to cover the address space.** The theoretical probability distribution is calculated by formula (17) which is represented as a solid line, and the simulation result is pointed by little circles.

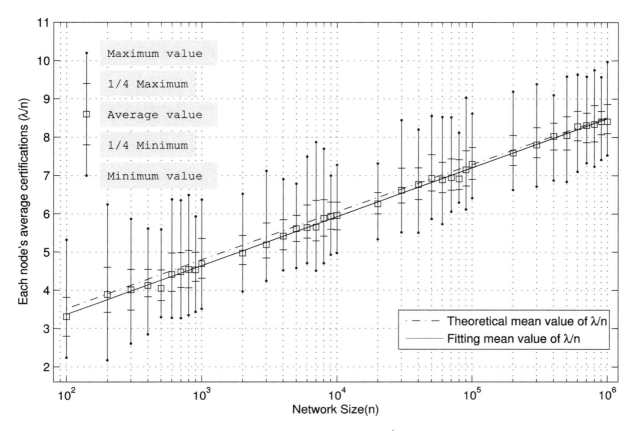

Figure 3. In different network size, the average number of certifications $\frac{\lambda}{n}$ every node saved. The horizontal coordinate represents the network size, and the vertical coordinate is the average number of certifications saved on every node (λ/n). For each network size n, the mean value, 1/4 maximum value, and 1/4 minimum value of 100 rounds tests are calculated.

K-rotation joining algorithm

Based on secure ID generating scheme, we will apply the PRG algorithm in this subsection. The key to applying PRG is to enforce the K-rotation(Unless otherwise noted, we always assume $K = 3$ in this paper) rules. Byzantine protocol can handle it well, but due to its cost, we propose to use an explicit CA to carry out the K-rotation rules. When a node joins, CA not only provides the signature to the node but also grants a certificate to its K-rotation joining process. The certification records a complete K-rotation process. Only the signature and certification are legal, can the neighbors of the joining node accept it.

Assuming the process of K-rotation is as follows: in the first round, the new node a substitutes its direct successor b. In the second round, node b is granted to a new position b', and b' will replace its direct successor c. In the third round, the node c is granted to a new position c', and directly inserted into the new position c'. The certification of the former K-rotation is represented as below:

$$cert = E[sig(a)\|sig(b)\|sig(b')\|sig(c)\|sig(c')\|T, K^-(u)] \quad (1)$$

where $sig(a)$ is the signature of a, $sig(b)$ is the old signature of node b, $sig(b')$ is the new signature of node b, and T is the timestamp when the certification is created. Meanwhile, we define the neighbour of node in address space as $[p - c\ln n, p + c\ln n]$, where n represents the total number of online nodes. With this preparation, we describe the K-rotation joining algorithm as follows:

Algorithm 1 the K-rotation Joining Algorithm.

Let a be a new node, u be CA.

1: a swaps public key with u, and requests to join the network;

2: u calculates the signature and ID of a, then finds the direct successor of a;

3: u swaps public key with b, and calculates the new signature of b and new ID number b';

4: u finds the direct successor of b';

5: u swaps public key with c, calculates the new signature of c and the ID number c' and the K-rotation Joining Replacement certification;

6: u sends new signature and certification to a, b and c;

We assume that the communication between nodes firstly needs to exchange their public keys through IKE. The hash function is used to digest the content of subsequent messages, and the digest encrypted by the private key is pegging back in messages.

Algorithm 0 follows the K-rotation rule. After the Algorithm 0, the nodes (a, b, c) gain new signatures and certifications. Neither old positions nor new positions of the nodes a,b,c can be predicted.

In the step 3 and 5 of algorithm 0, if the node b or c refuses to interact with the CA, i.e. u, CA will regard b or c as offline node, and let the next successor be the direct successor. With the help of the ID validation algorithm discussed later, the refusing nodes will be treated as illegal, and the remaining nodes will deport the refusing node from the network.

The steps which are vulnerable to be attacked are step 2 and 4, in which CA may probably not find the proper successor. To prevent this, CA can continuously ask the neighbors near a or b to verify the statements about successor. If CA finds some node lies, it can publish a new certificate to kick out the lying node.

ID Validating Algorithm

After running Algorithm 0, the new joining node and replaced nodes gain new signatures and certifications. By now these nodes do not really appear in the network topology. Only after the Stabilize Protocol of Chord is run, can other nodes in the network set up connections with them.

Although the adversary can not forge signature and ID, she may still accumulate a lot of signatures and certifications with just one attacking node from the time being. Most of these accumulated IDs have been replaced in K-rotation. If the adversary uses these replaced IDs to join the network through the stabilize protocol, she can violate the K-rotation rules. So we must find a method to patch this hole.

If the neighbour nodes save all previous certifications, when the attacking node tries to join the network again by using the replaced ID, the neighbour nodes then can see through the adversary's attempts after looking up saved certifications, and patch this hole. But it is unrealistic to completely save all old certifications.Do there other ways exist, which can significantly reduce the number of certification needed to save?

Notice that in algorithm 0, the node replaced by node a is its direct successor b, so there are no online nodes existing in range $(a,b]$. Similarly, there are no online nodes existing in range $(b',c]$. $(a,b]$ and $(b',c]$ are called as replacement intervals in this paper. When the adversary wants to let a node $e \in (a,b]$ join the network, then the node a and its neighbour nodes can use a's saved certification to deduce whether e is an expired ID and refuse the joining request of e.

Based on this idea, in this paper, neighbour nodes save recent certifications to verify whether an ID is expired. The next problem is how many certifications need to be saved in the neighbour nodes? If the replacement intervals of recent certifications can completely cover the neighbour area $[p-c\ln n, p+c\ln n]$, then the older certifications are not necessary to be saved. Thus the minimum number of recent certifications saved by neighbour is to cover the complete neighbour range.

On each node, a database S is set up to save all recent certifications within neighbour range, and it is required that the replacement intervals of the recent certifications can completely cover the neighbour range. The algorithm 0 is running on nodes to verify whether an ID is expired.

Algorithm 2 ID Validation algorithm.
Let S be the certification database, id be the node needed to be verified, $cert$ is the certification of id.

1: If id is not in the neighbour range, return illegal;
2: If S contains a certification newer than $cert$, and id is fallen into the replacement interval of the certification, then the id is illegal;
3: Otherwise, accept id as legal, and insert $cert$ into S.

In algorithm 0, first we need to check whether the id is within the neighbour range. If it is not, we mark it as an illegal id. If there is a certification in database S which covers this id, and the certification timestamp is newer than id, then mark this id illegal. The logical branch of step 3 in algorithm 0 contains: (1) $cert$ is newer than any other certifications in S; (2) id is not covered by S. The logical branch (1) corresponds to the new certification, while

(2) is probably because the certifications in database S can not completely cover the whole neighbour range.

Each node exchanges the database S periodically with its neighbours. If the timestamp of received certification is newer, the node inserts the certification into its local database S. If the replacement interval of the new inserted certification covers the replacement interval of the old ones, just delete the old one. Indeed, if one of the neighbour nodes is honest, the complete certification database can be inherited and propagated.

By using the ID validating algorithm with the Stabilize Protocol, we can verify whether a node is legal or not. We just neglect the request of illegal nodes, then the illegal nodes will be kicked out of the network.

Discussion

In algorithm 0, we use the recent certifications saved in database S to verify whether an ID is legal. It is required that the replacement intervals of all certifications should cover the neighbour range. Compared with the method of storing all certifications, the certification number in algorithm 0 is much less. However, if the number of certifications needed to save is still large, then the applying scheme of PRG proposed in this paper is still unpractical. In this section, we will analyze this problem.

We use another presentation to describe the considered problem: how many certifications are needed to completely cover the network address space? If the replacement interval is treated as segments, the problem is converted into a circle covering problem. Feller [19] has made an excellent summary on how to use equal-length segments to cover a circle. But not completely in accordance with what Feller describes, the length of covering segments is variable. Fortunately, there are many mathematicians trying to solve how to use random-length segments to cover a circle. Siegel [20] and Domb [21] use different methods to solve this problem. In this paper, we use Domb's method.

First we give Domb's conclusion. Assuming $P(l)$ is the probability for a circular arc with length l to be covered, we define the initial probability as $P_0(l)$, which represents the probability of that the starting point of a covering segment is fallen ahead one circle arc and the arc is covered. Meanwhile we introduce the intermediate function $v(l)$, which is defined as (7). And let the PDF of covering segments be $u(l)$. According to Domb [21], the probability that the circle is covered by random segments is:

$$P(l) = \int_0^l v(x)P(l-x)dx + P_0(l) \qquad (2)$$

Since $P(l)$ in (2) is a convolution, we then transform formula (2) by using Laplace's transformation and we get:

$$P(s) = \frac{P_0(s)}{1-V(s)} \qquad (3)$$

In the following, we will apply formula(2) and formula(3) to solve our problem. First we introduce two lemmas. Limited to the length of paragraph, we omit the proof of them.

Two Lemmas

In a unit circle whose circumference length is 1, we randomly insert α nodes. The probability of the number of nodes that appears on one arc and the interval between nodes obey the following distributions:

lemma 1 *If nodes randomly select ID in address space, then the node interval obeys negative exponential distribution, $P(l) = 1 - e^{-\alpha l}$.*

lemma 2 *If nodes randomly select ID in address space, then the number of nodes appearing in an arc obeys the Poisson distribution, $P(k) = \frac{(\alpha l)^k}{k!} e^{-\alpha l}$.*

According to lemma 1, the length of the replacement interval is a random variable, which obeys the negative exponential distribution with parameter n, where n is the network size. Thus the PDF and CDF of the replacement interval are respectively $u(l) = ne^{-nl}$ and $U(l) = 1 - e^{-nl}$. Let the number of total covering segments be λ, and the clockwise direction be positive. According to lemma 1, the starting location of every covering segment obeys the negative exponential distribution with parameter λ.

The Initial Distribution

By lemma 2, we get the initial distribution $P_0(l)$:

$$P_0(l) = \int_0^{1-l} e^{-\lambda(l+x)} \lambda dx \int_{l+x}^1 u(y)dy \qquad (4)$$

In formula(4), $e^{-\lambda(l+x)}$ represents that there are no starting points of covering segments in $(l+x)$, and λdx represents there is one starting point of covering segments appearing on the differential element dx, while $\int_{l+x}^1 u(y)dy$ represents all covering segments whose length exceeds $(l+x)$. Since the covering segments distribute in the interval $[0,1)$, the integral limit of x is from 0 to $(1-l)$. The formula (4) can be reduced as:

$$P_0(l) = \frac{\lambda}{\lambda+n} e^{-(\lambda+n)l} - e^{-(\lambda l+n)} + \frac{n}{\lambda+n} e^{-(\lambda+n)} \qquad (5)$$

According to formula(5), when $l \to \infty$, $P_0(l)$ converges to $\frac{n}{\lambda+n} e^{-(\lambda+n)}$. Using Laplace's transformation on $P_0(l)$ with $0 < l \le 1$, we get:

$$P_0(s) = \frac{\lambda(1 - e^{-(s+\lambda+n)})}{(s+\lambda+n)(\lambda+n)} - \frac{e^{-n} - e^{-(s+\lambda+n)}}{s+\lambda} \\ + \frac{n(e^{-(\lambda+n)} - e^{-(s+\lambda+n)})}{(\lambda+n)s} \qquad (6)$$

Intermediate Function

According to Domb [21], the intermediate function $v(l)$ is defined as:

$$v(l) = \lambda e^{-\lambda l}[1 - U(l)]e^{\lambda \int_0^l U(x)dx} \qquad (7)$$

Substitute it into the CDF $U(l)$ of covering segments:

$$v(l) = \lambda e^{-nl - \frac{\lambda}{n} + \frac{\lambda}{n}e^{-nl}}. \qquad (8)$$

Make Laplace's transformation on $v(l)$

$$V(s) = \int_0^\infty e^{-sl} \lambda e^{-nl - \frac{\lambda}{n} + \frac{\lambda}{n}e^{-nl}} dl = \lambda e^{-\frac{\lambda}{n}} \int_0^\infty e^{-(s+n)l} e^{\frac{\lambda}{n}e^{-nl}} dl \qquad (9)$$

According to formula (9), $V(s)$ exists. Since the solution of $1 - V(s) = 0$ is the pole of (3), and the position of pole can directly affect the time-domain properties, we must have detailed understanding of $V(s)$.

Limited to the length of this paper, we omit the detailed analysis on $V(s)$. After analysis, $1 - V(s) = 0$ only has solutions in the real axis. While $s \in R$, $V(s)$ is a monotone decreasing function. $V(0) = 1 - e^{-\frac{\lambda}{n}}$, $0 < V(0) < 1$; When $s \to \infty$, then $V(s) \to 0$; Thus the solution of $1 - V(s) = 0$ is on negative real axis. Assume the solution is $-\gamma$.

Covering Probability

Plugging the formula (6) and (9) into formula (3), we get:

$$P(s) = \frac{\frac{\lambda(1 - e^{-(s+\lambda+n)})}{(s+\lambda+n)(\lambda+n)} - \frac{e^{-n}(1 - e^{-(s+\lambda)})}{s+\lambda} + \frac{ne^{-(\lambda+n)}(1 - e^{-s})}{(\lambda+n)s}}{1 - \lambda e^{-\frac{\lambda}{n}} \int_0^\infty e^{-(s+n)l} e^{\frac{\lambda}{n}e^{-nl}} dl} \qquad (10)$$

In case of the complex form of formula(10), here we just consider its asymptotic solution. For a Laplace transformation, its pole position decides the time-domain transition process. In formula (10), there are four possible positions for pole: $-\lambda$, $-\lambda-n$, 0, $-\gamma$. Since n is the network size, λ is the number of covering segments, thus $\lambda > n$. In the formula (10), the coefficients of pole $-\lambda$ and 0 are both very little and these two poles can be neglected. Thus:

$$P(s) \approx \frac{\frac{\lambda(1 - e^{-(s+\lambda+n)})}{(s+\lambda+n)(\lambda+n)}}{1 - \lambda e^{-\frac{\lambda}{n}} \int_0^\infty e^{-(s+n)l} e^{\frac{\lambda}{n}e^{-nl}} dl} \qquad (11)$$

In order to further solute the asymptotic value of (11), using Domb's conclusion: when $l \gg 1/n$, where $1/n$ is the average value of covering segments, $V(s)$ is asymptotically equal to the intermediate function by using equal segments $1/n$ to cover the circle. This asymptotic intermediate function is [21]:

$$\widetilde{V}(s) = \frac{\lambda}{s+\lambda}(1 - e^{-\frac{s+\lambda}{n}}) \qquad (12)$$

When $s + \lambda e^{-\frac{s+\lambda}{n}} = 0$, where $s \in R$, let the solution be $\tilde{\gamma}$, where $\tilde{\gamma} = -nW(-\frac{\lambda}{n}e^{-\frac{\lambda}{n}})$, and $W(x) = xe^x$ is the Lambert-W function [22].

$$P(s) \approx \frac{\lambda(s+\lambda)(1 - e^{-(s+\lambda+n)})}{(\lambda+n)(s+\lambda+n)(s+\tilde{\gamma})} \qquad (13)$$

Expand the formula (13), and we get:

$$P(s) \approx \frac{\lambda(s+\lambda)}{(\lambda+n)(s+\lambda+n)(s+\widetilde{\gamma})} = \frac{\lambda}{\lambda+n}\frac{A}{s+\lambda+n}$$
$$+ \frac{B}{s+\widetilde{\gamma}}(1-e^{-(s+\lambda+n)}) \quad (14)$$

$$A = \frac{n}{\lambda+n-\widetilde{\gamma}}, B = \frac{\lambda-\widetilde{\gamma}}{\lambda+n-\widetilde{\gamma}}$$

Make Laplace Inversion Transformation on formula (14), and we get:

$$P(l) \approx \frac{\lambda}{\lambda+n}Ae^{-(\lambda+n)l}$$
$$+ Be^{-\widetilde{\gamma}l} - \frac{\lambda}{\lambda+n}e^{-(\lambda+n)}Ae^{-(\lambda+n)(l-1)} + Be^{-\widetilde{\gamma}(l-1)} \quad (15)$$

In the above formula, when $l\rightarrow 1$, all others items can be ignored. Thus:

$$P(l) \approx \frac{\lambda(\lambda-\widetilde{\gamma})}{(\lambda+n)(\lambda+n-\widetilde{\gamma})}e^{-l\widetilde{\gamma}} \quad (16)$$

Formula (17) is the probability when $l \gg 1/n$ and the circle with length 1 is covered. The problem this paper needs to consider is the probability when the unit circle is covered, thus $(l=1) \gg 1/n$. And in algorithm 0, every time when a new node joins the network, a certification will be generated, and each certification contains two replacement intervals, thus λ should be multiplied by 2. If let $\delta = \lambda/n$, we finally get:

$$P(1) \approx \frac{4\delta^2}{(2\delta+1)^2}e^{-\widetilde{\gamma}} \quad (17)$$

where $\widetilde{\gamma} = -nW(-2\delta e^{-2\delta})$

When the probability of formula(17) is 0.5, $4\delta^2 \approx (2\delta+1)^2$. Solving the formula $e^{-nW(-2\delta e^{-2\delta})} = 0.5$, then we get:

$$\delta \approx -\frac{1}{2}Re(W(\frac{0.6931}{n}e^{\frac{0.6931}{n}})) \quad (18)$$

where $Re()$ represents getting the real part, and the Lambert-W function gets the -1 side. Since $W(x) \approx \ln x - \ln\ln x$ [22], we get:

$$\delta \approx 0.1833 + 1.1513 * \lg n \quad (19)$$

Because every node needs to save the certifications of neighbours, according to the formular (19), we have the following theorem:

theorem 3 *In the scheme of this paper, the certification number saved on nodes asymptotically is $O(\log^2 n)$.*

By formula (17), when $n = 10^3, 10^4, 10^5, 10^6$, the probability with λ changes, as shown in Figure 1. In Figure 1, we can observe that 1) The λ/n value of every curve is not large. When $n = 10^6$, the

λ/n value is the largest, a little larger than 10; while λ/n represents the average number of certifications in every node. 2) In a network with size n, the probability to completely cover the address space increases to 0.9 in the narrow λ, which indicates that the capacity of the certification database S is changing in a narrow range. 3) The intervals of these four curves are almost the same in logarithmic coordinate, which indicates that with the network-size n increasing, the increasing amount of λ is almost proportion to $\lg n$. By (19), it is well explained.

With the above analysis, the average capacity of certification database S is not large. For a certain network size, S is changing in a very narrow range. Considering that every node should keep the certifications of neighbour nodes, the capacity of S is $O(\log^2 n)$.

Results

We use simulation tests to verify our analysis in this section. In the simulations, we select 32-bit unsigned number as the ID space, and use SHA1 algorithm to generate the random number. At the beginning of the simulation, first we generate n numbers of ID and let them join the network. After an experiment begins, we keep generating nodes and let them join the network, and we randomly choose an online node to make it leave the network, until all space is covered.

Some caution is needed to be taken here. At the time to select a random node to exit the network, we can not first generate a random ID and let the successor of the ID leave. The nodes chosen like this can not guarantee the uniform distribution [23].

From the results of 5000-time experiments, the range of λ/n is within $[4,11]$, and this range is not large, which indicates that in a network with $n = 10000$, the average number of certification (λ/n) to cover the address space is within range $[8c \ln n, 22c \ln n]$. The cost is acceptable.

The Distribution of λ/n

In this test, we try to verify whether the analysis on the probability distribution is correct. To do this, we count the frequency of the certifications λ to completely cover the whole address space. Select network size $n = 10000$, and take 5000 rounds tests and then collect the distribution condition of λ/n. The test result is shown in Figure 2. The horizontal cordinate is λ/n, and the vertical coordinate is frequency.

In Figure 2, the theoretical probability distribution is calculated by (17) which is represented as a solid line, and the simulation result is pointed by little circles. Observing the Figure 2, we can see that the simulation result and the theoretical result match well, which indicates that although the distribution function of λ/n is asymptotic, the asymptotic loss is little. So it is acceptable to make use of (17) to caculate the mean value $\bar{\Lambda}$, i.e., the capacity of the certification database.

The Number of Certifications in Different Network Size

In this subsection, we test the number of certifications to cover the whole address space in different network size. We use different network size to do the tests, from $n = 100$ to $n = 1000000$. For each network size, we take 100 times tests.

The test results are shown in Figure 3. The horizontal coordinate represents the network size, while the vertical coordinate is the average number of certifications saved on every node (λ/n). For each size n, we calculate the mean value, $1/4$ maximum value, and $1/4$ minimum value of 100 rounds tests.

Observing the Figure 3, with the increase of network size, the average number of certifications to save on each node is increasing too. And the average value of λ/n shows to be a linear growth under the logarithmic coordinate n. We fit the average curve of λ/n with the least squares.

$$\frac{\lambda}{n} = 1.2792 * \lg n + 0.8103 \qquad (20)$$

The linear fitting on λ/n is very close to the mean value. Compared (19) with (20), we can find that the difference between the coefficient of $\lg n$ is quite small. And in Figure 3, the theoretical mean curve calculated by (19) is very similar to the curve by (20).

Conclusions

In an open DHT network, it is difficult to defend the Sybil attack. The PRG algorithm requires that the number of nodes under the adversary's control can not exceed $1/4$ of totals. This condition can be easily satisfied when the DHT network size is very large. But how to carry out the K-rotation rules without being interrupted is a barrier to apply PRG.

Since the cost of the Byzantine algorithm is expensive, we propose to use an explicit CA to handle this problem. CA is used to send signatures and certifications to the joining nodes, which can guarantee that ID is verifiable and can not be forged. The certification records a complete K-rotation joining process, and it is the credential of nodes to enter the network. In order to prevent the adversary from using the expired IDs to join the network by Stabilize Protocol, we propose to make use of the replacement intervals of certifications to verify whether an ID is overdue. This ID validating algorithm requires that the saved certifications can completely cover the whole neighbour range, and the key problem is how many certifications are suitable. In this paper, we convert this key problem to covering a circle by random segments. We analyze the covering problem in details, and derive an asymptotic solution to it. The analysis and simulations show that the average number of certifications to be saved on each node is small, which is $O(\log^2 n)$, and indicates the scheme proposed in this paper is applicable.

Author Contributions

Conceived and designed the experiments: LR. Performed the experiments: YD. Analyzed the data: LR. Contributed reagents/materials/analysis tools: LR. Wrote the paper: XN.

References

1. Stoica I, Morris R, Liben-Nowell D, Karger D, Kaashoek M, et al. (2003) Chord: a scalable peerto-peer lookup protocol for internet applications. Networking, IEEE/ACM Transactions on 11: 17–32.
2. Rowstron A, Druschel P (2001) Pastry: Scalable, decentralized object location, and routing for large-scale peer-to-peer systems. In: Guerraoui R, editor, Middleware 2001, Springer Berlin Heidelberg, volume 2218 of *Lecture Notes in Computer Science*. 329–350.
3. Zhao B, Kubiatowicz J, Joseph A (2001) Tapestry: An infrastructure for fault-tolerant wide-area location and routing. Computer Science.
4. Ratnasamy S, Francis P, Handley M, Karp R, Shenker S (2001) A scalable content-addressable network. In: Proceedings of the 2001 conference on Applications, technologies, architectures, and protocols for computer communications. New York, NY, USA: ACM, SIGCOMM' 01, 161–172.
5. Douceur J (2002) The sybil attack. In: Druschel P, Kaashoek F, Rowstron A, editors, Peer-to-Peer Systems, Springer Berlin/Heidelberg, volume 2429 of *Lecture Notes in Computer Science*. 251–260.
6. Dabek F, Kaashoek MF, Karger D, Morris R, Stoica I (2001) Wide-area cooperative storage with cfs. In: Proceedings of the eighteenth ACM symposium on Operating systems principles. New York, NY, USA: ACM, SOSP '01, 202–215.
7. Lefebvre KR (2000) The added value of embassy in the digital world. Technical report, Wave Systems Corp.
8. Scheideler C (2005) How to spread adversarial nodes? rotate! In: Proceedings of the thirtyseventh annual ACM symposium on Theory of computing. New York, NY, USA: ACM, STOC '05, 704–713.
9. Awerbuch B, Scheideler C (2009) Towards a scalable and robust dht. Theory of Computing Systems 45: 234–260.
10. Castro M, Druschel P, Ganesh A, Rowstron A, Wallach DS (2002) Secure routing for structured peer-to-peer overlay networks. SIGOPS Oper Syst Rev 36: 299–314.
11. Yu H, Kaminsky M, Gibbons PB, Flaxman A (2006) Sybilguard: defending against sybil attacks via social networks. In: Proceedings of the 2006 conference on Applications, technologies, architectures, and protocols for computer communications. New York, NY, USA: ACM, SIGCOMM '06, 267–278.
12. Danezis G, Lesniewski-Laas C, Kaashoek M, Anderson R (2005) Sybil-resistant dht routing. In: di Vimercati S, Syverson P, Gollmann D, editors, Computer Security C ESORICS 2005, Springer Berlin/Heidelberg, volume 3679 of *Lecture Notes in Computer Science*. 305–318.
13. Bazzi R, Konjevod G (2007) On the establishment of distinct identities in overlay networks. Distributed Computing 19: 267–287.
14. Rowaihy H, Enck W, McDaniel P, La Porta T (2007) Limiting sybil attacks in structured p2p networks. In: INFOCOM 2007. 26th IEEE International Conference on Computer Communications. IEEE. 2596–2600.
15. Johansen H, Allavena A, van Renesse R (2006) Fireflies: scalable support for intrusion-tolerant network overlays. In: Proceedings of the 1st ACM SIGOPS/ EuroSys European Conference on Computer Systems 2006. New York, NY, USA: ACM, EuroSys' 06, 3–13.
16. Condie T, Kacholia V, Sankararaman S, Hellerstein J, Maniatis P (2006) Induced churn as shelter from routing-table poisoning. In: In Proc. 13th Annual Network and Distributed System Security Symposium (NDSS).
17. Fiat A, Saia J, Young M (2005) Making chord robust to byzantine attacks. In: Brodal G, Leonardi S, editors, Algorithms C ESA 2005, Springer Berlin/ Heidelberg, volume 3669 of *Lecture Notes in Computer Science*. 803–814.
18. King V, Saia J, Sanwalani V, Vee E (2006) Towards secure and scalable computation in peer-to-peer networks. In: Foundations of Computer Science, 2006. FOCS '06. 47th Annual IEEE Symposium on. 87–98.
19. Grubbs FE (1967) An introduction to probability theory and its applications. Technometrics 9: 342–342.
20. FSiegel A, Holst L (1982) Covering the circle with random arcs of random sizes. Journal of Applied Probability 19: 373–381.
21. Domb C (1989) Covering by random intervals and one-dimensional continuum percolation. Journal of Statistical Physics 55: 441–460.
22. Corless R, Gonnet G, Hare D, Jeffrey D, Knuth D (1996) On the lambertw function. Advances in Computational mathematics 5: 329–359.
23. King V, Lewis S, Saia J, Young M (2007) Choosing a random peer in chord. Algorithmica 49: 147–169.

14

Extracting the Globally and Locally Adaptive Backbone of Complex Networks

Xiaohang Zhang[1]*, Zecong Zhang[1], Han Zhao[1], Qi Wang[1], Ji Zhu[2]

1 School of Economics and Management, Beijing University of Posts and Telecommunications, Beijing, China, **2** Department of Statistics, University of Michigan, Ann Arbor, Michigan, United States of America

Abstract

A complex network is a useful tool for representing and analyzing complex systems, such as the world-wide web and transportation systems. However, the growing size of complex networks is becoming an obstacle to the understanding of the topological structure and their characteristics. In this study, a globally and locally adaptive network backbone (GLANB) extraction method is proposed. The GLANB method uses the involvement of links in shortest paths and a statistical hypothesis to evaluate the statistical importance of the links; then it extracts the backbone, based on the statistical importance, from the network by filtering the less important links and preserving the more important links; the result is an extracted subnetwork with fewer links and nodes. The GLANB determines the importance of the links by synthetically considering the topological structure, the weights of the links and the degrees of the nodes. The links that have a small weight but are important from the view of topological structure are not belittled. The GLANB method can be applied to all types of networks regardless of whether they are weighted or unweighted and regardless of whether they are directed or undirected. The experiments on four real networks show that the link importance distribution given by the GLANB method has a bimodal shape, which gives a robust classification of the links; moreover, the GLANB method tends to put the nodes that are identified as the core of the network by the k-shell algorithm into the backbone. This method can help us to understand the structure of the networks better, to determine what links are important for transferring information, and to express the network by a backbone easily.

Editor: Peter Csermely, Semmelweis University, Hungary

Funding: This work was partially supported by NSFC (Grant Nos: 71371034 and 71372194; www.nsfc.gov.cn), the National Basic Research Program of China (Grant No: 2012CB315805; www.973.gov.cn), the Program for NCET (Grant No: NCET-13-0687; www.1000plan.org/qrjh/channel/159), and the Youth Research and Innovation Program in Beijing University of Posts and Telecommunications (Grant No: 2012RC1006; www.bupt.edu.cn). The funders had no role in study design, data collection and analysis, decision to publish, or preparation of the manuscript.

Competing Interests: The authors have declared that no competing interests exist.

* E-mail: zhangXiaohang@bupt.edu.cn

Introduction

In recent years, complex networks have been investigated by scholars in many domains. The representation, analysis and modeling in complex network theory bring a new paradigm to research on some complex systems including the Internet, transportation systems, biological systems, and social systems [1]. One of the primary aims of complex network research is to reveal the structural characteristics of complex systems. Many emerging concepts, such as the small-world property [2], scale-free behavior [3], community structure [4], and fractality [5], form the basis of our understanding of complex network structure. Because the scales of networks are becoming larger, a more intuitive and efficient method is required to represent and analyze the complex networks. Reducing a large-scale network to an essential backbone can help to solve the conflicts between the large scale of the complex networks and the understanding of the network structure. The backbone of a network is a core component that is extracted by filtering redundant information from the network and preserving far fewer links and nodes from the original network.

The filtering methods for backbone extraction can be divided into two main categories: global methods and local methods. Some global methods use certain global measures to filter the links, such as the link betweenness-based method [6] and the link weight-based method [7]. These methods apply a global threshold on the weights or the betweenness of links in such a way that only those that exceed the threshold are preserved. These filters have been used in the study of functional networks that connect correlated human brain sites [8], food web resistance as a function of link magnitude [9], and mobile communications networks [7]. The link weight-based method, however, could neglect nodes that have a small strength (The strength of node i is defined as $s_i = \sum_{j \in \aleph_i} w_{ij}$, where w_{ij} is the weight of the link (i,j) and $\aleph_i$ is the set of neighbors of node i) because the introduction of a threshold induces a characteristics scale from the outside [10].

The link salience [11], another type of global method, defines the shortest-path tree $T(r)$ that summarizes the shortest paths from a reference node r to the remainder of the network and that is conveniently represented by a symmetric $N \times N$ matrix (N is the number of nodes in the network) that has the element $t_{ij}(r) = 1$ if the link (i,j) is part of at least one of the shortest paths and $t_{ij}(r) = 0$ if it is not. The central idea of the approach is based on the notion of the average shortest-path tree that is defined as

$$S = \langle T \rangle = \frac{1}{N} \sum_{r=1}^{N} T(r). \text{ The element } 0 \leq s_{ij} \leq 1 \text{ of the matrix } S$$

quantifies the fraction of the shortest-path trees that the link (i,j) participates in and denotes the salience of the link (i,j). Link salience is a robust approach to classifying network elements because the distribution of s, the link salience, exhibits a characteristic bimodal shape on the unit interval in many kinds of networks [11]. Link salience, however, tends to give an higher evaluation to the links being adjacent to low-degree nodes that often lie in the periphery of networks than the links being adjacent to high-degree nodes. For example, in Figure 1, link (i,p) is a part of the shortest-path tree $T(r)$ for all of the reference nodes, i.e., $s_{ip} = 1$, because (i,p) is the only path that connects node p to the remainder of the network. Thus, link (i,p) is always a part of the backbone extracted by the link salience method even though the link is meaningful only for node p to transfer information between it and the rest of the nodes.

The local methods use local measures to determine which links must be filtered, such as the disparity filter method [10] and the locally adaptive network sparsification (LANS) [12]. The disparity filter method introduces the normalized weight that corresponds to link (i,j) of a certain node i of degree k_i and is defined as $p_{ij} = w_{ij}/s_i$, where w_{ij} is the weight of the link, s_i is the strength of node i. The normalized weight is assumed to be produced by a random assignment from a uniform distribution; thus, the probability density function of p_{ij} is assumed to be $f(x; k_i) = (k_i - 1)(1 - x)^{k_i - 2}$. The backbone will include those links whose normalized weights satisfy the relation

$$a_{ij} = 1 - (k_i - 1)\int_0^{p_{ij}} (1 - x)^{k_i - 2} dx < \alpha \qquad \text{or}$$

$$a_{ji} = 1 - (k_j - 1)\int_0^{p_{ji}} (1 - x)^{k_j - 2} dx < \alpha, \text{ where } \alpha \text{ is a specified}$$

significance level. Here a_{ij} and a_{ji} denote significance of the link's normalized weight not following the uniform distribution. The local heterogeneity (Section 3.1) of a link's weight is the premise of the disparity filtering method [10].

The LANS method, for each node i and for any of its neighbors j, considers the fraction of non-zero links whose weights are less than or equal to p_{ij}, $\hat{F}(p_{ij}) = \frac{1}{|\aleph_i|}\sum_{m \in \aleph_i} \text{IND}\{p_{im} \leq p_{ij}\}$, where IND$\{\}$ is the indicator function, $|\aleph_i|$ is the number of neighbors of node i, and p_{ij} is the normalized weight of link (i,j). If $1 - \hat{F}(p_{ij})$ is less than a predetermined significance level α, the link (i,j) is locally significant and is included in the backbone network.

Although both of the local methods do not belittle some links that have small weights from a global view by considering the importance of the links in each specific node, we argue that they could ignore some links that have small weights with respect to the topological aspect. They assume that, for a certain node, its neighboring links (the links that connect to the node) with larger weights are more important. In many cases, however, local and global topological structures of a link determine how important the link is. For example, in Figure 2, although the weight of link (i,j) is greater than that of link (i,k), link (i,k) is more important than link (i,j) for node i because (i,k) is the path through which i can reach most of the other nodes. From the prospective of information transfer, link (i,k) can help node i send or receive information more effectively than link (i,j) can, because deleting link (i,k) could cause more damage than deleting link (i,j) for the information transfer of the network.

Because the local and global methods have advantages and disadvantages, in this study we aim to design a backbone extraction method that accounts for both the global and local topological structure of the networks. And the importance of links is synthetically determined by the weights of the links, the degree of the nodes, and the topological structure. The results of experiments on some real networks show that our propose method has some good characteristics.

Materials and Methods

In this study, we are inspired by the ideas of link salience and the disparity filter to propose a globally and locally adaptive network backbone (GLANB) extraction method. First, for each specific node, we compute the involvement of its neighboring links, which measures the fraction of the short paths connecting the node to the remainder of the network, which the links participate in. Second, we use a null hypothesis to determine whether each link is statistically important based on its involvement.

2.1 Link Involvement

We first consider a weighted, undirected and connected network. We define the length of the link (i,j) as $d_{ij} = 1/w_{ij}$, with w_{ij} being the weight of link (i,j), which is consistent with definition of the link length in the link salience method. In most networks the link weights denote the connection strength between nodes. For example, in social networks the link weights often denote the communication frequency between people. Thus, we assume that the links with high weights are important in our case, and we invert the weights to compute the link length that measures the distance between nodes. In practice, the formula of measuring link

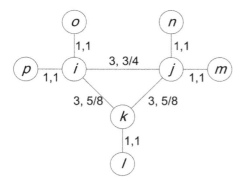

Figure 1. An undirected artificial network. The first number on the line is the value of the link weight, and the second number is the value of the link salience. Although the link (i,p) gets the largest value 1 of the link salience, it is only important for node p. The links (i,k) and (j,k) have the smallest value of the link salience, but they are in the core of the network.

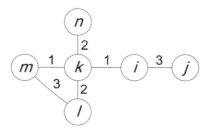

Figure 2. An undirected artificial network. The numbers on the lines denote the weights of the links. Although the weight of link (i,j) is greater than that of link (i,k), link (i,k) is more important for node i than link (i,j) is, because link (i,k) is the only path through which node i can reach the remainder of the network.

length should depend on the meaning of the weights. The length of a path that connects two terminal nodes (n_1, n_T) and that consists of $T-1$ links by a sequence of intermediate nodes n_i, and the link weight $w_{n_i n_{i+1}} > 0$ is defined as $l = \sum_{i=1}^{T-1} d_{n_i n_{i+1}}$. The shortest path minimizes the total distance l and can be interpreted as the most efficient route between its terminal nodes. The involvement I_{ij} of link (i,j) is defined as

$$I_{ij} = \frac{1}{N-1} \sum_{s=1, s \neq i}^{N} \frac{g_{is}^{(i,j)}}{g_{is}}, \qquad (1)$$

where N is the number of nodes in the network; $g_{is}^{(i,j)}$ is the number of shortest paths between node i and s that pass through the link (i,j); and g_{is} is the total number of shortest paths between node i and s. The involvement I_{ij} denotes how much the link (i,j) is involved in the most efficient connections between node i and the other nodes; thus, it can be a measure of the importance of link (i,j) for node i in the view of information transfer between node i and the remainder of the network. The larger the value of I_{ij} is, the more important link (i,j) is for node i. We can see that $\sum_{j \in \aleph_i} I_{ij} = 1$, where $\aleph_i$ is the set of neighbors of node i.

The involvement is different from the betweenness centrality. The betweenness of link (i,j) depends on the shortest paths between all pairs of nodes, but the involvement I_{ij} only depends on the shortest paths between the node i and the rest of the nodes since the definition of involvement I_{ij} is based on the idea what proportion of the rest of the nodes can connect the node i through the link (i,j). The involvement is also different from the salience because the involvement considers the multiple shortest paths between each pair of nodes, but the salience assumes that only one shortest path exists between a pair of nodes. That is why the GLANB can also be applied to unweighted networks that often have multiple shortest paths between each pair of nodes.

2.2 Statistical Importance (SI) of Links

We find that the involvement of links that are around a single node is distributed heterogeneously (see Section 3.1). We are interested in the links that have a significant involvement at each given node. However, the local heterogeneity of involvement could simply be produced by random fluctuations. Similar to the disparity filter method, we adopt a null model to compute the random expectation for the distribution of the involvements that is associated with the links of a certain node. The null hypothesis is that the involvement I that corresponds to a connection of a certain node of degree k is produced by a random assignment from a probability density function of $f(x; k)$. Because the links that are adjacent to a certain node with the degree of k should have the same chance under the random condition to connect the node to the remainder of the network, the mean of the involvement must satisfy the condition

$$E(x; k) = \frac{1}{k}, k \geq 2 \text{ and } x \in [0, 1]. \qquad (2)$$

Many probability density functions satisfy this condition and can be used to generate an involvement that is random and is based on specific assumptions. For example, if we assume that for each specific node that has the degree of k, its neighboring links independently participate in the shortest paths between the node and the remainder of the network with a probability of $1/k$; then, the involvement I obeys approximately the normal distribution

that has a mean of $1/k$ and a variance of $\frac{1}{k}\left(1 - \frac{1}{k}\right)/(N-1)$. Alternatively, we can assume that the involvement obeys the power law distribution $f(x) = \beta x^{\alpha}$ because for most complex networks, the degree and weight have been verified to follow power law distributions [1,3]. It is easy to obtain the probability density function $f(x; k) = \frac{1}{k-1} x^{-\frac{k-2}{k-1}}, k \geq 2$. Moreover, the involvement can be assumed to follow a uniform distribution, which is similar to what the disparity filter method has performed for the normalized weights of the links [10] and has the probability density function of $f(x; k) = (k-1)(1-x)^{k-2}$.

The GLANB measures the statistical importance SI_{ij} of link (i,j) by using a null model to calculate the probability in such a way that its involvement I_{ij} is compatible with the null hypothesis. The statistical importance SI_{ij} of link (i,j) is defined as

$$SI_{ij} = 1 - \int_0^{I_{ij}} f(x; k_i) dx, k_i \geq 2, \qquad (3)$$

where k_i is the degree of node i. In this study, the involvement is assumed to follow a uniform distribution, i.e., $f(x; k_i) = (k_i - 1)(1 - x)^{k_i - 2}$; thus, $SI_{ij} = (1 - I_{ij})^{k_i - 1}, k_i \geq 2$. To control the impact of the degree on the statistical importance, we add a parameter $c \geq 0$ to the formula, as follows:

$$SI_{ij} = (1 - I_{ij})^{(k_i - 1)^c}, k_i \geq 2. \qquad (4)$$

If $c = 0$, then the statistical importance SI_{ij} is determined only by I_{ij} and is not affected directly by the degree (I_{ij} can be affected indirectly by k_i because the shortest paths to node i are affected by k_i). As c increases, the impact of the degree becomes larger. The experimental results show some interesting characteristics of the GLANB method under different values of c (see Section 3).

The smaller the value of SI_{ij} is, the more significantly the link (i,j) is not compatible with a random distribution; furthermore, the link (i,j) can be considered more important due to the network-organizing principles. The final statistical importance of an undirected link (i,j) is the minimum of SI_{ij} and SI_{ji}. In the case when a node i of degree $k_i = 1$ is connected to a node j of degree $k_j > 1$, the statistical importance of link (i,j) is SI_{ji}. The GLANB can identify a backbone of a network by setting the significance level α for the SI (a link is included in the backbone if its SI is less than α) based on the distribution of SI (see Section 3.3), or identify the hierarchical backbones by setting different significance levels since the backbone under high significance level will contain the backbone under low significance level. The backbone includes the links that are statistically important according to the specified significance level and their terminal nodes.

2.3 Unweighted and Directed Networks

The GLANB method can be easily applied in unweighted networks. In this case, the weights of all of the links are treated as being equal; thus, the length of a path is the number of links that lie in the path.

To be applied in directed networks, the GLANB must be modified. The directed link (i,j) from starting node i to ending node j is either an out-link for node i or an in-link for node j. Thus, we define the out (in) involvement $I_{ij}^{(out)}$ ($I_{ij}^{(in)}$) of the directed link (i,j) separately as

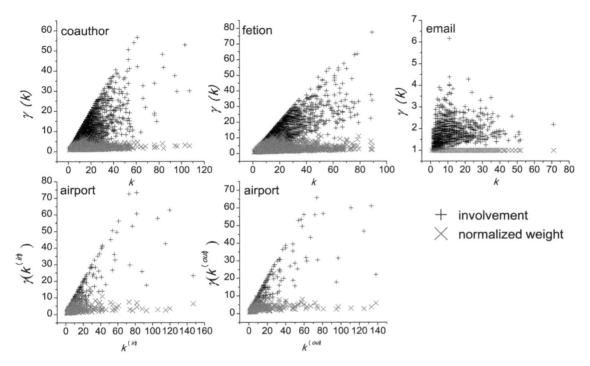

Figure 3. The local heterogeneity of the involvement and the normalized weight in four real networks. Each point in the figure denotes a node in the network. The local heterogeneity of the involvement for node i is defined as $\gamma_i(k_i) = k_i \sum_{j \in \aleph_i} I_{ij}^2$, where $\aleph_i$ is the set of neighbors of node i, k_i is the degree of node i, and I_{ij} is the involvement of link (i,j). The local heterogeneity of the normalized weight for node i is defined as $\gamma_i'(k_i) = k_i \sum_{j \in \aleph_i} (w_{ij}/s_i)^2$, where $s_i = \sum_{j \in \aleph_i} w_{ij}$ is the strength of node i. We can find that for all of the networks, the involvement is locally more heterogeneous than the normalized weight is.

$$I_{ij}^{(out)} = \frac{1}{|\aleph_i^{(out)}|} \sum_{s \in \aleph_i^{(out)}} \frac{g_{is}^{(i,j)}}{g_{is}} \text{ and}$$

$$I_{ij}^{(in)} = \frac{1}{|\aleph_j^{(in)}|} \sum_{s \in \aleph_j^{(in)}} \frac{g_{sj}^{(i,j)}}{g_{sj}}, \quad (5)$$

where $\aleph_i^{(out)}$ is the set of nodes that can be reached from node i through a directed path, and $\aleph_j^{(in)}$ is the set of nodes that can reach node j through a directed path; $|\aleph_i^{(out)}|$ denotes the size of $\aleph_i^{(out)}$; $g_{is}^{(i,j)}$ is the number of shortest paths from node i to s that pass through the link (i,j); and g_{is} is the total number of shortest paths from node i to s. The involvement $I_{ij}^{(out)}$ measures how much the link (i,j) is involved in the shortest paths from node i to the other nodes, and $I_{ij}^{(in)}$ measures how much the link (i,j) is involved in the shortest paths from the other nodes to node j.

The statistical importance of link (i,j) is composed of two parts, the in-importance $SI_{ij}^{(in)}$ and the out-importance $SI_{ij}^{(out)}$, which are defined from the viewpoint of the starting node i and the ending node j separately as

$$SI_{ij}^{(out)} = \left(1 - I_{ij}^{(out)}\right)^{\left(k_i^{(out)} - 1\right)^c}, k_i^{(out)} \geq 2 \text{ and}$$

$$SI_{ij}^{(in)} = \left(1 - I_{ij}^{(in)}\right)^{\left(k_j^{(in)} - 1\right)^c}, k_j^{(in)} \geq 2 \quad (6)$$

where $k_i^{(out)}$ is the out-degree of node i, $k_j^{(in)}$ is the in-degree of node j, and c is the control parameter. The final statistical importance of the directed link (i,j) is determined by the minimum of $SI_{ij}^{(out)}$ and $SI_{ij}^{(in)}$. Similar to the case of weighted and undirected networks, the GLANB can identify a backbone from unweighted or directed network by setting a significance level for SI based on the distribution of SI, or a hierarchical backbone by setting different significance levels for SI.

Results

To test the performance of the GLANB method, we apply it to four real-world networks, a collaboration network (coauthor) [13], an instant-message network (fetion), an email network (email) [14] and an airport traffic network (airport). We compare the obtained results with those obtained by the disparity filtering method and the link salience method. (1) The collaboration network is based on co-authorship of academic papers in the high-energy physics community from 1995–1999. Nodes represent individuals, and links measure the number of papers that were co-authored. The data are publicly available at http://www-personal.umich.edu/~mejn/netdata/. (2) The instant-message network is based on an instant-message tool, fetion, which is provided by Mobile Corporate. The nodes represent fetion users, and the links measure the number of messages sent between each pair of users. (3) The email network is an undirected and unweighted network. The nodes represent email users, and the links represent whether any communication exists between each pair of users. The email network data are available at http://deim.urv.cat/~aarenas/data/welcome.htm. (4) The airport traffic network is a weighted

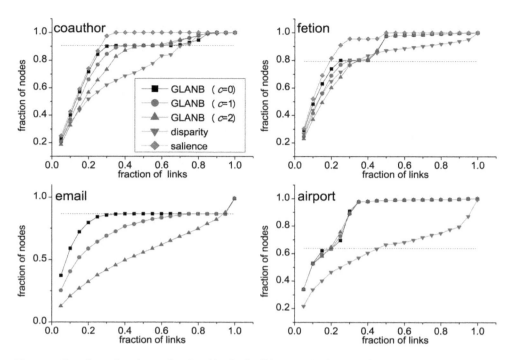

Figure 4. Fraction of nodes maintained in the backbones. The fraction of nodes is a function of the fraction of links retained by the filters. The dash lines correspond to the fraction of the nodes whose degree is greater than 1 in the networks.

and directed network. It measures global air traffic that is based on flight data that is provided by OAG Worldwide Ltd. (http://www. oag.com), and it includes all of the scheduled commercial flights in the world in 2011. The nodes represent airports worldwide. The link weights measure the total number of passengers that travel between a pair of airports by direct flights per year. This network is well represented in the literature [15,16,17]. In the experiments only the largest connected subnetworks of each of the networks are used. The backbone includes the links that are significantly important according to the extraction methods and their terminal nodes. Because the authors in [11] do not mention how the salience method deals with the directed or unweighted networks, we do not apply the salience method to the email and the airport networks.

3.1 Local Heterogeneity of the Link Involvement

The condition under which the null model can perform well is that for each node, its links' involvement shows heterogeneity. If this condition is not satisfied, then it is difficult to identify the important links through the GLANB method. To assess the effect of heterogeneities in the links' involvements at the local level, for each node i of degree k_i, one can calculate the function [18,19]

$$\gamma_i(k_i) = k_i Y_i(k_i) = k_i \sum_{j \in \aleph_i} I_{ij}^2, \qquad (7)$$

where $\aleph_i$ is the set of neighbors of node i and I_{ij} is the involvement of link (i,j).

As a standard indicator of measuring the concentration of data, the function $Y_i(k_i)$ has been extensively used in various domains, including ecology, economics, physics, and complex networks [10,19], where it is known as the disparity measure. Under perfect homogeneity, when all of the links share the same amount of the involvement of node i(i.e., $I_{ij} = 1/k_i$), $\gamma_i(k_i)$ equals 1 independently

of k_i, while in the case of perfect heterogeneity, when only one of the links carries the whole involvement of the node, the function is $\gamma_i(k_i) = k_i$. In this way, this function can be used as a preliminary indicator of the presence of local heterogeneity. When local heterogeneity of involvements exists, the GLANB can be more useful than in the case of homogeneity because the GLANB aims to identify the links whose involvements are significantly higher than other neighboring links'. To compare the involvement with the weights of the links, we also compute the heterogeneity of the normalized weights [10] by

$$\gamma_i'(k_i) = k_i \sum_{j \in \aleph_i} \left(\frac{w_{ij}}{s_i} \right)^2, \qquad (8)$$

where $s_i = \sum_{j \in \aleph_i} w_{ij}$ is the strength of node i. Figure 3 shows the local heterogeneity of the involvement and the normalized weight in the coauthor, fetion, email, and airport networks. We can find that for all of the networks, the involvement is locally more heterogeneous than the normalized weight is (Figure 3). These results indicate that applying the null model to the involvement can identify the statistically important links well.

3.2 Size of the Backbones

The main purpose of extracting backbones is to reduce the number of links in networks, while keeping more nodes. To measure the effects of these filtering methods on the extracted backbones, we analyze the relative sizes of the backbones as a function of the preserved fractions of the links when the network is filtered by the disparity filter, by the link salience and by the GLANB (Figure 4).

For the four real networks, the link salience method can preserve the largest fraction of nodes in the backbone, and the disparity filter method preserves the smallest (except when the fraction of links is less than 0.4 for the fetion network) when the same fraction of links is maintained. The results of the GLANB methods fall in between the disparity and the salience methods. We must note that for the salience method, all of the links that are adjacent to the nodes with a degree of 1 have the largest salience of 1, and preserving these links can retain at least one node. Thus, the link salience method can preserve the largest fraction of the nodes when filtering the networks.

We also find that in the backbone of the coauthor and fetion networks identified by the GLANB method at the specified values of control parameter c, the fraction of nodes stays approximately unchanged for an interval of the fraction of links when the fraction of nodes reaches the threshold that is the fraction of nodes with a degree greater than 1. For the email networks, this phenomenon also exists when $c=0$ or $c=1$. For the airport networks, this phenomenon exists when $c=0$. The interval of keeping unchanged is the longest for all of the networks when $c=0$ (Figure 4). The reason of the phenomenon is that for the nodes that have a degree of 1, the value of SI of their neighboring links is very close to 1; thus, these nodes are difficult to include in the backbone when the fraction of links in the backbone is not sufficiently large. Moreover, as the control parameter c increases, the growth curves of the fraction of nodes become relatively flat (Figure 4), because high value of c prefers the links that correspond to the nodes that have a high degree, and these links have a low value of SI. Preserving these links in the backbone cannot increase the fraction of nodes proportionally because some other links that could have been preserved in the backbone are more likely to share the same terminal nodes with them. Thus, these results indicate that the parameter c can control the size of extracted backbone by impacting the degrees of the nodes on the value of the involvement.

3.3 Robust Classification of Links Based on the Statistical Importance

Similar to the link salience measure [11], the surprising feature of the statistical importance SI is that the distribution $p(SI)$ exhibits a characteristic bimodal shape on the unit interval (Figure 5). The networks' links naturally accumulate at the boundaries and have a small fraction at intermediate values. The statistical importance thus successfully classifies network links into two groups: important ($SI \approx 0$) or non-important ($SI \approx 1$). Because a small fraction of links fall into the intermediate range, the resulting classification is not significantly sensitive to an imposed threshold. This circumstance is fundamentally different from some link centrality measures, such as weight and betweenness, which possess broad distributions and which require external and often arbitrary threshold parameters to perform meaningful classifications. The distribution of links' statistical relevance when measured by the disparity filter method shows a unimodal shape in the coauthor network or a flat distribution in the fetion network (Figure 5), which has the result that choosing the appropriate significance level α to filter links becomes difficult. For the GLANB method, as the control parameter c increases, the number of links with high importance increases (Figure 5). The reason is that the GLANB method with a high value of c favors the links that correspond to the nodes that have the degree $k>1$, and these links occupy a large proportion of total links.

3.4 K-shell distribution of links

To deeply explore the hierarchy of links in the backbones that are extracted by the GLANB, disparity filter and salience methods, we use the k-shell decomposition method to compare the topological distribution of extracted links. The k-shell decompo-

sition method is often used to identify the core and the periphery of the networks [20,21]. Although the k-shell method only takes into account the nodes' degree not the link weights, it provides a way to compare the backbone extraction methods from the view of topological structure. The process of the k-shell decomposition starts by removing all of the nodes that have one link (degree 1) only, until no more such nodes remain; then, it assigns them to the 1-shell. In the same manner, it recursively removes all of the nodes that have a degree of 2 (or less), creating the 2-shell. This process continues, increasing k until all of the nodes in the network have been assigned to one of the shells. The shells that have high indices lie in the core of the network. To assign all of the links to the shells, we define the shell index of a link as the minimum of its two terminal nodes' shell indices.

For the coauthor, fetion and email networks, we extract the top 10% important links based on the SI_{ij} of GLANB (from low to high), the a_{ij} of disparity filter (from low to high) and the s_{ij} of salience methods (from high to low) separately to analyze their distributions in terms of link-shells. Because the salience method ranks the links for which one terminal node has the degree of 1 as most important, and because both the disparity filter and the GLANB methods rank them as least important, we also exclude these links to extract the remaining top 10% important links based on the salience method (salience-E) to analyze the distribution. The distributions of the links in the range of the shell index are shown in Figure 6. We can see that compared with the disparity and salience methods, the GLANB ($c=2$) extracts more links that lie in the higher shells, i.e., the topological core of the networks. Especially for the salience method, most of the extracted links lie in the lower shells. This circumstance occurs because the links whose terminal nodes have a low degree tend to have a high salience. For example, the links that are adjacent to the nodes that have the degree of 1 have the highest salience of 1, which means that all of the links in the 1-shell are certain to be in the backbone that is extracted by the link salience method. For the salience-E method, most of the links still fall in the low shells, and the distribution almost coincides with that of the GLANB ($c=0$), which ignores the degree of the corresponding nodes in a similar way as the salience method. As the control parameter c increases, more links fall into the higher link-shells.

There are two reasons to explain why the GLANB ($c>0$) is more likely to extract links from the topological core of the networks than the other methods. One reason is that the backbone which is extracted by the GLANB ($c>0$) method does not include the links that are adjacent to the nodes that have a degree of 1. The second reason is that the null model depends on the degrees of the nodes. When I_{ij} stays unchanged, increasing the value of degree k_i can decrease the value of SI_{ij} in a power-law way (see formula 4). The larger the value of c is, the more greatly k_i affects SI_{ij}. Thus, some links that have a higher shell index would be in the backbone even though their involvement values are not very high. Furthermore, from Figure 3, we can see that the distribution of link involvements for the nodes that have a higher degree shows heterogeneity, which means that some links have both a high-degree terminal and a high involvement.

Discussion

The GLANB method accounts for both the global and local topology structure of the network when extracting the backbones. On the one hand, the involvement of each link is either a global measure (because it depends on the shortest paths that are determined by the global network structure and the link weights) or a local measure (because the sum of the involvements of the

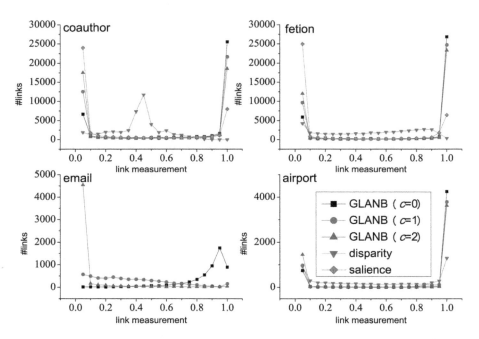

Figure 5. The distributions of the link salience, the link statistical importance and the disparity filtering importance. Link measurement refers to the values of the link salience, link statistical importance, and the disparity filtering importance that are given by the salience, GLANB and disparity methods separately. For the GLANB and disparity methods, the smaller values mean higher importance. For the salience method, the larger values mean higher importance.

links that are adjacent to any certain node has the value of 1). On the other hand, the null model that is adopted in GLANB is based on a local view because the probability density function depends on the degree of each certain node. Thus, the GLANB determines

the importance of the links by synthetically considering the topological structure, the weights of the links and the degrees of the nodes. In this method, the links that have a small weight but are important from the view of structure are not belittled.

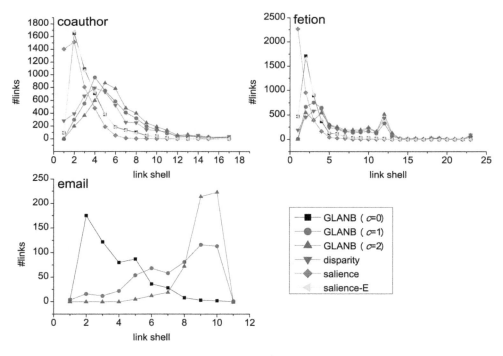

Figure 6. The distribution of links in link-shells. For the coauthor, fetion and email networks, we extract the top 10% important links, based on the GLANB, disparity filter and salience methods separately, to analyze their distributions in terms of link-shells. In addition, we also exclude the links that have degree of 1 to extract the remaining top 10% important links based on the salience method (salience-E) to analyze the distribution.

Furthermore, introducing the control parameter c into GLANB provides a way to adjust the impacts of the node degrees on the extracted backbones, which makes the backbone adaptive to the global structure and the local structure by changing the value of c. When $c \rightarrow 0$, the backbone mainly concentrates on the global structure. When the value of c becomes larger, the backbone is affected more greatly by the local structure. Another advantage is that the GLANB method can be applied to all types of networks regardless of whether they are weighted or unweighted and regardless of whether they are directed or undirected.

The computational complexity of the GLANB method is determined by the computation of the involvement and the statistical importance of the links. To compute the involvement, we must find all of the shortest paths between each pair of nodes, which results in the computational complexity being $O(NL + N^2 \ln(N))$ [22], where N is the number of nodes and L the number of links in the network. The computation of the statistical importance must scan all of the links to compute the degrees of the nodes and the SI of the links; thus, the computational complexity is $O(L)$. Because $L < N^2$, the computational complexity of GLANB is $O(NL + N^2 \ln(N))$. When the size of the network is very large, GLANB is not adaptable if it is executed on only a single computer. However, the computational environment has recently been changing dramatically. Parallel computation platforms are being used pervasively because of their low implementation costs and high performance. Because the GLANB method is based on each single node to measure the involvement and statistical importance of their neighboring links, it is easy to implement GLANB on a parallel platform.

The experiments on the real-world networks show some interesting results. First, the link involvements show local heterogeneity that arises from the topological structure of the networks and from the heterogeneous weight distributions because the shortest paths are determined by those two aspects. Moreover, the involvement is more heterogeneous in the weighted network than in the unweighted network (Figure 3). Second, the link importance distribution, which shows a bimodal shape, gives a robust classification of the links. The bimodal distribution comes from both the local heterogeneity of involvement and the null model that is adopted in GLANB. Third, as the fraction of links in the backbones increases, the size of the backbones that are extracted by the GLANB method first increases rapidly and then becomes almost unchanged, and at last, increases again. The GLANB method assesses the links that are adjacent to the nodes that have a degree of 1 as the least important; thus, as the number of links in the backbone increases, the size of the extracted backbone becomes unchanged for an interval when only the nodes with a degree of 1 are not included in the backbone. Fourth, the control parameter c can affect the size of the backbones. A larger value of c decreases the growth rate of the size of the backbone, because the links that are adjacent to the nodes that have a larger degree are favored, and they cannot efficiently add more nodes into the backbone. Fifth, the GLANB method tends to give more importance to the nodes that are in the core of the network than the other methods do. Especially as the control parameter c increases, more nodes in the core are included in the backbone. In practice, the choice of c value depends on what backbone is needed. The larger the value of c is, more likely the backbone includes the links that are adjacent to nodes with high degree and that are in the core of network from the view of k-shells, and more likely includes less nodes at preserving the same proportion of links.

The GLANB method aims to extract backbones from networks by filtering unimportant links, which can decrease the size of the network greatly. Thus, this method can help us to understand the structure of the networks better, to determine what links are important to transferring information, to express the network by a graph picture easily, and to control the network densities.

Author Contributions

Conceived and designed the experiments: XZ QW JZ. Performed the experiments: XZ ZZ HZ. Analyzed the data: XZ HZ ZZ. Contributed reagents/materials/analysis tools: XZ ZZ HZ. Wrote the paper: XZ QW JZ.

References

1. Newman M, Barabasi A-L, Watts DJ (2006) The structure and dynamics of networks. Princeton: Princeton University Press.
2. Watts DJ, Strogatz SH (1998) Collective dynamics of 'small-world' networks. Nature 393: 440–442.
3. Barabasi A-L, Albert R (1999) Emergence of scaling in random networks. Science (Washington D C) 286: 509–516.
4. Girvan M, Newman MEJ (2002) Community structure in social and biological networks. Proc Natl Acad Sci USA 99: 7821–7826.
5. Song C, Havlin S, Makse HA (2005) Self-similarity of complex networks. Nature 433: 392–395.
6. Goh K-I, Salvi G, Kahng B, Kim D (2006) Skeleton and fractal scaling in complex networks. Phys Rev Lett 96.
7. Zhang X, Zhu J (2013) Skeleton of weighted social network. Physica A 392: 1547–1556.
8. Eguiluz VM, Chialvo DR, Cecchi GA, Baliki M, Apkarian AV (2005) Scale-Free Brain Functional Networks. Phys Rev Lett 94: 018102.
9. Allesina S, Bodini A, Bondavalli C (2006) Secondary extinctions in ecological networks: Bottlenecks unveiled. Ecol Model 194: 150–161.
10. Serrano MA, Boguna M, Vespignani A (2009) Extracting the multiscale backbone of complex weighted networks. Proc Natl Acad Sci USA 106: 6483–6488.
11. Grady D, Thiemann C, Brockmann D (2012) Robust classification of salient links in complex networks. Nat Commun 3: 864.
12. Foti NJ, Hughes JM, Rockmore DN (2011) Nonparametric Sparsification of Complex Multiscale Networks. PLoS ONE 6.
13. Newman MEJ (2001) The structure of scientific collaboration networks. Proc Natl Acad Sci USA 98: 404–409.
14. Ruimera R, Danon L, Diaz-Guilera A, Giralt F, Arenas A (2003) Self-similar community structure in a network of human interactions. Phys Rev E 68: 065103.
15. Barrat A, Barthelemy M, Pastor-Satorras R, Vespignani A (2004) The architecture of complex weighted networks. Proc Natl Acad Sci USA 101: 3747–3752.
16. Guimera R, Mossa S, Turtschi A, Amaral LAN (2005) The worldwide air transportation network: Anomalous centrality, community structure, and cities' global roles. Proc Natl Acad Sci USA 102: 7794–7799.
17. Brockmann D, Hufnagel L, Geisel T (2006) The scaling laws of human travel. Nature 439: 462–465.
18. Almaas E, Kovacs B, Vicsek T, Oltvai ZN, Barabasi AL (2004) Global organization of metabolic fluxes in the bacterium Escherichia coli. Nature 427: 839–843.
19. Barthelemy M, Gondran B, Guichard E (2003) Spatial structure of the internet traffic. Physica A 319: 633–642.
20. Carmi S, Havlin S, Kirkpatrick S, Shavitt Y, Shir E (2007) A model of Internet topology using k-shell decomposition. Proc Natl Acad Sci USA 104: 11150–11154.
21. Kitsak M, Gallos LK, Havlin S, Liljeros F, Muchnik L, et al. (2010) Identification of influential spreaders in complex networks. Nat Phys 6: 888–893.
22. Brandes U (2001) A faster algorithm for betweenness centrality. J Math Sociol 25: 163–177.

15

Hierarchy Measure for Complex Networks

Enys Mones[1], Lilla Vicsek[2], Tamás Vicsek[1,3]*

1 Department of Biological Physics, Eötvös Loránd University, Budapest, Hungary, **2** Institute of Sociology and Social Policy, Corvinus University of Budapest, Budapest, Hungary, **3** Biological Physics Research Group of Hungarian Academy of Sciences, Budapest, Hungary

Abstract

Nature, technology and society are full of complexity arising from the intricate web of the interactions among the units of the related systems (e.g., proteins, computers, people). Consequently, one of the most successful recent approaches to capturing the fundamental features of the structure and dynamics of complex systems has been the investigation of the networks associated with the above units (nodes) together with their relations (edges). Most complex systems have an inherently hierarchical organization and, correspondingly, the networks behind them also exhibit hierarchical features. Indeed, several papers have been devoted to describing this essential aspect of networks, however, without resulting in a widely accepted, converging concept concerning the quantitative characterization of the level of their hierarchy. Here we develop an approach and propose a quantity (measure) which is simple enough to be widely applicable, reveals a number of universal features of the organization of real-world networks and, as we demonstrate, is capable of capturing the essential features of the structure and the degree of hierarchy in a complex network. The measure we introduce is based on a generalization of the m-reach centrality, which we first extend to directed/partially directed graphs. Then, we define the global reaching centrality (GRC), which is the difference between the maximum and the average value of the generalized reach centralities over the network. We investigate the behavior of the GRC considering both a synthetic model with an adjustable level of hierarchy and real networks. Results for real networks show that our hierarchy measure is related to the controllability of the given system. We also propose a visualization procedure for large complex networks that can be used to obtain an overall qualitative picture about the nature of their hierarchical structure.

Editor: Stefano Boccaletti, Technical University of Madrid, Italy

Funding: This work was supported by the EU FP7 COLLMOT Grant No: 227878. The funders had no role in study design, data collection and analysis, decision to publish, or preparation of the manuscript.

Competing Interests: The authors have declared that no competing interests exist.

* E-mail: vicsek@hal.elte.hu

Introduction

The last decade has witnessed an explosive growth of interest in the analysis of complex natural, technological and social systems that permeate many aspects of everyday life. These systems are typically made of many units. Complexity arises from either the structure of the interactions between very similar units or, alternatively, the units and the interactions themselves can have specific characteristics. In both cases, the abstract representation of a complex system can be achieved by a collection of nodes (units) and edges (representing interactions between the units) forming a network (or graph).

Research on networks has considerably profited from using both the standard and novel techniques developed in the field of statistical mechanics [1–3]. Although a remarkable body of knowledge has accumulated about the statistical properties of networks [4], a number of questions are still open. The issue of hierarchy has attracted the attention of a great number of social and natural scientists [5]. It has been argued that hierarchy is present in a wide range of complex systems: such as physical, chemical, biological, and social systems [6]. Recent empirical findings demonstrate that hierarchy is present in many of the related networks: in the dominant-subordinate hierarchy among animals [7], in the hierarchy of the leader-follower network of pigeon flocks [8], in rhesus macaque kingdoms [9], in the structure of the transcriptional regulatory network of *Escherichia coli* [10], or in a wide range of social and technological networks [5]. All of these examples suggest that hierarchy is an important feature of natural, artificial and social networks.

It is important to distinguish between the three major types of hierarchies: the *order*, the *nested* and the *flow* hierarchies. In case of an order hierarchy, hierarchy is regarded to be basically only an "ordered set", and it is understood to be "equivalent to an ordering induced by the values of a variable defined on some set of elements" [11] (i.e., generally there is no network behind this concept). In case of a nested hierarchy higher level elements consist of and contain lower level elements, or, as [12] has formulated "larger and more complex systems consist of and are dependent upon simpler systems and essential system-component entities". When a network is structured in a flow hierarchy (mostly directed graphs), the nodes can be layered in different levels so that the nodes that are influenced by a given node (are connected to it through a directed edge) are at lower levels.

Our observation is that the notions of "hierarchy" and the "level of hierarchy" are very closely related. In fact, without a proper measure of hierarchy the notion of hierarchy cannot be complete. Indeed, there are various definitions of hierarchy, or, in other words, there is no unique, widely accepted definition of the notion of hierarchy itself. Correspondingly, we propose that a good measure of hierarchy can serve as a starting point for finding the best definition of hierarchy.

In this paper, we are interested in flow hierarchy for the following reasons. First, order hierarchy is a single-valued function over the population and there is no underlying network of interactions attached to the hierarchy. Secondly, uncovering a nested hierarchy is analogous to community detection, for which there are known methods [13,14]. Finally, both order and nested hierarchies can be converted to flow hierarchies. In an order hierarchy, a directed edge can be assigned to each pair of adjacent members in the hierarchy and this produces a chain of directed edges. In a nested hierarchy, a virtual node is assigned to every subgraph, and if a subgraph contains another, then the two corresponding virtual nodes are connected with a directed link, which produces a flow hierarchy on the network of virtual nodes.

Among the many exciting questions related to hierarchy [5] is concerned with its origin. Several studies have approached this problem from a historical viewpoint [15,16] but without any quantitative description. The best known quantitative model for the evolution of hierarchies is the Bonabeau model [17]. According to this model, a hierarchy can emerge as the result of the outcomes of competitions between pairs of participating units, and a hierarchy itself is defined by a rank (*order*) assigned to each participating unit [17]. Another interesting result comes from game theory: simulations of prisoners dilemma type dynamics on adaptive networks showed that cooperation combined with imitation can lead to a hierarchical structure [18]. Note, however, that in this model every node can imitate at most one other, and therefore, the emerging hierarchy is by definition a directed tree.

Usually, a hierarchy is the consequence of the different roles, significances and histories of the nodes [17,19]. In other words, if the influence of the nodes on others (and thence, on the whole system) differs, then a hierarchy can emerge. Nodes with the strongest influence can denote the leaders of a group (as in the structure of a company or hidden groups [20,21]; or amongst homing pigeons [8]), central proteins in transcription regulatory networks [10,22] or opinion leaders [23,24]. These nodes can have a major impact on the system, and thus, finding them and quantifying the extent of hierarchy at the same time is an important step in the understanding of functionality and controlling of networks.

In most cases networks contain all sorts of edges (both directed and undirected, various edge weights [strength]) making the detection of hierarchy a difficult challenge. When one looks at real-life networks the picture is often much more complicated than for the simple treelike hierarchy: there can be (i) relations between entities on the same level, (ii) "shortcuts" when a step in the hierarchy is bypassed, (iii) ties which, instead of going downward on the hierarchy, go upward, (iv) even cycles of connected nodes [25] and (v) clusters [26], etc. It can even happen that some or all of the levels of hierarchy cannot be clearly defined (are not well-separated).

The hierarchy measures proposed so far have various undesirable properties that make their application to all classes of complex networks problematic: they (i) use free parameters that are unknown for many networks [20,27], (ii) quantify only the deviation of the network from the tree and penalize loops or multiple edges [28], and (iii) are applicable only to fully directed or fully undirected graphs [20,27–29]. Here we are aiming at introducing a measure which can be equally used for all sorts of networks and thus, used for uncovering universal features of the hierarchical organization of the relations within a complex system.

Visualizing the structure of networks has been a widely used approach to obtain a qualitative picture about some of their features (e.g., clusters/modules). At present, the hierarchical visualization of networks is mostly based on the Sugiyama method [30], which offers an informative and clear hierarchical layout for small networks. However, (i) for networks with more than 2–300

nodes the generated layout becomes difficult to understand; (ii) the meaning of the levels is not defined at all; (iii) independently of the presence or absence of a hierarchy in the given network, the method generates a hierarchical layout that is often misleading; (iv) all steps of the Sugiyama method are NP-complete or NP-hard [31,32], which makes the usage of several different heuristics necessary and thus, results become less well-defined.

Clearly, there is a need for (a) a measure of hierarchy that is free of the above-mentioned undesired properties and (b) a method for the hierarchical visualization of networks that is unbiased, unambiguous and easily applicable even to large graphs. Thus, the two main goals of our paper are to provide a universally applicable measure and a visualization technique of the hierarchical structure of complex large networks.

Results

Definition of the global reaching centrality

Unweighted directed networks. We are looking for a measure that is expected to satisfy the following natural and reasonable conditions:

1. Absence of free parameters and *a priori* metrics in the definition.
2. The definition should be for unweighted directed graphs (digraphs) and it should be easily extendable to both weighted and undirected graphs.
3. The hierarchy measure should be helpful for generating a layout of the graph.

To arrive at an appropriate definition, we quantify the concept of flow hierarchy, where nodes contribute to the dynamics of the system differently. We first define the *local reaching centrality* of node i in an unweighted directed graph, G, as the generalization of the *m-reach centrality* [33] to $m = N$ (where N is the number of nodes in G). The local reaching centrality, $C_R(i)$, of node i is the proportion of all nodes in the graph that can be reached from node i via outgoing edges. In other words, $C_R(i)$ is the number of nodes with a finite positive directed distance from node i divided by $N - 1$, i.e., the maximum possible number of nodes reachable from a given node. We aim to define hierarchy as a heterogeneous distribution of the local reaching centrality. Thus, in graph G we denote by C_R^{max} the highest local reaching centrality and define the *global reaching centrality* (GRC) as:

$$GRC = \frac{\sum_{i \in V} [C_R^{max} - C_R(i)]}{N - 1} \qquad (1)$$

Here, V denotes the set of nodes in G. For normalization, the sum is divided by $N - 1$, as this is the maximal value of the enumerator. In the $GRC = 1$ case the graph has only one node with nonzero local reaching centrality (i.e., it is a star graph). Throughout this paper, for the model networks and real networks we use this directed, unweighted type of C_R.

It is worth mentioning that in the special case of a tree graph, a recursive equation can be derived for $C_R(i)$. This equation has some formal similarities with the one for the *complexity measure* introduced by Huberman et al. [34,35], but with some important differences related to the motivation, details of the recursive equations involved, etc.

Weighted and undirected networks. Generalizations to weighted or undirected graphs are straightforward based on the definition of the local reaching centrality. For the generalization of the GRC to weighted directed graphs, we introduce a simple variant of the local reaching centrality:

$$C'_R(i) = \frac{1}{N-1} \sum_{j:0 < d^{out}(i,j) < \infty} \left(\frac{\sum_{k=1}^{d^{out}(i,j)} \omega_i^{(k)}(j)}{d^{out}(i,j)} \right) \qquad (2)$$

Here $d^{out}(i,j)$ is the length of the directed path that goes from i to j via out-going edges and $\omega_i^{(k)}(j)$ is the weight of the k-th edge along this path (link weight is assumed to be proportional to connection strength). If nodes i and j are connected by more than one directed shortest path, then the one with the maximum weight (i.e., maximum strength) should be used. This extension of the local reaching centrality measures the average weight of a given directed path starting from node i in a weighted directed graph. If we set $\omega_i^{(k)}(j) = 1$ for every i, j and k, then the original local reaching centrality (defined for unweighted directed graphs) is recovered.

To generalize the local reaching centrality to undirected unweighted graphs, we remove the $\sum_{k=1}^{d^{out}(i,j)} \omega_i^{(k)}(j)$ term from the previous definition and obtain

$$C''_R(i) = \frac{1}{N-1} \sum_{j:0 < d(i,j) < \infty} \frac{1}{d(i,j)} \qquad (3)$$

This quantity is very similar to the local *closeness centrality* defined by Sabidussi in [36]. In fact, this is equivalent to the generalization of the closeness centrality for disconnected graphs given by Opsahl [37].

Classical random networks

In order to demonstrate the basic features of the GRC, we briefly discuss its behavior for a few well-known network types. For Erdös–Rényi (ER) graphs [38,39], scale-free (SF) [40–42] graphs and directed trees (more precisely arborescences with random branching number [43,44]), the distribution of C_R is markedly different (the curves in Figure 1 are averages for 1000 random graphs of each type). In every case, the exponent for the SF networks was set to $\gamma = 2.5$. For the directed tree, the distribution follows a power-law that is distorted due to the random branching numbers. Directed trees have a maximally heterogeneous distribution of C_R, thus, based on our arguments above, they are maximally hierarchical. Note that the hierarchical tree (directed tree) has very few nodes with local reaching centrality close to 1.

This is in contrast with the ER and SF graphs in which most of the nodes have a large local reaching centrality. Since almost every node has the same centrality, the contribution of the nodes in Eq. 1 for the ER and SF graphs is negligible. Note that not only the GRC, but also the standard deviation of C_R increases with the heterogeneity of the graph. The values of GRC are shown in Table 1 together with the standard deviation of the distribution. However, the GRC itself is more suitable for quantifying the heterogeneity of the graph for two reasons. On the one hand, the accuracy of the standard deviation of C_R is worse than that of the GRC (it has larger deviation on the ensemble of graphs). On the other hand, the standard deviation of C_R is much smaller for the directed tree than for the ER, which is in contrast to our definition making the tree maximally hierarchical. In summary, we find that, based on their reaching centralities, ER graphs are not hierarchical at all, as expected, and SF graphs are slightly hierarchical.

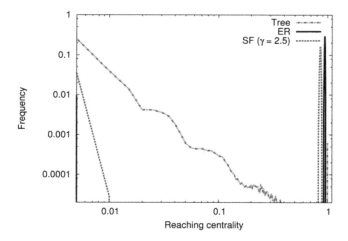

Figure 1. An adjustable hierarchical network with the different edge types. The blue edges belong to the original arborescence graph that is used as the backbone of the adjustable hierarchical (AH) network. There are three type of possible edges added to the graph: down edges (green), horizontal edges (orange) and up edges (red). They have different effects on the hierarchical structure of the directed tree. Down edges conserve the hierarchy, horizontal edges has a slight influence and up edges make strong changes in the structure.

Adjustable hierarchical network

We study the behavior of the GRC in a model with adjustable hierarchy as well (see Methods for a detailed description of the model). The parameter p tunes between the completely random and the totally hierarchical states. In the $p = 0$ limit, the topology of the AH graph is close to that of an ER graph, but, as one can see, the distribution of the local reaching centrality values of the AH is similar to that of the SF network (Figure 2): a little wider at small centralities than in the ER case. By increasing p, the distribution further widens around the origin and at $p = 1$, it resembles the one for the directed tree, but it is even closer to a power-law. The global reaching centrality as function of the parameter p is shown in Figure 3. The GRC monotonously increases with p and sweeps through the (0,1) interval in the synthetic model, indicating that it is suitable for measuring the level of hierarchy. As seen in the figures, the global reaching centrality at a given value of p is less for larger average degrees. This observation is confirmed with the results on ER and SF networks (Figure 4). For large densities the GRC vanishes for both the ER and the SF networks.

Table 1. Heterogeneity of the distribution of the local reaching centrality for different network types.

Graph	GRC	$s(C_R)$
ER	0.058 ± 0.005	0.222 ± 0.010
SF	0.127 ± 0.008	0.300 ± 0.009
Tree	0.997 ± 0.001	0.031 ± 0.004

The two measures of heterogeneity presented here are the global reaching centrality (*GRC*) and $\sigma(C_R)$ (standard deviation of C_R). Means and variances are shown for an ensemble of 1000 networks.

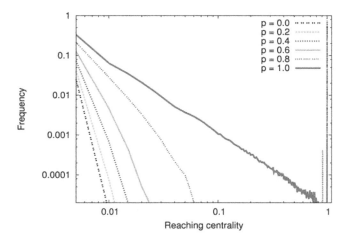

Figure 2. Distribution of the local reaching centrality for the adjustable hierarchical network. Distribution of the local reaching centrality in the adjustable hierarchical (AH) network model at different p parameter values. Each distribution is averaged over 1000 AH networks with $N=2000$ and $\langle k \rangle = 3$. The standard deviations of the distributions are comparable to the averages only for relative frequencies less than 0.002. Note that from the $p=0$ (highly random) to the $p=1$ (fully hierarchical) state the distribution changes continuously and monotonously with p.

Real networks

We now turn our attention to the hierarchical properties of real networks. The global reaching centralities for different types of networks are shown in Table 2. For each network we show the average degree ($\langle k \rangle$) and the GRC of the real network. It is important to point out that the direction of the edges in real networks had to be well-defined before calculating the reaching centrality. In every case, the networks were directed so that the source of an edge had a larger effect on the target than conversely. This choice of directedness originates in the observation that the higher a node is in the hierarchy, the more impact it has on the network. According to Table 2, the GRC can have values from a

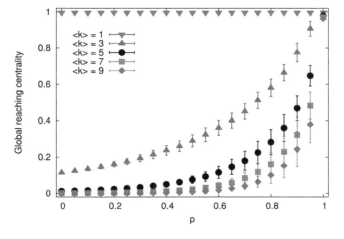

Figure 3. The global reaching centrality at different p values in the adjustable hierarchical model. All curves show averages over an ensemble of 1000 networks with $N=2000$ and different average degrees. Standard deviations grow with p, but they are clearly below the average values of the GRC. Note that for larger density, it is less likely to obtain the same level of hierarchy.

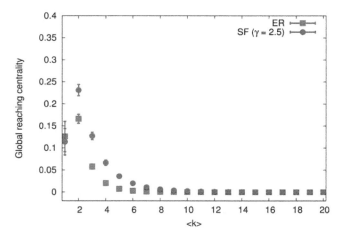

Figure 4. The global reaching centrality versus average degree in the Erdős–Rényi and scale-free networks. Dots show averages for 1000 graphs with $N=2000$ nodes. In the Erdős–Rényi and scale-free networks, standard deviations of the GRC are comparable with its averages only for $\langle k \rangle > 7$ and $\langle k \rangle > 12$, respectively.

broad range, depending on the average degree and the structure of the networks. For graphs with higher average degree, the GRC is usually smaller. This indicates that for a dense network it is harder to achieve a large reaching centrality, as seen with the ER, SF and AH graphs. The value of the GRC shows how hierarchical the structure of the network is. Food webs have the largest GRC and networks of intra-organizational trust have the smallest. This is in good agreement with the extremely low number of loops in food webs and the high number of loops in email-based organizational networks.

While the actual value of the GRC provides information about the hierarchical properties of the network, we can also compare the results to the randomized versions of the original networks to see how consistent the value we obtained is with the expectations. In order to do this, for each network we generated 100 random networks with the same degree (the details of randomization is explained in the Methods section): the mean values of the global reaching centralities for these randomized networks are shown in Table 2 (GRC^{rand}). The color of the networks' names indicates the relation of each original network to its randomized version: the names of statistically significantly (with a confidence interval of 98%) hierarchical networks are in red while the names of non-hierarchical ones (same confidence) are in blue. Apart from the actual GRC values, the comparison to randomized networks by GRC/GRC^{rand} shows slight differences between the analyzed network types. For the food webs GRC/GRC^{rand} is remarkably high. Although the electronic circuits have low GRC values, they are significantly more hierarchical than their randomized versions. In contrast, although the Internet networks have larger reaching centralities than most other listed networks, these values do not differ significantly from the values of the corresponding randomized networks. Also note that the regulatory networks are significantly less hierarchical, mostly because biochemical systems contain many feedbacks keeping the processes stabilized.

The emergence of hierarchy in many human-made organizations and networks raises the question whether conscious control over these systems plays a role in the origin of hierarchy? In order to investigate this question, we compared the global reaching centralities with the controllability of networks as defined by Liu et al. [45]. They show that the minimal number of *driver nodes* (N_D) is

Table 2. Hierarchical properties of real networks.

Type	Meaning of A→B	Network	N	$\langle k \rangle$	GRC	GRC^{rand}
Food web	A eats B	Ythan [48]	135	4.452	0.814	0.507
		Seagrass [49]	49	4.612	0.723	0.253
		LittleRock [50]	183	13.628	0.811	0.045
		GrassLand [48]	88	1.557	0.961	0.695
Electric	B depends on the value at A	s1488 [51]	667	2.085	0.482	0.298
		s1494 [51]	661	2.116	0.482	0.289
		s5378 [51]	2993	1.467	0.231	0.062
		s9234 [51]	5844	1.4	0.424	0.050
		s35932 [51]	17828	1.683	0.459	0.015
Metabolic	B is an end product of A	C. elegans [52]	1173	2.442	0.048	0.052
		E. coli [52]	2275	2.533	0.043	0.058
		S. cerevisiae [52]	1511	2.537	0.037	0.042
Neuronal	A synapse goes from A to B	C. elegans [53,54]	297	7.943	0.133	0.023
		Macaque brain [55]	45	10.289	0.000	0.000
Internet	A communicates with B	p2p-1 [56,57]	10876	3.677	0.598	0.597
		p2p-2 [56,57]	8846	3.599	0.600	0.599
		p2p-3 [56,57]	8717	3.616	0.607	0.605
Organization	B trusts in A	Enron [58,59]	156	10.699	0.038	0.044
		Consulting [60]	46	19.109	0.043	0.032
		Manufacturing [60]	34	18.935	0.013	0.013
	B knows A	Freemans-1 [61]	34	18.971	0.028	0.041
		Freemans-2 [61]	77	24.412	0.000	0.000
Trust	B trusts in A	WikiVote [62]	7115	14.573	0.494	0.534
		College [63,64]	32	3	0.275	0.273
		Prison [64,64]	67	2.716	0.172	0.111
Language	B follows A	English [65]	7724	5.992	0.128	0.238
		French [65]	9424	2.578	0.657	0.875
		Spanish [65]	12642	3.57	0.951	0.939
		Japanese [65]	3177	2.613	0.054	0.206
Regulatory	A regulates B	TRN-Yeast-1 [66]	4441	2.899	0.934	0.968
		TRN-Yeast-2 [67]	688	1.568	0.116	0.670
		TRN-EC [67]	419	1.239	0.261	0.679

We show the order (N), average degree ($\langle k \rangle$), and global reaching centrality for the original (GRC) and for the randomized networks (GRC^{rand}). References to data sources are included. Suits next to the GRC values show comparison to the randomized networks: whether the original networks are more hierarchical than their randomization (club suit) or they are more egalitarian (diamond suit) with a 98% confidence level. The meaning of edges is also indicated.

related to the maximum matching of the network and they also provide an algorithm for determining N_D. In a network with N nodes the relative number of driver nodes is $n_D^{Liu} = N_D/N$. Driver nodes are the nodes that have to be controlled in order to take full control over the network. Full control means that one can drive the system from any initial state to any other desired final state. Since the networks listed in Table 2 have different original functions (food web, electric, etc.), and in many cases their controllability and hierarchical properties are not yet well understood, we compared these two quantities separately within each group of networks. The Pearson correlations of the GRC and n_D^{Liu} are shown in Table 3. In most of the listed real networks, the correlation is above 0.5, which is a relatively small value but still indicates a weak relation between the two quantities. Next, we compared the hierarchy measure, GRC, to the ratio of driver nodes in our synthetic model. Interestingly, for high link densities

($\langle k \rangle \geq 5$) the ratio of driver nodes is very close to the value of the GRC and they differ significantly only for highly hierarchical graphs (i.e., for $p > 0.85$). In an easily (hardly) controllable network, i.e., where n_D is low (high), few (many) nodes need to be controlled for a total control over the network. According to the results shown in Table 3 for real graphs and the results with the synthetic model (for a wide range of p) the GRC and n_D^{Liu} are moderately positively correlated. In other words, *hierarchical networks are harder to control*. This result contradicts our initial intuitive concept that hierarchy emerges because it is the optimal structure with respect to controllability. This contradiction can be traced back to an assumption in the node-based definition of controllability given in [45] where each node is assumed to send the same signal to all of its neighbors. If, however, the network's dynamics is defined on the edges [46], then the definition of controllability differs from the definition by Liu et al. Therefore, as

Table 3. The Pearson correlation of the GRC and n_D defined by Liu et al.

Type of the networks	r(GRC,n_D^{Liu})
Regulatory	0.843
Trust	0.974
Food web	0.69
Metabolic	−0.225
Electric	0.503
Internet	0.632
Organizational	0.337
Language	0.933

With only one exception, all correlations are positive and many of them are above 0.6, i.e., the GRC and n_D^{Liu} are positively correlated.

an alternative, we compared hierarchy to controllability defined under the *switchboard dynamics* [46] (correlations are shown in Table 4). In the case of switchboard dynamics edges are controlled and nodes are simple devices converting the signals arriving on their in-edges to signals leaving on their out-edges. The driver nodes in this dynamics are those that one has to control for controlling the state of every edge. Based on the correlations between the GRC and the number of driver nodes, we conclude that *under the switchboard dynamics hierarchical networks are better controllable.*

To show how the generalized reaching centralities can be applied to undirected networks, we tested our method on the networks of terrorists investigated by Memon et al. Our results are similar to those of [21]: the top of the hierarchy related to the Bojinka case contains Isamudin and K. S. Mehmood (known as Mohammed). In the London Bombings network [21] found that the mastermind of the 7/7 bombings was H. R. Awsat; he was identified by our analysis (based on C''_R) as a leader and M. S. Khan and I. M. Said as additional important participants. These results suggest that the above extensions of the local reaching centrality are effective quantities for the description of undirected graphs.

Table 4. Pearson correlation of the GRC and n_D in the switchboard dynamics.

Type of the networks	r(GRC,n_D^{SBD})
Regulatory	−0.922
Trust	−0.983
Food web	−0.406
Metabolic	−0.916
Electric	−0.969
Internet	0.57
Organizational	−0.674
Language	−0.812

The correlations are all negative (except for the Internet networks) and most of them are very close to −1. Thus, under the switchboard dynamics the GRC (strength of hierarchy) and n_D^{SBD} are strongly negatively correlated.

Visualization of large networks

We use the method introduced in the Methods section for the hierarchical visualization of unweighted digraph by setting $x_i = C_R(i)$. Since the local reaching centrality takes discrete values on the graph, we use $z = \varepsilon$, that is, nodes that have local reaching centralities very close to each other are in the same level. Figure 5 shows the layout of various graphs. ER graphs have only two layers close to each other and most of their nodes are in the top layer indicating an almost equal impact of every node and the absence of hierarchy. As opposed to this, an arborescence has many layers, the distances between the layers vary and the layers contain different numbers of nodes. At the topmost layer there is only one node and it is far from the other nodes. This structure is due to the fact that the roles of nodes in the graph vary on a wide range, in other words, the distribution of the local reaching centrality is strongly heterogeneous. The hierarchical structure of an SF graph is between those of an ER graph and an arborescence: although it has only a few layers, these layers are clearly separated.

Note that different realizations (single graphs) of the same graph model (e.g., the SF model) usually have different hierarchical layouts. In order to eliminate this bias and to compare the graph models themselves (instead of single graphs from each model), we apply the hierarchical layouts of single graphs to define the drawing (image) of graph ensembles. To do this, first we rescale the hierarchical layout of each single graph to unit height and width and center it in the unit square (Figure 6). Next, we overlay the hierarchical layouts of graphs from the same model. For each graph model the result of this process is a density distribution of the nodes (in the unit square) averaged over the different realizations of the given model. Figure 7 shows graph ensemble drawings: the ER model is visualized as a thin horizontal line at the bottom of the box, while the SF model has more levels and it is similar to the AH(0.3) network. The ensemble of arborescences is visualized in a small concentrated region at the bottom of the unit square indicating the presence of many close levels. The transition from egalitarianism to hierarchy can be clearly seen on the visualization of the AH graphs. At small p (proportion of edges pointing to a lower level) there is mostly one level, then with increasing p more and more other levels emerge, and finally, the network splits into two groups of levels that are moving away from

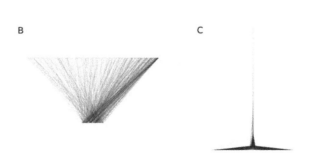

Figure 5. Visualization of three network types based on the local reaching centrality. Visualization of (A) an Erdös–Rényi (ER) network, (B) a scale-free (SF) network and (C) a directed tree with random branching number between 1 and 5. All three graphs have $N = 1000$ nodes and the ER and SF graphs have $\langle k \rangle = 3$. In each network z was set to $2/N$.

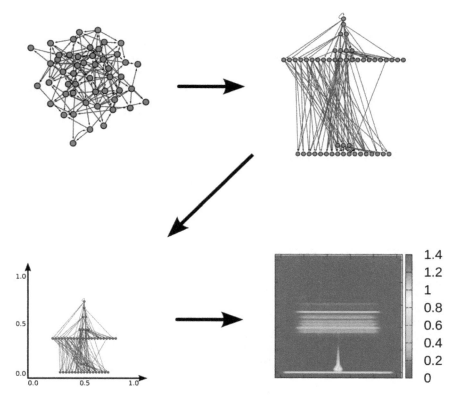

Figure 6. Diagram illustrating the process of visualizing an ensemble of networks. First, we compute the layout based on the selected x_i local quantity for each graph in the ensemble (top right). Next, we separate the levels logarithmically and scale each layout into the unit square (bottom left). Last, we overlay all rescaled layouts and plot the obtained density of nodes in the unit square (bottom right, see color scale also). In the heat maps, the color scale shows $\log(\log(\rho(x,y)+1)+1)$, where $\rho(x,y)$ is the average density of the ensemble.

each other. To illustrate the usefulness of our visualization method, we show results for four real graphs as well (Figure 8). The GrassLand network is highly hierarchical, while the Enron network is very egalitarian (only very few nodes are much lower than the majority). This is in good agreement with the global reaching centrality values. The electrical circuit and the biological regulatory network are between the two extreme cases. The first contains two major levels (further subdivided into smaller levels. In contrast, the regulatory network has only one wide bottom level and a few nodes in the top and they are close to each other.

Methods

Synthetic model

In order to show the behavior of GRC, we introduce a synthetic network model with tunable extent of hierarchy. The construction of the network is the following:

1. In a directed tree assign a level (ℓ) to every node. The level of the root node is equal to the number of levels. If and only if a node has level ℓ, then the level of its children will be $\ell-1$. These levels denote the natural layers in the hierarchy of the directed tree (the nodes at the bottom have $\ell=1$).

2. We put a given number of additional random directed edges in the graph according to the following rule. $1 - p$ proportion of the edges is totally random, i.e. we choose two nodes randomly (A and B) and if they are not already connected in the given ($A \rightarrow B$) direction, we connect them. By p proportion of the edges, we put the $A \rightarrow B$ edge only if $\ell_A > \ell_B$. In this way, p

proportion of the random edges will not change the hierarchical structure of the directed tree.

An example of a generated network with the different edge types is shown in Figure 9. Hereafter, we will refer to this synthetic model as the *adjustable hierarchical network* (AH).

Randomization of real networks

During the analysis of the results with real networks, we also calculated the GRC after randomizing them: first, we generated a random network with the same in and out degree distribution according to the configuration model. The generated network is further randomized in the following way: we choose two random edges ($A \rightarrow B$ and $C \rightarrow D$) and change the endpoints of them (so that we get $A \rightarrow D$ and $C \rightarrow B$). In every case, the number of rewired edge pairs was ten times the number of edges.

Visualization

We also propose a visualization method using an arbitrary local quantity on the graph. The algorithm is as follows:

1. Grade the nodes according to the local quantity x_i.

2. Add nodes to the first (lowermost) level of the layout in the increasing order of their x_i values as long as $\sigma_L < z \cdot \sigma_G$. Here σ_L is the standard deviation of x_i within the current (first) level, σ_G is the standard deviations of x_i within the whole graph, and z is an adjustable coefficient.

3. When $\sigma_L \geq z \cdot \sigma_G$ is reached, start a new level.

4. Repeat 2nd and 3rd steps until every node is put in levels.

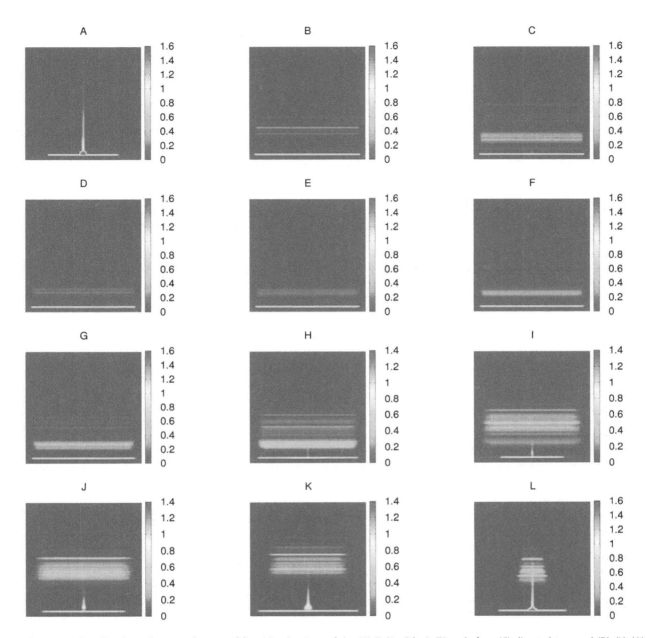

Figure 7. Visualization of network ensembles. Visualizations of the (A) Erdös–Rényi, (B) scale-free, (C) directed tree and (D)–(L) AH network ensembles (subfigures (D)–(L) are for different values of the model parameter: $p=0.1,\ldots,0.9$). In each case the color scale shows $\log(\log(\rho(x,y)+1)+1)$ where $\rho(x,y)$ is the density averaged over 1000 graphs. $N=2000$ and $\langle k\rangle=3$ were set. In every network, z was set to $3/N$. The corresponding GRC values are: 0.997 (A), 0.058 (B), 0.127 (C), 0.135 (D), 0.161 (E), 0.194 (F), 0.238 (G), 0.290 (H), 0.361 (I), 0.452 (J), 0.581 (K) and 0.775 (L).

5. For horizontal arrangement, align the center of every level to the same vertical line. In other words, in each level, the average of the horizontal positions of the nodes is the same:

$$X_{\ell_1}=X_{\ell_2}=0 \qquad \text{for all } \ell_1 \text{ and } \ell_2$$

Here, X_ℓ is the horizontal center of mass of level ℓ.

6. The levels are arranged vertically so that the distances between adjacent levels are proportional to the logarithm of the differences in the averages inside the corresponding levels, i.e.

$$(Y_{\ell+1}-Y_\ell) \quad \propto \quad \ln\left[\langle x\rangle_{\ell+1}-\langle x\rangle_\ell\right]$$

where Y_ℓ and is the vertical position of the ℓ-th level and $\langle x\rangle_\ell$ is the average of x_i inside this level. First, set the vertical distances of levels proportionally to the differences between their average values of x_i such that the smallest distance will be set to a given length (this length is the same as the horizontal distance between two adjacent nodes). Finally, set the distances to be proportional to the logarithm of the original differences so that the height of the graph is kept unchanged.

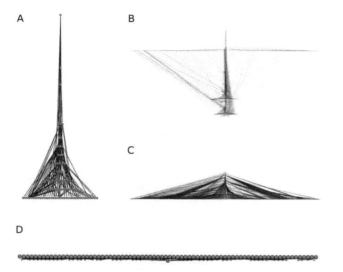

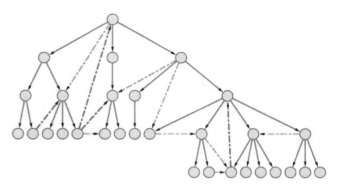

Figure 8. Visualization of real networks. The hierarchy-based visualization of (A) the GrassLand food web, (B) the electrical circuit benchmark s9234, (C) the transcriptional regulatory network of yeast and (D) the core of the Enron network. In every network z was set to $2/N$.

Figure 9. Distributions of the local reaching centrality for different network types. For each network type $N = 2000$ and for the Erdös–Rényi (ER) and scale-free (SF) networks $\langle k \rangle = 3$. All curves show averages of the distributions over an ensemble of 1000 graphs. Standard deviations are comparable with the averages only near the peaks in the ER and SF models. Although the standard deviations at the peaks are large, they do not change the positions of the peaks, and thus, do not affect the distributions.

In the above steps we use the standard deviation in order to get clearly different layouts for different distributions of x_i. In a network with a localized distribution of x_i the method produces few levels that are very close to each other. But if the distribution of x_i is non-localized, the network will have many levels and a large vertical extension. If the distribution of x_i is continuous, then we can use z to adjust the extent to which every level contributes to the total variance. In other words, for large graphs, z tunes the vertical extension of the layout. If the distribution of x_i is discrete, then we can assign a level to each of its different values, which is mathematically equivalent to $z = 0$. In practice, we set z to a sufficiently small value, ε.

Implementation

For the graph generations, randomizations and shortest path calculations presented in this paper, we used the already implemented functions in the *igraph* software package [47]. An open-source implementation of the local and global reaching centrality calculations is provided at http://hal.elte.hu/~enys/grc.htm.

Discussion

Hierarchy is an essential feature of many natural and human-made networks and therefore, it is of high importance to have a

measure quantifying it. Here we proposed a measure based on the assumption that the rank of the nodes should be related to their impact on the whole network, which is proportional to the number of all nodes reachable from them (local reaching centrality). The quantity we introduced, i.e., the global reaching centrality (GRC), measures the heterogeneity of the local reaching centrality distribution on the whole graph. In contrast to formerly proposed measures, the GRC does not penalize loops and undirected edges, but takes them into account by making bidirectionally connected pairs of nodes ($A{\rightarrow}B$, $B{\rightarrow}A$) equivalent in the hierarchy. There are neither free parameters in the method, nor optimization, and the ranks of the nodes are a natural result of the GRC. Since the controllability (according to the switchboard dynamics) and the extent of hierarchy are positively correlated, our calculations indicated that hierarchical structures are more easily controllable.

Acknowledgments

We thank Illés Farkas and Gábor Vásárhelyi for their helpful comments on the early version of the manuscript. We also thank Tamás Nepusz for his technical and theoretical advices and suggestions on the simulations.

Author Contributions

Conceived and designed the experiments: EM LV TV. Performed the experiments: EM. Analyzed the data: EM TV. Wrote the paper: EM LV TV.

References

1. Castellano C, Fortunato S, Loreto V (2009) Statistical physics of social dynamics. Phys Rev Lett 81: 591–646.
2. Vicsek T, Zafiris A (2010) Collective motion. arxiv:1010.5017.
3. Pastor-Satorras R, Vespignani A (2004) Evolution and Strcuture of the Internet. Cambridge: Cambridge University Press.
4. Albert R, Barabási AL (2002) Statistical Mechanics of Complex Networks. Phys Rev Lett 74: 47–97.
5. Pumain D, ed (2006) Hierarchy in Natural and Social Sciences. Dodrecht, The Netherlands: Springer. pp 1–12.
6. Huseyn L, Whetten DA (1984) The Concept of Horizontal Hierarchy and the Organization of Interorganizational Networks: a Comparative Analysis. Social Networks 6: 31–58.
7. Goessmann C, Hemelrijk C, Huber R (2000) The formation and maintenance of crayfish hierarchies: behavioral and self-structuring properties. Behavioral Ecology and Sociobiology 48: 418–428.
8. Nagy M, Ákos Z, Biro D, Vicsek T (2010) Hierarchical group dynamics in pigeon flocks. Nature 464: 890–893.
9. Fushing H, McAssey MP, Beisner B, McCowan B (2011) Ranking network of captive rhesus macaque society: A sophisticated corporative kingdom. PLoS ONE 6: e17817.
10. Ma HW, Buer J, Zeng AP (2004) Hierarchical structure and modules in the Escherichia coli transcriptional regulatory network revealed by a new top-down approach. BMC Bioinformatics 5: 199.
11. Lane D (2006) Hierarchy, complexity, society. Dodrecht, the Netherlands: Springer. pp 81–120.

12. Wimberley ET (2009) Nested ecology. The place of humans in the ecological hierarchy. Baltimore, MD: John Hopkins University Press.

13. Girwan M, Newman ME (2002) Community structure in social and biological networks. PNAS 99: 7821–7826.

14. Palla G, Derényi I, Farkas I, Vicsek T (2005) Uncovering the overlapping community structure of complex networks in nature and society. Nature 435: 814–818.

15. Smaje C (2000) Natural Hierarchies. The Historical Sociology of Race and Caste. Hoboken, NJ: Blackwell Publishers.

16. Dubreuil B (2010) Human Evolution and the Origins of Hierarchies. Cambridge: Cambridge University Press.

17. Theraulaz G, Bonabeau E, Deneubourg JL (1995) Self-organization of Hierarchies in Animal Societies: The Case of the Primitively Eusocial wasp Polistes dominulus Christ. Journal of Theoretical Biology 174: 313–323.

18. Eguíluz VM, Zimmermann MG, Cela-Conde CJ, Miguel MS (2005) Cooperation and the Emergence of Role Differentiation in the Dynamics off Social Networks. American Journal of Sociology 110: 977–1008.

19. Bonabeau E, Theraulaz G, Deneubourg JL (1999) Dominance Orders in Animal Societies: The Self-organization Hypothesis Revisited. Bulletin of Mathematical Biology 61: 727–757.

20. Rowe R, Creamer G, Hershkop S, Stolfo SJ (2007) Automated social hierarchy detection through email network analysis. In: WebKDD/SNA-KDD 07: Proceedings of the 9th WebKDD and 1st SNA-KDD 2007 workshop on Web mining and social network analysis ACM. pp 109–117.

21. Memon N, Larsen HL, Hicks DL, Harkiolakis N (2008) Detecting Hidden Hierarchy in Terrorist Networks: Some Case Studies. In: Proceedings of the IEEE ISI 2008 PAISI, PACCF, and SOCO international workshops on Intelligence and Security Informatics. New York: Springer-Verlag. pp 477–489.

22. Bhardwaj N, Kim PM, Gerstein MB (2010) Rewiring of transcriptional regulatory networks: hierarchy, rather than connectivity, better reflects the importance of regulators. Science Signaling 3.

23. Song X, Chi Y, Hino K, Tseng BL (2007) Identifying Opinion Leaders in the Blogosphere. In: Proceedings of the sixteenth ACM conference on Conference on information and knowledge man- agement ACM, CIKM '07. pp 971–974.

24. Mak V (2008) The Emergence of Opinion Leaders in Social Networks. Available: http://ssrn.com/abstract = 1157285. Accessed 2012 Feb 24.

25. Hummon NP, Fararo TJ (1995) Actors and networks as objects. Social Networks 17: 1–26.

26. Johnsen EC (1985) Network macrostructure models for the Davis-Leinhardt set of empirical sociomatrices. Social Networks 7: 203–224.

27. Carmel L, Haren D, Koren Y (2002) Drawing Directed Graphs Using One-Dimensional Optimization. Heidelberg: Springer. pp 193–206.

28. Krackhardt D (1994) Graph theoretical dimensions of informal organizatons. Mahwah, NJ: Lawrence Erlbaum Associates Inc.

29. Trusina A, Maslov S, Minnhagen P, Sneppen K (2004) Hierarchi measures in complex networks. Phys Rev Lett 92: 178702.

30. Sugiyama K, Tagawa S, Toda M (1981) Methods for visual understanding of hierarchical system structures. In: IEEE Transactions in Systems, Man and Cybernetics, volume 11. pp 109–125.

31. Garey MR, Johnson DS (1979) Computers and Intractability: A Guide to the Theory of NP-Completeness. New York: W. H. Freeman and Company.

32. Healy P, Nikolov NS (2004) Hierarchical drawind algorithms. St Helier, NJ: CRC Press.

33. Borgatti SP (2003) The Key Player Problem. Washington, D.C.: National Academy of Sciences Press. pp 241–252.

34. Huberman BA, Hogg T (1986) Complexity and adaption. Physica D 22: 376–384.

35. Ceccatto HA, Huberman BA (1988) The complexity of hierarchical systems. Physica Scripta 37: 145.

36. Sabidussi G (1966) The centrality index of a graph. Psychometrika 31: 581–603.

37. Opsahl T, Agneessens F, Skvoretz J (2010) Node centrality in weighted networks: Generalizing degree and shortest paths. Social Networks 32: 245–251.

38. Erdős P, Rényi A (1960) On the evolution of random graphs. Publ Math Inst Hung Acad Sci 5: 17–60.

39. Bollobás B (2001) Random Graphs. Cambridge: Cambridge University Press.

40. Barabási AL, Albert R (1999) Emergence of scaling in random networks. Science 286: 509–512.

41. Goh KI, Kahng B, Kim D (2001) Universal behavior of load distribution in scale-free networks. Phys Rev Lett 87.

42. Chung F, Lu L (2002) Connected component in random graphs with given expected degree sequences. Annual Combinatorics 6: 125–145.

43. Tutte WT (2001) Graph Theory. Cambridge: Cambridge University Press.

44. Grinstead CM, Snell JL (1997) Introduction to Probability, Second Revised Edition. Washington, D.C.: American Mathematical Society.

45. Liu YY, Slotine JJ, Barabási AL (2011) Controllability of complex networks. Nature 473: 167–173.

46. Nepusz T, Vicsek T (2011) Controlling edge dynamics in complex networks. arxiv:1112.5945.

47. Csárdi G, Nepusz T (2006) The igraph software package for complex network research. InterJournal Complex Systems 1695. Available: http://igraph.sf.net. Accessed 2012 Mar 8.

48. Dunne JA, Williams RJ, Martinez ND (2002) Food-web structure and network theory: The role of connectance and size. Proceedings of the National Academy of Sciences of the United States of America 99: 12917–22.

49. Christian RR, Luczkovich JJ (1999) Organizing and understanding a winter's seagrass foodweb network through effective trophic levels. Ecological Modelling 117: 99–124.

50. Martinez N (1991) Artifacts or attributes? Effects of resolution on the Little Rock Lake food web. Ecological Monographs 61: 367–392.

51. Source: http://courses.engr.illinois.edu/ece543/iscas89.html. Accessed 2012 Feb 24. Networks available at http://hal.elte.hu/~enys/data.htm. Accessed 2012 Feb 24.

52. Jeong H, Tombor B, Albert R, Oltvai ZN, Barabási AL (2000) The large-scale organization of metabolic networks. Nature 407: 651–4.

53. Achacoso TB, Yamamoto WS (1992) AY's Neuroanatomy of C. elegans for Computation. First edition. Boca Raton, FL: CRC Press.

54. Watts DJ, Strogatz SH (1998) Collective dynamics of 'small-world' networks. Nature 393: 440–2.

55. Négyessy L, Nepusz T, Kocsis L, Bazsó F (2006) Prediction of the main cortical areas and connections involved in the tactile function of the visual cortex by network analysis. European Journal of Neuroscience 23: 1919–1930.

56. Leskovec J, Faloutsos C (2005) Graphs over time: densification laws, shrinking diameters and possible explanations. In: Proceedings of the eleventh ACM SIGKDD international conference on Knowledge discovery in data mining ACM. pp 177–187.

57. Ripeanu M, Foster I, Iamnitchi A (2002) Mapping the Gnutella network: Properties of large-scale peer-to-peer systems and implications for system design. IEEE Internet Computing Journal 6: 50–57.

58. Leskovec J, Lang K, Dasgupta A, Mahoney M (2009) Community structure in large networks: Natural cluster sizes and the absence of large well-defined clusters. Internet Mathematics 6: 29–123.

59. Klimt B, Yang Y (2004) Introducing the Enron corpus.

60. Cross R, Parker A (2004) The Hidden Power of Social Networks. Boston, MA: Harvard Business School Press.

61. Freeman S, Freeman L (1979) Social science research reports 46. Technical report, University of California, Irvine, CA.

62. Leskovec J, Huttenlocher D, Kleinberg J (2010) Signed networks in social media. In: Proceedings of the 28th international conference on Human factors in computing systems ACM. pp 1361–1370.

63. Van Duijn MAJ, Huisman M, Stokman FN, Wasseur FW, Zeggelink EPH (2003) Evolution of sociology freshmen into a friendship network. Journal of Mathematical Sociology 27: 153–191.

64. Milo R, Itzkovitz S, Kashtan N, Levitt R, Shen-Orr S, et al. (2004) Superfamilies of evolved and designed networks. Science 303: 1538–42.

65. Cancho RF, Solé RV (2001) The small world of human language. Proceedings of the Royal Society of London Series B: Biological Sciences 268: 2261–2265.

66. Balaji S, Babu MM, Iyer LM, Luscombe NM, Aravind L (2006) Comprehensive analysis of combinatorial regulation using the transcriptional regulatory network of yeast. Journal of Molecular Biology 360: 213–27.

67. Milo R, Shen-Orr S, Itzkovitz S, Kashtan N, Chklovskii D, et al. (2002) Network motifs: simple building blocks of complex networks. Science 298: 824–7.

16

Mutual Information Rate and Bounds for It

Murilo S. Baptista[1]*, **Rero M. Rubinger**[2], **Emilson R. Viana**[3], **José C. Sartorelli**[4], **Ulrich Parlitz**[5,6], **Celso Grebogi**[1,7]

1 Institute for Complex Systems and Mathematical Biology, Scottish Universities Physics Alliance, University of Aberdeen, Aberdeen, United Kingdom, **2** Institute of Physics and Chemistry, Federal University of Itajubá, Itajubá, Brazil, **3** Instituto de Ciências Exatas, Departamento de F sica, Universidade Federal de Minas Gerais, Belo Horizonte, Brazil, **4** Institute of Physics, University of São Paulo, São Paulo, Brazil, **5** Biomedical Physics Group, Max Planck Institute for Dynamics and Self-Organization, Göttingen, Germany, **6** Institute for Nonlinear Dynamics, Georg-August-Universität Göttingen, Göttingen, Germany, **7** Freiburg Institute for Advanced Studies, University of Freiburg, Freiburg, Germany

Abstract

The amount of information exchanged per unit of time between two nodes in a dynamical network or between two data sets is a powerful concept for analysing complex systems. This quantity, known as the mutual information rate (MIR), is calculated from the mutual information, which is rigorously defined only for random systems. Moreover, the definition of mutual information is based on probabilities of significant events. This work offers a simple alternative way to calculate the MIR in dynamical (deterministic) networks or between two time series (not fully deterministic), and to calculate its upper and lower bounds without having to calculate probabilities, but rather in terms of well known and well defined quantities in dynamical systems. As possible applications of our bounds, we study the relationship between synchronisation and the exchange of information in a system of two coupled maps and in experimental networks of coupled oscillators.

Editor: Jesus Gomez-Gardenes, Universidad de Zarazoga, Spain

Funding: MSB was partially supported by the Northern Research Partnership, Alexander von Humboldt foundation, and the Engineering and Physical Sciences Research Council grant Ref. EP/I032606/1. The research leading to the results has received funding from the European Community? Seventh Framework Programme FP7/2007-2013 under grant agreement No. HEALTH-F2-2009-241526, EUTrigTreat. Furthermore, support by the Bernstein Center for Computational Neuroscience II G\"ottingen (BCCN grant 01GQ1005A, project D1) is acknowledged. RR, EV and JCS thanks the Brazilian agencies Coordenadoria de Aperfeiçoamento de Pessoal de Nível Superior, Conselho Nacional de Desenvolvimento Científico e Tecnológico, Fundação de Amparo à Pesquisa do estado de Minas Gerais and Fundação de Amparo à Pesquisa do Estado de São Paulo. The funders had no role in study design, data collection and analysis, decision to publish, or preparation of the manuscript.

Competing Interests: The authors have declared that no competing interests exist.

* E-mail: murilo.baptista@abdn.ac.uk

Introduction

Shannon's entropy quantifies information [1]. It measures how much uncertainty an observer has about an event being produced by a random system. Another important concept in the theory of information is the mutual information [1]. It measures how much uncertainty an observer has about an event in a random system **X** after observing an event in another random system **Y** (or vice-versa).

Mutual information (MI) is an important quantity because it quantifies not only linear and non-linear interdependencies between two systems or data sets, but also is a measure of how much information two systems exchange or two data sets share. Due to these characteristics, it became a fundamental quantity to understand the development and function of the brain [2,3], to characterise [4,5] and model complex systems [6–8] or chaotic systems, and to quantify the information capacity of a communication system [9]. When constructing a model of a complex system, the first step is to understand which are the most relevant variables to describe its behaviour. Mutual information provides a way to identify those variables [10].

However, the calculation of mutual information in dynamical networks or data sets faces three main difficulties[4,11–13]. Mutual information is rigorously defined for random memoryless processes, only. In addition, its calculation involves probabilities of significant events and a suitable space where probability is

calculated. The events need to be significant in the sense that they contain as much information about the system as possible. But, defining significant events, for example the fact that a variable has a value within some particular interval, is a difficult task because the interval that provides significant events is not always known. Finally, data sets have finite size. Probabilities computed from finite data sets are subjected to unavoidable sampling errors. As a consequence, mutual information can often be calculated with a bias, only [4,11–13].

In this work, we show how to calculate the amount of information exchanged per unit of time [Eq. (2)], the so called mutual information rate (MIR), between two arbitrary nodes (or group of nodes) in a dynamical network or between two data sets. Each node represents a d-dimensional dynamical system with d state variables. The trajectory of the network considering all the nodes in the full phase space is denoted by Σ and represents the "attractor", which in the following calculations is considered to be an asymptotic limiting set. Then, we propose an alternative method, similar to the ones proposed in Refs. [14,15], to calculate significant upper and lower bounds for the MIR in dynamical networks or between two data sets, in terms of Lyapunov exponents, expansion rates, and capacity dimension. These quantities can be calculated without the use of probabilistic measures. As possible applications of our bounds calculation, we describe the relationship between synchronisation and the exchange of information in small experimental networks of coupled Double-Scroll circuits.

In previous works of Refs. [14,15], we have proposed an upper bound for the MIR in terms of the positive Lyapunov exponents of the synchronisation manifold. As a consequence, this upper bound could only be calculated in special complex networks that allow the existence of complete synchronisation. In the present work, the proposed upper bound can be calculated to any system (complex networks and data sets) that admits the calculation of Lyapunov exponents.

We assume that an observer can measure only one scalar time series for each one of two chosen nodes. These two time series are denoted by X and Y and they form a bidimensional set $\Sigma_\Omega = (X, Y)$, a projection of the "attractor" into a bidimensional space denoted by Ω. To calculate the MIR in higher-dimensional projections Ω, see Information S1. To estimate the upper bound of the MIR in terms of Lyapunov exponents obtained from the reconstructed attractor of a scalar time-series see Information S1. Assume that the space Ω is coarse-grained in a square grid of N^2 boxes with equal sides ϵ, so $N = 1/\epsilon$.

Mutual information is defined in the following way [1]. Given two discrete random variables, $\mathbf{X}$ and $\mathbf{Y}$, each one produces events i and j with probabilities $P_X(i)$ and $P_Y(j)$, respectively, the joint probability between these events is represented by $P_{XY}(i,j)$. Then, mutual information is defined as

$$I_S = H_X + H_Y - H_{XY}. \qquad (1)$$

$H_X = -\sum_i P_X(i) \log[P_X(i)]$, $H_Y = -\sum_j P_Y(j) \log[P_Y(j)]$, and $H_{XY} = -\sum_{i,j} P_{XY}(i,j) \log[P_{XY}(i,j)]$. When using Eq. (1) to calculate the mutual information between the dynamical variables X and Y, the probabilities appearing in Eq. (1) are defined such that $P_X(i)$ is the probability of finding points in a column i of the grid, $P_Y(j)$ of finding points in the row j of the grid, and $P_{XY}(i,j)$ the probability of finding points in a box where the column i meets the row j of the grid.

The MIR was firstly introduced by Shannon [1] as a "rate of actual transmission" [16] and later more rigorously redefined in Refs. [17,18]. It represents the mutual information exchanged between two dynamical variables (correlated) per unit of time. To calculate the MIR, the two continuous dynamical variables are transformed into two discrete symbolic sequences X and Y. Then, the MIR is defined by

$$MIR = \lim_{n \to \infty} \frac{I_S(n)}{n}, \qquad (2)$$

where $I_S(n)$ represents the usual mutual information between the two sequences X and Y, calculated by considering words of length n. If $I_S(n)$ is calculated using log_2, the MIR in Eq. (2) has units of bits/symbol. If a discrete system is producing the symbols, the units of Eq. (2) are bits/iteration.

The MIR is a fundamental quantity in science. Its maximal value gives the information capacity between any two sources of information (no need for stationarity, statistical stability, memoryless) [19]. Therefore, alternative approaches for its calculation or for the calculation of bounds of it are of vital relevance. Due to the limit to infinity in Eq. (2) and because it is defined from probabilities, the MIR is not easy to be calculated especially if one wants to calculate it from (chaotic) trajectories of a large complex network or data sets. The difficulties faced to estimate the MIR from dynamical systems and networks are similar to the ones

faced in the calculation of the Kolmogorov-Sinai entropy, H_{KS} [20], (Shannon's entropy per unit of time). Because of these difficulties, the upper bound for H_{KS} proposed by Ruelle [21] in terms of the Lyapunov exponents and valid for smooth dynamical systems ($H_{KS} \leq \sum \lambda_i^+$, where λ_i^+ represent all the i positive Lyapunov exponents) or Pesin's equality [22] ($H_{KS} = \sum \lambda_i^+$) proved in Ref. [23] to be valid for the large class of systems that possess a SRB measure, became so important in the theory of dynamical systems. Our upper bound [Eq. (5)] is a result similar to the work of Ruelle, but instead we relate mutual information rate with Lyapunov exponents.

Our work is also similar to the work of Wissman-Jones-Binder [24] who have shown that upper and lower bounds for H_{KS} and the sum of the Lyapunov exponents can be calculated in terms of the mutual information, MI, of a trajectory. Their work, like ours, has shown a link between (conditional and joint) probabilities and a dynamical quantity, the Lyapunov exponents. We focus our attention to the relationship between MIR and Lyapunov exponents, Wissman and co-authors focus their attention in the relationship between MI and the Lyapunov exponents.

Results

One of the main results of this work (whose derivation can be seen in Sec. Methods) is to show that, in dynamical networks or data sets with fast decay of correlation, I_S in Eq. (1) represents the amount of mutual information between X and Y produced within a special time interval T, where T represents the time for the dynamical network (or data sets) to lose its memory from the initial state or the correlation to decay to zero. Correlation in this work is not the usual linear correlation, but a non-linear correlation defined in terms of the evolution of probabilities defined by space integrals, the quantity $C(T)$ in Eq. (9). Therefore, the mutual information rate (MIR), between the dynamical variables X and Y (or two data sets) can be estimated by

$$MIR = \frac{I_S}{T} \qquad (3)$$

In systems that exhibit sensitivity to initial conditions, e.g. chaotic systems, predictions are only possible for times smaller than this time T. This time has other meanings. It is the expected time necessary for a set of points belonging to an ϵ-square box in Ω to spread over Σ_Ω and it is of the order of the shortest Poincaré return time for a point to leave a box and return to it [25,26]. It can be estimated by

$$T \approx \frac{1}{\lambda_1} \log\left[\frac{1}{\epsilon}\right]. \qquad (4)$$

where λ_1 is the largest positive Lyapunov exponent measured in Σ_Ω. Chaotic systems can exhibit the mixing property (see Methods), and as a consequence the correlation $C(t)$ decays to zero, surely after an infinitely long time. The correlation of chaotic systems can also decay to zero for sufficiently large but finite $t = T$ (see Information S1). T can be interpreted to be the minimum time required for a system to satisfy the conditions to be considered as mixing. Some examples of physical systems that are proved to be mixing and have exponentially fast decay of correlation are nonequilibrium steady-state [27], Lorentz gases (models of diffusive transport of light particles in a network of heavier particles) [28], and billiards [29]. An example of a "real world" physical complex system that presents exponentially fast decay of correlation is plasma turbulence [30]. We do not expect that data coming from a "real world" complex system is rigorously mixing and has an exponentially fast decay of correlation. But, we expect that the data has a sufficiently fast decay of correlation (e.g. stretched exponential decay or polynomially fast decays), implying that the system has sufficiently high sensitivity to initial conditions and as a consequence $C(t) \cong 0$, for a reasonably small and finite time $t = T$

The other two main results of our work are presented in Eqs. (5) and (7), whose derivations are presented in Sec. Methods. An upper bound for the MIR is given by

$$I_C = \lambda_1 - \lambda_2 = \lambda_1(2 - D), \qquad (5)$$

where λ_1 and λ_2 represent the largest and the second largest Lyapunov exponent measured in Σ_Ω, if both exponents are positive. If the i-largest exponent is negative, then we set $\lambda_i = 0$. If the set Σ_Ω represents a periodic orbit, $I_C = 0$, and therefore there is no information being exchanged. The quantity D is defined as

$$D = - \frac{\log(N_C(t = T))}{\log(\epsilon)}, \qquad (6)$$

where $N_C(t = T)$ is the number of boxes that would be covered by fictitious points at time T. At time $t = 0$, these fictitious points are confined in an ϵ-square box. They expand not only exponentially fast in both directions according to the two positive Lyapunov exponents, but expand forming a compact set, a set with no "holes". At $t = T$, they spread over Σ_Ω.

A lower bound for the MIR is given by

$$I_C^l = \lambda_1(2 - \tilde{D}_0), \qquad (7)$$

where $\tilde{D}_0$ represents the capacity dimension of the set Σ_Ω

$$\tilde{D}_0 = \lim_{\epsilon \to 0} \left[- \frac{\log(\tilde{N}_C(\epsilon))}{\log(\epsilon)} \right], \qquad (8)$$

where $\tilde{N}_C$ represents the number of boxes in Ω that are occupied by points of Σ_Ω.

D is defined in a way similar to the capacity dimension, though it is not the capacity dimension. In fact, $D \leq \tilde{D}_0$, because $\tilde{D}_0$ measures the change in the number of occupied boxes in Ω as the space resolution varies, whereas D measures the relative number of boxes with a certain fixed resolution ϵ that would be occupied by the fictitious points (in Ω) after being iterated for a time T. As a consequence, the empty space in Ω that is not occupied by Σ_Ω does not contribute to the calculation of $\tilde{D}_0$, whereas it contributes to the calculation of the quantity D. In addition, $N_C \geq \tilde{N}_C$ (for any ϵ), because while the fictitious points form a compact set expanding with the same ratio as the one for which the real points expand (ratio provided by the Lyapunov exponents), the real set of points Σ_Ω might not occupy many boxes.

Methods

Mixing, Correlation Decay and Invariant Measures

Denote by $F^T(x)$ a mixing transformation that represents how a point $x \in \Sigma_\Omega$ is mapped after a time T into Σ_Ω, and let $\rho(x)$ to represent the probability of finding a point of Σ_Ω in x (natural invariant density). Let I_1' represent a region in Ω. Then, $\mu(I_1') = \int \rho(x) dx$, for $x \in I_1'$ represents the probability measure of

the region I_1'. Given two square boxes $I_1' \in \Omega$ and $I_2' \in \Omega$, if F^T is a mixing transformation, then for a sufficiently large T, we have that the correlation defined as

$$C(T) = \mu[F^{-T}(I_1') \cap I_2'] - \mu[I_1']\mu[I_2'], \qquad (9)$$

decays to zero, the probability of having a point in I_1' that is mapped to I_2' is equal to the probability of being in I_1' times the probability of being in I_2'. That is typically what happens in random processes.

Notice that $\mu[F^{-T}(I_1') \cap I_2']$ can be interpreted as a joint entropy defined by the probability of being at I_2' times the conditional probability (that defines elements in a transition matrix) of transferring from the set I_2' to I_1'.

If the measure $\mu(\Sigma_\Omega)$ is invariant, then $\mu([F^{-T}(\Sigma_\Omega)] = \mu(\Sigma_\Omega)$. Mixing and ergodic systems produce measures that are invariant.

Derivation of the Mutual Information Rate (MIR) in Dynamical Networks and Data Sets

We consider that the dynamical networks or data sets to be analysed present either the mixing property or have fast decay of correlations, and their probability measure is time invariant. If a system that is mixing for a time interval T is observed (sampled) once every time interval T, then the probabilities generated by these snapshot observations behave as if they were independent, and the system behaves as if it were a random process. This is so because if a system is mixing for a time interval T, then the correlation $C(T)$ decays to zero for this time interval. For systems that have some decay of correlation, surely the correlation decays to zero after an infinite time interval. But, this time interval can also be finite, as shown in Information S1.

Consider now that we have experimental points and they are sampled once every time interval T. If the system is mixing, then the probability $\tilde{P}_{XY}((i,j),(k,l))$ of the sampled trajectory to be in the box with coordinates (i,j) and then be iterated to the box (k,l) depends exclusively on the probabilities of being at the box (i,j), represented by $\tilde{P}_{XY}(i,j)$, and being at the box (k,l), represented by $\tilde{P}_{XY}(k,l)$.

Therefore, for the sampled trajectory, $\tilde{P}_{XY}((i,j),(k,l)) = \tilde{P}_{XY}(i,j)\tilde{P}_{XY}(k,l)$. Analogously, the probability $\tilde{P}_X((i),(k))$ (or $\tilde{P}_Y((j),(l))$) of the sampled trajectory to be in the column i (or row j) of the grid and then be iterated to the column k (or row l) is given by $\tilde{P}_X((i),(k)) = \tilde{P}_X(i)\tilde{P}_X(k)$ (or $\tilde{P}_Y((j),(l)) = \tilde{P}_Y(j)\tilde{P}_Y(l)$).

The MIR of the experimental non-sampled trajectory points can be calculated from the mutual information of the sampled trajectory points $\tilde{I}_S$ that follow itineraries of length n:

$$MIR = \lim_{n \to \infty} \frac{\tilde{I}_S(n)}{nT}, \qquad (10)$$

Due to the absence of correlations of the sampled trajectory points, the mutual information for these points following itineraries of length n can be written as

$$\tilde{I}_S(n) = n[\tilde{H}_X(n = 1) + \tilde{H}_Y(n = 1) - \tilde{H}_{XY}(n = 1)], \qquad (11)$$

where $\tilde{H}_X(n = 1) = -\sum_i \tilde{P}_X(i) \log[\tilde{P}_X(i)]$, $\tilde{H}_Y(n = 1) = -\sum_j \tilde{P}_Y(j) \log[\tilde{P}_Y(j)]$, and $\tilde{H}_{XY}(n = 1) = -\sum_{i,j} \tilde{P}_{XY}(i,j) \log[\tilde{P}_{XY}(i,j)]$, and $\tilde{P}_X(i)$, $\tilde{P}_Y(j)$, and $\tilde{P}_{XY}(i,j)$ represent the probability of the sampled trajectory points to be in the column i of the grid, in the row j of the grid, and in the box (i,j) of the grid, respectively.

Due to the time invariance of the set Σ_Ω assumed to exist, the probability measure of the non-sampled trajectory is equal to the probability measure of the sampled trajectory. If a system that has a time invariant measure is observed (sampled) once every time interval T, the observed set has the same natural invariant density and probability measure of the original set. As a consequence, if Σ_Ω has a time invariant measure, the probabilities $P_X(i)$, $P_Y(j)$, and $P_{XY}(i,j)$ (used to calculate I_S) are equal to $\tilde{P}_X(i)$, $\tilde{P}_Y(j)$, and $\tilde{P}_{XY}(i,j)$.

Consequently, $\tilde{H}_X(n=1)=H_X$, $\tilde{H}_Y(n=1)=H_Y$, and $\tilde{H}_{XY}(n=1)=H_{XY}$, and therefore $\tilde{I}_S(n)=nI_S$. Substituting into Eq. (10), we finally arrive to $MIR=\dfrac{I_S}{T}$ in Eq. (3), where I_S between two nodes is calculated from Eq. (1).

Therefore, in order to calculate the MIR, we need to estimate the time T for which the correlation of the system approaches zero and the probabilities $P_X(i)$, $P_Y(j)$, $P_{XY}(i,j)$ of the experimental non-sampled experimental points to fall in the column i of the grid, in the row j of the grid, and in the box (i,j) of the grid, respectively.

We demonstrate the validity of Eqs. (10) and (11) by showing that $\tilde{I}_S(n=2)=2\tilde{I}_S(n=1)$, which leads to Eq. (3). For the following demonstration, (i,j) (or (k,l)) represents a box in the subspace Ω placed at coordinates (i,j), meaning a square of sides ε whose lower left corner point is located at $((i-1)\epsilon,(j-1)\epsilon)$. Then, i (or k) represents a column with width ϵ in Ω whose left side is located at $(i-1)\epsilon$ (or $(k-1)\epsilon$) and j (or l) represents a row with width ϵ in Ω whose bottom side is located at $(j-1)\epsilon$ (or $(l-1)\epsilon$).

If the system is mixing for a time T, then the probability of having points in a box (i,j) and going to another box (k,l), i.e., $P_{XY}(F^{-T}(k,l)\cap(i,j))$ can be calculated by

$$P_{XY}[F^{-T}(k,l)\cap(i,j)]=\tilde{P}_{XY}((i,j),(k,l))=\tilde{P}_{XY}(i,j)\tilde{P}_{XY}(k,l), \quad (12)$$

Notice that $P_{XY}[F^{-T}(k,l)\cap(i,j)]$ is a joint entropy that is equal to $\tilde{P}_{XY}((i,j),(k,l))$, and could be written as a function of conditional probabilities: $\tilde{P}_{XY}((i,j),(k,l))=\tilde{P}_{XY}(i,j)\tilde{P}_{XY}((i,j)|(k,l))$, where $\tilde{P}_{XY}((i,j)|(k,l))$ represents the conditional probability of being transferred from the box (i,j) to the box (k,l).

The same can be done to calculate the probability of having points in a column i that are mapped to another column k, i.e. $\tilde{P}_X((i),(k))$, or of having points in a row j that are mapped to another row l, i.e. $\tilde{P}_X((j),(l))$. If the system is mixing for a time T, then

$$P_X[F^{-T}(k)\cap(i)]=\tilde{P}_X((i),(k))=\tilde{P}_X(i)\tilde{P}_X(k) \quad (13)$$

and

$$P_Y[F^{-T}(l)\cap(j)]=\tilde{P}_Y((j),(l))=\tilde{P}_Y(j)\tilde{P}_Y(l) \quad (14)$$

for the rows. Notice that $P_X(i)=\sum_{j=1}^{N}P_{XY}(i,j)$ and $P_Y(j)=\sum_{i=1}^{N}P_{XY}(i,j)$.

The order-2 Mutual information of the sampled points can be calculated by.

$$\tilde{I}_S(n=2)=$$

$$\sum_{i,j=1}^{N}\sum_{k,l=1}^{N}\tilde{P}_{XY}((i,j),(k,l))\log\left[\frac{\tilde{P}_{XY}((i,j),(k,l))}{\tilde{P}_X((i),(k))\tilde{P}_Y((j),(l))}\right], \quad (15)$$

where $\sum_{i,j=1}^{N}=\sum_{i=1}^{N}\sum_{j=1}^{N}$. $\tilde{I}_S(n=2)$ measures the MI of points that follow an itinerary of one iteration, points that are in a box and are iterated to another box. Substituting Eq. (12) in Eq. (15) we arrive at

$$\tilde{I}_S(n=2)=\sum_{i,j=1}^{N}\sum_{k,l=1}^{N}\tilde{P}_{XY}(i,j)\tilde{P}_{XY}(k,l)$$

$$\times\left(\log[\tilde{P}_{XY}(i,j)]+\log[\tilde{P}_{XY}(k,l)]-\right.$$
$$\left.\log[\tilde{P}_X((i),(k))]-\log[\tilde{P}_Y((j),(l))]\right). \quad (16)$$

Then, substituting (13) and (14) in Eq. (16), and using the fact that $\sum_{i,j}\tilde{P}_{XY}(i,j)=1$ and $\sum_{k,l}\tilde{P}_{XY}(k,l)=1$, we arrive at

$$\tilde{I}_S(n=2)=2\sum_{i,j=1}^{N}\tilde{P}_{XY}(i,j)\log[\tilde{P}_{XY}(i,j)]-$$

$$\sum_{i,j=1}^{N}\sum_{k,l=1}^{N}\tilde{P}_{XY}(i,j)\tilde{P}_{XY}(k,l)\left(\log[\tilde{P}_X(i)]+\log[\tilde{P}_X(k)]+\right.$$
$$\left.\log[\tilde{P}_Y(j)]+\log[\tilde{P}_Y(l)]\right) \quad (17)$$

Re-organizing the terms we arrive at

$$\tilde{I}_S(n=2)=2\sum_{i,j=1}^{N}\tilde{P}_{XY}(i,j)\log[\tilde{P}_{XY}(i,j)]$$

$$-\sum_{k,l=1}^{N}\tilde{P}_{XY}(k,l)\sum_{i=1}^{N}\log[\tilde{P}_X(i)]\sum_{j=1}^{N}\tilde{P}_{XY}(i,j)+\ldots, \quad (18)$$

where ... represents other terms that are similar to the term appearing in the last hand-side part of the previous equation. Using the fact that $\sum_{j=1}^{N}\tilde{P}_{XY}(i,j)=\tilde{P}_X(i)$, we arrive at

$$\tilde{I}_S(n=2)=$$

$$2\sum_{i,j=1}^{N}\tilde{P}_{XY}(i,j)\log[\tilde{P}_{XY}(i,j)]-\sum_{i=1}^{N}\log[\tilde{P}_X(i)]\tilde{P}_X(i)+\ldots, \quad (19)$$

which can then be written as

$$\tilde{I}_S(n=2)=2\sum_{i,j=1}^{N}\tilde{P}_{XY}(i,j)\log[\tilde{P}_{XY}(i,j)]$$

$$-\sum_{i=1}^{N}\tilde{P}_X(i)\log[\tilde{P}_X(i)]-\sum_{j=1}^{N}\tilde{P}_Y(j)\log[\tilde{P}_Y(j)]-$$

$$\sum_{k=1}^{N}\tilde{P}_X(k)\log[\tilde{P}_X(k)]-\sum_{l=1}^{N}\tilde{P}_Y(l)\log[\tilde{P}_Y(l)]. \quad (20)$$

Since $\sum_{i=1}^{N} \tilde{P}_X(i) \log[\tilde{P}_X(i)] = \sum_{k=1}^{N} \tilde{P}_X(k) \log[\tilde{P}_X(k)]$ and $\sum_{j=1}^{N} \tilde{P}_Y(j) \log[\tilde{P}_Y(j)] = \sum_{l=1}^{N} \tilde{P}_Y(l) \log[\tilde{P}_Y(l)]$, we finally arrive at that $\tilde{I}_S(n=2) = 2\tilde{I}_S(n=1)$. Similar calculations can be performed to state that $\tilde{I}_S(n) = n\tilde{I}_S(n=1)$. As previously discussed, $\tilde{I}_S(n=1) = I_S$, which lead us to Eq. (3).

Derivation of an Upper (I_C) and Lower (I_C^l) Bounds for the MIR

Consider that our attractor Σ is generated by a 2d expanding system with constant Jacobian that possesses two positive Lyapunov exponents λ_1 and λ_2, with $\lambda_1 \geq \lambda_2$. $\Sigma \in \Omega$. Imagine a box whose sides are oriented along the orthogonal basis used to calculate the Lyapunov exponents. Then, points inside the box spread out after a time interval t to $\epsilon\sqrt{2}\exp^{\lambda_1 t}$ along the direction from which λ_1 is calculated. At $t = T$, $\epsilon\sqrt{2}\exp^{\lambda_1 T} = L$, which provides T in Eq. (4), since $L = \sqrt{2}$. These points spread after a time interval t to $\epsilon\sqrt{2}\exp^{\lambda_2 t}$ along the direction from which λ_2 is calculated. After an interval of time $t = T$, these points spread out over the set Σ_Ω. We require that for $t \leq T$, the distance between these points only increases: the system is expanding.

Imagine that at $t = T$, fictitious points initially in a square box occupy an area of $\epsilon\sqrt{2}\exp^{\lambda_2 T} L = 2\epsilon^2 \exp^{(\lambda_2 + \lambda_1)T}$. Then, the number of boxes of sides ϵ that contain fictitious points can be calculated by $N_C = 2\epsilon^2 \exp^{(\lambda_1 + \lambda_2)T} / 2\epsilon^2 = \exp^{(\lambda_1 + \lambda_2)T}$. From Eq. (4), $N = \exp^{\lambda_1 T}$, since $N = 1/\epsilon$.

We denote with a lower-case format, the probabilities $p_X(i)$, $p_Y(j)$, and $p_{XY}(i,j)$ with which fictitious points occupy the grid in Ω. If these fictitious points spread uniformly forming a compact set whose probabilities of finding points in each fictitious box is equal, then $p_X(i) = 1/N$ ($= \frac{1}{N_C}\frac{N_C}{N}$), $p_Y(j) = 1/N$, and $p_{XY}(i,j) = 1/N_C$. Let us denote the Shannon entropy of the probabilities $p_X(i)$, $p_Y(j)$ and $p_{XY}(i,j)$ as h_X, h_Y, and h_{XY}, respectively. The mutual information of the fictitious trajectories after evolving a time interval T can be calculated by $I_S^u = h_X + h_Y - h_{XY}$. Since, $p_X(i) = p_Y(j) = 1/N$ and $p_{XY}(i,j) = 1/N_C$, then $I_S^u = 2\log(N) - \log(N_C)$. At $t = T$, we have that $N = \exp^{\lambda_1 T}$ and $N_C = \exp^{(\lambda_1 + \lambda_2)T}$, leading us to $I_S^u = (\lambda_1 - \lambda_2)T$. Therefore, defining, $I_C = I_S^u / T$, we arrive at $I_C = \lambda_1 - \lambda_2$.

We define D as

$$D = -\frac{\log(N_C(t=T))}{\log(\epsilon)}, \qquad (21)$$

where $N_C(t=T)$ being the number of boxes that would be covered by fictitious points at time T. At time $t = 0$, these fictitious points are confined in an -square box. They expand not only exponentially fast in both directions according to the two positive Lyapunov exponents, but expand forming a compact set, a set with no "holes". At $t = T$, they spread over Σ_Ω.

Using $\epsilon = \exp^{-\lambda_1 T}$ and $N_C = \exp^{(\lambda_1 + \lambda_2)T}$ in Eq. (21), we arrive at $D = 1 + \frac{\lambda_2}{\lambda_1}$, and therefore, we can write that $I_C = \lambda_1 - \lambda_2 = \lambda_1(2 - D)$, as in Eq. (5).

To calculate the maximal possible MIR, of a random independent process, we assume that the expansion of points is uniform only along the columns and rows of the grid defined in the space Ω, i.e., $P_X(i) = P_Y(j) = 1/N$, (which maximises H_X and H_Y), and we allow $P_{XY}(i,j)$ to be not uniform (minimising H_{XY}) for all i and j, then

$$I_S(\epsilon) = -2\log(\epsilon) + \sum_{i,j} P_{XY}(i,j) \log[P_{XY}(i,j)]. \qquad (22)$$

Since $T(\epsilon) = -1/\lambda_1 \log(\epsilon)$, dividing $I_S(\epsilon)$ by $T(\epsilon)$, taking the limit of $\epsilon \to 0$, and reminding that the information dimension of the set Σ_Ω in the space Ω is defined as $\tilde{D}_1 = \lim_{\epsilon \to 0} \frac{\sum_{i,j} P_{XY}(i,j) \log[P_{XY}(i,j)]}{\log(\epsilon)}$, we obtain that the MIR is given by

$$I_S/T = \lambda_1(2 - \tilde{D}_1). \qquad (23)$$

Since $\tilde{D}_1 \leq \tilde{D}_0$ (for any value of ϵ), then $\lambda_1(2 - \tilde{D}_1) \geq \lambda_1(2 - \tilde{D}_0)$, which means that a lower bound for the maximal MIR [provided by Eq. (23)] is given by $I_C^l = \lambda_1(2 - \tilde{D}_0)$, as in Eq. (7). But $D \leq \tilde{D}_0$ (for any value of ϵ), and therefore I_C is an upper bound for I_C^l.

To show why I_C is an upper bound for the maximal possible MIR, assume that the real points Σ_Ω occupy the space Ω uniformly. If $\tilde{N}_C > N$, there are many boxes being occupied. It is to be expected that the probability of finding a point in a column or a row of the grid is $P_X(i) = P_Y(j) \cong 1/N$, and $P_{XY}(i,j) \cong 1/\tilde{N}_C$. In such a case, $MIR \cong I_C^l$, which implies that $I_C \geq MIR$. If $\tilde{N}_C < N$, there are only few boxes being sparsely occupied. The probability of finding a point in a column or a row of the grid is $P_X(i) = P_Y(j) \cong 1/\tilde{N}_C$, and $P_{XY}(i,j) \cong 1/\tilde{N}_C$. There are $\tilde{N}_C$ columns and rows being occupied by points in the grid. In such a case, $I_S \cong 2\log(\tilde{N}_C) - \log(\tilde{N}_C) \cong \log(\tilde{N}_C)$. Comparing with $I_S^u = 2\log(N) - \log(N_C)$, and since $\tilde{N}_C < N$ and $N_C \geq \tilde{N}_C$, then we conclude that $I_S^u \geq I_S$, which implies that $I_C \geq MIR$.

Notice that if $P_{XY}(i,j) = p_{XY}(i,j) = 1/N_C$ and $\tilde{D}_1 = \tilde{D}_0$, then $I_S/T = I_C^l = I_C$.

Expansion Rates

In order to extend our approach for the treatment of data sets coming from networks whose equations of motion are unknown, or for higher-dimensional networks and complex systems which might be neither rigorously chaotic nor fully deterministic, or for experimental data that contains noise and few sampling points, we write our bounds in terms of expansion rates defined in this work by

$$e_k(t) = 1/\tilde{N}_C \sum_{i=1}^{\tilde{N}_C} \frac{1}{t} \log[L_k^i(t)], \qquad (24)$$

where we consider $k = 1,2$. $L_1^i(t)$ measures the largest growth rate of nearby points. In practice, it is calculated by $L_1^i(t) = \frac{\Delta}{\delta}$, with δ representing the largest distance between pairs of points in an ϵ-square box i and Δ representing the largest distance between pairs of the points that were initially in the ϵ-square box but have spread out for an interval of time t. $L_2^i(t)$ measures how an area enclosing points grows. In practice, it is calculated by $L_2^i(t) = \frac{A}{\epsilon^2}$, with ϵ^2 representing the area occupied by points in an ϵ-square box, and A the area occupied by these points after spreading out for a time interval t. There are $\tilde{N}_C$ boxes occupied by points which are taken into consideration in the calculation of $L_k^i(t)$. An order-k

expansion rate, $e_k(t)$, measures on average how a hypercube of dimension k exponentially grows after an interval of time t. So, e_1 measures the largest growth rate of nearby points, a quantity closely related to the largest finite-time Lyapunov exponent [31]. And e_2 measures how an area enclosing points grows, a quantity closely related to the sum of the two largest positive Lyapunov exponents. In terms of expansion rates, Eqs. (4) and (5) read

$$T = \frac{1}{e_1} \log\left[\frac{1}{\epsilon}\right] \text{ and } I_C = e_1(2 - D),$$ respectively, and Eqs. (6) and

(7) read $D(t) = \frac{e_2(t)}{e_1(t)}$ and $I_C^l = e_1(2 - \tilde{D}_0)$, respectively.

From the way we have defined expansion rates, we expect that $e_k \leq \sum_{i=1}^{k} \lambda_i$. Because of the finite time interval and the finite size of the regions of points considered, regions of points that present large derivatives, contributing largely to the Lyapunov exponents, contribute less to the expansion rates. If a system has constant Jacobian, is uniformly hyperbolic, and has a constant natural measure, then $e_k = \sum_{i=1}^{k} \lambda_i$.

There are many reasons for using expansion rates in the way we have defined them in order to calculate bounds for the MIR. Firstly, because they can be easily experimentally estimated whereas Lyapunov exponents demand more computational efforts. Secondly, because of the macroscopic nature of the expansion rates, they might be more appropriate to treat data coming from complex systems that contain large amounts of noise, data that have points that are not (arbitrarily) close as formally required for a proper calculation of the Lyapunov exponents. Thirdly, expansion rates can be well defined for data sets containing very few data points: the fewer points a data set contains, the larger the regions of size ϵ need to be and the shorter the time T is. Finally, expansion rates are defined in a similar way to finite-time Lyapunov exponents and thus some algorithms used to calculate Lyapunov exponents can be used to calculate our defined expansion rates.

Results and Discussion

MIR and its Bounds in Two Coupled Chaotic Maps

To illustrate the use of our bounds, we consider the following two bidirectionally coupled maps.

$$X_{n+1}^{(1)} = 2X_n^{(1)} + \rho X_n^{(1)^2} + \Sigma(X_n^{(2)} - X_n^{(1)}), \text{mod } 1$$

$$X_{n+1}^{(2)} = 2X_n^{(2)} + \rho X_n^{(2)^2} + \Sigma(X_n^{(1)} - X_n^{(2)}), \text{mod } 1 \quad (25)$$

where $X_n^{(i)} \in [0,1]$. If $\rho = 0$, the map is piecewise-linear and quadratic, otherwise. We are interested in measuring the exchange of information between $X^{(1)}$ and $X^{(2)}$. The space Ω is the unit square. The Lyapunov exponents measured in the space Ω are the Lyapunov exponents of the set Σ_Ω that is the chaotic attractor generated by Eqs. (25).

The quantities I_S/T, I_C, and I_C^l are shown in Fig. 1 as we vary Σ for $\rho = 0$ (A) and $\rho = 0.1$ (B). We calculate I_S using in Eq. (1) the probabilities $P_{XY}(i,j)$ in which points from a trajectory composed of 2,000,000 samples fall in boxes of sides $\epsilon = 1/500$ and the probabilities $P_X(i)$ and $P_Y(j)$ that the points visit the intervals $[(i-1)\epsilon, i\epsilon[$ of the variable $X_n^{(1)}$ or $[(j-1)\epsilon, j\epsilon[$ of the variable $X_n^{(2)}$, respectively, for $i,j = 1, \ldots, N$. When computing I_S/T, the quantity T was estimated by Eq. (4). Indeed for most values of Σ, $I_C \geq I_S/T$ and $I_C^l \leq I_S/T$.

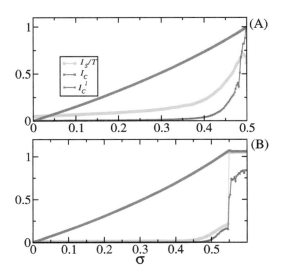

Figure 1. Results for two coupled maps. I_S/T [Eq. (3)] as (green online) filled circles, I_C [Eq. (5)] as the (red online) thick line, and I_C^l [Eq. (7)] as the (blue online) crosses. In (A) $\rho = 0$ and in (B) $\rho = 0.1$. The units of I_S/T, I_C, and I_C^l are [bits/iteration].

For $\Sigma = 0$ there is no coupling, and therefore the two maps are independent from each other. There is no information being exchanged. In fact, $I_C = 0$ and $I_C^l \cong 0$ in both figures, since $D = \tilde{D}_0 = 2$, meaning that the attractor Σ_Ω fully occupies the space Ω. This is a remarkable property of our bounds: to identify that there is no information being exchanged when the two maps are independent. Complete synchronisation is achieved and I_C is maximal, for $\Sigma > 0.5$ (A) and for $\Sigma \geq 0.55$ (B). A consequence of the fact that $D = \tilde{D}_0 = 1$, and therefore, $I_C = I_C^l = \lambda_1$. The reason is because for this situation this coupled system is simply the shift map, a map with constant natural measure; therefore $P_X(i) = P_Y(j)$ and $P_{XY}(i,j)$ are constant for all i and j. As usually happens when one estimates the mutual information by partitioning the phase space with a grid having a finite resolution and data sets possessing a finite number of points, I_S is typically larger than zero, even when there is no information being exchanged ($\Sigma = 0$). Even when there is complete synchronisation, we find non-zero off-diagonal terms in the matrix for the joint probabilities causing I_S to be smaller than it should be. Due to numerical errors, $X^{(1)} \cong X^{(2)}$, and points that should be occupying boxes with two corners exactly along a diagonal line in the subspace Ω end up occupying boxes located off-diagonal and that have at least three corners off-diagonal. Due to such problems, I_S/T is underestimated by an amount of $\lambda_1 \frac{3}{N} \approx 0.18\lambda_1$, resulting in a value of approximately $I_S/T = 0.82\lambda_1$, close to the value of I_S/T shown in Fig. 1(A), for $\Sigma = 0.5$. The estimation of the lower bound I_C^l in (B) suffers from the same problems.

Our upper bound I_C is calculated assuming that there is a fictitious dynamics expanding points (and producing probabilities) not only exponentially fast but also uniformly. The "experimental" numerical points from Eqs. (25) expand exponentially fast, but not uniformly. Most of the time the trajectory remains in 4 points: (0,0), (1,1), (1,0), (0,1). That is the main reason of why I_C is much larger than the estimated real value of the *MIR*, for some coupling strengths. If two nodes in a dynamical network behave in the same way the fictitious dynamics does, these nodes would be able to exchange the largest possible amount of information.

We would like to point out that one of the main advantages of calculating upper bounds for the MIR (I_S/T) using Eq. (5) instead of actually calculating I_S/T is that we can reproduce the curves for I_C using much less number of points (1000 points) than the ones (2,000,000) used to calculate the curve for I_S/T. If $\rho=0$, $I_C=-\ln(1-\Sigma)$ can be calculated since $\lambda_1=\ln(2)$ and $\lambda_2=\ln(2-2\Sigma)$.

MIR and its Bounds in Experimental Networks of Double-Scroll Circuits

We illustrate our approach for the treatment of data sets using a network formed by an inductorless version of the Double-Scroll circuit [32]. We consider four networks of bidirectionally diffusively coupled circuits (see Fig. 2). Topology I in (A) represents two bidirectionally coupled circuits, Topology II in (B), three circuits coupled in an open-ended array, Topology III in (C), four circuits coupled in an open-ended array, and Topology IV in (D), coupled in a closed array. We choose two circuits in the different networks (one connection apart) and collect from each circuit a time-series of 79980 points, with a sampling rate of $\delta=80.000$ samples/s. The measured variable is the voltage across one of the circuit capacitors, which is normalised in order to make the space Ω to be a square of sides 1. Such normalisation does not alter the quantities that we calculate. The following results provide the exchange of information between these two chosen circuits. The values of ϵ and t used to course-grain the space Ω and to calculate e_2 in Eq. (24) are the ones that minimise $|N_C(T,e_2)-\tilde{N}_C(\epsilon)|$ and at the same time satisfy $N_C(T,e_2)\geq\tilde{N}_C(\epsilon)$, where $N_C(T,e_2)=\exp^{Te_2(t)}$ represents the number of fictitious boxes covering the set Σ_Ω in a compact fashion, when $t=T$. This optimisation excludes some non-significant points that make the expansion rate of fictitious points to be much larger than it should be. In other words, we require that e_2 describes well the way most of the points spread. We consider that t used to calculate e_k in Eq. (24) is the time points initially in an ϵ-side box to become at most apart by $0.8L$. That guarantees that nearby points in Σ_Ω are expanding in both directions within the time interval $[0,T]$. Assuming that $t=T$ is calculated by measuring the time points initially in an ϵ-side box to be at most apart by $[0.4L, 0.8L]$ produces already similar results. If $t=T$ is calculated by measuring the time points become at least apart by $0.8L$, the set Σ_Ω might not be only expanding. T might be overestimated.

I_S has been estimated by the method in Ref. [33]. Since we assume that the space Ω where mutual information is being measured is 2D, we will compare our results by considering in the method of Ref. [33] a 2D space formed by the two collected scalar signals. In the method of Ref. [33] the phase space is partitioned in regions that contain 30 points of the continuous trajectory. Since that these regions do not have equal areas (as it is the case for I_C and I_C^l), in order to estimate T we need to imagine a box of sides ϵ_k, such that its area ϵ_k^2 contains in average 30 points. The area occupied by the set Σ_Ω is approximately given by $\epsilon^2\tilde{N}_C$, where $\tilde{N}_C$ is the number of occupied boxes. Assuming that the 79980 experimental data points occupy the space Ω uniformly, then on average 30 points would occupy an area of $\dfrac{30}{79980}\epsilon^2\tilde{N}_C$. The square root of this area is the side of the imaginary box that would occupy 30 points. So, $\epsilon_k=\sqrt{\dfrac{30}{79980}\tilde{N}_C}\epsilon$. Then, in the following, the "exact" value of the MIR will be considered to be given by

I_S/T_k, where T_k is estimated by $T_k=-\dfrac{1}{e_1}\log(\epsilon_k)$.

The three main characteristics of the curves for the quantities I_S/T_k, I_C, and I_C^l (appearing in Fig. 3) with respect to the coupling strength are that (i) as the coupling resistance becomes smaller, the coupling strength connecting the circuits becomes larger, and the level of synchronisation increases leading to an increase in I_S/T_k, I_C, and I_C^l, (ii) all curves are close, (iii) and as expected, for most of the resistance values, $I_C>I_S/T_k$ and $I_C^l\leq I_S/T_k$. The two main synchronous phenomena appearing in these networks are almost synchronisation (AS) [34], when the circuits are almost completely synchronous, and phase synchronisation (PS) [35]. For the circuits considered in Fig. 3, AS appears for the interval $R\in[0,3]$ and PS appears for the interval $R\in[3,3.5]$. Within this region of resistance values the exchange of information between the circuits becomes large. PS was detected by using the technique from Refs. [36,37].

MIR and its Upper Bound in Stochastic Systems

To analytically demonstrate that the quantities I_C and I_S/T can be well calculated in stochastic systems, we consider the following stochastic dynamical toy model illustrated in Fig. 4. In it points within a small box of sides ϵ (represented by the filled square in Fig. 4(A)) located in the centre of the subspace Ω are mapped after one iteration ($n=1$, $n\in\mathbb{N}$) of the dynamics to 12 other neighbouring boxes. Some points remain in the initial box. The points that leave the initial box go to 4 boxes along the diagonal line and 8 boxes off-diagonal along the transverse direction. Boxes along the diagonal are represented by the filled squares in Fig. 4(B) and off-diagonal boxes by filled circles. At the second iteration ($n=2$), the points occupy other neighbouring boxes, as illustrated in Fig. 4(C), and at a time T ($T\in\mathbb{R}$) the points occupy the attractor Σ and do not spread any longer. For iterations n larger than T, the points are somehow reinjected inside the region of the attractor. We consider that this system is completely stochastic, in the sense that no one can precisely determine the location of where an initial condition will be mapped. The only information is that points inside a smaller region are mapped to a larger region.

At the iteration n, there will be $N_d=2^{1+n}+1$ boxes occupied along the diagonal (filled squares in Fig. 4) and $N_t=2nN_d-C(\tilde{n})$ (filled circles in Fig. 4) boxes occupied off-diagonal (along the transverse direction), where $C(\tilde{n})=0$ for $\tilde{n}=0$, and $C(\tilde{n})>0$ for

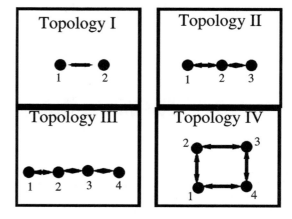

Figure 2. Black filled circles represent a Chua's circuit and the numbers identify each circuit in the networks. Coupling is diffusive. We consider 4 topologies: 2 coupled Chua's circuit (A), an array of 3 coupled circuits, an array of 4 coupled circuits, and a ring formed by 4 coupled circuits.

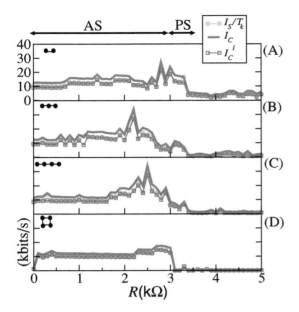

Figure 3. Results for experimental networks of Double-Scroll circuits. On the left-side upper corner pictograms represent how the circuits (filled circles) are bidirectionally coupled. I_S/T_k as (green online) filled circles, I_C as the (red online) thick line, and I_C^l as the (blue online) squares, for a varying coupling resistance R. The unit of these quantities shown in these figures is (kbits/s). (A) Topology I, (B) Topology II, (C) Topology III, and (D) Topology IV. In all figures, $\tilde{D}_0$ increases smoothly from 1.25 to 1.95 as R varies from $0.1k\Omega$ to $5k\Omega$. The line on the top of the figure represents the interval of resistance values responsible to induce almost synchronisation (AS) and phase synchronisation (PS).

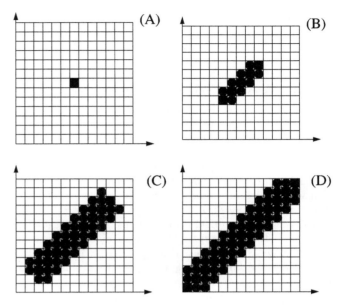

Figure 4. This picture is a hand-made illustration. Squares are filled as to create an image of a stochastic process whose points spread according to the given Lyapunov exponents. (A) A small box representing a set of initial conditions. After one iteration of the system, the points that leave the initial box in (A) go to 4 boxes along the diagonal line [filled squares in (B)] and 8 boxes off-diagonal (along the transverse direction) [filled circles in (B)]. At the second iteration, the points occupy other neighbouring boxes as illustrated in (C) and after an interval of time $n = T$ the points do not spread any longer (D).

$\tilde{n} \geq 1$ and $\tilde{n} = n - T - \alpha$. α is a small number of iterations representing the time difference between the time T for the points in the diagonal to reach the boundary of the space Ω and the time for the points in the off-diagonal to reach this boundary. The border effect can be ignored when the expansion along the diagonal direction is much faster than along the transverse direction.

At the iteration n, there will be $N_C = 2^{1+n} + 1 + (2^{1+n} + 1)2n - C(\tilde{n})$ boxes occupied by points. In the following calculations we consider that $N_C \cong 2^{1+n}(1 + 2n)$. We assume that the subspace Ω is a square whose sides have length 1, and that $\Sigma \in \Omega$, so $L = \sqrt{2}$. For $n > T$, the attractor does not grow any longer along the off-diagonal direction.

The largest Lyapunov exponent or the order-1 expansion rate of this stochastic toy model can be calculated by $N_d(n)\exp^{\lambda_1} = N_d(n+1)$, which takes us to

$$\lambda_1 = \log(2). \quad (26)$$

Therefore, the time T, for the points to spread over the attractor Σ, can be calculated by the time it takes for points to visit all the boxes along the diagonal. It can be calculated by $\epsilon\sqrt{2}\exp^{\lambda_1 T} = \sqrt{2}$, which take us to

$$T = -\frac{\log(\epsilon)}{\lambda_1} = -\frac{\log(\epsilon)}{\log(2)}. \quad (27)$$

The quantity D can be calculated by $D = \dfrac{\log(N_C)}{\log(N)}$, with $n = T$. Neglecting $C(\tilde{n})$ and the 1 appearing in N_C due to the initial box, we have that $N_C \cong 2^{1+T}[1 + 2^T]$. Substituting in the definition of D, we obtain $D = \dfrac{(1+T)\log(2) + \log(1 + 2^T)}{-\log(\epsilon)}$. Using T from Eq. (27), we arrive at

$$D = 1 + r, \quad (28)$$

where

$$r = -\frac{\log(2)}{\log(\epsilon)} - \frac{\log(1 + 2^T)}{\log(\epsilon)} \quad (29)$$

Placing D and λ_1 in $I_C = \lambda_1(2 - D)$, gives us

$$I_C = \log(2)(1 - r). \quad (30)$$

Let us now calculate I_S/T. Ignoring the border effect, and assuming that the expansion of points is uniform, then $P_{XY}(i,j) = 1/N_C$ and $P_X(i) = P_Y(j) = 1/N = \epsilon$. At the iteration $n = T$, we have that $I_S = -2\log(\epsilon) - \log(N_C)$. Since $N_C \cong 2^{1+T}[1 + 2^T]$, we can write that $I_S = -2\log(\epsilon) - (1 + T)\log(2) - \log(1 + 2^T)$. Placing T from Eq. (27) into I_S takes us to $I_S = -\log(2) - \log(\epsilon) - \log(1 + 2^T)$. Finally, dividing I_S by T, we arrive that

$$\frac{I_S}{T} = \log(2)\left[1 + \frac{\log(2)}{\log(\epsilon)} + \frac{\log(1+2^T)}{\log(\epsilon)}\right]$$

$$= \log(2)(1-r). \tag{31}$$

As expected from the way we have constructed this model, Eq. (31) and (30) are equal and $I_C = \dfrac{I_S}{T}$.

Had we included the border effect in the calculation of I_C, denote the value by I_C^b, we would have obtained that $I_C^b \geq I_C$, since λ_2 calculated considering a finite space Ω would be either smaller or equal than the value obtained by neglecting the border effect. Had we included the border effect in the calculation of I_S/T, denote the value by I_S^b/T, typically we would expect that the probabilities $P_{XY}(i,j)$ would not be constant. That is because the points that leave the subspace Ω would be randomly reinjected back to Ω. We would conclude that $I_S^b/T \leq I_S/T$. Therefore, had we included the border effect, we would have obtained that $I_C^b \geq I_S^b/T$.

The way we have constructed this stochastic toy model results in $D \cong 1$. This is because the spreading of points along the diagonal direction is much faster than the spreading of points along the off-diagonal transverse direction. In other words, the second largest Lyapunov exponent, λ_2, is close to zero. For stochastic toy models which produce larger λ_2, one could consider that the spreading along the transverse direction is given by $N_t = N_d 2^{\alpha n} - C(\tilde{n})$, with $\alpha \in [0,1]$.

Expansion Rates for Noisy Data with Few Sampling Points

In terms of the order-1 expansion rate, e_1, our quantities read $I_C = e_1(2-D)$, $T = \dfrac{1}{e_1}\log\left[\dfrac{1}{\epsilon}\right]$, and $I_C^l = e_1(2-\tilde{D}_0)$. In order to show that our expansion rate can be used to calculate these quantities, we consider that the experimental system is being observed in a one-dimensional projection and points in this projection have a constant probability measure. Additive noise is assumed to be bounded with maximal amplitude η, and having constant density.

Our order-1 expansion rate is defined as

$$e_1(t) = 1/\tilde{N}_C \sum_{i=1}^{\tilde{N}_C} \frac{1}{t}\log[L_1^i(t)]. \tag{32}$$

where $L_1^i(t)$ measures the largest growth rate of nearby points. Since all it matters is the largest distance between points, it can be estimated even when the experimental data set has very few data points. Since, in this example, we consider that the experimental noisy points have constant uniform probability distribution, $e_1(t)$ can be calculated by

$$e_1(t) = \frac{1}{t}\log\left[\frac{\Delta+2\eta}{\delta+2\eta}\right]. \tag{33}$$

where $\delta+2\eta$ represents the largest distance between pair of experimental noisy points in an ϵ-square box and $\Delta+2\eta$ represents the largest distance between pair of the points that were initially in the ϵ-square box but have spread out for an interval of time t. The experimental system (without noise) is responsible to make points that are at most δ apart from each other to spread to at most to Δ apart from each other. These points spread out exponentially fast according to the largest positive Lyapunov exponent λ_1 by

$$\Delta = \delta \exp^{\lambda_1 t}. \tag{34}$$

Substituting Eq. (34) in (33), and expanding log to first order, we obtain that $e_1 = \lambda_1$, and therefore, our expansion rate can be used to estimate Lyapunov exponents.

Conclusions

We have shown a procedure to calculate mutual information rate (MIR) between two nodes (or groups of nodes) in dynamical networks and data sets that are either mixing, or exhibit fast decay of correlations, or have sensitivity to initial conditions, and we have proposed significant upper (I_C) and lower (I_C^l) bounds for it, in terms of the Lyapunov exponents, the expansion rates, and the capacity dimension.

Since our upper bound is calculated from Lyapunov exponents or expansion rates, it can be used to estimate the MIR between data sets that have different sampling rates or experimental resolution or between systems possessing a different number of events. For example, suppose one wants to understand how much information is exchanged between two time-series, the heart beat and the level of CO_2 in the body. The heart is monitored by an EEG that collects data with a high-frequency, whereas the monitoring of the CO_2 level happens in a much lower frequency. For every m points collected from an EEG one could collect $n << m$ points in the monitoring of the CO_2 level. Assuming that the higher-frequency variable (the heart beat) is the one that contributes mostly for the sensibility to the initial conditions, then the larger expansion rate (or Lyapunov exponent) can be well estimated only using this variable. The second largest expansion rate (or Lyapunov exponent) can be estimated by the composed subspace formed by these two measurements, but only the measurements taken simultaneously would be considered. Therefore, the estimation of the second largest expansion rate would have to be done using less points than the estimation used to obtain the largest. In the calculation of the second largest expansion rate, it is necessary to know the largest exponent. If the largest is correctly estimated, then the chances we make a good estimation of the second largest increases, even when only a few points are considered. With the two largest expansion rates, one can estimate I_C, the upper bound for the MIR.

Additionally, Lyapunov exponents can be accurately calculated even when data sets are corrupted by noise of large amplitude (observational additive noise) [38,39] or when the system generating the data suffers from parameter alterations ("experimental drift") [40]. Our bounds link information (the MIR) and the dynamical behaviour of the system being observed with synchronisation, since the more synchronous two nodes are, the smaller λ_2 and D_0 will be. This link can be of great help in establishing whether two nodes in a dynamical network or in a complex system not only exchange information but also have linear or non-linear interdependences, since the approaches to measure the level of synchronisation between two systems are reasonably well known and are been widely used. If variables are synchronous in a time-lag fashion [35], it was shown in Ref. [16] that the MIR is independent of the delay between the two processes. The upper bound for the MIR could be calculated by measuring the Lyapunov exponents of the network (see Information S1), which are also invariant to time-delays between the variables.

If the MIR and its upper bounds are calculated from an "attractor" that is not an asymptotic limiting set but rather a transient trajectory, these values should typically differ from the values obtained when the "attractor" is an asymptotic limiting set. The dynamical quantities calculated, e.g., the Lyapunov exponents, expansion rates, and the fractal dimension should be interpreted as finite time quantities.

In our calculations, we have considered that the correlation of the system decays to approximately zero after a finite time T. If after this time interval the correlation does not decay to zero, we expect that I_S will be overestimated, leading to an overestimated value for the MIR. That is so because the probabilities used to calculate I_S will be considered to have been generated by a random system with uncorrelated variables, which is not true. However, by construction, the upper bound I_C is larger than the overestimated MIR.

Supporting Information

Information S1

Acknowledgments

M. S. Baptista would like to thank A. Politi for discussions concerning Lyapunov exponents and N. R. Obrer for discussions concerning MI and MIR.

Author Contributions

Conceived and designed the experiments: MSB RR EV JCS. Performed the experiments: RR EV JCS. Analyzed the data: MSB RR EV JCS UP. Contributed reagents/materials/analysis tools: MSB RR EV JCS UP. Wrote the paper: MSB RR EV JCS UP CG. Computer simulations: MSB. Analytical calculations: MSB. Analysis of analytical calculations: MSB UP.

References

1. Shannon CE (1948) A Mathematical Theory of Communication. Bell System Technical Journal 27: 379–423.
2. Strong SP, Koberle R, de Ruyter van Steveninck RR, Bialek W (1998) Entropy and Information in Neural Spike Trains. Phys. Rev. Lett. 80: 197–200.
3. Sporns O, Chialvo DR, Kaiser M, Hilgetag CC (2004) Organization, development and function of complex brain networks. Trends in Cognitive Sciences. 8: 418–425.
4. Palus M, Komárek V, Procházka T, Hrncir Z, Sterbova K (2001) Synchronization and information ow in EEGs of epileptic patients. IEEE Engineering in Medicice and Biology Sep/Oct: 65–71.
5. Donges JF, Zou Y, Marwan N, Kurths J (2009) Complex networks in climate dynamics. Eur. Phys. J. 174: 157–179.
6. Fraser AM, Swinney HL (1986) Independent coordinates for strange attractors from mutual information. Phys. Rev. A 33: 1134–1140.
7. Kantz H, Schreiber T (2004) Nonlinear Time Series Analysis. Cambridge: Cambridge University Press.
8. Parlitz U (1998) Nonlinear Time-Series Analysis, in Nonlinear Modelling - Advanced Black-Box techniques. The Netherlands: Kluwer Academic Publishers.
9. Haykin S (2001) Communication Systems. New York: John Wiley & Sons.
10. Rossi F, Lendasse A, François D, Wertz V, Verleysen M (2006) Mutual information for the selection of relevant variables in spectrometric nonlinear modelling. Chemometrics and Intelligent Laboratory Systems, 80: 215–226.
11. Paninski L (2003) Estimation of entropy and mutual information. Neural Computation 15: 1191–1253.
12. Steuer R, Kurths J, Daub CO, Weckwerth W (2002) The Mutual Information: Detecting and evaluating dependencies between variables. Bioinformatics 18: S231–S240.
13. Papana A, Kugiumtzis D, (2009) Evaluation of Mutual Information Estimators for Time Series. Int. J. Bifurcation and Chaos 19: 4197–4215.
14. Baptista MS, Kurths J (2008) Information transmission in active channels. Phys. Rev. E 77: 026205–1–026205–13.
15. Baptista MS, de Carvalho JX, Hussein MS (2008) Optimal network topologies for information transmission in active networks. PloS ONE 3: e3479.
16. Blanc JL, Pezard L, Lesne A (2011) Delay independence of mutual-information rate of two symbolic sequences. Phys. Rev. E 84: 036214–1–036214–9.
17. Dobrushin RL (1959) General formulation of Shannon's main theorem of information theory. Usp. Mat. Nauk. 14: 3–104; transl: Amer. Math. Soc. Translations, series 2 33: 323–438.
18. Gray RM, Kieffer JC (1980) Asymptotically mean stationary measures. IEEE Transations on Information theory IT-26: 412–421.
19. Verdú S, Han TS (1994) A general formula for channel capacity. IEEE Trans. Information Theory 40: 1147–1157.
20. Kolmogorov AN (1958) A new metric invariant of transient dynamical systems and automorphisms in Lebesgue spaces. Dokl. Akad. Nauk SSSR 119: 861–864; (1959) Entropy per unit time as a metric invariant of automorphisms. Dokl. Akad. Nauk SSSR 124: 754–755.
21. Ruelle D (1978) An inequality for the entropy of differentiable maps. Bol. Soc. Bras. Mat. 9: 83–87.
22. Pesin YaB (1977) Characteristic Lyapunov exponents and smooth ergodic theory. Russ. Math. Surveys 32: 55–114.
23. Ledrappier F, Strelcyn JM (1982) A proof of the estimate from below in Pesin's entropy formula. Ergod. Theory Dyn. Syst. 2: 203–219.
24. Wissman BD, McKay-Jones LC, Binder PM, (2011) Entropy rate estimates from mutual information. Phys. Rev. E 84: 046204–1–046204–5.
25. Gao JB (1999) Recurrence Time Statistics for Chaotic Systems and Their Applications. Phys. Rev. Lett. 83: 3178–3181.
26. Baptista MS, Eulalie N, Pinto PRF, Brito M, Kurths J (2010) Density of first Poincaré returns, periodic orbits, and Kolmogorov-Sinai entropy. Phys. Lett. A 374: 1135–1140.
27. Eckmann JP (2003) Non-equilibrium steady states. arXiv:math-ph/0304043.
28. Sinai YaG (1970) Dynamical systems with elastic reections. Ergodic properties of dispersing billiards. Russ. Math. Surv. 25: 137–189.
29. Chernov N, Young LS (2001) Decay of correlations for Lorentz gases and hard balls. Encycl. Of Math. Sc., Math. Phys. II 101: 89–120.
30. Baptista MS, Caldas IL, Heller MVAP, Ferreira AA (2001) Onset of symmetric plasma turbulence. Physica A, 301: 150–162.
31. Dawson S, Grebogi C, Sauer T, Yorke JA (1994) Obstructions to Shadowing When a Lyapunov Exponent Fluctuates about Zero. Phys. Rev. Lett. 73: 1927–1930.
32. Albuquerque HA, Rubinger RM, Rech PC, (2007) Theoretical and experimental time series analysis of an inductorless Chuas circuit. Physics D 233: 66–72.
33. Kraskov A, Stogbauer H, Grassberger P (2004) Estimating mutual information. Phys. Rev. E 69: 066138-1-066138-16.
34. Femat R, Soís-Perales G (1999) On the chaos synchronization phenomena. Phys. Lett. A 262: 50–60.
35. Pikovsky A, Rosenblum M, Kurths J (2001) Synchronization: A Universal Concept in Nonlinear Sciences. Cambridge: Cambridge University Press.
36. Baptista MS, Pereira T, Kurths J (2006) Upper bounds in phase synchronous weak coherent chaotic attractors. Physica D 216: 260–268.
37. Pereira T, Baptista MS, Kurths J (2007) General framework for phase synchronization through localized sets. Phys. Rev. E 75: 026216–1–026216–12.
38. Mera ME, Morán M (2009) Reduction of noise of large amplitude through adaptive neighborhoods. Phys. Rev E 80: 016207–1–016207–8.
39. Gao JB, Hu J, Tung WW, Cao YH, Distinguishing chaos from noise by scale-dependent Lyapunov exponent. Phys. Rev. E 74: 066204–1–066204–9.
40. Stefański A (2008) Lyapunov exponents of systems with noise and uctuating parameters. Journal of Theoretical and Applied Mechanics 46: 665–678.

17

Robustness Elasticity in Complex Networks

Timothy C. Matisziw[1,2,3]*, **Tony H. Grubesic**[4], **Junyu Guo**[1]

1 Department of Civil and Environmental Engineering, University of Missouri, Columbia, Missouri, United States of America, 2 Department of Geography, University of Missouri, Columbia, Missouri, United States of America, 3 Informatics Institute, University of Missouri, Columbia, Missouri, United States of America, 4 Geographic Information Systems and Spatial Analysis Laboratory, College of Information Science and Technology, Drexel University, Philadelphia, Pennsylvania, United States of America

Abstract

Network robustness refers to a network's resilience to stress or damage. Given that most networks are inherently dynamic, with changing topology, loads, and operational states, their robustness is also likely subject to change. However, in most analyses of network structure, it is assumed that interaction among nodes has no effect on robustness. To investigate the hypothesis that network robustness is not sensitive or elastic to the level of interaction (or flow) among network nodes, this paper explores the impacts of network disruption, namely arc deletion, over a temporal sequence of observed nodal interactions for a large Internet backbone system. In particular, a mathematical programming approach is used to identify exact bounds on robustness to arc deletion for each epoch of nodal interaction. Elasticity of the identified bounds relative to the magnitude of arc deletion is assessed. Results indicate that system robustness can be highly elastic to spatial and temporal variations in nodal interactions within complex systems. Further, the presence of this elasticity provides evidence that a failure to account for nodal interaction can confound characterizations of complex networked systems.

Editor: Stefano Boccaletti, Technical University of Madrid, Italy

Funding: This research is supported in part by the National Science Foundation (0908030 and 0718091). Any opinions, findings, and conclusions or recommendations expressed in this material are those of the author(s) and do not necessarily reflect the views of the National Science Foundation. Portions of this work are also supported by the National Academies Keck Futures Initiative Complex Systems grant CS05. The funders had no role in study design, data collection and analysis, decision to publish, or preparation of the manuscript.

Competing Interests: The authors have declared that no competing interests exist.

* E-mail: matisziwt@missouri.edu

Introduction

The structural and operational characteristics of many types of networks, particularly those representing physical, biological, chemical and social systems are highly dynamic and subject to constant change [1–4]. Networks exhibit periods of growth, decline, adjustment and equilibrium, expressed as changes to their structure (i.e. topology) and use (i.e. the magnitude of interaction or flow between pairs of nodes). As a result, the ability to effectively characterize the robustness of networks to the deletion of arcs and/or nodes is a tremendous analytical challenge requiring the consideration of both the structural and operative states of a network over time.

Much of the research on characterizing network dynamics focuses on structural change of systems over time, emphasizing network growth via preferential attachment [5–7] or copying [8], together with scaling [6,9–10], design considerations [11], decline [12] and vulnerability to failure [13–15]. Likewise, research that assesses network robustness typically addresses the problem from a structural perspective, emphasizing various measures of connectivity and performance [9,11,16–18]. As a result, these types of approaches primarily *describe* a structural state of the network, assuming that interaction or flow among all pairs of nodes is equivalent in magnitude and value to the system. However, in most networks, the level of interaction between any pair of nodes can vary in response to changes in the demand or need for interaction between the pair. For instance, the number of commuters between two cities can vary based on cost of travel, time of day, day of week, services available, etc [19]. Individuals in

a social network such as Facebook do not require (or want) connectivity with all other individuals in the network. Likewise, every species in a food web does not consume equivalently at every trophic level. Unfortunately, relatively little research has been devoted to understanding how variations in interaction among network nodes can affect a network's robustness [20–22]. One reason for the overwhelming focus on network structure is that measuring interaction among network nodes is a substantial practical and analytical challenge in itself. Fortunately, new scientific developments continue to yield nodal interaction data of increasing resolution and quality, increasing prospects for more sophisticated assessments of network structure and operation [23–26]. Thus, many research areas are now better positioned to exploit these spatial relationships in their analysis and move beyond the overgeneralizations inherent to structural analysis. To investigate the hypothesis that network robustness is not sensitive or elastic to the level of interaction (or flow) among network nodes, this paper explores the impacts of network disruption, namely arc deletion, over a temporal sequence of observed nodal interactions for a large Internet backbone system. In particular, a mathematical programming approach is used to identify exact bounds on robustness to arc deletion for each epoch of nodal interaction. Elasticity of the identified bounds relative to the magnitude of arc deletion is then assessed.

Evaluations of network robustness are typically premised on the extent to which a network is impacted by a disruptive or disassembly mechanism, such as those triggering the deletion or loss of network arcs and nodes [12,14]. Networks that experience lower levels of disruption from such events are considered to be more robust. One common way of modeling a disruptive mechanism is through the deletion of network elements in a manner that is representative of the assumed process (e.g. random deletion of nodes) [12]. Once an element (or a set of elements) is deleted, the resulting impact to the network's performance (i.e. decreases in efficiency, connectivity, capacity, interaction, etc.) can be assessed [9]. A network's robustness is therefore intimately linked with the mechanism of disruption assumed to impact the network and how the resulting disruption is measured.

Given the diversity of networks that have been studied, many mechanisms of disruption have been modeled, giving rise to a tremendous range of methodological options for characterizing and interpreting robustness [18,27]. Murray et al. [27] provide a basic typology of these methods using four broad categories: 1) scenario specific, 2) strategy specific, 3) simulation, and 4) mathematical modeling. Each of these categories is structured to reflect the way that deletion scenarios (sets of arcs and nodes deleted) are identified. Scenario specific methods are focused on analyzing the impact of a single or very limited selection of deletion scenarios that are presumed to be targeted by a deletion mechanism. Modeling the network effects of an airport closure (i.e. nodal deletion) due to local or regional weather conditions is considered a scenario-specific approach in this typology. Strategy specific methods identify scenarios where a deletion mechanism is assumed to logically order and sequentially delete network elements in some fashion. For instance, nodes might be ranked in decreasing order of their perceived value (e.g. based on some structural characteristic such as degree) to the deletion mechanism to establish the sequence of deletion [9,20]. Similar to the scenario specific methods, strategy specific approaches assume that scenarios selected by the disruptive mechanism can be precisely determined using simple rules and ranking metrics. As a result, both scenario specific and strategy specific methods for evaluating network robustness typically consider a relatively limited set of deletion scenarios. However, this can be problematic, because even in small networks, an enormous range of potential deletion scenarios exist whose contribution to network robustness remains unexplored. As a result, evaluation, comparison and benchmarking of robustness is limited to only those deletion scenarios identified, rather than a broader spectrum of potential scenarios [18,27–29]. Simulation methods attempt to provide a more detailed characterization of robustness by identifying a larger sample of potential deletion scenarios and assessing their relative value. That is, simulation attempts to relax the rules guiding deletion and account for the wide range of scenarios available to a deletion mechanism. However, unless all potential scenarios of deletion are completely enumerated, the full extent of network robustness remains unknown. This is of particular concern since the deletion scenarios to which the network is least robust may not be identified [18,27–29]. To address this issue, mathematical modeling techniques have been developed to establish the exact mathematical bounds on robustness (i.e. robustness to the most disruptive mechanism and the least disruptive mechanism) [22,28–35]. These mathematical programming approaches, widely known as "interdiction" models, have been developed to identify optimal ways of deleting or degrading network elements by explicitly modeling the objective(s) of the deletion mechanism without constraining the order in which the elements are selected for deletion. In other words, it is assumed that a mechanism optimizes its capability for deletion by assessing the simultaneous impact of the deletion scenario on a network's robustness. In this sense, one bound on robustness can be viewed as the level of disruption caused by a deletion mechanism that optimally targets a set of arcs and/or nodes such that network performance is maximally

degraded. That is, no other scenario of deletion targeting the same number of arcs and nodes would result in greater disruption to network performance than the bounding scenario. Since these bounds represent a mathematically optimal benchmark on network robustness, the relative impacts of all other scenarios of arc/node deletion (regardless of the underlying mechanism) can be evaluated consistently and without bias with respect to the bounds. Sadly, little attention has been given to mathematical bounds on robustness since they are extremely difficult to provably identify due to the combinatorics and interdependencies inherent to complex networks [22,35]. Consider, for example, a network with 400 nodes and a mechanism targeting eight nodes for deletion. Combinatorially, the mechanism in this case would have C_8^{400} (or 15 quadrillion) feasible scenarios of simultaneous node deletion to choose from. In order to provably identify the scenario bounding robustness of a network this size, the impact of each of these scenarios would need to be evaluated in some fashion. Clearly, while this type of network is not particularly large by today's standards, the associated computational challenges for evaluating robustness on a system this size are daunting. Regardless, since the mathematical bounds on robustness yield valuable context for robustness measures associated with any other mechanism of deletion, they are ideal for testing the sensitivity of network robustness to changes in nodal interaction as will be examined next. First, a mathematical programming approach for deriving bounds on network robustness to arc deletion given observations of nodal interaction over time is detailed. This modeling framework is then applied to a large Internet backbone system, for which a temporal sequence of nodal interactions was obtained. After robustness bounds are determined, elasticity of the identified bounds relative to the magnitude of arc deletion is assessed.

Methods

Provided a network G with N nodes and A arcs in epoch t $(G_t(N_t,A_t))$ and level of interaction or flow f_{ijt} between each pair of nodes $i \in N_t, j \in N_t$, the total nodal interaction supported by the network can be expressed as $\Omega_t = \sum_{i \in N_t} \sum_{j \in N_t} f_{ijt}$. Let p denote the number of arcs to be targeted by the deletion mechanism and let X_{ijt}^k represent the deletion mechanism's decision to act on each arc $(i,j) \in A_t$ in scenario k (where, $X_{ijt}^k = 1.0$ if arc (i,j) is selected for deletion; $X_{ijt}^k = 0.0$ otherwise). Thus, in any feasible scenario of arc deletion k in epoch t, $\sum_{(i,j) \in A_t} X_{ijt}^k = p$. Numerous such scenarios k (entire set denoted K_{pt}) exist given the combinatorial nature of the problem as described earlier. Given any scenario of deletion k, the impact on connectivity or the presence of a path between a pair of nodes can then be referenced as the variable Z_{ijt}^k where, $Z_{ijt}^k = 0.0$ if connectivity between nodes i and j is present, and $Z_{ijt}^k = 1.0$ if no path is available between the nodal pair. Thus, interaction between a pair of nodes can only be facilitated whenever at least one path between the two nodes exists (i.e. $Z_{ijt}^k = 0.0$). The total nodal interaction inhibited by a scenario of arc deletion can then be denoted $\hat{\Omega}_t^{pk} = \sum_{i \in N_t} \sum_{j \in N_t} f_{ijt} Z_{ijt}^k$. If K_{pt} accounts for all feasible scenarios of p-arc deletion, the state of maximally inhibited nodal interaction is then induced by the scenario k where $\hat{\Omega}_t^{pk} = \text{maximize}_{k \in K_{pt}} \hat{\Omega}_t^{pk}$. Therefore, a lower bound on network robustness in epoch t is then the level of nodal interaction supported by the network (or non-inhibited) given a scenario of maximal disruption or $\Gamma_t^p = \Omega_t - \text{maximize}_{k \in K_{pt}} \hat{\Omega}_t^{pk}$

[22,36]. In practice, the identification of arc deletion scenarios that provably $\underset{k\in K_{pt}}{\text{maximize}}\ \hat{\Omega}_t^{pk}$ is a computational challenge, necessitating efficient optimization approaches and solution techniques [22,30–31,35]. In order to identify a bounding scenario of arc deletion, a mathematical programming problem can be structured based on the model of [22]. Let $k = *$ delineate the scenario of deletion resulting in maximal inhibition of nodal interaction to be sought and let M_{ijt} be the set of nodes v incident to node i through which node j can be reached via non-cyclic paths.

$$Maximize\ \hat{\Omega}_t^{p*} = \sum_{i\in N_t}\sum_{j\in N_t} f_{ijt} Z_{ijt}^* \qquad (1)$$

Subject to:

$$\sum_{(i,j)\in A_t} X_{ijt}^* = p \qquad (2)$$

$$X_{ijt}^* - Z_{ijt}^* \geq 0 \qquad \forall(i,j)\in A_t \qquad (3)$$

$$X_{ivt}^* + Z_{vjt}^* - Z_{ijt}^* \geq 0 \qquad \forall i\in N_t, j\in N_t, v\in M_{ijt}, v\neq j \qquad (4)$$

$$X_{ijt}^* = \{0,1\} \qquad \forall(i,j)\in A_t \qquad (5)$$

$$Z_{ijt}^* = \{0,1\} \qquad \forall i\in N_t, j\in N_t$$

Model Objective (1) is to identify a network state where total nodal interaction is maximally inhibited. If the nodal interaction variable f_{ijt} is omitted, Objective (1) would then be to maximally inhibit structural connectivity. Constraint (2) states that a scenario must be found that involves the deletion of exactly p arcs. Constraints (3) and (4) state that connectivity between a pair of nodes can only be completely inhibited if *no* paths between the nodal pair are available after arc deletion. That is, *any* path between a pair of nodes can provide connectivity until one or more of the arcs participating in the path are deleted. Given this constraint structure, *all* potential paths of movement between each nodal pair are considered in the modeling framework (not just the shortest or some subset of paths) [22]. Constraints (5) ensure that the decisions made by the model are binary-integer in nature. Given the linear-integer structure of this model, it can be solved using techniques such as branch-and-bound [37], available in many commercial optimization software packages. Once solved, the variables $X_{ijt}^* = 1.0$ will indicate which arcs are selected for deletion and the variables $Z_{ijt}^* = 1.0$ will indicate which nodal pairs are no longer connected given the optimal scenario of arc deletion. Network robustness to the most disruptive mechanism of p-arc deletion can then be reported as $\Gamma_t^p = \Omega_t - \hat{\Omega}_t^{p*}$.

Once a network's robustness has been characterized, the sensitivity or elasticity of robustness to changes in the magnitude of arc deletion p can be evaluated. The elasticity of robustness in epoch t can be approximated as $E_{\Gamma_t^p,p} = |\%\Delta\Gamma_t^p/\%\Delta p|$ for any change in robustness relative to the corresponding change in p using standard midpoint elasticity calculations [38]. Given this formulation of elasticity, values greater than 1.0 represents increasing returns to scale, where changes in network robustness

are very sensitive to changes in the magnitude of arc deletion. In other words, a larger elasticity indicates greater potential for a mechanism to efficiently degrade network performance. Conversely, robustness elasticity less than 1.0 indicates decreasing returns to scale, where changes in network robustness are less sensitive to changes in the magnitude of arc deletion. Simply put, a lower sensitivity means that the network can better withstand the effects of a disruptive mechanism.

Results

The concept of robustness elasticity is illustrated using the Internet2 backbone network for which observations of nodal interaction were recorded [39]. Topology and levels of nodal interaction for this Internet system were observed at network routers. When this study was conducted, 372 routers (nodes) and 495 fiber linkages (arcs) defined the backbone structure (Figure 1). Thus, in this network there are 138,384 nodal pairs (372×372) that can potentially interact with one another (sending/receiving data in this example). Data (i.e. bytes) transmitted between network nodes was recorded over a 24 hour period. Given the amount of data collected, network traffic is aggregated into six epochs for subsequent analysis. Table 1 shows a summary of network activity in the analysis epochs. Over the course of the day sampled, some level of data transmission is observed between 70,685 unique pairs of nodes (routers). Therefore, only around 51% of the nodal pairs in the network required connectivity on this day. The number of nodal pairs interacting varies considerably throughout the day with a high of 62,200 pairs engaged in the movement of nearly 24% of the day's data in the 12 pm–4 pm epoch (all times are in U.S. Eastern Standard Time) to a low of 47,913 pairs supporting only 8% of the day's interaction in the 4 am–8 am epoch (Table 1). In this paper, bounds on robustness for scenarios of arc deletion ranging from $p = 1$ (deletion of a single arc) to $p = 20$ (simultaneous deletion of 20 arcs) for each of the six epochs are sought. To accomplish this, a total of 120 instances to the optimization model (1)-(5) are generated to derive twenty bounding scenarios for each of the six epochs. Each of the 120 modeling instances is then solved to optimality using IBM's ILOG CPLEX v12.1.0, a commercial optimization solver. Using the optimal deletion scenarios, the Internet network's robustness to arc loss (Γ_t^p) can then be evaluated.

Table 2 details the bounds on robustness for each epoch for the different levels of p-arc deletion assessed. To better visualize the nature of these bounds, Figure 2 illustrates the scenario of seven arc deletion ($p = 7$) identified by the optimization approach as maximally inhibiting nodal interaction in the 8 am–12 pm epoch. The seven arcs comprising this optimal scenario constitute a cutset, fragmenting the network into two subgraphs. In this particular epoch, this cutset inhibits 33.7% of all nodal interaction (66.3% interaction is non-inhibited). Therefore, while nodes in the same subgraph (i.e. Denver and New York) are still connected and can interact, nodes in different subgraphs (i.e. New York and Los Angeles) are no longer connected and all interaction among them has been inhibited. In order to more clearly illustrate the spatial distribution of inhibited nodal interaction, Figures 3–4 depict the backbone network and the percent of interaction inhibited at each node (deleted arcs are not shown). Figure 3 details the level of nodal interaction inhibited in the 8 am–12 pm epoch due to the optimal deletion scenario of seven arcs shown in Figure 2. As highlighted in Figure 3, many nodes in California, Oregon, Nevada, and Arizona experience higher levels of disruption given that most of their interaction was with nodes in the Eastern subgraph. Many of the nodes in the Eastern subgraph display

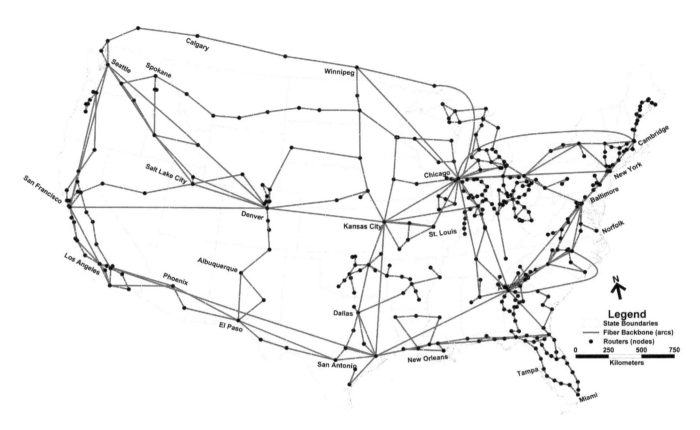

Figure 1. Internet2 backbone.

lower levels of disruption on average, indicating they required little or no connectivity with the Western subgraph in this epoch. Interestingly, there are some non-intuitive pockets of nodes elsewhere in the network (e.g. Maine) that too experience significantly degraded levels of interaction – likely a function of their demand for interaction with Western nodes during this epoch. Figure 4 depicts the percent degradation in nodal interaction at network nodes in the 8 pm–12 am epoch. In this case, the seven deleted arcs maximally inhibiting nodal interaction (36.9% of total interaction inhibited; 63.1% non-inhibited) are primarily located in the Northeastern portion of the network comprising a completely different scenario from that shown in Figure 2. The resulting spatial distribution of disruption varies considerably among network nodes. While interaction between many nodal pairs experiences little to no reduction, interaction

among other nodes (i.e. those in the Northeastern region where arc deletion occurred) is severely diminished. Although very distant from the deleted arcs, significant levels of inhibited nodal interaction can be observed in Wisconsin, California, Georgia, as well as many other locales. While the *number* of arcs deleted in the 8 pm–12 am and 8 am–12 pm epochs is the same ($p = 7$), the *set* of arcs selected for deletion in each epoch are very different as is the impact of their deletion on nodal interaction. These changes in the role of the network arcs and in the spatial distribution of nodal interaction disrupted highlight the remarkable sensitivity of network robustness, both in time and space, to arc deletion. This finding is clear evidence that network robustness is indeed dependent on the spatial and temporal organization of interacting nodes within a network.

Figure 5 summarizes the derived bounds on network robustness from Table 2 for those epochs most robust (maximum) and least robust (minimum) to optimal *p*-arc deletion. In this Figure, the robustness of the other four epochs, though not shown for clarity, falls somewhere between these extrema. Without identification of these bounds, the relationship of a deletion mechanism to a most disruptive or 'worst-case' mechanism is impossible to assess. As shown, the bounds on robustness can range significantly within each epoch. For example, given the simultaneous deletion of two arcs ($p = 2$), the 12 pm–4 pm epoch is when the network is least robust, respective to the other epochs, where 83.8% nodal interaction not inhibited. Conversely, the 4 am–8 am epoch is the most robust, where 85.3% interaction is not inhibited. Although the difference in robustness between these two epochs for $p = 2$ is rather small, it becomes more pronounced as the number of arcs deleted increases. Consider, for example, an eight arc deletion scenario ($p = 8$). In this instance, the network is most

Table 1. Summary of observed nodal interaction by epoch.

Epoch	Interacting Node Pairs	% Daily Interaction
12 am–4 am	50,516	11
4 am–8 am	47,913	8
8 am–12 pm	60,168	19
12 pm–4 pm	62,202	24
4 pm–8 pm	59,741	22
8 pm–12 am	54,777	17
Day Total	70,685 Unique Pairs	100

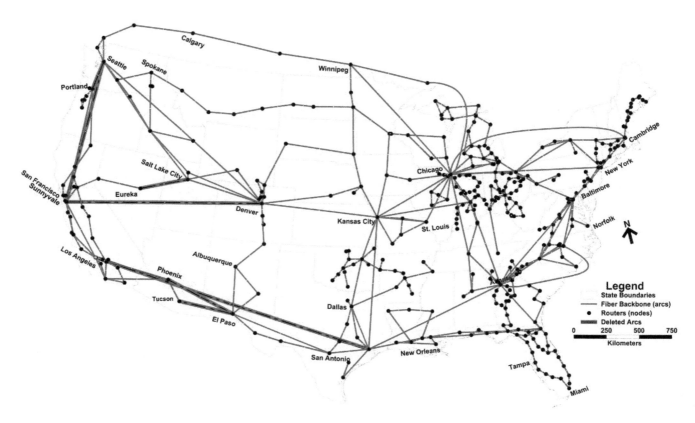

Figure 2. Seven arc deletion scenario bounding robustness 8 am–12 pm.

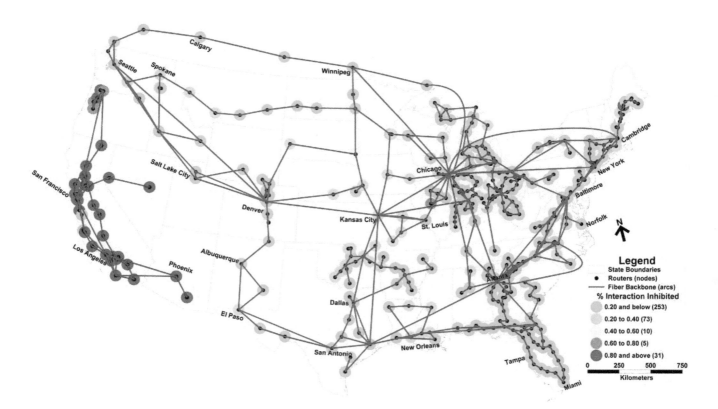

Figure 3. Maximally inhibited nodal interaction: 8 am–12 pm.

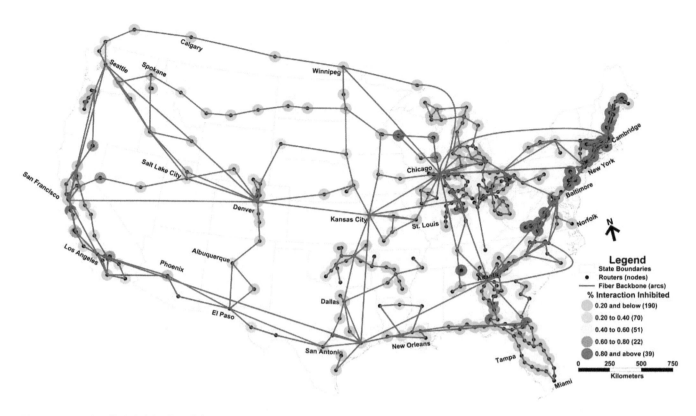

Figure 4. Maximally inhibited nodal interaction: 8 pm–12 am.

Table 2. Bounds on robustness (% non-inhibited nodal interaction) to p-arc deletion by epoch.

p	12 am–4 am	4 am–8 am	8 am–12 pm	12 pm–4 pm	4 pm–8 pm	8 pm–12 am
0	100.00	100.00	100.00	100.00	100.00	100.00
1	95.16	93.66	96.00	96.52	95.51	95.23
2	84.60	85.30	84.38	83.83	84.60	84.88
3	79.92	79.08	81.23	80.74	80.64	81.04
4	74.35	75.89	76.34	76.66	75.15	72.72
5	69.68	70.12	73.21	73.59	71.60	68.89
6	67.05	67.16	71.18	70.97	68.71	66.90
7	64.53	63.93	66.30	62.18	62.81	63.07
8	45.35	42.28	37.41	38.71	42.80	47.71
9	42.35	39.75	35.06	36.77	40.63	44.84
10	35.65	34.36	28.84	29.28	33.32	36.14
11	32.80	32.25	27.25	27.72	31.47	33.76
12	27.88	28.53	23.84	24.61	26.29	27.83
13	25.84	26.50	22.19	23.07	24.83	26.38
14	24.23	24.42	21.12	21.76	23.12	22.95
15	21.08	20.77	19.71	20.72	21.67	20.82
16	19.43	19.09	18.71	19.14	19.97	19.14
17	17.64	17.46	16.63	17.32	18.16	17.30
18	15.56	15.89	15.06	15.58	16.32	15.75
19	13.93	14.35	13.01	13.58	14.42	14.12
20	12.98	13.12	12.42	13.04	13.61	13.42

robust in the 8 pm–12 am epoch, where 47.7% of nodal interaction is not inhibited. However, the network is least robust to the deletion of eight arcs during the 8 am–12 pm epoch where only 37.4% nodal interaction is not inhibited. As expected, larger magnitudes of arc deletion (larger p) are met by lower levels of robustness within a single epoch. However, it is noted that this tendency does not necessarily carry over *between* epochs as depicted in multiple cases in Figure 5. For instance, network robustness is much higher for the deletion of nine arcs ($p = 9$) in the 8 pm–12 am epoch than it is for the loss of 8 arcs ($p = 8$) in the 8 am–12 pm epoch. This behavior is clear evidence of the influence that variations in nodal interaction can have on characterizations of robustness. In particular, changing patterns of nodal interaction can affect how the network is used to facilitate these interactions. Further, the arc deletion scenarios comprising the bounds on robustness can vary in arc composition both between *and* within epochs as highlighted in the previous example. That is to say that an arc contributing to a scenario of p-arc deletion bounding network robustness may not be included in bounding scenarios for other magnitudes of arc deletion given the interdependencies among network nodes.

To better illustrate the relationship between the sets of arcs involved in bounding scenarios, Figure 6 displays Dice's Coefficient [40], a measure of set similarity, for the sets of deleted arcs maximally inhibiting interaction in the 8 pm–12 am epoch. This matrix depicts the percent similarity in the arcs selected for deletion between any pair of bounding scenarios. For instance, row one of the matrix describes the extent to which the single arc deleted in the $p = 1$ scenario is also deleted in the other deletion scenarios. Thus, as detailed in row one of the matrix, the single arc deleted in the scenario bounding $p = 1$ is not selected for deletion in the scenarios bounding $p = 2, 4, 6, 8–10, 12,$ and $14–19$; hence, bearing no similarity with them. However, the arc selected for

deletion in $p = 1$ is also selected for deletion in scenarios where $p = 3, 5, 7, 11, 13,$ and 20. Row eight of the matrix indicates that none of the eight arcs deleted in the optimal $p = 8$ scenario are deleted in the $p = 1–7$ scenarios. Yet, many of the arcs selected for deletion in the $p = 8$ scenario are also selected for deletion in other bounding scenarios, such as is the case for $p = 10–14$ (at least 80% similarity in the arcs selected for deletion). Since the set of arcs characterizing robustness in one epoch may differ so significantly from those characterizing robustness in other epochs, these results provide further evidence that dynamics in nodal interaction give rise to variations in the importance of arcs to the network.

Figure 7 illustrates robustness elasticity for the network relative to each unit change in arc deletion magnitude over the six epochs of observed nodal interaction. In essence, this is a relative measure of robustness sensitivity to changes in magnitude of arc deletion (p). As illustrated by Figure 7, robustness elasticity (on the y-axis) varies substantially given unit increases in p. This particular network is relatively non-elastic ($E_{\Gamma_t^p, p} < 1.0$) when arc deletion magnitudes are low (e.g. increase from $p = 1$ to $p = 2$ or from $p = 6$ to $p = 7$). One reason for this is that unit changes between smaller values of p will result in a greater percent change in disruptive magnitude when compared to unit changes between larger values of p. For example, when moving from $p = 1$ to $p = 2$, the network experiences a large percent decrease in robustness (over 11%). However, the percent change in p is also relatively large (over 66%), resulting in low elasticity. That said, most instances exhibit a much smaller change in robustness relative to the magnitude of arc deletion. The non-elastic nature of robustness at these magnitudes of arc deletion can be seen as indicative as greater network resistance to a disruptive mechanism or greater effort needed by the mechanism to maximally inhibit nodal interaction. However, an increase from $p = 7$ to $p = 8$ indicates a clear bifurcation point, where increasing returns to scale ($E_{\Gamma_t^p, p} \geq 1.0$) are realized. This

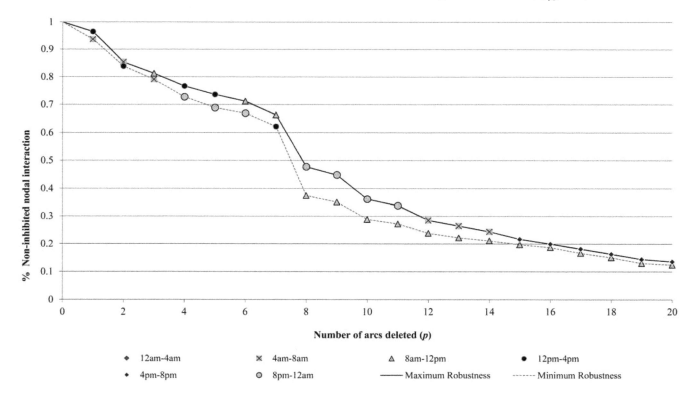

Figure 5. Epochs with maximum and minimum robustness for bounding scenarios of p-arc deletion.

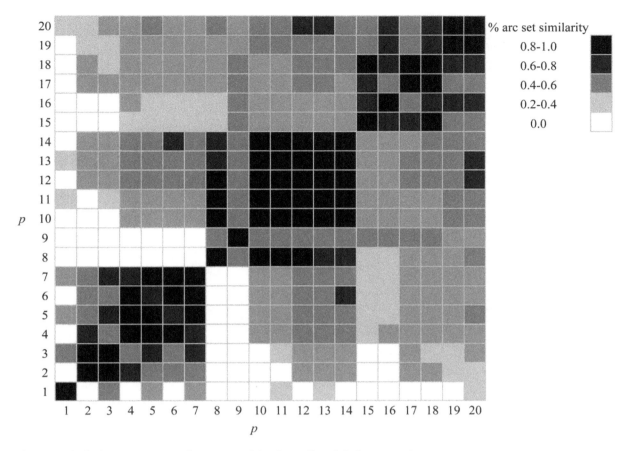

Figure 6. Similarity among sets of arcs comprising bounding deletion scenarios.

greater elasticity can be viewed as a decrease in resistance to a particular mechanism of disruption or alternatively, as an increase in the efficiency with which a mechanism of disruption can degrade the network's performance. In contrast to the previous example, this bifurcation is due to a relatively large percent change in robustness that accompanies a relatively small change in arc deletion magnitude between $p = 7$ to $p = 8$. In the 8 pm to 12 am epoch, robustness is decreased nearly 24% given an increase from $p = 7$ to $p = 8$. In the 8 am–12 pm epoch, robustness is decreased nearly 44% given an increase from $p = 7$ to $p = 8$. This is a major difference and again points to the dynamic nature of both networks and their robustness properties. While the network's robustness in both periods is very sensitive to a small change in the number of arcs deleted, robustness in the 8 am–12 pm epoch displays a considerably higher level of sensitivity to this change. Although the 8 am–12 pm is the most robust to the deletion of seven arcs, this slight increase in the number of arcs deleted results in the 8 am–12 pm epoch being the least robust to a $p = 8$ scenario (Figure 5). In general, it is observed that after larger decrease in robustness, such as that accompanying the increase from $p = 7$ to $p = 8$, robustness elasticity tends to briefly diminish, fluctuating between non-elasticity and elasticity. As shown in Figure 7, there is considerable variation among the epochs as to which one is the most elastic or least elastic over the increases in p considered. In most cases though, all six epochs do together tend toward relative elasticity or non-elasticity for each increase in p. However, in a few instances, change in arc deletion magnitude results in elasticity in one epoch while resulting in relative non-elasticity in others.

Discussion

To effectively capture and describe network robustness with respect to changes in the distribution of nodal interaction in a network, one significant challenge is to ensure that measures of robustness are consistent and comparable under the range of operational states experienced by a system. The identification of exact mathematical bounds on robustness facilitates unbiased comparisons of nodal interaction across different network states (i.e. epochs). However, the identification of these mathematical extrema (i.e. bounding scenarios) is difficult given the multifaceted and non-intuitive interdependencies defining complex networks. These exact bounds are essential for providing a comparative benchmark for other measures of network robustness identified through modeling other mechanisms of network change [18,27–32]. This is particularly important since many mechanisms of network change have been proposed and in many cases, their characterizations of robustness relative to one another tend to lack consistency within and between networks [18,27–28]. Thus, the ability to assess the proximity of a network's robustness to any other mechanism of p-arc or node deletion relative to the bounding mechanism will certainly add great analytical strength in evaluations of robustness.

The modeling approach detailed in this paper complements existing work in several ways. First, it allows one to simultaneously evaluate network structure as well as performance (e.g. interaction inhibited), two of the most important facets of network robustness. Second, this approach considers all unique paths between nodal pairs when determining connectivity, eliminating the need to use

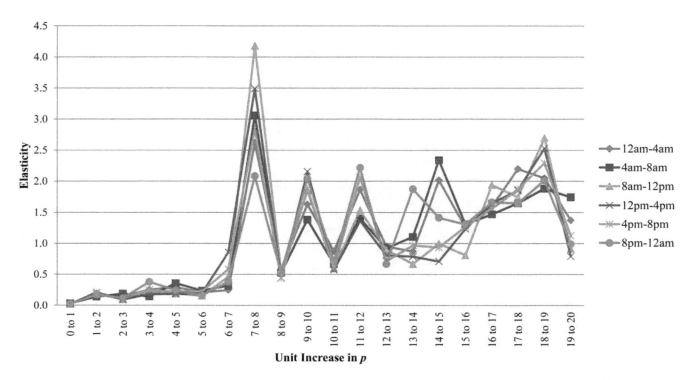

Figure 7. Robustness elasticity.

simple approximations for connectivity (e.g. nodal degree) or to further generalize network structure. Computationally, the model structure also represents an improvement over similar structures given that it requires fewer constraints to represent the network, enhancing its ability to be solved to optimality. Since optimal solutions can be identified using this modeling framework, the results are consistent and provide an objective benchmark for all potential deletion scenarios. Finally, although applied to an Internet system in this paper, the modeling framework is system agnostic and can be adapted to any network.

Bounds on robustness to arc deletion are identified for a large Internet network for six different epochs of observed nodal interaction. While network structure is held constant over this sequence of network activity, the level of interaction among pairs of nodes varies considerably as does the robustness to arc deletion. The results presented here demonstrate that robustness can be highly elastic over the spatial and temporal dimensions of a network and is particularly sensitive to variations in nodal interaction. The results also indicate that the set of arcs selected for deletion in the bounding scenarios can be dramatically different in arc composition given different magnitudes of arc deletion as well as different states (i.e. epochs) of nodal interaction. This is a critical finding since it provides firm evidence that the

'importance' of an arc or node in a network cannot assumed to be constant over different magnitudes of deletion. This is particularly true in cases where nodal interaction is dynamic. Given that characterizations of robustness can display such spatial and temporal variation, it is imperative to carefully consider how nodal interaction within complex systems is represented in analyses and how the selected representation of interaction might impact the evaluation of network robustness. This is especially important when the analysis results are used to inform planning decisions on where to invest financial and human resources to improve a network's robustness to arc and/or node deletion.

Acknowledgments

We thank David Ripley at Indiana University for providing the raw Internet2 data.

Author Contributions

Conceived and designed the experiments: TCM THG JG. Performed the experiments: TCM THG JG. Analyzed the data: TCM THG JG. Contributed reagents/materials/analysis tools: TCM THG JG. Wrote the paper: TCM THG JG.

References

1. Snijders TAB (2001) The statistical evaluation of social network dynamics. Sociol Methodol 31(1): 361–395.
2. Benda L, Poff NL, Miller D, Dunne T, Reeves G, et al. (2004) The network dynamics hypothesis: how channel networks structure riverine habitats. BioScience 54(5): 413–427.
3. Argollo de Menezes M, Barabasi AL (2004) Separating internal and external dynamics of complex systems. Phys Rev Lett 93: 068701.
4. Behrends C, Sowa ME, Gygi SP, Harper JW (2010) Network organization of the human autophagy system. Nature 466: 68–77.
5. Price D de S (1976) A general theory of bibliometric and other cumulative advantage processes. J Amer Soc Inform Sci 27: 292–306.
6. Barabasi AL, Albert R (1999) Emergence of scaling in random networks. Science 286: 509.
7. D'Souza RM, Borgs C, Chayes JT, Berger N, Kleinberg RD (2007) Emergence of tempered preferential attachment from optimization. Proc Natl Acad Sci USA 104(15): 6112–6117.
8. Kumar R, Raghavan P, Rajagopalan S, Sivakumar D, Tomkins A, et al. (2000) Stochastic models for the web graph. In Proceedings of the 41st Annual Symposium on Foundations of Computer Science. FOCS, Redondo Beach, CA, USA. IEEE CS Press, 57–65.
9. Albert R, Jeong H, Barabási AL (2000) The internet's achilles' heel: error and attack tolerance of complex networks. Nature 406: 378–382.

10. Caldarelli G (2007) Scale-Free Networks. Oxford University Press, Oxford.
11. Doyle JC, Alderson DL, Li L, Low S, Roughan M, et al. (2005) The "robust yet fragile" nature of the Internet. Proc Natl Acad Sci USA 102(41): 14497–14502.
12. Saavedra S, Reed-Tsochas F, Uzzi B (2008) Asymmetric disassembly and robustness in declining networks. Proc Natl Acad Sci USA 105(43): 16466–16471.
13. Rinaldi SM, Peerenboom JP, Kelly TK (2001) Identifying, understanding and analyzing critical infrastructure interdependencies. IEEE Control Systems Magazine December: 11–25.
14. Watts DJ (2002) A simple model of global cascades on random networks. Proc Natl Acad Sci USA 99: 5766–5771.
15. McDaniels T, Chang S, Peterson K, Mikawoz J, Reed D (2007) Empirical framework for characterizing infrastructure failure interdependencies. Journal of Infrastructure Systems 13(3): 175–184.
16. Watts DJ, Strogatz SH (1998) Collective dynamics of 'small-world' networks. Nature 393: 440–442.
17. Pastor-Satorras R, Vespignani A (2000) Epidemic spreading in scale-free networks. Phys Rev Lett 86: 3200–3203.
18. Grubesic TH, Matisziw TC, Murray AT, Snediker D (2008) Comparative approaches for assessing network vulnerability. International Regional Science Review 31(1): 88–112.
19. Fotheringham AS, O'Kelly ME (1989) Spatial interaction models: formulations and applications. University of Michigan: Kluwer Academic Publishers.
20. Holme P, Kim BJ, Yoon CN., Han SK (2002) Attack vulnerability of complex networks. Phys Rev E 65: 056109.
21. Kurant M, Thiran P (2006) Extraction and analysis of traffic and topologies of transportation networks. Phys Rev E 74: 036114.
22. Matisziw TC, Murray AT (2009) Modeling s-t path availability to support disaster 23. vulnerability assessment of network infrastructure. Computers & Operations Research 36(1): 16–26.
23. Meloni S, Arenas A, Moreno Y (2009) Traffic-driven epidemic spreading in finite-size scale-free networks. Proc Natl Acad Sci USA 106(40): 16897–16902.
24. Ito T, Chiba T, Ozawa R, Yoshida M, Hattori M, et al. (2001) A comprehensive two-hybrid analysis to explore the yeast protein interactome. Proc Natl Acad Sci USA 98: 4569–4574.
25. Deville Y, Gilbert D, van Helden, J Wodak, SJ (2003) An overview of data models for the analysis of biochemical pathways. Brief Bioinform 4(3): 246–259.
26. Lazer D, Pentland A, Adamic L, Sinan A, Barabasi A-L, et al. (2009) Computational social science. Science 323: 721–723.
27. Murray AT, Matisziw TC, Grubesic TH (2008) A methodological overview of network vulnerability analysis. Growth & Change 39(4): 573–592.
28. Snediker DE, Murray AT, Matisziw TC (2008) Decision support for network disruption mitigation. Decis Support Syst 44: 954–969.
29. Matisziw TC, Murray AT, Grubesic TH (2009) Exploring the vulnerability of network infrastructure to disruption. Annals of Regional Science 43: 307–321.
30. Wollmer R (1964) Removing arcs from a network. Oper Res 12: 934–40.
31. Myung Y-S, Kim H (2004) A cutting plane algorithm for computing k-edge survivability of a network. European Journal of Operational Research 156: 579–589.
32. Church RL, Scaparra MP, Middleton RS (2004) The median and covering facility interdiction problems. Ann Assoc Am Geogr 94: 491–502.
33. Alderson DL (2008) Catching the "network science" bug: insight and opportunity for the operations researcher. Oper Res 56(5): 1047–1065.
34. Willinger W, Alderson D, Doyle JC (2009) Mathematics and the internet: a source of enormous confusion and great potential. Notices of the AMS 56(5): 586–599.
35. Shen S, Smith JC (2011) Polynomial-time algorithms for solving a class of critical node problems on trees and series-parallel graphs. Networks DOI: 10–1002/net.20464.
36. Matisziw TC, Murray AT (2009) Connectivity change in habitat networks. Landsc Ecol 24(1): 89–100.
37. Land AH, Doig AG (1960) An automatic method of solving discrete programming problems. Econometrica 28(3): 497–520.
38. Allen RG (1933) The concept of arc elasticity of demand: I. Review of Economic Studies 1(3): 226–29.
39. Grubesic TH, Matisziw TC, Ripley DAJ (2011) Approximating the geographical characteristics of Internet activity. Journal of Urban Technology 18(1): 51–71.
40. Dice LR (1945) Measures of the amount of ecologic association between species. Ecology 26(3): 297–302.

18

Benchmarking Undedicated Cloud Computing Providers for Analysis of Genomic Datasets

Seyhan Yazar[1], George E. C. Gooden[1], David A. Mackey[1,2], Alex W. Hewitt[1,2,3]*

1 Centre for Ophthalmology and Visual Science, University of Western Australia, Lions Eye Institute, Perth, Western Australia, Australia, 2 School of Medicine, Menzies Research Institute Tasmania, University of Tasmania, Hobart, Tasmania, Australia, 3 Centre for Eye Research Australia, University of Melbourne, Department of Ophthalmology, Royal Victorian Eye and Ear Hospital, Melbourne, Victoria, Australia

Abstract

A major bottleneck in biological discovery is now emerging at the computational level. Cloud computing offers a dynamic means whereby small and medium-sized laboratories can rapidly adjust their computational capacity. We benchmarked two established cloud computing services, Amazon Web Services Elastic MapReduce (EMR) on Amazon EC2 instances and Google Compute Engine (GCE), using publicly available genomic datasets (*E.coli* CC102 strain and a Han Chinese male genome) and a standard bioinformatic pipeline on a Hadoop-based platform. Wall-clock time for complete assembly differed by 52.9% (95% CI: 27.5–78.2) for *E.coli* and 53.5% (95% CI: 34.4–72.6) for human genome, with GCE being more efficient than EMR. The cost of running this experiment on EMR and GCE differed significantly, with the costs on EMR being 257.3% (95% CI: 211.5–303.1) and 173.9% (95% CI: 134.6–213.1) more expensive for *E.coli* and human assemblies respectively. Thus, GCE was found to outperform EMR both in terms of cost and wall-clock time. Our findings confirm that cloud computing is an efficient and potentially cost-effective alternative for analysis of large genomic datasets. In addition to releasing our cost-effectiveness comparison, we present available ready-to-use scripts for establishing Hadoop instances with Ganglia monitoring on EC2 or GCE.

Editor: Maureen J. Donlin, Saint Louis University, United States of America

Funding: This work was supported by funding from the BrightFocus Foundation, the Ophthalmic Research Institute of Australia and a Ramaciotti Establishment Grant. CERA receives operational infrastructure support from the Victorian government. The funders had no role in study design, data collection and analysis, decision to publish, or preparation of the manuscript.

Competing Interests: The authors have declared that no competing interests exist.

* Email: hewitt.alex@gmail.com

Introduction

Through the application of high-throughput sequencing, there has been a dramatic increase in the availability of large-scale genomic datasets [1]. With reducing sequencing costs, small and medium-sized laboratories can now easily amass many gigabytes of data. Given this dramatic increase in the volume of data generated, researchers are being forced to seek efficient and cost-effective measures for computational analysis [2]. Cloud computing offers a dynamic means whereby small and medium-sized laboratories can rapidly adjust their computational capacity, without concern about its physical structure or ongoing maintenance [3–6]. However, transitioning to a cloud environment presents with unique strategic decisions [7], and although a number of general benchmarking results are available (http://serverbear.com/benchmarks/cloud; https://cloudharmony.com/; Accessed 2014 Aug 7), there has been a paucity of comparisons of cloud computing services specifically for genomic research.

We undertook a performance comparison on two established cloud computing services: Amazon Web Services EMR on Amazon EC2 instances and GCE. Paired-end sequence reads of publicly available genomic datasets (*Escherichia coli* CC102 strain and a Han Chinese male genome) were analysed using Crossbow, a genetic annotation tool, on Hadoop-based platforms with equivalent system specifications [8–10]. A standard analytical pipeline was run simultaneously on both platforms multiple times (Figure 1 and 2). The performance metrics of both platforms were recorded using Ganglia, an open-source high performance computing monitoring system [11].

Results

Wall-clock time for complete mapping and SNP calling differed by 52.9% (95% CI: 27.5–78.2) and 53.5% (95% CI: 34.4–72.6) for *E.coli* and human genome alignment and variant calling, respectively, with GCE being more efficient than EMR. Table 1 displays the key metrics for data analysis using both services. The proportion of central processing unit (CPU) usage by Crossbow differed between platforms when aligning and SNP calling each genome, with GCE having better utilisation as the genome size increased. There was considerably more free memory on GCE for the smaller *E.coli* dataset and on EMR for larger human genome runs. The CPU idle percentage, the percentage of time where the CPU was idle without waiting for disk input/output (I/O), was greater on EMR for the human genome while CPU waiting for I/O (WIO) was considerably lower on the same platform. The CPU idle and CPU WIO percentages were both significantly higher on EMR for the *E.coli* genome. The cost of running this Crossbow

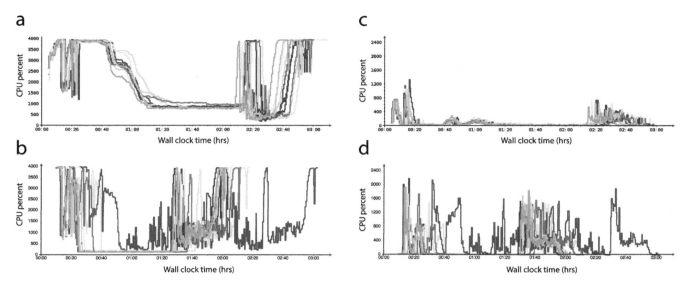

Figure 1. Comparison of undedicated cloud computing performances. The panel includes results of Amazon Web Services Elastic MapReduce (EMR) on Amazon EC2 instances (panels a & c) versus Google Compute Engine (GCE) (panels b & d) for human genome alignment and variant calling. In this 40 node cluster the total CPU percent for CPU idle (a and b) and waiting for disk input/output (c and d) is displayed. Note the greater consistency in performance of Crossbow, though generally longer wall clock times for complete analysis, on EMR compared to GCE.

pipeline on EMR and GCE also differed significantly (p<0.001), with the costs on EMR being 257.3% (95% CI: 211.5–303.1) and 173.9% (95% CI: 134.6–213.1) more expensive than GCE for *E.coli* and human assemblies, respectively. For ~36x coverage of a human genome, at a current sequencing cost of ~US$1000, the median cost for computation on GCE was US$29.81 (range: US$28.86 to US$45.99), whilst on EMR with a fixed hourly rate it was US$69.60 (range: US$69.60 to US$92.80).

Although runtime variability was inevitable and present in both platforms when assembling each genome, GCE had a considerably greater variability with the larger human genome compared to EMR (coefficient of variation $(COV)_{EMR} = 4.48\%$ vs - $COV_{GCE} = 16.72\%$). We identified a single outlier in run time

on GCE during the human genome analysis. This occurred due to the virtual cluster having a slower average network connection (1.55 MB/s compared to the average of the other GCE clusters of 2.02 MB/s) and a higher CPU WIO percentage than the average for the other GCE runs (9.56% versus 3.52%). The variation in cluster performance likely reflects an increase in network congestion amongst GCE servers.

Runtime predictably is an important issue in undedicated cloud computing. The existing workload of the cloud at the time of service usage is one of the main determinants of variability in runtime of undedicated services [12]. In our benchmarking, EMR was more consistent, though slower, in overall wall-clock time compared to GCE. This may suggest that GCE is more susceptible

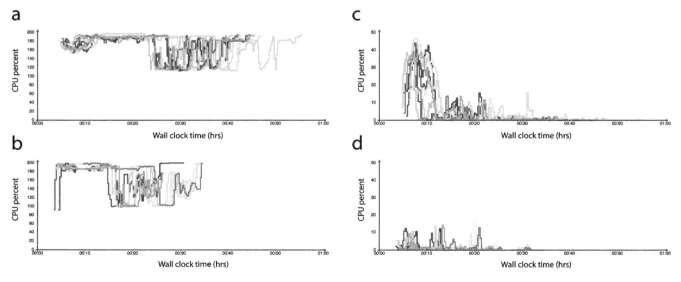

Figure 2. Comparison of undedicated cloud performance of Amazon Web Services Elastic MapReduce (EMR) on Amazon EC2 instances (panels a & c) versus Google Compute Engine (GCE) (panels b & d) for *E.coli* genome alignment and variant calling. In this two node cluster the total CPU percent for CPU idle (a and b) and waiting for disk input/output (c and d) is displayed. Note the shorter wall clock times for complete analysis on GCE compared to EMR.

Table 1. Comparison of performance metrics for genomic alignment and SNP calling.

Metric	E.coli Genome			Human Genome		
	EMR (n = 10)	GCE (n = 10)	p-value*	EMR (n = 10)	GCE (n = 10)	p-value*
Wall clock time (mean)	0:46:30	0:31:50	<0.001	2:58:24	2:14:12	<0.001
Pre-processing short reads time (mean)	0:14:37	0:12:46	0.109	0:07:29	0:06:23	0.116
Alignment with Bowtie time (mean)	0:07:04	0:05:03	<0.001	1:51:06	1:15:07	0.003
Calling SNPs with SOAPsnp time (mean)	0:05:05	0:02:51	<0.001	0:35:31	0:29:31	0.033
Post-processing time (mean)	0:04:51	0:00:57	<0.001	0:01:23	0:01:03	<0.001
CPU user (mean %)	17.44±1.30	22.31±3.14	<0.001	43.80±1.87	58.05±6.20	<0.001
CPU idle (mean %)	72.75±1.23	65.76±4.63	<0.001	47.48±2.30	22.17±3.14	<0.001
CPU wio (mean %)	3.88±1.06	0.70±0.16	<0.001	1.86±0.19	4.54±1.82	0.001
Bytes in (MB/sec)	1.15±0.09	2.12±0.42	<0.001	1.58±0.07	2.00±0.19	<0.001
Memory free (GB)	2.19±0.13	6.17±0.42	<0.001	0.91±0.07	0.70±0.03	<0.001

All times are presented as hr:min:sec and remaining metrics are shown as mean ± standard deviation.
*Calculated by paired t-test.

to server congestion than EMR; though service usage data is difficult to obtain.

Discussion

Our findings confirm that cloud computing is an efficient and potentially cost-effective alternative for analysis of large genomic datasets. Cloud computing offers a dynamic, economical and versatile solution for large-scale computational analysis. There have been a number of recent advances in bioinformatic methods utilising cloud resources [4,9,13], and our results suggest that a standard genomic alignment is generally faster in GCE compared to EMR. The time differences identified could be attributed to the hardware used by the Google and Amazon for their cloud services. Amazon offers a 2.0 GHz Intel Xeon Sandy Bridge CPU, whilst Google uses a 2.6 GHz Intel Xeon Sandy Bridge CPU. This clock speed variability is considered the main contributing factor to the difference between the two undedicated platforms. It must also be noted that the resource requirements of Ganglia may have had a small impact on completion times [11].

There are a number of technical differences between GCE and EMR, which are important to consider when running standard bioinformatic pipelines. Running Crossbow on Amazon Web Services was simplified by an established support service, which provides an interface for establishing and running Hadoop clusters (Text S1). In contrast, there is currently no built-in support for GCE in Crossbow (Text S2). The current process to run a Crossbow job on GCE requires users to complete various steps such as installing and configuring the required software on each node in the cluster, transferring input data onto the Hadoop Distributed File System (HDFS), downloading results from the HDFS and terminating the cluster on completion. All of these steps are automatically performed by Crossbow on EMR. Python scripts offering similar functionality for GCE that Crossbow provides for EMR were created and are available (https://github.com/hewittlab/Crossbow-GCE-Hadoop).

While our findings confirm that cloud computing is an attractive alternative to the limitations imposed by the local environment, it is noteworthy that better performance metrics and lower cost were found with GCE compared to its established counterpart,

Amazon's EMR. Currently, a major limitation of these services remains at the initial transfer of large datasets onto the hosted cloud platform [14]. To circumvent this in the future, sequencing service providers are likely to directly deposit data to a designated cloud service provider, thereby eliminating the need for the user to double handle the data transfer [15]. Once this issue is resolved, it is foreseen that demand for these services is likely to increase considerably, given the low cost, broad flexibility and good customer support for cloud services [15]. The development of

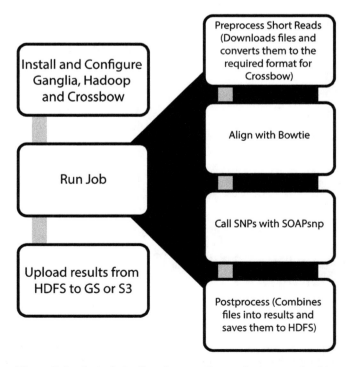

Figure 3. Analytical pipeline demarcating each step required to complete the Crossbow job in the cloud.

Table 2. Specification of used computational nodes for each system.

	Virtual Cores	Memory (GB)	Included Storage (GB)	Price (USD/Hour)^
Amazon Elastic Compute Cloud (EC2) + Elastic MapReduce (EMR) [c1.xlarge]	8	7	4×420	$0.640
Google Compute Engine [n1-highcpu-8]	8	7.2	0#	$0.352

^Date accessed: April to June 2014; prior to this period, pricing was $0.700 and $0.520 in Amazon and Google respectively.
#for each instance we added the minimum storage quota of 128 GB.

additional tools specific to genomic analysis in the cloud, which offer flexibility in choice of providers, is clearly required.

Methods

Datasets and Analytical Pipeline

We benchmarked two platforms by a single job that completed read alignment and variant calling stages of next generation sequencing analysis simultaneously on two independent cloud platforms. To investigate the impact of data size on undedicated cluster performance, one small (*Escherichia coli* CC102 strain (3 GB SRA file; Accession: SRX003267) and one large (a Han Chinese male genome (142 GB Fastq files; Accession: ERA000005) publicly available genomic dataset was selected for analysis [8,10]. For each job in this experiment, a parallel workflow was designed using Crossbow. This workflow included the following four steps: (1) Download and conversion of files; (2) Short read alignment with Bowtie; (3) SNP call with SOAPsnp; and (4) Combination of the results (Figure 3). Crossbow was the preferred genetic annotation tool in this experiment, as it has built in support for running via Amazon's EMR and Hadoop clusters [16].

Cluster construction and architecture

Instances were simultaneously established on Amazon's EMR (http://aws.amazon.com/ec2/; Accessed 2014 Aug 7) and GCE (http://cloud.google.com/products/compute-engine.html; Accessed 2014 Aug 7). Undedicated clusters were optimized by selection of computational nodes as suggested for Crossbow [9]. Nodes with equivalent specifications were selected for each system (Table 2), these being c1.xlarge node in EMR and the closest specification node n1-highcpu-8 in GCE. For the *E.coli* genome, two nodes (one master and one slave) were used on each platform. On the other hand, for the human genome, the cluster was built with 40 nodes (one master and 39 slaves). As GCE did not provide any included storage for each instance, a 128 GB drive (the default storage quota provided by GCE) was added for each node. This was at the additional cost of $0.04/GB/Month or $0.000056/GB/Hour (Jan to June 2014).

Each cluster was run using Apache Hadoop, an open-source implementation of the MapReduce algorithm [17]. MapReduce was used to organise distributed servers, manage the communication between servers and provide fault tolerance allowing tasks to be performed in parallel [18].

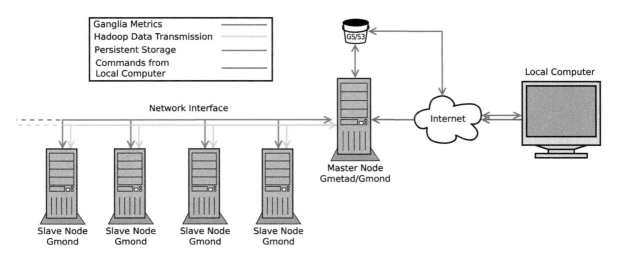

Figure 4. Directions and types of network transfers in our cloud-computing model. There are a variety of different network transfers between the nodes for each of the services in use in our model. Hadoop requires a bidirectional transmission of data between the master node and the slave nodes. This is required to coordinate the parallel processing of the cluster, and to allow for data transfer between nodes. Ganglia uses a unidirectional connection from the slave nodes to the master node to transfer the recorded metrics for storage and visualization. The persistent storage (provided by Amazon S3 (Simple Storage Service) or Google Storage, or an alternative method such as an FTP server) is accessed via the master node. The master node uses it to download input files for Crossbow, such as the manifest file and the reference Jar, and to use for persistent storage of the results of the Crossbow job as the instances destroy their storage on termination. Our local computer can also access the persistent storage via the Internet to allow access to upload the input files, or to download the results. The local computer needs to access the master node to initiate Crossbow. In EMR, this is replaced by a web interface and a JavaScript Object Notation Application Programming Interface (JSON API). In GCE, the user is required to remotely log in via Secure Shell (SSH) to commence the job.

To explore the effect of network activity differences between the platforms, each job was run simultaneously; same day (including weekdays and weekends) and same time. Detailed description of the set up and scripts to run the jobs can be found in Text S1 and Text S2.

Cluster Monitoring

In both EMR and GCE, multiple components of cloud infrastructure including CPU utilisation, memory usage and network speeds were monitored and recorded for each node using Ganglia. The default setting of Ganglia for distributing incoming requests is multicast mode; however, since EMR and GCE environments do not currently support multicast Ganglia, it was configured in unicast mode (Figure 4). The metric output files constructed in.rrd format were converted into.csv format with a Perl script (Text S3). For comparison between performance and costs between platforms, the Student t-test was undertaken using the statistical software R (R Foundation for Statistical Computing version 3.0.2; http://www.r-project.org/). In the analysis, cost of each run was calculated using current pricing (June 10th 2014); however, all *E.coli* runs and one human genome run were performed prior to a recent decrease in price on both platforms.

The COV for runtime variability was calculated as the ratio of the standard deviation to the mean time (mins) for each system.

Supporting Information

Text S1   Uploading data and setting up an Amazon Web Services Elastic MapReduce (EMR) cluster.

Text S2   Scripts for configuration and running jobs on Google Compute Engine (GCE).

Text S3   Transformation of metric outputs from. RRD to. CSV format.

Author Contributions

Conceived and designed the experiments: SY AWH. Performed the experiments: SY GECG. Analyzed the data: SY GECG. Contributed reagents/materials/analysis tools: DAM AWH. Contributed to the writing of the manuscript: SY GECG DAM AWH.

References

1. Marx V (2013) Biology: The big challenges of big data. Nature 498: 255–260.
2. Patro R, Mount SM, Kingsford C (2014) Sailfish enables alignment-free isoform quantification from RNA-seq reads using lightweight algorithms. Nat Biotechnol 32: 462–464.
3. Schatz MC, Langmead B, Salzberg SL (2010) Cloud computing and the DNA data race. Nat Biotechnol 28: 691–693.
4. Angiuoli SV, White JR, Matalka M, White O, Fricke WF (2011) Resources and Costs for Microbial Sequence Analysis Evaluated Using Virtual Machines and Cloud Computing. PLoS ONE 6: e26624.
5. Fusaro VA, Patil P, Gafni E, Wall DP, Tonellato PJ (2011) Biomedical Cloud Computing With Amazon Web Services. PLoS Comput Biol 7: e1002147.
6. Drake N (2014) Cloud computing beckons scientists. Nature 509: 543–544.
7. Marx V (2013) Genomics in the clouds. Nat Meth 10: 941–945.
8. Parkhomchuk D, Amstislavskiy V, Soldatov A, Ogryzko V (2009) Use of high throughput sequencing to observe genome dynamics at a single cell level. Proc Natl Acad Sci USA 106: 20830–20835.
9. Langmead B, Schatz MC, Lin J, Pop M, Salzberg SL (2009) Searching for SNPs with cloud computing. Genome Biol 10: R134.
10. Wang J, Wang W, Li R, Li Y, Tian G, et al. (2008) The diploid genome sequence of an Asian individual. Nature 456: 60–65.
11. Massie ML, Chun BN, Culler DE (2004) The ganglia distributed monitoring system: design, implementation, and experience. Parallel Comput 30: 817–840.
12. Schad J, Dittrich J, Quiané-Ruiz J-A (2010) Runtime measurements in the cloud: observing, analyzing, and reducing variance. Proceedings VLDB Endowment 3: 460–471.
13. Onsongo G, Erdmann J, Spears MD, Chilton J, Beckman KB, et al. (2014) Implementation of Cloud based Next Generation Sequencing data analysis in a clinical laboratory. BMC Res Notes 7: 314.
14. Schadt EE, Linderman MD, Sorenson J, Lee L, Nolan GP (2010) Computational solutions to large-scale data management and analysis. Nat Rev Genet 11: 647–657.
15. Stein LD (2010) The case for cloud computing in genome informatics. Genome Biol 11: 207.
16. Crossbow project homepage. Available: http://bowtie-bio.sourceforge.net/crossbow/index.shtml. Accessed 2014 Aug 7.
17. Hadoop - Apache Software Foundation project homepage. Available: http://hadoop.apache.org/. Accessed 2014 Aug 7.
18. Dean J, Ghemawat S (2008) MapReduce. Commun ACM 51: 107–113.

19

Control Centrality and Hierarchical Structure in Complex Networks

Yang-Yu Liu[1,2], Jean-Jacques Slotine[3,4], Albert-László Barabási[1,2,5]*

1 Center for Complex Network Research and Department of Physics, Northeastern University, Boston, Massachusetts, United States of America, **2** Center for Cancer Systems Biology, Dana-Farber Cancer Institute, Boston, Massachusetts, United States of America, **3** Nonlinear Systems Laboratory, Massachusetts Institute of Technology, Cambridge, Massachusetts, United States of America, **4** Department of Mechanical Engineering and Department of Brain and Cognitive Sciences, Massachusetts Institute of Technology, Cambridge, Massachusetts, United States of America, **5** Department of Medicine, Brigham and Women's Hospital, Harvard Medical School, Boston, Massachusetts, United States of America

Abstract

We introduce the concept of control centrality to quantify the ability of a single node to control a directed weighted network. We calculate the distribution of control centrality for several real networks and find that it is mainly determined by the network's degree distribution. We show that in a directed network without loops the control centrality of a node is uniquely determined by its layer index or topological position in the underlying hierarchical structure of the network. Inspired by the deep relation between control centrality and hierarchical structure in a general directed network, we design an efficient attack strategy against the controllability of malicious networks.

Editor: Yamir Moreno, University of Zaragoza, Spain

Funding: This work was supported by the Network Science Collaborative Technology Alliance sponsored by the United States Army Research Laboratory under Agreement Number W911NF-09-2-0053; the Defense Advanced Research Projects Agency under Agreement Number 11645021; the Defense Threat Reduction Agency award WMD BRBAA07-J-2-0035; and the generous support of Lockheed Martin. The funders had no role in study design, data collection and analysis, decision to publish, or preparation of the manuscript.

Competing Interests: The authors have declared that no competing interests exist.

* E-mail: alb@neu.edu

Introduction

Complex networks have been at the forefront of statistical mechanics for more than a decade [1–4]. Studies of them impact our understanding and control of a wide range of systems, from Internet and the power-grid to cellular and ecological networks. Despite the diversity of complex networks, several basic universal principles have been uncovered that govern their topology and evolution [3,4]. While these principles have significantly enriched our understanding of many networks that affect our lives, our ultimate goal is to develop the capability to control them [5–17].

According to control theory, a dynamical system is controllable if, with a suitable choice of inputs, it can be driven from any initial state to any desired final state in finite time [18–20]. By combining tools from control theory and network science, we proposed an efficient methodology to identify the minimum sets of driver nodes, whose time-dependent control can guide the whole network to any desired final state [12]. Yet, this minimum driver set (MDS) is usually not unique, but one can often achieve multiple potential control configurations with the same number of driver nodes. Given that some nodes may appear in some MDSs but not in other, a crucial question remains unanswered: what is the role of each individual node in controlling a complex system? Therefore the question that we address in this paper pertains to the importance of a given node in maintaining a system's controllability.

Historically, various types of centrality measures of a node in a network have been introduced to determine the relative importance of the node within the network in appropriate circumstances. For

example, the degree centrality, closeness centrality [21], betweenness centrality [22], eigenvector centrality [23,24], PageRank [25], hub centrality and authority centrality [26], routing centrality [27], and so on. Here, we introduce control centrality to quantify the ability of a single node in controlling the whole network. Mathematically, control centrality of node i captures the dimension of the controllable subspace or the size of the controllable subsystem when we control node i *only*. This agrees well with our intuitive notion about the "power" of a node in controlling the whole network. We notice that control centrality is fundamentally different from the concept of control range, which quantifies the "duty" or "responsibility" of a node i in controlling a network *together with other driver nodes* [28].

Results

Control Centrality

Consider a complex system described by a directed weighted network of N nodes whose time evolution follows the linear time-invariant dynamics.

$$\dot{\mathbf{x}}(t) = \mathbf{A}\mathbf{x}(t) + \mathbf{B}\mathbf{u}(t) \qquad (1)$$

where $\mathbf{x}(t) = (x_1(t), x_2(t), \cdots, x_N(t))^{\mathrm{T}} \in \mathbb{R}^N$ captures the state of each node at time t. $\mathbf{A} \in \mathbb{R}^{N \times N}$ is an $N \times N$ matrix describing the weighted wiring diagram of the network. The matrix element $a_{ij} \in \mathbb{R}$ gives the strength or weight that node j can affect node i. Positive (or negative) value of a_{ij} means the link $(j \rightarrow i)$ is excitatory (or inhibitory).

$\mathbf{B} \in \mathbb{R}^{N \times M}$ is an $N \times M$ input matrix $(M \leq N)$ identifying the nodes that are controlled by the time dependent input vector $\mathbf{u}(t) = (u_1(t), u_2(t), \cdots, u_M(t))^{\mathrm{T}} \in \mathbb{R}^M$ with M independent signals imposed by an outside controller. The matrix element $b_{ij} \in \mathbb{R}$ represents the coupling strength between the input signal $u_j(t)$ and node i. The system (1), also denoted as $(\mathbf{A}, \mathbf{B})$, is controllable if and only if its controllability matrix $\mathbf{C} = (\mathbf{B}, \mathbf{AB}, \cdots, \mathbf{A}^{N-1}\mathbf{B}) \in \mathbb{R}^{N \times NM}$ has full rank, a criteria often called Kalman's controllability rank condition [18]. The rank of the controllability matrix $\mathbf{C}$, denoted by $\mathrm{rank}(\mathbf{C})$, provides the dimension of the controllable subspace of the system $(\mathbf{A}, \mathbf{B})$ [18,19]. When we control node i only, $\mathbf{B}$ reduces to the vector $\mathbf{b}^{(i)}$ with a single non-zero entry, and we denote $\mathbf{C}$ with $\mathbf{C}^{(i)}$. We can therefore use $\mathrm{rank}(\mathbf{C}^{(i)})$ as a natural measure of node i's ability to control the system: if $\mathrm{rank}(\mathbf{C}^{(i)}) = N$, then node i alone can control the whole system, i.e. it can drive the system between any points in the N-dimensional state space in finite time. Any value of $\mathrm{rank}(\mathbf{C}^{(i)})$ less than N provides the dimension of the subspace i can control. In particular if $\mathrm{rank}(\mathbf{C}^{(i)}) = 1$, then node i can only control itself.

The precise value of $\mathrm{rank}(\mathbf{C})$ is difficult to determine because in reality the system parameters, i.e. the elements of $\mathbf{A}$ and $\mathbf{B}$, are often not known precisely except the zeros that mark the absence of connections between components of the system [29]. Hence $\mathbf{A}$ and $\mathbf{B}$ are often considered to be structured matrices, i.e. their elements are either fixed zeros or independent free parameters [29]. Apparently, $\mathrm{rank}(\mathbf{C})$ varies as a function of the free parameters of $\mathbf{A}$ and $\mathbf{B}$. However, it achieves the maximal value for all but an exceptional set of values of the free parameters which forms a proper variety with Lebesgue measure zero in the parameter space [30,31]. This maximal value is called the *generic rank* of the controllability matrix $\mathbf{C}$, denoted as $\mathrm{rank}_{\mathrm{g}}(\mathbf{C})$, which also represents the generic dimension of the controllable subspace. When $\mathrm{rank}_{\mathrm{g}}(\mathbf{C}) = N$, the system $(\mathbf{A}, \mathbf{B})$ is *structurally controllable*, i.e. controllable for almost all sets of values of the free parameters of $\mathbf{A}$ and $\mathbf{B}$ except an exceptional set of values with zero measure [29,30,32,33]. For a single node i, $\mathrm{rank}_{\mathrm{g}}(\mathbf{C}^{(i)})$ captures the "power" of i in controlling the whole network, allowing us to define the *control centrality* of node i as

$$C_{\mathrm{c}}(i) \equiv \mathrm{rank}_{\mathrm{g}}(\mathbf{C}^{(i)}). \qquad (2)$$

The calculation of $\mathrm{rank}_{\mathrm{g}}(\mathbf{C})$ can be mapped into a combinatorial optimization problem on a directed graph $G(\mathbf{A}, \mathbf{B})$ constructed as follows [31]. Connect the M input nodes $\{u_1, \cdots, u_M\}$ to the N state nodes $\{x_1, \cdots, x_N\}$ in the original network according to the input matrix $\mathbf{B}$, i.e. connect u_j to x_i if $b_{ij} \neq 0$, obtaining a directed graph $G(\mathbf{A}, \mathbf{B})$ with $N + M$ nodes (see Fig. 1a and b). A state node j is called *accessible* if there is at least one directed path reaching from one of the input nodes to node j. In Fig. 1b, all state nodes $\{x_1, \cdots, x_7\}$ are accessible from the input node u_1. A *stem* is a directed path starting from an input node, so that no nodes appear more than once in it, e.g. $u_1 \rightarrow x_1 \rightarrow x_5 \rightarrow x_7$ in Fig. 1b. Denote with G_{s} the *stem-cycle disjoint* subgraph of $G(\mathbf{A}, \mathbf{B})$, such that G_{s} consists of stems and cycles only, and the stems and cycles have no node in common (highlighted in Fig. 1b). According to Hosoe's theorem [31], the generic dimension of the controllable subspace is given by

$$\mathrm{rank}_{\mathrm{g}}(\mathbf{C}) = \max_{G_{\mathrm{s}} \in G} |E(G_{\mathrm{s}})| \qquad (3)$$

with G the set of all stem-cycle disjoint subgraphs of the accessible part of $G(\mathbf{A}, \mathbf{B})$ and $|E(G_{\mathrm{s}})|$ the number of edges in the subgraph G_{s}. For example, the subgraph highlighted in Fig. 1b, denoted as $G_{\mathrm{s}}^{\mathrm{max}}$, contains the largest number of edges among all possible stem-cycle disjoint subgraphs. Thus, $C_{\mathrm{c}}(1) = \mathrm{rank}_{\mathrm{g}}(\mathbf{C}^{(1)}) = 6$, which is the number of red links in Fig. 1b. Note that $\mathrm{rank}_{\mathrm{g}}(\mathbf{C}^{(1)}) = 6 < N = 7$, the whole system is therefore not structurally controllable by controlling x_1 only. Yet, the nodes covered by the $G_{\mathrm{s}}^{\mathrm{max}}$ highlighted in Fig. 1b, e.g. $\{x_1, x_2, x_3, x_4, x_5, x_7\}$, constitute a structurally controllable subsystem [33]. In other words, by controlling node x_1 with a time dependent signal $u_1(t)$ we can drive the subsystem $\{x_1, x_2, x_3, x_4, x_5, x_7\}$ from any initial state to any final state in finite time, for almost all sets of values of the free parameters of $\mathbf{A}$ and $\mathbf{B}$ except an exceptional set of values with zero measure. In general $G_{\mathrm{s}}^{\mathrm{max}}$ is not unique. For example, in Fig. 1b we can get the same cycle $x_2 \rightarrow x_3 \rightarrow x_4 \rightarrow x_2$ together with a different stem $u_1 \rightarrow x_1 \rightarrow x_5 \rightarrow x_6$, which yield a different $G_{\mathrm{s}}^{\mathrm{max}}$ and thus a different structurally controllable subsystem $\{x_1, x_2, x_3, x_4, x_5, x_6\}$. Both subsystems are of size six, which is exactly the generic dimension of the controllable subspace. Note that we can fully control each subsystem individually, yet we cannot fully control the whole system.

The advantage of Eq.(3) is that $\max_{G_{\mathrm{s}} \in G} |E(G)|$ can be calculated via linear programming [34], providing us an efficient numerical tool to determine the control centrality and the structurally controllable subsystem of any node in an arbitrary complex network (see Fig. S1).

Distribution of Control Centrality

We first consider the distribution of control centrality. Shown in Fig. 2 is the distribution of the normalized control centrality $(c_{\mathrm{c}}(i) \equiv C_{\mathrm{c}}(i)/N)$ for several real networks. We find that for the intra-organization network, $P(c_{\mathrm{c}})$ has a sharp peak at $c_{\mathrm{c}} = 1$, suggesting that a high fraction of nodes can individually exert full control over the whole system (Fig. 2a). In contrast, for company-ownership network, $P(c_{\mathrm{c}})$ follows an approximately exponential distribution or a very short power-law distribution (Fig. 2d), indicating that most nodes display low control centrality. Even the most powerful node, with $c_{\mathrm{c}} \sim 0.01$, can control only one percent of the total dimension of the system's full state space. For other networks $P(c_{\mathrm{c}})$ displays a mixed behavior, indicating the coexistence of a few powerful nodes with a large number of nodes that have little control over the system's dynamics (Fig. 2b,c). Note that under full randomization, turning a network into a directed Erdös-Rényi (ER) random network [35,36] with number of nodes (N) and number of edges (L) unchanged, the c_{c} distribution changes dramatically. In contrast, under degree-preserving randomization [37,38], which keeps the in-degree (k_{in}) and out-degree (k_{out}) of each node unchanged, the c_{c} distribution does not change significantly. This result suggests that $P(c_{\mathrm{c}})$ is mainly determined by the underlying network's degree distribution $P(k_{\mathrm{in}}, k_{\mathrm{out}})$. (Note that similar results were also observed for the minimum number of driver nodes [12] and the distribution of control range [28].) This result is very useful in the following sense: $P(k_{\mathrm{in}}, k_{\mathrm{out}})$ is easy to calculate for any complex network, while the calculation of $P(c_{\mathrm{c}})$ requires much more computational efforts (both CPU time and memory space). Studying $P(c_{\mathrm{c}})$ for model networks of prescribed $P(k_{\mathrm{in}}, k_{\mathrm{out}})$ will give us qualitative understanding of how $P(c_{\mathrm{c}})$ changes as we vary network parameters, e.g. mean degree $\langle k \rangle$. See Fig. S7 for more details.

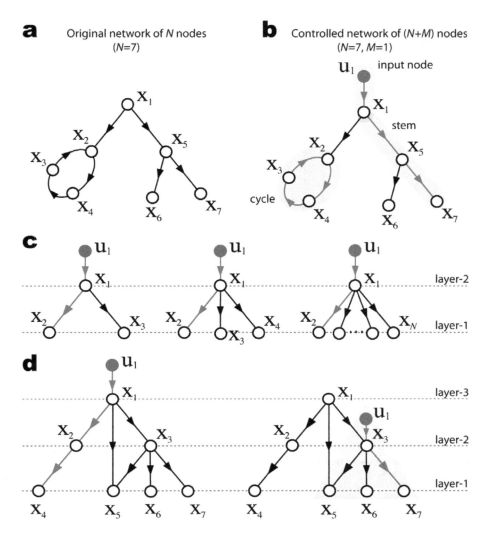

Figure 1. Control centrality. (a) A simple network of $N=7$ nodes. (b) The controlled network is represented by a directed graph $G(\mathbf{A},\mathbf{B})$ with an input node u_1 connecting to a state node x_1. The stem-cycle disjoint subgraph G_s (shown in red) contains six edges, which is the largest number of edges among all possible stem-cycle disjoint subgraphs of the directed graph $G(\mathbf{A},\mathbf{B})$ and corresponds to the generic dimension of controllable subspace by controlling node x_1. The control centrality of node 1 is thus $C_c(1)=6$. (c) The control centrality of the central hub in a directed star is always 2 for any network size $N \geq 2$. (d) The control centrality of a node in a directed acyclic graph (DAG) equals its layer index. In applying Hosoe's theorem, if not all state nodes are accessible, we just need to consider the accessible part (highlighted in green) of the input node(s).

Control Centrality and Topological Features

To understand which topological features determine the control centrality itself, we compared the control centrality for each node in the real networks and their randomized counterparts (denoted as rand-ER and rand-Degree). The lack of correlations indicates that both randomization procedures eliminate the topological feature that determines the control centrality of a given node (see Fig. S2). Since accessibility plays an important role in maintaining structural controllability [29], we conjecture that the control centrality of node i is correlated with the number of nodes $N_r(i)$ that can be reached from it. To test this conjecture, we calculated $N_r(i)$ and $C_c(i)$ for the real networks shown in Fig. 2, observing only a weak correlation between the two quantities (see Fig. S3). This lack of correlation between $N_r(i)$ and $C_c(i)$ is obvious in a directed star, in which a central hub (x_1) points to $N-1$ leaf nodes $(x_2, \cdots, x_N)$ (Fig. 1c). As the central hub can reach all nodes, $N_r(1)=N$, suggesting that it should have high control centrality. Yet, one can easily check that the central hub has control

centrality $C_c(1)=2$ for any $N \geq 2$ and there are $N-1$ structurally controllable subsystems, i.e. $\{x_1, x_2\}, \cdots, \{x_1, x_{N-1}\}$. In other words, by controlling the central hub we can fully control each leaf node individually, but we cannot control them collectively.

Note that in a directed star each node can be labeled with a unique *layer index*: the leaf nodes are in the first layer (bottom layer) and the central hub is in the second layer (top layer). In this case the control centrality of the central hub equals its layer index (see Fig. 1c). This is not by coincidence: we can prove that for a directed network containing no cycles, often called a directed acyclic graph (DAG), the control centrality of any node equals its *layer index*.

$$C_c(i)=l_i. \tag{4}$$

Indeed, lacking cycles, a DAG has a unique *hierarchical structure*, which means that each node can be labeled with a unique layer

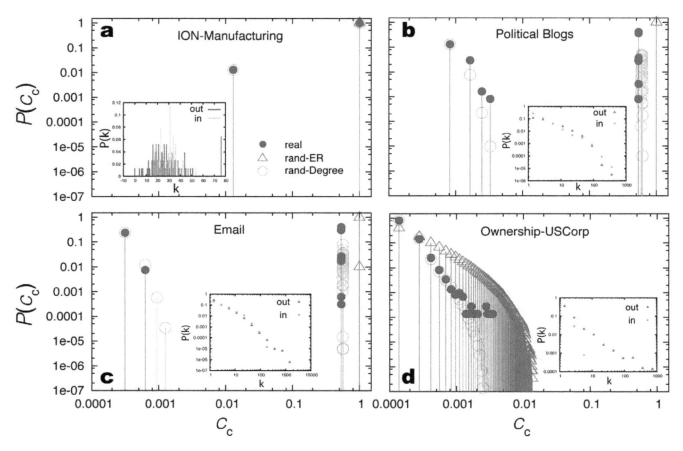

Figure 2. Distribution of normalized control centrality of several real-world networks (blue) and their randomized counterparts: rand-ER (red), rand-Degree (green), plotted in log-log scale. (a) Intra-organizational network of a manufacturing company [49]. (b) Hyperlinks between weblogs on US politics [50]. (c) Email network in a university [51]. (d) Ownership network of US corporations [52]. In- and out-degree distributions for each network are shown in the insets. See Table 1 for other network characteristics.

index (l_i), calculated using a recursive labeling algorithm [39]: (1) Nodes that have no outgoing links ($k_{out}=0$) are labeled with layer index 1 (bottom layer). (2) Remove all nodes in layer 1. For the remaining graph identify again all nodes with $k_{out}=0$ and label them with layer index 2. (3) Repeat step (2) until all nodes are labeled. As the DAG lacks cycles, each subgraph in the set G of the directed graph $G(\mathbf{A},\mathbf{b}^{(i)})$ consists of a stem only, which starts from the input node pointing to the state node i and ends at a state node in the bottom layer, e.g. $u_1 \to x_1 \to x_2 \to x_4$ in Fig. 1d. The number of edges in this stem is equal to the layer index of node i, so $\text{rank}_g(\mathbf{C}^{(i)}) = C_c(i) = l_i$. Therefore in DAG the higher a node is in

the hierarchy, the higher is its ability to control the system. Though this result agrees with our intuition to some extent, it is surprising at the first glance because it indicates that in a DAG the control centrality of node i is only determined by its topological position in the hierarchical structure, rather than any other importance measures, e.g. degree or betweenness centrality. This result also partially explains why driver nodes tend to avoid hubs [12]. (Note that similar phenomena about have been observed in other problems, e.g. networked transportation [40], synchronization [41] and epidemic spreading [42]).

Despite the simplicity of Eq. (4), we cannot apply it directly to real networks, because most of them are not DAGs. Yet, we note that any directed network has a underlying DAG structure based on the strongly connected component (SCC) decomposition (see Fig. S4). A subgraph of a directed network is *strongly connected* if there is a directed path from each node in the subgraph to every other node. The SCCs of a directed network G are its maximal strongly connected subgraphs. If we contract each SCC to a single supernode, the resulting graph , called the *condensation* of G, is a DAG [43]. Since a DAG has a unique hierarchical structure, a directed network can then be assigned an underlying hierarchical structure. The layer index of node i can be defined to be the layer index of the corresponding supernode (i.e. the SCC that node i belongs to) in . With this definition of l_i, it is easy to show that $C_c(i) \geq l_i$ for general directed networks (see Fig. S6 for more details). Furthermore, for an edge ($i \to j$) in a general directed

Table 1. Real networks analyzed in the paper.

name	N	L	$\langle k \rangle$	r	c
ION-Manufacturing [49]	77	2,228	57.9	−0.017	0.244
Political blogs [50]	1,224	19,025	31.1	−0.196	0.174
Email network [51]	3,188	39,256	24.6	−0.240	0.128
Ownership-USCorp [52]	7,253	6,726	1.9	−0.181	0.004

For each network, we show its name and reference; number of nodes (N) and edges (L); mean degree ($\langle k \rangle$); degree correlation (r) [4]; and clustering coefficient (c) [53], respectively.

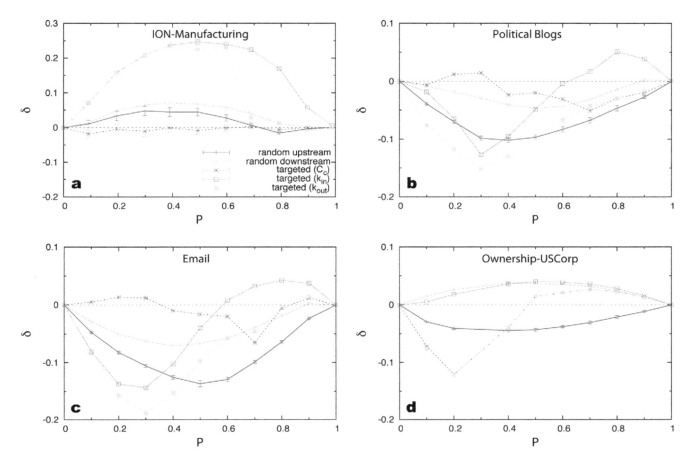

Figure 3. The impact of different attack strategies on network controllability with respective to the random attack.
$\delta \equiv [\mathrm{rank}_g^{\mathrm{Strategy}-j}(\mathbf{C}') - \mathrm{rank}_g^{\mathrm{Random}}(\mathbf{C}')]/N$ with $\mathrm{rank}_g^{\mathrm{Strategy}-j}(\mathbf{C}')$ represents the generic dimension of controllable subspace after removing a P fraction of nodes using strategy-j. The nodes are removed according to six different strategies. (Strategy-0) Random attack: randomly remove P fraction of nodes. (Strategy-1 or 2) Random upstream (or downstream) attack: randomly choose P fraction of nodes, randomly remove one of their upstream neighbors (or downstream neighbors). The results are averaged over 10 random choices of P fraction of nodes with error bars defined as s.e.m. Lines are only a guide to the eye. (Strategy-3,4, or 5) Targeted attacks: remove the top P fraction of nodes according to their control centralities (or in-degrees or out-degrees).

network, if node i is topologically "higher" than node j (i.e. $l_i > l_j$), then $C_c(i) > C_c(j)$. Since $C_c(i)$ has to be calculated via linear programming which is computationally more challenging than the calculation of l_i, the above results suggest an efficient way to calculate the lower bound of $C_c(i)$ and to compare the control centralities of two neighboring nodes. Note that if $l_i > l_j$ and there is no directed edge $(i \rightarrow j)$ in the network, then in general one cannot conclude that $C_c(i) > C_c(j)$ (see Fig. S5 for more details).

Attack Strategy

Our finding on the relation between control centrality and hierarchical structure inspires us to design an efficient attack strategy against malicious networks, aiming to affect their controllability. The most efficient way to damage the controllability of a network is to remove all input nodes $\{u_1, u_2, \cdots, u_M\}$, rendering the system completely uncontrollable. But this requires a detailed knowledge of the control configuration, i.e. the wiring diagram of $G(\mathbf{A}, \mathbf{B})$, which we often lack. If the network structure ($\mathbf{A}$) is known, one can attempt a *targeted attack*, i.e. rank the nodes according to some centrality measure, like degree or control centrality, and remove the nodes with highest centralities [44,45]. Though we still lack systematic studies on the effect of a targeted

attack on a network's controllability, one naively expects that this should be the most efficient strategy. But we often lack the knowledge of the network structure, which makes this approach unfeasible anyway. In this case a simple strategy would be *random attack*, i.e. remove a randomly chosen P fraction of nodes, which naturally serves as a benchmark for any other strategy. Here we propose instead a *random upstream attack* strategy: randomly choose a P fraction of nodes, and for each node remove one of its incoming or upstream neighbors if it has one, otherwise remove the node itself. A *random downstream attack* can be defined similarly, removing the node to which the chosen node points to. In undirected networks, a similar strategy has been proposed for efficient immunization [45] and the early detection of contagious outbreaks [46], relying on the statistical trend that randomly selected neighbors have more links than the node itself [47,48]. In directed networks we can prove that randomly selected upstream (or downstream) neighbors have more outgoing (or incoming) links than the node itself. Thus a random upstream (or downstream) attack will remove more hubs and more links than the random attack does. But the real reason why we expect a random upstream attack to be efficient in a directed network is because $C_c(i) \geq C_c(j)$ for most edges $(i \rightarrow j)$, i.e. the control centrality of the starting node is usually no less than the ending node of a directed edge (see Fig. S8). In DAGs, for any edge $(i \rightarrow j)$, we have strictly $C_c(i) > C_c(j)$. Thus, the upstream neighbor of a node is expected to play a more important or equal role in control than the node itself, a result deeply rooted in the nature of the control problem, rather than the hub status of the upstream nodes.

To show the efficiency of the random upstream attack we compare its impact on fully controlled networks with several other strategies. We start from a network that is fully controlled ($\text{rank}_g(\mathbf{C}) = N$) via a minimum set of N_D driver nodes. After the attack a P faction of nodes are removed, denoting with $\text{rank}_g(\mathbf{C}')$ the dimension of the controllable subspace of the damaged network. We calculate $\text{rank}_g(\mathbf{C}')$ as a function of P, with P tuned from 0 up to 1. Since the random attack serves as a natural benchmark, we calculate the difference of $\text{rank}_g(\mathbf{C}')$ between a given strategy and the random attack, denoted as $\delta = [\text{rank}_g^{\text{Strategy}-j}(\mathbf{C}') - \text{rank}_g^{\text{Random}}(\mathbf{C}')]/N$. Obviously, the more negative is δ, the more efficient is the strategy compared to a fully random attack. We find that for most networks random upstream attack results in $\delta < 0$ for $0 < P < 1$, i.e. it causes more damage to the network's controllability than random attack (see Fig. 3b,c,d). Moreover, random upstream attack typically is more efficient than random downstream attack, even though in both cases we remove more hubs and more links than in the random attack. This is due to the fact that the upstream (or downstream) neighbors are usually more (or less) "powerful" than the node itself.

The efficiency of the random upstream attack is even comparable to targeted attacks (see Fig. 3). Since the former requires only the knowledge of the network's local structure rather than any knowledge of the nodes' centrality measures or any other global information (i.e. the structure of the $\mathbf{A}$ matrix) while the latter rely heavily on them, this finding indicates the advantage of the random upstream attack. The fact that those targeted attacks do not always show significant superiority over the random attacks is intriguing and would be explored in future work. Notice that for the intra-organization network all attack strategies fail in the sense that δ is either positive or very close to zero (Fig. 3a). This is due to the fact this network is so dense (with mean degree $\langle k \rangle \approx 58$) that we have $C_c(i) = C_c(j) = N$ for almost all the edges $(i \rightarrow j)$. Consequently, both random upstream and downstream attacks are not efficient and the C_c-targeted attack shows almost the same impact as the random attack. This result suggests that when the network becomes very dense its controllability becomes extremely robust against all kinds of attacks, consistent with our previous result on the core percolation and the control robustness against link removal [12]. We also tested those attack strategies on model networks (see Fig. S9, S10 and S11). The results are qualitatively consistent with what we observed in real networks.

Discussion

In sum, we study the control centrality of single node in complex networks and find that it is related to the underlying hierarchical structure of networks. The presented results help us better understand the controllability of complex networks and design an efficient attack strategy against network control. Due to the duality of controllability and observability [18,19], a similar centrality measure can be defined to quantify the ability of a single node in observing the whole system, i.e. inferring the state of the whole system.

Supporting Information

Figure S1 Calculation of control centrality (or the generic dimension of the controllable subspace). (a) The original controlled system is represented by a digraph $G(A,B)$. (b) The modified digraph $G'(A,B)$ used in solving the linear programming. Dotted and solid lines are assigned with weight $w_{ij} = 0$ and 1, respectively. The maximum-weight cycle partition is shown in red, which has weight 3, corresponding to the generic dimension of controllable subspace by controlling node x_1 or equivalently the control centrality of node x_1.

Figure S2 Control centrality of nodes in several real-world networks and their randomized counterparts: rand-ER (red), rand-Degree (green). (a) Intra-organizational network of a manufacturing company. (b) Hyperlinks between weblogs on US politics. (c) Email network in a university. (d) Ownership network of US corporations.

Figure S3 Control centrality vs. the number of reachable nodes. The real networks are the same as used in Fig. S2.

Figure S4 Any directed network has a underlying hierarchical structure. (a) A directed network of 50 nodes. There are seven SCCs highlighted in different colors. The nodes are colored according to their control centrality. The edge $(i \rightarrow j)$ is colored in green, red, or blue if $C_c(i)$ is larger than, smaller than, or equal to $C_c(j)$, respectively. For all edges with $l_i > l_j$, we have $C_c(i) > C_c(j)$. But this is not true for general node pairs $\{i, j\}$. (b) The condensation of the network in (a) is a DAG with three layers. Each node in the DAG represents a SCC in the original network.

Figure S5 Even if a lower node is accessible from a higher node, it is still possible that the control centrality of the higher node is smaller than or equal to the lower one.

Figure S6 Control centrality as a function of layer index in several real-world networks. The real networks are the same as used in Fig. S2. Symbol ('+') represents the average value of C_c with error bar defined as the C_c range, i.e. $[C_c^{\min}, C_c^{\max}]$, for all the nodes in the same layer of the largest connected component of the network. Dotted lines represents $C_c(i) = l_i$.

Figure S7 Variation of the hierarchical structure and its impact on the distribution of control centrality. (a) Number of layers (N_L). (b) Size of the giant SCC. Both ER and SF networks are generated from the Chung-Lu model with $N = 10^4$ and the results are averaged over 100 realizations with error bars defined as s.e.m. Dotted lines are only a guide to the eye. (c,d,e) Distribution of control centrality for ER networks at different $\langle k \rangle$ values ($\langle k \rangle = 1,2,8$).

Figure S8 Fraction of edges $(i \rightarrow j)$ which satisfy $C_c(i) > C_c(j)$. Fractions of edges $(i \rightarrow j)$ with $C_c(i) > C_c(j)$, $C_c(i) < C_c(j)$, and $C_c(i) = C_c(j)$, are denoted as $f_>$, $f_<$, and $f_=$, respectively. Both ER and SF networks are generated from the Chung-Lu model with $N = 10^3$ and the results are averaged over 100 realizations with error bars defined as s.e.m. Dotted lines are only a guide to the eye. (a) ER network. (b) SF network with $\gamma = 2.5$. (c) SF network with $\gamma = 2.1$.

Figure S9 Impact of different attack strategies on network controllability. $\text{rank}_g^{\text{Strategy}-j}(C')$ represents the generic dimension of controllable subspace after removing a P fraction of nodes using strategy-j. The nodes are removed according to 10 different strategies (see text). Both ER and SF networks are generated from the Chung-Lu model with $N = 10^3$ and the results are averaged over 10 random choices of P fraction of nodes with error bars defined as s.e.m. Lines are only a guide to the eye.

Figure S10 Impact of different attack strategies on network controllability with respect to random attack. $\delta \equiv [\mathrm{rank}_{\mathrm{g}}^{\mathrm{Strategy}-j}(C') - \mathrm{rank}_{\mathrm{g}}^{\mathrm{Strategy}-0}(C')]/N$ denotes the generic dimension difference of the controllable subspace after removing a P fraction of nodes using strategy-j and random attack. The more negative is δ, the more efficient is the strategy compared to a random attack. Symbols are the same as used in Fig. S9.

Figure S11 Impact of different attack strategies on network connectivity. n_{lc} represents the normalized size of the largest connected component of the network after removing a P fraction of nodes. The nodes are removed according to 10 different strategies (see text). Both ER and SF networks are generated from the Chung-Lu model with $N = 10^3$ and the results are averaged over 10 random choices of P fraction of nodes with error bars defined as s.e.m. Lines are only a guide to the eye.

Author Contributions

Conceived and designed the experiments: Y-YL J-JS A-LB. Wrote the paper: Y-YL A-LB. Analyzed the empirical data and did the analytical and numerical calculations: Y-YL. Edited the manuscript: J-JS.

References

1. Albert R, Barabási AL (2002) Statistical mechanics of complex networks. Rev Mod Phys 74: 47–97.
2. Newman M, Barabási AL, Watts DJ (2006) The Structure and Dynamics of Networks. Princeton: Princeton University Press.
3. Barabási AL, Albert R (1999) Emergence of scaling in random networks. Science 286: 509.
4. Watts DJ, Strogatz SH (1998) Collective dynamics of 'small-world' networks. Nature 393: 440–442.
5. Wang XF, Chen G (2002) Pinning control of scale-free dynamical networks. Physica A 310: 521–531.
6. Tanner HG (2004) On the controllability of nearest neighbor interconnections. Decision and Control, 2004 CDC 43rd IEEE Conference on 3: 2467–2472.
7. Sorrentino F, di Bernardo M, Garofalo F, Chen G (2007) Controllability of complex networks via pinning. Phys Rev E 75: 046103.
8. Yu W, Chen G, Lü J (2009) On pinning synchronization of complex dynamical networks. Automatica 45: 429–435.
9. Lombardi A, Hörnquist M (2007) Controllability analysis of networks. Phys Rev E 75: 056110.
10. Rahmani A, Ji M, Mesbahi M, Egerstedt M (2009) Controllability of multi-agent systems from a graph-theoretic perspective. SIAM J Control Optim 48: 162–186.
11. Mesbahi M, Egerstedt M (2010) Graph Theoretic Methods in Multiagent Networks. Princeton: Princeton University Press.
12. Liu YY, Slotine JJ, Barabási AL (2011) Controllability of complex networks. Nature 473: 167–173.
13. Liu YY, Slotine JJ, Barabási AL (2011) Few inputs reprogram biological networks (reply). Nature 478: E4–E5.
14. Egerstedt M (2011) Complex networks: Degrees of control. Nature 473: 158–159.
15. Nepusz T, Vicsek T (2012) Controlling edge dynamics in complex networks. Nature Physics 8: 568–573.
16. Cowan NJ, Chastain EJ, Vilhena DA, Freudenberg JS, Bergstrom CT (2011) Nodal dynamics determine the controllability of complex networks. arXiv: 11062573v3.
17. Wang WX, Ni X, Lai YC, Grebogi C (2012) Optimizing controllability of complex networks by minimum structural perturbations. Phys Rev E 85: 1–5.
18. Kalman RE (1963) Mathematical description of linear dynamical systems. J Soc Indus and Appl Math Ser A 1: 152.
19. Luenberger DG (1979) Introduction to Dynamic Systems: Theory, Models, & Applications. New York: John Wiley & Sons.
20. Slotine JJ, Li W (1991) Applied Nonlinear Control. Prentice-Hall.
21. Sabidussi G (1966) The centrality index of a graph. Psychometrika 31.
22. Freeman L (1977) A set of measures of centrality based upon betweenness. Sociometry 40.
23. Bonacich P (1987) Power and centrality: A family of measures. American Journal of Sociology 92: 1170–1182.
24. Bonacich P, Lloyd P (2001) Eigenvector-like measures of centrality for asymmetric relations. Social Networks 23: 191–201.
25. Brin S, Page L (1998) The anatomy of a large-scale hypertextual web search engine. In: Seventh International World-Wide Web Conference (WWW 1998).
26. Kleinberg JM (1999) Authoritative sources in a hyperlinked environment. J ACM 46: 604–632.
27. Dolev S, Elovici Y, Puzis R (2010) Routing betweenness centrality. J ACM 57: 25: 1–25: 27.
28. Wang B, Gao L, Gao Y (2012) Control range: a controllability-based index for node significance in directed networks. Journal of Statistical Mechanics: Theory and Experiment 2012: P04011.
29. Lin CT (1974) Structural controllability. IEEE Trans Auto Contr 19: 201.
30. Shields RW, Pearson JB (1976) Structural controllability of multi-input linear systems. IEEE Trans Auto Contr 21: 203.
31. Hosoe S (1980) Determination of generic dimensions of controllable subspaces and its application. IEEE Trans Auto Contr 25: 1192.
32. Dion JM, Commault C, van der Woude J (2003) Generic properties and control of linear structured systems: a survey. Automatica 39: 1125–1144.
33. Blackhall L, Hill DJ (2010) On the structural controllability of networks of linear systems. In: 2nd IFAC Workshop on Distributed Estimation and Control in Networked Systems. 245–250.
34. Poljak S (1990) On the generic dimension of controllable subspaces. IEEE Trans Auto Contr 35: 367.
35. Erdős P, Rényi A (1960) On the evolution of random graphs. Publ Math Inst Hung Acad Sci 5: 17–60.
36. Bollobás B (2001) Random Graphs. Cambridge: Cambridge University Press.
37. Maslov S, Sneppen K (2002) Specificity and stability in topology of protein networks. Science 296: 910–913.
38. Milo R, Shen-Orr S, Itzkovitz S, Kashtan N, Chklovskii D, et al. (2002) Network motifs: Simple building blocks of complex networks. Science 298: 824–827.
39. Yan KK, Fang G, Bhardwaj N, Alexander RP, Gerstein M (2010) Comparing genomes to computer operating systems in terms of the topology and evolution of their regulatory control networks. Proc Natl Acad Sci USA.
40. Yan G, Zhou T, Hu B, Fu ZQ, Wang BH (2006) Efficient routing on complex networks. Physical Review E 73.
41. Motter AE, Zhou C, Kurths J (2005) Network synchronization, diffusion, and the paradox of heterogeneity. Phys Rev E 71: 016116.
42. Yang R, Zhou T, Xie YB, Lai YC, Wang BH (2008) Optimal contact process on complex networks. Phys Rev E 78: 066109.
43. Harary F (1994) Graph Theory. Westview Press.
44. Albert R, Jeong H, Barabási AL (2000) Error and attack tolerance of complex networks. Nature 406: 378–382.
45. Cohen R, Havlin S, ben Avraham D (2003) Efficient immunization strategies for computer networks and populations. Phys Rev Lett 91: 247901.
46. Christakis NA, Fowler JH (2010) Social network sensors for early detection of contagious outbreaks. PLoS ONE 5: e12948.
47. Feld SL (1991) Why your friends have more friends than you do. Am J Soc 96: 1464.
48. Newman MEJ (2003) Ego-centered networks and the ripple effect. Soc Netw 25: 83.
49. Cross R, Parker A (2004) The Hidden Power of Social Networks. Boston, MA: Harvard Business School Press.
50. Adamic LA, Glance N (2005) The political blogosphere and the 2004 us election. Proceedings of the WWW-2005 Workshop on the Weblogging Ecosystem.
51. Eckmann JP, Moses E, Sergi D (2004) Entropy of dialogues creates coherent structures in e-mail traffic. Proc Natl Acad Sci USA 101: 14333.
52. Norlen K, Lucas G, Gebbie M, Chuang J (2002) Eva: Extraction, visualization and analysis of the telecommunications and media ownership network. Proceedings of International Telecommunica- tions Society 14th Biennial Conference, Seoul Korea.
53. Newman MEJ (2002) Assortative mixing in networks. Phys Rev Lett 89: 208701.

20

Using Networks To Understand Medical Data: The Case of Class III Malocclusions

Antonio Scala[1,2]*, Pietro Auconi[1,3], Marco Scazzocchio[1], Guido Caldarelli[1,2,4], James A. McNamara[5,6,7,8], Lorenzo Franchi[5,9]

1 Istituto dei Sistemi Complessi Udr "La Sapienza", Roma, Italy, 2 London Institute of Mathematical Sciences, London, United Kingdom, 3 Private Practice of Orthodontics, Rome, Italy, 4 NATWORKS Unit for the Study of Natural Networks, IMT Lucca Institute for Advanced Studies, Lucca, Italy, 5 Department of Orthodontics and Pediatric Dentistry, School of Dentistry, The University of Michigan, Ann Arbor, Michigan, United States of America, 6 Department of Cell and Developmental Biology, School of Medicine, The University of Michigan, Ann Arbor, Michigan, United States of America, 7 Center for Human Growth and Development, The University of Michigan, Ann Arbor, Michigan, United States of America, 8 Private Practice of Orthodontics, Ann Arbor, Michigan, United States of America, 9 Department of Orthodontics, The University of Florence, Florence, Italy

Abstract

A system of elements that interact or regulate each other can be represented by a mathematical object called a network. While network analysis has been successfully applied to high-throughput biological systems, less has been done regarding their application in more applied fields of medicine; here we show an application based on standard medical diagnostic data. We apply network analysis to Class III malocclusion, one of the most difficult to understand and treat orofacial anomaly. We hypothesize that different interactions of the skeletal components can contribute to pathological disequilibrium; in order to test this hypothesis, we apply network analysis to 532 Class III young female patients. The topology of the Class III malocclusion obtained by network analysis shows a strong co-occurrence of abnormal skeletal features. The pattern of these occurrences influences the vertical and horizontal balance of disharmony in skeletal form and position. Patients with more unbalanced orthodontic phenotypes show preponderance of the pathological skeletal nodes and minor relevance of adaptive dentoalveolar equilibrating nodes. Furthermore, by applying Power Graphs analysis we identify some functional modules among orthodontic nodes. These modules correspond to groups of tightly inter-related features and presumably constitute the key regulators of plasticity and the sites of unbalance of the growing dentofacial Class III system. The data of the present study show that, in their most basic abstraction level, the orofacial characteristics can be represented as graphs using nodes to represent orthodontic characteristics, and edges to represent their various types of interactions. The applications of this mathematical model could improve the interpretation of the quantitative, patient-specific information, and help to better targeting therapy. Last but not least, the methodology we have applied in analyzing orthodontic features can be applied easily to other fields of the medical science.

Editor: Angel Sánchez, Universidad Carlos III de Madrid, Spain

Funding: The authors have no support or funding to report.

Competing Interests: Pietro Auconi and James A. Mcnamara work in a private practice of orthodontics, i.e: Studio Auconi in Rome, Italy, and McNamara Orthodontics, Ann Arbor, Michigan, respectively. There are no patents, products in development or marketed products to declare.

* E-mail: antonio.scala@phys.uniroma1.it

Introduction

A general way to understand complex biological systems is to represent them using the simplest units of architecture. Such patterns of local and global interconnection are called *networks*. A network, or in more formal mathematical language, a *graph*, is a simplified representation that reduces a system to an abstract structure capturing the basis of connection pattern of the system [1,2]. The simplest possible network representation reduces the system's elements to *nodes* ("*vertices*") and their pairwise relationships to *links* ("*edges*") connecting pairs of nodes. Links represent functional interactions or anatomical relationships between the nodes, such as "catalyze", or "binds to", or "is converted to", or "shift" [3,4]. The network's inference and analysis refers to information on the identity and the state of the elements of a system to their functional relationships and to the extraction of biological insight and predictions. A multitude of studies have shown that meaningful biological properties can be extracted by network analysis [5,6].

An important advancement in network science has been the possibility of identifying and localizing sub-networks of functional modules (*motifs*) in complex systems [7]. The decomposition of large networks into distinct components, or modules, has to be regarded as a major approach to deal with the complexity of large biological networks. A motif refers to a group of physically or functionally connected components (nodes in graph) that work together to achieve the desired biological function. These organized sets of interactions are capable of local ordering, function, process information, and presumably act as regulators of growth and development in determining auxologic choices between homeostasis and plasticity [8–10].

Already applied in biomedical areas such as genetics, molecular biology, microbiology, and epidemiology, networks often have revealed surprising and unanticipated biological and functional insights, delineating the possibility of a new, holistic approach in scientific investigation. This approach ideally aims to define and analyze the interrelationship of *all* the elements in a biomedical system in order to understand how a system works in ever changing conditions (a new discipline called "*Systems Biology*") [11]. An apparently more modest but not less important task is to apply such an approach to the ordinary data sets used in medical practice; in particular, we will produce an example based on standard orthodontic data.

Network analysis has been applied recently to orthodontics to detect and visualize the most interconnected clinical, radiographic, and functional data pertaining to the orofacial system [12]. In particular, by considering phenotypic, functional, and radiographic characteristics it has been shown that different kinds of dentofacial malocclusions correspond to different network structures (a malocclusion is a misalignment of teeth or incorrect relation between the teeth of the two dental arches).

During the diagnostic process to establish the objectives, strategies, priorities and sequences of treatment, the orthodontist has to identify and locate the critical points of malocclusion [13]. Among malocclusions, the more severe is the so-called Class III malocclusion, often associated with the protrusion of the lower dental arch (Fig. 1). Class III malocclusion in growing subjects is characterized by a complex combinations of skeletal features (*e.g.* a shorter and more retrusive maxilla, an excess of lower anterior face height, a shorter anterior cranial base length, a more acute cranial base angle) with multiple dentoalveolar compensatory processes (*e.g.* proclined maxillary incisors, retroclined mandibular incisors) [14–18]. The management of the architectural and structural Class III network parameters forces the orthodontist to collect clinical and radiographic data sets on craniofacial characteristics, growth, and function. The paradox of daily orthodontic practice is that these data sets may bring more disorientation than understanding of the main problem of the patient [19]. With the aim of identifying pathognomonic traits of severity for Class III malocclusion, Freer [20] found that labiolingual spread and overjet were the most critical variables, while Stellzig-Eisenhauer et al [19] focused attention on the individualized combination of palatal plane angle, inclination of lower incisors, and Wits appraisal, but no morphologic trait was shown to be indicative of potential Class III development [20–23].

The craniofacial region can be regarded as a complex system that grows and remodels itself following an intricate network of auxologic forces, distortive processes and/or compensatory mechanisms [18]. Complex systems are dynamic systems that present with the capacity of self-organizing a large number of interacting elements in a non-linear fashion (*e.g.* forests, ants, flocks of birds, financial markets, the immune system) [3]. In order to understand the function of a biological organization it often is beneficial to conceptualize it as a systems of interacting elements and to define the dynamic behavior of these components [1,11]. The global behavior of complex systems cannot be explained solely on the basis of a single physical law, or the behavior of individual elements. The cooperation of the elements determines the overall behavior and provides properties that can be totally unrelated to the individual components of the system ("more is different"). The system must be analyzed in its entirety, as a coherent unit: it is pattern that matters [24,25].

The aim of this study is to show how "network thinking" and network modeling leads to a systemic analysis of standard diagnostic data under a different perspective that digs out previously undiscovered information. In particular, we will identify the physiological and/or pathological characteristics in a large cross-sectional sample of 532 female Class III subjects on the basis of a model derived from network analysis.

Methods

Objectives

The aim of this study is to apply conjunctly statistical analysis with network tools and methodologies to Class III malocclusion features' longitudinal (i.e. time varying) datasets in order to uncover the systemic importance of such features and to

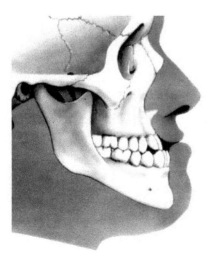

Figure 1. Class III malocclusion with protrusion of the lower dental arch.

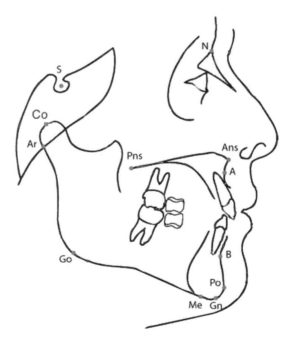

Figure 2. Cephalogram reference points. Most of the cephalometric landmarks are either angles or normalized linear distances. As an example, SN-GoGn is an angle between anterior cranial base and mandibular plane. The 21 cephalometric landmarks analyzed in the paper correspond to the standard set of features analyzed in orthodontics (see Table 1).

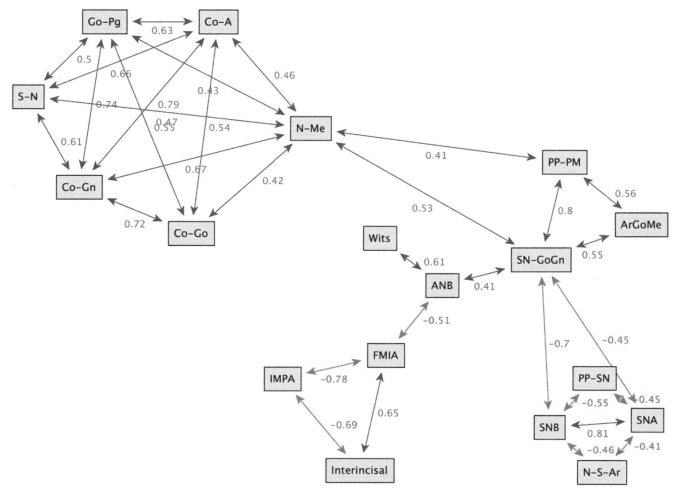

Figure 3. Graph obtained from the cephalometric data of 240 female Class III patients between 7 and 10 years of age (group G1).
The highly connected nodes N-Me (anterior facial height) and SN-GoGn (divergence between the anterior cranial base and mandibular body) work as bridges, i.e. they connect separate sub-graphs. The graph highlights a division between the cephalometric parameters: linear (upper left nodes: Go-Pg, Co-A, S-N, Co-Gn, Co-Gn, N-Me), angular parameters (upper right: PP-PM, SN-Go-Gn, Ar-Go-Me) and adaptive dentoalveolar parameters (lower left: IMPA; FMIA, Interincisal).

individuate the possible emergence of features' subset driving the orofacial development of Class III malocclusion

Participants

This study analyzed the pretreatment lateral cephalometric records of 532 untreated Class III Caucasian female patients collected from the Department of Orthodontics of the University of Florence, Italy, and from the Graduate Orthodontic Program at the University of Michigan, Ann Arbor, Michigan. All these subjects was enrolled previously in large descriptive estimates of craniofacial growth in Class III malocclusion [14,23,26]. The age range was between 6 years 4 months to 17 years 3 months.

To be included in this study, the female patients had to satisfy all of the following inclusion criteria:

- Caucasian ancestry;
- no orthopedic/orthodontic treatment prior to cephalogram;
- diagnosis of Class III malocclusion based on anterior cross-bite, accentuated mesial step relationships of the primary second

molars, permanent first molar relationship of at least one half cusp Class III;
- no congenitally missing or extracted teeth.

Description of Procedures or Investigations undertaken

The subjects were examined separately in four age groups: Group G1 (from 7 to 10 years) 240 subjects, Group G2 (from 11 to 12 years) 89 subjects, Group G3 (from 13 to 14 years) 105 subjects, and Group G4 (from 15 to 17 years) 98 subjects.

The cephalometric analysis required the digitization of 21 landmarks on the tracing of each cephalogram (Fig. 2). The error of the method for the cephalometric measurements was evaluated by repeating the measures in 100 randomly selected cephalograms. Error was on average 0.6° for angular measures and 0.9 mm for linear measures.

Ethics

All data used in this study have been previously published as referenced in the methods section. Written informed consent was obtained from the patients' parents as part of their orthodontic

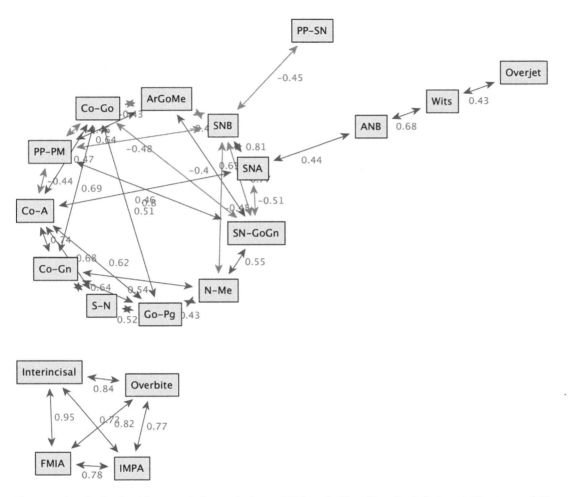

Figure 4. Graph obtained from cephalometric data of 90 female Class III patients between 11 years and 12 years of age (group G2). The graph is composed by two characterized groups: structural (upper group) and dentoalveolar adaptive (lower group of four nodes).

treatment. The approval of an Ethical Committee was not sought as all data analysed were collected as part of routine orthodontic pre-treatment diagnosis.

Statistical methods

We analize the correlation matrices among the 21 cephalographic landmarks considered by using complex netwoks. First we calculate (using KNIME [27]) for each pair of features their sample Pearson correlation coefficient $r_{xy} = (<xy> - <x><y>)/s_x s_y$, where x,y are the numerical values of the landmarks, $<...>$ indicates sample means and s_x, s_y are their sample standard deviations. Each r_{xy} can be considered as the weight of a link between x and y; the associated network therefore is a complete graph, *i.e.* a network where every node is connected to every other node. Such correlation graphs already have been considered in other applications of network theory, like finance and genomics [28,29]; in order to dig out the information present in the whole correlation matrix and sort out relevant features with their global correlations, some filtering has to be applied. Our choice is to use a cutoff to correlation values in order to consider only the most significant correlations [12]; therefore we consider two features (the nodes of our graphs) to be linked if $|r_{xy}| > 0.40$. Notice that at difference with most previous studies in networks, we do not discard negative correlations: this is a critical point when analyzing

any complex systems where important relations, as a negative feedback, naturally would show up as significantly high negative correlations.

Networks have been visualized using the software yEd [30] with the standard layout; the choice of filtering at $|r_{xy}| > 0.40$ reduces the complexity of the system and permitted the identification of many characteristics just by visual inspection. In particular, it is very easy to identify *bridge nodes*, i.e. nodes whose absence would split the graphs in two or more separate parts. Bridge nodes are important both because they allow to detect separate subsystems (sets of highly correlated features) and because they represent the connection among such subsystems.

Furthermore, to investigate the presence of functional modules, we have searched for motifs in our filtered networks. Motifs searches are potentially valuable tools to predict unknown interactions involving 3–5 nodes (rarely more than 6). These organized sets of interactions are capable of higher order functions (such as amplification), and hence probably represent the functional capabilities within the network. They provide balance between modules through signaling gates (*i.e.* negative feedforward motifs), favoring plasticity (open-gate configuration), or homeostasis (closed- gate configuration). We have focused on the presence of *cliques* (subsets where each of node is connected to every other node) as they naturally represent the presence of a

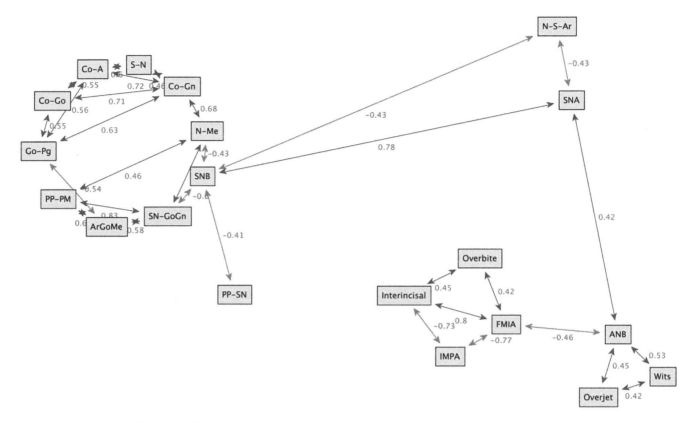

Figure 5. Graph obtained from cephalometric data of 105 female Class III patients between 13 and 14 years of age (group G3). The main bridge node is S-N-B (longitudinal position of the maxillary arch) divides the structural nodes from the ones representing dentoalveolar adaptive and mixed features.

subsystem acting as a whole: in fact, every feature in such a subsystem is interrelated. To individuate the presence of clicques, we have employed the Power Graphs plugin [31] in the software Cytoscape [32].

Results

Figures 3, 4, 5, 6 illustrate the correlation networks of the cephalometric characteristics of 532 Class III female patients, from 7 to 17 years of age. In all ages considered, the most-connected nodes are those related to vertical skeletal features (N-Me, SN-GoGn, PP-PM). These vertical parameters always are connected with those of mandibular sagittal nodes (SNB, GoPg). These strong patterns of interaction are observed for all ages considered. Due to the persistence of such network topology in all age groups, these highly connected nodes can be regarded as the key features in the growth of female Class III subjects.

Further results come from the Power Graph analysis of the networks. With the aim of defining the possible clinical relevance of these orthodontic network patterns, the patients were differentiated into two cephalometric categories using Wits appraisal of jaw disharmony, a simple method whereby the severity of degree of anteroposterior jaw displasia may be measured on a lateral cephalometric head film. The two class consist of "mild" and "severe" Class III patients (Wits appraisal greater than −3 mm and Wits appraisal smaller or equal to −3 mm, respectively) [19]. The visual network inspection of these "mild" and "severe" Class III patients (group G4) reveals several interesting characteristics:

1. the networks of the "mild" patients exhibits a balanced node pattern (Fig. 7a);
2. in the "severe" patients group, we find a preponderance of maxillomandibular divergence nodes (related to the vertical development of the craniofacial system) and mandibular sagittal nodes (related to the horizontal prominence of the chin), with poor balance of adaptive nodes (Fig. 7b).

Discussion

Instead of searching single or multiple dentoskeletal radiographic predictors variables, our work attempts to delineate the overall dentofacial organizing principles, the functional dynamics, and the regulatory growth principles of Class III malocclusion. The cephalometric data of a large retrospective cohort of 532 Class III female subjects, in mixed and permanent dentition, were analyzed through a combination of multivariate computational techniques: networks analysis of correlation matrices and search for regulatory motifs. These high-throughput techniques allow the extraction and identification of new biological insight from data regarding several related topics of importance during the Class III craniofacial growth such as robustness, adaptation, time progression, and structural stability.

Understanding structure-dynamics relationships in networks is a major goal of complex system research. In several biomedical fields, the analysis of interaction dynamics of the components may be useful to capture the essential behavior of the system, to understand higher-order biological function, and also to facilitate prediction responses [9,25].

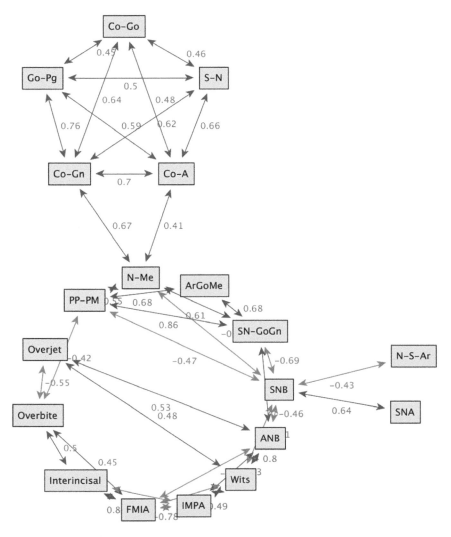

Figure 6. Graph obtained from cephalometric data of 99 female Class III patients between 15 and 17 years of age (group G4). The graph is divided into two groups clearly inter-connected via the bridge N-Me (anterior facial height).

General principles behind the relationships between orthodontic structure and dynamics still are lacking, in part due to the scarcity of sufficiently general formalism to study structure and dynamics within a common framework. When a complex system is investigated using network analysis, the network map often shows groups of nodes only weakly connected, alternating with groups of highly connected nodes. Many aspects of the inherent complexity of nature follow a pattern that is the same in many contexts (from biology to ecology, sociology, financial markets, etc.). Among the network of connections, very few nodes have many links ("hubs"), while the majority of the remainder are characterized by few or very few links. These hubs govern the entire system through preferential interactions, facilitating the movement of information, creating shortcuts between distant nodes, helping to create a robust network ("*small world networks*") that can adapt to environmental stresses [4,24].

A previous investigation illustrated the more compact network Class III malocclusion structure as regard to Class I and II when considering phenotypic, functional, and radiographic characteristics [12]. The results of the current study showed that, in the interrelationship of Class III skeletal elements, the "*driver nodes*"

that presumably guide the growth of the orofacial system are located in the interplay between maxillomandibular divergence (PP-PM, NS-Go-Gn) and mandibular sagittal nodes (Go-Gn, Co-Gn). This structural organization, reflected in the network topology, probably constrains the range of dynamical behaviors available to the system during the generative process of the malocclusion. Our data confirm the observation of Bui et al. [21] regarding the generative process of Class III malocclusion observed in a retrospective cohort of 309 patients: the most important cephalometric variables reflect the anteroposterior and vertical imbalance during growth, rather than specific Class III craniofacial structures.

Malocclusions are isoforms of biological complexity. The network of functional and morphologic characteristics of the orofacial system causes diffuse connections of strict interdependence. Any therapeutic intervention applied to a part of the system, invariably has an impact on other structures. For example, the decision to open the bite by rotating the mandible clockwise must take into account the concomitant effects on the vertical dimension, on the convexity of face, and on the potential divergence of the occlusal plane [13,17].

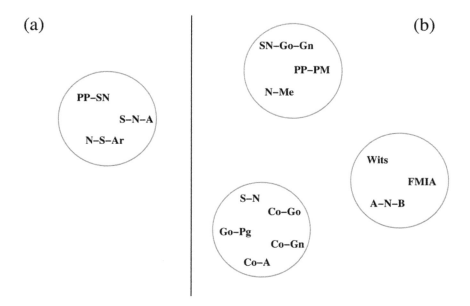

(a)   (b)

Figure 7. Cliques (motifs) individuated by the Power Graphs analysis for female patients (15–17 years) with mild Class III malocclusion (panel A) and with severe Class III malocclusion (panel B). Mild Class III patients show a single clique of only three structural nodes (SNA, N-S-Ar, PP-SN). Severe Class III patients show the presence of three separate cliques: mandibular sagittal nodes (S-N,...), maxillomandibular divergence nodes (N-Me,...) and adaptive nodes (Wits,..). The comparison between the two figures indicates that severe Class III patients are characterized by the presence of groups of strongly inter-correlated features, i.e. tend to act as a single whole system.

Once the pattern of a malocclusion has been identified, it becomes easier to analyze the force flow in the orofacial network, to define the local functional entities involved (in Graph theory, *motifs*) and localize signaling gates that provide among between modules, rather than taking solely into consideration the morphological characteristics of the system [8].

Table 1. The 21 cephalometric variables employed in our study.

SN	anteroposterior length of the cranial base
Wits	Wits appraisal
Co-A	midfacial length as distance from Co to A
Co-Gn	mandibular length as distance from Co to Gn
Ar-Go	mandibular ramus height
NS-GoGn	divergence of the mandibular plane relative to the anterior cranial base
NS-Ar	saddle angle
ArGoMe	gonial angle
SNA	anteroposterior maxillary position to the anterior cranial base
SNB	anterorposterior mandibular position to the anterior cranial base
IMPA	angle between the lower incisor with the mandibular plane
ANB	anteroposterior relation of the maxilla and the mandible
Interincisal	angle between the axis of the upper and the lower incisor
PP-SN	inclination of the palatal plane in relation to anterior cranial base
PP-PM	inclination of the palatal plane in relation to the mandible plane
NMe	anterior facial height
FMIA	angle between the axis of the lower incisor and the Frankfort plane
Overbite	Vertical distance between the incisal edges of the most protrusive maxillary and mandibular central incisors.
Overjet	Horizontal distance between the incisal edge of the most protrusive maxillary central incisors and the most facial aspect of the crown of the most protrusive mandibular central incisor
Go-Pg	distance between gonion and pogonion points
Co-Go	distance between condylion and gonion points

Most of the cephalometric variables are angles or distances derived from the cephalometric reference landmarks (Fig. 2).

The present study shows that during the growth process of Class III malocclusion the skeletal vertical and sagittal growth features (SN-GoGn, PP-PM) are central in the interacting network of the system components: these nodes can be considered the "driver nodes" for the growth of the orofacial system. The ability of the orofacial system to function as an integrate unit may arise from the balance of activities between the modules: this may be the core design principle revealed by orthodontic network analysis. Network analysis revealed that the patients with more unbalanced cephalometric features ("severe patients") present a network topology with a preponderance of the skeletal nodes and minor relevance of adaptive dentoalveolar nodes. In the "mild" patient group, the network topology showed a greater balance between skeletal and adaptive craniofacial features. In the patients with more pronounced radiographic Class III features, we have identified two subnetworks of strong functional interaction (cliques). As observed in several metabolic pathways, these subnetworks are recognized as critical elements of biological organization [7,8]; they work as feed-forward loops, with high capacity of anticipatory regulation as opposed to the homeostatis effects of feed-back loops. Such analysis confirms the importance of considering the co-occurrence of the interrelated morphologic features, reinforcing the hypothesis that these sites of co-occurrence of the overall interrelated morphologic features are more suitable to indicate the favorable or unfavorable progression of this type of disharmony respect to the individual orthodontic features. Presumably, the convergence of the orthodontic therapeutic approaches into these modules allows the clinician to maximize results and to shorten treatment times.

Computational technology has proved to be most useful in the handling of mass data (in the present case, a set of cephalometric measurements). As orthodontic studies shift from local description to system analysis, we need to identify the design principles of large craniofacial features networks. The limitations of viewing the head region in two dimensions only are well known. However, postnatal growth differences and the high incidence and magnitude of anteroposterior and vertical dentofacial abnormalities render this record useful for characterizing the overall morphology of the growing orofacial system.

The result of the present study indicate that, in their most basic abstraction level, the orofacial radiographic characteristics can be represented as networks using nodes to represent orthodontic characteristics, and edges to represent their various types of interactions. A substantial portion of the Class III issues during growth is driven by only a few nodes. By linking radiographic data and phenotypes to clinical characteristics in a causal or correlative manner, these observations may contribute to the construction of a model that provides a theoretical framework of the reciprocal interaction between organizing craniofacial pathways, growth, and malocclusion.

In conclusion, due to their generality, the application of network mathematical models could increase the interpretation of quantitative, patient-specific information and help to better targeting of therapy not only in orthodontics but also in other medical fields.

Acknowledgments

P. Auconi and M. Scazzocchio thank Matthias Reimann for help and support with the Power Graphs plugin.

Author Contributions

Conceived and designed the experiments: AS PA MS GC JAM LF. Performed the experiments: AS PA MS GC JAM LF. Analyzed the data: AS PA MS GC JAM LF. Contributed reagents/materials/analysis tools: AS PA MS GC JAM LF. Wrote the paper: AS PA MS GC JAM LF.

References

1. Albert R (2007) Network inference, analysis, and modelling in systems biology. The Plant Cell 19: 3327–3338.
2. Barabàsi A-L, Oltvai ZN (2004) Network biology: under standing the cell's functional organisation. Nat Rev Genet 5: 101–113.
3. Caldarelli G (2007) Scale-free networks. Complex webs in nature and technology. Oxford: Oxford Univ Press.
4. Newman MEJ (2006) Modularity and community structure in networks. Proc Natl Acad Sci USA 103: 8577–8582.
5. Barabasi A-L (2009) Scale-free networks: a decade and beyond. Science 325: 412–413.
6. Barrat A, Barthelemy M, Pastor-Satorras, Vespignani A (2004) The architecture of complex weighted networks. Proc Natl Acad Sci USA 101: 3747–3752.
7. Royer L, Reimann M, Andreopulos B, Schroeder M (2008) Unraveling protein networks with power graph analysis. PLoS Comput Biol 4: 1–8.
8. Ma'ayan A, Blitzer RD, Iyngegar R (2004) Toward predictive models of mammalian cells. Annu Rev Biophys Biomol Struct 34: 319–349.
9. Mesarovic MD, Sreenath SN, Keene JD (2004) Search for organising principles: understanding in system biology. Sys Biol 1: 19–27.
10. Janes KA, Yaffe MB (2006) Data-driven modelling of signal-transduction networks. Nat Mol Cell Biol 7: 820–828.
11. Kitano H (2002) Systems Biology: a brief overview. Science 295: 1662–1664
12. Auconi P,Caldarelli G, Scala A, Ierardo G, Polimeni A(2011) A network approach to orthodontic diagnosis. Orthod Craniofac Res 14: 189–197.
13. Staley RN (1995) Orthodontic diagnosis and treatment plan. In: Bishara SE Textbook of Orthodontics. Philadelphia: WB Saunders Co. pp. 98–113.
14. Baccetti T, Reyes BC, McNamara JA (2005) Gender differences in Class III malocclusion. Angle Orthod 75: 510–520.
15. Battagel JM (1994) The identification of Class III malocclusions by discriminand analysis. Eur J Orthod 16: 71–80.
16. Betzemberger D, Ruf S, Panchez H (1999) The compensatory mechanism in high angle malocclusions: a comparison of subjects in the mixed and permanent dentition. Angle Orthod. 69: 27–32.
17. Franchi L, Baccetti T, McNamara JA (1998) Cephalometric floating norms for north American adults. Angle Orthod 68: 497–502.
18. Solow B (1980) The dentoalveolar compensatory mechanism: background and clinical implications. Br J Orthod 7: 145–151.
19. Stellzig-Eisenhauer A, Lux CJ, Schuster G (2002) Treatment decision in adult patients with Class III malocclusion: orthodontic therapy or orthognatic surgery? Am J Orthod Dentofacial Orthop 122: 27–38.
20. Freer T J (1973) Selection of predictor variables in assessing the severity of malocclusion. Am J Orthod 64: 155–161.
21. Bui C, King T, Proffit W, Frazier-Bowers S (2006) Phenotypic characterization of Class III patients. Angle orthod 76: 564–569.
22. Sanborn R T (1955) Differences between the facial skeletal pattern of Class III malocclusion and normal occlusion. Angle Orthod 24:208–219.
23. Reyes BC, Baccetti T, McNamara JA (2006) An estimate of craniofacial growth in Class II malocclusion. Angle orthod 76: 577–584.
24. Buchanan M, Caldarelli G (2010) A networked world. Phys. World 23: 22–23.
25. Zhu X, Gerstein M, Snyder M (2007) Getting connected: analysis and principles of biological networks. Gene Dev 21: 1010–1024.
26. Baccetti T, Reyes BC and McNamara JA Jr. (2007) Craniofacial changes in Class III malocclusion as related to skeletal and dental maturation. Am J Orthod Dentofacial Orthop. 132(2):171.e1–171.e12
27. Berthold M R, Cebron N, Dill F, Gabriel T R, Kotter T et al. (2007), "KNIME: The Konstanz Information Miner", in "Studies in Classification, Data Analysis, and Knowledge Organization", Springer ISBN = 978-3-540-78239-1, ISSN = 1431-8814 http://www.knime.org/ last accessed on 29 Aug 2012
28. Bonnanno G, Caldarelli G, Lillo F, and Mantegna R N (2003) Topology of correlation-based minimal spanning trees in real and model markets. Phys Rev E (68): 046103
29. Langfelder P, Horvath S (2008) WGCNA: an R package for weighted correlation network analysis, BMC Bioinformatics (9): 559. Published online 2008 December 29. doi: 10.1186/1471-2105-9-559
30. http://www.yworks.com/en/products_yed_about.html last accessed on 29 Aug 2012
31. http://wiki.cytoscape.org/CyOog last accessed on 29 Aug 2012
32. Smoot M, Ono K, Ruscheinski J, Wang PL, Ideker T (2011) Cytoscape 2.8: new features for data integration and network visualization. Bioinformatics (27): 431–432. Published online 2010 December 12.

21

A Heuristic Placement Selection of Live Virtual Machine Migration for Energy-Saving in Cloud Computing Environment

Jia Zhao[1,2], Liang Hu[2], Yan Ding[2], Gaochao Xu[2], Ming Hu[1]*

1 College of Computer Science and Engineering, ChangChun University of Technology, Changchun, China, **2** College of Computer Science and Technology, Jilin University, Changchun, China

Abstract

The field of live VM (virtual machine) migration has been a hotspot problem in green cloud computing. Live VM migration problem is divided into two research aspects: live VM migration mechanism and live VM migration policy. In the meanwhile, with the development of energy-aware computing, we have focused on the VM placement selection of live migration, namely live VM migration policy for energy saving. In this paper, a novel heuristic approach PS-ES is presented. Its main idea includes two parts. One is that it combines the PSO (particle swarm optimization) idea with the SA (simulated annealing) idea to achieve an improved PSO-based approach with the better global search's ability. The other one is that it uses the Probability Theory and Mathematical Statistics and once again utilizes the SA idea to deal with the data obtained from the improved PSO-based process to get the final solution. And thus the whole approach achieves a long-term optimization for energy saving as it has considered not only the optimization of the current problem scenario but also that of the future problem. The experimental results demonstrate that PS-ES evidently reduces the total incremental energy consumption and better protects the performance of VM running and migrating compared with randomly migrating and optimally migrating. As a result, the proposed PS-ES approach has capabilities to make the result of live VM migration events more high-effective and valuable.

Editor: Fengfeng Zhou, Shenzhen Institutes of Advanced Technology, China

Funding: This work is supported by the National Natural Science Foundation of China (Grant No. 61133011), the Natural Science Foundation of Jilin (Grant No. 20101525), the Jilin Provincial Education Office (Jilin Provincial Educational and Scientific Program [2010] No. 85), the Natural Science Foundation of Jilin (Grant No. 20101533) and the Jilin Provincial Education Office (Jilin Provincial Educational and Scientific Program [2010] No. 103. The funders had no role in study design, data collection and analysis, decision to publish, or preparation of the manuscript.

Competing Interests: The authors have declared that no competing interests exist.

* Email: zhaiyj049@sina.com

Introduction

In green cloud computing, live VM migration technology [1] has always been playing a critical role. It not only contributes to implement cloud computing systems such as Infrastructure as a Service architecture [2,3] but also is the embody of elasticity and flexibility of the green cloud computing idea. Also, the maintenance management can be achieved through live VM migration technology in green cloud computing data centers, in which there exist many occasions needing live VM migrtion events. For instance, all VMs of some host probably need to be migrated out on account of a shut-down requirement of the host. Some VMs of a host probably need to be migrated out because of a load balancing requirement, a re-allocation requirement or other goals etc. Whenever a VM is ready to be migrated, generally there are large number of available hosts which can accommodate it and meet its resource requirements in the current cloud data centers. Traditionally, the migration target of the VM will be chosen randomly from these available hosts and then one can automatically or manually move the VM to the target host. It is obviously that the way to randomly selecting a target host for a live VM migration isn't efficient in any way.

In the contemporary society, large number of data centers working worldwide are having huge energy consumption, whose impact on environments is evident and considerable. Many researchers have been attempting to propose effective approaches with energy consumption of data centers minimized while ensuring the desired QoS (Quality of Service). With the rapid development of cloud computing and green computing, an array of researchers have focused their attention on green cloud data centers based on cloud computing and virtualized technologies and aiming to minimize energy consumption. This paper has focused on live VM migration policy for energy saving in this context of green cloud data centers. In virtualized green cloud data centers, there are always plenty of VMs needing to be migrated for certain goals. These migrant VMs, however, have many valid target hosts to select from. It is generally acknowledged that only one target host is most suitable for the VM in the aspect of minimizing the total incremental energy consumption in cloud data center. It is the proposed objective to pick out the optimal target hosts of migrant VMs.

Varieties of existing works have presented some heuristic algorithms to find optimal solutions aiming to minimize energy consumption. The basic idea is that the controllers have searched for a best policy by using their proposed algorithms on the basis of the current situation and history of a cloud data center. The problems of convergence and local optimization have been challenging the research direction. On the other hand, we know that a data center doesn't have abilities in predicting the size and type of the next workloads. As a consequence, the optimal policy which the proposed algorithms have found out over a short period of time isn't necessarily the optimal solution over a long period of time. In a word, the global best which of some VM the proposed algorithms have found out in an algorithm cycle may be a local best in a long-term process. Moreover, since the capability with which the current random migration policy and optimal migration policy adapt to a dynamic cloud environment isn't excellent enough, they may cause many failure events of live VM migration in a real and dynamic cloud environment. To address these problems, this paper has put forward a novel heuristic approach PS-ES, which employs the improved PSO method and utilizes the idea of SA to achieve a long-term energy saving optimization. Besides, a parameter, which can make the proposed PS-ES have capability to self-adapt to a dynamic cloud environment, is introduced into PS-ES to improve the performance of live VM migration. That is, the failure rate of VM migration is decreased. Compared to migrating a VM randomly and optimally, the proposed PS-ES has decreased more incremental energy consumption and failure events of live VM migration to contribute to achieving better green cloud data centers.

The rest of the paper is organized as follows. In Section 2, we present the related work of our proposed approach aiming to green cloud data center and the reasonable prerequisites are shown clearly. In Section 3, the analysis of the problem proposed in this paper and its formulation are given. In Section 4, the algorithm and implementation of PS-ES are introduced in detail. In Section 5, the experimental results and analysis on CloudSim platform are given. Finally, in Section 6, we summarize the full paper and future work is put forward.

Related Work

At present, the proposed problem concerning finding an appropriate target host for a live VM migration in terms of the objective of minimizing the total incremental energy consumption from the perspective of a long period of time has not been widely researched in the related fields. Most researchers, however, have focused on some problems similar to the proposed problem in this paper. Some researchers have focused on the direction targeting other problems of minimizing the incremental energy consumption by utilizing the technology of live VM migration in cloud data centers. Similarly, some researchers have been studying the direction which utilizes live VM migration technology to move these VMs in order to fulfill the requirement of performance and workload limitation while minimizing the energy drawn by a cloud data center. Most of them, in fact, are just to find an optimal host for each VM, which will be migrated or be created in it with the energy drawn by cloud data centers minimized. Ergo, the related work of the kind of problems of green cloud data centers will be discussed briefly in this section.

Rusu et al. in [4] have proposed a novel energy saving and cluster-level approach, which has abilities in dynamically reconfiguring the cluster to reduce energy consumption in the case that the load is decreased. The proposed approach includes two important components: the front end manager and the local manager. The front end manager is in charge of monitoring the cluster consisting of many hosts. In terms of a given system load, when the front end manager finds that some hosts should be turned on or off, the local managers of the corresponding hosts will take advantage of DVFS (Dynamic Voltage and Frequency Scaling) technology to save energy. The approach depends on the table of values and needs computing offline. Besides, the proposed system should have made use of consolidation technology through live VM migration and thus to duly turn off some hosts for better energy saving. As a result, its on/off policy and performance may not be effective enough.

In literature [5], Srikantaiah et al. have focused on the problem of dynamic consolidation of applications used for serving small stateless requests in cloud data centers to minimize energy consumption. The proposed problem is abstracted as a multidimensional bin packing problem. The authors have proposed a heuristic approach to address the defined bin packing problem. Its main idea is to minimize the sum of the Euclidean distances between the current allocations to the optimal point at each host. By using the proposed approach, the application workload will be allocated to a host once a request to executing a new application is received. If all active hosts do not have capabilities enough to process the current workload, a new host will be switch on while re-allocating all the workloads by utilizing the proposed approach in an arbitrary order. The proposed approach is suitable for heterogeneous environments. However, there exist some deficiencies in the proposed approach. It can only work well under the circumstances that the resource requirements of all applications are known in advance and can't be changed. The performance and energy overhead not considered by the authors are caused by migration of state-full applications between nodes. Besides, the frequent switching servers on/off also results in significant costs which are not negligible for a real-world system.

In literature [6], Verma et al. has focused on reducing energy consmption of cloud data centers by utilizing application placement achieved by live VM migration while ensuring minimizing migration cost. A novel application placement architecture pMapper is proposed by the authors. In pMapper, there are three major components given. A performance manager is used to dynamically resize VMs. A energy manager is achieved through CPU throttling. And a migration manager is in charge of identifying the target host for migration by using a knowledge base. The authors have presented that it is not necessary for energy-aware scheduling approaches to estimate energy consumption values. As long as the scheduling algorithms have capabilities to pick out the host which can relatively minimize the total incremental energy consumption due to a new VM being placed, it can schedule the given VM to the fit host. The proposed pMapper architecture minimizes energy and migration costs with keeping the performance. Our approach is based on a heuristic approach which exploits the concept of minimizing the total incremental energy owing to the new VM migrations. Our proposed architecture is simple and doesn't need any knowledge base to achieve significant reduction in the energy consumption.

Bo Li et al. in [7] have presented a novel approach EnaCloud. It has aimed to achieve a energy-efficient cloud platform by utilizing live application placement. Like pMapper, the application is also encapsulated in a VM in EnaCloud to support its live migration to make the number of running hosts minimized in order to save energy. EnaCloud has modeled the VM placement problem as a bin packing problem and proposed a heuristic algorithm to obtain the better solution. Besides, a novel over-provision method is presented to deal with the varying resource requirements of VMs encapsulating applications. Although this method can reduce extra operation overhead due to the changes of resource demands, it has risk to optimizing this problem. That is, it has possibility to result in more overhead and cost.

Jeyarani et al. [8] have proposed SAPSO (self-adaptive particle swarm optimization) for efficient virtual machine provisioning in cloud aimed at that when mapping a set of VM instances onto a set of servers from a dynamic resource pool, the total incremental energy drawn upon the mapping is minimal and does not compromise the performance objectives. The advantage of the proposed solution is obvious. It has focused on not only improving the performance of workload facilitating the cloud consumers but also developing the energy efficient data center management to facilitate cloud providers. However, the approach still may be inefficient and cause some additional events and costs from a long-term perspective as it doesn't take the future workload into account. Our proposed algorithm PS-ES is a heuristic approach which is based on PSO, one of swarm intelligence algorithms and introduces the SA (Simulated Annealing) idea into it.

Gaochao Xu et al. [9] present a novel heuristic approach named PS-ABC. Its algorithm consists of two parts. One part is that it combines the artificial bee colony (ABC) idea with the uniform random initialization idea, the binary search idea, and Boltzmann selection policy to achieve an improved ABC-based approach with better global exploration's ability and local exploitation's ability. The other part is that it uses the Bayes theorem to further optimize the improved ABC-based process to faster get the final optimal solution. The whole approach achieves a longer-term efficient optimization for power saving. However, it is by achieving the more accurate solution of the current problem window that its longer-term energy saving optimization effect is reached. It doesn't take the whole problem into consideration from the long-term operation perspective of a cloud data center. Although it has relatively achieved the global optimization in an algorithm cycle, it may get a local optimal result from the long-term operation of cloud data centers. As a result, the proposed PS-ES in this paper has the better energy saving effect than PS-ABC from a long-term operation of cloud data centers.

In this paper, PS-ES has a prerequisite. PS-ES aims to pick out the target host of each of the n migrant VMs from all m available hosts. It is assumed that each VM's target host picked out by PS-ES will be not the host that the VM is moved out from. The algorithm provides a live VM migration policy aiming to green cloud data centers. Therefore, the fact that the VM should be moved out for its reason is the premise of our approach. Since a VM needs to be migrated from its source host, its candidate hosts will not include its source host. Otherwise, it does not need the current migration event. What is more is that a host both needs move out VMs while having ability in receiving VMs is impossible and non-objective within a time window Δt. It can be seen that, for all the migrant VMs, the hosts, each of which is the source host of some migrant VM, will not be the target hosts. Therefore, the proposed prerequisite is rational and natural. The performance and efficiency of PS-ES will not be affected by it.

Results and Discussion

1. The Proposed Problem

In cloud data centers based on the IaaS architecture, the running VMs always have some requirements of live migration for some reasons in physical hosts. Determing the target host is the indispensable step of live VM migration. And the number of the available target hosts of a migrant VM is more than one. Besides, the varying placement selections of available target hosts will also lead to the different energy consumption. As a consequence, it is necessary for IaaS cloud data centers based on virtualized technologies to have a high-efficient energy saving placement selection policy for migrating the migrant VMs into the

appropriate physical hosts. In this paper, the proposed problem is the live migration policy problem of VM placement selection of available target physical hosts.

2. Problem Formulation

The proposed problem can be formulated as migrating n VMs accumulated within a time window **Δt** into m available candidate physical hosts. An n-dimensional vector is utilized to represent a solution of the proposed problem. The target host No. of the migrant VM which the location of an element of the vector represents is the value on the element. It is assumed that there exist m available physical hosts in the resource pool of the cloud data center for the current problem window. The m hosts are heterogeneous and dynamic while using space shared allocation policy. The states of the hosts are changed dynamically in real time in the light of the corresponding workloads. The problem can be stated as follows. Search out a VM-host set **PS** of placement selections so as to minimize the total incremental energy consumption caused by the migrated VMs onto the corresponding physical hosts while maximizing the performance by fulfilling the resource requirements of maximum number of VMs. A four tuple $S = \{$**PH, VM, E, PS**$\}$ for the proposed problem scenario is defined. **PH** is a set of **m** available physical hosts denoted by **PH** **(m, t)** = $\{$**PH$_1$, PH$_2$, PH$_3$ ..., PH$_m$**$\}$, available at migrating start time **t**. **VM** is a set of **n** VMs denoted by **VM (n, t, Δt)** = $\{$**VM$_1$, VM$_2$, VM$_3$, ..., VM$_n$**$\}$ accumulated within a time window **Δt**. **E (m, t)** = $\{$**E$_1$, E$_2$, ..., E$_m$**$\}$ is the energy consumption by the **m** physical hosts in resource pool. It is obvious that the proposed problem has a host of solutions which meet the performance constraints of the VM requests. That is, it is a multimodal problem having more than one placement selection to select from. Consequently, finding all of **o** candidate placement selections capable of maximizing the performance and then finding which among minimizes the energy consumption are supposed to be the objective. In the first place, a metric τ_r denoting resource fulfillment requirement is defined as follows to meet the performance demand above all.

$$\tau_r = \sum_{i=1}^{n} \sum_{j=1}^{m} \chi_i^j, \quad \begin{matrix} i \in \{1,2,3,\ldots,n\}, j \in \{1,2,3,\ldots,m\} \\ r \in \{1,2,3,\ldots,s\} \end{matrix} \quad (1)$$

where χ_i^j marks the placement selection of **i**th VM on the **j**th host and is defined as following. The total number of placement selections is represented as **s**.

$$\chi_i^j =$$

$$\begin{cases} 1 \\ if\ VM_i\ has\ been\ allocated\ to\ Host_j\ and\ rcrVM_i \leq acrHost_j,\ i \in \{1,2,3,\ldots,n\} \\ 0 \\ if\ VM_i\ has\ been\ allocated\ to\ Host_j\ and\ rcrVM_i > acrHost_j,\ j \in \{1,2,3,\ldots,m\} \\ Invalid \\ if\ VM_i\ has\ not\ been\ allocated\ to\ Host_j \end{cases} \quad (2)$$

where the minimized computing resource requirements of **i**th VM and the available computing resource of **j**th host are represented by **rcrVM$_i$** and **acrHost$_j$** respectively. **o** placement selections with maximum τ_r values are picked out from all **s** placement selections and **PS [m, n, o, t]** denotes them.

The next metric is designed on the energy consumption. Let **PS [m, n, r, t+t$_0$ (k)]** represent the migration of successive VMs, **r** represents any one in **o** placement selections and an integer **k** is utilized to represent a stage, increasing with successive migrating. A reasonable case in point may be that if **k** is 5, the fifth VM can be migrated to the host marked at the fifth location of the **r** vector through the proposed approach. **PS [m, n, r, t+t₀ (k)]** r∈{1,2,3,...,o} denotes the **o** placement selections at stage **k** and π_k^r represents the corresponding energy consumption. It means that, having migrated the **k**th VM to its target host in terms of **r** placement vector, the total energy consumption is π_k^r in the cloud data center. Similarly, it is of great ease to deduce the meaning of π_{k-1}^r. This paper can obtain these parameters of π_k^r through utilizing simulation platform in the following experiments. Thus far, the incremental energy consumption is defined by the equation (3), on account of migrating **PS [m, n, r, t+t₀ (k)]** as for previous migration stage **PS [m, n, r, t+t₀ (k−1)]**.

$$\Delta\varsigma = \pi_k^r - \pi_{k-1}^r; \quad r \in \{1,2,3,\dots,o\} \tag{3}$$

The objective is optimal energy conversation and thus the following $\delta\varsigma$ is supposed to be minimized to get the optimal solution obtained and it can be represented as following.

$$\delta\varsigma = \sum_{k=1}^{n} \left(\pi_k^r - \pi_{k-1}^r\right); \quad r \in \{1,2,3,\dots,o\} \tag{4}$$

Eventually, τ_r is maximized for fulfilling performance requirements to greatest extent and then $\delta\varsigma$ is minimized for better energy saving effect by the proposed PS-ES approach.

3. Performance Evaluation

An array of experiments are designed and conducted to experimentally evaluate the performance of the proposed PS-ES approach in this section. The energy saving effect of PS-ES from the long-term point of view and the performance on the failure rate of migration events are verified. Moreover, other two experiments are performed to make a related parameter tested and obtain the optimal power management policy, which contributes to balancing the energy cost and penalty cost due to performance violation while minimizing the total cost. The CloudSim toolkit/platform [10], as an event driven simulator, which can make it possible to calculate the total energy consumption caused by cloud data centers during the simulation period by providing a class including the methods getPower(), is utilized to simulate dynamic cloud data centers since it can create various types of entities dynamically in real time and enables to remove data center objects at runtime. These features have achieved simulating dynamic cloud environment where the varying components and entities can join, fail, or leave the system at random [10]. On the CloudSim platform, the proposed PS-ES approach is compared with random migration policy, the optimal migration policies based on PSO and the optimal migration policy PS-ABC [9] on energy consumption and the number of invalid VM migration events. Four different kinds of experiments to evaluate and test the proposed PS-ES approach have been made It can be manifested from the final experimental results that the proposed PS-ES approach has a better energy saving effect while having a better execution performance. Notably, PS-ES has presented the stability and the excellent execution performance under the circumstance of plenty of live VM migration events.

3.1 Experimental Scenarios. To evaluate and test the proposed PS-ES approach, we have designed and made simulation experiments on the CloudSim platform. The simulated cloud data center is constructed as a resource pool comprising 100 hosts,

which have varying computing resource available. Live VM migration requests are simulated by CloudSim. The CloudSim platform has 24 batches of VM migration requests created. Each batch accommodates 13 requests generated with different resource requirements and randomly belonging to different physical hosts. During the simulation experiments, the proposed PS-ES migration policy has been running to receive live VM migration requests while getting resource information of available physical hosts at the end of each Δt.

3.2 Evaluate Energy Consumption on Varying Approaches. PS-ES is compared with Random-Migration, DAPSO and PS-ABC on energy consumption in the long-term operation process of the simulated cloud data center to evaluate the efficiency and available of PS-ES in energy conservation for the placement selection of live VM migration events in the experiment scenario. In this experiment, Δt is set as 600 seconds and the migration events of each batch are uniformly distributed within an hour, which includes 6Δts. Besides, the host's resource change rate is set as 1 time per half an hour. It can be seen from **Fig. 1** that apart from the cloud data center executing Random-Migration, the cloud data center executing PS-ES consumes more energy than the cloud data centers executing PS-ABC and DAPSO after fortnight on ground that the latter two approaches have brilliant global convergence in an algorithm cycle. Although the proposed PS-ES approach isn't worse than them, it has made the migrant VMs be migrated into the corresponding optimal target hosts with a certain probability and thus to cause the result that PS-ES has a more energy consumption at the beginning stage.

As illustrated in **Fig. 1**, the cloud data center executing PS-ES has better energy conservation effect since it consumes less total energy than the other three approaches after four weeks. According to the overall trend, the fact that the cloud data center executing Random-Migration migration policy has increasingly growing incremental energy consumption between two weeks can be seen. The reason for this fact is that the Random-Migration policy doesn't enable to self-adapt to the dynamic cloud environment and thus it is likely to result in that more migration events are generated while picking out inappropriate target physical hosts in energy consumption at random.Since the cloud data centers executing DAPSO and PS-ABC have the migrant VMs migrated to the optimal target hosts for energy conservation in an algorithm cycle, they have the relatively less total energy consumed in the first fortnight. They, however, have only made the current problem optimized rather than taken this proposed problem into consideration from the perspective of cloud data centers' long-term operations. Accordingly, their current optimization is very likely to make the next problem cause more consumption and harder to optimize. On the other hand, the proposed PS-ES approach hasconsidered the proposed energy-saving problem from the higher perspective rather than solely been limited to achieving the global optimization of the current problem cycle by heuristic algorithms such PA-ABC.

3.3 Test the Failure Rate in VM Migration Events. The dynamic cloud environment is carried out by the CloudSim platform through dynamically triggering a range of shut-down events or failure events of physical hosts within the interval time of the placement selection in the experiment scenario. Quite a few failures events in VM migration may be produced on account of the corresponding physical hosts' non-availability. The proposed PS-ES approach is compared with Random-Migration, the optimal migration policy achieved by StdPSO and PS-ABC on failure rate in VM migration events as illustrated in **Fig. 2**. It can be seen that, compared to PS-ABC and PS-ES, greater failure rate of VM migration events is caused by the cloud data centers executing Random-Migration and StdPSO under the varying number of VM migration requests. This is because that Random-Migration and StdPSO can't have the corresponding adjustment with the environment changed and thus to result in that their memory data is outdated. Conversely, the Boltzmann selection policy and Bayes theorem are introduced the PS-ABC migration policy and consequently it has abilities to efficiently respond to changing circumstances within the interval time. However, it isn't as excellent as the proposed PS-ES approach. The fundamental reason for that PS-ABC can have relatively less failure number of VM migration events is that it has the excellent optimization and iteration mechanisms and isn't that it aims at achieve this goal. By contrast, it is to self-adapt the dynamic cloud environment that the proposed PS-ES policy utlizes the DAPSO idea. Beside, the introduction of the SA method with the probability idea in PS-ES makes it have higher adaptability. Obviously, the proposed PS-ES should be much more efficient than PS-ABC in detecting the host failures during the interval as well as have a fit adjustment in a better manner by dynamically searching out the new available hosts that can meet the resource requirements of the VM migration requests.

3.4 Comparison of the Failure Rate in VM Migration with Fixed and Variable Evaporation Factor. In this experimental scenario, we will evaluate one of the most important parameters of PS-ES, the evaporation factor **Z** which makes the proposed approach self-adaptive placement selecting in a dynamic cloud environment. As shown in **Fig. 3**, the experiment shows the impact of fixed and self-increased evaporation factor on the performance of PS-ES in a highly dynamic cloud resource pool. With the rising of the rate of failure of hosts, the rate of failure in VM migrations is recorded. The runs will be tested with fixed evaporation and self-increased evaporation factor. For the fixed evaporator factor, since the capability with which PS-ES adapts to a dynamic environment is also within a certain range, the number of failure in VM migration events will increase with the rising of the rate of failure of hosts. Whereas for the self-increased evaporator factor, the capability with which PS-ES adapts to a dynamic environment is getting stronger and thus can be aware of

the failure of hosts and make the rate of failure in VM migrations lower. It shows that the adjustments in evaporation factor according to the rate of resource changing in a dynamic cloud environment reduce the rate of failure in VM migrations.

3.5 Test the Incremental Energy Consumption under Different Load. The incremental energy consumption of DAPSO, PS-ABC and PS-ES is compared in a cloud data center with varying percentage of load in this experimental scenario. The load mentioned in this experiment does not refer to the load in a physical host but the load of the whole cloud data center. In **Fig. 4**, X axis denotes the varying percentage of load in the same cloud data center while Y axis represents the percentage of the incremental energy consumption. It can be observed in **Fig. 4** that PS-ES has the relatively less incremental energy consumption than that of PS-ABC and DAPSO under increasing load. PS-ABC and DAPSO have nearly identical performance in the experiment since their efficiency and optimization degree of processing large-scale problems are similar in the cloud data center. It is well-known that the heavier the load is, the greater impact the solution of the current problem has on the future problem. Obviously, PS-ES not only has better optimization effect in the current problem but also makes better preparation for the coming problems than PS-ABC with no such excellent features in it since it has achieved the SA idea.

3.6 Evaluate Power Management Policies. The auxiliary experiment is presented and conducted to pick out the optimal power management policy which has a tradeoff between the energy cost and penalty cost due to SLA (Service Level Agreements) while having abilities to relatively minimize the total cost of energy cost and penalty cost of performance violation in the cloud data center implementing PS-ES. Since live VM migration requests are time critical VM events and the cloud service provider should meet strict SLA compliance, any violations in SLA will cause penalty cost based on performance loss of VMs on the provider of a cloud data center. It can be well-understood that the performance loss is likely to be caused by energy conservation, live VM migration events, lack of network bandwidth and throughput etc. This paper, however, has not focused on these problems

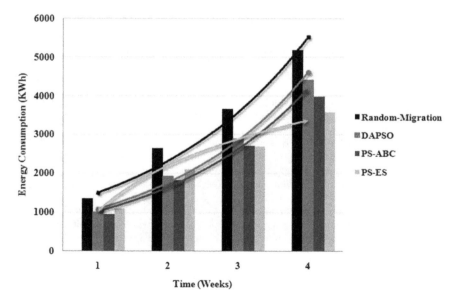

Figure 1. This figure has four kinds of bars, which respectively represent the energy consumption of Random-Migration, DAPSO, PS-ABC and PS-ES. The four approaches are compared in four time points on energy consumption. The trend line are also added to this figure. The amount of energy consumption is measured by KWh (KiloWatt hour).

directly. This experiment is performed to solely find out a better power mangement policy applicable to the cloud environment implementing the proposed PS-ES to balance the cost of energy consumption and penalty cost due to SLA violation and thus to make the total cost minimized. There are, generally, four power policies available for cloud data centers to select from. As is well known, they are On/Off, Single-DSS, Multiple-SS and Single-SSS respectively. As illustrated in **Fig. 5**, the Multiple-SS power management policy leads to the better tradeoff between energy cost and penalty cost as well as have the relatively better total cost of both them. The experimental result can be analyzed. For the On/Off policy, all idle hosts are switched off. Obviously, it can give the optimal energy saving effect but causes the high penalty cost. The single-DSS policyswitchs all idle hosts to deep sleep state, where an increase in the energy consumption cost is caused. Although the penalty cost declines significantly, its tradeoff effect is insufficient and thus the total cost is relatively more. Single-SSS makes all idle hosts switched to shallow sleep state. Almost no penalty cost is generated as SLA violation is absent in this policy. On the contrary, the policy causes the enormous increase in the energy consumption cost. The Multiple-SS policy keeps some of the idle hosts in deep sleep and others in shadow sleep state according to a short-term prediction technology. It can dynamically switch the state of a physical host in terms of the workloads in real time in cloud data centers. To sum up, the Multiple-SS policy is picked out as the optimal power management policy in cloud data centers implementing PS-ES.

Discussion

It is noticeable that there exists an interesting problem in the proposed PS-ES approach. It is obvious that a candidate solution vector of the proposed problem is supposed to be denoted as a sequence of integers that represent these candidate hosts in the cloud data center. The PSO-based approaches, however, initialize

their swarms at random in PS-ES. Furthermore, the velocity function of the particles has some random coefficients which are limited between 0 and 1. Accordingly, even though each element of a particle is limited to the Integer type during the implementation, the problem that the solution vectors aren't integers still exists. To address this problem, PS-ES employs the SPV (Smallest Position Value) rules presented by in [11,12] rather than limit all the elements to the Integer type. In a word, each particle's vector given by the classical PSO algorithm can be converted to a valid solution vector fit for the proposed problem through the SPV rules. The process of applying the SPV rules into the proposed PS-ES approach can be understood as following. First, these candidate hosts in the cloud data center are numbered from 0 to $m-1$. Second, after the velocity and position vectors of each particle are initialized randomly, all the elements of each position vector are sorted in ascending order and then are numbered from 0 to $n-1$ as well as have a modulo operation of m. A reasonable case in point may be given. Within a time window Δt, there are six VMs to be migrated in a cloud resource pool, in which four physical hosts are available currently. If a candidate solution vector $(-1.21, 3.29, 1.26, -0.12, 4.76, 0.78)$ is generated in the process of iterations, it will be converted to $(0, 4, 3, 1, 5, 2)$ firstly and then to $(0, 0, 3, 1, 1, 2)$. At this point, the solution vector is meaningful and available. In PS-ES, all the position vectors refer to the vectors which the original vectors have been converted to according to the SPV rules.

Starting from this intuition, the PS-ES algorithm which aims at live VM migration events gives consideration to both a short-term optimization and a long-term optimization to save more energy. To achieve this goal, the proposed approach utilizes the improved PSO algorithm to search this global optimal solution in order to optimize the current problem situation. And then it takes use of SA idea to optimize the future problem situation. To illustrate our problem, we give an example as shown in **Fig. 6**.

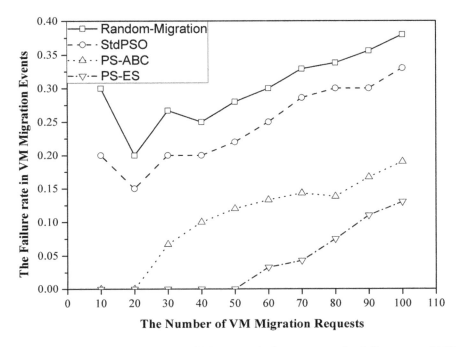

Figure 2. This figure consists of four kinds of curves, which respectively represent the failure rate of VM migration events of Random-Migration, StdPSO, PS-ABC and PS-ES. X axis denotes the number of VM migration requests. Y axia denotes the failure rate in VM migration events. The failure rate is equal to that the failure number of VM migration events is divided by the number of VM migration requests.

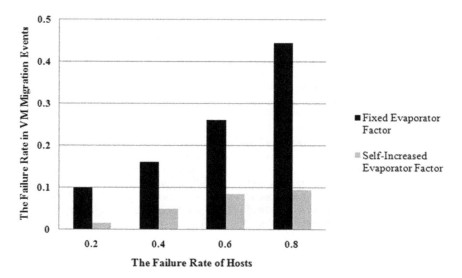

Figure 3. This figure has two kinds of bars, which respectively represent the failure rate on VM migration events in PS-ES with fixed evaporator factor and self-increased evaporator factor.

In (a), a resource pool consists of three hosts. The rated power of all the hosts is the same. There are two VMs running in host 0. In the first time window Δt, VM 0 with a light computing workload in the host 0 sends a migration request for some reason. The current problem caused during the first Δt is finding out the optimal target host of VM 0 to minimize the increment energy consumption. As is well known, the host node with a larger 'performance per watt' will consume less energy in the case of dealing with the same load. While the percentage of load of a host is beyond a critical value, it will reach its performance bottleneck. After that, the host's performance will degrade significantly during dealing with the next load. The consumed energy will increase in the case of dealing with the same load. Therefore, the host with a stronger computing power which shows that it has a better 'performance per watt' in the case that the rated power is the same will cause the less increase of energy consumption. Therefore, the optimal solution of the current problem is host 1. That is, VM 0 will be migrated to host 1 optimally. After the second time window

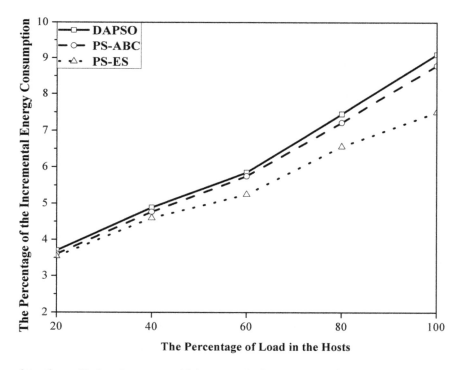

Figure 4. This figure has three kinds of curves, which respectively represent the percentage of the incremental energy consumption of DAPSO, PS-ABC and PS-ES with the percentage of load in the hosts increasing. X axis denotes the percentage of load in the hosts. Y axis denotes the percentage of the incremental energy consumption.

Δt, VM 1 needs to be migrated. At this time, if the host 1 has not been able to accommodate it, it will have to be migrated to host 2 with the weak computing power. We know that the energy consumption is to increase rapidly when a host with weak computing power deals with a relatively heavy workload. In other words, starting from the time when a host begins to feel the pressure caused by dealing with its workload, the energy consumption caused by the host will suddenly increase rapidly and be significantly affected by the increase of workload. In fact, if VM 0 is not migrated onto host 1 but onto host 2 after the first time window Δt, VM 1 will be migrated onto host 1. At this moment, both host 1 and host 2 won't feel the pressure during dealing with their own workload. It is obvious that the latter incremental energy consumption is less from a long-term point of view.

In (b), we give a specific instance in order to further illustrate another situation of this problem. The numbers in VM 0 and VM 1 represent their required computing resource and the numbers in host 1 and host 2 represent their available computing resource. After a time window Δt, VM 0 needs to be migrated for some reason. The current problem caused during the first Δt is finding out the optimal target host of VM 0 to minimize the increment energy consumption. Host 1 has stronger computing power as it has more computing resource. As previously mentioned, the optimal solution of the current problem should be host 1. That is, VM 0 will be migrated to host 1 optimally. After the second time window Δt, VM 1 needs to be migrated. At this point, the available resource of host 1 and host 2 isn't enough to accommodate VM 1. This situation will cause a new migration event that VM 0 is migrated from host 1 to host 2. This will increase energy consumption and cost. The incremental energy consumption caused by a new migration event is much larger than that caused by only running a VM. This is because a VM is always running regardless of migrating or not. The migration cost has

caused a net increase of energy consumption. Thus, if VM 0 is migrated onto host 2 after the first Δt, the result will be better after the second time window Δt. In another word, the host 1 is a global optimal solution for the current situation. However, it is a local optimal solution for a long-term view. After all, our goal is to achieve better energy saving during the long-term operation of a cloud data center but not only the current and short-term energy saving. After realizing these facts, under the background that the future is unpredictable we think of taking advantage of the SA idea to further optimize this problem. Let the VMs be probabilistically moved to suboptimal host which may be its optimal host from a long-term view in the future. From the long-term and global point of view, compared to optimally migrating and randomly migrating, this approach can further minimize the increment energy consumption.

To achieve this idea of the proposed PS-ES, the global search of optimal solution is still important at the end of every time window Δt as it is the research basis of the problem. It firstly should have ability in finding the optimal solution for the current Δt. And then it can proceed further. We employ the PSO algorithm to search the optimal solution. Thus, one can see that the PSO-based algorithm is our main algorithm. To improve the performance and accuracy of the PSO algorithm, we also introduce the SA idea into the PSO algorithm to optimize its global search and avoid being trapped into the local optima. Generally, the PSO algorithm only returns a global optimal solution at last. However, in our proposed approach we need not only the global optimal solution but also the available local optimal solutions. Moreover, we also need obtain the reasonable probability value of each solution. To address the two problems, we take two reasonable, effective and simple ways. Based on the PSO's characteristics that the global best vector of every round of iteration actually represents a solution of every round of iteration and is gradually converged to the optimal solution of the last round of iteration, the last several rounds of

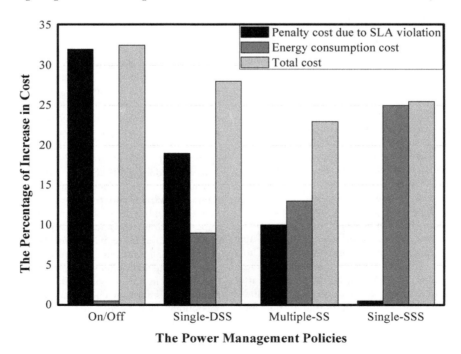

Figure 5. This figure has three kinds of bars, which respectively represent the percentage of increase on penalty cost due to SLA violation, energy consumption cost and total cost under varying power management policies of On/Off, Single-DSS, Multiple-SS and Single-SSS.

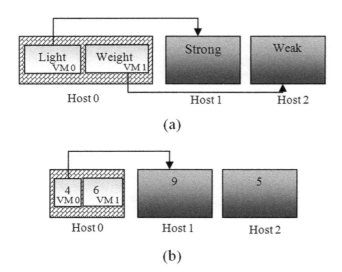

Figure 6. This example has shown two kinds of live VM migration situations. In (a), the situation represents that in cloud data centers there exists the fact that sometimes the VMs with the weight are migrated to the hosts with weak computing power in contrast to the VMs with the light, which are migrated to the hosts with strong computing power. In (b), the situation is similar to that in (a).

global best solution vectors can be regarded as the optimal solution and several suboptimal solutions. Thus, we present a parameter **N**. The PS-ES will preserve the last **N** global best vectors of the PSO-based algorithm to obtain the optimal solution and the available suboptimal solutions. Put simply, the PSO process of the proposed approach doesn't return a solution vector but a solution matrix. At this time, each migrant VM has obtained its **N** solutions which constitute a column vector of that matrix. For any VM, the majority of these solutions should be the optimal solution and the minority should be the suboptimal solutions as well as few solutions may be the unreasonable solutions. Subsequently, for a VM, the probability of its each solution is obtained by calculating its frequency according to the Probability Theory and Mathematical Statistics. To filter out the individual unreasonable solutions, the Expectation and Standard Deviation are calculated. If the Absolute Value of the difference between a solution and the Expectation is larger than the Standard Deviation, the solution should be filtered out. The sum of the probabilities of all the unreasonable solutions is assigned to others solutions proportionally. Now, the optimal solution, the suboptimal solutions and their probabilities have been obtained. To achieve a probabilistic migration, we utilize a probability wheel and a random pointer. The greater probability will have a larger sector which the pointer is more likely to stop within. In a specific implementation, each sector is represented as an interval **(a, b]** included in **[0, 1]**. The pointer is represented as a random number between 0 and 1. The solution which the interval which the random number belongs to represents is the final solution of a VM. Each VM has found its target host of live migration so far. Each target host is found neither randomly nor for the current optimization but for achieving a long-term optimization on energy saving according to the SA idea. Thus, compared to them, the PS-ES approach is more efficient and meaningful.

In a cloud data center, there are many functional modules and system architectures running together for the different purposes. Many systems are managing the cloud environment at the same time. So, for each system, the environment and resource which

they are facing are dynamic. During the running of an algorithm of any system, its objects and environment may have been changed. Therefore, the design of the PS-ES algorithm should adapt to a cloud environment with dynamic resource. The PS-ES employs a dynamic adaptive PSO (DAPSO) for monitoring and automatically reacting to the changes in a cloud environment. DAPSO is proposed in [13] to search out the changing optimal solution in a dynamic and noisy cloud computing environment. It doesn't need any centralized control and only needs to update the memory of each particle. DAPSO has achieved dynamically adapting to the changed cloud environment by adjusting personal best fitness value of each particle. In the classical PSO, each particle will compare the fitness value of its current location with that of its personal best location in each round of iteration. If the current fitness value doesn't have any improvement, its personal best fitness value will not be changed; if not, the personal best fitness value will be changed to the current fitness value. Nevertheless in the DAPSO, if the current fitness value doesn't have any improvement, its personal best fitness also will be changed according to the equation (5).

$$P(i+1) = \begin{cases} p(i) * Z & f(X(i+1)) \le P(i) * Z \\ f(X(i+1)) & f(X(i+1)) > P(i) * Z. \end{cases} \qquad (5)$$

The parameter **Z** is called the evaporation factor and its value is between 0 and 1 [14]. Each particle has the same evaporation factor. However, the updating frequency of each particle may be different. The past personal best fitness value and the current fitness value of a particle determine its updating frequency. Its main idea is that if the current fitness value of a particle continuously doesn't have any improvement through using its previous searching experience, its personal best value will gradually be evaporated and decrease at the rate of the evaporation factor **Z**. Eventually, the personal best fitness value will be lower than the fitness value of the particle's current location and the best fitness value will be replaced by the particle's current fitness value corresponding to the changed cloud environment [15]. The fitness value which in the changed environment is generated later will become its personal best fitness value by using the evaporation factor. For doing so, the PSO algorithm can be self-adaptive for the changing of cloud environment and makes the particles respond the changing of cloud environment as well as make the PSO process match the reality. Besides, it has ability in sensing the new powered on hosts and recently powered off hosts and considering this updated information. Thus, it can also optimize our proposed approach further.

In the proposed PS-ES, there are many parameters, most of which have great influences on the proposed algorithm. The number **MaximumofIteration** of iteration of the PSO process and the number **N** of the returned solution vectors are two important parameters and their values are related to the efficiency of PS-ES. For instance, if **MaximumofIteration** is too large and **N** is too small relatively, the probability with which the optimal solution is the final solution is closed to 100%. It will make the SA idea invalid in our approach. On the contrary, if **Maximumo-fIteration** is not large enough and **N** isn't small relatively, several suboptimal solutions may appear and each has a big probability. This will make our approach inefficient and inaccurate as well as make the proposed idea invalid. Therefore, the two values need to be researched further to optimize the algorithm. In the proposed approach, **MaximumofIteration** is set to 200 and **N** is set to 50. Also, the initial temperature **T** of the SA and its attenuation factor **α** are another two important parameters. **T** should be initialized to an enough big value and it makes the corresponding algorithm have a stronger global search in the early iteration. Then **T** is gradually decreased by using **α**, as makes the search process gradually converged to an optimal solution in the later iteration. Thus, the values of **T** and **α** are important for the SA idea. They should be set to the appropriate values as much as possible.

Let us consider the obtained probability values of solutions mentioned above in the view of Probability Theory and Statistics. By many direct observations and experiments, we have discovered that for any VM, the Probability Distribution of its solutions yields to random Poisson distribution. Here we will analyze this phenomenon theoretically. Firstly we know that when a random event occurs at a fixed average instantaneous rate λ randomly and independently, the number of occurrences of this event within a unit time should approximately yield to Poisson distribution. From a long-term view, the migration event of some VM occurs at a relatively fixed average instantaneous rate randomly. For this VM, each available target host is independent each other and the probability with which any available host is selected as the target host should be the same. Therefore, if a VM is migrated according to the traditional policy of random migration, from the view of a long-term operation (A large number of **Δt**) of a cloud data center, the number of times for which a VM has been migrated to a certain host should approximately yield to Poisson distribution. Similarly, for the PS-ES approach, in a time window **Δt**, each VM has a solution space whose size is **N**. It can be easy to deduce that in the solution space, the number of each solution should also yield to Poisson distribution. Thus, the obtained probabilities values above approximately yield to Poisson distribution in the probability figure. From the side, this fact also shows the mathematical background and theoretical basis of the proposed problem and PS-ES approach as well as further demonstrates its rationality.

Methods

1. The Proposed System Architecture

In the paper, the system architecture of PS-ES is proposed as illustrated in **Fig. 7**, in which the position of the controller PS-ES for migration placement selections can be seen and its interaction with other entities is clear [16]. Within a time window **Δt**, live VM migration requests will be accumulated by the Monitor while the current available amount of computing resource such as CPUs, memory, storage and network bandwidth etc. as well as energy consumption is updated. After a time window **Δt**, these information will be transferred to the PS-ES controller, where the placement policy is supposed to be generated by utilizing the proposed PS-ES approach and obtained information. Subsequently, the generated migration solution will be sent to Migration Controller, which is in charge of executing live migration of these VMs. Eventually, the VMs are migrated into their target hosts.

2. Solution Representation

Aiming to achieve an efficient PSO-based approach for picking out the optimal vector of target hosts of all migrant VMs accumulated within a time window **Δt**, the problem of solution representation is the primary problem since it reflects a direct relationship between the proposed problem domain and the proposed approach [11]. It is well-known that when applying a PSO-based approach to solve a problem, a particle is generally denoted as a solution of the specific problem. In this paper, the proposed problem is concerned about migrating **n** VMs into **m** physical hosts and is an **n**-dimensional problem. Thus, a particle (solution) can be represented as an **n**-dimensional vector. Each of its elements has a discrete set of possible placement selection and is limited to **m**. In the proposed PSO-based approach, the position

vector is denoted as $x_i^k = \left(x_{i1}^k, \quad x_{i2}^k, \quad \ldots, \quad x_{ij}^k, \quad \ldots, \quad x_{iD}^k \right)$, where x_{ij}^k represents the position of **j**th dimension (the **j**th migrant VM) of **i**th particle (the **i**th possible solution vector) in **k**th generation. The velocity vector is denoted by $v_i^k = \left(v_{i1}^k, \quad v_{i2}^k, \quad \ldots, \quad v_{ij}^k, \quad \ldots, \quad v_{iD}^k \right)$, where v_{ij}^k represents the velocity in **j**th dimension of **i**th particle in **k**th generation. The personal best position vector is denoted by $pBest_i^l = \left(pB_{i1}^l, \quad pB_{i2}^l, \quad \ldots, \quad pB_{iD}^l \right)$ and represents the ever best position of each particle so far. The global best position vector is denoted by $gBest^g = \left(gB_1^g, \quad gB_2^g, \quad \ldots, \quad gB_D^g \right)$ and represents the obtained best position of the entire population so far.

3. The Main Idea of PS-ES

Its main idea can be divided into two aspects. On the one hand, from the point of view of a time window **Δt**, we introduce the SA idea into the PSO algorithm to find out the better global optimal solution and improve the accuracy of PSO global search. On the other hand, from the point of view of a long-term operation of a cloud data center, we have found the fact that the optimal placement searched out in the current time window may be a local optima in a long-term process as the next some VM may be more suitable this host. However, we can't predict the future VM migration requests. Thus, we again introduce the SA idea into the long-term process. That is, the migrant VM is not necessarily moved to the optimal host but may be moved into some suboptimal host with a certain probability for achieving a long-term optimization. To achieve this optimization, the probability theory and the probability wheel idea is also introduced to the proposed approach.

4. The Implementation of PS-ES

In this section, we describe the specific process of PS-ES. Details are as follows:

Find the optimal target host of each VM. the PS-ES module receives all required information and begins running the algorithm. First, the parameters required by the approach are initialized. The PSO performs the first round of iteration. The initial velocity vector and position vector is initialized randomly. The fitness value of each particle is obtained by using the fitness function (1) & (2). The PSO sets personal best position vector $pBest_i^l$ of each particle as its current position and sets personal best value of each particle as its current fitness value. The PSO sets global best position vector $gBest^g$ of the population as the position where the particle has corresponding best personal best value among all the particles and sets global best value as the corresponding fitness value. Second, the PSO begins performing the loop of iteration process from the second round of iteration. Each particle updates its velocity and position by using the formulas of PSO but isn't moved to the new position temporarily. The variation **ΔE** of the fitness value between the next position and the current position is obtained for the SA. If the variation **ΔE** is larger than or equal to 0, the particle should be moved to the new position; if not, according to the SA idea, the particle neither is moved to the new particle undoubtedly nor isn't moved to the new position undoubtedly but is moved to the new position with the probability of **exp (ΔE/KT)**. Subsequently, each particle is annealed and cooled. That is, **T** is attenuated as **αT**, where **α** is the attenuation factor. Now the position of each particle has been fixed in the current iteration, so each particle compares its current fitness value with its personal best value. If better, updates it; if not, does nothing. If there is more than one particle with maximum

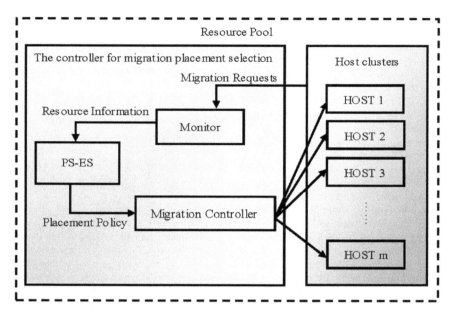

Figure 7. In this figure of PS-ES's architecture, the right part represents the set of available physical hosts, where a plenty number of VMs are running. In the left part, the controller consists of three modules of Monitor, PS-ES and Migration Controller. It implies that the proposed architecture's processing flow.

fitness value, the final particle with the minimum value of function (4) is found. Subsequently, the global best value is updated. The inertia weight ω is updated as $\omega*\exp(-\textbf{iteration})$. If the termination condition of the maximum number **MaximumofIteration** of iteration is met, the loop of iteration ends; if not, the algorithm begins the next round of iteration. Finally, when it ends, the particle with global best value is the solution particle. In another word, the global best vector $gBest^g$ is the solution vector.

Find the final placement of each VM. in order to obtain some available suboptimal solutions, the approach will record the last **N** global best vector of the last **N** rounds of iteration of the PSO algorithm. We can regard the **N** vectors as an **N*n** of matrix, each of the **n** column vectors of which represents **N** solutions of the place selection of the corresponding VM. We consider that the **N** solutions consists of the optimal, the suboptimal and unreasonable solutions. The unreasonable solutions ought to be very few and may also not exist. For a migrant VM, we can find a probability of every kind of solution by using the **N** solutions. And the expectation and standard deviation of the solutions are also found by using the equations (6) & (7).

$$E(X) = X_1 * p(X_1) + X_2 * p(X_2) + \ldots\ldots + X_N * p(X_N) \quad (6)$$

$$\sigma = \sqrt{\frac{1}{N}\sum_{i=1}^{N}(X_i - E(X))^2} \quad (7)$$

One can find out the reasonable solution by using the expectation and standard deviation as well as assign the probabilities of the unreasonable solutions to other solutions proportionately. If the sum of the probabilities of all unreasonable solutions is $\textbf{\textit{M}}$, the probability of each available solution is converted to $\textbf{1/1}-\textbf{\textit{M}}$ times as the original probability. At this point, each migrant VM has a probability wheel as shown in **Fig. 8**. A pointer randomly rotates on the probability wheel. The host which the area where

the pointer finally stops represents is the final target host. In the specific implementation, a random number limited between 0 and 1 can be used to find the final target host by finding the range within which the random number is. It is understandable that the probability of the optimal host is much larger than that of the suboptimal hosts. However, each migrant VM may be moved to suboptimal host with a certain probability. It is obvious that with the SA idea the approach is more efficient than randomly migrating and optimally migrating from a long-term's point of view as it can be understood as reaching a compromise between migrating optimally and randomly as well as achieving a long-term optimization relatively. At last, each migrant VM has the final target host. An **n** dimension of solution vector is returned.

Conclusions

In this paper, a novel placement selection policy of live VM migration PS-ES is proposed and we give its main idea, implementation and evaluation. It employs the improved PSO-based approach and the Simulated Annealing idea. In the improved PSO-based approach, we introduce the limitation of maximum velocity, the adaptive adjustment policy of inertia weight ω, the dynamic adaptive PSO idea and simulated annealing idea into the classic PSO algorithm to achieve optimizing the PSO algorithm to search out the global optimal solution. In the proposed PS-ES, we have utilized the Simulated Annealing idea for twice. For the first time, it is used to optimize the PSO process to improve the performance and efficiency. For the second time, it is as the second part of the PS-ES approach for optimizing the whole approach. Also, aiming to connect the improved PSO-based algorithm and simulated annealing process, we take use of the Probability Theory and Mathematical Statistics as well as the characteristics of the algorithm itself to obtain and process data. We have discovered a noteworthy theoretical phenomenon that the probability values which are used for the SA idea approximately yield to Possion distribution. It has shown that the proposed PS-ES approach has the strong mathematical

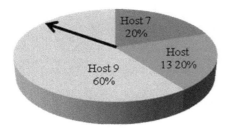 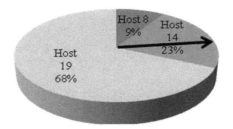

Figure 8. The figure is presented to show how to utilize the SA idea to PS-ES. These two pie charts describe that PS-ES obtains the final target host of a VM by selecting the solutions with a certain probability value.

basis. PS-ES achieves the high-efficiency of energy consumption and the stability of requirement performance. It not only minimizes the incremental energy consumption of a cloud data center but also minimizes the number of failure in VM migration events relatively. What is more, it aims at achieving the better energy conservation from a long-term view of operation of a cloud data center and protects the performance of VM running. In the proposed PS-ES approach, there are some open problems which need be studied further and experience problems which need many experiments to gradually get a better solution. The **T** value of the SA idea is an experience problem and needs perform several experiments to obtain a fit value with the condition that **T** makes $\exp(-\Delta E/KT)$ close to 1 at the beginning. The **N** value of our approach is also an experience problem. Its situation has been clarified above. It is set to 50 in this paper. Both the attenuation factor **α** value and the evaporation factor **Z** value are the open problems.

To evaluate the PS-ES approach, we have conducted several experiments on the CloudSim platform. Firstly, in the comparison experiment of Random-Migration, DAPSO, PS-ABC and PS-ES in Energy Consumption, the PS-ES approach has the least incremental energy consumption from a long-term view of operation of the cloud data center. Secondly, in the comparison experiment of the number of failures in VM migration events, the PS-ES approach has the less number of failures in VM migration events than that of random migration and optimal migration. Thirdly, in the comparison experiment of the failure rate in VM migration with fixed and variable evaporation factor, the result has shown that the increased evaporation factor has the better capability to adapt to a dynamic cloud environment. Eventually, in the experiment of testing the incremental energy consumption under different load, the result has shown that under both the light and heavy load, the PS-ES approach shows the relatively better

energy saving effect. Aiming to get the optimal policy management policy which can balance the energy cost and penalty cost due to performance violation in cloud data centers executing PS-ES, an auxiliary experiment is designed and performed and proved that the multiple-SS policy is supposed to the best selection. It can be observed through the final experimental results that PS-ES, as a placement selection policy of live VM migration for energy conservation, is efficient and have a great significance towards green cloud data centers.

In the next work, we plan to further study energy saving optimization for live VM migration policy with such optimization processes that as many physical hosts as possible are shut down. Subsequently, we will take the network situation into consideration in the process of picking out physical hosts. The connectivity between physical nodes will be studied. Furthermore, since the PS-ES approach proposed in this paper is aiming to the local domain, we intend to extend the PS-ES idea to several cross-domain cloud data centers so as to deeply match the demanding in real world.

Acknowledgments

This work is supported by the National Natural Science Foundation of China (Grant No. 61133011), the Natural Science Foundation of Jilin (Grant No. 20101525), the Jilin Provincial Education Office (Jilin Provincial Educational and Scientific Program [2010] No. 85), the Natural Science Foundation of Jilin (Grant No. 20101533) and the Jilin Provincial Education Office (Jilin Provincial Educational and Scientific Program [2010] No. 103).

Author Contributions

Conceived and designed the experiments: LH GX JZ YD. Performed the experiments: JZ YD LH GX. Analyzed the data: JZ YD MH. Contributed reagents/materials/analysis tools: MH. Wrote the paper: JZ YD MH.

References

1. Barham P, Dragovic B, Fraser K, Hand S, Harris T, et al. (2003) Xen and the Art of Virtualization. ACM SIGOPS Operating Systems Review 37(5): 164–177.

2. Li Y, Li W, Jiang C (2010) A Survey of Virtual Machine System: Current technology and future trends. Proceedings of the 3th International Symposium on Electronic Commerce and Security. Guangzhou, Guangdong: IEEE press. pp. 332–336.

3. Armbrust M, Fox A, Griffith R, Joseph A, Katz R, et al. (2010) Above the Clouds: A View of Cloud Computing. Communications of the ACM 53(4): 50–58.

4. Rusu C, Ferreira A, Scordino C, Watson A (2006) Energy Efficient Real-time Heterogeneous Server Clusters. Proceedings of IEEE Real-Time and Embedded Technology and Applications Symposium. San Jose, California: IEEE press. pp. 418–428.

5. Srikantaiah S, Kansal A, Zhao F (2009) Energy Aware Consolidation for Cloud Computing. Energy 10(20): 30–40.

6. Verma A, Ahuja P, Neogi A (2008) PMapper: Power and Migration Cost Aware Application Placement in Virtualized Systems. Proceedings of the 9th ACM/

IFIP/USENIX International Conference on Middleware. New York: Spinger-Verlag. pp. 243–264.

7. Li B, Li J, Huai J, Wo T, Li Q (2009) EnaCloud: An Energy-Saving Application Live Placement Approach for Cloud Computing Environments. Proceedings of IEEE International Conference on Cloud Computing. Bangalore, India: IEEE press. pp. 17–24.

8. Jeyarani R, Nagaveni N, Vasanth RR (2011) Self Adaptive Particle Swarm Optimization for Efficient Virtual Machine Provisioning in Cloud. International Journal of Intelligent Information Technology 7(2): 25–44.

9. Gaochao X, Yan D, Jia Z, Liang H, Xiaodong F (2013) A Novel Artificial Bee Colony Approach of Live Virtual Machine Migration Policy Using Bayes Theorem. The Scientific World Journal 2013(2013): 369209.

10. Calheiros RN, Ranjan R, Beloglazov A, De Rose CA, Buyya R (2011) Cloudsim: A Toolkit for Modeling and Simulation of Cloud Computing Environments and Evaluation of Resource Provisioning Algorithms. Software: Practice and Experience 41(1): 23–50.

11. Tasgetiren MF, Sevkli M, Liang YC, Gencyilmaz G (2004) Particle Swarm Optimization Algorithm for Permutation Flowshop Sequencing Problem. Lecture Notes in Computer Science 3172: 382–389.

12. Tasgetiren MF, Sevkli M, Liang YC, Gencyilmaz G (2004) Particle Swarm Optimization Algorithm for Single-machine Total Weighted Tardiness Problem. Proceedings of 2014 Congress on Evolutionary Computation. Portland, Oregon: IEEE press. pp. 1412–1419.

13. Carlislie A, Dozler G (2002) Tracking Changing Extrema with Adaptive Particle Swarm Optimizer. Proceedings of the 5th Biannual World Automation Congress. Orlando, Florida: IEEE press. pp. 265–270.

14. Shi YH, Eberhart RC (1998) Parameter Selection in Particle Swarm Optimization. Proceedings of the 7th Annual Conference on Evolutionary Programming. Berlin: Springer. pp. 591–600.

15. Hu X, Eberhart RC (2002) Adaptive Particle Swarm Optimization: Detection and Response to Dynamic Systems. Proceedings of the World Congress on Computational Intelligence. Honolulu, HI: IEEE press. pp. 1666–1670.

16. Jeyarani R, Vasanth RR, Nagaveni N (2009) Implementation of Efficient Light Weight Internal Scheduler for High Throughput Grid Environment. Proceedings of the National Conference on Advanced Computing in Computer Applications. Coimbatore, INDIA. pp. 283–289, 2009.

22

SIMPLEX: Cloud-Enabled Pipeline for the Comprehensive Analysis of Exome Sequencing Data

Maria Fischer[1]*, Rene Snajder[1,2], Stephan Pabinger[1], Andreas Dander[1,2], Anna Schossig[3], Johannes Zschocke[3], Zlatko Trajanoski[1], Gernot Stocker[1]*

1 Division for Bioinformatics, Biocenter, Innsbruck Medical University, Innsbruck, Austria, 2 Oncotyrol, Center for Personalized Cancer Medicine, Innsbruck, Austria, 3 Division of Human Genetics, Biocenter, Innsbruck Medical University, Innsbruck, Austria

Abstract

In recent studies, exome sequencing has proven to be a successful screening tool for the identification of candidate genes causing rare genetic diseases. Although underlying targeted sequencing methods are well established, necessary data handling and focused, structured analysis still remain demanding tasks. Here, we present a cloud-enabled autonomous analysis pipeline, which comprises the complete exome analysis workflow. The pipeline combines several in-house developed and published applications to perform the following steps: (a) initial quality control, (b) intelligent data filtering and pre-processing, (c) sequence alignment to a reference genome, (d) SNP and DIP detection, (e) functional annotation of variants using different approaches, and (f) detailed report generation during various stages of the workflow. The pipeline connects the selected analysis steps, exposes all available parameters for customized usage, performs required data handling, and distributes computationally expensive tasks either on a dedicated high-performance computing infrastructure or on the Amazon cloud environment (EC2). The presented application has already been used in several research projects including studies to elucidate the role of rare genetic diseases. The pipeline is continuously tested and is publicly available under the GPL as a VirtualBox or Cloud image at http://simplex.i-med.ac.at; additional supplementary data is provided at http://www.icbi.at/exome.

Editor: Gajendra P. S. Raghava, CSIR-Institute of Microbial Technology, India

Funding: This work was funded by GENAU Bioinformatics Network (BIN III), by the "Bioinformatics Tyrol" project of the "Standortagentur Tyrol," and by the COMET Center ONCOTYROL. The funders had no role in study design, data collection and analysis, decision to publish, or preparation of the manuscript.

Competing Interests: The authors have declared that no competing interests exist.

* E-mail: maria.fischer@i-med.ac.at (MF); gernot@stocker.bz (GS)

Introduction

During the last years, the rapid development of next generation sequencing (NGS) technologies [1–3] sustainably extended the possibilities of scientific work in biology and medicine but, at the same time, confronted researchers with an overwhelming flood of data. Different sequencing platforms became available (e.g. Roche 454 FLX [4], Illumina Genome Analyzer [5], and SOLiD system) and increased the discrepancy of being able to generate sequence data and extracting relevant information out of performed experiments even more. Hand in hand with the increase of sequencing throughput, the cost per base dropped from $10 in 1985 [6] to fractions of cents in 2011 [7] and made large scale studies including whole-genome approaches affordable.

Although the costs of human whole-genome sequencing dropped significantly, it still remains a time consuming and expensive method. Therefore, exome sequencing proved to be a valuable alternative for the investigation of several diseases including rare Mendelian disorders [8,9]. In this approach, only the protein coding regions of the DNA are sequenced, which contain around 180,000 exons and form approximately one percent of the human genome [10]. Exome sequencing studies primarily aim at the discovery of single nucleotide polymorphisms (SNPs) and deletion/insertion polymorphisms (DIPs) to identify disease-causing variants in clinical samples, as it is assumed that about 85% of these mutations can be found in protein coding regions [11].

The current bottleneck of NGS projects is not mainly the sequencing of DNA itself, but lies in the structured way of data management and the targeted computational analysis of experiments [12]. The coordinated, systematic storage and backup of data is still challenging to most laboratories, and many dedicated analysis methods require deep methodological knowledge and a powerful computational infrastructure. Recently, the introduction of cloud computing has created new possibilities to analyze NGS data at reasonable costs [12,13], especially for laboratories lacking a dedicated bioinformatics infrastructure. Still, the facilitation of exome-seq analysis by developing comprehensive and intuitive software suites is one of the main goals of bioinformaticians working with NGS data.

To this end, several NGS analysis pipelines were published [14–19] that are suitable for the investigation of exome-seq data. However, they either do not cover the complete analysis workflow or require the fulfillment of cumbersome and tediousness prerequisites. Especially the installation and configuration of analysis tools and databases are challenging tasks for most inexperienced users. Moreover, based on the diversity and the lack of standards for NGS analysis, many different tools and data formats were introduced, posing a problem when combining different methods to conclude the analysis and obtain biological meaningful results [12]. The selection of adequate tools, applying appropriate parameters, and combining them to a streamlined analysis pipeline is a challenge which is often underestimated and requires advanced bioinformatics skills.

To overcome these challenges, an automatized pipeline, called SIMPLEX, for analyzing exome sequencing data has been developed. The pipeline is able to handle single-end (SE) as well as paired-end (PE) data and is able to process input data encoded in nucleotide space or color space. SIMPLEX combines published and in-house developed applications and is continuously, automatically tested. To facilitate the analysis of exome-seq data, especially in small scale laboratories, the pipeline is offered as a fully functional VirtualBox image that requires no additional installation of tools and databases. Furthermore, the pipeline provides a transparent usage of the high performance computing (HPC) infrastructure and offers quick access through a dedicated Cloud image.

Methods

Pipeline Overview

SIMPLEX is a comprehensive pipeline for investigating exome SE and PE sequencing data generated by deep sequencing devices from Illumina and ABI SOLiD. It exposes a wide variety of parameters to offer great flexibility for analyzing data according to the given biological problem and, at the same time, provides a well chosen set of standard parameters for unversed users. SIMPLEX requires as input the raw sequence reads, their corresponding base calling quality values, and a list of genomic positions specifying the complete exome. A default exome pipeline analysis with SIMPLEX includes all steps depicted in Figure 1 and is elaborated in the following.

Input Files

The pipeline is able to handle different input file formats which result from combining specific library preparation protocols with various sequencing platforms. Data produced by Illumina devices need to be in FASTQ file format (Sanger, Solexa, or Illumina 1.3+, see [20]) whereas ABI SOLiD data require to be given in two separate files - csfasta and qual files, both in FASTA format. For all platforms PE information must be given by adding additional files representing the second reads in pair.

Read Quality Control and Preprocessing

This part of the pipeline generates a basic overview on raw sequence reads, handles conversion to standardized file formats, and enhances the overall read quality by sophisticated filtering and read trimming. All analysis steps conducted within this component are highly customizable to meet the needs of different sequencing devices and library preparation methods. An overview is shown in the first step of Figure 1.

The first component handles either the conversion of Solexa and Illumina 1.3+ FASTQ format into Sanger FASTQ or the preparation of ABI SOLiD data to be readable by the sequence aligner. Next, read characteristics and read quality characteristics are calculated and exported as PDF report. Amongst other information, the report depicts the read length distribution, base call and base call quality distribution, and characteristics of unidentified base calls.

The read trimmer step is used to truncate FASTQ entries based on a given read length, nucleotide, or quality value. Furthermore, read filters can be applied to eliminate short or error prone sequence reads. The pipeline offers a *length filter*, a *quality filter*, and

an *unidentified read call filter*, which can be applied sequentially on the provided data.

After filtering and trimming, quality statistics are created once more, which allow researchers to get a complete, appealing overview of performed read quality improvements.

Sequence Alignment and Refinement

After the reads were preprocessed and low quality reads were filtered out, the sequence alignment software BWA [21] individually aligns the remaining reads to the chosen reference genome (see step two of Figure 1). Before executing the alignment process, it is important to consider the characteristics of the sequencing platform (nucleotide or color space) because specific alignment indices for the reference genome are required [22]. However, the indexing has to be performed only once for each reference genome and hereby generated indices are already included in the pipeline for widely used organisms.

Multiple local realignment around mutations. The initial alignment of sequence reads includes alignment artifacts due to the suboptimal characteristics of single alignment algorithms. Therefore, multiple local realignment around putative deletions and insertions (DIPs) is necessary to correct for alignment artifacts by minimizing the number of mismatching bases across all reads. SIMPLEX uses the realignment algorithm of the Genome Analysis Toolkit (GATK) [15], which has been optimized in-house to analyze reads in parallel. Since multiple local realignment is very time consuming, only sites likely requiring a realignment are processed.

Base quality recalibration. Systematic bias introduced by the initial base calling quality calculations are corrected using the base quality score recalibrator of GATK. It corrects the co-variation of the assigned quality value considering (i) the position within the sequence read, (ii) preceding and current nucleotide calls, and (iii) the probability of mismatching the reference genome. After performing base quality recalibration, the pipeline creates summarizing reports of this step.

Alignment filtering. Using the improved quality values, a critical filtering step removes unmapped and improperly paired reads. Furthermore, it detects unwanted PCR-duplicates and excludes reads which do not overlap with exonic regions of the reference genome. These filters can be fine-tuned by setting individual parameters.

Alignment Statistics

The third step (see Figure 1) calculates several analysis statistics that are useful for evaluating data quality and alignment results before performing variant detection. All parts of this section are applied on reads which passed all precedent filters. The *BAM statistics* module provides a quick summary of the performed alignment, including total number of reads, number of mapped and unmapped reads, and read coverage in relation to the genome size. *Alignment summary metrics* report high level metrics about the alignment, such as median read length, deletions/insertions rate, and number of bases of high quality aligned reads. Furthermore, the pipeline reports *insert size metrics* that are useful to evaluate the insert size distribution of PE data.

Variant Detection

The next analysis component (step four in Figure 1) deals with the identification of variants and is aimed at refining all variant calls to improve accuracy. In order to facilitate the search for recessive or dominant causes, variants are divided into homo- and heterozygous mutations. DIP calling, SNP identification, and variant score recalibration are carried out by GATK.

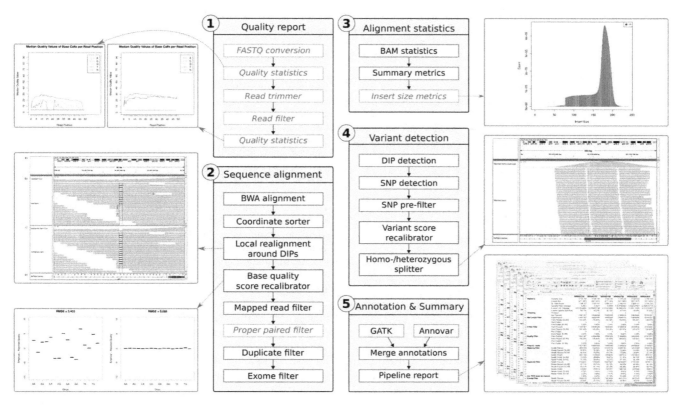

Figure 1. Schematic overview. The SIMPLEX analysis pipeline contains five major steps (blue boxes), which are further divided into several components. Mandatory components are depicted in black, optional in gray. The first step of the pipeline includes calculations of quality statistics on raw and processed reads, and applies filters and trimmers on sequenced reads (quality report). Afterwards, the pipeline aligns the processed reads to a reference genome (sequence alignment), performs alignment statistics and region filtering (alignment statistics), and detects variants resulting in a list of potential disease driver candidates (variant detection). Output files can be visualized using standard genome viewers. At the end, the pipeline automatically annotates variants, generates a detailed summary report, and combines calculated results including key figures in a structured way (annotation & summary).

DIP caller. DIPs are detected by combining multiple sources, such as the number of reads covering a DIP site, read mapping qualities, and mismatch counts. Next, this initial set of DIP calls is filtered to remove false positives. The generated results are reported as Variant Call Format (VCF)-, as text (TXT)-, and as Browser Extensible Data (BED) files, which can be displayed in Genome Browser tracks. In order to accelerate DIP identification, the pipeline evenly divides the input data and executes DIP calling in parallel.

SNP caller. A raw set of SNP calls is determined by comparing the reference genome with the consensus sequence, which was previously deferred from the read alignment information by a Bayesian identifier. To improve runtime performance, SNP positions close to previously identified DIPs are ignored during sequence comparison. The identified SNPs are reported in VCF file format and are separated in homozygous and heterozygous variants. The subsequent SNP filter masks ambiguous SNP calls to create an improved SNP call set. This set is used as training data for variant score recalibration, which aims at improving the biological variant estimation.

Mutation Annotation

Variant annotation is a two-step process, that comprises (1) adding information to already known mutations and (2) providing de-novo information for unknown variants.

The first component (see step five in Figure 1) uses the annotation function of GATK to add annotation information from existing databases and public resources. Amongst others, variants are annotated with RefSeq name [23], RefSeq hyperlink, GO term [24], KEGG [25], and dbSNP [26] information.

The second component applies the summarize_annovar function of ANNOVAR [27] on all variant files. In addition to adding information for known mutations (e.g.: allele frequencies as determined by the 1000 genomes project), the method uses inheritance models to deduce the exonic function of unknown variants. Furthermore, it reports normalized scores for identified variants from numerous tools (SIFT, PolyPhen2, PhyloP, MutationTaster, LRT), which try to predict the severity of mutations.

Finally, results from both annotation components are merged together into a structured and easily readable, tab delimited file.

Pipeline Report Generation

The last component of the pipeline collects summary information from log and result files generated during the pipeline run and outputs the report as an MS-Excel file (see step five of Figure 1). The first section contains informative key figures regarding the alignment including *exome size, genome and exome fold coverage, exome capture specificity*, and *estimated PCR duplicates by chance*.

Next, the performance of all applied filters is reported including percentage values of passed and filtered reads. Summarizing information about detected DIPs contains figures such as the number of deletions, insertions, DIPs associated with RefSeq, and the number of DIPs in coding regions. The final section summarizes information about all identified SNPs.

Pipeline Architecture

The methodological basis of the pipeline consists of a Java Enterprise Edition web service (JClusterService), which forms a dynamically extensible calculation back end and provides all necessary functionality to the pipeline users. This in-house developed API allows the delegation of numerical intensive calculations to a HPC infrastructure, which can be located in a dedicated server room or in a public cloud environment.

The pipeline client, which can be started on a regular office PC, transfers the raw sequencing data over secure web access to the calculation back-end and coordinates the parallel execution of analysis steps. Already completed result files are transferred back to the client workstation, and available summary information is collected throughout the complete pipeline run. The client side can be terminated during execution and easily restarted with the same parameters in order to continue the previously interrupted run. The service allows multiple users to perform multiple analyses at the same time and secures access to data by a central usermanagement system.

The client needs an adequate network connection to the server which is hosting JClusterService and an installed Java Runtime Environment. Since the result files of the pipeline can be several gigabytes, e.g. if mapped reads are fetched from the calculation back-end, increased storage capacity on the client side might be an additional requirement.

Cloud Computing

A cloud image including SIMPLEX and all required programs has been created within Amazon's Elastic Compute Cloud (EC2). This way, anyone with an Amazon EC2 account can instantiate the image with little to no effort and can run SIMPLEX without local compute facilities or advanced technical know-how. The EC2 cloud instantaneously provides the pipeline users with the full set of functions required to analyze exome sequencing data.

The cloud image is based on CloudBioLinux [28] and uses Galaxy CloudMan [29] to offer a straightforward and secured webinterface for the configuration and dynamic allocation of resources. Additional compute nodes or storage space can easily be added, and SIMPLEX can immediately make full use of the provided resources.

Once started, the user has the choice to either transfer the data manually to the cloud storage to analyze it with SIMPLEX, or call the pipeline client from a local machine, which will then automatically transfer the raw data to the cloud image and fetch the desired results.

Application Usage

The pipeline is currently controlled through a command line interface, where input files and pipeline parameters can be specified. Although only a few parameters are required to run SIMPLEX, there is a large number of optional parameters that allow in- depth customization for specific biological questions (Table 1 and Table S1 provide a list of mandatory and all available parameters, respectively).

The complete software installation can be downloaded as a VirtualBox image or is available as EC2 Cloud image. No further installation is required. The VirtualBox image can be run on any system that has at least 4 CPU cores and more than 4GB of main memory. To achive a reasonable performance, an

installation on an HPC infrastructure or (if the former is not available) the use of the EC2 Cloud image is recommended.

A detailed user manual is available in the supplementary section (see Supplementary Material S1), where all functions and parameters are explained, including how to use the SIMPLEX VirtualBox and Cloud image.

Results

The presented autonomous pipeline for investigating exome sequencing data, SIMPLEX, allows researchers to analyze data generated by Illumina and ABI SOLiD NGS devices. It supports SE and PE data and takes advantage of HPC infrastructures or the EC2 Cloud to perform intensive calculations in a timely manner. The pipeline requires sequence reads, their corresponding base calling quality values, and a list of exon positions specifying the complete exome as input. The manifold results of the pipeline include a detailed summary report, files that can be used for viewing mapping results in Genome Browsers, and annotated lists of variants, which can be easily opened with office programs (see Table 2).

Evaluation of the Pipeline

To assess the performance on real biological data, we downloaded raw sequencing data generated by a study of the Kabuki syndrome [9] from the Sequence Read Archive (phs000295.v1.p1). The study comprised 42 runs, both SE and PE, from 10 different patients produced by Illumina Genome Analyzer II. All reads were mapped to the human genome primary assembly from the Genome Reference Consortium GRCh37NCBI (hg19). The results of the evaluation are described below and summarized in Table 3.

A performance summary of the pipeline is depicted in Table 4, listing descriptive values for the runtime for SE and PE analysis runs. All samples were analyzed in parallel on a HPC infrastructure with 128 cores and 1 TB of memory.

Read preprocessing. Initial read preprocessing included the components *read-trimming* (truncating 5′ and 3′ Ns of a read, and removing base calls flagged by the Read Segment Quality Control Indicator), *min-length-filter* (filters out reads shorter than 25), *n-max-filter* (removes reads with more than five percent unidentified base calls), and *quality-filter* (filters out reads with more than five percent unreliable base calls). On average, 98% of SE and 100% of PE reads passed all preprocessing steps, indicating that raw files had already been preprocessed before publication (see Supplementary Material S2 for detailed results).

Alignment. BWA was started with the default parameter set followed by several filters. On average, 63% of SE and 54% PE reads could be mapped to the human genome. PE reads were subsequently applied to a proper-paired-filter where 79% of the reads passed the filter. Duplicate filtering removed 12% of SE and 4% of PE reads. After all exome-filtering steps, 23% of SE and 16% of PE *raw* reads remained for variant detection.

Variant detection. Variant detection identified on average 14,926 raw SNPs, 6,357 filtered SNPs, and 471 DIPs for SE, as well as 17,858 raw SNPs, 7,875 filtered SNPs, and 402 DIPs for PE reads. The calculated transition-transversion ratio for SNPs ranged from 2.15 to 3.58 with an average of 3.32.

Mutation annotation. Variants were annotated with additional information using the GATK annotator and the ANNO-VAR software. On average 83% of all SNPs were referenced to dbSNP and 99% of all DIPs had an association to the RefSeq database. Furthermore, we identified 64,670 unique loss-of-function (nonsynonymous or frameshift) mutations in all in-

Table 1. Mandatory pipeline parameters.

Parameter	Name	Description
-c	command	which pipeline should be run (*exomeSE* or *exomePE*)
-od	output directory	directory where result files are stored
-genP	genome prefix	prefix of the reference genome (e.g. hg18, hg19)
-I	input files	list of files containing raw sequence reads[1]
-sfeb	SAM exome option	bed file determining the exone regions
-dsP	dip splitter option	percentage to distinguish between homo- and heterozygous DIPs
-k	Cluster profile	configuration file to access the cluster service

Listed are all parameters that need to be specified when starting the pipeline.
[1] If PE data is given, the file names need to end with _R1 or _R2.

vestigated samples. Moreover, 24,093 variants were annotated as either missense or nonsense mutations.

Pipeline report generation. All automatically generated summary reports were combined into a single document (see Table S2). Amongst other key figures reported, the exome capture specificity was 37.7% for SE reads and 30.2% for PE reads. Exome fold coverage was reported to be 13.2 fold for SE and 17.5 fold for PE. Moreover, we identified that 18.8% of exons (as specified by CCDS [30]) were not covered (<1x) by SE runs, whereas around 7% had a coverage above 20 fold (SE). PE runs did on average not cover 25% of the exome, but approximately 21% were highly covered.

Discussion

SIMPLEX is a novel pipeline for the consistent analysis of exome sequencing data, covering the complete workflow from read filtering and mapping to annotated lists of detected variants. Due to its support for SE and PE data in nucleotide and color space, it is universally applicable to several different platforms and biological problems. Since the installation of all required analysis tools and the targeted analysis itself are still daunting tasks for many researchers, SIMPLEX is provided as a ready to use VirtualBox image and a fully configured Cloud image, which allows users to quickly and comfortably add more computational power. Detected variants are annotated with additional information, including multiple scores which are useful for getting more accurate functional predictions of mutations [31]. The output format was adapted to be easily viewable in standard office software, and a detailed summary report lists several key figures and results of the analysis run.

In principal, it is possible to extend SIMPLEX to support the analysis of whole-genome data by simply changing a few configuration parameters. However, since currently many labs (especially smaller ones) are focusing on exome sequencing data due to the lower data amount and straightforward interpretation of the results, we focused on this data type and included specific steps such as filtering exonic regions, calculation of exome capture specificity, and detection of poorly captured exons.

Selection of Tools

All external tools that are integrated into SIMPLEX were carefully selected and thoroughly evaluated. Several programs for the read preprocessing steps were tested for their suitability, including TileQC [32], PIQA [33], CANGS [34], and SolexaQA [35]. At the time of development none of them supported both Illumina and ABI SOLiD platforms, and therefore did not qualify for incorporation into the pipeline. As a result, new preprocessing components were developed in-house, which are capable of handling SE and PE reads from Illumina and ABI SOLiD platforms.

Alignment of reads is performed by the Burrows-Wheeler based aligner BWA [21] as it is accurate, fast, open-source and supports gapped as well as quality scored alignment [22]. Furthermore, it is capable of analyzing sequences encoded in nucleotide and color space, handles SE and PE reads, and was selected by the 1000 genome project to map the reads obtained for the *full project* [36]. Other alignment programs such as MAQ [37], SOAP [38], Bowtie [39], and ELAND [40] were ruled out after thorough investigation, as they were either slower than BWA (MAQ, SOAP) or did not support gapped alignment (Bowtie, ELAND). Furthermore, recent studies show that BWA offers superior alignment

Table 2. Description of output files.

Name	Format	Description
read qualities	pdf	read quality statistics report available for raw and refined reads
read alignment	bam, bai	result files of alignment and alignment filtering steps
insert size distribution	png	insert size histogram (provided for PE data only)
exon counts	tsv	number of covering reads and fold coverage per exon
mutations	vcf, tsv	list of detected mutations
summary report	tsv, xlsx	detailed report of the analysis including several key figures

Listed are key intermediate and final results that are created by the pipeline.

Table 3. Detailed results of SIMPLEX evaluation.

	SE Samples	PE samples
reads passed preprocessing	98%	100%
reads mappable	63%	54%
reads used for variant detection	23%	16%
number of raw SNPs	14,926	17,858
number of filtered SNPs	6,357	7,875
number of DIPs	473	402
raw SNPs in dbSNP	92%	76%
filtered SNPs in dbSNP	99%	98%
DIPs with RefSeq association	99%	99%
raw loss-of-function SNPs	1,181	4,098
filtered loss-of-function SNPs	593	1329
loss-of-function DIPs	47	96
missense/nonsens raw SNPs	737	1,562
missense/nonsens filtered SNPs	497	1,098

Listed are key figures (in avg.) for SE and PE samples.

Table 4. Runtime summary for Kabuki syndrome study.

Statistic	SE Samples	PE samples
mean pipeline runtime	12:39	21:19
median pipeline runtime	12:54	24:59
longest pipeline runtime	15:14	26:37
shortest pipeline runtime	07:39	05:13
mean longest step (local realignment)	02:45	06:59
mean alignment duration	02:50	04:52
mean SNP calling duration	00:05	00:06

Listed are overall and key runtime statistics (in hours).

runtime and memory usage while still providing satisfactory mapping results [41,42].

Post processing is done either by GATK or by a custom made component which performs several filtering steps. First, it applies mapping and properly-paired filters, followed by PCR duplicate removal and exome filtering. Results of each filtering step are documented in log files and are assembled in a summary report.

GATK was chosen for variant calling, as it supports several NGS platforms and is suitable for both, individual and multi sample, analyses. In addition, the toolkit is shipped with a set of additional SNP analysis tools, including SNP quality evaluation, SNP filtering, and standardized downstream recalibration of variant quality scores. Moreover, it has already been successfully used in large-scale projects like the 1000 Genomes Project [36] and The Cancer Genome Atlas [5]. Amongst other applications tested, SNPseeker [43] is limited to a certain NGS platform, whereas CRISP [44] is only capable of handling pooled sequencing data. Although SAMtools [45] and SOAPsnp [46] are equipped for single sample analysis and multi-platform support, they do not provide functionality to detect the novelty status of SNP calls.

Additional information for detected variants, such as RefSeq names, GO ids, and KEGG ids, are added using the GATK annotator. However, as those annotations depend on existing dbSNP ids, they are not suitable for newly discovered variations. Therefore, SIMPLEX includes Annovar [27] to add additional information for unknown mutations. Annovar was assessed to be superior to other competitors as it comprehends annotations from several databases, provides frequent updates, and is easily extendable. Amongst other evaluated annotation tools, SAAPdb [47] is currently not maintained, *SeattleSeq Annotation* is not available for local installation, and SNPs3D [48] is only available for registered users. The Sequence Variant Analyser [49] does provide several annotations, but is designed as a standalone graphical application and lacks variant scores which are provided by Annovar.

Comparison with Existing Software

Currently several NGS analysis pipelines are available which differ in their provided feature sets and functionality [14–18,50]. In contrast to several existing pipelines, SIMPLEX is delivered as a fully set up VirtualBox image, which eliminates the arduous installation and setup process of required analysis programs. Furthermore, none of the published pipelines are capable of providing multiple user support and, to the best of our knowledge, none offers the possibility to use current Cloud technologies for data analysis. SIMPLEX covers a complete exome analysis workflow, starting with the analysis of raw sequencing data and ultimately leading to well annotated lists of detected variants. In contrast to other analysis pipelines, detailed summary reports are created at numerous stages which help to quickly evaluate the quality of the sequencing runs and provide an overview of the performed analyses. A comparison overview between pipelines is depicted in Table 5 and Table S3.

Discussion of Pipeline Evaluation

The performance assessment of the presented pipeline was done with data from the Kabuki study described by [9]. It demonstrated that the application is able to successfully analyze 42 samples in parallel, while still achieving good runtime results (see Table 4). Comparison figures show that more SE reads (63%) than PE reads (54%) could be mapped and more SE reads (23%) than PE reads (16%) were on target.

After the initial analysis, we checked for MLL2 loss-of-function mutations in each individual which could be observed in 8 out of 10 subjects (see Table S4). This number is comparable to the results of the Kabuki study which identified mutations in MLL2 in 9 out of 10 individuals. Furthermore, additional standard Auto-annovar analysis labeled MLL2 as a possible candidate mutation in 5 out of 10 individuals (see Tables S5 and S6).

Conclusion

We have developed and validated SIMPLEX, a highly configurable pipeline for the analysis of NGS exome data, covering the complete workflow from sequence alignment to SNP/DIP identification and variant annotation. Due to the pipeline's flexible design SIMPLEX is supporting SE and PE data as well as input from various sequencing platforms. The pipeline is optimized for HPC infrastructures and can be used in the Amazon EC2 Cloud to speed up the analysis process. Complex methods and commands are abstracted from investigators to facilitate the use of NGS technologies in laboratories even without a specialized bioinformatics staff. SIMPLEX outputs highly readable reports including summary documents that list key figures such as *exome coverage, filtering results*, or *exome capture specificity*. All detected variants

Table 5. Comparison of exome analysis tools.

Criteria	SIMPLEX	ngs- backbone[a]	GATK[b]	inGAP[c]	SeqGene[d]	GAMES[e]	TREAT[f]	Atlas2[g]
Free of charge	✓	✓	✓	✓	✓	✓	✓	✓
SE/PE data handling	✓/✓	✓/−	✓/✓	✓/✓	n.m.	✓/✓	✓/✓	✓/✓
NS/CS data handling	✓/✓	✓/✓	✓/✓	✓/−	n.m.	✓/✓	✓/−	✓/✓
Alignment	✓	✓	-	✓	✓	-	✓	-
Variant annotation	✓	-	✓	-	✓	✓	✓	-
Highly customizable	✓	✓	✓	-	✓	✓	✓	-
PCR duplicate handling	✓	-	-	-	-	✓	-	-
Homo−/heterozygosity	✓/✓	−/−	✓/✓	−/−	✓/✓	−/−	✓/✓	✓/✓
Quality reports	✓	✓	✓	-	✓	-	✓	-
Summary reports	✓	-	-	✓	-	✓	-	-
HPC support	✓	✓	✓	-	-	-	✓	-
Cloud support	✓	-	-	-	-	-	✓	✓
Graphical user interface	-	-	-	✓	-	-	-	✓
Multi user support	✓	-	-	-	-	-	-	-
Standalone	✓	✓	✓	✓	✓	✓	✓	✓
Web service	✓	-	-	-	-	-	-	-

Compared are several key features of currently available non-commercial exome sequencing analysis pipelines.
n.m. ... not mentioned.
a) [14].
b) [15].
c) [16].
d) [17].
e) [18].
f) [50].
g) [19].

are annotated with additional information allowing researchers to easily and quickly discriminate silent mutations from variants that are potentially causing diseases. Furthermore, result files can be used in downstream analyses to additionally identify driver mutations using tools such as Auto-Annovar or VAAST [51]. SIMPLEX combines proven analysis tools with a set of newly developed methods, which are all optimized toward the selection of statistically and functionally significant genetic events. Moreover, the pipeline can be smoothly extended to include additional methods, such as Varscan [52]. In addition, it is generally possible to use SIMPLEX with different organisms and we have outlined all needed steps to include additional species in the user manual. The complete application is continuously tested and is distributed in ready-to-use virtual images that can be easily deployed in the Cloud.

Due to the modular design of the pipeline, it is possible to integrate any command line tool by simply extending a XML file and creating a few Java wrapper classes (for detailed information see the user manual). The whole pipeline code is open-source and can be extended to one's needs. We hope to encourage the community to create extensions and submit them to the productive development branch. Regarding the long-term use and sustainability of the pipeline, the application is under heavy use in clinical research environment, which guarantees active development and improvements.

In conclusion, SIMPLEX is a tool designed to be readily used for life science researchers to quickly obtain biological insight into genetic events investigated by exome sequencing. The presented system was successfully applied in a recent study to elucidate the cause of the rare genetic disease epileptic encephalopathy and amelogenesis imperfecta (Kohlschütter-Tönz syndrome) [53].

Supporting Information

Table S1   SIMPLEX parameters and their description.

Table S2   Kabuki syndrome study summary.

Table S3   Comparison of SIMPLEX, Atlas, and Treat pipelines.

Table S4   Kabuki syndrome study - SNV statistics grouped by individuals.

Table S5   Kabuki syndrome study - unique occurrences of MLL2.

Table S6   Kabuki syndrome study - summary of auto-annovar results.

Supplementary Material S1   SIMPLEX user manual.

Supplementary Material S2   QA report after raw sequence preprocessing for sample SRR063831.

Author Contributions

Analyzed the data: MF RS SP AD GS. Contributed reagents/materials/analysis tools: MF RS SP AD ZT GS. Wrote the paper: MF RS SP AD GS. Designed the software: MF RS GS. Implemented the software: MF RS

SP AD GS. Contributed considerably to improve the revised version of the paper, provided additional data sets, helped evaluating and interpreting the pipeline results, and contributed to the manuscript: JZ AS.

References

1. Mardis ER (2008) Next-generation dna sequencing methods. Annu Rev Genomics Hum Genet 9: 387–402.
2. Metzker ML (2009) Sequencing technologies - the next generation. Nat Rev Genet: –.
3. Shendure J, Ji H (2008) Next-generation dna sequencing. Nat Biotechnol 26: 1135–1145.
4. Margulies M, Egholm M, Altman WE, Attiya S, Bader JS, et al. (2005) Genome sequencing in microfabricated high-density picolitre reactors. Nature 437: 376–380.
5. Bentley DR (2006) Whole-genome re-sequencing. Curr Opin Genet Dev 16: 545–552.
6. Pettersson E, Lundeberg J, Ahmadian A (2009) Generations of sequencing technologies. Genomics 93: 105–111.
7. Wetterstrand K. Dna sequencing costs: Data from the nhgri large-scale genome sequencing program. Available at: www.genome.gov/sequencingcosts. Accessed 2011 Aug.
8. Ku CS, Naidoo N, Pawitan Y (2011) Revisiting mendelian disorders through exome sequencing. Hum Genet 129: 351–370.
9. Ng SB, Bigham AW, Buckingham KJ, Hannibal MC, McMillin MJ, et al. (2010) Exome sequencing identifies mll2 mutations as a cause of kabuki syndrome. Nat Genet 42: 790–793.
10. Ng SB, Turner EH, Robertson PD, Flygare SD, Bigham AW, et al. (2009) Targeted capture and massively parallel sequencing of 12 human exomes. Nature 461: 272–276.
11. Choi M, Scholl UI, Ji W, Liu T, Tikhonova IR, et al. (2009) Genetic diagnosis by whole exome capture and massively parallel dna sequencing. Proc Natl Acad Sci U S A 106: 19096–19101.
12. Schadt EE, Linderman MD, Sorenson J, Lee L, Nolan GP (2010) Computational solutions to large-scale data management and analysis. Nat Rev Genet 11: 647–657.
13. McPherson JD (2009) Next-generation gap. Nat Methods 6: S2–S5.
14. Blanca JM, Pascual L, Ziarsolo P, Nuez F, Cañizares J (2011) ngs backbone: a pipeline for read cleaning, mapping and snp calling using next generation sequence. BMC Genomics 12: 285.
15. DePristo MA, Banks E, Poplin R, Garimella KV, Maguire JR, et al. (2011) A framework for variation discovery and genotyping using next-generation dna sequencing data. Nat Genet 43: 491–498.
16. Qi J, Zhao F, Buboltz A, Schuster SC (2010) ingap: an integrated next-generation genome analysis pipeline. Bioinformatics 26: 127–129.
17. Deng X (2011) Seqgene: a comprehensive software solution for mining exome- and transcriptomesequencing data. BMC Bioinformatics 12: 267.
18. Sana ME, Iascone M, Marchetti D, Palatini J, Galasso M, et al. (2011) Games identifies and annotates mutations in next-generation sequencing projects. Bioinformatics 27: 9–13.
19. Challis D, Yu J, Evani US, Jackson AR, Paithankar S, et al. (2012) An integrative variant analysis suite for whole exome next-generation sequencing data. BMC Bioinformatics 13: 8.
20. Cock PJA, Fields CJ, Goto N, Heuer ML, Rice PM (2010) The sanger fastq file format for sequences with quality scores, and the solexa/illumina fastq variants. Nucleic Acids Res 38: 1767–1771.
21. Li H, Durbin R (2009) Fast and accurate short read alignment with burrows-wheeler transform. Bioinformatics : –.
22. Li H, Homer N (2010) A survey of sequence alignment algorithms for next-generation sequencing. Brief Bioinform 11: 473–483.
23. Pruitt KD, Tatusova T, Maglott DR (2005) Ncbi reference sequence (refseq): a curated nonredundant sequence database of genomes, transcripts and proteins. Nucleic Acids Res 33: D501–D504.
24. Ashburner M, Ball CA, Blake JA, Botstein D, Butler H, et al. (2000) Gene ontology: tool for the unification of biology. the gene ontology consortium. Nat Genet 25: 25–29.
25. Kanehisa M, Goto S, Kawashima S, Nakaya A (2002) The kegg databases at genomenet. Nucleic Acids Res 30: 42–46.
26. Sherry ST, Ward MH, Kholodov M, Baker J, Phan L, et al. (2001) dbsnp: the ncbi database of genetic variation. Nucleic Acids Res 29: 308–311.
27. Wang K, Li M, Hakonarson H (2010) Annovar: functional annotation of genetic variants from high-throughput sequencing data. Nucleic Acids Res 38: e164.
28. Chapman B. Next generation sequencing information management and analysis system for galaxy. Available: http://bcbio.wordpress.com/2011/01/11/next-generation-sequencing-information-management-and-analysis-system-for-galaxy/. Accessed 2011 Oct.
29. Afgan E, Baker D, Coraor N, Chapman B, Nekrutenko A, et al. (2010) Galaxy cloudman: delivering cloud compute clusters. BMC Bioinformatics 11: S4.
30. Pruitt KD, Harrow J, Harte RA, Wallin C, Diekhans M, et al. (2009) The consensus coding sequence (ccds) project: Identifying a common protein-coding gene set for the human and mouse genomes. Genome Res 19: 1316–1323.
31. Liu X, Jian X, Boerwinkle E (2011) dbnsfp: A lightweight database of human nonsynonymous snps and their functional predictions. Hum Mutat 32: 894–899.
32. Dolan PC, Denver DR (2008) Tileqc: a system for tile-based quality control of solexa data. BMC Bioinformatics 9: 250–250.
33. Martinez-Alcantara A, Ballesteros E, Feng C, Rojas M, Koshinsky H, et al. (2009) Piqa: Pipeline for illumina g1 genome analyzer data quality assessment. Bioinformatics: –.
34. Pandey RV, Nolte V, Schlotterer C (2010) Cangs: a user-friendly utility for processing and analyzing 454 gs-x data in biodiversity studies. BMC Res Notes 3: 3–3.
35. Cox MP, Peterson DA, Biggs PJ (2010) Solexaqa: At-a-glance quality assessment of illumina second-generation sequencing data. BMC Bioinformatics 11: 485–485.
36. Genomes Project Consortium (2010) A map of human genome variation from population-scale sequencing. Nature 467: 1061–1073.
37. Li H, Ruan J, Durbin R (2008) Mapping short dna sequencing reads and calling variants using mapping quality scores. Genome research 18: 1851.
38. Li R, Li Y, Kristiansen K, Wang J (2008) Soap: short oligonucleotide alignment program. Bioinformatics 24: 713.
39. Langmead B, Trapnell C, Pop M, Salzberg S (2009) Ultrafast and memory-efficient alignment of short dna sequences to the human genome. Genome Biol 10: R25.
40. Illumina Inc. Available: http://www.illumina.com/. Accessed 2012 Feb.
41. Bao S, Jiang R, Kwan W, Wang B, Ma X, et al. (2011) Evaluation of next-generation sequencing software in mapping and assembly. J Hum Genet 56: 406–414.
42. Ruffalo M, Laframboise T, Koyutrk M (2011) Comparative analysis of algorithms for nextgeneration sequencing read alignment. Bioinformatics 27: 2790–2796.
43. Druley TE, Vallania FLM, Wegner DJ, Varley KE, Knowles OL, et al. (2009) Quantification of rare allelic variants from pooled genomic dna. Nat Methods 6: 263–265.
44. Bansal V (2010) A statistical method for the detection of variants from next-generation resequencing of dna pools. Bioinformatics 26: i318–i324.
45. Li H, Handsaker B, Wysoker A, Fennell T, Ruan J, et al. (2009) The sequence alignment/map format and samtools. Bioinformatics 25: 2078–2079.
46. Li R, Li Y, Fang X, Yang H, Wang J, et al. (2009) Snp detection for massively parallel whole-genome resequencing. Genome Res 19: 1124–1132.
47. Cavallo A, Martin ACR (2005) Mapping snps to protein sequence and structure data. Bioinformatics 21: 1443–1450.
48. Yue P, Melamud E, Moult J (2006) Snps3d: candidate gene and snp selection for association studies. BMC Bioinformatics 7: 166.
49. Ge D, Ruzzo EK, Shianna KV, He M, Pelak K, et al. (2011) Sva: software for annotating and visualizing sequenced human genomes. Bioinformatics 27: 1998–2000.
50. Asmann YW, Middha S, Hossain A, Baheti S, Li Y, et al. (2012) Treat: a bioinformatics tool for variant annotations and visualizations in targeted and exome sequencing data. Bioinformatics 28: 277–278.
51. Yandell M, Huff C, Hu H, Singleton M, Moore B, et al. (2011) A probabilistic disease-gene finder for personal genomes. Genome Res 21: 1529–1542.
52. Koboldt DC, Chen K, Wylie T, Larson DE, McLellan MD, et al. (2009) Varscan: variant detection in massively parallel sequencing of individual and pooled samples. Bioinformatics 25: 2283–2285.
53. Schossig A, Wolf NI, Fischer C, Fischer M, Stocker G, et al. (2012) Mutations in rogdi cause kohlschtter-tnz syndrome. Am J Hum Genet 90: 701–707.

23

Structural Controllability of Complex Networks Based on Preferential Matching

Xizhe Zhang[1]*, **Tianyang Lv**[2,3,4], **XueYing Yang**[1], **Bin Zhang**[1]

1 College of Information Science and Engineering, Northeastern University, Shenyang, China, **2** College of Computer Science and Technology, Harbin Engineering University, Harbin, China, **3** College of Computer Science and Technology, Tsinghua University, Beijing, China, **4** Audit Research Institute, National Audit Office, Beijing, China

Abstract

Minimum driver node sets (MDSs) play an important role in studying the structural controllability of complex networks. Recent research has shown that MDSs tend to avoid high-degree nodes. However, this observation is based on the analysis of a small number of MDSs, because enumerating all of the MDSs of a network is a #P problem. Therefore, past research has not been sufficient to arrive at a convincing conclusion. In this paper, first, we propose a preferential matching algorithm to find MDSs that have a specific degree property. Then, we show that the MDSs obtained by preferential matching can be composed of high- and medium-degree nodes. Moreover, the experimental results also show that the average degree of the MDSs of some networks tends to be greater than that of the overall network, even when the MDSs are obtained using previous research method. Further analysis shows that whether the driver nodes tend to be high-degree nodes or not is closely related to the edge direction of the network.

Editor: Sergio Gómez, Universitat Rovira i Virgili, Spain

Funding: This work is sponsored by the Fundamental Research Funds for the Central Universities of China under grant number N120404011; the Natural Science Foundation of China under grant numbers 60903009, 60903080, and 71272216; the National Key Technology Research and Development Program of the Ministry of Science and Technology of China under grant number 2012BAH08B02; and the Supporting Plan Project for Youth Scholar Backbone of General Colleges and Universities of Heilongjiang under grant number 1253G017. The funders had no role in study design, data collection and analysis, decision to publish, or preparation of the manuscript.

Competing Interests: The authors have declared that no competing interests exist.

* Email: zhangxizhe@ise.neu.edu.cn

Introduction

Controlling complex systems is a critical topic in many applications. A system is called controllable if it can be driven from any initial state to any desired state in a finite time. Previous researches have usually adopted a complex network as the fundamental model to analyze the topological structure [1–3], the evolving model [4–6], and the dynamic behavior [7–9] of complex systems.

However, we still lack a thorough understanding of how to control complex networks. According to the control theory, a linear time-invariant system whose states are determined by the following equation:

$$\frac{dx(t)}{dt} = Ax(t) + Bu(t) \quad (1)$$

where the vector $\boldsymbol{x}(t) = (x_1(t), \ldots, x_N(t))^T$, denotes the state of N nodes in the network at time t, A is the transpose of the adjacency matrix of the network, B is the input matrix that defines how control signals are inputted to the network, and $\boldsymbol{u}(t) = (u_1(t), \ldots, u_H(t))^T$ represents the H input signals at time t. A node whose control signal is directly inputted is called a driver node. The minimum sets of driver nodes to control a network are called the minimum driver nodes sets (MDSs).

Lin [10] presented a network representation of linear time-invariant systems and stated that the system is structurally controllable if and only if the network can be spanned by cacti structures. Commault [11] proved that the minimal signals need to control a network can be obtained by maximal matching [12] of network. Based on above works, Liu [13] developed an analysis tool to study the controllability of an arbitrary complex directed network, and found that MDSs tend to be composed of low-degree nodes in both real and model networks.

However, the maximum matching of a network is usually not unique [14], and thus neither are the MDSs. Previous studies [15–19] have only randomly sampled MDSs and analyzed a small number of the MDSs of a network because enumerating all possible maximum matchings is in the class of #P problem [20]. Therefore, the past researches have not been sufficient to arrive at a convincing conclusion about whether MDSs tend to avoid high degree nodes or not.

In this paper, we propose a preferential matching algorithm to find some MDSs with desired degree properties. To find these MDSs, the algorithm arranges the matching order of the nodes according to their degree rank. Because low-ranking nodes have higher probabilities of being driver nodes, the obtained MDSs tend to be composed of the high- or medium-degree nodes of the network. The algorithm can also be applied to obtain the MDSs with other topological properties.

By using the preferential matching algorithm, we found that there were some MDSs composed mainly of high- and medium-degree nodes in some networks. Moreover, in some networks, the average degree of the MDSs tended to be greater than that of the overall network, even if the MDSs were obtained using the previous random-matching method.

We conclude that there are networks that favor low-degree MDSs and other networks that favor high-degree MDSs. To find the underlying reason for this phenomenon, we designed a directed BA model for model networks and a reversal strategy for the edge direction for real networks. The experimental results showed that the MDSs of the network tended to be composed of high-degree nodes if the majority of the edges of a network were pointing from high-degree nodes to low-degree nodes; otherwise, the MDSs of the network tended to be composed of low-degree nodes. Therefore, whether the driver nodes tended to be high degree or not was closely related to the edge direction of the network.

Preferential Matching Algorithm

First, we will briefly introduce the basic concepts of maximum matching. For a directed network G, $V(G)$ is the node set and $E(G)$ is the edge set, with $N = |V|$ and $L = |E|$. A set of edges in G is called a matching M if no two edges in M have a node in common. A node v_i is matched by M if there is an edge of M pointing to v_i, otherwise v_i is unmatched. A path P is said to be M-alternating if the edges of P are alternately in and not in M. An M-alternating path P that starts and ends at the unmatched nodes is called an M-augmenting path. A matching with the maximum number of nodes is called a maximum matching M^*. A matching M is called a perfect matching if all of the nodes of G are matched by M.

The minimum input theorem [38] proves that if there is a perfect matching in a network, the number of driver nodes is one, otherwise the number of driver nodes is equal to the number of unmatched nodes with respect to any maximum matchings. And the driver nodes are unmatched nodes. The size of the maximum matching M^* is denoted $|M^*|$. The minimum number of driver nodes is thus

$$n_D = \max\{N - |M^*|, 1\} \qquad (2)$$

Based on this theorem, the MDSs can be obtained by finding the maximum matchings of a network. Therefore, it is critical to find all of the maximum matchings. Previous maximum matching algorithms, such as Hopcroft-Karp [12] and the Hungarian algorithm [21], are based on the theorem proposed by Berge [22]. That theorem proves that M^* is a maximum matching if and only if there is no augmenting path in G relative to M^*. Therefore, the basic idea of the maximum matching algorithm is as follows: first, find an augmenting path from each unmatched node by current matching M (initially $M = \varphi$), then obtain an expanded matching M'. Repeat the first and the second steps until no augmenting path exists. The final matching is a maximum matching. Using this process, once a node v_i becomes a matched node, it will be matched by the final maximum matching and won't be a driver node.

Therefore, if we deliberately arrange the matching order of nodes according to the order of degree, we would find MDSs with a desired degree property such as finding some high-degree MDSs, particularly when a network has many maximum matchings. However, the matching order of nodes is determined by the time when a node first appears in the augmenting path, but the time is hard to be pre-decided. It is possible that a node with a high degree appears very early in an augmenting path, even if it is arrange to be the last one as the start of augmenting paths. For example, we can sort the nodes as $\{v_0, v_1, v_2, v_3, v_4, v_5, v_6\}$ in the ascending order by degree and treat this order as the input sequence to select the unmatched start node in finding an augmenting path. But we may find an augmenting path P $v_0 \rightarrow v_4 \rightarrow v_5 \rightarrow v_6$ at the very first step. Although the path starts from v_0 with the lowest degree, it contains the highest degree nodes v_4, v_5 and v_6 and these nodes cannot be the driver nodes of the final MDSs. Thus, the matching order of the nodes would be quite different from the degree order of the nodes, and the MDSs with a desired degree property could not be easily found.

To overcome this problem, we designed an iterative preferential matching method. We sort the nodes as $\{v_0, v_1, ... v_n\}$ in the ascending order by degree and denote m as the number of preferential matching nodes. The method starts from the sub graph H_0 with the lowest-degree node ranked first; at each

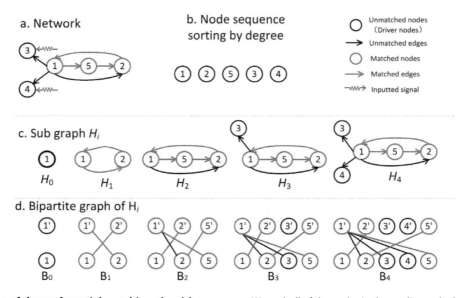

Figure 1. Illustration of the preferential matching algorithm process. We rank all of the nodes in descending order by degree, and the driver nodes are nodes v_3 and v_4 that are the last two of the sequence.

Table 1. Overview of real networks and the statistical results of their MDSs.

Type	Name	N	L	$<k>$	$\overline{<k^D>}$	$[<k^P_{min}>, <k^P_{max}>]$	n_D	λ_D
Trust	Wiki-Vote [23]	7115	103689	29.15	9.66	[9.66,9.66]	4736	0.67
Food Web	Grassland [24]	88	137	3.11	2.67	[2.20,3.02]	46	0.52
	Little Rock [25]	183	2494	27.26	15.39	[14.79,15.83]	99	0.54
Food Web	Seagrass [26]	49	226	9.22	8.06	[6.46,11.08]	13	0.27
	Ythan [24]	135	601	8.90	7.43	[4.86,9.67]	69	0.51
	Florida [27]	128	2106	32.91	24.86	[16.1,36.6]	30	0.23
	Mondego [28]	46	400	17.39	12.47	[9.26,12.58]	19	0.41
Power Grid	USpowerGrid [29]	4941	13188	10.68	2.73	[2.06,3.50]	575	0.12
Neuronal	C. elegans [29]	306	2345	15.33	5.6	[3.36,16.47]	58	0.19
	Hep-th [30]	27770	352807	25.41	9.45	[7.96,11.64]	5994	0.22
Citation	Zewall [31]	6752	54233	16.064	17.55	[4.99,25.02]	2427	0.36
	Kohonen [31]	4470	12731	5.696	5.73	[2.67,6.3]	2812	0.63
WWW	Polblogs [32]	1224	16718	27.32	12.41	[4.12,17.41]	418	0.34
Internet	P2P-1 [33]	10876	39994	7.36	6.92	[2.67,9.45]	6004	0.55
Social-Communication	UClonline [34]	1899	20296	21.38	6.75	[1.72,13.76]	614	0.32
Regulatory	TRN-Yeast-1 [35]	4441	12873	5.80	5.85	[3.18,5.95]	4284	0.96
Companies	Eva [36]	8497	6726	1.584	1.59	[1.36,1.61]	7194	0.85
Literary	Literature [37]	35	81	4.628	4.72	[4.46,5.46]	13	0.37
Trade	World_trade [38]	80	998	24.95	26.93	[10.46,47.33]	24	0.3

$<k>$ is the average degree of a network, n_D is the size of a MDS, $\lambda_D = n_D/N$, $<k^D>$ is the average degree of the MDS, $\overline{<k^D>}$ is the average value of $<k^D>$ for all of the obtained MDSs, and $<k^P_{min}>$ and $<k^P_{max}>$ are the maximum and the minimum values $<k^P>$ of all of the MDSs obtained by the preferential matching method under a different preferential matching number m.

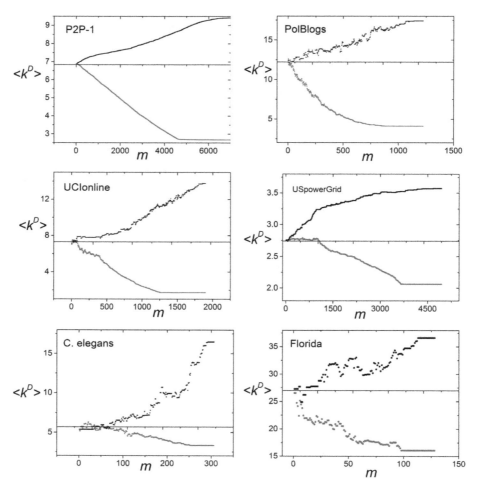

Figure 2. Relationship of $<k^D>$ of a MDS versus the preferential matching number m. The results above the solid line show the value of $<k^D>$ when nodes are sorted in ascending order by degree. The results below the solid line show the value of $<k^D>$ when nodes are sorted in descending order by degree.

iterative step i, the sub graph H_i will be extended by adding the node with the i-th rank, and the maximum matching of H_i is calculated based on the previously obtained maximum matching of H_{i-1}. We repeat this procedure until the sub graph H_i is equal to the whole network or until m preferential nodes have been added. Details of the preferential matching method are as follows:

1. Sort nodes as $\{v_0, v_1, ...v_n\}$, $H_0 = \{v_0\}$, $M^*_0 = \varphi$, $i = 1$;
2. Set $H_i = H_{i-1} + \{v_i\}$ and find a maximum matching M^*_i of H_i based on M^*_{i-1}, $i = i+1$;
3. Repeat step 2 until $i = m$;
4. If $m < N$, find the resulting maximum matching M^* of G based on M^*_m; else M^*_m is the resulting maximum matching of G, and the MDS is composed of the unmatched nodes with respect to M^*.

An example of the proposed method is shown in Figure 1.

We obtain a maximum matching of G in the step 4. And, as with current algorithms [12,21], once v_i is matched in the process, it must be matched by the resulting maximum matching. The proposed method ensures that we can find the maximum number of matched nodes of H_i from the first i ranking nodes and that a high-degree node will not be matched in early steps because the node is not included in the early sub-graphs. Therefore, we can

make the matching order of the nodes as similar as possible to the predefined order of degrees. Thus, high-degree nodes will have a higher probability of being the driver nodes. However, the order of arrangement has no influence on some particular nodes, for instance the nodes with zero in-degree must be driver nodes no matter what the input order is.

Experimental Results and Analysis

To analyze the degree property of MDSs, we selected 21 real networks that belong to 12 categories, including trust networks, food networks, electric networks, neuronal networks, citation networks, the World Wide Web, the internet, social communication networks and social organization networks. Table 1 shows the average degree of a network $<k>$, the size of the networks' MDSs n_D, and the fraction of driver nodes $\lambda_D = n_D/N$.

First, we find the MDSs with the desired high-degree property based on the preferential matching algorithm. Let $<k^D>$ be the average degree of the MDSs obtained under a different number m of preferential nodes, and let $<k^D_{max}>$ and $<k^D_{min}>$ be the maximum and the minimum $<k^D>$ of all of the obtained MDSs, respectively. Figure 2 shows the variation in $<k^D>$ versus m in the real and model networks. Obviously, the preferential matching method can find MDSs with the preferred high-degree property,

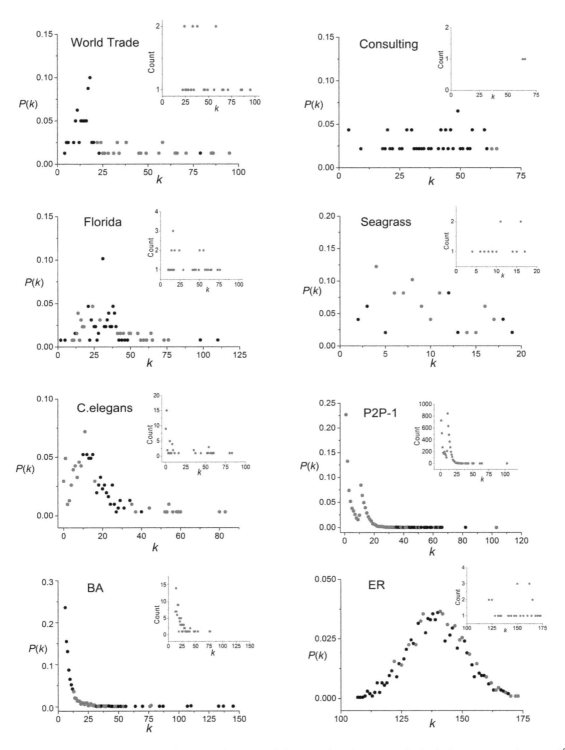

Figure 3. Degree distribution of driver nodes in real and model networks. The MDS with the highest average degree $<k^D_{max}>$ was computed by using the preferential matching method. Each point corresponds to the set of nodes with the specific degree k, the black point means that no node with the degree k appeared in the result MDS and the red point means that some nodes with the degree k appeared in the result MDS. The inset graph shows the degree distribution of all driver nodes of the MDS with $<k^D_{max}>$.

and the high-degree property becomes clearer with the increment of m. If the nodes are sorted in ascending order according to degree, $<k^D>$ will increase with m to the upper bound $<k^D_{max}>$;

if the nodes are sorted in descending order according to degree, $<k^D>$ will decrease with m to the lower bound $<k^D_{min}>$.

From Table 1 and Figure 2, a basic observation was that the MDSs were structurally diverse: the $<k^D>$ of many networks

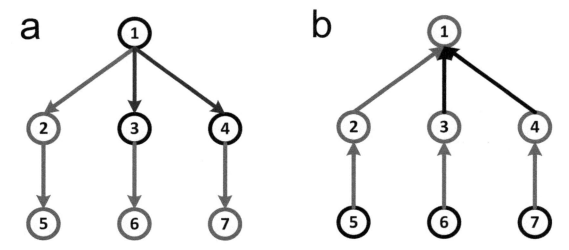

Figure 4. Two simple networks with $<k> = 1.857$. Red nodes and edges are matched by a maximum matching. Black nodes and edges are driver nodes and unmatched edges. The average degrees of the MDSs of networks (a) and (b) are 2.33 and 1, respectively.

varied widely. Thus, the different MDSs of the same network could have quite different degree properties. Moreover, $<k^D_{max}>$ was greater than $<k>$ in many networks, such as the *Grassland*, *Seagrass*, *Ythan*, and *Florida* networks. Therefore, we were able to find the MDSs whose $<k^D>$ was greater than the average degree of the network.

To further verify the above observation, we analyzed the degree distribution of driver nodes of the MDSs with high $<k^D>$. We computed the MDS with the highest average degree $<k^D_{max}>$ by using the preferential matching method. Figure 3 shows the results of some real and model networks. In Figure 3, each point corresponds to the set of nodes with the specific degree k. The black point means that no node with the degree k appears in the result MDS, and the red point means that some nodes with the

degree k appear in the result MDS. The inset graph shows the degree distribution of all driver nodes of the MDS with $<k^D_{max}>$. Therefore, if all red points have high degree, the MDS tends to be composed of high-degree nodes. It can be seen from Figure 3 that there do exist the MDS mainly composed of high- or medium-degree nodes in some networks. Taking the *world-trade*[38] network as an example, 66.2% of its nodes have $k \leq 20$, but none of these low-degree nodes appeared in the result MDS; meanwhile, 88.9% of the rest high-degree nodes with $k > 20$ appeared in the MDS. Similar results can be observed in the *BA* and *ER* networks. However, not all networks had the MDS mainly composed of high-degree nodes. The MDS with $<k^D_{max}>$ of some networks was composed of the nodes with degree ranging from the lowest degree to the highest, such as the *seagrass* [26], *florida* [27] and *c*.

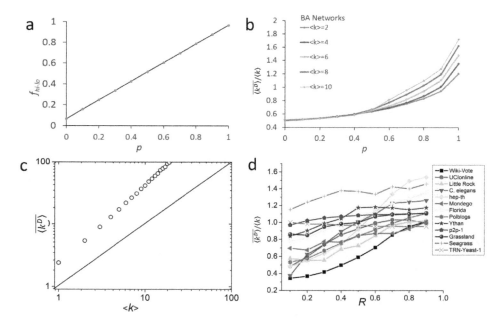

Figure 5. Edge direction strongly influences the average degree of MDSs. (a) The fraction f_{hi-lo} and the probability p have a clear linear relation in directed BA networks; (b) the ratio of $\overline{<k^D>}$ and $<k>$ increase with p in directed BA networks; (c) the $\overline{<k^D>}$ of all directed BA networks is always greater than $<k>$ when $p = 1$; (d) the ratio of $\overline{<k^D>}$ to $<k>$ increases with the reversal probability R in real networks.

elegans [29] networks, while the MDS with $<k^D_{max}>$ of other networks was mainly composed of the low-degree nodes, such as the *P2P*-1 [33] network.

Second, we tried to prove that the average degree of the MDSs of some networks tended to be greater than that of the overall networks, even if the MDSs were obtained using the previous random matching method. In the experiment, we randomly sampled 10,000 different MDSs of each network. Table 1 shows the average value $\overline{<k^D>}$ of the average degree of all of the sampled MDSs because the average degree of the different MDSs varied. We found that the $\overline{<k^D>}$ of some networks, such as the *Zewail*, *world trade* and *literature* networks, were greater than or equal to $<k>$ even when using the previous sample method [13].

Finally, these experimental results provoked us to explain why the driver nodes of some networks tended to be low degree while others were not. According to the minimum input theorem, a driver node is not pointed to by any matched edge. Therefore, if the majority of edges of a network point from high-degree nodes to low-degree nodes, the MDSs tend to be composed of high-degree nodes. Otherwise, the MDSs tend to be composed of low-degree nodes. Figure 4 gives an example where two networks have the same topology except that the directions of their edges are opposite. The edges of the network in Figure 4(a) are pointing to the low-degree nodes, while the edges in Figure 4(b) are pointing to the high-degree nodes. Therefore, they have very different MDSs. The driver nodes of network Figure 4(a) are v_1, v_3 and v_4 and have the highest degrees, while the driver nodes of network Figure 4(b) are v_5, v_6 and v_7, which have the lowest degrees.

Therefore, we believe that the node composition of the MDSs is closely related to the direction of the edges in a network. To verify this hypothesis, we designed a revised BA model to generate directed networks. The model was the same as the classical BA model [39] except that the direction of a newly added edge is determined by the following rule: the direction of the new edge points from an existing old node v_{old} to a new node v_{new} with probability p, and the probability of pointing in the opposite direction is $1-p$. Therefore, if p is large enough, the edges of a high-degree node v_{old} will have a high probability of pointing to other nodes. The result of this arrangement is that the edges of a generated network tend to point from high-degree nodes to low-degree nodes, so the high degree nodes are more likely to be the source nodes [40], which must receive the control signal from outside. We calculated the fraction f_{hi-lo} of edges that pointed from high-degree nodes to low-degree nodes in a directed BA network. Figure 5(a) shows the linear relation between f_{hi-lo} and p.

Then, we randomly calculated 10,000 MDSs of several directed BA networks using the Hopcroft-Karp algorithm. Figure 5(b) shows the average degree of the MDSs $\overline{<k^D>}$ increases with p. When $p = 0.5$, which means that the direction of the edges are randomly decided, $\overline{<k^D>}$ is much less than $<k>$; as p increases to close to 1, $\overline{<k^D>}$ gradually becomes greater than $<k>$; and in Figure 5(c), when $p = 1$, the $\overline{<k^D>}$ of all of the directed BA networks is always greater than $<k>$.

We also verified this hypothesis in the real networks. Due to the complexity of degree correlation in real directed networks [41], there may be no obvious relationship between $\overline{<k^D>}$ and f_{hi-lo} in different real networks. Therefore, we designed the following edge-reversal strategy to verify this hypothesis: for an edge $v_i \rightarrow v_j$, if $k_i < k_j$, then reverse the edge direction to $v_j \rightarrow v_i$ with probability R. Similarly to the directed BA model, if R is large enough, the edges of a high-degree node will have a high probability of pointing to a low-degree node. Figure 5(d) shows $\overline{<k^D>}$ versus R. We can see that if the original $\overline{<k^D>}$ of a network is less than $<k>$, the $\overline{<k^D>}$ increases gradually with the increase of R and becomes greater than or equal to the $<k>$ of the network. However, for a few networks such as *TRN-Yeast*-1, the average degree of the MDSs will decrease with R. This finding suggests that other topological factors also influence the degree properties of MDSs, although the direction of the edges may be a major factor.

Discussion

The minimal driver nodes set can be obtained by finding the maximal matching of network. However, the MDSs of a network are not unique, and have very different topological features exist. Thus, one important research direction in the controllability of complex networks is analyzing the topological features of all of the possible MDSs.

However, enumerating all of the MDSs is in the class of #P problem, so we tried to find the MDSs with specific topological features. Our contribution in this paper was twofold. First, we proposed a MDS-discovery method based on preferential matching. This method could effectively find a MDS with a high average degree by arranging the matching sequence of nodes based on the order of their degree. Furthermore, we were able sort nodes by any desired property and found a MDS satisfying that property. The algorithm also showed the promise for finding a MDSs that satisfy application-specific constraints. For instance, if some nodes cannot be driver nodes in practice, we let these nodes be matched with high priority in the preferential matching process; thus, a MDS without these nodes can be obtained if such a MDS exists.

Second, we found that whether driver nodes tended to be low degree was closely related to the direction of edges. If the majority of edges pointed to low-degree nodes, control signals were required to transfer from high-degree nodes to low-degree nodes; thus, the MDSs tended to be composed of high-degree nodes.

Future research will investigate all of the possible MDSs and analyze the degree distribution of the driver nodes of networks. In this manner, we may discover an optimal strategy for finding MDSs that satisfy specific constraints.

Author Contributions

Conceived and designed the experiments: XZ TL. Performed the experiments: XY BZ. Contributed reagents/materials/analysis tools: XZ TL. Wrote the paper: XZ TL.

References

1. Fortunato S (2010) Community detection in graphs. Physics Reports 486: 75–174.
2. Ghoshal G, Barabasi AL (2011) Ranking stability and super-stable nodes in complex networks. Nature Communications 2.
3. Karsai M, Kivela M, Pan RK, Kaski K, Kertesz J, et al. (2011) Small but slow world: How network topology and burstiness slow down spreading. Physical Review E 83.
4. Papadopoulos F, Kitsak M, Serrano MÁ, Boguná M, Krioukov D (2012) Popularity versus similarity in growing networks. Nature 489: 537–540.
5. Barabási AL, Albert R (1999) Emergence of scaling in random networks. Science 286: 509–512.
6. Watts DJ (1999) Networks, dynamics, and the small-world phenomenon. American Journal of Sociology 105: 493–527.
7. Vespignani A (2012) Modelling dynamical processes in complex socio-technical systems. Nature Physics 8: 32–39.
8. Stanoev A, Smilkov D, Kocarev L (2011) Identifying communities by influence dynamics in social networks. Physical Review E 84: 046102.
9. Palla G, Barabasi AL, Vicsek T (2007) Quantifying social group evolution. Nature 446: 664–667.

10. Lin CT (1974) Structural controllability. IEEE Transactions on Automatic Control, 19: 201–208.
11. Commault C, Dion JM, van der Woude JW (2002) Characterization of generic properties of linear structured systems for efficient computations. Kybernetika, 38(5): 503–520.
12. Hopcroft JE, Karp RM (1973) An n5/2 algorithm for maximum matchings in bipartite. SIAM J. Comput. 2: 225–231.
13. Liu YY, Slotine JJ, Barabasi AL (2011) Controllability of complex networks. Nature 473: 167–173.
14. Zdeborova L, Mezard M (2006) The number of matchings in random graphs. J. Stat. Mech. 05, 05003.
15. Wang WX, Ni X, Lai YC (2012) Optimizing controllability of complex networks by minimum structural perturbations. Physical Review E 85: 026115(5).
16. Müller FJ, Schuppert A (2011) Few inputs can reprogram biological networks. Nature 478: E4–E4.
17. Nepusz T, Vicsek T (2012) Controlling edge dynamics in complex networks. Nature Physics 8: 568–573.
18. Yan G, Ren J, Lai YC, Lai CH, Li B (2012) Controlling complex networks: How much energy is needed? Physical Review Letters 108: 218703.
19. Cowan NJ, Chastain EJ, Vilhena DA, Freudenberg JS, Bergstrom CT (2012) Nodal Dynamics, Not Degree Distributions, Determine the Structural Controllability of Complex Networks. PLoS ONE 7(6): e38398. doi:10.1371/journal.pone.0038398.
20. Valiant LG (1979) The complexity of computing the permanent. Theoretical Computer Science: 8(2), 189–201.
21. Kuhn HW (1955) The Hungarian method for the assignment problem. Naval research logistics quarterly 2: 83–97.
22. Berge C (1957) Two theorems in graph theory. Proceedings of the National Academy of Sciences of the United States of America 43: 842–844.
23. Leskovec J, Lang KJ, Dasgupta A, Mahoney MW (2009) Community structure in large networks: Natural cluster sizes and the absence of large well-defined clusters. Internet Mathematics 6: 29–123.
24. Dunne JA, Williams RJ, Martinez ND (2002) Food-web structure and network theory: the role of connectance and size. Proceedings of the National Academy of Sciences 99: 12917–12922.
25. Martinez ND (1991) Artifacts or attributes? Effects of resolution on the Little Rock Lake food web. Ecological Monographs: 367–392.
26. Christian RR, Luczkovich JJ (1999) Organizing and understanding a winter's seagrass foodweb network through effective trophic levels. Ecological Modelling 117: 99–124.
27. Ulanowicz RE, DeAngelis DL (2005) Network Analysis of Trophic Dynamics in South Florida Ecosystems. US Geological Survey Program on the South Florida Ecosystem: 114.
28. Patrıcio J, Ulanowicz R, Pardal M, Marques J (2004) Ascendency as an ecological indicator: a case study of estuarine pulse eutrophication. Estuarine, Coastal and Shelf Science 60: 23–35.
29. Watts D, Strogatz S (1998) Collective Dynamics of Small-World Networks. Nature 393: 440–442.
30. Leskovec J, Kleinberg J, Faloutsos C (2005) Graphs over time: densification laws, shrinking diameters and possible explanations. ACM SIGKDD International Conference on Knowledge Discovery and Data Mining (KDD): 177–187.
31. Pajek datasets website (2001) Available: http://vlado.fmf.uni-lj.si/pub/networks/data/cite/default.htm. Accessed 2014 Oct 15.
32. Adamic LA, Glance N (2005) The political blogosphere and the 2004 US election: divided they blog. Proceedings of the WWW-2005 Workshop on the Weblogging Ecosystem: 36–43.
33. Leskovec J, Kleinberg J, Faloutsos C (2007) Graph evolution: Densification and shrinking diameters. ACM Transactions on Knowledge Discovery from Data 1: 2.
34. Opsahl T, Panzarasa P (2009) Clustering in weighted networks. Social networks 31: 155–163.
35. Balaji S, Babu MM, Iyer LM, Luscombe NM, Aravind L (2006) Comprehensive analysis of combinatorial regulation using the transcriptional regulatory network of yeast. Journal of Molecular Biology 360: 213–227.
36. Norlen K, Lucas G, Gebbie M, Chuang J (2002) EVA: Extraction, visualization and analysis of the telecommunications and media ownership network. Proceedings of International Telecommunications Society 14th Biennial Conference (ITS2002), Seoul Korea, August 2002.
37. De Nooy W (1999) A literary playground: Literary criticism and balance theory. Poetics 26: 385–404.
38. Smith DA, White DR (1992) Structure and dynamics of the global economy: Network analysis of international trade 1965–1980. Social Forces 70: 857–893.
39. Barabási AL, Albert R (1999) Emergence of scaling in random networks. Science 286: 509–512.
40. Ruths J, Ruths D (2014) Control Profiles of Complex Networks. Science 343, 1373–1376. DOI:10.1126/science.1242063.
41. Foster JG, Foster DV, Grassberger P, Paczuski M (2010) Edge direction and the structure of networks. Proceedings of the National Academy of Sciences 107.24: 10815–10820.

24

A Service Brokering and Recommendation Mechanism for Better Selecting Cloud Services

Zhipeng Gui[1,2], **Chaowei Yang**[1]*, **Jizhe Xia**[1], **Qunying Huang**[1], **Kai Liu**[1], **Zhenlong Li**[1], **Manzhu Yu**[1], **Min Sun**[1], **Nanyin Zhou**[1], **Baoxuan Jin**[1]

1 NSF Spatiotemporal Innovation Center, George Mason University, Fairfax, Virginia, United States of America, **2** School of Remote Sensing and Information Engineering, Wuhan University, Wuhan, Hubei Province, China

Abstract

Cloud computing is becoming the new generation computing infrastructure, and many cloud vendors provide different types of cloud services. How to choose the best cloud services for specific applications is very challenging. Addressing this challenge requires balancing multiple factors, such as business demands, technologies, policies and preferences in addition to the computing requirements. This paper recommends a mechanism for selecting the best public cloud service at the levels of Infrastructure as a Service (IaaS) and Platform as a Service (PaaS). A systematic framework and associated workflow include cloud service filtration, solution generation, evaluation, and selection of public cloud services. Specifically, we propose the following: a hierarchical information model for integrating heterogeneous cloud information from different providers and a corresponding cloud information collecting mechanism; a cloud service classification model for categorizing and filtering cloud services and an application requirement schema for providing rules for creating application-specific configuration solutions; and a preference-aware solution evaluation mode for evaluating and recommending solutions according to the preferences of application providers. To test the proposed framework and methodologies, a cloud service advisory tool prototype was developed after which relevant experiments were conducted. The results show that the proposed system collects/updates/records the cloud information from multiple mainstream public cloud services in real-time, generates feasible cloud configuration solutions according to user specifications and acceptable cost predication, assesses solutions from multiple aspects (e.g., computing capability, potential cost and Service Level Agreement, SLA) and offers rational recommendations based on user preferences and practical cloud provisioning; and visually presents and compares solutions through an interactive web Graphical User Interface (GUI).

Editor: Moncho Gomez-Gesteira, University of Vigo, Spain

Funding: This research is supported by FGDC (G13PG00091), Microsoft Research, NSF (PLR-1349259, IIP-1338925, CNS-1117300). The funders had no role in study design, data collection and analysis, decision to publish, or preparation of the manuscript.

Competing Interests: The authors have declared that no competing interests exist.

* Email: cyang3@gmu.edu

Introduction

As a new computing paradigm, cloud computing provides the capability of delivering elastic and virtually unlimited computing capacity as the 5th utility [1]. The proliferation of cloud computing technologies is exemplified by the number of cloud vendors and their services, has produced numerous options for cloud users, and at the same time brings the complexities and challenges for selecting cloud service.

Applications and scientific research benefit from the virtually unlimited resources of cloud computing to meet the increasingly complicated and challenging requirements for computing resources [2–5]. Public cloud services provide convenience, including reducing the initial time investment and learning curve for building cloud solutions for users with limited knowledge on cloud computing. However, it is still a challenge to select the most suitable solution to deploy and configure applications due to the following reasons:

- **Application requirements**: different application features (e.g., data volume, data production rate, data transfer and updating, communication, computing intensities) result in varying computational intensity (e.g., data intensity, computing intensity, communication intensity) and disparate computing resource requirements (e.g., CPU, memory, storage, and network bandwidth).

- **Business expectations**: applications and potential users of the applications differ, which result in different budget investments (fee constraints) and expectations of cloud services. Meanwhile, various pricing models (e.g., on demand/reserved/bidding mode), pricing items (e.g., VM, dedicated server, storage, IP, network, software packages, custom services) and business strategies further complicate the selection.

- **Capacity provisioning**: commercial and open-source cloud services adopt different IT technologies (e.g., virtualization, storage) and have unique strengths and weaknesses. The learning curve to fully understand these technologies is steep.

- **Cloud information collection and process**: to compare cloud services, users "march" through multiple websites individually to collect the required information and conduct assessments manually (e.g., cost analysis). This manual process is time-consuming.

The interweaving of these factors makes cloud service selection problematic. It is not only a technical issue but a decision-making problem, involving trade-offs among business expectations, investment cost, capacity provisioning, application requirements, rules and policies [6]. Making a sensible and correct decision is not easy for all levels of experienced users as applications, options and platforms can vary significantly.

There is valuable research on cloud service measurement, simulation, evaluation, brokering, and state-of-the-art cloud advisory systems. However, for specific applications, there is no comprehensive research integrating application preferences/ constraints, computational features, and real-world cloud resource provisioning to assist with the generation, comparison and recommendation of cloud solutions. This research proposes a brokering and recommendation mechanism coupled with a corresponding tool to assist users to compare and select cloud solutions. Such a system leverages the following capabilities: 1) automatically collect heterogeneous cloud information from different cloud services and depict a uniform information model; 2) generate specific configuration solutions by aggregating different cloud resources for target applications (i.e., cloud solutions) based on users' preferences and constraints; 3) evaluate and recommend cloud solutions by leveraging multiple selection criteria (e.g., potential cost and the fitness upon computational requirements and features). Based on such a mechanism, a cloud advisory tool with integrated computing experiences and knowledge is capable of recommending cloud solutions for achieving both cost-efficiency and high performance. Each of these cardinal features is the basis for Section 1 of this paper. The remainder is organized as follows: Section 2 reviews related work; Section 3 introduces the methodologies and system architecture; Section 4 reports the implementation of the prototypes, experiment and results; and Section 5 concludes the paper and discusses future research and development.

Related Work

2.1 Cloud Service Measurement, Simulation and Evaluation

Cloud metrics (http://collaborate.nist.gov/twiki-cloud-computing/ bin/view/CloudComputing/RATax_CloudMetrics) is the foundation for cloud measurements, evaluation, and selection to assist cloud consumers to compare and understand the advantages and disadvantages of cloud services. Research has been conducted on establishing cloud metrics [7–9] and metrics-based evaluation algorithms [10,11]. Specifically, Repschläger et al. [8] proposed a provider independent classification model with six target dimensions to compare IaaS providers. Martens et al. [9] summarized a maturity evaluation model for cloud services with nine different characteristics (e.g., SLAs, scalability, auditability, security). The degree of maturity is calculated using the weighted average of the criteria. National Institute for Standards and Technology (NIST) cloud Reference Architecture and Taxonomy Working Group (RATax WG) created a Cloud Metrics Sub Group to explore open issues and establish a consistent and operable measurement to enable stakeholders to communicate efficiently by standardizing the criteria and associated models [13]. The Cloud Service Measurement Initiative Consortium (CSMIC, http://csmic.org/) developed the Service Measurement Index (SMI) to define global measures for cloud service [14]. Despite progress, further efforts are needed to define consistent, reusable, and operational models to support comprehensive and objective measurements of cloud services [15].

A performance and application-based mechanism is best to evaluate open-source cloud solutions and commercial cloud services [16,17]. CloudCmp [18] is a performance comparison tool developed to measure elastic computing, persistent storage and networking services. To investigate the readiness of public cloud services for supporting scientific computing, Jackson et al. [19] tested the performance of Amazon web services using eight selected high performance computing applications. Iosup et al. [20] conducted many-tasks performance analysis on four services of Amazon EC2, GoGrid, ElasticHosts and Mosso. Farley et al. [21] investigated the performance heterogeneity of supposedly identical instances and explored heterogeneity-aware placement strategies to find better-performing instances. Huang et al. [22] evaluated the readiness of open-source cloud solutions for supporting geospatial applications. The basic features and performances of three open source cloud software (i.e., Open-Nebula, Eucalyputus and CloudStack) were compared in terms of cloud resource operation and geoscience application [22].

Simulation provides theoretical approaches to assist cloud service selection. CloudSim [23] is a toolkit to model and simulate a cloud computing environment. The toolkit provides a repeatable, controllable and cost-free environment for cloud customers to test their applications. CloudMIG [24,25] is a simulation-based environment and user interface to evaluate cloud deployment options for supporting cloud migration. CloudMIG compares cloud service solutions and checks conformance and simulate workloads for envisioned cloud-based target architectures. Moreover, a genetic algorithm to optimize software deployment and reconfiguration rules is proposed [26] based upon CloudMIG, which relies on architecture analysis of target software. In order to capture code structures and their dependencies, and to check potential constraints violation in cloud environment, all source codes and dependent libraries must be imported and analyzed in CloudMIG. The code analysis process is time-consuming and introduces code privacy issues.

To help end users understand their Return On Investment (ROI), cost models were developed to estimate potential cost composition and utilization of imbalanced factors. Li et al. [27] developed an amortization and utilization models to calculate cloud Total Cost of Ownership (TCO) and Utilization Cost, respectively. Andrzejak [28] proposed a probabilistic model for optimizing monetary costs, performance and reliability given application requirements and dynamic conditions. The model helps consumers bid optimally on Amazon EC2 Spot Instances (http://aws.amazon.com/ec2/spot-instances/). A dynamic resource allocation algorithm [29] based on Model Predictive Control (MPC) best matches cloud customer demand with supply and price. The method maximizes the provider's ROI while minimizing energy cost.

The research provides theoretical methods to measure, simulate and evaluate cloud services. More specifically, the cloud metrics comprehensively measures cloud service. Simulation is a mechanism to study clouds' behaviors, capacities and status.

Performance analysis compares cloud solutions in a quantitative manner but rarely consider user preferences, constraints and computational features. To address this problem, we designed an operational service classification model for comparing different services and propose an application requirement schema to represent application-specific requirements and user preferences. However, there is no comprehensive consideration of application owner's preferences/constraints, computational feature of target applications and real-world cloud resource provisioning. The mechanism to integrate these methodologies for assisting generation, comparison and recommendation of cloud configuration solutions has not been systematically investigated.

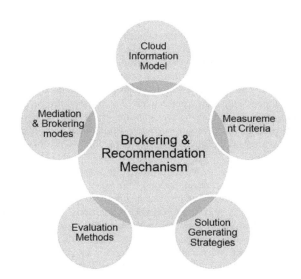

Figure 1. Building blocks of cloud brokering and recommendation mechanism.

2.2 Cloud Brokering Mechanism

Current cloud offerings have the following deficiencies [30]: limited scalability of single cloud service; lack of interoperability among cloud services; and no built-in business service management support. The brokering approach efficiently mediates, advertises and integrates heterogeneous cloud information and resources from different cloud providers.

The Reservoir model [30] draws a blue-print to open federate cloud services. In this architecture, cloud providers dynamically partner with each other to create an infinite IT resource pool while preserving their individual autonomy in making technological and

business management decisions. Buyya et al. [31] proposed the utility-oriented federal cloud computing environment InterCloud, supporting auto-scaling across multiple vendor clouds. InterCloud dynamically expands and contracts to handle sudden changes in service demands. It consistently achieves QoS targets under various workload, resource and network conditions. To achieve a federate cloud framework still requires further development of tightly-coupled mechanisms and agreements to manipulate and integrate resources from multiple providers.

Goscinski and Brock [32] proposed a systematic method to publish, discover and select cluster resources by establishing a Resources Via Web Service framework (RVWS) using Service-Oriented Architecture (SOA). Under this framework, a cluster is encapsulated as a stateful web service using Web Service Resource Framework (WSRF) and is published through a dynamic discovery broker. The client queries and selects matched cluster based on resource states (e.g., free disk, free memory, CPU usage) and cluster characteristics (e.g., core number, core speed, hardware architecture). This framework provides an efficient method to monitor and manipulate the cluster through a web service interface. Although the proposed method is extendable to other cloud resources, most public cloud services do not yet provide such a mechanism to publicly describe and publish their resource offerings for discovery and selection. Furthermore, the real-time states of computing infrastructures may be non-transparent to the public [33].

These brokering mechanisms and federation frameworks mediates and integrates cloud services. However, the interoperability environment is too immature to achieve seamless and flexible integration. The specifications and initiatives for advertising, mediating, manipulating and orchestrating cloud services are at early stage. As such, declaring stateless resource provisioning through web pages/APIs is the primary channel to share cloud information. The method to efficiently collect and fuse cloud information from heterogeneous sources is a practical and critical.

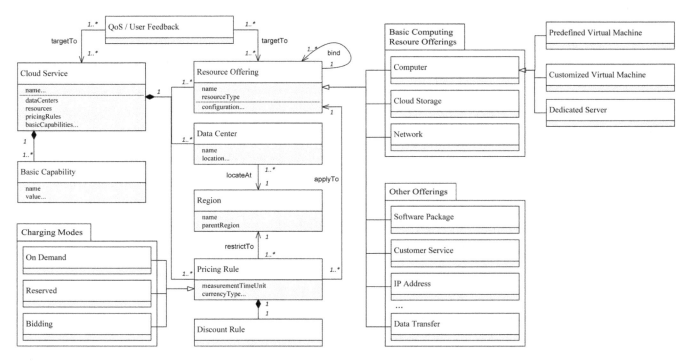

Figure 2. High-level hierarchy of cloud information model.

We propose a unified cloud information model and related collecting methods.

2.3 State-of-the-Art Cloud Advisory System

Cloud advisory websites simplify the search and comparison of cloud service by integrating information through one-stop portals. Service filtering and user reviews are two widely-supported basic functions. The former uses a feature-based (e.g., technology characteristics) filtering function to facilitate service matching, while the latter provides an approach to collect user feedback and conduct experience-based ratings. Data Center Map (http://www.datacentermap.com/cloud.html) combines a map-based visualization function and feature-based filter function. The map view visualizes the geographical distribution of data centers and IaaS cloud servers through Google Maps, where users search resources in certain regions, browse profiles, grade and conduct reviews. FindTheBest (http://cloud-computing.findthebest.com/) provides purchasing guidance and explains basic factors and concepts in cloud service selection. Furthermore, it personalizes ranking rules by allowing users to specify the important factors (e.g., compatible OS, control interface, support features, cost).

Third-party auditing provides a trustable understanding of the performance, reliability, and consistency of cloud services. Global Provider Viewer (https://cloudsleuth.net/global-provider-view) is a web-based tool for collecting and visually analyzing the performance and availability of PaaS and IaaS in a near real-time manner. It continuously monitors the top cloud services globally *via* Internet backbone locations by running a sample web application for each of the cloud services. The response time and availability of cloud services are analyzed at multiple geographical (e.g., global, continental, regional, city) and time (e.g., hours, days, months) scales. To better support visual analytics, multiple display methods (e.g., map view, linear series diagram, data tables) are integrated through web Rich Internet Application (RIA) technologies. The adopted quality monitoring method is proper for typical web applications. In order to comprehensively evaluate cloud services for different applications (e.g., scientific computing, business transactions), an elaborate auditing and monitoring architecture needs to be designed.

The developments of cloud service monitoring tools and advisory websites facilitate the measurement and comparison of cloud services. Besides collecting cloud information and visually comparing cloud services, an advisory system should generate application-specific configuration solutions upon real cloud provisioning and provide recommendations on specific application requirements and user preferences. To address this need, we developed a preference-aware solution evaluation model. The model predicts cost, measures VM computational capability and conducts an overall evaluation based on the importance of selected criteria.

In summary and to assist cloud service selection, a systematic brokering and recommendation framework is needed. This framework should integrate cloud information from multiple cloud providers, and create/evaluate solutions based on the application owners' requirements. We propose such a framework and introduce the corresponding models, methods and architecture. Instead of assessing cloud at service level, this research focuses on concrete configuration solutions (finer granularity) for applications upon application owners' requirements and real public cloud service (both IaaS and PaaS) resource offerings. The prototype generates feasible solutions, calculates potential cost, and evaluates/makes recommendations based on proposed models. The solutions give valuable references for specific applications in cloud adoption. The proposed framework and methods provide conceptual guidelines for designing and developing relevant advisory systems.

Methodologies & System Architecture

To establish a systematic recommendation mechanism and to develop advisory systems sequentially, sophisticated methods and technologies should be developed (Fig. 1) that have the five charcateristics First, a unified cloud information model is essential to synthesize and depict heterogeneous cloud information. Second, mediation and brokering modes provide approaches to mediate and integrate information from different sources (e.g., cloud providers, auditors, consumers). Third, a model of measurement criteria facilitates solution filtering and evaluation by measuring capabilities of cloud services/solutions in qualitative and quantitive terms. Four, solution strategies determine modes and rules to

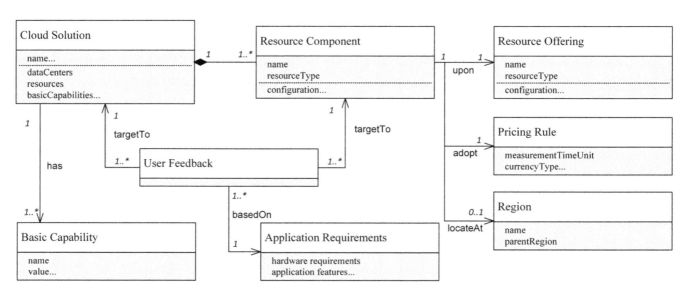

Figure 3. Structure of cloud solution.

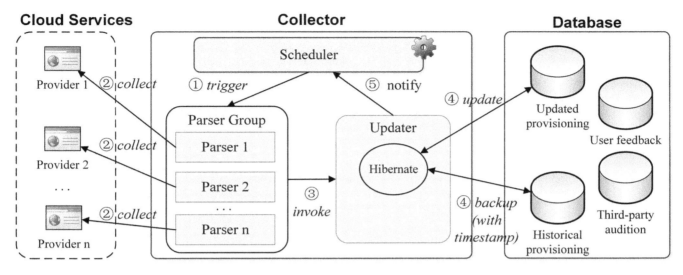

Figure 4. Structure and updating workflow of cloud collector.

generate solutions. And five, evaluation methods provide effective and preference-aware approaches to rank cloud solutions according to users' requirements.

3.1 A Unified Cloud Information Model

To evaluate cloud solutions, information needs to be fused, including resource offerings and pricing rules published by cloud providers, performance monitored by third-party audits and

feedback from cloud users. The information originates from heterogeneous sources and is expressed differently. Even for widely-used public cloud services, different terminologies and expressions describe their provisioning, so a uniform and sophisticated information model is essential to manage heterogeneous information.

By generalizing information provided by ten public cloud services (section 4.3), audit performance and user feedback for

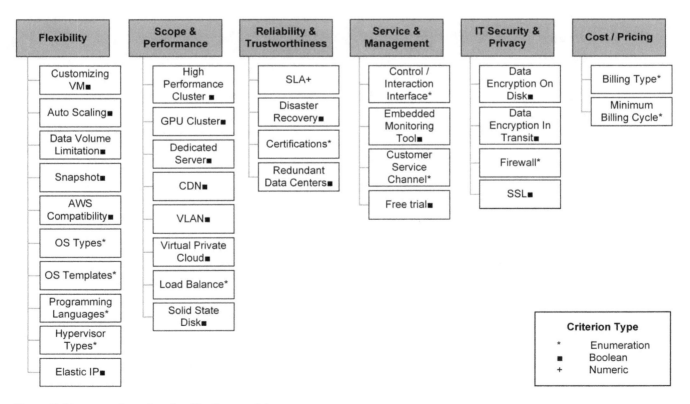

Figure 5. Structure of service classification model.

Table 1. Parameters of application requirement schema.

Category/Source	Category Item	Description	Value Expression
Hardware Requirements/User specified or Predefined default values according to application type	VM Number +	expected machine number	<min, prefer>
	RAM +	physical memory size per machine (GB)	<min, prefer>
	CPU Core +	core number per machine	<min, prefer>
	CPU Speed +	speed of each core (GHz)	<min, prefer>
	Local Disk Size +	physical storage space per machine (GB)	<min, prefer>
	Bandwidth +	expected network speed (Mb/s)	<min, prefer>
	VM GeoLocation *	machine location constraint/preference	Region_ID
	Cloud Storage GeoLocation *	cloud storage location constraint/preference	Region_ID
	Hybird Solution ∎	whether cloud resources can come from different providers	true/false
Application Features/User specified or generated according to intensity features	Application Type *	types of the target application	AppType_ID
	OS Type *	required operating system to run, the application	OS_ID
	Application Size +	application size (after extra disk space) installation/deployment)	$<\mu, \sigma>$ or $<\mu$, min, max>
	Extra Local Disk Size +	local data and switching space	$<\mu, \sigma>$ or $<\mu$, min, max>
	VM Ingress Traffic +	ingress speed for each (virtual) machine (Mbps)	$<\mu, \sigma>$ or $<\mu$, min, max>
	VM Egress Traffic +	egress speed for each (virtual) machine (Mbps)	$<\mu, \sigma>$ or $<\mu$, min, max>
	Traffic Among VMs +	communication speed between machines	$<\mu, \sigma>$ or $<\mu$, min, max>
	Concurrent Access Number +	concurrent access number to the application	$<\mu, \sigma>$ or $<\mu$, min, max>
	Use Cloud Storage ∎	whether use cloud storage to store data	true/false
	Cloud Data Volume +	potential data volume used on cloud storage	$<\mu, \sigma>$ or $<\mu$, min, max>
	Storage Ingress Traffic +	data transfer-in speed for cloud storage (Mbps)	$<\mu, \sigma>$ or $<\mu$, min, max>
	Storage Egress Traffic +	data transfer-out speed for cloud storage (Mbps)	$<\mu, \sigma>$ or $<\mu$, min, max>
	VM to Storage Traffic +	communication from machine to storage (Mbps)	$<\mu, \sigma>$ or $<\mu$, min, max>
	Storage to VM Traffic +	communication from storage to machine (Mbps)	$<\mu, \sigma>$ or $<\mu$, min, max>
	Data Durability *	reliability demand for data stored on cloud storage	durability type
Payment Preferences/User specified	Rental Time +	time period to rental cloud resources	[t1, t2]
	Fee Constraint +	acceptable maximum monetary cost	upperBound
	Billing Type *	Pay as you go/subscription/bidding/...	BillingType_ID

cloud solution generation and evaluation, we propose a cloud information mode whose high-level hierarchy is illustrated (Fig.2). The top level element is Cloud Service, a service provided by a specific vendor. A *Cloud Service* is composed of four components: *Data Center*, *Basic Capability*, *Resource Offering* and *Pricing Rule*. The *Data Centers* are the physical allocation of Cloud Infrastructure and is an indicator for applications which need to meet geo-location related policy restrictions by avoiding cross boundary issues. *Basic Capabilities* describe technical (e.g., VLAN, data encryption, hypervisor type) or business modes (e.g., reserved or bidding pricing) that determine if the service is supported. These indicators can be used as filtering criteria. A *Resource Offering* depicts a physical/virtual resource, function or service provided by a cloud provider, which may be charged by usage or not at all. It is divided into basic computing resource offerings (i.e., computer, cloud storage, network) and complementary offerings (e.g., software package, OS template, customer service, snapshot/imaging/data backup/data transfer functions). To support differ-

ent charging modes, the model defines three sub-types of Pricing Rules (i.e., on demand, reserved bidding modes). A *Pricing Rule* specifies a charging mode for a certain resource offering in a certain region because charging modes are geo-location related. Each rule has an associated measurement time unit and currency type. A resource offering may provide multiple charging modes. To support different charging modes, the model defines three sub-types of Pricing Rules (i.e., on demand, reserved and bidding modes).

Association relations are significant in this mode for several reasons. First, the Data Center and pricing rule are associated with Regional object as they are location related. Second, third-party Quality of Service (QoS) and user feedback are linked with cloud services or concrete resource offerings instead of being added as list properties. This makes the connection more flexible since the QoS and feedback are user-specific and changing frequently. Third, the setting of pricing rules and resource offering modes depends on the providers' business strategies, technical status and specific application demands, and different cloud services have different settings. For instances, services may offer multiple resources in batches as binding resources, whereas others offer them separately. To address this problem, the model describes basic Resource Offerings at an atomic resource level allowing them to be combined with each other through association relations. In summary, through an extendable hierarchical structure and associations among components, the information model is used for multiple cloud services.

Based on the above model, a cloud solution that users could adopt for their applications is expressed as a composition of multiple resource components (Fig. 3). A resource component is a resource offering at a certain region and with certain pricing rules. Resource components of a single solution can be provided by different services (e.g., hybrid solution in which cloud storage is envisioned by different providers). A solution can inherit basic capabilities from resource providers and the resourcing offerings.

3.2 Collecting and Managing Cloud Service Information

Collecting and managing up-to-date and heterogeneous cloud information from different cloud providers are critical for a cloud service recommendation system.

3.2.1 Collecting Cloud Service Information. Normally, the pricing rules and resource offerings of cloud services are frequently adjusted and published on the cloud providers' websites. Only a few providers offer web service-based APIs and specifications to the public. To automatically collect the information in a near real-time manner, we adopt a combined strategy of web page parsing and web APIs invocation. A proposed structure and interactions of an information collector are illustrated in Figure 4. A scheduler triggers update events on a daily basis and invokes the parsers in parser group. The parsers collect information through either web page parsing or web APIs invocation. For each cloud service, a dedicated parser translates collected information into entities and relations in the cloud information model. An updater inserts collected information into the database.

3.2.2 Storage and Update of Cloud Information. The database contains four components (Fig. 4) as follows: user feedback for recording user reviews and grades; third-party audition for storing the performance summaries from auditors; updated provisioning for storing the latest information collected from cloud providers; and historical provisioning for recording every change in cloud provisioning for further analysis. To avoid redundancy, only changed atomic items are updated. For example, once the on-demand tenant price of a certain VM type changes, the price of related *Pricing Rule* in update provisioning is updated, after which a new *Pricing Rule* record associated with updating timestamp is inserted into historical provisioning. To avoid complex SQL operation on inserting, updating and retrieving, Hibernate is used to manipulate the information model and database.

3.3 Service Filtering Using an Operable Service Classification Model

The service classification model are criteria organized with hierarchical tree structures to measure capabilities, limits and offerings of cloud services in logical and/or operable criterion layers (Fig. 5). The logical layer is a series of dimensions which describes capabilities demanded conceptually and which contain operational criteria. An operational criterion corresponds to a measureable and comparable atomic indicator describing a service-level feature of the cloud provider independently from any concrete service offering (e.g., existing certifications and IT infrastructure characteristics).

Six dimensions of the model (Fig. 3) based on relevant cloud metrics [7,8,14] were selected. First flexibility is a cardinal feature of cloud service, having the advantage of agility and scalability compared to traditional solutions. Within this characteristic, ten criteria are used for standardization of API, fertility of selectably predefined OS and software, customization of hardware and software, and scalability of capability offering. Second, *scope and performance* measures computational performance using a group of hardware/software criteria. Three, reliability and trustworthiness define how certain the customer is served as promised by the cloud provider. Trustworthiness is measured *via* provider's infrastructure features (e.g., disaster recovery, certifications, redundant sites). Four, service and management addresses features that determine the convenience of cloud service usages, including types and friendliness of user interfaces, auxiliary service options (e.g., monitoring, reporting) and customer service channels. Five, IT security and privacy are security related technical indicators. Six, cost/price addresses monetary consideration, including billing and penalty models.

These dimensions cover the most important aspects of cloud measurement, and the criteria are from well-accepted technical concepts [7,8,10,12–14] and popular cloud services (section 4.3.1). Most criteria are qualitative, indicating whether a function/ capability is supported or which types it supports. Thus, users with some cloud experiences can specify their service filtering rules. In addition, the model is not limited to the selected dimensions and criteria but can be expanded. Using these criteria, cloud providers are compared, classified and filtered. The model guarantees that the filtered services meet the user's demands at the service level. Meanwhile, service filtering makes cloud solution generation (next step) more efficiently since solutions are generated through qualified services only instead of all services.

3.4 Solution Generating with an Application-Dependent Requirement Description Schema

After selecting preferred and qualified cloud service, generating configuration and deployment solutions are the next task. So the generated cloud solutions match the requirements of specific applications, an elaborate requirement description at the application level is needed. We proposed an application-dependent requirement description schema (Table 1) consisting of three hardware requirements, application features and payment preferences.

Three features of this table are relevant. First, the hardware requirements specify the qualified hardware configuration to run the application. For numeric parameters, the minimum and preferred configurations are required. Second, application features describe the software requirements and computational features. The numeric parameters are derived from statistical values (e.g., mean value or μ, standard deviation or σ, minimum value or *min* and maximum value or *max*) because of the inherent uncertainty and statistical features. Three, in payment preference, rental times are modeled as a time range (from minimum to maximum), while fee constraint is expressed as the acceptable maximum monetary cost.

The function of criteria in service classification model is service filtering. The parameters in the application requirement schema depict the application-specific requirements in detail. More parameters are quantitative and fine-grained. Based on the schema, the cloud solutions can be generated using qualified resource offerings (e.g., VM types, cloud storage types). Moreover,

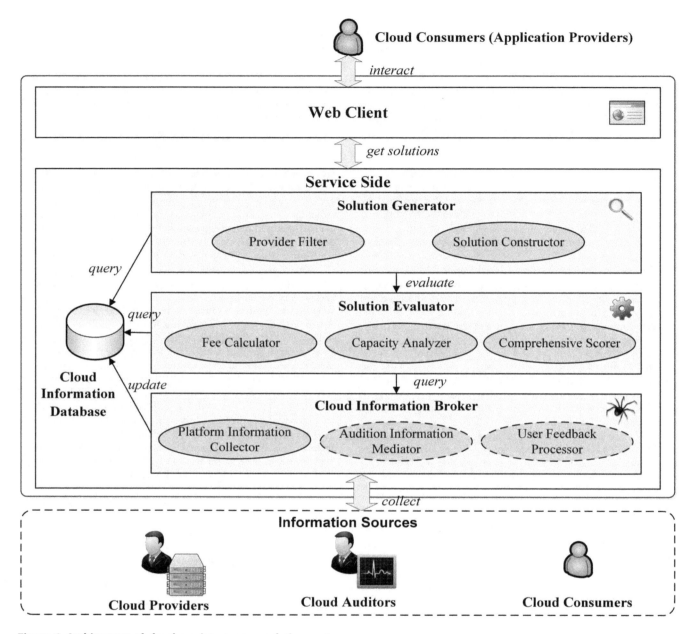

Figure 6. Architecture of cloud service recommendation system.

the schema provides essential information for potential rental fee prediction and analysis on computational intensity features.

3.5 Preference-Aware Solution Evaluation Mode

Cloud solution selection is a Multi-Objective Decision Making (MODM) [34] process [11,12] and in which multiple criteria (e.g., fee, SLA, performance, customer service) are objectives. In selecting multiple objectives, there is always a trade-off as one objective may influence/compromise another (i.e., Pareto efficiency). No universal evaluation principle maximizes the satisfactions to all requirements. Moreover, individual users have different preferences for their objectives. Accordingly, we propose a preference-aware evaluation, in which users select options to interactively change the importance of other objectives according

to their preferences; and importantly this interactive evaluation and ranking happens "on-the-fly".

In this paper, six criteria for demonstrated objectives are selected as follows: fee cost, VM computing capacity, SLA, user feedback, customer services and software ecosystem. Fee cost is the potential monetary cost for cloud services, and VM computing capacity measures the computational capability of the adopted individual VM. The SLA is the service-level agreement announced by cloud providers, while user feedback collects user, experience-based evaluation information complementing third-party measurement based methods. Customer service measures the convenience and quality of customer service. And finally, software ecosystem measures the fertility of software products provided by the cloud or contributed by third parties and the maturity of the software resource market of the cloud provider. To further define this

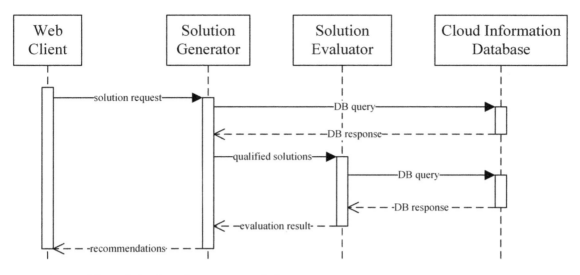

Figure 7. Interaction workflow of cloud service recommendation.

criteria, each is assigned a level of importance as follows: *Unimportant*, *Less important*, *Moderate*, *Important* and *Very Important*. To make sure the selected cloud solution is balanced with the multiple objectives, Eq. (1) is adopted:

$$S_i = \Pi_{j=1}^{k} S_{i,j}^{j} \quad (0 \leq s_{i,j}, S_i \leq 1) \qquad (1)$$

The S_i is the synthesized cumulative score for solution I and K is the number of objectives. The $s_{i,j}$ is the normalized score of the jth objective for solution I, and w_j is the importance of objective j. The predefined weights are 0, 0.3, 0.5, 1 and 2 for *Unimportant*, *Less important*, *Moderate*, *Important* and *Very Important*, in series. Given this equation, if all objectives are important, any one objective with a low score causes a low cumulative score for the solution. Conversely, if one objective is unimportant to the user, the score of this one objective does not affect the cumulative score. Therefore, this equation reflects user preferences on objective importance and helps balance the objectives. The scores of fee cost, VM computing capacity and user feedback for each solution are dynamically calculated in the solution evaluation stage, whereas the others are service level objectives calculated in

advance. Specifically, the user feedback score is calculated by summarizing the collected grades (about involved cloud services and resources) from third-party cloud advisory systems. The SLA is collected from cloud providers' websites, and customer service is measured by counting the service channel types and collecting user feedback. The software ecosystem score is calculated by counting the type and number of provisioned software. The calculation of fee cost and VM computing capacity are discussed in the following subsections.

3.5.1 Fee prediction. The ROI is a determining factor in cloud service/solution selection. To choose cost-effective solutions that meet users' budget constraints, a model is needed to predict monetary cost for each solution. Although variation exists on modes of resource offerings and billing for different cloud providers, a general model is proposed (Eq. 2):

$$Total_{fee}(t) = VM_{fee} + DataTransfer_{fee} + Software_{fee} \\ + Support_{fee} + Other_{fee} \qquad (2)$$

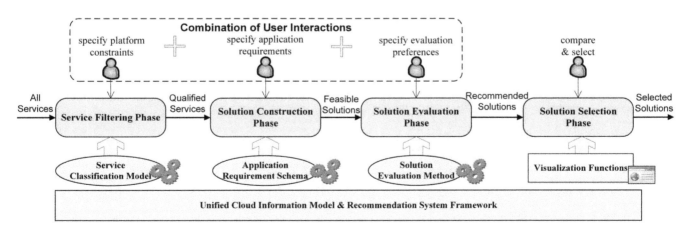

Figure 8. Workflow of four-phase recommendation framework.

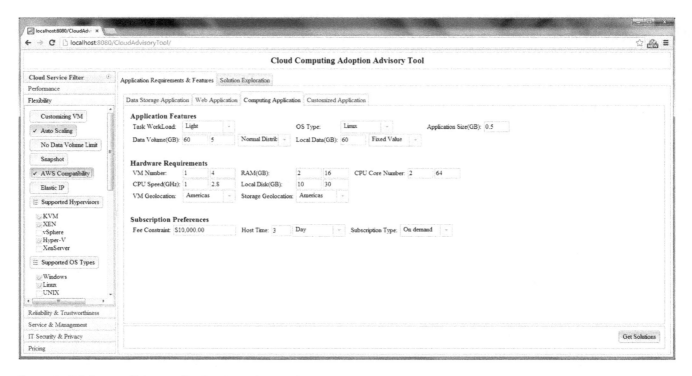

Figure 9. GUI for specifying application & service requirement.

The model's parameters are defined as follows: total fee (Total$_{fee}$) is a function of rental time t; VM$_{fee}$ is the fee spent on VMs tenancy; Storage$_{fee}$ is the fee for employing cloud storage or cloud databases (e.g., SQL Azure); DataTransfer$_{fee}$ is the potential service fee for data transfer; Support$_{fee}$ is the customer service fee; Software$_{fee}$ is the license fee or the fee charged for using extra software packages not included in basic software stack of a VM (e.g., Hadoop, SQL Server); Other$_{fee}$ includes fees for elastic IP

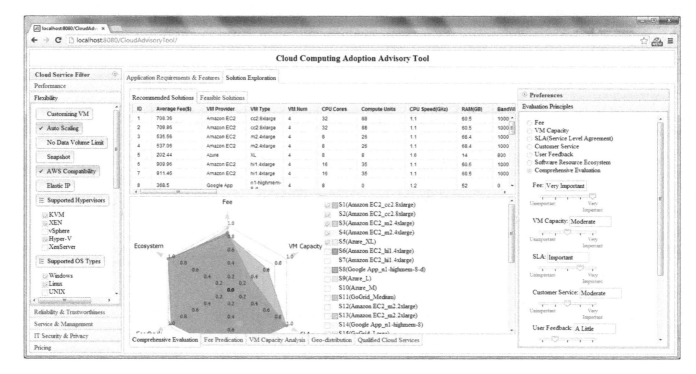

Figure 10. GUI for cloud solution exploration.

ID	Average Fee($)	VM Provider	VM Type	VM Num	CPU Cores	Compute Units	CPU Speed(GHz)	RAM(GB)	BandWidth(Mbps)	Local Disk(GB)	OS Type	VM Service Mode	Storage Provider
1	708.36	Amazon EC2	cc2.8xlarge	4	32	88	1.1	60.5	10000	3370	Linux	Shared	Amazon EC2
2	709.86	Amazon EC2	cc2.8xlarge	4	32	88	1.1	60.5	10000	3370	Linux	Shared	Amazon EC2
3	535.56	Amazon EC2	m2.4xlarge	4	8	26	1.1	68.4	1000	1690	Linux	Shared	Amazon EC2
4	537.06	Amazon EC2	m2.4xlarge	4	8	26	1.1	68.4	1000	1690	Linux	Shared	Amazon EC2
5	202.44	Azure	XL	4	8	8	1.6	14	800	2644	WhatEver	Shared	Azure
6	909.96	Amazon EC2	hi1.4xlarge	4	16	35	1.1	60.5	10000	2048	Linux	Shared	Amazon EC2
7	911.46	Amazon EC2	hi1.4xlarge	4	16	35	1.1	60.5	10000	2048	Linux	Shared	Amazon EC2
8	368.5	Google App	n1-highmem-8-d	4	8	0	1.2	52	0	3540	WhatEver	Shared	Google App
9	110.28	Azure	L	4	4	4	1.6	7	400	1284	WhatEver	Shared	Azure
10	64.2	Azure	M	4	2	2	1.6	3.5	200	624	WhatEver	Shared	Azure
11	63.24	GoGrid	Medium	4	2	2	2	2	1024	100	WhatEver	Shared	GoGrid

Figure 11. Data tables for recommended solutions and all feasible solutions.

address, extra network services (e.g., exclusive Content Delivery Network), and communication/processing/responding to different requests from others.

A cloud utilization fee is usually charged as a function of usage. The mutability of cloud usage may incur an uncertainty for the utilization fee, making it difficult to offer a precise prediction. To address this, a treat fee is introduced as a mean value with an estimated range (from potential minimum to maximum fee). Using the statistical values in the application requirement model, a rational range (e.g., $[max\{0, \mu - 3\sigma\}, \mu + 3\sigma]$ or $[min, max]$) for each application feature parameter is defined. Upon the ranges, the potential cloud disk usage and data transfer volume are calculated, and, total range and mean fees are calculated by summing the different fee components.

Based on the total fee, fee scores are calculated (Eq. 3) and normalized (Eq. 4).

$$s_i' = a * u_i(fee) + b * (max_i(fee) - min_i(fee)) \qquad (3)$$

$$s_i = (max_{i=1}^{n}\{s_i'\} - s_i')/(max_{i=1}^{n}\{s_i'\} - min_{i=1}^{n}\{s_i'\}) \qquad (4)$$

For a cloud solution, $u_i(fee)$, $min_i(fee)$ and $max_i(fee)$ are the mean fee and two boundaries of the fee range in series, while a and b are weights. The n is the number of generated solution candidates. As the range interval is minimized, the predicted fee becomes more stable and mutability is reduced. Thus, the solution

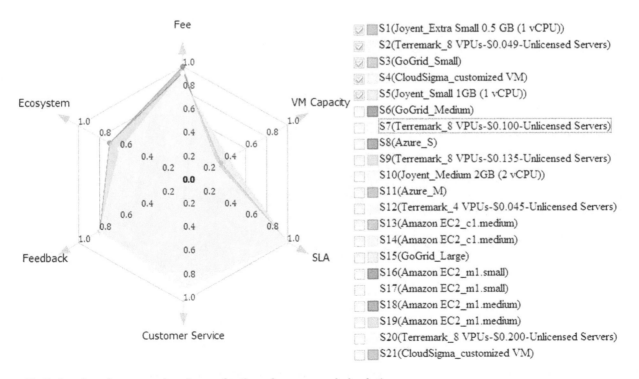

Figure 12. Rader chart for comprehensive evaluation of recommended solutions.

with a low mean cost and small range interval (low standard deviation) is a good solution.

3.5.2 VM computational capability. The computational capability of a computing resource dictates its feasibility for individual applications. Multiple applications have a range of computational intensity features reflecting different hardware requirements.

To match the most suitable VM hardware configuration to the application features from numerous potential solutions, a computational capability measurement model is proposed based on the Technique for Order of Preference by Similarity to Ideal Solution (TOPSIS) [35,36]. Six hardware indicators measure computation-

al capability: *CPU core number, CPU speed, computing unit, RAM size, local disk size and bandwidth.* The first four are for computing performance. Local disk size measures VM storage capacity, whereas bandwidth measures network I/O performance.

The six indicators are normalized and weighed using Eq. (5):

$$v_{i,j} = w_j * \frac{v'_{i,j} - \min_{i=1}^{n}\{v'_{i,j}\}}{\max_{i=1}^{n}\{v'_{i,j}\} - \min_{i=1}^{n}\{v'_{i,j}\}} \quad j = \{1,...,m\} \quad (5)$$

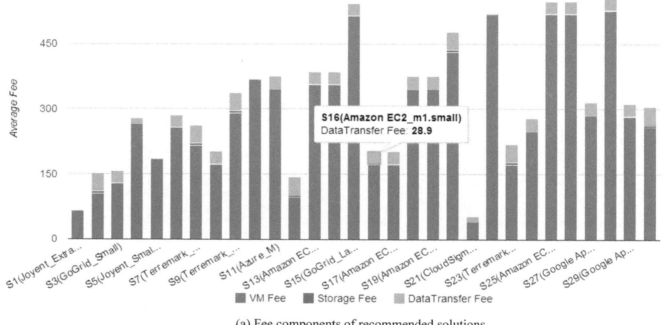

(a) Fee components of recommended solutions

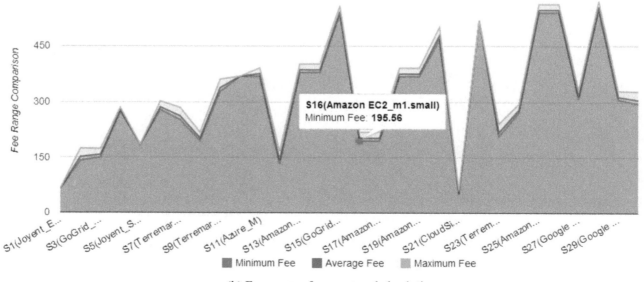

(b) Fee range of recommended solutions

Figure 13. Potential fee ranges of recommended solutions: (a) fee components of recommended solutions; (b) fee range of recommended solutions.

With $v'_{i,j}$ as the value of jth indicator for the ith cloud solution, m as the number of indicators, and w_j as the importance of the indictor j for specific application (subject to). $\sum_{j=1}^{m} w_j = 1$ The weights are determined using Analytical Hierarchical Process (AHP) [12] and application intensity features.

$$s_i = d_i^- / (d_i^- + d_i^*) \quad 1 \leq i \leq n \tag{6}$$

Since each of these selected indicators is positive (i.e., the higher value, the better the indicator), the positive ideal weighted value (v_j^*) and negative ideal weighted value (v_j^-) for indicator j are the largest and smallest weighted values in all solutions, respectively. The score s_i of each cloud solution i is calculated using Eq. (6) by considering the distances to positive and negative ideal solutions, calculated using Eq. (7) and (8), respectively.

$$d_i^* = [\sum_{j=1}^{m} (v_j^* - v_{i,j})^2]^{1/2} \quad 1 \leq i \leq n \tag{7}$$

$$d_i^- = [\sum_{j=1}^{m} (v_j^- - v_{i,j})^2]^{1/2} \quad 1 \leq i \leq n \tag{8}$$

The higher the score value, the better the computational capabilities for a given application. The proposed model makes the computational capability of solutions quantitatively comparable. More specifically, the weighing mechanism introduces the indicator importance by considering different application scenarios, and the distances to positive and negative ideal solutions reflects the relative advantages and disadvantages on computing capacities of a solution in all solution candidates.

Implementation and Experiments

4.1 System Architecture and Workflow

To implement, integrate and verify the proposed models, methods and technologies, the following architecture of cloud service recommendation system and recommendation workflow are proposed.

4.1.1 Architecture. The architecture is based on the following components (Fig. 6):

The *Web Client* controls user interactions and provides solution presentation and visualization functions to assist in cloud solution selection. The server side includes four components: *Solution Generator*; *Solution Evaluator*; *Cloud Information Broker*; and *Cloud Information Database*. The *Solution Generator* generates feasible cloud solutions as a function of user inputs. It contains two sub-components: a *Service Filter* selects qualified cloud service from all service candidates according to service-level restrictions; and a *Solution Constructor* constructs feasible solutions based on application requirements and qualified services generated by the *Service Filter*. The *Solution Evaluator* assesses the suitability of the generated solutions according to application requirements and user's selection preferences. While a *Fee Calculator* calculates the potential fee cost, a *Capacity Analyzer* analyzes computational capacity. A *Comprehensive Scorer* grades and ranks solutions by counting multiple factors, and a *Cloud Information Broker* collects and integrates information from different sources and updates the *Cloud Information Database*. *Service Information Collector* collects information from cloud providers (see section 3.2). The *Audition Information Mediator* gathers and grades performance monitoring information from third-party auditors, and the *User Feedback Processor* collects feedbacks from cloud consumers (under development). Finally, the *Cloud Information Database* stores collected cloud information (e.g., pricing rules, configuration scheme, capability declarations, user feedbacks).

In the process of cloud service recommendation, *Web Client*, *Solution Generator*, *Solution Evaluator* and *Cloud Information Database* work collaboratively (Fig. 7). The *Cloud Information Broker* performs independently of this process. After user inputs are sent to the server side, the *Service Filter* is engaged, after which the *Solution Constructor* generates solutions with filtered services. When solutions are generated, *solution evaluator* evaluates all qualified solution. The *Fee calculator* and *Capacity Analyzer* work simultaneously (see section 3.5). Subsequently, the *Comprehensive scorer* ranks each solution by leveraging multiple criteria, including cost and VM capacity score.

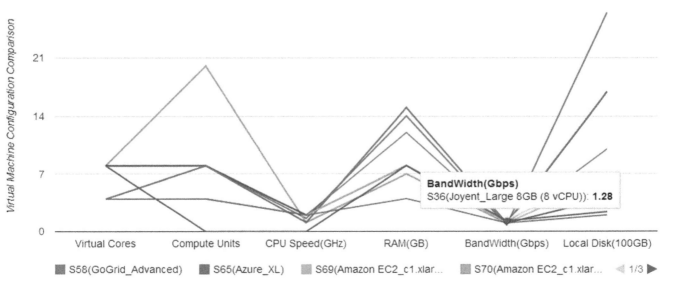

Figure 14. Virtual machine hardware configuration for recommended solutions.

Figure 15. Data center distribution of cloud services.

4.1.2 A four-phase recommendation workflow. With rational workflow, appropriate interaction and visualization technologies, the ease of using the solution evaluation and selection becomes commonplace. Based on this consideration, a four-phase recommendation workflow is proposed (Fig. 8).

The unified cloud information model and a system framework are the bases of the entire recommendation workflow. At the service filtering phase, the service classification model specifies the service level requirements and constraints/filters the cloud services. At the solution construction phase, application level requirements are described using the application requirement schema; these codify rules for generating solutions from qualified services. Subsequently, solutions are evaluated and recommended based on users' evaluation preferences. And in the final phase, the users compare solutions through a visualization-enhanced web GUI.

4.2 Web GUI Design and Visualization Functions

An intuitive, interactive, and straight-forward graphic user interface (GUI) is essential for better cloud solution selection. A well-designed GUI improves user experience and helps convey important information to assist decision-making [37]. This is especially true for the web-based applications [38,39]. In this prototype, the Dojo toolkit (http://dojotoolkit.org/) and widgets are selected to define the GUI and layout, while Google Maps/ Charts provide visualization and interaction function.

4.2.1 Categorizing requirements input panels. To conduct a reliable evaluation, comprehensive requirements and preferences on applications and cloud services are essential. However, the process of complicated parameter input frustrates many users. User-friendly GUI, input wizards and tooltips simplify this process. An expandable service filtering panel - "Cloud Service Filter" (the left side panel in Fig. 9) allows experts to customize service level demands and constraints. Four application requirement input panels (tabs on the center of Fig. 9) are defined according to application types, as the same application type may have similar requirements. The *Data Storage Application Tab* stores simple cloud-based data where no application needs to be deployed. The *Web Application Tab* is for small-to-medium scale web applications, such as geospatial web portals and web services (e.g., web map services). The *Computing Application Tab* is for computing intensive requirements (e.g., dust storm forecasting, [22]). For experts who have a sufficient knowledge of the features of target application and cloud computing, the *Customized*

ID	Name	Description	Service Type	Hypervisor	Web Site
1	Amazon EC2	Amazon EC2 Cloud	IaaS	XEN	http://aws.amazon.com/
2	Azure	Microsoft Windows Azure	IaaS,PaaS	Hyper-V	http://www.windowsazure.com/
3	Google App	Google App Engine Cloud	IaaS,PaaS,SaaS	KVM	https://cloud.google.com/
4	OpSource	OpSource Cloud	IaaS	vSphere	http://www.opsource.net/
5	Joyent	Joyent Cloud	IaaS	KVM	http://joyent.com/
6	Rackspace	Rackspace Cloud	IaaS	XEN;XenServer	http://www.rackspace.com/
7	CloudSigma	CloudSigma Cloud	IaaS	KVM	http://www.cloudsigma.com/
8	GoGrid	GoGrid Cloud	IaaS	XEN	http://www.gogrid.com/
9	Terremark	Terremark Worldwide Cloud	IaaS	vSphere	http://www.terremark.com/

Figure 16. Data table of qualified cloud services.

Table 2. Selected features of the ten public cloud services.

Service Name\ Features	HPC/GPU Cluster	Dedicated Server	VM Customization	Data Encryption	Global Data Center	Web-based Control Interface	Disaster Recovery	Minimum Billing Cycle	Auto-Scaling
Amazon EC2	X	X		X	X	X	X	1 h	X
Microsoft Azure	X			X	X	X	X	1 h	
Google App	X			X	X	X	X	1 min.	X
FlexiScale*			✓					1 h	
OpSource		X	X		X	X	X	1 h	
Joyent		X		X	X			1 h	X
Rackspace		X		X	X	X	X	1 h	X
CloudSigma			X	X	X	X		5 min	
GoGrid		X			X	X		1 h	X
Terremark		X			X	X	X	1 h	X

*FlexiScale provides partial VM customization by re-sizing the memory and disk size.

Application Tab is a panel to specify elaborate requirements and from which the system can generate more reliable evaluations and recommendations. The value input parameters are predefined and dynamically adjusted according to the application type and user inputs in the tabs.

4.2.2 Visualization and interaction for selecting cloud solutions. To intuitively present and compare cloud solutions, multiple visualization and interactive methods are nested within the solution exploration GUI (Fig. 10), and these have six features. The first is data tables to exhibit solutions in detail (e.g., configurations, potential fee components, scores for objectives). The table *Recommended Solution* lists the solutions, whereas the *Feasible Solution* identifies all filtered feasible solutions (Fig. 11). A column-based re-sorting function allows one to compare solutions based on a variety of attributes. The second feature is the Comprehensive Evaluation Radar Chart (Fig. 12), which reveals the advantages and disadvantages of each solution by tabulating scores of evaluation objectives for the user-selected solutions. The third feature - Fee Charts (Average/Minimum/Maximum fee chart and fee range comparison chart) - (Fig. 13) compares potential fee ranges of for each solution. By visualizing the major fee components (e.g., VM fee, storage fee. data transfer fee), the users intuitively understands the percentages that each part costs. The fourth feature is the (line series based) Virtual Machine Configuration Chart (Fig. 14) in which one can compare VM computational capability parameters. The fifth feature - Geo-Distribution Maps (Fig. 15) - illustrates the geographical distribution of computing infrastructures (e.g., data centers) and potential end users of target applications using a map context. The geo-location information helps providers leverage spatial factors of resource allocation for cloud service selection. The sixth and final feature is the table of qualified Cloud services (Fig. 16), which is a brief description of general information of the selected services used in generating solutions.

Interactions are designed to make these visualization methods intuitive. Evaluating and ranking solutions "on-the-fly" allow users to adjust evaluation preferences at any time using the evaluation preference panel (right side panel, Fig. 10), which updates the solution tables and charts Moreover, users can specify the solution number and specific comparing solutions in charts. Finally, users can interact in data visualization either in tables or maps. Selecting a solution from the solution table, the data centers of the solution are highlighted. After the data center is clicked and the window displays the map, a brief introduction of the data center is offered and provides the URL of the cloud provider's website. Through the URL, users check the details and contact the cloud provider.

By leveraging the advancements of visualization technologies and web GUI design, the presentation and comparison of cloud solutions emerges as an intuitive feature for better supporting selection. Meanwhile, the user interaction becomes simple and efficient. Comparing many contemporary cloud advisory systems, the major feature of proposed prototype is its application-specified configuration of solutions and methods to help visualize, compare and evaluate solutions. Besides the map-based cloud infrastructure visualization function (Data Center Map) and the service features and user preferences based comparison functions (adopted by FindTheBest), the proposed prototype offers a preference-aware comprehensive evaluation function so users can specify their preferences "on-the-fly". Potential usage fee predication and computational capability measurement functions are also integrated. In contrast to developing a desktop-based simulation system to analyze the frameworks and codes of target applications (e.g., CloudMIG), a web-based advisory system is proposed. This system recommends cloud solutions by leveraging user-specified applica-

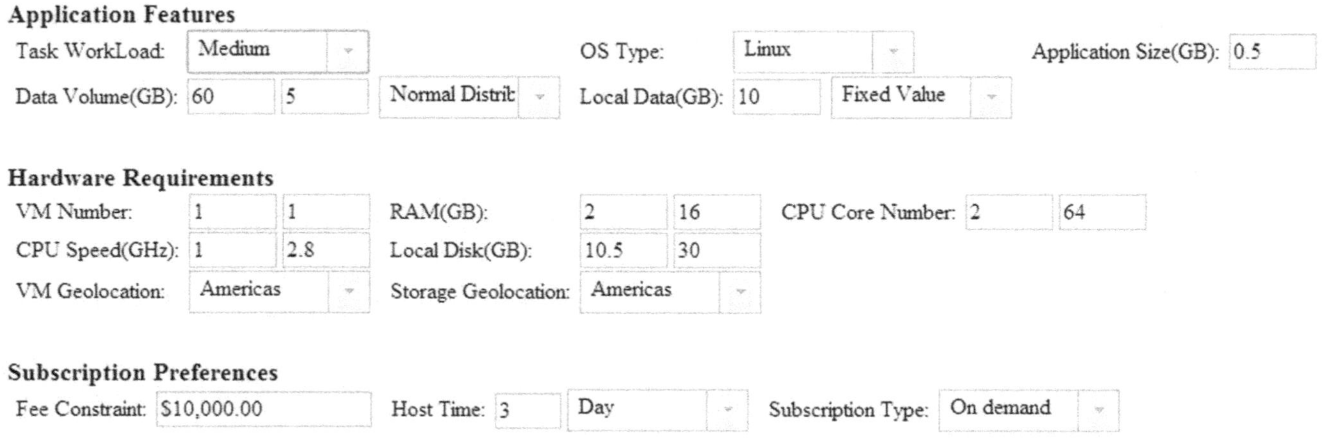

Application Features

Task WorkLoad: Medium   OS Type: Linux   Application Size(GB): 0.5

Data Volume(GB): 60   5   Normal Distrib   Local Data(GB): 10   Fixed Value

Hardware Requirements

VM Number: 1   1   RAM(GB): 2   16   CPU Core Number: 2   64

CPU Speed(GHz): 1   2.8   Local Disk(GB): 10.5   30

VM Geolocation: Americas   Storage Geolocation: Americas

Subscription Preferences

Fee Constraint: $10,000.00   Host Time: 3   Day   Subscription Type: On demand

Figure 17. Requirements for demonstrated computing application.

tion requirements, constraints and real-world cloud service provisioning.

4.3 Feasibilities of the Proposed Methods

4.3.1 Effectiveness of service filtering method. From ten mainstream public cloud services their provisioning and pricing information were collected using the proposed cloud information broker. These services differ on business scales and adopt a range of technologies/strategies in cloud computing (Table 2).

Based on table 2, these services have disparate assets and capabilities. For example, distinct minimum billing cycles range from 1 min to 1 h. Three services (Google App, Amazon EC2 and Microsoft Azure) provide HPC support but currently only EC2 offers GPU Cluster. Three services support VM configuration customization function. Using the systematic service classification model and critical features, a qualified cloud service can be quickly identified. Subsequently, additional processes on cloud solution generation and evaluation handled by other modules will become efficient.

4.3.2 Requirement-driven solution generation. The application requirement description schema guarantees the generated solutions taking into consideration hardware requirements, OS types and geo-location restriction. Taking the following computing application (with medium workload) scenario as an example (Fig. 17), the minimum hardware configuration per task is a machine with >2 GB RAM and 2 CPU core. The application runs on Linux and needs 0.5 GB local disk. Furthermore, the task requires the VM to have >10 GB local disk to host local data and ~60 GB cloud storage to inventory the final result. The Americas is the geo-location restriction on VM and cloud storage. The user wants to host and run the task for 3 days.

According to the requirements, 94 feasible cloud solutions from nine cloud service providers (excluding FlexiScale which does not have a cloud infrastructure in Americas) are generated. If the minimum hardware configuration is changed to 16 GB RAM and 8-core, 43 solutions remain, less than half of the original. If the user changes the geo-location of VM and storage to Asia, 27 solutions from five vendors (EC2, Azure, Google App, Rackspace and Terremark) are generated. Solution generation is also affected by the parameters of computational features. For example, concurrent access intensity of a web application determines not only the network configurations of a cloud solution but even the instance number or scaling strategies. The task workload of a

computing application can determine the hardware configuration of VMs.

4.3.3. Preference-sensitive solution evaluation. Solutions are dynamically assessed and ranked according to the importance of evaluation objectives. Therefore, the recommended solutions reflect the users' preferences. This approach is applied to a real cloud solution and the first ten recommended solutions for three different preferences are illustrated (Fig. 18) using the computing application scenario. The results with default preference (i.e., importance of fee, VM capacity, SLA, customer service, user feedback software resource ecosystem set as "very important", "moderate", "important", "moderate", "a little" and "unimportant", in series) (Fig. 18a). The same analysis but including a fee is illustrated in Fig. 18 (b) while the results with the inclusion of a VM capacity are shown in Fig. 18 (c).

In summary, this dynamic and interactive ability to test the role of user's preference "on the fly" is a significant advancement to help users explore more effectively their assumption and thus accelerate their research initiatives by considering different priorities.

4.3.4 Accuracy of fee prediction. Fee prediction is critical to end users as significant deviation on fee prediction dramatically affects the decision making on cloud solution selection. To validate the utility of the proposed method, the practical cloud usage and fee cost of a global accessible web application, GEOSS Clearinghouse (CLH) [40], on Amazon EC2 were analyzed. The application is a core component of Global Earth Observation System of Systems (GEOSS) Common Infrastructure for supporting geospatial data discovery and utilization. By 06 May 2013, 105 catalogues and 125,000metadata have been registered in the CLH and shared among 140 countries [41]. The application uses an m1.large Linux instance in the US East region and adopts a pay-as-you-go billing. The monthly cloud usage of CLH from July 2011 to October 2012 is summarized by analyzing log files and Amazon billing statements (Table 3). From this information, predictions can be offered of the monthly fee cost from November 2012 to April 2013 (6 months).

The predicted results (Fig. 19) show that the monthly average prediction error and standard deviation between real fee and predicated mean fee was 3.46% and 3.57%, respectively. December 2012 had largest predication error because that month had extreme EBS I/O requests (305,235,693). The range between predicted minimum and maximum fee and most of the errors were

ID	Average Fee($)	VM Provider	VM Type	VM Num	CPU Cores	Compute Units	CPU Speed(GHz)	RAM(GB)	BandWidth(Mbps)	Local Disk(GB)	OS Type	VM Service Mode	Storage Provider	St
1	191.08	Amazon EC2	cc2.8xlarge	1	32	88	1.1	60.5	10000	3370	Linux	Shared	Amazon EC2	
2	192.58	Amazon EC2	cc2.8xlarge	1	32	88	1.1	60.5	10000	3370	Linux	Shared	Amazon EC2	
3	147.88	Amazon EC2	m2.4xlarge	1	8	26	1.1	68.4	1000	1690	Linux	Shared	Amazon EC2	
4	64.94	Azure	XL	1	8	8	1.6	14	800	2644	WhatEver	Shared	Azure	
5	149.38	Amazon EC2	m2.4xlarge	1	8	26	1.1	68.4	1000	1690	Linux	Shared	Amazon EC2	
6	241.48	Amazon EC2	hi1.4xlarge	1	16	35	1.1	60.5	10000	2048	Linux	Shared	Amazon EC2	
7	242.98	Amazon EC2	hi1.4xlarge	1	16	35	1.1	60.5	10000	2048	Linux	Shared	Amazon EC2	
8	105.53	Google App	n1-highmem-8-d	1	8	0	1.2	52	0	3540	WhatEver	Shared	Google App	
9	41.9	Azure	L	1	4	4	1.6	7	400	1284	WhatEver	Shared	Azure	
10	30.38	Azure	M	1	2	2	1.6	3.5	200	624	WhatEver	Shared	Azure	

(a) Results with default evaluation preference

ID	Average Fee($)	VM Provider	VM Type	VM Num	CPU Cores	Compute Units	CPU Speed(GHz)	RAM(GB)	BandWidth(Mbps)	Local Disk(GB)	OS Type	VM Service Mode	Storage Provider
70	21.24	Joyent	Medium 2GB (2 vCPU)	1	2	0	0	2	1280	60	Linux	Shared	Joyent
52	20.12	CloudSigma	customized VM	1	2	0	1	0.5	100	10.5	WhatEver	Shared	CloudSigma
68	26.28	Joyent	Medium 4GB (4 vCPU)	1	4	0	0	4	1280	120	Linux	Shared	Joyent
54	23.44	OpSource	customized VM	1	2	0	1	0.5	100	10.5	WhatEver	Shared	OpSource
47	27.05	Google App	n1-highcpu-2	1	2	0	1.2	1.8	0	0	WhatEver	Shared	Google App
44	29.35	Google App	n1-highcpu-2-d	1	2	0	1.2	1.8	0	870	WhatEver	Shared	Google App
11	29.8	GoGrid	Medium	1	2	2	2	2	1024	100	WhatEver	Shared	GoGrid
38	30.16	Amazon EC2	c1.medium	1	2	5	1.1	1.7	500	350	Linux	Shared	Amazon EC2
10	30.38	Azure	M	1	2	2	1.6	3.5	200	624	WhatEver	Shared	Azure
59	34.92	Joyent	Large 8GB (8 vCPU)	1	8	0	0	8	1280	240	Linux	Shared	Joyent

(b) Results by only consider fee

ID	Average Fee($)	VM Provider	VM Type	VM Num	CPU Cores	Compute Units	CPU Speed(GHz)	RAM(GB)	BandWidth(Mbps)	Local Disk(GB)	OS Type	VM Service Mode	Storage Provider
1	191.08	Amazon EC2	cc2.8xlarge	1	32	88	1.1	60.5	10000	3370	Linux	Shared	Amazon EC2
2	192.58	Amazon EC2	cc2.8xlarge	1	32	88	1.1	60.5	10000	3370	Linux	Shared	Amazon EC2
6	241.48	Amazon EC2	hi1.4xlarge	1	16	35	1.1	60.5	10000	2048	Linux	Shared	Amazon EC2
7	242.98	Amazon EC2	hi1.4xlarge	1	16	35	1.1	60.5	10000	2048	Linux	Shared	Amazon EC2
51	307.11	CloudSigma	customized VM	1	64	0	2.8	4	1000	30	WhatEver	Shared	CloudSigma
79	540.49	OpSource	customized VM	1	64	0	2.8	4	1000	30	WhatEver	Shared	OpSource
3	147.88	Amazon EC2	m2.4xlarge	1	8	26	1.1	68.4	1000	1690	Linux	Shared	Amazon EC2
5	149.38	Amazon EC2	m2.4xlarge	1	8	26	1.1	68.4	1000	1690	Linux	Shared	Amazon EC2
36	210.6	Joyent	Dedicated 80GB (16 vCPU)	1	16	0	0	80	1280	2048	Linux	Shared	Joyent
93	1218.28	GoGrid	Elite	1	12	12	2	48	1024	294	WhatEver	Dedicated	GoGrid

(c) Results by only consider VM capacity

Figure 18. Recommended solutions with different evaluation preferences: (a) results with default evaluation preference; (b) results by only considering fee; (c) results by only considering VM capacity.

introduced by uncertainty of data transfer, storage volume and I/O operations, whereas the prediction on VM fee is relatively accurate since the CPU hours were stable. Therefore, if cloud usage is relatively stable, prediction the fee will be accurate. This is especially true for the applications which do not involve spatiotemporal dynamics on cloud usages. For web applications, the changes on user access intensities may dramatically impact fee prediction due to the changes in data transfer, storage and VM usages. Auto scaling may also influence fee prediction by introducing uncertainty on used CPU hours. Therefore, it is difficult to predict with precision the short-time (e.g., days) behavior and fee. However, for a long-time tenancy, the proposed model provides acceptable predictive estimates of fees. Furthermore, analyzing the long-time behaviours and spatiotemporal

dynamics of the target application, the patterns of application feature parameters can be obtained. Based on that, the fee model may produce more reliable predictions.

Conclusions and Future Work

This paper introduces a comprehensive framework and associated methodologies for brokering and recommending cloud services for application owners. Instead of only providing capabilities to compare the functional/non-functional properties, cost and ranking of cloud services at service level (coarse-granule), a novel method is proposed to generate, evaluate and recommend cloud service at the level of solution configuration (fine-granule). Four major conclusions are offered from this research.

Table 3. Monthly cloud usage of CLH (July 2011– October 2012).

Features	Mean	Standard Deviation	Minimum	Maximum
CPU h per day (h)	24	0	24	24
EBS data size (GB)	193.305	35.349	160	287.325
EBS I/O requests	53650312.19	100360034	102942	307766613
EBS snapshot size (GB)	3.727	0.038	3.609	3.739
Data In-Transfer (GB)	17.146	28.534	1.321	111.451
Data Out-Transfer (GB)	20.407	48.026	0.213	204.174
Data Transfer (Regional) (GB)	5.507	6.738	0.147	27.143

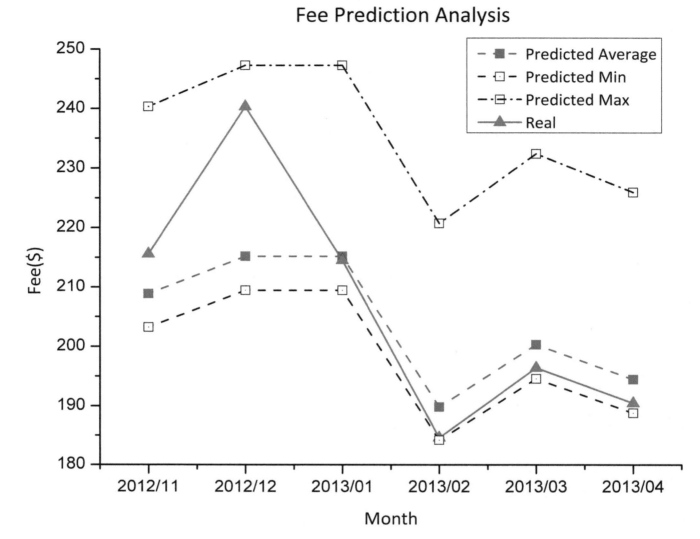

Figure 19. Monthly cloud usage fee predication analysis for CLH in EC2.

First, To unify and integrate heterogeneous and multi-source cloud information from different cloud providers, auditors and consumers, a unified cloud information model is proposed. This model describes different cloud information and their relationships including service offerings, pricings, infrastructure distributions, basic features and capabilities, user feedback, and auditing.

Second, to categorize and refine user requirements and preferences for better supporting solution generation, an operational service classification model and an application-dependent requirement description schema are proposed. The former filters cloud services based on service-level features and constraints, while the latter depicts hardware requirements, application features and subscription preferences in detail. The integration of the two models provides an approach to create a user-requirement-qualified cloud solution.

Third, to comprehensively and flexibly evaluate generated cloud solutions, a user preference-aware and dynamic changeable solution evaluation mode is proposed. A fee prediction and VM computing capacity measurement method are defined to support the proposed evaluation method. By using these methods, solution

can be evaluated and sorted according to user's preferences based on multiple evaluation criteria.

Four, to validate the feasibility of the proposed methods, an architecture and prototype of cloud advisory system is introduced. This system collects and updates cloud information from cloud providers' website using the proposed collecting mechanism. The adopted web visualization and interaction technologies facilitate the integration, presentation and comparison of cloud information and solutions, and make these functions easily accessible to users.

To further improve and expand the proposed brokering and recommendation capabilities, the direction of future research should target the following:

Integrating performance monitoring information

Third-party audition information can help the advisory system make more reliable recommendations by providing near real-time availability, performance status and grades from long-time monitoring and analysis. Therefore, the mechanism to broker/collect, manage and utilize the performance information in the recommendation workflow should be investigated.

Investigating a cloud information update mechanism and specifications

The web page parsing-based collecting method inevitably introduces unwanted issues such as timeliness. The recommendation system cannot guarantee all gathered provisioning information reflects the latest conditions. Another issue is the expensive cost for parser maintenance since the URL and content of the web pages may frequently change. In the future, it is proposed that one utilize the notification mechanism by cloud providers to trigger collecting information in a timely manner. Furthermore, formal and semantic-aided web service specifications for describing and querying heterogeneous cloud information are emerging needs to improve interoperability and brokering capabilities.

Improving solution generation strategies and evaluation methods

Currently, the proposed system only provides static configured solutions (i.e., without considering scaling-up and scaling-down scenarios). To create solutions with dynamically changeable configuration strategies for different scenarios, more studies and experiments are required on real applications to learn their computational characteristics, spatiotemporal dynamics and requirements. This may also result in collaborate with third-party

tools (e.g., CloudSim) to simulate cloud resource provisioning and consumption.

Creating solutions for private and hybrid clouds

Private and hybrid cloud services, which provide more freedom and privacy of open cloud, are two major features of cloud computing. Therefore, evaluating cloud solutions with open-source cloud management software and private/hybrid cloud environments is needed. This should investigate relevant evaluation mechanisms and methodologies, and a means to integrate them into the proposed recommendation framework.

Acknowledgments

Dr. George Taylor proofed an earlier version of the paper. The research and manuscript preparation were conducted at George Mason University.

Author Contributions

Conceived and designed the experiments: CY ZG QH. Performed the experiments: ZG KL JX ZL MS CY. Analyzed the data: ZG CY KL MY BJ. Contributed reagents/materials/analysis tools: KL ZL NZ. Wrote the paper: ZG CY JX.

References

1. Buyya R, Yeo CS, Venugopal S, Broberg J, Brandic I (2009) Cloud computing and emerging IT platforms: Vision, hype, and reality for delivering computing as the 5th utility. Future Generation computer systems, 25: 599–616.
2. Vecchiola C, Pandey S, Buyya R (2009) High-performance cloud computing: A view of scientific applications. in: 10th International Symposium on Pervasive Systems, Algorithms, and Networks (ISPAN), pp.4–16.
3. Lee CA (2010) A perspective on scientific cloud computing. in: Proc. of the 19th ACM International Symposium on High Performance Distributed Computing, pp.451–459.
4. Yang C, Goodchild M, Huang Q, Nebert D, Raskin R, et al. (2011) Spatial cloud computing: How can geospatial sciences use and help to shape cloud computing. International Journal of Digital Earth, 4: 305–329.
5. Yang C, Xu Y, Nebert D (2013) Redefining the possibility of digital Earth and geosciences with spatial cloud computing. International Journal of Digital Earth, 6: 1–16.
6. Gui Z, Xia J, Zhou N, Huang Q (2013) How to choose cloud computing: towards a cloud computing cost model. in: Yang C, Huang Q, Li Z, Xu C, Liu K (Eds.), Spatial Cloud Computing: A Practical Approach, CRC Press/ Taylor & Francis, 304p.
7. Subashini S, Kavitha V (2011) A survey on security issues in service delivery models of cloud computing. Journal of Network and Computer Applications, 34: 1–11.
8. Repschläger J, Wind S, Zarnekow R, Turowski K (2011) Developing a Cloud Provider Selection Model. in: Proc. of Enterprise Modelling and Information Systems Architectures (EMISA 2011), pp.163–176.
9. Zeng W, Zhao Y, Zeng J (2009) Cloud service and service selection algorithm research. in: Proc. of the first ACM/SIGEVO Summit on Genetic and Evolutionary Computation, ACM, pp.1045–1048.
10. Martens B, Teuteberg F, Gräuler M (2011) Design and implementation of a community platform for the evaluation and selection of cloud computing services: A market analysis. in: Proc. of European Conference on Information Systems.
11. Hussain FK, Hussain OK (2011) Towards multi-criteria cloud service selection. in: 2011 Fifth International Conference on Innovative Mobile and Internet Services in Ubiquitous Computing (IMIS), pp.44–48.
12. Garg SK, Versteeg S, Buyya R (2011) SMICloud: A framework for comparing and ranking cloud services. in: 2011 Fourth IEEE International Conference on Utility and Cloud Computing (UCC), pp.210–218.
13. Badger L, Grance T, Patt-Corner R, Voas J (2012) Cloud Computing Synopsis and Recommendations. NIST Special Publication, 800: 146.
14. CSMIC (2013) SMI Framework Version 2.0 Draft for Public Review. Available: http://csmic.org/wp-content/uploads/2013/08/SMI_Overview_1308151.pdf. Accessed 2014 August 4.
15. NIST (2009) Cloud Service Metrics Description (Draft), Rev 2.3d17, NIST Cloud Computing Reference Architecture. Available: http://collaborate.nist. gov/twiki-cloud-computing/pub/CloudComputing/RATax_CloudMetrics/ RATAX-CloudServiceMetricsDescription-DRAFT-v2-3d17_20140430-internal-dist-v2.docx. Accessed 2014 August 4.
16. Stantchev V (2009) Performance evaluation of cloud computing offerings. in: Third International Conference on Advanced Engineering Computing and Applications in Sciences (ADVCOMP' 09), pp.187–192.
17. Wang YA, Huang C, Li J, Ross KW (2011) Estimating the performance of hypothetical cloud service deployments: A measurement-based approach. in: Proc. IEEE INFOCOM, pp.2372–2380.
18. Li A, Yang X, Kandula S, Zhang M (2010) CloudCmp: comparing public cloud providers. in: Proc. of the 10th ACM SIGCOMM conference on Internet measurement, ACM, pp.1–14.
19. Jackson KR, Ramakrishnan L, Muriki K, Canon S, Cholia S, et al. (2010) Performance analysis of high performance computing applications on the amazon web services cloud. in: IEEE Second International Conference on Cloud Computing Technology and Science (CloudCom), pp.159–168.
20. Iosup A, Ostermann S, Yigitbasi MN, Prodan R, Fahringer T, et al. (2011) Performance analysis of cloud computing services for many-tasks scientific computing. IEEE Transactions on Parallel and Distributed Systems, 22: 931–945.
21. Farley B, Juels A, Varadarajan V, Ristenpart T, Bowers KD, et al. (2012) More for your money: Exploiting performance heterogeneity in public clouds. In: Proc. of the Third ACM Symposium on Cloud Computing, ACM, 14p.
22. Huang Q, Yang C, Liu K, Xia J, Xu C, et al. (2013) Evaluating Open-source Cloud Computing Solutions for Geosciences. Computers & Geosciences, 59: 41–52.
23. Calheiros RN, Ranjan R, Beloglazov A, De Rose CA, Buyya R (2011) CloudSim: a toolkit for modeling and simulation of cloud computing environments and evaluation of resource provisioning algorithms. Software: Practice and Experience, 41: 23–50.
24. Frey S, Hasselbring W (2011) The CloudMIG Approach: Model-Based Migration of Software Systems to Cloud-Optimized Applications. International Journal on Advances in Software, 4: 342–353.
25. Frey S, Hasselbring W, Schnoor B (2012) Automatic Conformance Checking for Migrating Software Systems to Cloud Infrastructures and Platforms. Journal of Software: Evolution and Process, 25: 1089–1115.
26. Frey S, Fittkau F, Hasselbring W (ICSE 2013) Search-Based Genetic Optimization for Deployment and Reconfiguration of Software in the Cloud. in: 35th International Conference on Software Engineering, San Francisco, CA, USA, pp.512–521.
27. Li X, Li Y, Liu T, Qiu J, Wang F (2009) The method and tool of cost analysis for cloud computing. in: IEEE International Conference on Cloud Computing, pp.93–100.
28. Andrzejak A, Kondo D, Yi S (2010) Decision model for cloud computing under SLA constraints. IEEE International Symposium on Modeling, Analysis & Simulation of Computer and Telecommunication Systems (MASCOTS). Miami Beach, FL, USA.
29. Zhang Q, Zhu Q, Boutaba R (2011) Dynamic resource allocation for spot markets in cloud computing environments. in: Fourth IEEE International Conference on Utility and Cloud Computing (UCC 2011), Victoria, NSW, pp.178–185.

30. Rochwerger B, Breitgand D, Levy E, Galis A, Nagin K, et al. (2009) The reservoir model and architecture for open federated cloud computing. IBM Journal of Research and Development, 53: 4–1.
31. Buyya R, Ranjan RN (2010) Calheiros, Intercloud: Utility-oriented federation of cloud computing environments for scaling of application services. In Hsu CH, Yang LT, Park JH, Yeo SS (Eds.), Algorithms and architectures for parallel processing, Lecture Notes in Computer Science, Vol. 6081, pp.13–31.
32. Goscinski A, Brock M (2010) Toward dynamic and attribute based publication, discovery and selection for cloud computing. Future Generation Computer Systems, 26: 947–970.
33. Catteddu D, Hogben G (2010) Cloud Computing: Benefits, risks and recommendations for information security. Springer Berlin Heidelberg, 125p.
34. Hwang CL, Masud ASM (1979) Multiple objective decision making-methods and applications. Lecture Notes in Economics and Mathematical Systems, vol. 164, Berlin: Springer-Verlag, 351p.
35. Hwang CL, Yoon K (1981) Multiple Attribute Decision Making: Methods and Applications. New York: Springer-Verlag, 333p.
36. Hwang CL, Lai YJ, Liu TY (1993) A new approach for multiple objective decision making. Computers and Operational Research 20: 889–899.
37. Galitz WO (2007) The essential guide to user interface design: an introduction to GUI design principles and techniques. third ed., Wiley. 835p.
38. Nerurkar U (2001) Web user interface design, forgotten lessons. IEEE Software, 18: 69–71.
39. Van Schaik P, Ling J (2008) Modelling user experience with web sites: Usability, hedonic value, beauty and goodness. Interacting with Computers, 20: 419–432.
40. Liu K, Yang C, Li W, Li Z, Wu H, et al. (2011) The GEOSS Clearinghouse High Performance Search Engine. 19th International Conference on Geoinformatics, Shanghai, China.
41. Huang Q, Yang C, Nebert D, Liu K, Wu H (2010) Cloud computing for geosciences: deployment of GEOSS clearinghouse on Amazon's EC2, Proc. of the ACM SIGSPATIAL International Workshop on High Performance and Distributed Geographic Information Systems, pp. 35–38.

Permissions

List of Contributors

Shuai Ding, Kai-Le Zhou and Shan-Lin Yang
School of Management, Hefei University of Technology, Hefei, P.R. China
Key Laboratory of Process Optimization and Intelligent Decision-Making, Ministry of Education, Hefei, P.R. China

Chen-Yi Xia
Tianjin Key Laboratory of Intelligence Computing and Novel Software Technology and Key Laboratory of Computer Vision and System (Ministry of Education), Tianjin University of Technology, Tianjin, P.R. China

Jennifer S. Shang
The Joseph M. Katz Graduate School of Business, University of Pittsburgh, Pittsburgh, Pennsylvania, United States of America

Konrad J. Karczewski, Guy Haskin Fernald and Alicia R. Martin
Biomedical Informatics Training Program, Stanford University School of Medicine, Stanford, California, United States of America
Department of Genetics, Stanford University School of Medicine, Stanford, California, United States of America

Michael Snyder
Department of Genetics, Stanford University School of Medicine, Stanford, California, United States of America

Nicholas P. Tatonetti
Department of Biomedical Informatics, Columbia University, New York, New York, United States of America

Joel T. Dudley
Department of Genetics and Genomic Sciences, Mount Sinai School of Medicine, New York, New York, United States of America

Tina Šantl-Temkiv
Department of Environmental Science, Aarhus University, Roskilde, Denmark
Microbiology Section, Department of Bioscience, Aarhus University, Aarhus, Denmark
Stellar Astrophysics Centre, Department of Physics and Astronomy, Aarhus University, Aarhus, Denmark

Kai Finster
Microbiology Section, Department of Bioscience, Aarhus University, Aarhus, Denmark
Stellar Astrophysics Centre, Department of Physics and Astronomy, Aarhus University, Aarhus, Denmark

Thorsten Dittmar
Max Planck Research Group for Marine Geochemistry, Institute for Chemistry and Biology of the Marine Environment, University of Oldenburg, Oldenburg, Germany

Bjarne Munk Hansen and Ulrich Gosewinkel Karlson
Department of Environmental Science, Aarhus University, Roskilde, Denmark

Runar Thyrhaug
Department of Biology, University of Bergen, Bergen, Norway

Niels Woetmann Nielsen
Danish Meteorological Institute, Copenhagen, Denmark

Stephan Bialonski and Klaus Lehnertz
Department of Epileptology, University of Bonn, Bonn, Germany
Helmholtz Institute for Radiation and Nuclear Physics, University of Bonn, Bonn, Germany
Interdisciplinary Center for Complex Systems, University of Bonn, Bonn, Germany

Martin Wendler
Fakultät für Mathematik, Ruhr-Universität Bochum, Bochum, Germany

Samuel V. Angiuoli
Institute for Genome Sciences (IGS), University of Maryland Baltimore, Baltimore, Maryland, United States of America
Center for Bioinformatics and Computational Biology, University of Maryland, College Park, Maryland, United States of America

James R. White, Malcolm Matalka, Owen White and W. Florian Fricke
Institute for Genome Sciences (IGS), University of Maryland Baltimore, Baltimore, Maryland, United States of America

Wei-Chun Chung
Institute of Information Science, Academia Sinica, Taipei, Taiwan
Department of Computer Science and Information Engineering, National Taiwan University, Taipei, Taiwan
Research Center for Information Technology Innovation, Academia Sinica, Taipei, Taiwan

Chien-Chih Chen
Institute of Information Science, Academia Sinica, Taipei, Taiwan
Department of Computer Science and Information Engineering, National Taiwan University, Taipei, Taiwan

Jan-Ming Ho
Institute of Information Science, Academia Sinica, Taipei, Taiwan
Research Center for Information Technology Innovation, Academia Sinica, Taipei, Taiwan

Chung-Yen Lin, Wen-Lian Hsu, Yu-Chun Wang, Chih-Wei Huang and Yu-Jung Chang
Institute of Information Science, Academia Sinica, Taipei, Taiwan

D. T. Lee
Institute of Information Science, Academia Sinica, Taipei, Taiwan
Department of Computer Science and Information Engineering, National Taiwan University, Taipei, Taiwan
Department of Computer Science and Information Engineering, National Chung Hsing University, Taichung, Taiwan

Feipei Lai
Department of Computer Science and Information Engineering, National Taiwan University, Taipei, Taiwan

Muhammad Shiraz, Abdullah Gani, Raja Wasim Ahmad, Syed Adeel Ali Shah and Ahmad Karim
Center for Mobile Cloud Computing (C4MCC), Faculty of Computer Science and Information Technology, University of Malaya, Kuala Lumpur, Malaysia

Zulkanain Abdul Rahman
Department of History, Faculty of Arts and Social Sciences, University of Malaya, Kuala Lumpur, Malaysia

Xiao Fan Liu, Michael Small and Chi K. Tse
Department of Electronic and Information Engineering, The Hong Kong Polytechnic University, Hung Hom, Kowloon, Hong Kong

Xiao-Ke Xu
Department of Electronic and Information Engineering, The Hong Kong Polytechnic University, Hung Hom, Kowloon, Hong Kong
School of Communication and Electronic Engineering, Qingdao Technological University, Qingdao, People's Republic of China

Hugh P. Shanahan
1 Department of Computer Science, Royal Holloway, University of London, Egham, Surrey, United Kingdom

Anne M. Owen
Department of Mathematical Sciences, University of Essex, Wivenhoe Park, Colchester, United Kingdom

Andrew P. Harrison
Department of Mathematical Sciences, University of Essex, Wivenhoe Park, Colchester, United Kingdom
Department of Biological Sciences, University of Essex, Wivenhoe Park, Colchester, United Kingdom

Lu Gao and Yumin Wang
School of Life Sciences and Technology, Xidian University, Xi'an, China

Liaojun Patng
School of Life Sciences and Technology, Xidian University, Xi'an, China
Department of Computer Science, Wayne State University, Detroit, Michigan, United States of America

Huixian Li
Department of Computer Science, Wayne State University, Detroit, Michigan, United States of America
School of Computer Science and Engineering, Northwestern Polytechnical University, Xi'an, China

Giulia Menichetti and Daniel Remondini
Department of Physics and Astronomy and INFN Sez. Bologna, Bologna University, Bologna, Italy

Pietro Panzarasa
School of Business and Management, Queen Mary University of London, London, United Kingdom

Raúl J. Mondragón
School of Electronic Engineering and Computer Science, Queen Mary University of London, London, United Kingdom

Ginestra Bianconi
School of Mathematical Sciences, Queen Mary University of London, London, United Kingdom

Daniele Santoni and Fabio Cumbo
Institute for System Analysis and Computer Science "Antonio Ruberti", National Research Council, Rome, Italy

Paola Paci
Institute for System Analysis and Computer Science "Antonio Ruberti", National Research Council, Rome, Italy
SysBio Centre for Systems Biology, Milan and Rome, Italy

Luisa Di Paola
Faculty of Engineering, Università CAMPUS BioMedico, Roma, Italy

Alessandro Giuliani
Environment and Health Department, Istituto Superiore di Sanità, Roma, Italy

LiYong Ren, XiaoWen Nie and YuChi Dong
School of Computer Science & Engineering, University of Electronic Science and Technology of China, ChengDu, China

Xiaohang Zhang, Zecong Zhang, Han Zhao and Qi Wang
School of Economics and Management, Beijing University of Posts and Telecommunications, Beijing, China,

Ji Zhu
Department of Statistics, University of Michigan, Ann Arbor, Michigan, United States of America

Enys Mones
Department of Biological Physics, Eötvös Loránd University, Budapest, Hungary

Lilla Vicsek
Institute of Sociology and Social Policy, Corvinus University of Budapest, Budapest, Hungary

Tamás Vicsek
Department of Biological Physics, Eötvös Loránd University, Budapest, Hungary
Biological Physics Research Group of Hungarian Academy of Sciences, Budapest, Hungary

Murilo S. Baptista
Institute for Complex Systems and Mathematical Biology, Scottish Universities Physics Alliance, University of Aberdeen, Aberdeen, United Kingdom

Rero M. Rubinger
Institute of Physics and Chemistry, Federal University of Itajubá, Itajubá, Brazil

Emilson R. Viana
Instituto de Ciências Exatas, Departamento de F sica, Universidade Federal de Minas Gerais, Belo Horizonte, Brazil

José C. Sartorelli
Institute of Physics, University of São Paulo, São Paulo, Brazil

Ulrich Parlitz
Biomedical Physics Group, Max Planck Institute for Dynamics and Self-Organization, Göttingen, Germany
Institute for Nonlinear Dynamics, Georg-August-Universität Göttingen, Göttingen, Germany

Celso Grebogi
Institute for Complex Systems and Mathematical Biology, Scottish Universities Physics Alliance, University of Aberdeen, Aberdeen, United Kingdom
Freiburg Institute for Advanced Studies, University of Freiburg, Freiburg, Germany

Junyu Guo
Department of Civil and Environmental Engineering, University of Missouri, Columbia, Missouri, United States of America
Timothy C. Matisziw
Department of Civil and Environmental Engineering, University of Missouri, Columbia, Missouri, United States of America
Department of Geography, University of Missouri, Columbia, Missouri, United States of America
Informatics Institute, University of Missouri, Columbia, Missouri, United States of America

Tony H. Grubesic
Geographic Information Systems and Spatial Analysis Laboratory, College of Information Science and Technology, Drexel University, Philadelphia, Pennsylvania, United States of America

Seyhan Yazar and George E. C. Gooden
Centre for Ophthalmology and Visual Science, University of Western Australia, Lions Eye Institute, Perth, Western Australia, Australia

David A. Mackey
Centre for Ophthalmology and Visual Science, University of Western Australia, Lions Eye Institute, Perth, Western Australia, Australia
School of Medicine, Menzies Research Institute Tasmania, University of Tasmania, Hobart, Tasmania, Australia

Alex W. Hewitt
Centre for Ophthalmology and Visual Science, University of Western Australia, Lions Eye Institute, Perth, Western Australia, Australia
School of Medicine, Menzies Research Institute Tasmania, University of Tasmania, Hobart, Tasmania, Australia
Centre for Eye Research Australia, University of Melbourne, Department of Ophthalmology, Royal Victorian Eye and Ear Hospital, Melbourne, Victoria, Australia

Yang-Yu Liu
Center for Complex Network Research and Department of Physics,Northeastern University, Boston, Massachusetts, United States of America
Center for Cancer Systems Biology, Dana-Farber Cancer Institute, Boston, Massachusetts, United States of America

Jean-Jacques Slotine
Nonlinear Systems Laboratory, Massachusetts Institute of Technology, Cambridge, Massachusetts, United States of America
Department of Mechanical Engineering and Department of Brain and Cognitive Sciences, Massachusetts Institute of Technology, Cambridge, Massachusetts, United States of America

Albert-László Barabási
Center for Complex Network Research and Department of Physics,Northeastern University, Boston, Massachusetts, United States of America
Center for Cancer Systems Biology, Dana-Farber Cancer Institute, Boston, Massachusetts, United States of America
Department of Medicine, Brigham and Women's Hospital, Harvard Medical School, Boston, Massachusetts, United States of America

Antonio Scala
Istituto dei Sistemi Complessi Udr "La Sapienza", Roma, Italy
London Institute of Mathematical Sciences, London, United Kingdom

Pietro Auconi
Istituto dei Sistemi Complessi Udr "La Sapienza", Roma, Italy
Private Practice of Orthodontics, Rome, Italy

Marco Scazzocchio
Istituto dei Sistemi Complessi Udr "La Sapienza", Roma, Italy

Guido Caldarelli
Istituto dei Sistemi Complessi Udr "La Sapienza", Roma, Italy
London Institute of Mathematical Sciences, London, United Kingdom
NATWORKS Unit for the Study of Natural Networks, IMT Lucca Institute for Advanced Studies, Lucca, Italy

James A. McNamara
Department of Orthodontics and Pediatric Dentistry, School of Dentistry, The University of Michigan, Ann Arbor, Michigan, United States of America
Department of Cell and Developmental Biology, School of Medicine, The University of Michigan, Ann Arbor, Michigan, United States of America
Center for Human Growth and Development, The University of Michigan, Ann Arbor, Michigan, United States of America
Private Practice of Orthodontics, Ann Arbor, Michigan, United States of America

Lorenzo Franchi
Department of Orthodontics and Pediatric Dentistry, School of Dentistry, The University of Michigan, Ann Arbor, Michigan, United States of America
Department of Orthodontics, The University of Florence, Florence, Italy

Jia Zhao
College of Computer Science and Engineering, ChangChun University of Technology, Changchun, China
College of Computer Science and Technology, Jilin University, Changchun, China

Liang Hu, Yan Ding and Gaochao Xu
College of Computer Science and Technology, Jilin University, Changchun, China

Ming Hu
College of Computer Science and Engineering, ChangChun University of Technology, Changchun, China

Maria Fischer, Stephan Pabinger, Zlatko Trajanoski and Gernot Stocker
Division for Bioinformatics, Biocenter, Innsbruck Medical University, Innsbruck, Austria

Rene Snajder and Andreas Dander
Division for Bioinformatics, Biocenter, Innsbruck Medical University, Innsbruck, Austria
Oncotyrol, Center for Personalized Cancer Medicine, Innsbruck, Austria

Anna Schossig and Johannes Zschocke
Division of Human Genetics, Biocenter, Innsbruck Medical University, Innsbruck, Austria

Xizhe Zhang, XueYing Yang and Bin Zhang
College of Information Science and Engineering, Northeastern University, Shenyang, China

Tianyang Lv
College of Computer Science and Technology, Harbin Engineering University, Harbin, China
College of Computer Science and Technology, Tsinghua University, Beijing, China
Audit Research Institute, National Audit Office, Beijing, China

Zhipeng Gui
NSF Spatiotemporal Innovation Center, George Mason University, Fairfax, Virginia, United States of America
School of Remote Sensing and Information Engineering, Wuhan University, Wuhan, Hubei Province, China

Chaowei Yang, Jizhe Xia, Qunying Huang, Kai Liu, Zhenlong Li, Manzhu Yu, Min Sun, Nanyin Zhou and Baoxuan Jin
NSF Spatiotemporal Innovation Center, George Mason University, Fairfax, Virginia, United States of America

Index

CPSIA information can be obtained
at www.ICGtesting.com
Printed in the USA
BVHW06*1517100518
515857BV00002BA/97/P